Lecture Notes in Computer Science 15194

The series Lecture Notes in Computer Science (LNCS), including its subseries Lecture Notes in Artificial Intelligence (LNAI) and Lecture Notes in Bioinformatics (LNBI), has established itself as a medium for the publication of new developments in computer science and information technology research, teaching, and education.

LNCS enjoys close cooperation with the computer science R & D community, the series counts many renowned academics among its volume editors and paper authors, and collaborates with prestigious societies. Its mission is to serve this international community by providing an invaluable service, mainly focused on the publication of conference and workshop proceedings and postproceedings. LNCS commenced publication in 1973.

Oleg Kiselyov
Editor

Programming Languages and Systems

22nd Asian Symposium, APLAS 2024
Kyoto, Japan, October 22–24, 2024
Proceedings

Editor
Oleg Kiselyov
Tohoku University
Sendai, Miyagi, Japan

ISSN 0302-9743 ISSN 1611-3349 (electronic)
Lecture Notes in Computer Science
ISBN 978-981-97-8942-9 ISBN 978-981-97-8943-6 (eBook)
https://doi.org/10.1007/978-981-97-8943-6

This Springer imprint is published by the registered company Springer Nature Singapore Pte Ltd.
The registered company address is: 152 Beach Road, #21-01/04 Gateway East, Singapore 189721, Singapore

Preface

This volume contains the proceedings of the Twenty-Second Asian Symposium on Programming Languages and Systems—APLAS 2024—held during October 22–24, 2024, in Kyoto, Japan.

APLAS brings together programming language researchers, practitioners and implementors *worldwide*, to present and discuss the latest results and exchange ideas in all areas of programming languages and systems. The list of topics includes, among others: programming paradigms and styles; methods and tools to specify and reason about programs and languages; programming language foundations; methods and tools for implementation; concurrency and distribution; applications and case studies.

APLAS is organized by the Asian Association for Foundation of Software (AAFS), founded by Asian researchers in cooperation with many researchers from Europe and the USA. Past APLAS symposiums were held in Taipei ('23), Auckland ('22), Chicago ('21), Fukuoka ('20), Bali ('19),Wellington ('18), Suzhou ('17), Hanoi ('16), Pohang ('15), Singapore ('14), Melbourne ('13), Kyoto ('12), Kenting ('11), Shanghai ('10), Seoul ('09), Bangalore ('08), Singapore ('07), Sydney ('06), Tsukuba ('05), Taipei ('04) and Beijing ('03) after three informal workshops.

The call for papers attracted 37 submissions, two of which were desk-rejected. The rest were reviewed double-blind: we aimed to keep the identities out of the picture during the whole review process. Each submission received three reviews. In addition, for some submissions, we sought opinions of external experts, whose prompt and very helpful comments were greatly appreciated.

At the end of the review period, the authors had 50 hours to respond to the reviews. The PC has considered the responses and decided on acceptance. In many cases, the reviews were augmented to account for the responses and to summarize the PC discussion. Quite a number of responses clarified the submission and resolved the reviewers' concerns. In some other cases, unfortunately, the responses did not address all the concerns and questions raised in the reviews.

No numerical targets were set for acceptance. The only criterion was a submission being understandable, interesting and instructive to the audience and publishable in the proceedings, after perhaps only *minor* revisions. After careful and thorough discussions, the Program Committee accepted 18 submissions.

The symposium program also included three invited talks, by Albert Cohen (Google), Naoki Kobayashi (University of Tokyo: joint with ATVA 2024) and Sukyoung Ryu (KAIST, South Korea).

Furthermore, APLAS 24 included a student research competition and the associated poster session, as well as the APLAS-NIER post-conference workshop (October 25, 2024). This year, APLAS was co-located with the 22nd International Symposium on Automated Technology for Verification and Analysis (ATVA).

APLAS 2024 continued the tradition of recognizing the best paper submitted to the symposium. I am delighted to announce that the Best Paper award for APLAS 2024 went to

Benedikt Ahrens, Peter LeFanu Lumsdaine, Paige Randall North Comparing semantic frameworks of dependently sorted algebraic theories

Putting together APLAS 2024 was a team effort. First of all, I would like to thank the authors of the submitted papers and the presenters of the invited talks. Without the program committee, there would have been no program either, and I am very grateful to the PC members for their hard work. Complementing the PC were external reviewers, whose contribution is gratefully acknowledged. I am indebted to the General Chair Jacques Garrigue for his advice, encouragement and support throughout the process. This year APLAS was held in cooperation with ATVA, whose organizing committee—in particular, General Chair Ichiro Hasuo—has shared the burden. They were invaluable in setting up the conference and making sure everything ran smoothly.

We gratefully acknowledge Takashi Suwa for the design of the conference logo, which can be seen on the cover.

Finally, thanks are due to Silver Sponsors *DENSO* and *Mitsubishi Electric*; Organizational Sponsor *The Kyoto University Foundation* and the Award Sponsor *Springer*.

September 2024 Oleg Kiselyov

Organization

General Chair

Jacques Garrigue	Nagoya University, Japan

Program Chair

Oleg Kiselyov	Tohoku University, Japan

Program Committee

Beniamino Accattoli	Inria and Ėcole Polytechnique, France
Pierre-Évariste Dagand	IRIF/CNRS, France
Silvia Ghilezan	University of Novi Sad, Mathematical Institute SASA, Serbia
Fritz Henglein	DIKU and Deon Digital, Denmark
Mirai Ikebuchi	Kyoto University, Japan
Patrik Jansson	Chalmers University of Technology and University of Gothenburg, Sweden
Oleg Kiselyov	Tohoku University, Japan
Hsiang-Shang 'Josh' Ko	Academia Sinica, Taiwan
Daan Leijen	Microsoft Research, USA
Martin Lester	University of Reading, UK
Fredrik Nordvall Forsberg	University of Strathclyde, UK
Matija Pretnar	University of Ljubljana, Slovenia
Peter Schachte	University of Melbourne, Australia
Sven-Bodo Scholz	Radboud University, Netherlands
Philipp Schuster	University of Tübingen, Germany
Taro Sekiyama	NII, Japan
Amir Shaikhha	University of Edinburgh, UK
Pavle Subotic	Fantom Foundation, Serbia
Yong Kiam Tan	Institute for Infocomm Research, A*STAR, Singapore
Kazunori Ueda	Waseda University, Japan
Yuting Wang	Shanghai Jiao Tong University, China
Ki Yung Ahn	Hannam University, South Korea

External Reviewers

Arthur Azevedo de Amorim
Jacques Garrigue
Mario Carneiro
Ugo Dal Lago
Xing Li

Contents

Type Theory and Semantic Frameworks

Comparing Semantic Frameworks for Dependently-Sorted Algebraic Theories

Benedikt Ahrens[1,4(✉)], Peter LeFanu Lumsdaine[2], and Paige Randall North[1,3,4]

[1] Delft University of Technology, Delft, The Netherlands
p.r.north@uu.nl
[2] Stockholm University, Stockholm, Sweden
p.l.lumsdaine@math.su.se
[3] Utrecht University, Utrecht, The Netherlands
[4] University of Birmingham, Birmingham, England
b.p.ahrens@tudelft.nl

Abstract. Algebraic theories with dependency between sorts form the structural core of Martin-Löf type theory and similar systems. Their denotational semantics are typically studied using categorical techniques; many different categorical structures have been introduced to model them (contextual categories, categories with families, display map categories, etc.) Comparisons of these models are scattered throughout the literature, and a detailed, big-picture analysis of their relationships has been lacking. We aim to provide a clear and comprehensive overview of the relationships between as many such models as possible. Specifically, we take *comprehension categories* as a unifying language, and show how almost all established notions of model embed as sub-2-categories (usually full) of the 2-category of comprehension categories.

Keywords: dependent types · categorical semantics

1 Introduction

Algebraic theories with dependency between their sorts—that is, the *generalised algebraic theories* of Cartmell [12], and similar frameworks—are of interest both in their own right, and as the structural core of richer type theories such as Martin-Löf type theory [30] and its many extensions, Makkai's First Order Logic with Dependent Sorts [29], and others.

The semantics of such systems are usually studied via categorical abstractions. A veritable zoo of these have been considered: contextual categories [11], categories with attributes [11], display map categories [38], categories with families [15], type-categories [34], comprehension categories [23], C-systems [43], B-systems [41], natural models [5], clans [25], and more. Comparisons between

O. Kiselyov (Ed.): APLAS 2024, LNCS 15194, pp. 3–22, 2024.
https://doi.org/10.1007/978-981-97-8943-6_1

many of these have been given in the literature; more are well-known in folklore, and some may be considered too obvious to need spelling out.

However, no accessible overview of this landscape exists. Here, we aim to give a clear summary of the relationships between these different structures for easy reference at a glance. What comparison functors connect different kinds of structures? When are these comparisons equivalences? And when they are not, how significant is the difference?

Summary of results We take the 2-category of *comprehension categories* [23] and pseudo maps as a unified general setting; most other models considered in the literature turn out to embed as certain sub-2-categories theoreof.

The bulk of this paper consists of laying out these embeddings, the comparisons between them, and their properties. The models fall naturally into two groups: first (Sect. 3) those where types are represented as certain "display maps", and second (Sect. 4) those where types are a primitive notion, such as contextual categories and categories with families.

The resulting relationships are summarised in Figs. 1 and 2. The classes of comprehension categories used are defined in Definition 7 below; most are to be read as conditions either on the fibration of types (*split*, *discrete*, etc.) or on the comprehension functor (*fully faithful*, *injective on objects*, etc.).

One flea throughout is whether a terminal object is assumed; many but not all models assume this, often independently of more significant differences. In the summary diagrams we suppress this point, but later we note its inclusion or omission more carefully.

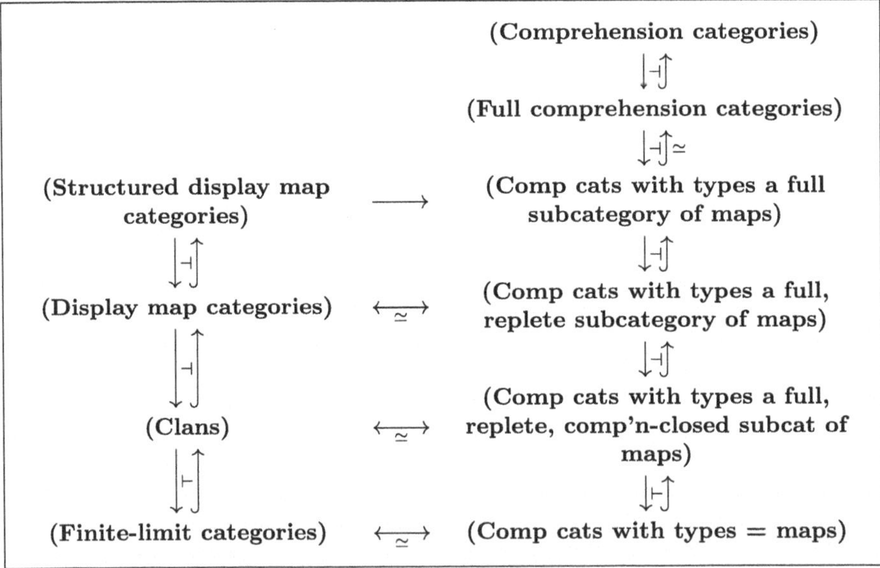

Fig. 1. Models with types as display maps (Sect. 3)

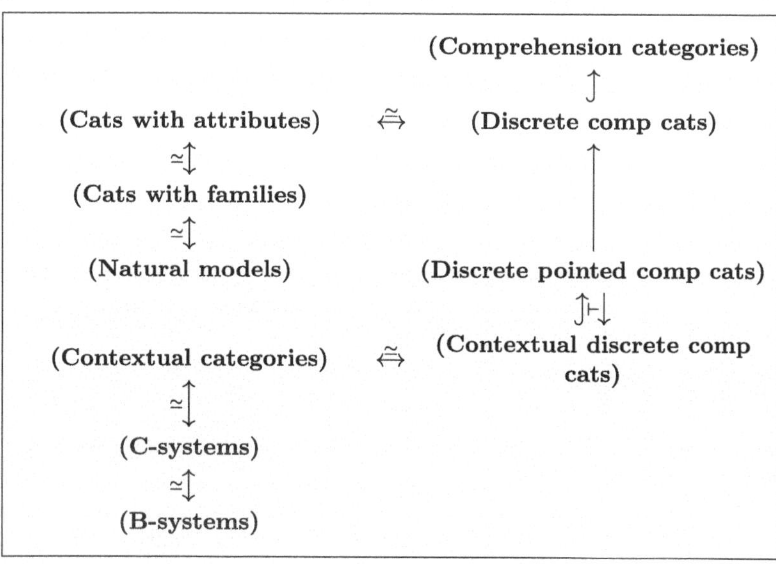

Fig. 2. Models with types as a primitive (Sect. 4)

Prerequisites Any reader familiar with at least one of the notions of model we survey (categories with families, display map categories, clans, etc.) should be able to follow this paper. For background on several such models, and their motivation for interpreting dependent type theories, we recommend Hofmann [21] and Jacobs [23].

The 2-categorical language we rely on is minimal—mostly just 2-categories themselves, and equivalences and adjunctions between them. All our 2-categories and functors are strict; we sometimes view 1-categories as locally discrete 2-categories. For a breezy introduction covering all these, see Power [35].

2 Comprehension Categories: A Broad Church

Comprehension categories were introduced by Jacobs [23] as a common generalisation of earlier models of type dependency. As he intended, they form a good common home in which to compare those notions and others introduced since. In this section we set up the 2-categories of comprehension categories into which we will later embed the other notions considered, along with key constructions and properties of comprehension categories for later use.

2.1 2-Categories of Comprehension Categories

Definition 1. A *comprehension category* consists of (1) a category $\mathcal{C}$ (whose objects we call *contexts*); (2) a fibration $\mathcal{T} \xrightarrow{p} \mathcal{C}$ (of *types*); and (3) a functor

$\mathcal{T} \xrightarrow{\chi} \mathcal{C}^{\rightarrow}$ (*comprehension*); such that (4) χ lies strictly over $\mathcal{C}$, in that $\mathrm{cod} \circ \chi = p$, and is cartesian, i.e. sends p-cartesian maps to pullback squares.

$$\begin{array}{ccc} \mathcal{T} & \xrightarrow{\chi} & \mathcal{C}^{\rightarrow} \\ & {\scriptstyle p}\searrow \quad \swarrow{\scriptstyle \mathrm{cod}} & \\ & \mathcal{C} & \end{array}$$

We write the comprehension $\chi(A)$ of a type $A \in \mathcal{T}_\Gamma$ as $\Gamma.A \longrightarrow A$ (where $\mathcal{T}_\Gamma$ denotes the fiber $p^{-1}\Gamma$). We often refer to a comprehension category $(\mathcal{C}, \mathcal{T}, p, \chi)$ just as $\mathcal{C}$, and so on for other structures.

Definition 2.

1. A *pseudo map* $(F, \bar{F}, \varphi) : (\mathcal{C}, \mathcal{T}, p, \chi) \to (\mathcal{C}', \mathcal{T}', p', \chi')$ of comprehension categories consists of a functor $F : \mathcal{C} \to \mathcal{C}'$; a functor $\bar{F} : \mathcal{T} \to \mathcal{T}'$ lying (strictly) over F, and sending p-cartesian maps to p'-cartesian maps; and a natural isomorphism $\varphi : \chi'\bar{F} \cong F^{\rightarrow}\chi$ lying (strictly) over the identity natural transformation on F (so φ witnesses that F preserves context extension up to isomorphism):

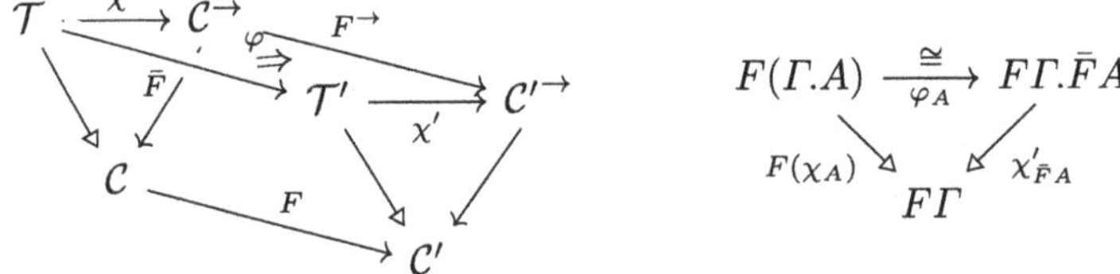

2. A *strict map* is a pseudo map which preserves context extension on the nose; that is, $\chi'\bar{F} = F^{\rightarrow}\chi$, and φ is the identity.

Remark 3. Strict maps of comprehension categories are considered by Blanco [9]. The earliest source for pseudo maps we know is Curien–Garner–Hofmann ([14], §5.1).[1] We agree with the latter authors that *maps* of comprehension categories should mean "pseudo map" by default; but in the present paper, we will generally explicitly specify whether maps are pseudo or strict.

Definition 4. A *transformation* of pseudo maps $(F, \bar{F}, \varphi) \Longrightarrow (G, \bar{G}, \gamma)$ consists of a natural transformation $\alpha : F \Longrightarrow G$, and another $\bar{\alpha} : \bar{F} \Longrightarrow \bar{G}$ lying (strictly) over α, such that for each $A \in \mathcal{T}_\Gamma$ we have $\gamma_A \chi'(\bar{\alpha}_A) = \alpha_{\Gamma.A}\varphi_A$.

Definition 5. We write $\mathbf{CompCat}^{\mathrm{ps}}$ (or just $\mathbf{CompCat}$) for the 2-category of comprehension categories, pseudo maps, and transformations; $\mathbf{CompCat}^{\mathrm{str2}}$ for the 2-category of comprehension categories, strict maps, and transformations; and $\mathbf{CompCat}^{\mathrm{str1}}$ for the 1-category of comprehension categories and strict maps.

[1] Note however that their *strict* maps are stronger than ours, strictly preserving chosen cleavings on the fibration of types.

Definition 6. Let $(\mathcal{C}, \mathcal{T}, p, \chi)$ be a comprehension category, and $\Gamma \in \mathcal{C}$ any object. The *contextual slice* $\mathcal{C} /\!\!/ \Gamma$ is the comprehension category in which:

1. objects of $\mathcal{C} /\!\!/ \Gamma$ are finite sequences $(A_0, \ldots, A_{n-1})$ in which $A_k \in \mathcal{T}_{\Gamma.A_0 \ldots A_{k-1}}$, for each $0 \leq k < n$;
2. maps $(A_0, \ldots, A_{n-1}) \to (B_0, \ldots, B_{m-1})$ are maps
$$\Gamma.A_0 \ldots A_{n-1} \to \Gamma.B_0 \ldots B_{m-1}$$
in the slice $\mathcal{C}/\Gamma$;
3. the new fibration of types is the pullback of $\mathcal{T}$ along the functor $\mathcal{C} /\!\!/ \Gamma \to \mathcal{C}$ sending $(A_0, \ldots, A_{n-1})$ to the context extension $\Gamma.A_0, \ldots, A_{n-1}$;
4. the new comprehension is given by $(A_0, \ldots, A_{n-1}).B := (A_0, \ldots, A_{n-1}, B)$, with the evident projection $\chi(B)$.

This construction is given for display map categories by Taylor ([39], Def. 8.3.8), and for categories with attributes by Kapulkin and Lumsdaine ([26], Def. 2.4).

We can now delineate various important subclasses of comprehension categories, and notation for the resulting full sub-2-categories of **CompCat**:

Definition 7. A comprehension category $(\mathcal{C}, \mathcal{T}, p, \chi)$ is called:

1. *full* if χ is fully faithful (with the 2-category of these denoted $\mathbf{CompCat}_{\mathrm{full}}$);
2. *subcategorical* if χ is a full subcategory inclusion, i.e. full, faithful, and injective on objects ($\mathbf{CompCat}_{\mathrm{sub}}$);
3. *replete* (assuming it is subcategorical) if $\mathcal{T}$ is a replete subcategory of $\mathcal{C}^{\to}$ ($\mathbf{CompCat}_{\mathrm{repl}}$);
4. *composition-closed* (assuming subcategorical) if $\mathcal{T}$ is closed under composition and includes identities ($\mathbf{CompCat}_{\mathrm{sub,compcl}}$);
5. *trivial* if χ is an identity ($\mathbf{CompCat}_{\mathrm{triv}}$);
6. *discrete* if p is a discrete fibration ($\mathbf{CompCat}_{\mathrm{disc}}$);
7. *split* if p is a split fibration ($\mathbf{CompCat}_{\mathrm{spl}}$).

These subscripts combine in the obvious ways: for instance, $\mathbf{CompCat}_{\mathrm{full,spl}}$ is the 2-category of full comprehension categories with a subcategory inclusion.

We also sometimes restrict the maps in the split case: we say a map of split comprehension categories is *split* if it preserves the chosen splitting on the nose, and denote the resulting sub-2-category $\mathbf{CompCat}^{\mathrm{spl}}_{\mathrm{spl}}$.

Lastly we consider some notions which also add restrictions on the maps:

Definition 8. A *pointed* comprehension category **CompCat** is one equipped with a distinguished object $\diamond \in \mathcal{C}$; a map is pointed (resp. strictly pointed) if it preserves $\diamond$ up to specified isomorphism (resp. on the nose); a transformation is pointed if its value at $\diamond$ commutes with the given isomorphism. We write $\mathbf{CompCat}^{\mathrm{ps}}_{\diamond}$, $\mathbf{CompCat}^{\mathrm{str2}}_{\diamond}$ for the resulting 2-categories.

A pointed comprehension category is *rooted* if its distinguished object is terminal (so written 1) and the map $\mathcal{C} /\!\!/ 1 \to \mathcal{C}$ is essentially surjective (that is, every object is isomorphic to some context extension of 1); and *contextual* if $\mathcal{C}\between 1 \to \mathcal{C}$ is moreover bijective on objects (and hence an isomorphism) (so every object is *uniquely* expressible as an extension of 1). We write $\mathbf{CompCat}_{\mathrm{rtd}}$, $\mathbf{CompCat}_{\mathrm{cxl}}$ for the resulting full sub-2-categories of $\mathbf{CompCat}_{\diamond}$.

Remark 9. Many of these conditions are not invariant under equivalence of categories, as they involve on-the-nose equality of objects. In each case, one can of course generalise them to a property closed under equivalence; we work with the present versions since they correspond most naturally and tightly to the other structures we are comparing—display map categories, categories with attributes, and so on.

Remark 10. Why do we insist on 2-categories? 1-categories are technically simpler, and are used in much of the literature on these structures; e.g., Blanco [9] compares 1-categories of categories with attributes, contextual categories, and comprehension categories. Abstractly, experience from category theory suggests that categorical structures should always be analysed 2-categorically. But, as they should be, these abstract considerations are justified by applications.

A comprehensive analysis must include pseudo maps, since maps between non-syntactic comprehension categories are often not strict; and even when they are (usually in the cases where strict maps are equivalent to pseudo maps, because the source is contextual or the target replete, cf. Corollary 47, Theorem 16), the strictness may be lost if for instance we pass to strictifications to interpret syntax as done by Hofmann [20].

Once we admit pseudo maps, however, we must also admit some 2-cells to keep the resulting (1- or 2-) category well-behaved. For instance, the syntactic contextual category of a type theory is typically 1-categorically initial in a 1-category of models with strict maps [10, 36], and bicategorically initial in a 2-category of pseudo maps, but *not* initial in either sense in a 1-category of pseudo maps.

3 Frameworks with Types as Certain Maps

In this section, we consider frameworks where types are represented as certain maps of a category—*display maps*.

These first appear in work of the Cambridge group (Hyland, Pitts, and Taylor) from the late eighties [22, 38], with some variation in details and terminology. We primarily follow recent literature in our terminology, but note historical differences in usage.

We consider three main notions, successively broadening the franchise of display maps by imposing stronger closure conditions:

1. *display map categories* (and their *structured* variant), assuming just closure under pullback;
2. *clans*, adding closure under composition and identities;
3. *finite-limit categories*, the limiting case in which all maps are display.

3.1 Display Map Categories

Definition 11 (Hyland–Pitts ([22], §2.2), Taylor ([39], Def. 8.3.2)). A *display map category*[2] is a category $\mathcal{C}$ together with a replete (i.e. isomorphism-invariant) subclass $\mathcal{D} \subseteq \mathrm{mor}(\mathcal{C})$ of maps (called *display maps* and written $\longrightarrow\!\!\triangleright$), such that display maps pull back along arbitrary maps; that is, for any display map d and map f into its target, there is some display map f^*d that is a pullback of d along f:

$$\begin{array}{ccc} \cdot & \dashrightarrow & \cdot \\ {\scriptstyle f^*d}\,\downarrow\!\triangledown & \lrcorner & \downarrow\!\triangledown\,{\scriptstyle d} \\ \cdot & \xrightarrow[f]{} & \cdot \end{array} \tag{1}$$

We call such a $\mathcal{D}$ a *class of display maps* in $\mathcal{C}$.

Example 12. ([39] Ex. 8.3.6e) A map is called *carrable* if it admits pullbacks along arbitrary maps, as in Diagram (1). Given any class D of carrable maps in a category $\mathcal{C}$, its closure under pullbacks $\mathcal{D}$ gives a class of display maps in $\mathcal{C}$.

Example 13. (Awodey–Warren [6]) Important natural examples are given by *weak factorization systems* and their *algebraic* variants. Given a category with a (possibly algebraic) weak factorisation system, we take the display maps to be the right maps of the wfs (often called *fibrations*), which are always stable under pullback. In particular, in any Quillen model category, the fibrations form a class of display maps, yielding as instances Kan fibrations in the category of simplicial sets, or Hurewicz or Serre fibrations in the category of topological spaces.

Lemma 14. *Any display map category $(\mathcal{C}, \mathcal{D})$ gives a comprehension category $(\mathcal{C}, \mathcal{D}, \mathrm{cod} \circ \iota, \iota)$ where $\iota : \mathcal{D} \hookrightarrow \mathcal{C}^{\to}$ is the inclusion of $\mathcal{D}$ viewed as a full subcategory of $\mathcal{C}^{\to}$.*

Proof. The assumed pullbacks ensure that $\mathcal{D} \to \mathcal{C}$ is a fibration, and ι cartesian.

Definition 15. A map of display map categories is a functor preserving display maps and pullbacks thereof; a transformation of these is simply a natural transformation between functors. Write **DMC** for the resulting 2-category.

Theorem 16. *Lemma 14 lifts to give an isomorphism and an equivalence*

$$\mathbf{DMC} \cong \mathbf{CompCat}^{\mathrm{str2}}_{\mathrm{repl}} \equiv \mathbf{CompCat}_{\mathrm{repl}}$$

where these denote the 2-categories of comprehension categories whose comprehension is a replete subcategory inclusion, with strict and pseudo maps respectively (but with all 2-cells in both cases).

---

[2] These appear in Hyland–Pitts ([22], §2.2) as classes satisfying "**stability**", and in Taylor ([39], Def. 8.3.2) as *classes of displays*.

Proof. It is clear that Lemma 14 underlies a 2-functor $\mathbf{DMC} \to \mathbf{CompCat}$, whose image consists of precisely the replete subcategorical comprehension categories. It remains to show that it is 2-fully-faithful, and its image on 1-cells consists precisely of the strict maps.

Given display map categories $(\mathcal{C}, \mathcal{D})$, $(\mathcal{C}', \mathcal{D}')$, a map of comprehension categories $(\mathcal{C}, \mathcal{D}, \mathrm{cod} \circ \iota, \iota) \to (\mathcal{C}', \mathcal{D}', \mathrm{cod} \circ \iota', \iota')$ amounts to a functor $F : \mathcal{C} \to \mathcal{C}'$ together with a functor $\bar{F} : \mathcal{D} \to \mathcal{D}'$, preserving cartesian morphisms (i.e. pullback squares as in Diagram (1)) together with natural isomorphisms $\varphi_d : \bar{F}d \cong d$. Such data $\bar{F}$, φ certainly implies (by repleteness of $\mathcal{D}$) that F preserves display maps and their pullbacks, hence is a map in **DMC**. Conversely, given that F is such a map, suitable $\bar{F}$, φ are given by $F^{\to}|_{\mathcal{D}}$ and the identity isomorphism (yielding a strict map of comprehension categories), and any other such $(\bar{F}, \varphi)$ are uniquely isomorphic to these.

Finally, 2-cells in **CompCat** are pairs $(\alpha, \bar{\alpha}) : (F, \bar{F}, \varphi) \to (G, \bar{G}, \gamma)$; but since the comprehension of $(\mathcal{C}', \mathcal{D}')$ is fully faithful, any such α uniquely determines a suitable $\bar{\alpha}$.

This theorem justifies regarding display map categories precisely as replete subcategorical comprehension categories.

Theorem 17. *The following inclusions of subcategories of comprehension categories have left adjoints or are equivalences, as shown below.*

$$\mathbf{CompCat}_{\mathrm{repl}} \underset{\hookrightarrow}{\overset{\longleftarrow}{\simeq}} \mathbf{CompCat}_{\mathrm{sub}} \underset{\hookrightarrow}{\overset{\longleftarrow}{\simeq}} \mathbf{CompCat}_{\mathrm{full}} \underset{\hookrightarrow}{\overset{\longleftarrow}{\perp}} \mathbf{CompCat}$$

Proof. Starting on the right with the inclusion $\mathbf{CompCat}_{\mathrm{full}} \hookrightarrow \mathbf{CompCat}$, the left adjoint "fullification" sends a comprehension category $(\mathcal{C}, \mathcal{T}, p, \chi)$ to $(\mathcal{C}, \mathcal{T}_\chi, p', \chi')$ where $\mathcal{T} \to \mathcal{T}_\chi \to [\chi']\mathcal{C}^{\to}$ is the factorisation of χ as identity-on-objects followed by fully faithful; concretely $\mathcal{T}_\chi$ has the objects of $\mathcal{T}$, but arrows induced by χ from $\mathcal{C}^{\to}$. Isomorphisms of hom-categories making this a (strict 2-)adjunction follow formally from the fact that (bijective-on-objects, fully faithful) forms an orthogonal factorization system on **Cat** ([28], §4(a))]:

$$\begin{aligned} &\mathbf{CompCat}_{\mathrm{full}}((\mathcal{C}_1, (\mathcal{T}_1)_\chi, p_1', \chi_1'), (\mathcal{C}_2, \mathcal{T}_2, p_2, \chi_2)) \\ &\qquad \cong \mathbf{CompCat}((\mathcal{C}_1, \mathcal{T}_1, p_1, \chi_1), (\mathcal{C}_2, \mathcal{T}_2, p_2, \chi_2)) \end{aligned}$$

The middle inclusion $\mathbf{CompCat}_{\mathrm{sub}} \hookrightarrow \mathbf{CompCat}_{\mathrm{full}}$ has a left adjoint given by factoring a fully faithful comprehension functor $\chi : \mathcal{T} \to \mathcal{C}^{\to}$ by its image subcategory $\mathrm{im}\,\chi$; this again gives a strict 2-adjunction, but now moreover a biequivalence, since the unit map $(\mathcal{C}, \mathcal{T}, p, \chi) \to (\mathcal{C}, \mathrm{im}\,\chi, \iota, \mathrm{cod})$ is an equivalence in **CompCat**.

Finally, $\mathbf{CompCat}_{\mathrm{sub}} \hookrightarrow \mathbf{CompCat}_{\mathrm{repl}}$ has a left adjoint sending a subcategory inclusion $\mathcal{T} \hookrightarrow \mathcal{C}^{\to}$ to its repletion $\mathrm{repl}\,\mathcal{T} \hookrightarrow \mathcal{C}$. Again, the unit maps are equivalences, and we have an isomorphism of hom-categories giving a strict 2-adjunction:

$$\begin{aligned}&\mathbf{CompCat}_{\mathrm{repl}}((\mathcal{C}_1, \mathrm{repl}\, \mathcal{T}_1, p_1', \chi_1'), (\mathcal{C}_2, \mathcal{T}_2, p_2, \chi_2)) \\ &\qquad\qquad \equiv \mathbf{CompCat}_{\mathrm{sub}}((\mathcal{C}_1, \mathcal{T}_1, p_1, \chi_1), (\mathcal{C}_2, \mathcal{T}_2, p_2, \chi_2))\end{aligned}$$

Structured Display Map Categories The repleteness condition on display maps is occasionally dropped. The resulting notion is relatively little-used, and seems to enjoy few advantages, perhaps because (as we argue below) their natural maps are "wrong".

Definition 18 (Taylor ([39], Def. 8.3.2)). A *display structure* on a category $\mathcal{C}$ is a class of maps $\mathcal{D} \subseteq \mathrm{mor}(\mathcal{C})$, again called *display maps*, such that display maps admit all pullbacks as in Diagram (1) above. A *structured display map category* (sDMC) is a category equipped with a display structure.

Remark 19. Taylor ([39], Def. 8.3.2) couples repleteness with the question of chosen pullbacks versus existence. The latter point matters mainly under a more fine-grained constructive analysis than we aim for; see also Remark 24 below.

Example 20. The category of sets with subset inclusions as display maps forms an sDMC.

The obvious notion of maps is the same as for DMC's.

Definition 21. Let **sDMC** denote the 2-category whose objects are structured display map categories, 1-cells are functors preserving display maps and pullbacks of display maps, and 2-cells are natural transformations.

Like DMC's, sDMC's may be regarded as certain comprehension categories.

Theorem 22. *There is an isomorphism* $\mathbf{sDMC} \cong \mathbf{CompCat}^{\mathrm{str2}}_{\mathrm{sub}}$ *where the latter 2-category consists of full comprehension categories where* χ *is a subcategory inclusion, and with strict maps as 1-cells.*

In contrast to Theorem 16, pseudo and strict maps do not agree for sDMC's:

Example 23. Take $\mathcal{C}$ to be the full subcategory of **FinSet** on $\{0, 1, 2\}$, with injections as display maps. With any choice of pullbacks, this gives an sDMC.

Take $\mathcal{C}'$ to be similar but with two isomorphic copies of 1, so with objects $\{0, 1, 1', 2\}$. As displays, take all injections, except for maps $1 \to 2$, where we make the left point $l : 1 \to 2$ a display map, and the right point $r' : 1' \to 2$, but *not* $r : 1 \to 2$ or $l' : 1' \to 2$. Pullbacks for a display structure can still be chosen: whenever a pullback yields a point-inclusion into 2, either l or r' will suffice.

$\mathcal{C}$ and $\mathcal{C}'$ have equivalent repletions, so are equivalent via pseudo maps. However, no equivalence $F : \mathcal{C} \to \mathcal{C}'$ can strictly preserve display maps, since $Fl, Fr : F1 \to F2$ would give distinct parallel display maps from either 1 or $1'$ to 2. So not every pseudo map $\mathcal{C} \to \mathcal{C}'$ is isomorphic to a strict one.

Remark 24. If we take sDMC's to include chosen pullbacks, and additionally require maps of sDMC's to preserve these on the nose (the definition of *interpretations* in Taylor ([39], Def. 8.3.2) is unclear on this point), then these correspond to maps of *cloven* comprehension categories strictly preserving the cleaving, and so diverge even further from the pseudo maps.

Theorem 25. *The inclusion* $\mathbf{DMC} \hookrightarrow \mathbf{sDMC}$*, or equivalently* $\mathbf{CompCat}^{\mathrm{str2}}_{\mathrm{repl}} \hookrightarrow \mathbf{CompCat}^{\mathrm{str2}}_{\mathrm{sub}}$*, has a left adjoint.*

Proof. The left adjoint is given by repletion, as in Theorem 17.

Rooted Display Map Categories Relatively little changes when we add roots.

Definition 26. ([39], **Rem. 8.3.9**) A (possibly structured) display map category is *rooted* if $\mathcal{C}$ has a terminal object, and all morphisms to the terminal object are composites of display maps and isomorphisms. (In the non-structured case, repleteness renders the isomorphisms redundant.)

Let $\mathbf{DMC}_{\mathrm{rtd}}$ be the (non-1-full) sub-2-category of $\mathbf{DMC}$ consisting of rooted display map categories, maps additionally preserving terminal objects, and all transformations.

Example 27. Weak factorisation systems, considered as display map categories following Example 13, are often rooted: for instance, those coming from model categories with all objects fibrant, such as **Top** with either Serre or Hurewicz fibrations. When this fails, such as the Kan model structure on simplicial sets, we may still restrict to the full subcategory of fibrant objects (Kan complexes) to recover rootedness.

This notion of rootedness agrees with rootedness for comprehension categories as given in Definition 8:

Theorem 28. *Theorems 16, 17, 22 and 25 remain true with rootedness added, with one caveat: the "strict" 2-categories should take maps that are strict on comprehension categories, but not necessarily strictly rooted.*

We do not restate them in full here; they are summarised in Fig. 4 below.

3.2 Clans

Definition 29 (Taylor ([38], §4.3.2)). A *clan*[3] is a rooted display map category $(\mathcal{C}, \mathcal{D})$ where $\mathcal{D}$ is closed under composition and contains all identities.

[3] This name is due to Joyal ([25], Def. 1.1.1); in fact these are the original *classes of display maps* of Taylor ([38], §4.3.2).

Example 30. Display map categories arising from weak factorization systems as in Examples 13 and 27 are always closed under composition and identities, so are clans whenever they are rooted, i.e. when all objects are fibrant.

Write **Clan** for the 2-category of clans, as a full sub-2-category of $\mathbf{DMC}_{\mathrm{rtd}}$.

Theorem 31. $\mathbf{Clan} \cong \mathbf{CompCat}^{\mathrm{str2}}_{\mathrm{rtd,repl,compcl}} \simeq \mathbf{CompCat}_{\mathrm{rtd,repl,compcl}}$.

Proof. Immediate by restriction of

$$\mathbf{DMC}_{\mathrm{rtd}} \cong \mathbf{CompCat}^{\mathrm{str2}}_{\mathrm{rtd,repl}} \equiv \mathbf{CompCat}_{\mathrm{rtd,repl}}$$

from Theorem 28 (so again, "strict" maps here preserve comprehension strictly, but not necessarily the root).

Theorem 32. *The inclusions*

$$\mathbf{CompCat}^{\mathrm{str22}}_{\mathrm{(rtd,)repl,compcl}} \hookrightarrow \mathbf{CompCat}^{\mathrm{str22}}_{\mathrm{(rtd,)repl}}$$

have a left adjoint (in four versions: rooted and unrooted, strict and unstrict); hence so does the inclusion $\mathbf{Clan} \hookrightarrow \mathbf{DMC}_{\mathrm{rtd}}$.

Proof. We take first the least restrictive case,

$$\mathbf{CompCat}_{\mathrm{repl,compcl}} \hookrightarrow \mathbf{CompCat}_{\mathrm{repl}} \simeq \mathbf{DMC}$$

The left adjoint sends a display map category $(\mathcal{C}, \mathcal{D})$ to $(\mathcal{C}, \overline{\mathcal{D}})$, where $\overline{\mathcal{D}}$ is the closure of $\mathcal{D}$ under composition. It is straightforward to check this gives a (strict 2-)adjoint, and does not interact with either rootedness or strictness of maps, so restricts to give the other adjoints desired.

3.3 Finite-Limit Categories

Finite limit categories (also called *left exact* or *lex* categories) are longest-established notion we consider, predating dependent sorts, and with a literature too deep and wide to comprehensively survey. Logically they model *essentially algebraic theories*, which may be presented syntactically in several ways (see, for instance, [17], ([2], 3.D), [33]) or categorically by *sketches* [27]. They correspond under Gabriel–Ulmer duality [1,18] to *locally finitely presentable categories.* Good surveys are given by Adámek and Rosický [2] and Johnstone ([24] D1–2).

Definition 33. We write **Lex** for the 2-category of categories with finite limits, functors preserving finite limits, and natural transformations.

Definition 34. A finite-limit category $\mathcal{C}$ determines a clan $(\mathcal{C}, \mathrm{mor}(\mathcal{C}))$, with all morphisms taken as display maps.

Recall that a comprehension category is called *trivial* if its fibration of types is precisely its codomain fibration.

Lemma 35. $\mathbf{Lex} \cong \mathbf{CompCat}^{\mathrm{str2}}_{\mathrm{rtd,triv}} \equiv \mathbf{CompCat}_{\mathrm{rtd,triv}}$.

Proof. The construction of Definition 34 evidently underlies a 2-functor $\mathbf{Lex} \hookrightarrow \mathbf{Clan}$; this is 2-fully faithful, since preserving pullbacks and the terminal object implies preserving all finite limits. Then composing with the isomorphism $\mathbf{Clan} \cong \mathbf{CompCat}^{\mathrm{str2}}_{\mathrm{rtd,repl,compcl}}$, the image is precisely $\mathbf{CompCat}_{\mathrm{rtd,triv}}$.

Theorem 36. *The inclusion* $\mathbf{Lex} \hookrightarrow \mathbf{Clan}$*, or, equivalently, the inclusion* $\mathbf{CompCat}_{\mathrm{rtd,triv}} \hookrightarrow \mathbf{CompCat}_{\mathrm{rtd,repl,compcl}}$*, has a right adjoint.*

Proof. The right adjoint sends a clan $(\mathcal{C}, \mathcal{D})$ to the full category $\mathcal{C}_{\mathrm{sep}} \subseteq \mathcal{C}$ of objects whose diagonal is a display map ("*separated* objects").

All maps in $\mathcal{C}_{\mathrm{sep}}$ are display in $\mathcal{C}$ (if Y is separated, any $f : X \to Y$ is the composite of $(f \times Y)^* \Delta_Y : X \twoheadrightarrow X \times Y$ and $\pi_2 : X \times Y \twoheadrightarrow Y$), and finite products and equalisers in $\mathcal{C}_{\mathrm{sep}}$ are direct to construct; so $\mathcal{C}_{\mathrm{sep}}$ is lex and the inclusion $(\mathcal{C}_{\mathrm{sep}}, \mathcal{C}_{\mathrm{sep}}{}^{\to}) \to (\mathcal{C}, \mathcal{D})$ is a map of clans; and any other map from a trivial clan to $(\mathcal{C}, \mathcal{D})$ certainly factors uniquely through $\mathcal{C}_{\mathrm{sep}}$. The higher-dimensional parts of the adjunction follow essentially formally.

4 Frameworks with Types as Primitive

We turn our attention now to frameworks in which types are not merely certain maps, but a primitive notion. Compared to the models of Sect. 3, those of this section reflect the syntax of type theory more precisely, but are correspondingly further from the natural organisation of more "mathematical" models.

The main group consists of several very closely related notions, essentially reformulations of each other with slightly different emphasis and permitting different generalisations: categories with attributes [11,31], (split) type-categories [7,34], categories with families [15], and natural models [5].[4] These models may be (and have been) viewed either as *discrete* or as *full split* comprehension categories.

Finally, we reach a venerable and authoritative notion: the *contextual categories* of Cartmell [11]. This too has enjoyed several later reformulations as C-systems [43] and B-systems [3,41].

4.1 Categories with Families, and Equivalents

We first consider categories with attributes, since they make the comparison with comprehension categories most straightforward.

Definition 37 (Cartmell ([11], §3.2), Moggi ([31], Def. 6.2)). A *category with attributes (CwA)*[5] consists of a category $\mathcal{C}$; a presheaf $\mathrm{Ty} : \mathcal{C}^{\mathrm{op}} \to \mathbf{Set}$;

[4] As the Swedish saying goes, *kärt barn har många namn.*

[5] The original CwA's of Cartmell ([11], §3.2) also included further structure corresponding to type-constructors. This was stripped down to the present definition by Pitts ([34], Def. 6.9) (there called *type-categories*) and Moggi ([31], Def. 6.2), and most subsequent literature has followed suit.

a functor $(-.-) : \int_{\mathcal{C}} \mathrm{Ty} \to \mathcal{C}$; and a natural transformation $p : (-.-) \to \pi_1$, cartesian in that its naturality squares are pullbacks.

$$\begin{array}{ccc} \Gamma'.f^*A & \xrightarrow{f.A} & \Gamma.A \\ {\scriptstyle p_{f^*A}}\downarrow & \lrcorner & \downarrow{\scriptstyle p_A} \\ \Gamma' & \xrightarrow{f} & \Gamma \end{array}$$

A *(strict) map* of CwA's is a homomorphism of them considered as essentially algebraic structures in the evident way; equivalently, a functor $F : \mathcal{C} \to \mathcal{C}'$ and natural transformation $\bar{F} : \mathrm{Ty} \to \mathrm{Ty}' \cdot F$, commuting on the nose with $(-.-)$ and p.

A *pseudo map* consists of F and $\bar{F}$ as in a homomorphism and a natural isomorphism $\varphi : F-.- \cong F-.\bar{F}-$, commuting with p in that $p_F A \varphi_{\Gamma,A} = F p_A$ for all Γ, A. A *transformation* of pseudo maps $\alpha : (F, \bar{F}, \varphi) \to (G, \bar{G}, \psi)$ is a natural transformation $\alpha : F \to G$, such that for each Γ, A, $(\alpha_\Gamma)^*(\bar{G}A) = \bar{F}A$ and $\alpha_{G\Gamma.A}\psi\Gamma, A = \varphi_{\Gamma,A}\alpha_\Gamma.\bar{F}A$.

We write $\mathbf{CwA}^{\mathrm{str1}}$ for the 1-category of CwA's with strict maps, and $\mathbf{CwA}^{\mathrm{ps}}$ for their 2-category with pseudo maps and transformations.

Most literature considers just the 1-category of strict maps; we know no source presenting pseudo maps for CwA's, though they must be intended in for instance the "suitable 2-category" of ([7], Rem. 2.2.2).

It is clear, as noted from the beginning by Jacobs ([23], Ex. 4.10), that categories with attributes simply "are" discrete comprehension categories; precisely, we have:

Proposition 38. $\mathbf{CwA}^{\mathrm{str1}} \equiv \mathbf{CompCat}^{\mathrm{str1}}_{\mathrm{disc}}$, *and* $\mathbf{CwA}^{\mathrm{ps}} \equiv \mathbf{CompCat}^{\mathrm{ps}}_{\mathrm{disc}}$.

Proof. This comes down to the classical equivalence between presheaves and discrete fibrations. The 1-categorical version is presented in Blanco ([9], Thm. 2.3); the 2-categorical version is similarly direct.

They may be alternatively viewed as full split comprehension categories:

Proposition 39. $\mathbf{CwA}^{\mathrm{str1}} \equiv \mathbf{CompCat}^{\mathrm{str1,spl}}_{\mathrm{full,spl}}$ *and* $\mathbf{CwA}^{\mathrm{ps}} \equiv \mathbf{CompCat}^{\mathrm{ps,spl}}_{\mathrm{full,spl}}$.
Note that even in the pseudo version we restrict to split maps, i.e. strictly preserving chosen lifts.

Proof. Both equivalences are direct, using fullification in one direction (as in Theorem 17), and taking the discrete core of a split fibration in the other. The 1-categorical equivalence is presented by Blanco ([9], Thm. 2.4).

CwA's were reformulated by Dybjer to make *terms*, a core component of the syntax of type theory, equally primitive in the semantics:

Definition 40 (Dybjer ([15], Def. 1)). A *category with families (CwF)* consists of a category $\mathcal{C}$; a presheaf Ty on $\mathcal{C}$; a presheaf Tm on $\int_{\mathcal{C}} \mathrm{Ty}$; and for each $\Gamma \in \mathcal{C}$ and $A \in \mathrm{Ty}(\Gamma)$, an object $\Gamma.A$ and map $p_A : \Gamma.A \to \Gamma$ *representing* $\mathrm{Tm}(A, \Gamma)$ in the sense of a certain universal property.

A *strict map* of CwF's consists of a functor and suitable natural transformations on Ty and Tm, preserving the chosen extensions $\Gamma.A$, p_A on the nose. These are the only maps considered by Dybjer [15] and most literature; we denote their 1-category by $\mathbf{CwF}^{\mathrm{str1}}$.

A *weak map*[6] of CwF's ([8], Def. 14) consists of the same data, but preserving context extensions in the weaker sense that their images satisfy the same universal property in the target CwF. With a suitable notion of transformation, we denote their 2-category $\mathbf{CwF}^{\mathrm{wk}}$.

A *pseudo map* of CwF's ([13], Def. 9) is weaker still, preserving reindexing of types and terms only up to coherent isomorphism. With transformations as defined there, we denote the 2-category of these by $\mathbf{CwF}^{\mathrm{ps}}$.

Proposition 41.

1. $\mathbf{CwF}^{\mathrm{str1}} \equiv \mathbf{CwA}^{\mathrm{str1}}$;
2. $\mathbf{CwF}^{\mathrm{wk}} \equiv \mathbf{CwA}^{\mathrm{ps}}$;
3. $\mathbf{CwF}^{\mathrm{ps}} \equiv \mathbf{CompCat}^{\mathrm{ps}}_{\mathrm{full,spl}}$. *(Note we use split comprehension categories here, but do not restrict to split maps.)*

Proof. The core comparison between CwF's and CwA's is given by Hofmann ([21], §3.2) (and formalised by Ahrens, Lumsdaine, and Voevodsky [4]); checking this extends to the claimed equivalences is routine.

Natural models [5,16] are a further reformulation of categories with families, especially fruitful in paving the way for the massive generalisation by Uemura [40].

Definition 42. A *natural model* consists of a category $\mathcal{C}$, and a pair of objects in $\hat{\mathcal{C}}$ connected by a map $p : \mathrm{Tm} \to \mathrm{Ty}$, which is *representable* in that the pullback of any representable along it is a representable, and *structured* if it is equipped with a choice of such pullbacks.

A *pseudo map* of these is a functor $F : \mathcal{C} \to \mathcal{C}'$, and a commutative square from p to F^*p' in $\hat{\mathcal{C}}$, such that F sends the representing pullbacks of p to representing pullbacks of F; a transformation of these is a natural transformation $\alpha : F \to F'$ commuting with the given squares to F^*p', G^*p'. A map of structured natural models is *strict* if it preserves the chosen representations on the nose.

We write $\mathbf{NatMod}^{\mathrm{ps}}$ for the 2-category of natural models with pseudo maps and transformations, and $\mathbf{NatMod}^{\mathrm{str1}}$ for the 1-category of structured natural models and strict maps.

These maps are defined by Newstead ([32], §2.3) (with the strict as default); it is direct that the comparisons between natural models and CwFs given by Awodey ([5], Prop. 2) extend to equivalences:

Proposition 43. $\mathbf{NatMod}^{\mathrm{str1}} \equiv \mathbf{CwF}^{\mathrm{str1}}$, *and* $\mathbf{NatMod}^{\mathrm{ps}} \equiv \mathbf{CwF}^{\mathrm{wk}}$.

[6] We would call these pseudo, but it would clash with both ([8], Def. 14) and ([13], Def. 9).

Finally, Van den Berg and Garner ([7], Def. 2.2.1) borrow the "type-category" terminology for CwA's from Pitts ([34], Def. 6.9) but call them *split type-categories*, and use *type-categories* for a slightly weaker, non-split notion. Type-categories in this sense, with the right natural definitions of maps and 2-cells, are straightforwardly shown equivalent to full comprehension categories.

4.2 Contextual Categories, and Equivalents

Contextual categories are introduced in Cartmell's dissertation ([11], §2). The definition is rather lengthy; we recall it roughly, and quickly replace it with a much simpler reformulation.

Definition 44 (Cartmell ([11], §2.2)). A *contextual category* consists of (1) a category $\mathcal{C}$ equipped with a distinguished terminal object 1; (2) a tree structure on ob$\mathcal{C}$ with root 1; (3) for each non-root object A, a "projection" map p_A from A to its parent; (4) and pullbacks of projections along arbitrary maps to projections $f^*p_A = p_{f^*A}$, strictly functorial in that $1^*A = A$, $(fg)^*A = g^*f^*A$.

A homomorphism of contextual categories is a functor commuting on the nose with all the given structure.

The comparison with categories with attributes is direct, and implicit already in Cartmell's work ([11], §3.2). Call a category with attributes *contextual* if it is so in the sense of Definition 7, when viewed as a discrete comprehension category: that is, each object is uniquely expressible as a context extension of the terminal object.

Proposition 45. *The 1-category* **CxlCat** *of contextual categories and homomorphisms is equivalent to the 1-category* $\mathbf{CwA}^{\mathrm{str1}}_{\mathrm{cxl}}$ *of contextual CwA's and strict maps, and hence to the 1-category* $\mathbf{CompCat}^{\mathrm{str1}}_{\mathrm{disc,cxl}}$ *of discrete, contextual comprehension categories and strict maps.*

The reader may have wondered why for contextual categories, unlike all other notions, we have only introduced strict maps and a 1-category thereof. This is because in the contextual case, it genuinely makes no difference:

Proposition 46. *If* $\mathcal{C}, \mathcal{D}$ *are pointed comprehension categories,* $\mathcal{C}$ *is contextual, and the point of* D *is terminal, then the inclusion* $\mathbf{CompCat}^{\mathrm{str1}}_{\diamond}(\mathcal{C}, \mathcal{D}) \to \mathbf{CompCat}^{\mathrm{ps}}_{\diamond}(\mathcal{C}, \mathcal{D})$ *is an equivalence; in particular,* $\mathbf{CompCat}^{\mathrm{ps}}_{\diamond}(\mathcal{C}, \mathcal{D})$ *is essentially discrete.*

Proof. Any pseudo map $F : \mathcal{C} \to \mathcal{D}$ may be modified to an isomorphic strict map F', by induction on the contextual "length" of objects of $\mathcal{C}$; likewise by induction, any (pointed) transformation of pseudo maps $\alpha : F \to G$ is uniquely determined by F and G.

This implies that for contextual categories, unlike CwA's and similar models, the 1-category of strict maps agrees with the 2-category of pseudo maps, so there is no need to consider pseudo maps or transformations explicitly.

Corollary 47. $\mathbf{CxlCat} \equiv \mathbf{CompCat}^{\mathrm{ps}}_{\mathrm{disc,cxl}} \equiv \mathbf{CompCat}^{\mathrm{str1}}_{\mathrm{disc,cxl}}$.

In this case we drop the superscripts and write just $\mathbf{CompCat}_{\mathrm{disc,cxl}}$. It is straightforward moreover to check:

Proposition 48. *The "contextual core" construction* $\mathcal{C} \mapsto \mathcal{C} \between \diamond$ *gives right (1- and strict 2-)adjoints to the subcategory inclusions* $\mathbf{CxlCat} \hookrightarrow \mathbf{CompCat}^{\mathrm{ps}}_{\mathrm{disc},\diamond}$, $\mathbf{CxlCat} \hookrightarrow \mathbf{CompCat}^{\mathrm{str1}}_{\mathrm{disc},\diamond}$.

Later reformulations of contextual categories include the *C-systems* of Voevodsky ([42], Def. 2.1) (emphasising them as set-level rather than categorical structures); the *B-systems* of Voevodsky [41] (an alternative organisation of the dependency between sorts); and the $\{w, p, s\}$-*GATs* of Garner [19] (elucidating their combinatorial structure). In each case, the key parts of an equivalence of 1-categories with **CxlCat** are sketched in the cited works introducing them; an equivalence of 1-categories of C- and B-systems is presented explicitly by Ahrens, Emmenegger, North, and Rijke ([3], Thm. 4.1).

5 Conclusion

Summary of results We can now recapitulate the summary diagrams from the introduction more precisely. Figures 3 and 4 summarise the notions where types are certain maps, in the rooted and unrooted versions respectively; Fig. 5 similarly summarises the notions with primitive types.

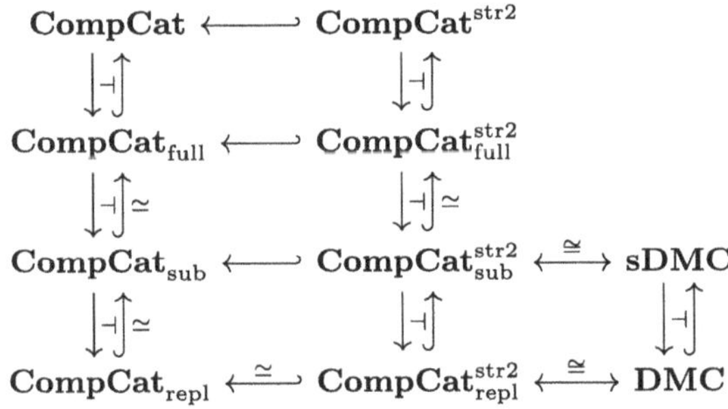

Fig. 3. Notions with types as maps, unrooted

Related work This is not the first article to compare these sorts of structures.

An important early survey is Blanco [9], very comparable to the present work but purely 1-categorical and narrower in scope: Blanco relates categories with attributes, contextual categories, and a version of display map categories by embedding them into the (1-)category of comprehension categories and strict maps.

Similarly, Subramaniam ([37], §1.4) compares 1-categories of various categorical structures including Lawvere theories and contextual categories.

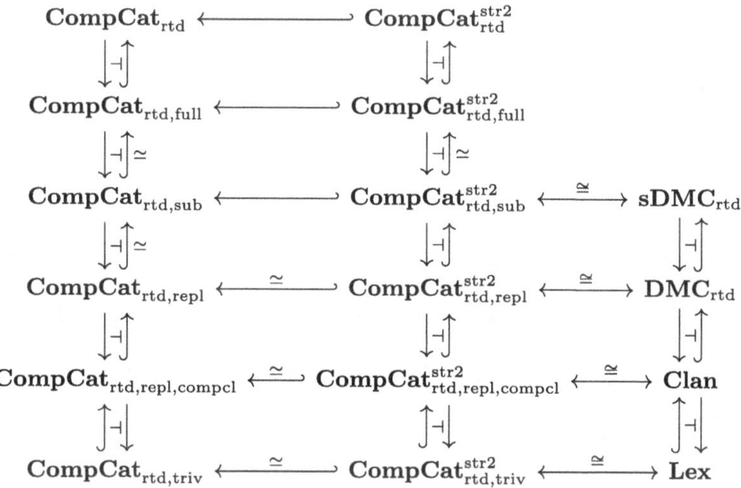

Fig. 4. Notions with types as maps, rooted

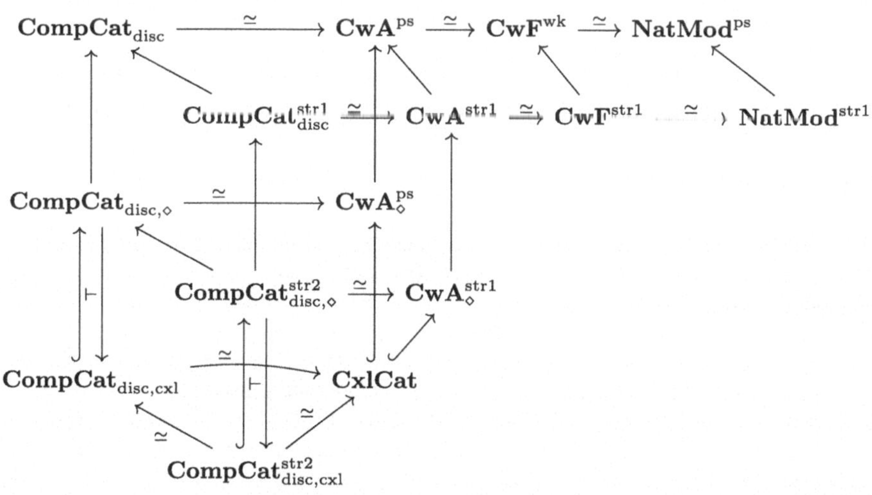

Fig. 5. Notions with types primitive

Ahrens, Lumsdaine, and Voevodsky [4] compare (split) type categories, categories with families, and relative universe categories, working in univalent type theory and (enabled by this) comparing the *types* of these structures, without considering morphisms.

Open questions Firstly, we have deliberately avoided distinguishing between structure and property, in several places. One could refine our analysis to take these choices into account.

Secondly, we have been agnostic about the foundations we work in. However, the 1-categorical analysis given in Sect. 4 relies on a setting where equality of objects of a category is available, e.g., a set-theoretic setting, or using set-based categories in univalent foundations. It would be interesting to analyse the relationship between these structures using *univalent categories* in univalent foundations, where equality of objects is not available.

There is an interesting interplay between the first and second question. Working with univalent categories would, in many cases, make the previous question of structure vs. property moot: since *essentially unique* structure is actually unique (up to identity) in univalent categories, such structure *is* property. For instance, for univalent categories, cloven fibrations coincide with fibrations, chosen pullbacks coincide with pullbacks merely existing, etc. That is, in univalent categories, the choices mentioned in the first open question, and glossed over in this paper, do not arise.

Acknowledgements. The work presented in this article benefited greatly from meetings and visits supported by COST Action CA20111 EuroProofNet, funded by COST (European Cooperation in Science and Technology), https://www.cost.eu. The second author was also supported by the Knut and Alice Wallenberg Foundation project "Type Theory for Mathematics and Computer Science" (PI Thierry Coquand). This material is based upon work supported by the Air Force Office of Scientific Research under award number FA9550-21-1-0334.

References

1. Adámek, J., Hébert, M., Rosický, J.: On essentially algebraic theories and their generalizations. Algebra Universalis **41**(3), 213–227 (1999). https://doi.org/10.1007/s000120050111
2. Adámek, J., Rosický, J.: Locally presentable and accessible categories, London Mathematical Society Lecture Note Series, vol. 189. Cambridge University Press, Cambridge (1994). https://doi.org/10.1017/CBO9780511600579
3. Ahrens, B., Emmenegger, J., North, P.R., Rijke, E.: B-systems and C-systems are equivalent. The Journal of Symbolic Logic p. 1-9 (2023). https://doi.org/10.1017/jsl.2023.41
4. Ahrens, B., Lumsdaine, P.L., Voevodsky, V.: Categorical structures for type theory in univalent foundations. Logical Methods in Computer Science **14**(3), 1–18 (9 2018). https://doi.org/10.23638/LMCS-14(3:18)2018
5. Awodey, S.: Natural models of homotopy type theory. Math. Struct. Comput. Sci. **28**(2), 241–286 (2018). https://doi.org/10.1017/S0960129516000268
6. Awodey, S., Warren, M.A.: Homotopy theoretic models of identity types. Math. Proc. Cam. Phil. Soc. **146**(1), 45–55 (2009). https://doi.org/10.1017/S0305004108001783
7. van den Berg, B., Garner, R.: Topological and simplicial models of identity types. ACM Trans. Comput. Log. **13**(1), Art. 3, 44 (2012). https://doi.org/10.1145/2071368.2071371
8. Birkedal, L., Clouston, R., Mannaa, B., Møgelberg, R.E., Pitts, A.M., Spitters, B.: Modal dependent type theory and dependent right adjoints. Math. Structures Comput. Sci. **30**(2), 118–138 (2020). https://doi.org/10.1017/s0960129519000197

9. Blanco, J.: Relating categorical approaches to type dependency (1991), masters thesis, Univ. Nijmegen
10. de Boer, M.: A proof and formalization of the initiality conjecture of dependent type theory (2020), http://www.diva-portal.org/smash/record.jsf?pid=diva2%3A1431287 licentiate thesis, Stockholm University
11. Cartmell, J.: Generalised algebraic theories and contextual categories. Ph.D. thesis, Oxford (1978)
12. Cartmell, J.: Generalised algebraic theories and contextual categories. Ann. Pure Appl. Logic **32**(3), 209–243 (1986)
13. Clairambault, P., Dybjer, P.: The biequivalence of locally cartesian closed categories and Martin-Löf type theories. Math. Structures Comput. Sci. **24**(6), e240606, 54 (2014). https://doi.org/10.1017/S0960129513000881
14. Curien, P., Garner, R., Hofmann, M.: Revisiting the categorical interpretation of dependent type theory. Theor. Comput. Sci. **546**, 99–119 (2014). https://doi.org/10.1016/J.TCS.2014.03.003
15. Dybjer, P.: Internal type theory. In: Berardi, S., Coppo, M. (eds.) Types for proofs and programs (Torino, 1995). Lecture Notes in Comput. Sci., vol. 1158, pp. 120–134. Springer, Berlin (1996). https://doi.org/10.1007/3-540-61780-9_66
16. Fiore, M.: Discrete generalised polynomial functors (2012), http://www.cl.cam.ac.uk/~mpf23/talks/ICALP2012.pdf, slides from talk given at ICALP 2012
17. Freyd, P.: Aspects of topoi. Bull. Aust. Math. Soc. **7**(1), 1–76 (1972). https://doi.org/10.1017/S0004972700044828
18. Gabriel, P., Ulmer, F.: Lokal präsentierbare Kategorien. Lecture Notes in Mathematics, vol. 221. Springer-Verlag, Berlin-New York (1971). https://doi.org/10.1007/BFb0059396
19. Garner, R.: Combinatorial structure of type dependency. J. Pure Appl. Algebra **219**(6), 1885–1914 (2015). https://doi.org/10.1016/j.jpaa.2014.07.015
20. Hofmann, M.: On the interpretation of type theory in locally Cartesian closed categories. In: Computer science logic (Kazimierz, 1994), Lecture Notes in Comput. Sci., vol. 933, pp. 427–441. Springer, Berlin (1995). https://doi.org/10.1007/BFb0022273
21. Hofmann, M.: Syntax and semantics of dependent types. In: Semantics and logics of computation (Cambridge, 1995), Publ. Newton Inst., vol. 14, pp. 79–130. Cambridge Univ. Press, Cambridge (1997). https://doi.org/10.1017/CBO9780511526619.004
22. Hyland, J.M.E., Pitts, A.M.: The theory of constructions: categorical semantics and topos-theoretic models. In: Categories in computer science and logic (Boulder, CO, 1987), Contemp. Math., vol. 92, pp. 137–199. Amer. Math. Soc., Providence, RI (1989). https://doi.org/10.1090/conm/092/1003199
23. Jacobs, B.: Comprehension categories and the semantics of type dependency. Theoret. Comput. Sci. **107**(2), 169–207 (1993). https://doi.org/10.1016/0304-3975(93)90169-T
24. Johnstone, P.T.: Sketches of an elephant: a topos theory compendium, Oxford Logic Guides, vol. 43,44. The Clarendon Press Oxford University Press, New York (2002)
25. Joyal, A.: Notes on clans and tribes (2017), https://arxiv.org/abs/1710.10238, unpublished notes
26. Kapulkin, K., Lumsdaine, P.L.: Homotopical inverse diagrams in categories with attributes. J. Pure Appl. Algebra **225**(4), Paper No. 106563, 44 (2021). https://doi.org/10.1016/j.jpaa.2020.106563

27. Kelly, G.M.: On the essentially-algebraic theory generated by a sketch. Bull. Austral. Math. Soc. **26**(1), 45–56 (1982). https://doi.org/10.1017/S0004972700005591
28. Lucatelli Nunes, F., Sousa, L.: On lax epimorphisms and the associated factorization. J. Pure Appl. Algebra **226**(12), 107126 (2022). https://doi.org/10.1016/j.jpaa.2022.107126. https://www.sciencedirect.com/science/article/pii/S0022404922001220
29. Makkai, M.: First order logic with dependent sorts, with applications to category theory (1995), http://www.math.mcgill.ca/makkai/folds/foldsinpdf/FOLDS.pdf
30. Martin-Löf, P.: Intuitionistic type theory, Studies in Proof Theory. Lecture Notes, vol. 1. Bibliopolis, Naples (1984)
31. Moggi, E.: A category-theoretic account of program modules. Math. Structures Comput. Sci. **1**(1), 103–139 (1991). https://doi.org/10.1017/S0960129500000074
32. Newstead, C.: Algebraic models of dependent type theory. Ph.D. thesis, Carnegie Mellon University (2018), https://arxiv.org/abs/2103.06155
33. Palmgren, E., Vickers, S.J.: Partial horn logic and Cartesian categories. Ann. Pure Appl. Logic **145**(3), 314–353 (2007). https://doi.org/10.1016/j.apal.2006.10.001
34. Pitts, A.M.: Categorical logic. In: Handbook of Logic in Computer Science, vol. 5, pp. 39–128. Oxford Univ. Press, New York (2000). https://doi.org/10.1093/oso/9780198537816.001.0001
35. Power, J.: 2-categories. Tech. Rep. NS-98-7, Basic Research in Computer Science, Aarhus (Aug 1998), https://www.brics.dk/NS/98/7/index.html
36. Streicher, T.: Semantics of type theory: Correctness, completeness, and independence results. Progress in Theoretical Computer Science, Birkhäuser, Boston, MA (1991). https://doi.org/10.1007/978-1-4612-0433-6
37. Subramaniam, C.L.: From dependent type theory to higher algebraic structures. Ph.D. thesis, Université Paris Diderot (2021). https://doi.org/10.48550/arXiv.2110.02804
38. Taylor, P.: Recursive Domains, Indexed Category Theory and Polymorphism. Ph.D. thesis, University of Cambridge (1986), https://www.paultaylor.eu/domains/recdic.pdf
39. Taylor, P.: Practical foundations of mathematics, Cambridge Studies in Advanced Mathematics, vol. 59. Cambridge University Press, Cambridge (1999), https://www.paultaylor.eu/~pt/prafm/
40. Uemura, T.: A general framework for the semantics of type theory. Math. Struct. Comput. Sci. **33**(3), 134–179 (2023). https://doi.org/10.1017/S0960129523000208
41. Voevodsky, V.: B-systems (2016), https://www.math.ias.edu/Voevodsky/files/files-annotated/Dropbox/Unfinished_papers/Type_systems/Notes_on_Type_Systems/Bsystems/B_systems_current.pdf, unpublished manuscript, revision of arXiv:1410.5389
42. Voevodsky, V.: Subsystems and regular quotients of C-systems. In: A panorama of mathematics: pure and applied, Contemp. Math., vol. 658, pp. 127–137. Amer. Math. Soc., Providence, RI (2016). https://doi.org/10.1090/conm/658/13124
43. Voevodsky, V.: C-system of a module over a Jf-relative monad. J. Pure Appl. Algebra **227**(6), 107283 (2023). https://doi.org/10.1016/j.jpaa.2022.107283

Random-Access Lists, from EE to FP

Titouan Quennet and Pierre-Évariste Dagand(✉)

Université Paris Cité, CNRS, IRIF, Paris, France
pierre@evr.ist

Abstract. Numerical representations, which were popularized by Okasaki in his seminal book [1], decouple the design of data-*types* into, first, a choice of a data-*structure* encoding a suitable numerical system, followed by decorating this structure with as many pieces of *data* as specified by the underlying numerical system. This paper ambitions to apply McBride's theory of *ornaments* [2] to explore a structural interpretation of numerical representation. In particular, we propose a journey from Electronic Engineering —computing with binary numbers— to Functional Programming —implementing a persistent random-access list datatype.

1 Introduction

Ornaments [2] were introduced to dependently-typed programmers as a means to rationalize the development of inductive families. It grew out of the observation that the notion of a "data-type" in a dependently-typed programming language (called an "inductive family" in type theory) can be decomposed into a "data-structure" —a recursive skeleton— onto which is grafted a "data-logic" —witnessing some evidence and asserting propositional invariants. This technology exploits a key affordance of modern, dependently-typed programming languages: dependent pattern-matching. Having embedded the logic into the data, one automatically benefits from strong invariants during pattern-matching. The perennial example is the type of vectors, *i.e.* lists indexed by their length. Pattern-matching on a vector reveals not only information about its value but also about its overall length.

The structuring role of ornaments is also at play in proof assistants based on dependent types, such as Coq. Although less critical in this setting, it is frequent for Coq users to define an ML-style inductive type (*e.g.*, the type of lists) onto which an inductive relation is specified (*e.g.*, the predicate `NoDup` in the Coq standard library), so as to *a posteriori* delineate a particular subset of values. This decomposition was, for example, exploited by Dagand et al. [3] to relate inductive types, inductive predicates, and decision procedures so as to coerce data from one presentation to the other at run-time.

The seminal example of an ornament is the trinity between Peano natural numbers (where natural numbers are inductively presented as either zero or the successor of a natural number), lists (inductively presented as either nil or a

O. Kiselyov (Ed.): APLAS 2024, LNCS 15194, pp. 23–41, 2024.
https://doi.org/10.1007/978-981-97-8943-6_2

cons-cell of some data and another list), and vectors (the inductive family of lists indexed by their length). Interestingly, the relationship between Peano naturals and lists is also studied at the opening of Okasaki [1] chapter on "Numerical representations" (Chap. 9). Indeed, the gist of numerical representations is to derive data-types (and their operations) out of data-structures encoding a numerical system (and their operations).

For instance, the number "11" is written $\mathbb{0b}{\cdot}1{\cdot}0{\cdot}1{\cdot}1$ in binary, with the kth digit being interpreted as a coefficient multiplied by the base 2^k. If we associate, say, a complete leaf binary tree of height h to each digit 1 at position h, we could represent the sequence of 11 elements $[a_0; a_1; a_2; \ldots; a_{10}]$ (in that order) as follows:

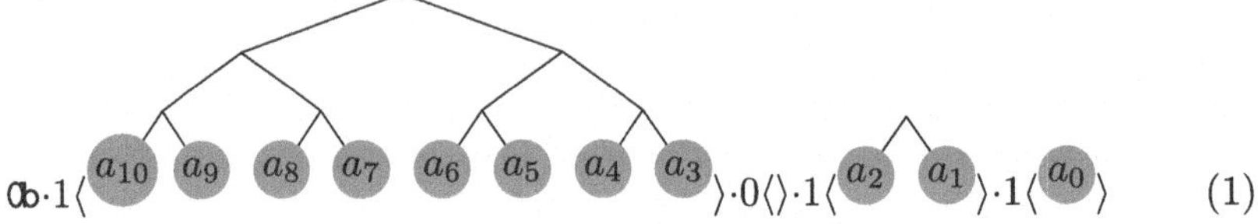

(1)

where the digits 1 have been ornamented so as to store a binary tree.

Set in the heart of the nineties, Okasaki's book is not concerned with data-logics: invariants are stated and proved on paper. However, read through the glass of ornaments, numerical representations offer an interesting challenge to our research program: how far reaching is the "data-structure + data-logics" principle in this setting? What are the limits of the exercise, if any?

At the turn of the millennium, Hinze [4] exploited the expressiveness offered by nested types [5] in Haskell to capture the structural invariants of numerical representations [6]. Some of these techniques have recently been adapted in Agda [7] while, independently, Montin et al. [8] have studied linked nested data-types in Coq.

However, nested types seem to go against the grain of dependent type-theory: working with nested types deprive us from the powerful induction principles offered by inductive families. Defining a recursive program becomes an act of faith where one must constantly struggle to see the tree through a forest of binary products. As a consequence, there has been several efforts to explore numerical representations using inductive families as a more amenable vehicle. An early result is the work of [9], implementing binomial heaps (offering `push` and `pop` operations) from binary numbers with digits 0 and 1. Still in Agda, Swierstra [10] has implemented random-access lists (offering `cons` and `lookup` operations) from binary numbers with digits 0 and 1.

A sketch of a general framework for calculating data-structures from lookups have been proposed by Hinze and Swierstra [11] in terms of Napierian logarithms, using binary numbers with digits 1 and 2 as a running example. Similarly, Dagand et al. [12] sketched a universe of numerical representations, compatible with a type-theoretic presentation but without dwelling on the implementation and specification of supporting operations.

Aside from the aesthetic value of the exercise (which is quite endearing, one must admit!), numerical representations represent an inspiring take on data-type design: we are given a compositional toolbox, by which one chooses a structure (the numerical system), a container of suitable cardinality and, voilà, we get a set of operations with a strong and clear specification with respect to its cardinality.

In the present work, we set our sights onto random-access lists, built upon binary numbers with digits 0 and 1. Unlike previous work, we shall strive to implement all the operations suggested by Okasaki [1]: `cons`, `hd`, `tl`, `lookup`, `update` and `drop`. This is first and foremost a *pedagogical* exercise for the intellectual delight of our reader, who will enjoy the thrill of getting their neurons for Boolean arithmetic to fire together with the neurons for functional programming. From a practical standpoint, one must caution that, performance-wise, such a representation suffers from uncontrolled ripple carry (discussed further in Sect. 2.2) while better behaved alternatives (such as binary numbers with digits 1 and 2) exist [4, 11].

Another pedagogical choice has been to adopt an idealized notation for an hypothetical programming language based on type theory. The underlying technical development has been carried in the Coq proof assistant[1], following an extrinsic approach (based on inductive relations and their decidability to justify uniqueness of identity proof). However, we felt that the quality of the exposition would have suffered from an unfiltered presentation of the Coq artefact.

First, notationally, indo-arabic numbers are written in a right-to-left manner, *i.e.* with their most-significant digit first (on the left) and least-significant digit last (on the right). This goes against usage in most programming languages, where prefix-based inductive constructors will force a left-to-right style. Second, the objects we study are of interest beyond their current incarnation in Coq: putting proofs aside, functional programmers at large will undoubtedly meet some neat programming puzzles in the following. Finally, an idealized notation allows for some poetic license, which we hope our reader will indulge us with. Following mathematical usage, we have tried to maximize our signal-to-noise ratio by dispensing with unnecessary syntactic details so as to better focus on semantic insights. We relate our on-paper presentation with the Coq development through hyperlinks, denoted by the symbol 🐓, to the documentation automatically generated from our library.

Our contributions are the following:

- we give an inductive definition of binary numbers with digits 0 and 1, together with their operations and canonicity properties (Sect. 2). Driven by our extreme care to preserve structural invariants, we unearth a finely chiseled type for the operation testing whether a binary number is greather than another one ;
- we go through the folklore definition of complete leaf binary tree to introduce key notions from the theory of ornaments, focusing on structural invariants (Sect. 3). We deviate from traditional presentations of ornaments by adopting an extrinsically-typed approach, hence offering a different perspective on the topic ;

[1] Available at https://github.com/tquennet/random-access-list.

- we show how binary numbers can be ornamented with binary trees and their operations lifted to recover the usual programming interface of random-access list (Sect. 4), *i.e.* it cons like a list and support efficient (logarithmic) lookup and update like a random-access structure. Crucially, we observe that lookup and update but also drop, which deletes the first k elements of a random-access list, are intimately connected: all emanate from the "greater than" operation on binary number and, in fact, can be derived from a single operation, dubbed open. As a consequence, our implementation relies solely on the underlying, inductive structure of types and never resort to counting, in contrast to Okasaki [1] that resorted to machine integers and their arithmetic to implement indexing.

In truth, we simply hope that our readers will be transported, as the binary operations and ourselves did, through the delicate interplay between structure and logical invariants that are at play in the following.

2 Binary Numbers

We start our journey with the most bare-bones (and, in fact, cruelly naïve) representation of binary numbers. For now, we make no assumption about the intended semantics of binary numbers: in particular, we shall not attempt to control for trailing zeros at the most-significant position(s).

Being semantics-agnostic allows us to present the type of binary numbers as the combination of a binary choice of digits, either 0 or 1

$$\begin{aligned} &\textsf{type Bit} : \star \triangleq \\ &\quad \mid \textsf{0} : \textsf{Bit} \\ &\quad \mid \textsf{1} : \textsf{Bit} \end{aligned} \qquad (🐓)$$

together with a generic notion of dense representation of numbers, as snoc-lists of digits in a any base D

$$\begin{aligned} &\textsf{type Num}\ (D : \star) : \star \triangleq \\ &\quad \mid \textsf{0b} : \textsf{Num}\ D \\ &\quad \mid (ds : \textsf{Num}\ D) \cdot (d : D) : \textsf{Num}\ D \end{aligned} \qquad (🐓)$$

We thus have binary numbers as a straightforward inductive type

$$\begin{aligned} &\textsf{Bin} : \star \\ &\textsf{Bin} \triangleq \textsf{Num Bit} \end{aligned} \qquad (🐓)$$

For example, this type is inhabited by the likes of "0b", "0b·1", "0b·1·0", "0b·1·1" but also, somewhat problematically, "0b·0", "0b·0·0" and for example "0b·0·0·1".

Expounding the type Num allows us to factor out various notions of iterations over digits through 2 combinators: its functorial action Num-mapi and its foldable Num-fold, whose types are as follows:

$$\mathsf{Num\text{-}mapi} : \{A\, B : \star\}(f : \mathbb{N} \to A \to B)(as : \mathsf{Num}\, A) \to \mathsf{Num}\, B \qquad (🐓)$$

$$\mathsf{Num\text{-}fold} : \{M : \star\}\{\mathsf{Monoid}\, M\}(ms : \mathsf{Num}\, M) \to M \qquad (🐓)$$

Operationally, Num-mapi maps a function $f\ k$ for each coefficient k of the number, starting from $k = 0$ for the least-significant digit. Num-fold reduces over an arbitrary monoid M. This lets us abstract away the notion of "indexed iteration over all digits" and put forward any non-trivial recursive computations over numbers (for which we will explicitly appeal to recursion). In this paper, our monoid of choice will often be $(\mathbb{N}, +, 0)$, the set of natural numbers with addition and 0. The composition of Num-mapi f with Num-fold is shortened as

$$\mathsf{Num\text{-}foldMap} : \{A\, M : \star\}\{\mathsf{Monoid}\, M\}(f : \mathbb{N} \to A \to M)(as : \mathsf{Num}\, A) \to M \qquad (🐓)$$

If we specialize Num-foldMap to the monoid $\star$ (with identity being the unit type and product being the Cartesian product), we obtain the predicate

$$\mathsf{Num\text{-}mapi}^{\square} : \{A : \star\}(P : \mathbb{N} \to A \to \star)(as : \mathsf{Num}\, A) \to \star \qquad (🐓)$$

that asserts that P holds everywhere in as. This corresponds to the "below" predicate transformer [13] for the type Num, *i.e.* the predicative counterpart of the functoriality of Num.

The "semantics" of binary numbers is traditionally (*e.g.*, in the Coq standard library [14]) given through a recursive function such as

$$\begin{aligned}
&\mathsf{Bin{\Rightarrow}\mathbb{N}}\ (bs : \mathsf{Bin}) : \mathbb{N}\\
&\mathsf{Bin{\Rightarrow}\mathbb{N}}\ \mathsf{0b} \triangleq 0\\
&\mathsf{Bin{\Rightarrow}\mathbb{N}}\ (bs{\cdot}0) \triangleq 2 \times (\mathsf{Bin{\Rightarrow}\mathbb{N}}\ bs)\\
&\mathsf{Bin{\Rightarrow}\mathbb{N}}\ (bs{\cdot}1) \triangleq 2 \times (\mathsf{Bin{\Rightarrow}\mathbb{N}}\ bs) + 1
\end{aligned} \qquad (🐓)$$

However, such a definition goes against our ambition to identify and preserve the structure of binary numbers. Here, the weight of the k-th digit of a number is muddled in a stack of k pending multiplications by 2. Besides, we resort to recursion —the GOTO of functional programming— without effecting any computational change to the underlying Num structure. Instead, we prefer the following (equivalent) definition

$$\begin{aligned}
&\mathsf{Bit{\Rightarrow}\mathbb{N}}\ (k : \mathbb{N})(b : \mathsf{Bit}) : \mathbb{N}\\
&\mathsf{Bit{\Rightarrow}\mathbb{N}}\ k\ 0 \triangleq 0 \times 2^k\\
&\mathsf{Bit{\Rightarrow}\mathbb{N}}\ k\ 1 \triangleq 1 \times 2^k
\end{aligned} \qquad (🐓)$$

$$\begin{aligned}
&\mathsf{Bin{\Rightarrow}\mathbb{N}}\ (bs : \mathsf{Bin}) : \mathbb{N}\\
&\mathsf{Bin{\Rightarrow}\mathbb{N}}\ bs \triangleq \mathsf{Num\text{-}foldMap}\ \mathsf{Bit{\Rightarrow}\mathbb{N}}\ bs
\end{aligned} \qquad (🐓)$$

which will turn into a structural property in Sect. 4.1.

We recover the intended semantics of binary numbers written right-to-left, following common usage:

$$\begin{aligned} \mathsf{Bin{\Rightarrow}\mathbb{N}}\ \mathsf{0b} &= 0 \\ \mathsf{Bin{\Rightarrow}\mathbb{N}}\ (\mathsf{0b}{\cdot}1) &= 1 \\ \mathsf{Bin{\Rightarrow}\mathbb{N}}\ (\mathsf{0b}{\cdot}1{\cdot}0) &= 2 \\ \mathsf{Bin{\Rightarrow}\mathbb{N}}\ (\mathsf{0b}{\cdot}1{\cdot}1) &= 3 \\ \mathsf{Bin{\Rightarrow}\mathbb{N}}\ (\mathsf{0b}{\cdot}1{\cdot}0{\cdot}0) &= 4 \end{aligned}$$

including warts and all, namely the lack of canonicity of this representation with respect to trailing 0s:

$$\begin{aligned} \mathsf{Bin{\Rightarrow}\mathbb{N}}\ (\mathsf{0b}{\cdot}0) &= 0 \\ \mathsf{Bin{\Rightarrow}\mathbb{N}}\ (\mathsf{0b}{\cdot}0{\cdot}0) &= 0 \\ \mathsf{Bin{\Rightarrow}\mathbb{N}}\ (\mathsf{0b}{\cdot}0{\cdot}1) &= 1 \end{aligned}$$

Type theorists, with their obsession for equality, are quite rightfully keen to avoid such a naïve definition. Instead, they would favor an inductive definition that either enforce the most-significant bit to be 1, such as in the Coq standard library [15], or they would represent binary numbers with digits "1" and "2", dispensing with the digit "0" altogether, such as in the Agda standard library [16].

2.1 Canonicity

Following the lead of type theorists, we identify the set of canonical representatives of binary numbers. Since we are proceeding after the fact, we resort to a pair of inductive predicates:

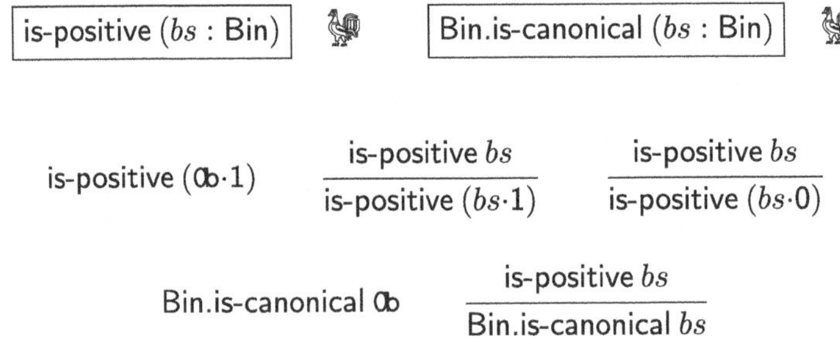

which state that a binary number bs is canonical (Bin.is-canonical bs) if it is either null or stricly positive (is-positive bs). Being positive amounts to having a most-significant bit set to 1.

Cast in an ornamental framework [2], these inductive predicates are induced by algebraic ornamentation of the type Bin with the pair of Boolean functions deciding the canonicity and strict positivity of a binary number [3]. We thus automatically obtain the decidability of this predicate and, as a consequence, the unicity of its identity proofs (which, to a programmer, is quite a relief: dependently-typed pattern-matching over canonical binary numbers is admissible, even in the absence of axiom K [17]).

Remark that the inhabitants of Bin refined by the predicate Bin.is-canonical are isomorphic to a purely inductive definition, as in the Coq standard library:

```
Inductive positive : Set :=
  | xI : positive -> positive
  | xO : positive -> positive
  | xH : positive.
```

```
Inductive N : Set :=
  | N0 : N
  | Npos : positive -> N.
```

This is indeed a very reasonable implementation of binary numbers. In the present work, we strive to balance clarity of exposition and generality, hinting at the fact that our techniques and results reach beyond binary numbers. This was our motivation for expounding the type Num. The refinement-based approach follows this line of thought: we specialize the generic representation (based on Num) with a domain-specific data-logic, here tailored to binary numbers with digits 0 and 1. While different "terms and conditions" would apply for other numerical systems, the same process of characterizing canonical forms through algebraic ornamentation by a decision procedure is at work.

Given any binary number, we can turn it into an equivalent canonical binary number by trimming away potential trailing 0s:

$$\begin{array}{lll} \mathsf{normalize}\ (bs : \mathsf{Bin}) : \mathsf{Bin} & & \\ \mathsf{normalize}\ 0\mathsf{b} & \triangleq 0\mathsf{b} & \\ \mathsf{normalize}\ (bs{\cdot}1) & \triangleq \mathsf{normalize}\ bs{\cdot}1 & \\ \mathsf{normalize}\ (bs{\cdot}0) & \triangleq 0\mathsf{b} & \text{if normalize } bs = 0\mathsf{b} \\ \mathsf{normalize}\ (bs{\cdot}0) & \triangleq \mathsf{normalize}\ bs{\cdot}0 & \text{otherwise} \end{array}$$

(🐓)

We easily prove that normalize preserves the semantics ($\mathsf{Bin}{\Rightarrow}\mathbb{N} \circ \mathsf{normalize} = \mathsf{Bin}{\Rightarrow}\mathbb{N}$) and produces canonical numbers (we have Bin.is-canonical (normalize bs) for any number bs).

2.2 Operations

We can now equip our numerical system with the usual arithmetic operations, starting with increment.

Increment. We recover the definition we are all familiar with from attending Computer Architecture in our Bachelor years:

$$\begin{array}{ll} \mathsf{inc}\ (bs : \mathsf{Bin}) : \mathsf{Bin} & \\ \mathsf{inc}\ 0\mathsf{b} & \triangleq 0\mathsf{b}{\cdot}1 \\ \mathsf{inc}\ (bs{\cdot}0) & \triangleq bs{\cdot}1 \\ \mathsf{inc}\ (bs{\cdot}1) & \triangleq (\mathsf{inc}\ bs){\cdot}0 \end{array}$$

(🐓)

One easily shows that it preserves the canonicity of its argument and rightfully implements the expected semantics ($\mathsf{Bin}{\Rightarrow}\mathbb{N} \circ \mathsf{inc} = (1+) \circ \mathsf{Bin}{\Rightarrow}\mathbb{N}$).

Interestingly, we also have that *canonical* binary numbers are generated by 0_b and inc. In type theoretic terms, this means that the type Bin satisfies Peano's induction principle, meaning that we have the property

$$\begin{aligned}
&\forall P : \mathsf{Bin} \to \star.\\
&\quad P\, 0_b \to\\
&\quad (\forall bs : \mathsf{Bin}.\ \mathsf{Bin.is\text{-}canonical}\, bs \to P\, bs \to P\, (\mathsf{inc}\, bs)) \to\\
&\qquad \forall bs : \mathsf{Bin}.\ \mathsf{Bin.is\text{-}canonical}\, bs \to P\, bs
\end{aligned} \qquad (🐓)$$

Decrement. For the implementation of decrement, we resort to a failure monad $\mathfrak{m} : \star \to \star$ so as to distinguish an integer underflow (namely, upon failing to decrement 0_b) from normal operation, where we may have to propagate a borrow (namely, upon decrementing a number of the form $bs{\cdot}0$):

$$\begin{aligned}
&\mathsf{dec}\,(bs : \mathsf{Bin}) : \mathfrak{m}\,\mathsf{Bin}\\
&\mathsf{dec}\,0_b \triangleq \mathsf{fail}\ \text{"underflow"}\\
&\mathsf{dec}\,(0_b{\cdot}1) \triangleq \mathsf{return}\ 0_b\\
&\mathsf{dec}\,(bs{\cdot}1) \triangleq \mathsf{return}\,(bs{\cdot}0)\\
&\mathsf{dec}\,(bs{\cdot}0) \triangleq \mathsf{let!}\ bs' = \mathsf{dec}\,bs\ \mathsf{in}\ bs'{\cdot}1
\end{aligned} \qquad (🐓)$$

Explicitly signaling the underflow is key to preserve canonicity: the absorption of the leading 0s is implicitly performed by the monadic composition (bind) of the failure monad, denoted "let! – = – in –" here.

Our implementation is proved correct in a typical "partial correctness" manner: if dec successfully produces a binary number then that number is canonical. In our effect-generic setting, "partial correctness" amounts to asking for the monad $\mathfrak{m}$ to provide a predicate lifting [18,19]

$$\mathfrak{m}^{\Box} : \forall P : A \to \star.\ \forall ma : \mathfrak{m}\,A.\ \to \star$$

On the Maybe monad, this corresponds exactly to its "below" predicate, which is trivially true upon failure and asserts that P must hold upon success.

Note that, once again, a trained algorithmist would certainly be staggered by the extreme naivety of these binary numbers: inc suffers from logarithmic carry propagation while dec suffers from logarithmic borrow propagation. If both were to enter into a resonant mode (*e.g.*, being used in a non-monotonic counter), the algorithmic complexity would be rather poor. A well-trodden path [4] consists in adopting a numerical representation with constant-time increment and decrement, such as Myers' skew binary numbers [20]. Whilst being out of the scope of the present work, the same thought process applies there too.

Decidable total order. Over canonical binary numbers, equality is easily decided: by construction, two numbers are equal if and only they have the same canonical representation. To implement comparison, we definitely part ways with the Electronic Engineering department: having the luxury of manipulating words of fixed bit-width, our esteemed colleagues would build their digital comparator cascading from the most significant bit to the least significant bit [21].

In the Mathematically-Structured Programming department, we are working with an inductive, least-significant-bit-first presentation of binary numbers. As a consequence, our implementation is continuation-based —so as to reach the most significant bits and carry the results back to least significant bits— and it has to do some additional work to identify which word has the shortest bit-width, if any.

Because programming in type-theory is also the art of collecting evidence, we shall strive to make the result of our comparison function as informative as possible: if we have bs greater than bs' (denoted $\mathsf{gt}\ bs\ bs'$), then this means that we can split bs into a pair of a shortest canonical prefix $0b \cdot 1 \cdot p$ (least-significant bits) and longest suffix s (most-significant bits, *i.e.*, we have $bs = s \cdot 1 \cdot p$) such that there exists a number $0b \cdot k$ verifying $bs' + 1 + 0b \cdot k = 1 \cdot p$. Note that p itself is not binary number, rather it is the *one-hole context* [22,23] of a binary number, *i.e.* a sequence of bits in cons form. Similarly, it is more natural to determine k from least-significant bit to most-significant bit order, so it comes "inside out" as well. We conveniently denote by $bs \cdot sb$ the act of "plugging" the binary number bs under a one-hole context sb: indeed, this is nothing but a concatenation of bits.

We thus define an operation

$$\mathsf{gt} : (bs\ bs' : \mathsf{Bin}) \to \mathfrak{m}\ \{s : \mathsf{Bin}; p : \mathsf{List\ Bit}; k : \mathsf{List\ Bit}\}$$

such that the result triple s, p, and k, if it is defined, satisfy the above specification. We remark, in particular, that $1 + 0b \cdot k$ corresponds to the result of the subtraction of bs by bs'. From gt, we thus derive a binary subtraction operation

$$\mathsf{sub} : (bs\ bs' : \mathsf{Bin}) \to \mathfrak{m}\ \mathsf{Bin}$$

The implementation of gt, linked above, proceeds by incrementally moving the zipper over bs towards its most significant bits, until exhaustion of the bits of bs' *and* reaching the closest non-$\mathsf{0}$ bit of bs. This separates bs into canonical prefixes and suffices. Besides, we accumulate the bits of the subtraction, propagating borrows to the most-significant bits when necessary.

3 Interlude: Complete Binary Tree

The insight of numerical *representations* consists in ornamenting the data-structure corresponding to a number system (in our case: binary numbers) with a data container of suitable cardinality (in our case: powers-of-2 elements).

Luckily for us, this is an Introduction to Functional Programming classics: binary tree, which we define as follows

$$\begin{aligned}
&\mathsf{type\ Tree}\ (A : \star) : \star \triangleq \\
&\quad \mid \mathsf{leaf}\ (a : A) : \mathsf{Tree}\ A \\
&\quad \mid \mathsf{node}\ (l\ r : \mathsf{Tree}\ A) : \mathsf{Tree}\ A
\end{aligned}$$

In the remainder, we should dispense with the polymorphic quantification over the set A. Our treatment is parameterized over this type.

Computing the cardinality of a binary tree is standard:

$$\begin{aligned}
&\mathsf{Tree.card}\ (t : \mathsf{Tree}\ A) : \mathbb{N}\\
&\mathsf{Tree.card}\ (\mathsf{leaf}\ a) \triangleq 1\\
&\mathsf{Tree.card}\ (\mathsf{node}\ l\ r) \triangleq \mathsf{Tree.card}\ l + \mathsf{Tree.card}\ r
\end{aligned}$$

(🐓)

However, our interest in binary trees is narrower than this: we are specifically interested in trees whose cardinality is a power of 2. One way to achieve this is to constrain our binary tree to be complete, *i.e.* the height of the left and right subtrees of every node must be equal:

$$\boxed{\mathsf{Tree.is\text{-}valid}\ (h : \mathbb{N})\ (t : \mathsf{Tree}\ A)}$$ 🐓

$$\mathsf{Tree.is\text{-}valid}\ 0\ (\mathsf{leaf}\ a) \qquad \frac{\mathsf{Tree.is\text{-}valid}\ h\ l \qquad \mathsf{Tree.is\text{-}valid}\ h\ r}{\mathsf{Tree.is\text{-}valid}\ (h+1)\ (\mathsf{node}\ l\ r)}$$

Doing so, we have that

$$\forall\, h : \mathbb{N}.\ \forall\, t : \mathsf{Tree}\ A.\ \mathsf{Tree.is\text{-}valid}\ h\ t \to \mathsf{Tree.card}\ t = 2^h$$ (🐓)

Note that one could have chosen other data-structures to this effect, such as binomial trees and pennant trees. For our purposes in the present work (Sect. 4), complete binary trees are amply sufficient.

Create. Initializing a valid tree of height h from a single element is a straightforward recursive process:

$$\begin{aligned}
&\mathsf{Tree.create}\ (a : A)(h : \mathbb{N}) : \mathsf{Tree}\ A\\
&\mathsf{Tree.create}\ a\ 0 \triangleq \mathsf{leaf}\ a\\
&\mathsf{Tree.create}\ a\ (n+1) \triangleq \mathsf{let!}\ t = \mathsf{Tree.create}\ a\ n\ \mathsf{in}\ \mathsf{node}\ t\ t
\end{aligned}$$

(🐓)

Lookup. Given a valid binary tree of height h, a list of bits of length h designates a specific element of the tree:

$$\begin{aligned}
&\mathsf{Tree.lookup}\ (t : \mathsf{Tree}\ A)(k : \mathsf{List\ Bit}) : \mathfrak{m}\ A\\
&\mathsf{Tree.lookup}\ (\mathsf{leaf}\ a)\ [] \triangleq \mathsf{return}\ a\\
&\mathsf{Tree.lookup}\ (\mathsf{node}\ l\ _)\ (0 :: k) \triangleq \mathsf{Tree.lookup}\ l\ k\\
&\mathsf{Tree.lookup}\ (\mathsf{node}\ _\ r)\ (1 :: k) \triangleq \mathsf{Tree.lookup}\ r\ k\\
&\mathsf{Tree.lookup}\ _\ _ \triangleq \mathsf{fail}
\end{aligned}$$

(🐓)

Note that, because we are following an extrinsic approach, we have to prove *a posteriori* that Tree.lookup will in fact always succeeds on a conjunction of a valid tree and an index in the correct range. Similarly, we can update the value stored at a particular index in a tree of suitable height through

$$\mathsf{Tree.update} : (t : \mathsf{Tree}\ A)(k : \mathsf{List\ Bit})(a : A) \to \mathfrak{m}\ (\mathsf{Tree}\ A)$$ (🐓)

At this stage of the presentation, we thus have a numerical system based on binary numbers (Num) and a data-structure representing collections of powers-of-2 elements (Tree). It is time to put 0b10 and 2^h together!

4 Random-Access List

The first step consists in extending individual Bits with the data-container Tree. To do so, we ornament the former with a data-extension of the latter:

$$\begin{aligned}&\mathsf{type\ ArrayBit}\ (A:\star):\star \triangleq\\ &\quad|\ 0\langle\rangle : \mathsf{ArrayBit}\ A\\ &\quad|\ 1\langle(t:\mathsf{Tree}\ A)\rangle : \mathsf{ArrayBit}\ A\end{aligned}$$ (🐓)

which comes with an ornamental (forgetful) map:

$$\begin{aligned}&\mathsf{ArrayBit{\Rightarrow}Bit}\ (mt : \mathsf{ArrayBit}) : \mathsf{Bit}\\ &\mathsf{ArrayBit{\Rightarrow}Bit}\ 0\langle\rangle \triangleq 0\\ &\mathsf{ArrayBit{\Rightarrow}Bit}\ 1\langle t\rangle \triangleq 1\end{aligned}$$ (🐓)

Note that, much as Bit was equivalent to $\mathbb{B}$, ArrayBit is essentially an option type. Hence the rather unsurprising ornamentation [24]. For conciseness, we shall exploit the functoriality and foldability of ArrayBit, seen as an option type.

$$\mathsf{ArrayBit.foldMap} : \{A\ M : \star\}\{\mathsf{Monoid}\ M\}(f : A \to M)(mt : \mathsf{ArrayBit}\ A) \to M$$ (🐓)

The ornamentation lifts functorially across the data-type Num, yielding both the type of random-access lists and a forgetful map to the underlying binary number:

$$\begin{aligned}&\mathsf{ArrayList}\ (A:\star):\star\\ &\mathsf{ArrayList}\ A \triangleq \mathsf{Num}\ (\mathsf{ArrayBit}\ A)\end{aligned}$$ (🐓)

$$\begin{aligned}&\mathsf{ArrayList{\Rightarrow}Bin}\ (as : \mathsf{ArrayList}\ A) : \mathsf{Bin}\\ &\mathsf{ArrayList{\Rightarrow}Bin}\ as \triangleq \mathsf{Num\text{-}mapi}\ (\lambda\ \_.\ \mathsf{ArrayBit{\Rightarrow}Bit})\ as\end{aligned}$$ (🐓)

The number of elements stored in a random-access list corresponds to the sum the elements stored in each individual binary tree:

$$\begin{aligned}&\mathsf{ArrayList.card}\ (as : \mathsf{ArrayList}\ A) : \mathbb{N}\\ &\mathsf{ArrayList.card}\ as \triangleq \mathsf{Num\text{-}foldMap}\ (\lambda\ \_.\ \mathsf{ArrayBit.foldMap\ Tree.card})\ as\end{aligned}$$ (🐓)

4.1 Validity and Canonicity

Obviously, we would expect the cardinality of a random-access list (as computed by ArrayList.card) to correspond to the value of the underlying binary number (as computed by Bin⇒ℕ ∘ ArrayList⇒Bin). However, this is only true if the height of the underlying binary trees grow accordingly to the power-of-2 coefficients, as specified by Bit⇒ℕ and Bin⇒ℕ.

To enforce this data-logic, we algebraically ornament the type ArrayBit with the recursive function Bit⇒ℕ and functorially lift this predicate over to Num. This produces the following inductive predicates:

$$\boxed{\mathsf{ArrayBit.is\text{-}valid}\ (h : \mathbb{N})\ (mt : \mathsf{ArrayBit})} \qquad \boxed{\mathsf{ArrayList.is\text{-}valid}\ (as : \mathsf{ArrayList})}$$

$$\mathsf{ArrayBit.is\text{-}valid}\ h\ 0\langle\rangle \qquad \frac{\mathsf{Tree.is\text{-}valid}\ h\ t}{\mathsf{ArrayBit.is\text{-}valid}\ h\ 1\langle t\rangle} \qquad \frac{\mathsf{Num\text{-}mapi}^{\square}\ \mathsf{ArrayBit.is\text{-}valid}\ as}{\mathsf{ArrayList.is\text{-}valid}\ as}$$

Under this proviso that a random-access list as satisfies ArrayList.is-valid as, we indeed have that Bin⇒ℕ (ArrayList⇒Bin as) = ArrayList.card as (🐓). However, much like our original definition of Bin, this representation suffers from a lack of canonicity: for instance, there is an infinite number of representations of the empty list. We recover canonicity by simply enforcing canonicity of the underlying numerical structure:

$$\boxed{\mathsf{ArrayList.is\text{-}canonical}\ (as : \mathsf{ArrayList})}$$

$$\frac{\mathsf{Bin.is\text{-}canonical}\ (\mathsf{ArrayList{\Rightarrow}Bin}\ as)}{\mathsf{ArrayList.is\text{-}canonical}\ as}$$

The random-access lists we shall consider will have to be both valid and canonical. We package both invariant in an overarching predicate, the composition [9], also-called the pull-back [24] of both data-logics:

$$\boxed{\mathsf{is\text{-}well\text{-}formed}\ (as : \mathsf{ArrayList})}$$

$$\frac{\mathsf{ArrayList.is\text{-}canonical}\ as \qquad \mathsf{ArrayList.is\text{-}valid}\ as}{\mathsf{is\text{-}well\text{-}formed}\ as}$$

4.2 Operations

While the process of turning binary numbers into an operational object required careful thought and semantics considerations (Sect. 2.2), providing random-access list with operations amounts to, first, finding an operational counterpart in the world of binary numbers and, then, figuring out where the data stored in the binary trees must be transferred to, so as to preserve validity and semantics.

As explained by Okasaki [1], we expect a rather uneventful journey when it comes to initializing a random-access list of a given size (ArrayList.create), adding an element to a list (cons) or project it out its head and tail (respectively, hd and tl). The crux of the matter concerns the implementation of the logarithmic lookup and update operations (respectively, lookup and update). Luckily, there turns out to be a single abstraction (open) underpinning both abstractions and this abstraction has an interesting counterpart on the numerical side.

Create. Initializing a random-access list of a given cardinality is dual to converting a random-access list back to a binary number with ArrayList⇒Bin: it consists in turning the digit 1 into a constructor $1\langle - \rangle$ with a binary tree of 2^h elements.

$$\begin{aligned}
&\mathsf{ArrayBit.create}(a : A)(h : \mathbb{N})(b : \mathsf{Bit}) : \mathsf{ArrayBit}\ A\\
&\mathsf{ArrayBit.create}\ a\ h\ 0 \triangleq 0\langle\rangle\\
&\mathsf{ArrayBit.create}\ a\ h\ 1 \triangleq 1\langle \mathsf{Tree.create}\ a\ h\rangle
\end{aligned}$$

$$\begin{aligned}
&\mathsf{ArrayList.create}(a : A)(bs : \mathsf{Bin}) : \mathsf{ArrayList}\ A\\
&\mathsf{ArrayList.create}\ a\ bs \triangleq \mathsf{Num\text{-}mapi}\ (\mathsf{ArrayBit.create}\ a)\ bs
\end{aligned}$$

Given a binary number in canonical form, this results in a well-formed random-access list. In particular, the following diagram commutes:

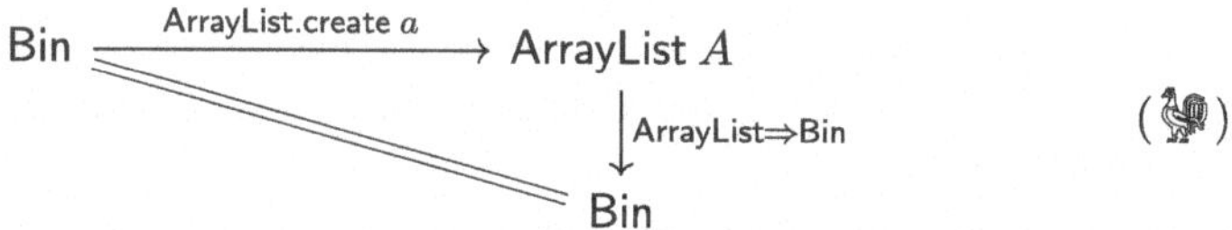

Cons. The implementation of inc (Sect. 2.2, page 29) turns into a blueprint laying out the recursive definition of the insertion of a valid tree t of height h (*i.e.*, satisfying Tree.is-valid h t) into a valid random-access list $\mathbb{0}\mathsf{b}\cdot \ldots \cdot as_1 \cdot as_0$ of the corresponding weights (*i.e.*, satisfying ArrayBit.is-valid $h\ as_0$, ArrayBit.is-valid $(h+1)\ as_1$, *etc.*.). The only novelty here is having to manipulate trees, with the occasional carry from one digit to a twice bigger node at the next digit:

$$\begin{aligned}
&\mathsf{cons\text{-}tree}\ (t : \mathsf{Tree}\ A)(as : \mathsf{ArrayList}\ A) : \mathsf{ArrayList}\ A\\
&\mathsf{cons\text{-}tree}\ t\ \mathbb{0}\mathsf{b} &&\triangleq \mathbb{0}\mathsf{b}\cdot 1\langle t\rangle\\
&\mathsf{cons\text{-}tree}\ t\ (as\cdot 0\langle\rangle) &&\triangleq as\cdot 1\langle t\rangle\\
&\mathsf{cons\text{-}tree}\ t\ (as\cdot 1\langle t'\rangle) &&\triangleq (\mathsf{cons\text{-}tree}\ (\mathsf{node}\ t'\ t)\ as)\cdot 0\langle\rangle
\end{aligned}$$

Note that we are careful to put the cons-ed tree t *to the right* of the tree t', which was already there. The relation between cons-tree and inc amounts to the following commuting diagram:

$$\begin{array}{ccc}
\mathsf{ArrayList} & \xrightarrow{\mathsf{cons\text{-}tree}\ t} & \mathsf{ArrayList}\\
\big\downarrow{\scriptstyle \mathsf{ArrayList}\Rightarrow\mathsf{Bin}} & & \big\downarrow{\scriptstyle \mathsf{ArrayList}\Rightarrow\mathsf{Bin}}\\
\mathsf{Bin} & \xrightarrow{\mathsf{inc}} & \mathsf{Bin}
\end{array}$$

Functional ornaments [25] and their later evolutions [26] offered the promise to assist this process of lifting a recursive definition (here, inc) to an ornamented version of its input and output types (here, cons-tree) while guaranteeing commutativity with respect to forgetful maps (here, ArrayList⇒Bin). For readability, we chose to expound the actual definition rather than appealing to automation.

To simplify the programming interface, we expose the cons operator instead

$$\text{cons}\,(a : A)(as : \text{ArrayList}\,A) : \text{ArrayList}\,A$$
$$\text{cons}\,a\,as \triangleq \text{cons-tree}\,(\text{leaf}\,a)\,as$$

(🐓)

whose invariant is more simply stated as: given a well-formed random-access list as (*i.e.*, satisfying is-well-formed as) and a single element a, cons a as produces a well-formed random-access list whose cardinality has been increased by 1.

As for binary numbers, having implemented 0b and cons, we can prove that well-formed random-access list satisfy the usual induction principle for lists, that is we have:

$$\begin{aligned}&\forall P : \text{ArrayList}\,A \to \star.\\ &\quad P\,0b \to\\ &\quad (\forall a : A.\,\forall as : \text{ArrayList}\,A.\ \text{is-well-formed}\,as \to P\,as \to P\,(\text{cons}\,a\,as)) \to\\ &\qquad \forall as : \text{ArrayList}\,A.\ \text{is-well-formed}\,as \to P\,as\end{aligned}$$

(🐓)

Uncons. The dual operation consists in removing the head of the random-access list. Once again, we rely on the implementation of dec as a blueprint for the recursive definition:

$$\begin{aligned}&\text{uncons}\,(as : \text{ArrayList}\,A) : \mathfrak{m}\,(\text{Tree}\,A \times \text{ArrayList}\,A)\\ &\text{uncons}\,0b \triangleq \text{fail "underflow"}\\ &\text{uncons}\,(0b\cdot 1\langle t\rangle) \triangleq \text{return}\,(t\,,\,0b)\\ &\text{uncons}\,(as\cdot 1\langle t\rangle) \triangleq \text{return}\,(t\,,\,as\cdot 0\langle\rangle)\\ &\text{uncons}\,(as\cdot 0\langle\rangle) \triangleq \text{let!}\,(\text{node}\,t\,t'\,,\,as') = \text{uncons}\,as\ \text{in}\ (t'\,,\,as'\cdot 1\langle t\rangle)\end{aligned}$$

(🐓)

subject to an ornamental invariant relating the cardinality of the input random-access list to the cardinality of the (potential) output random-access list in terms of dec:

$$\begin{array}{ccc}\text{ArrayList} & \xrightarrow{\text{uncons}} & \mathfrak{m}\,(\text{Tree}\,A \times \text{ArrayList}\,A)\\ \downarrow{\scriptstyle \text{ArrayList}\Rightarrow\text{Bin}} & & \downarrow{\scriptstyle \mathfrak{m}^{\rightarrow}(\text{ArrayList}\Rightarrow\text{Bin}\circ\text{proj}_2)}\\ \text{Bin} & \xrightarrow{\text{dec}} & \mathfrak{m}\,\text{Bin}\end{array}$$

(🐓)

Compared to dec, the only novelty here consists in splitting binary nodes so as to materialize the borrow from a more significant bit to a least significant bit.

Starting from a well-formed random-access list (whose least significant bit has order 0), we are guaranteed that the first component of the pair is a tree t satisfying Tree.is-valid 0 t, which, by inversion of the validity predicate, means that it is necessarily a leaf a. We expose the following, simpler interface instead:

$$\text{hd}\,(as : \text{ArrayList}\,A) : \mathfrak{m}\,A$$
$$\text{hd}\,as \triangleq \text{let!}\,(\text{leaf}\,a\,,\,\_) = \text{uncons}\,as\ \text{in}\ a$$

(🐓)

$$\text{tl}\,(as : \text{ArrayList}\,A) : \mathfrak{m}\,(\text{ArrayList}\,A)$$
$$\text{tl}\,as \triangleq \text{let!}\,(\text{leaf}\,\_\,,\,as') = \text{uncons}\,as\ \text{in}\ as'$$

(🐓)

Open. The insertion and update operations over random-access list have the following types:

$$\mathsf{lookup} : (as : \mathsf{ArrayList}\ A)(bs : \mathsf{Bin}) \to \mathfrak{m}\ A$$
$$\mathsf{update} : (as : \mathsf{ArrayList}\ A)(bs : \mathsf{Bin})(a : A) \to \mathfrak{m}\ (\mathsf{ArrayList}\ A)$$

In both cases, we must first identify to which non-zero digit of the input list as —if it exists— one must look into so as to further navigate into the associated binary tree in order to find either the element to return (in the case of lookup) or to replace it (in the case of update).

How should we determine whether this position exists? As a matter of fact, this corresponds exactly to the definition of gt (Sect. 2.2, page 9), where the first argument is ornamented from a binary number to a random-access list while keeping the second argument unchanged. Ornamenting the result types gives

$$\mathsf{open} : (as : \mathsf{ArrayList}\ A)(bs : \mathsf{Bin}) \to \mathfrak{m} \begin{Bmatrix} s : \mathsf{ArrayList}\ A; \\ t : \mathsf{Tree}\ A; \\ p : \mathsf{List}\ (\mathsf{ArrayBit}\ A); \\ k : \mathsf{List}\ \mathsf{Bit} \end{Bmatrix} \qquad (🐓)$$

that witnesses the fact that —if bs is smaller than as— the list as can be split into a canonical prefix $1\langle t\rangle{\cdot}p$ (where t is a tree of height h) and a suffix s (*i.e.*, $as = s{\cdot}1\langle t\rangle{\cdot}p$). Besides, $\mathbb{0}\mathsf{b}{\cdot}k$ represents the difference between as and bs: we have $bs + 1 + \mathbb{0}\mathsf{b}{\cdot}k = 1{\cdot}(\mathsf{ArrayList}{\Rightarrow}\mathsf{Bin}\ p)$. A direct consequence is that $\mathbb{0}\mathsf{b}{\cdot}k$ denotes a number in the range $\{0, 1, \ldots, 2^h - 1\}$.

Let us illustrate this decomposition on our earlier example of an 11-elements random-access list (Eq. 1, p. 2). If we open this list at index 6, we obtain:

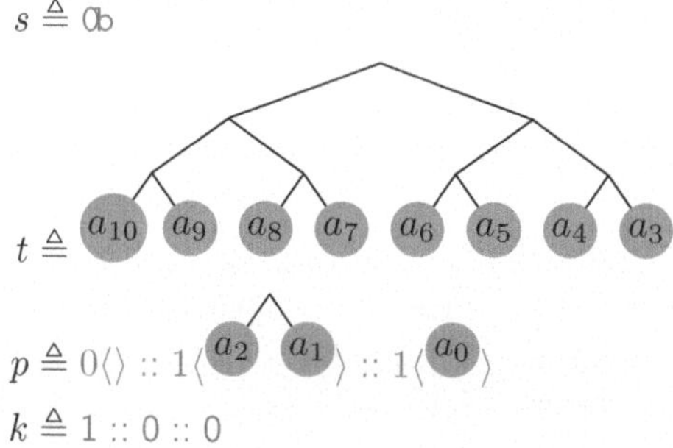

Effectively, k encodes a dissection [27] of the binary tree t: k identifies a specific element of t, where the bit 0 is interpreted as "move to left subtree" and the bit 1 as "move to right subtree". On the left and in blue, are elements which were cons-ed *later* and, on the right and in red, elements which were cons-ed *earlier*:

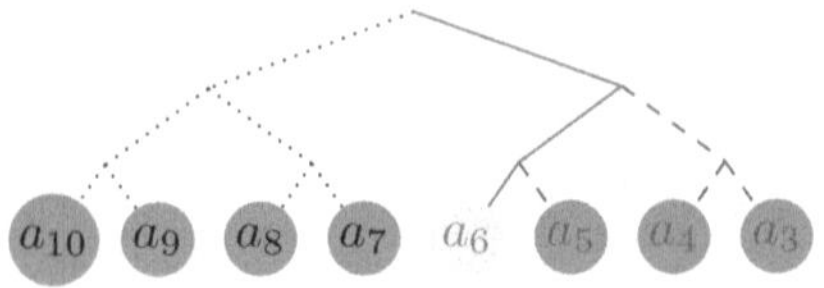

Note that $\mathbb{0b}{\cdot}k = \mathbb{0b}{\cdot}1{\cdot}0{\cdot}0$ denotes the number 4: indeed, the designated element is the 4th leaf of the tree, counting from right-to-left!

The structural ties between open and gt is summarized by this commuting diagram:

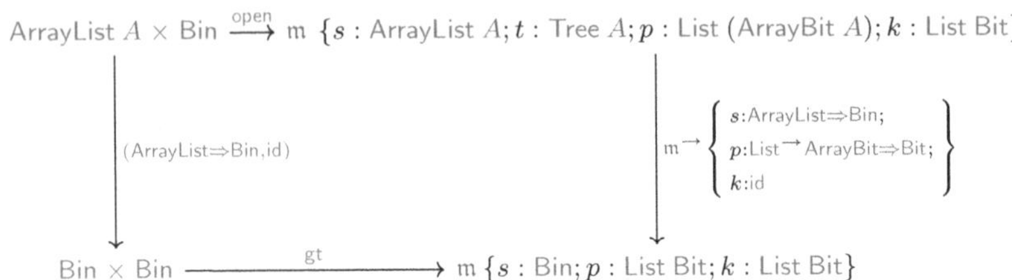

Lookup. Using open, it becomes easier to extract the nth element (in cons-order) of a random-access list as: it is the element designated by k in the binary tree t. To reach this element, we navigate the binary tree according to its path, coded in binary (Sect. 3, page 32):

```
lookup (as : ArrayList A)(bs : Bin) : m A
lookup as bs ≜ let! {_ ; t ; _ ; k} = open as bs in
                 Tree.lookup t k
```

Update. The zipper over random-access list really shines in the implementation of update: it allows us to perform the update of the designated tree and then plug this updated tree back into an otherwise unchanged random-access list:

```
update (as : ArrayList A)(bs : Bin)(a : A) : m A
update as bs a ≜ let! {s ; t ; p ; k} = open as bs in
                 let! t′ = Tree.update t k a in
                 return s·1⟨t′⟩·p
```

Drop. Okasaki [1] left as an exercise to the reader the task of implementing drop, which remove the first bs elements of a random-access list as. Once again, we rely on open to deliver a zipper-based decomposition capturing the state "as at index bs". However, whilst the most-significant bits s of as will carry over as-is to the resulting list, we have to rebalance the fragment consisting of the last $k + 1$ elements cons-ed in that tree t (*i.e.*, the k elements to the left of the designated element and the designated element itself) onto a new prefix. The simplest way to achieve this is to first unload the k elements to the left of the designated value (keeping this value aside for the moment) in a the one-hole context of a random-access list. Computing this structure is straightforward: it is coded upon k itself! This corresponds to the following operation:

$$\begin{array}{ll}\mathsf{Tree.scatter}\ (t : \mathsf{Tree}\ A)(bs : \mathsf{List\ Bit}) : \mathfrak{m}\ (A \times \mathsf{List}\ (\mathsf{ArrayBit}\ A)) & \\ \mathsf{Tree.scatter}\ (\mathsf{leaf}\ a)\ [] & \triangleq \mathsf{return}\ (a\ ,\ []) \\ \mathsf{Tree.scatter}\ (\mathsf{node}\ lt\ rt)\ (1 :: bs) & \triangleq \mathsf{let!}\ (a\ ,\ p) = \mathsf{Tree.scatter}\ rt\ bs\ \mathsf{in}\ (a\ ,\ 1\langle lt\rangle :: p) \\ \mathsf{Tree.scatter}\ (\mathsf{node}\ lt\ \_)\ (0 :: bs) & \triangleq \mathsf{let!}\ (a\ ,\ p) = \mathsf{Tree.scatter}\ lt\ bs\ \mathsf{in}\ (a\ ,\ 0\langle\rangle :: p)\end{array}$$

(🐓)

This operation returns the value at the designated element (a) together with the new prefix p of k elements. The random-access list $s{\cdot}0\langle\rangle{\cdot}p$ is almost the desired result but we are short of one element: a. We must cons it to the overall list (which may lead to cascading overflows up to the separating $0\langle\rangle$):

$$\begin{array}{l}\mathsf{drop}\ (as : \mathsf{ArrayList}\ A)(bs : \mathsf{Bin}) : \mathfrak{m}\ (\mathsf{ArrayList}\ A) \\ \mathsf{drop}\ as\ bs \triangleq \mathsf{let!}\ \{s\ ;\ t\ ;\ \_\ ;\ k\} = \mathsf{open}\ as\ bs\ \mathsf{in} \\ \qquad\qquad \mathsf{let!}\ (a\ ,\ p') = \mathsf{Tree.scatter}\ t\ k\ \mathsf{in} \\ \qquad\qquad \mathsf{return}\ (\mathsf{cons}\ a\ (s{\cdot}0\langle\rangle{\cdot}p'))\end{array}$$

(🐓)

4.3 Equational Theory 🐓

Proving the equational theory of random-access list is "business as usual", with the notable exception that 1. we can rely on the ornamental projection to binary number whenever necessary (*e.g.*, to characterize out-of-bound accesses as binary overflow) and 2. the trio of operations lookup, update and drop rely on a single, common abstraction open. Developing the equational theory through open thus immediately yields results that apply to lookup, update as well as drop.

5 Conclusion

This journey from binary numbers to random-access lists raises some interesting questions, which we side-stepped here thanks to carefully-crafted definitions and *a posteriori* proofs that our craft was correct. This suggests that we are relying on some implicit invariants, which we recovered after the fact through sheer stubbornness. An intrinsic presentation would have been much less forgiving. In fact, all our attempts at giving a maximally-ornamented intrinsic presentation of random-access list in Agda have failed so far. A maximally-ornamented intrinsic random-access list is a random-access list indexed by the binary number encoding its size: by construction, any operation on those is ornamentally-correct. However, our experience has been that it can be extremely challenging (quite an understatement!) to work with pattern-matching to get through recursive steps. The work of Hinze and Swierstra [11] is an obvious inspiration for future work: in their work, the authors have expounded some of the implicit invariants at play between the type of indices and data-types supporting such indices.

The present work is part of a larger, on-going effort to offer a generic representation suitable for all numerical representations [12]: it provides an example of a dense data-structure with non-trivial canonicity property. In the future, we shall explore representations based on sparse (following Okasaki's terminology) number systems, such as Myers' skewed binary numbers [20] and integrate these various systems into a unified library.

Our presentation relied extensively on ornaments as a conceptual apparatus but did not use it as an effective tool. Whenever ornamentation manifests itself, we manually roll our own according to the ornamental blueprints on paper. With proper language support [9,25,26], we would have avoided this extra legwork. However, to the best of our knowledge, existing ornament library or ornament-processing systems are still too verbose given our pedagogical intents in the present work.

Acknowledgments. Our interest in these questions was rekindled thanks to inspiring discussions with Catherine Dubois, Amélie Ledein and Mathieu Montin. We are grateful to them for their time and enthusiasm. We also thank Adrien Guatto as well as the anonymous referees for their insightful comments and for their relentless efforts to maintain high standards of seriousness in academic writing.

References

1. Chris Okasaki. *Purely functional data structures.* Cambridge University Press, 1999. ISBN 978-0-521-66350-2
2. Conor McBride. Ornamental algebras, algebraic ornaments. Manuscript available online, 2010. URL http://personal.cis.strath.ac.uk/~conor/pub/OAAO/Ornament.pdf
3. Dagand, P.É., Tabareau, N., Tanter, É.: Foundations of dependent interoperability. J. Funct. Program. **28**, e9 (2018). https://doi.org/10.1017/S0956796818000011
4. Hinze, R.: Manufacturing datatypes. J. Funct. Program. **11**(5), 493–524 (2001). https://doi.org/10.1017/S095679680100404X
5. Richard S. Bird and Lambert G. L. T. Meertens. Nested datatypes. In Johan Jeuring, editor, *Mathematics of Program Construction, MPC'98, Marstrand, Sweden, June 15-17, 1998, Proceedings*, volume 1422 of *Lecture Notes in Computer Science*, pages 52–67. Springer, 1998. https://doi.org/10.1007/BFb0054285
6. Ralf Hinze. Numerical representations as higher-order nested datatypes. Technical Report IAI-TR-98-12, Institut für Informatik III, Universität Bonn, 1998. URL https://www.cs.ox.ac.uk/ralf.hinze/publications/IAI-TR-98-12.ps.gz
7. Samuel Klumpers. Generic numerical representations as ornaments. Master's thesis, Utrecht University, 2023. URL https://studenttheses.uu.nl/handle/20.500.12932/45670
8. Mathieu Montin, Amélie Ledein, and Catherine Dubois. Libndt: Towards a formal library on spreadable properties over linked nested datatypes. In Jeremy Gibbons and Max S. New, editors, *Proceedings Ninth Workshop on Mathematically Structured Functional Programming, MSFP@ETAPS 2022, Munich, Germany, 2nd April 2022*, volume 360 of *EPTCS*, pages 27–44, 2022. https://doi.org/10.4204/EPTCS.360.2

9. Ko, H.-S., Gibbons, J.: Programming with ornaments. J. Funct. Program. **27**, e2 (2017). https://doi.org/10.1017/S0956796816000307
10. Swierstra, W.: Heterogeneous binary random-access lists. J. Funct. Program. **30**, e10 (2020). https://doi.org/10.1017/S0956796820000064
11. Hinze, R., Swierstra, W.: Calculating datastructures. In Mathematics of Program Construction MPC (2022). https://doi.org/10.1007/978-3-031-16912-0_3
12. Pierre-Evariste Dagand, Pierre Letouzey, and Ellenor Fatemeh Taghayor. Rough Pearl: Manufacturing Cons-Cells. In *35es Journées Francophones des Langages Applicatifs (JFLA 2024)*, 2024. URL https://inria.hal.science/hal-04406422
13. Conor McBride, Healfdene Goguen, and James McKinna. A few constructions on constructors. In Jean-Christophe Filliâtre, Christine Paulin-Mohring, and Benjamin Werner, editors, *Types for Proofs and Programs, International Workshop, TYPES 2004, Jouy-en-Josas, France, December 15-18, 2004, Revised Selected Papers*, volume 3839 of *Lecture Notes in Computer Science*, pages 186–200. Springer, 2004. https://doi.org/10.1007/11617990_12
14. Coq standard library. Binary numbers: `to_nat`, 2024a. Module `NArith.BinNatDef` (l.367-371)
15. Coq standard library. Binary numbers, 2024b. Module `Numbers.BinNums` (l.21-24)
16. Agda standard library. Binary numbers, 2024. Module `Data.Nat.Binary.Base` (l.29-32)
17. Hedberg, M.: A coherence theorem for Martin-Löf's type theory. J. Funct. Program. **8**(4), 413–436 (1998)
18. Sam Lindley and Ian Stark. Reducibility and tt-lifting for computation types. In Pawel Urzyczyn, editor, *Typed Lambda Calculi and Applications, 7th International Conference, TLCA 2005, Nara, Japan, April 21-23, 2005, Proceedings*, volume 3461 of *Lecture Notes in Computer Science*, pages 262–277. Springer, 2005. https://doi.org/10.1007/11417170_20
19. Kenji Maillard. *Principles of Program Verification for Arbitrary Monadic Effects. (Principes de la Vérification de Programmes à Effets Monadiques Arbitraires).* PhD thesis, École Normale Supérieure, Paris, France, 2019. URL https://tel.archives-ouvertes.fr/tel-02416788
20. Myers, E.W.: An applicative random-access stack. Inf. Process. Lett. **17**(5), 241–248 (1983). https://doi.org/10.1016/0020-0190(83)90106-0
21. Texas Instruments. CMOS 4-bit magnitude comparator. 2003
22. Gérard P. Huet. The zipper. *J. Funct. Program.*, 7(5), 1997. https://doi.org/10.1017/S0956796897002864
23. Conor McBride. The Derivative of a Regular Type is its Type of One-Hole Contexts. Available at http://strictlypositive.org/diff.pdf, 2001
24. Dagand, P.É.: The essence of ornaments. J. Funct. Program. **27**, e9 (2017). https://doi.org/10.1017/S0956796816000356
25. Dagand, P.É., McBride, C.: Transporting functions across ornaments. J. Funct. Program. **24**(2–3), 316–383 (2014). https://doi.org/10.1017/S0956796814000069
26. Thomas Williams and Didier Rémy. A principled approach to ornamentation in ML. *Proc. ACM Program. Lang.*, 2(POPL):21:1–21:30, 2018. https://doi.org/10.1145/3158109
27. Conor McBride. Clowns to the left of me, jokers to the right (pearl): dissecting data structures. In George C. Necula and Philip Wadler, editors, *Proceedings of the 35th ACM SIGPLAN-SIGACT Symposium on Principles of Programming Languages, POPL 2008, San Francisco, California, USA, January 7-12, 2008*, pages 287–295. ACM, 2008. https://doi.org/10.1145/1328438.1328474

Generic Reasoning of the Locally Nameless Representation

Yicheng Ni and Yuting Wang(✉)

Shanghai Jiao Tong University, Shanghai, China
yuting.wang@sjtu.edu.cn

Abstract. When reasoning about properties of languages represented in the locally nameless style, a significant set of lemmas about binding structure and substitutions is needed. Such lemmas either need to be manually proved or generated from some language specifications, each time a particular object language is dealt with. We present an approach to deriving those lemmas which can be generically applied to different languages. Our approach is based on Locally Nameless Sets (LNS). It extends the theory of LNS with additional generic operations and axioms on binding structure, from which lemmas about the locally nameless representation can be described and proved without any assumption on the language syntax. Therefore, for any language satisfying the given axioms, which can be proved by straightforward induction, these lemmas are automatically proved. We implement a library for supporting our generic reasoning in Coq with built-in automation and demonstrate its effectiveness by proving equivalence properties of the simply-typed λ-calculus and the compactness theorem for PCF.

Keywords: Locally nameless representation · Generic reasoning · Coq

1 Introduction

The treatment of binding structure and variables is a fundamental issue in reasoning about programming languages, especially when formalizing these languages and proofs in proof assistants [4]. Various kinds of techniques have been proposed for formalizing meta-theory of programming languages. The de Bruijn indices [11] use numerical indices to represent variables. The locally named representation [16] and the locally nameless representation [9] explicitly divide variables into bound variables and free variables. The higher-order abstract syntax [18] encodes binding structure of object languages with the binders of the meta-language. The second-order abstract syntax [13,14] combines intrinsically-typed encoding with initial algebra semantics.

The locally nameless representation employs de Bruijn indices to represent bound variables, thereby reducing α-equivalence to syntactic equivalence, and employs explicit names to represent free variables, thereby avoiding shift operations in substitutions. Moreover, the locally nameless representation employs

O. Kiselyov (Ed.): APLAS 2024, LNCS 15194, pp. 42–62, 2024.
https://doi.org/10.1007/978-981-97-8943-6_3

co-finite quantification in inductively-defined propositions to avoid renaming free variables in inductive reasoning [3,9]. All these benefits make the locally nameless representation attractive in formalizing programming languages and logics, especially when the formalizing system cannot directly support the higher-order abstract syntax because of the rich function space in its meta-logic (e.g., Coq). Indeed, various formalization projects built in conventional proof systems have adopted the locally nameless representation for the above reason [2,7,28].

The overhead of using locally nameless representation is still significant. A non-trivial amount of lemmas about the locally nameless representation must be proved when formalizing a language [23]. These proofs depend on the syntax of the object language, meaning that they need to be redone every time a new language is introduced or the constructs of the language change. To reduce this overhead, tools have been developed to automatically generate the above lemmas from language specifications. For instance, LNgen takes as input language definitions written in the specification language Ott [25] and generates their locally nameless representation together with a set of lemmas for this representation (and their proofs) in Coq [5]. However, this approach incurs dependency on external tools such that the basic formalization of syntax is not fully controlled by users. Moreover, the generated lemmas may be insufficient for our needs. In this case, we either have to update the tools or prove the missing lemmas manually.

Our goal is to explicitly capture the essential proof structures of lemmas for the locally nameless representation so that the structured proofs can be reused for different languages independent of their syntax. This idea is initiated by Locally Nameless Sets (LNS), an equational axiomatization for the locally nameless representation [21]. In LNS, locally nameless terms are represented as a set of abstract elements equipped with abstract opening and closing operations for converting de Bruijn indices into free variables, and vice versa. By assuming axioms for opening and closing operations, a set of lemmas about these operations can be derived. They are generic in the sense that, for any language satisfying the axioms, the instances of the lemmas are established immediately. Based on these axioms and lemmas, *generic reasoning* about the formalized languages in proof assistants becomes possible, much like generic programming.

However, the vanilla LNS is insufficient to support generic reasoning in any non-trivial formal reasoning because the opening and closing operations are not enough for manipulating language constructs. In this work, we develop an approach to generically reasoning about the locally nameless representation based on the ideas of LNS. Our contributions include the following:

Table 1. Comparison of Operations for Manipulating Binding Structure

	opening	closing	open-term	substitution	morphism
LNS	✓	✓	✗	✗	●
Our Approach	✓	✓	✓	✓	✓

- Formalized theory for generic reasoning of the locally nameless representation. As described in Table 1, on top of the abstract set with opening and closing operations, we add two new abstract operations, open-term and substitution, and extend *morphisms* (abstract functions that commute with the opening and closing operations described in LNS). By assuming generic axioms for open-term, substitution and morphisms, key properties of the locally nameless representation (as described by Charguéraud [9]) can be proved ignorant of the concrete syntax of object languages. Any object language satisfying the axioms will get these properties for free. We realize the above operations, axioms and lemmas as a generic reasoning library in Coq.
- Non-trivial applications of our generic reasoning library to formalized meta-theory of programming languages, including verification of program equivalence for the simply typed λ-calculus (STLC) and proving the compactness theorem for PCF [22] (both adapted from the classic proofs on paper [15]). These examples demonstrate that our library is sufficient for practical reasoning about binding structures in the locally nameless representation, and that a large part of such formal reasoning can be automated by simply adding the derived lemmas into the hint database of Coq. Moreover, the axioms for STLC and PCF can be proved by straightforward inductions which are mostly automated. Therefore, they provide strong evidence that our library can effectively support formalization of programming languages in general.

The generic reasoning library and its applications can be found at https://zenodo.org/doi/10.5281/zenodo.13352783. The rest of the paper is organized as follows. We first introduce the background of locally nameless representation in §2. We discuss the challenges for adopting the locally nameless representation and the existing approaches in §3. We then present the theory for generic reasoning of the locally nameless representation—which is formalized as a Coq library—in §4. We further discuss the applications of our formalized theory in §5. We present the evaluation of our applications in §6 and discuss the related work in §7. Finally, we conclude in §8.

2 Locally Nameless Representation

We give an introduction to the locally nameless representation (which we call LNR in the remaining discussions) with the encoding of the untyped λ-calculus, which is defined as follows:

$$t := x \mid \lambda x.t_1 \mid (t_1\ t_2)$$

Variables in LNR are explicitly divided into bound variables, represented by de Bruijn indices, and free variables, represented by explicit names:

$$t := i \mid x \mid \lambda.t_1 \mid (t_1\ t_2)$$

For example, the term $\lambda x.(y\ x)$ is written as $\lambda.(y\ 0)$.

2.1 Opening and Closing

Opening and closing are two key operations on locally nameless terms [9]. An opening operation $\{i \to x\}t$ replaces all occurrences of the index i in term t with the free variable x. When a λ-abstraction is encountered, the target i should be shifted to $i+1$ before the recursion of the opening operation. For example, $\{0 \to z\}\lambda.(y\ 1) = \lambda.\{1 \to z\}(y\ 1) = \lambda.(y\ z)$. We shall write t^x for $\{0 \to x\}t$. Dual to opening, the closing operation $\{i \leftarrow x\}t$ converts all the occurrences of the free variable x in term t into the index i. For example, $\{0 \leftarrow x\}\lambda.(0\ x) = \lambda.\{1 \leftarrow x\}(0\ x) = \lambda.(0\ 1)$. We shall write t/x for $\{0 \leftarrow x\}t$.

2.2 Freshness and Locally Closedness

The freshness predicate $x \notin \mathit{fv}(t)$ states that x is not a free variable of t, where the fv function is recursively defined as follows:

$$\mathit{fv} := i \mapsto \emptyset \mid x \mapsto \{x\} \mid (t_1\ t_2) \mapsto \mathit{fv}(t_1) \cup \mathit{fv}(t_2) \mid \lambda.t \mapsto \mathit{fv}(t)$$

The locally closedness predicate $(\mathit{lc}\ t)$ states that t contains no unbound de Bruijn indexes; we call t a locally closed term. lc is defined inductively:

$$\frac{}{\mathit{lc}\ x}\ \text{LC-VAR} \qquad \frac{\mathit{lc}\ t_1 \quad \mathit{lc}\ t_2}{\mathit{lc}\ (t_1\ t_2)}\ \text{LC-APP} \qquad \frac{\boxed{\forall x \notin L,}\ \mathit{lc}\ (t^x)}{\mathit{lc}\ \lambda.t}\ \text{LC-ABS}$$

The rule LC-ABS employs a co-finite quantification (in the dashed box), which generates stronger induction hypotheses in inductive reasoning [9], to describe locally closed abstractions: if there exists a finite set L of variables s.t. for all $x \notin L$, t^x is locally closed, then $\lambda.t$ is locally closed.

2.3 Substitution and Open-Term

The dynamics of λ-calculus is captured by the β-reduction rule which is based on capture-avoiding substitution:

$$((\lambda x.t_1)t_2) \to_\beta [x \mapsto t_2]t_1.$$

We assume that we are only working with locally closed terms. Then, a substitution $[x \mapsto u]t$ simply replaces all occurrences of x in t with u—the α-conversion for capture-avoiding substitution is unnecessary. Combining substitution with opening, β-reduction in the LNR can be stated as:

$$((\lambda.t_1)\ t_2) \to_\beta [x \mapsto t_2](t_1^x) \qquad \text{where } x \notin \mathit{fv}(t_1) \wedge \mathit{lc}\ \lambda.t_1 \wedge \mathit{lc}\ t_2.$$

To avoid introducing a temporary variable x for substitution, a generalized opening operation called *open-term* (written as $\{i \mapsto t_2\}t_1$ in this paper) is proposed to directly replace de Bruijn indices in t_1 with term t_2 [9]. The notation $t_1^{t_2}$ is used for $\{0 \mapsto t_2\}t_1$. With open-term, β-reduction can be stated as:

$$((\lambda.t_1)\, t_2) \rightarrow_\beta \{0 \mapsto t_2\}t_1 \text{ with } lc\ \lambda.t_1 \wedge lc\ t_2.$$

We can represent open-term with substitution and opening : $\{0 \mapsto t_2\}t_1 = [x \mapsto t_2](\{0 \rightarrow x\}t_1)$ (where $x \notin fv(t_1)$), which is useful in reasoning.

3 Challenges and Our Approach

3.1 Challenges for Adopting LNR

Several challenges exist when reasoning with LNR. First, in most of the reasoning, we must maintain the locally closedness relation to exclude terms with unbound de Bruijn indices since these terms do not correspond to any term in the original language. Second, since the locally nameless operations (including opening, closing and open-term) are used in the statics and dynamics of the language (e.g., typing judgment and reduction relation, see below), we must manipulate terms mixing substitution and the locally nameless operations; for example, we need to rewrite terms with opening applied first and then substitution to terms with substitution applied first and then opening.

We give examples to show formal reasoning with LNR and its challenges. We will see that a set of locally nameless lemmas listed in Fig. 1 are essential in the reasoning. In each example below, we illustrate the extra subgoals brought by LNR in the proof and the corresponding locally nameless lemmas to solve them.

subst_lc:	$lc\ e_1 \wedge lc\ e_2$	$\Rightarrow lc\ ([x \mapsto e_1]e_2)$
subst_open:	$lc\ e_1$	$\Rightarrow [x \mapsto e_1](e_2^{e_3}) = ([x \mapsto e_1]e2)^{[x \mapsto e_1]e_3}$
subst_open_var:	$x \neq y \wedge lc\ u$	$\Rightarrow [x \mapsto u](t^y) = ([x \mapsto u]t)^y$
subst_intro:	$x \notin fv(t)$	$\Rightarrow t^u = [x \mapsto u]t^x$
subst_fresh:	$x \notin fv(e_2)$	$\Rightarrow [x \mapsto e_1]e_2 = e_2$
subst_as_close_open:	$lc\ e_2$	$\Rightarrow [x \mapsto e_1]e_2 = (e_2/x)^{e_1}$
open_term_lc:	$lc\ e_1$	$\Rightarrow e_1 = e_1^{e_2}$
lc_open_term:	$(\forall x \notin L, lc\ e_1^x) \wedge lc\ e_2$	$\Rightarrow lc\ e_1^{e_2}$

Fig. 1. Locally nameless lemmas for binding structure and substitution

The first example is proving that the call-by-value reduction (written as $\rightarrow_{cbv}$) in the untyped λ-calculus is congruent under substitution.

$$\frac{lc\ \lambda.t}{value\ \lambda.t}\ \text{V-ABS} \qquad \frac{lc\ \lambda.t \quad value\ u}{((\lambda.t)\ u) \rightarrow_{cbv} t^u}\ \text{RED-BETA}$$

$$\frac{t_1 \rightarrow_{cbv} t_1' \quad lc\ t_2}{(t_1\ t_2) \rightarrow_{cbv} (t_1'\ t_2)} \text{ RED-APP1} \qquad \frac{value\ t_1 \quad t_2 \rightarrow_{cbv} t_2'}{(t_1\ t_2) \rightarrow_{cbv} (t_1\ t_2')} \text{ RED-APP2}$$

Theorem 1. *If $t \rightarrow_{cbv} t'$ and $lc\ u$, then $[x \mapsto u]t \rightarrow_{cbv} [x \mapsto u]t'$.*

The proof is by induction on $t \rightarrow_{cbv} t'$. In the RED-APP1 and RED-APP2 cases, the goal can be proved by the induction hypothesis. In the RED-BETA case, the goal can be proved by the distributive property of substitution.

Compared with the proof on paper, the formal proof in LNR has the following additional goals. First, because lc is used in RED-APP1 and RED-APP2, we must prove $lc\ [x \mapsto u]t_2$ and $lc\ [x \mapsto u]t_1$, which can be done with lemma *subst_lc* in Fig. 1. Second, open-term is used in RED-BETA so that we must prove $([x \mapsto u]t)^{[x \mapsto u]t_2} = [x \mapsto u](t^{t_2})$, which can be done with *subst_open* in Fig. 1.

The next two examples are properties about type safety of the simply-typed λ-calculus. First, we define types and typing judgment of STLC. The types are built from the base type and arrow types: $\tau := nat \mid \tau_1 \rightarrow \tau_2$. The typing judgment for STLC $\Gamma \vdash t : \tau$ are derived by the following rules:

$$\frac{(x : \tau) \in \Gamma}{\Gamma \vdash x : \tau} \text{ T-VAR} \qquad \frac{\Gamma \vdash t_1 : \tau_1 \rightarrow \tau_2 \quad \Gamma \vdash t_2 : \tau_1}{\Gamma \vdash (t_1\ t_2) : \tau_2} \text{ T-APP}$$

$$\frac{\forall x \notin L, \Gamma; x : \tau_1 \vdash t^x : \tau_2}{\Gamma \vdash \lambda.t : \tau_1 \rightarrow \tau_2} \text{ T-ABS}$$

Lemma 1. *If $\Gamma; x : \tau' \vdash t : \tau$ and $\Gamma \vdash u : \tau'$, then $\Gamma \vdash [x \mapsto u]t : \tau$.*

The proof of Lemma 1 is by induction on $\Gamma; x : \tau' \vdash t : \tau$. The differences between the formal proof and the proof on paper lie in the T-ABS case. In the formal reasoning, we need to manipulate terms mixing substitution with opening. We have $\Gamma; y : \tau_1 \vdash [x \mapsto u]t^y : \tau_2$ and need to prove $\Gamma; y : \tau_1 \vdash ([x \mapsto u]t)^y : \tau_2$. The remaining goal becomes $[x \mapsto u]t^y = ([x \mapsto u]t)^y$, which can be solved by lemma *subst_open_var* in Fig. 1.

Theorem 2 (Preservation). *If $\Gamma \vdash t : \tau$ and $t \rightarrow_{cbv} t'$, then $\Gamma \vdash t' : \tau$.*

The proof of Theorem 2 is by induction on $t \rightarrow_{cbv} t'$. We focus on the RED-BETA case where $t = ((\lambda.t)\ v)$ and $t' = t^v$. The goal becomes typing judgment on terms containing the open-term operation $\Gamma \vdash t^v : \tau$. To apply Lemma 1, we use lemma *subst_intro* in Fig. 1 to convert t^v to $[x \mapsto v]t^x$. The remaining reasoning follows the proof on paper.

The remaining lemmas in Fig. 1 are used in the derivation of the lemmas mentioned above and more complicated reasoning. *subst_fresh* and *open_term_lc* are used to derive *subst_intro* and *subst_open*. *subst_as_close_open* is useful for dealing with mixed representation of name binding (e.g., reasoning about contextual equivalence in our Coq development). *lc_open_term* provides a way to directly prove the locally closedness for terms containing the open-term operation (e.g., terms after β-reduction).

Problems The proofs of the locally nameless lemmas depend on the language syntax. Consequently, every time we define a new language or modify the current language, the proofs for locally nameless lemmas must be redone. For example, the proof of the freshness lemma $a \notin fv(t_1\ t_2) \Rightarrow a \notin fv(t_1)$ relies on the definition of *fv*, which is recursively defined on the structure of the terms. Moreover, the proof of the lemma $lc\ (t_1\ t_2) \Rightarrow lc\ t_1$ depends on the rule LC-APP. Furthermore, the proofs of the locally nameless lemmas in Fig. 1 also depend on the syntax:

- *subst_fresh* and *subst_open* are proved by induction on the syntax of terms.
- *open_term_lc* and *subst_lc* are proved by induction on predicate *lc*.
- The remaining lemmas in Fig. 1 are derived from the former four lemmas. The proof of *subst_as_close_open* depends on *subst_intro*, which can be derived from *subst_fresh* and *subst_open*; *subst_open_var* is a special case of *subst_open*; *lc_open_term* can be derived from *subst_lc* and *subst_intro*.

$$
\begin{aligned}
\{i \to a\}\{i \to b\}t &= \{i \to b\}t && (\mathbf{OC_1})\\
\{i \leftarrow a\}\{j \leftarrow a\}t &= \{j \leftarrow a\}t && (\mathbf{OC_2})\\
\{i \leftarrow a\}\{i \to a\}t &= \{i \leftarrow a\}t && (\mathbf{OC_3})\\
\{i \to a\}\{i \leftarrow a\}t &= \{i \to a\}t && (\mathbf{OC_4})\\
i \neq j \Rightarrow \{i \to a\}\{j \to b\}t &= \{j \to b\}\{i \to a\}t && (\mathbf{OC_5})\\
a \neq b \Rightarrow \{i \leftarrow a\}\{j \leftarrow b\}t &= \{j \leftarrow b\}\{i \leftarrow a\}t && (\mathbf{OC_6})\\
i \neq j \land a \neq b \Rightarrow \{i \to a\}\{j \leftarrow b\}t &= \{j \leftarrow b\}\{i \to a\}t && (\mathbf{OC_7})
\end{aligned}
$$

Fig. 2. Axioms for opening and closing

3.2 Existing Approaches

Two approaches, named LNgen and the locally nameless sets (LNS), are proposed to solve the problems discussed above.

LNgen LNgen takes definitions of languages written in Ott as input and generates corresponding definitions in locally nameless syntax together with a set of locally nameless lemmas (including specifications and proofs) in Coq.

Locally Nameless Sets Locally nameless sets generically derive locally nameless lemmas by assuming axioms for abstract terms and operations. The basic idea is to use generic properties of LNR to describe concrete locally nameless lemmas. The generic properties have underlying algebraic structure, which is captured by LNS. Suppose we have abstract sets $\mathbf{X}, \mathbf{N}$ and $\mathbf{A}$ (with $\mathbf{N}$ and $\mathbf{A}$ being disjoint), and two abstract functions *open* and *close* with type $\mathbf{N} \times \mathbf{A} \times \mathbf{X} \to \mathbf{X}$. Given $(i, a, t) \in \mathbf{N} \times \mathbf{A} \times \mathbf{X}$, $open\ i\ a\ t$ denotes $\{i \to a\}t$ and $close\ i\ a\ t$ denotes $\{i \leftarrow a\}t$. A set $\mathbf{X}$ equiped with opening and closing operations is called an *opening-closing set* (called an *oc-set* in [21]).

Given an oc-set $\mathbf{X}$, the freshness and locally closedness relations are defined:

$$a \# t := \{0 \leftarrow a\}t = t$$
$$i \succ t := \forall j \geq i, \exists a \in \mathbf{A}, \{j \to a\}t = t$$

Here, $a \# t$ is equivalent to $a \notin fv(t)$. $i \succ t$ denotes that t only contains de Bruijn index less than i. Therefore, $0 \succ t$ is equivalent to $lc\ t$ [21].

The critical observation made in LNS is that the properties of opening and closing operations can be reasoned about based on *equational* axioms, instead of inductive definitions of language syntax. This enables generic reasoning of object languages independent of their concrete syntax. Fig. 2 lists some of the axioms proposed in LNS [21] (note that we use bold fonts to highlight axioms). $\mathbf{OC_1}$ and $\mathbf{OC_2}$ state the properties that the outer opening and closing operations are overshadowed by the inner ones, while $\mathbf{OC_3}$ and $\mathbf{OC_4}$ state the properties that the outer operations are overwritten by the inner ones. $\mathbf{OC_5}, \mathbf{OC_6}$ and $\mathbf{OC_7}$ describe the commutative properties of opening and closing. It is worth noting that we exclude $\mathbf{OC_8}$ and $\mathbf{OC_9}$, which express renaming (atom-to-atom) and re-indexing (index to index) in LNS but found not useful in our formalization.

With these axioms, lemmas about opening and closing in Fig. 3 can be derived with equational reasoning [21]. *lc_open* and *ge_closed* are lemmas about locally closedness for opening and closing (LCOC); *open_lc*, *open_any_atom* and *close_any_index* are lemmas about rewriting for opening and closing (ROC); *fresh_close* describes freshness for opening and closing (FOC). The derived lemmas are *generic* since they are described and proved without any assumption on the language syntax.

lc_open:	$(i+1) \succ t$	$\Rightarrow i \succ \{i \to a\}t$	(LCOC)
ge_closed:	$j \geq i \wedge i \succ t$	$\Rightarrow j \succ t$	(LCOC)
open_lc	$i \succ t$	$\Rightarrow \{i \to a\}t = t$	(ROC)
open_any_atom:	$\{i \to a\}t = t$	$\Rightarrow \{i \to b\}t = t$	(ROC)
close_any_index:	$\{i \leftarrow a\}t = t$	$\Rightarrow \{j \leftarrow a\}t = t$	(ROC)
fresh_close:		$\Rightarrow a \# (\{i \leftarrow a\}t)$	(FOC)

Fig. 3. Derived Lemmas about Opening and Closing

Morphisms A morphism $f : \mathbf{X} \to \mathbf{Y}$ of oc-sets is a function from the set $\mathbf{X}$ to the set $\mathbf{Y}$ that commutes with the opening and closing operations:

$$f(\{i \to a\}t) = \{i \to a\}(f\ t)\ (\mathbf{M_{11}})$$
$$f(\{i \leftarrow a\}t) = \{i \leftarrow a\}(f\ t)\ (\mathbf{M_{12}})$$

Morphisms have good properties on freshness and locally closedness, marked respectively as FM and LCM:

$$mph\_preserves\_fr : a \# t \Rightarrow a \# f\ t\ (FM)$$
$$mph\_preserves\_lc : i \succ t \Rightarrow i \succ f\ t\quad (LCM)$$

Similar to the lemmas about opening and closing, properties of morphisms can be *equationally* derived independent of the implementation of the morphisms [21].

Limitations of the Existing Approaches

LNgen First, LNgen generates definitions and lemmas according to the specifications in Ott, which makes it difficult for users to modify the definitions or add more locally nameless lemmas. Furthermore, LNgen does not really solve the problem of repeating proving locally nameless lemmas. Essentially, it generates a copy of lemmas for each language. Once LNgen is updated, we must rerun the tool to get a new copy of the lemmas.

LNS As we have discussed above and as summarized in Table 1, properties about opening and closing operations can already be proved generically with the vanilla theory of LNS. However, properties in Fig. 1 are about open-term and substitution which LNS cannot handle. Moreover, there are no generic properties in LNS corresponding to the lemmas about the freshness predicate and locally closedness predicate in §2. For example, the statement $lc\ (t_1\ t_2)$ can be constructed with $lc\ t_1$ and $lc\ t_2$ by rule LC-APP, which seems underivable in LNS since concrete language constructs are involved.

3.3 Our Approach

We present an approach to generically reason about the locally nameless representation based on its equational axiomatization in LNS. First, we observe that generic properties for open-term and substitutions can be derived from a similar set of generic axioms. Second, we observe that the constructs of the language correspond to instances of morphisms in LNS. Therefore, it is possible to generically derive properties about constructs of languages by reasoning about morphisms. In particular, we discover that basic morphisms can be generalized to derive more generic properties of the locally nameless representation (e.g., properties of *lc* and *fv*).

As a result, our approach can generically derive a series of locally nameless lemmas, reducing the burden of proving all the locally nameless properties to a fixed set of axioms for the locally nameless operations.

4 Formalized Theory for Generic Reasoning

In this section, we introduce our generic reasoning approach, through which the locally nameless lemmas discussed in §3.1 can be generically derived. We have implemented a library for supporting our generic reasoning approach in Coq.

4.1 Overview of the Formalized Theory

Our theory follows the idea of LNS. Instead of proving the concrete locally nameless lemmas for each language, we propose generic properties, which are equivalent to concrete ones, and reason about them without any assumption on specific syntax. The overview of the approach is shown in Table 2. The columns are abstract operations, the rows are generic properties and each cell is an identifier for classification. The abstract operations include opening, closing, open-term, substitution and morphisms. The generic properties are systematically divided into four categories: axioms, freshness lemmas, locally closedness lemmas and rewriting lemmas. Each cell is a label to classify the generic properties. For example, LCOT stands for locally closedness lemmas for open-term.

First, based on LNS (the second and third columns in grey), we add abstract open-term and substitution operations, propose axioms for them and generically derive the locally nameless lemmas in Fig. 1, which corresponds to the fourth and fifth columns in Table 2. In our reasoning, *subst_lc* and *open_term_lc* (which were proved by induction on the locally closedness relation) can be derived from our axioms without induction on syntax, therefore are generically applicable to any language satisfying the axioms (see details below).

Second, we reason about generalized morphisms and instantiate them with language constructs to generically derive properties which are equivalent to the derivation rules of *fv* and *lc* described in §2. Also, we define morphisms which commute with the substitution operation and derive commutative properties about multi-substitution for abstract constructs. The generic reasoning about morphisms corresponds to the sixth column in Table 2.

Table 2. Overview of the generic reasoning approach

	Opening	Closing	Open-term	Substitution	Morphism
Axiom	**OC**	**OC**	**OT**	**S**	**M**
Freshness	FOC	FOC	$\emptyset$	$\emptyset$	FM
Locally closedness	LCOC	LCOC	LCOT	LCS	LCM
Rewriting	ROC	ROC	ROT	RS	RM

Let X represent OC (opening and closing), OT (open-term), S (substitution) and M (morphism). **X** (X in bold) are axioms for X (e.g., **OC** are axioms for Opening and Closing). F{X}, LC{X} and R{X} are freshness, locally closedness, and rewriting lemmas for X, respectively.

4.2 Open-term and Substitution

We add abstract *open-term* and *substitution* operations into our generic reasoning approach. Suppose we have abstract sets $\mathbf{N}$, $\mathbf{A}$ and $\mathbf{X}$, *open-term* is a function of type $\mathbf{N} \times \mathbf{X} \times \mathbf{X} \to \mathbf{X}$ and *substitution* is a function of type $\mathbf{A} \times \mathbf{X} \times \mathbf{X} \to \mathbf{X}$. Additionally, auxiliary function *fvar* with type $\mathbf{A} \to \mathbf{X}$ is introduced. Given $i \in \mathbf{N}, a \in \mathbf{A}$ and $t_1, t_2 \in \mathbf{X}$, *open-term* $i\ t_1\ t_2$ denotes $\{i \mapsto t_1\}t_2$ and *substitution* $a\ t_1\ t_2$ denotes $[a \mapsto t_1]t_2$.

Our goal is to generically derive the locally nameless lemmas in Fig. 1. For this, Fig. 1 is abstracted into the axioms in Fig. 4 and lemmas in Fig. 5 independent of concrete syntax of languages because of the use of abstract operations. Axioms $\mathbf{S_1}$ and $\mathbf{S_2}$ are equivalent to the lemmas *subst_fresh* and *subst_open* in Fig. 1, respectively. Lemmas in Fig. 5 (with i instantiated with 0) are equivalent to the remaining lemmas in Fig. 1. The remaining **S** and **OT** axioms are properties about the algebraic structure of abstract substitution and open-term.

Now, we show the generic lemmas in Fig. 5 can be derived by applying the axioms in Fig. 4 without mentioning any concrete syntax. Therefore, the reasoning process (hence the derived lemmas) is applicable to any concrete language.

$$\{i \mapsto u\}\{i \to a\}t = \{i \to a\}t \quad (\mathbf{OT_1})$$
$$i \succ u \Rightarrow \{i \to a\}\{i \mapsto u\}t = \{i \mapsto u\}t \quad (\mathbf{OT_2})$$
$$i \neq j \wedge i \succ u \Rightarrow \{i \to a\}\{j \mapsto u\}t = \{j \mapsto u\}\{i \to a\}t \quad (\mathbf{OT_3})$$
$$\{i \mapsto fvar\ a\}t = \{i \to a\}t \quad (\mathbf{OT_4})$$
$$a \# t \Rightarrow [a \mapsto u]t = t \quad (\mathbf{S_1})$$
$$i \succ u \Rightarrow [x \mapsto u](\{i \mapsto t_2\}t_1) = \{i \mapsto ([x \mapsto u]t_2)\}([x \mapsto u]t_1) \quad (\mathbf{S_2})$$
$$[a \mapsto t]\,(fvar\ a) = t \quad (\mathbf{S_3})$$
$$b \neq a \Rightarrow [a \mapsto t](fvar\ b) = fvar\ b \quad (\mathbf{S_4})$$

Fig. 4. Axioms for Open-term and Substitution

open_term_lc:	$i \succ t$	$\Rightarrow t = \{i \mapsto y\}t$	(ROT)
lc_open_term:	$(i+1) \succ t \wedge i \succ y$	$\Rightarrow i \succ \{i \mapsto y\}t$	(LCOT)
subst_intro:	$x \# t \wedge i \succ u$	$\Rightarrow \{i \mapsto u\}t = [x \mapsto u](\{i \to x\}t)$	(RS)
subst_lc:	$i \succ t \wedge i \succ u$	$\Rightarrow i \succ [x \mapsto u]t$	(LCS)
subst_as_close_open:	$i \succ u \wedge i \succ t$	$\Rightarrow [x \mapsto u]t = \{i \mapsto u\}\{i \leftarrow x\}t$	(RS)
subst_open_var:	$y \neq x \wedge 0 \succ u$	$\Rightarrow ([x \mapsto u]t)^y = [x \mapsto u](t^y)$	(RS)

Fig. 5. Derived Lemmas about Open-term and Substitution

open_term_lc and *lc_open_term* are properties about open-term. As mentioned in §2, open-term is a generalized version of opening. We observe that *open_term_lc* and *lc_open_term* are generalized version of *open_lc* and *lc_open* in Fig. 3, and that the derivation of former lemmas follows the derivation of latter ones. Therefore, the required axioms for open-term (**OT** in Fig. 4) generalize axioms for opening (**OC** in Fig. 2). First, to derive *open_term_lc*, assuming $i \succ t$ we need to show $t = \{i \mapsto y\}t$. By $i \succ t$ we have $\{i \rightarrow a\}t = t$. By replacing t in the goal with $\{i \rightarrow a\}t$, we are left to prove $\{i \rightarrow a\}t = \{i \mapsto y\}\{i \rightarrow a\}t$, which is exactly the axiom $\mathbf{OT_1}$. Second, to derive *lc_open_term*, we follow a proof similar to that of *lc_open* which depends on the axioms $\mathbf{OC_1}$ and $\mathbf{OC_5}$ in Fig. 2. For that, we generalize $\mathbf{OC_1}$ and $\mathbf{OC_5}$ to $\mathbf{OT_2}$ and $\mathbf{OT_3}$, respectively. $\mathbf{OT_2}$ states that the outer opening is overshadowed if the inner open-term does not introduce indexes greater than i. $\mathbf{OT_3}$ states that opening and open-term are commutative.

The remaining lemmas about substitution in Fig. 5 can also be derived from the abstract axioms and lemmas without depending on the language syntax. First, *subst_intro*, *subst_as_close_open* and *subst_open_var* can be derived from $\mathbf{S_1}$ and $\mathbf{S_2}$, which follows the derivation discussed in §3.1; auxiliary axioms ($\mathbf{OT_4}, \mathbf{S_3}$ and $\mathbf{S_4}$) are used to relate the abstract operations involved in the reasoning. Second, the derivation of *subst_lc* differs from the proof in §3.1. Instead of induction on the locally closedness relation, it can be proved with full use of the axioms and lemmas about opening, closing, open-term and substitution.

4.3 Generalization of Morphisms

As described in §2.2, the definitions of the freshness predicate $x \notin fv(t)$ and the locally closedness predicate $lc\ t$ depend on the syntax of the language, which facilitates reasoning properties for language constructs. For example, if we have $x \notin fv(t_1)$ and $x \notin fv(t_2)$, it is straightforward to get $x \notin fv(\mathbf{app}\ t_1\ t_2)$ by the definition of *fv*, where $\mathbf{app}\ t_1\ t_2$ is the term of application. Also, if we have $lc\ t_1$ and $lc\ t_2$, it is easy to derive $lc\ (\mathbf{app}\ t_1\ t_2)$ by LC-APP.

Since general reasoning has no assumptions on the language syntax, we cannot derive the freshness and locally closedness lemmas about language constructs by defining *lc* and *fv*. However, we discover that the language constructs satisfy the axioms for morphisms. The properties for these constructs are equivalent to the rules defined in *lc* and *fv*. We generalize the definition of morphisms, reason about them and generically derive properties for language constructs as follows:

- *Binary morphisms* abstract language constructs requiring two sub-terms (e.g.,**app**). We generically derive freshness and locally closedness properties for **app**, which are equivalent to the rule in *fv* and rule LC-APP respectively.
- *Shift-morphisms* abstract language constructs with binders (e.g.**abs**). Similarly, freshness and locally closedness properties can be derived for **abs**.
- *Injective morphisms* are proposed to derive the inversion property of the freshness and locally closedness rules. For example, with injective morphisms we can derive the inversion of rule LC-APP for the construct **app**.
- *Substitution morphisms* capture abstract functions that commute with the substitution operation. By substitution morphisms, we can generically derive commutative properties about multi-substitution for language constructs.

Binary morphisms We define binary morphisms to represent abstract construct **app**. A binary morphism $g : \mathbf{X} \times \mathbf{X} \to \mathbf{X}$ is a function of arity 2 that commutes with opening and closing operations:

$$g(\{i \to a\}t_1)(\{i \to a\}t_2) = \{i \to a\}(g\, t_1\, t_2)\ (\mathbf{M_{21}})$$
$$g(\{i \leftarrow a\}t_1)(\{i \leftarrow a\}t_2) = \{i \leftarrow a\}(g\, t_1\, t_2)\ (\mathbf{M_{22}})$$

Just as unary morphisms in LNS, binary morphisms have similar properties on freshness and locally closedness relation:

$$\textit{bimph\_preserves\_fr} : a \# t_1 \wedge a \# t_2 \Rightarrow a \# g\, t_1\, t_2\ (FM)$$
$$\textit{bimph\_preserves\_lc} : i \succ t_1 \wedge i \succ t_2 \Rightarrow i \succ g\, t_1\, t_2 \quad (LCM)$$

According to the implementation of opening and closing in [9], it is trivial to prove **app** is a binary morphism. Therefore, we have $a \# t_1 \wedge a \# t_2 \Rightarrow a \# \mathbf{app}\ t_1\ t_2$, which is equivalent to the statement $x \notin \mathit{fv}(t_1) \wedge x \notin \mathit{fv}(t_2) \Rightarrow x \notin \mathit{fv}(\mathbf{app}\ t_1\ t_2)$ in the classic LNR. Also, we have $0 \succ t_1 \wedge 0 \succ t_2 \Rightarrow 0 \succ \mathbf{app}$ $t_1\ t_2$, which is equivalent to the statement $\mathit{lc}\, t_1 \wedge \mathit{lc}\, t_2 \Rightarrow \mathit{lc}\ (\mathbf{app}\ t_1\ t_2)$.

Shift-morphisms We define shift-morphisms to capture properties for constructs containing λ binders. A shift-morphism $h : \mathbf{X} \to \mathbf{X}$ is a function that commutes and shifts the index with opening and closing operations:

$$h(\{(i+1) \to a\}t) = \{i \to a\}(h\, t)\ (\mathbf{M_{31}})$$
$$h(\{(i+1) \leftarrow a\}t) = \{i \leftarrow a\}(h\, t)\ (\mathbf{M_{32}})$$

Shift-morphisms have properties:

$$\textit{smph\_preserves\_fr} : a \# t \Rightarrow a \# h\, t \qquad (FM)$$
$$\textit{smph\_preserves\_lc} : (i+1) \succ t \Rightarrow i \succ h\, t\ (LCM)$$

Suppose we have a construct **abs** and **abs** t is the abstraction form in the locally nameless syntax, it is trivial to prove **abs** is a shift-morphism. Therefore, we have $a \# t \Rightarrow a \# \mathbf{abs}\ t$ and $(i+1) \succ t \Rightarrow i \succ \mathbf{abs}\ t$. The latter one is a generalized property of the rule LC-ABS in §2.2.

Injective morphisms In classic LNR, it is trivial to prove $\mathit{lc}\ t_1$ if we have $\mathit{lc}\ (t_1\ t_2)$, which is the inversion of the rule LC-APP in §2.2. We can add injectivity to the above morphisms to generically derive similar inversion lemmas. For example, an injective unary morphism $f : \mathbf{X} \to \mathbf{X}$ is a morphism such that:

$$\forall t_1, t_2 \in \mathbf{X}, f\ t_1 = f\ t_2 \Rightarrow t_1 = t_2 (\mathbf{M_4})$$

Injective unary morphisms have good inversion properties on freshness and locally closedness:

$$\textit{injmph\_inverses\_fr} : a \# f\ t \Rightarrow a \# t\ (FM)$$
$$\textit{injmph\_inverses\_lc} : i \succ f\ t \Rightarrow i \succ t \quad (LCM)$$

To prove *injmph_inverses_fr*, by the definition of morphisms and $a \# (f\ t)$, we have $f(\{0 \leftarrow a\}t) = \{0 \leftarrow a\}(f\ t) = f\ t$. By injectivity, we have $\{0 \leftarrow a\}t = t$, which is exactly $a \# t$. The proof of *injmph_inverses_lc* follows a similar pattern.

Similarly, injective binary morphism and injective shift-morphism can be defined to get their corresponding inversion properties. To instantiate injective morphisms with constructs of languages, we discover that injectivity is a property for free of the constructs.

Substitution morphisms In LNR, language constructs commute with the substitution operation. For example, $\mathbf{abs}([x \mapsto u]t) = [x \mapsto u](\mathbf{abs}\ t)$, which is exactly the definition of substitution. Multi-substitutions can be defined on top of substitutions and equational lemmas for multi-substitutions can be proved. For example, the lemma $\widehat{\gamma}(\mathbf{abs}\ e) = \mathbf{abs}\ (\widehat{\gamma}(e))$, which states that multi-substitutions commute with the construct **abs**, is proved by induction on the substitution list γ. Similar lemmas must be proved for each construct of the language.

We discover that by defining morphisms commuting with substitution rather than opening and closing, the above equational lemmas can be derived generically. A substitution morphism $f : \mathbf{X} \to \mathbf{X}$ is a function commuting with substitution:

$$f([x \mapsto u]t) = [x \mapsto u](f\ t)\ (\mathbf{M_5})$$

We can derive that a substitution morphism f commutes with multi-substitutions:

$$substmph\_commutes\_msubst : f\ (\widehat{\gamma}(t)) = \widehat{\gamma}(f\ t)\ (RM)$$

The lemma can be proved by induction on the list γ. By the definition of substitution, it is obvious that all constructs are substitution morphisms.

5 Case Study

In this section, we show two applications of our generic reasoning library, including verification of program equivalence for STLC and proving the compactness theorem for PCF (both adapted from [15]). For each language, first we define its syntax and the locally nameless operations. After proving that the operations satisfy the axioms in our generic reasoning library, instances of the generic lemmas discussed in §4 will be automatically generated for the specific language. Then, we can reason about the meta-theory of the language.

In our development, we observe that the formal proofs are similar to the proofs on paper. Furthermore, a large part of formal reasoning about LNR can be automated by simply adding the derived lemmas into the hint database of Coq and the remaining goals can be solved by applying the lemmas in our library.

5.1 Program Equivalence of STLC

Instantiation of STLC The instantiation of STLC is the process of defining the syntax and locally nameless operations, and proving axioms stated in the generic reasoning library. The definitions follow the style described by Charguéraud [9]. The axioms for opening, closing, open-term and substitution can be proved by simple induction on the structure of the STLC terms and the axioms for morphisms can be proved by simplification. For example, the proof of axiom $\mathbf{OT_1}$: $\{i \mapsto u\}\{i \to a\}t = \{i \to a\}t$ (where t, u are terms of STLC and $\{i \to a\}, \{i \mapsto u\}$ are implementation of the opening and open-term operations) is by induction on the structure of t.

Formalization Two program equivalences are involved in the verification – contextual equivalence, written $\Gamma \vdash e \cong e' : \tau$, and logical equivalence, written $\Gamma \vdash e \sim e' : \tau$. Contextual equivalence means that given any *well-typed* evaluation context, two terms always evaluate to the same value under the context. Logical equivalence is defined in the following example. Our goal is to show $\Gamma \vdash e \cong e' : \tau$ iff $\Gamma \vdash e \sim e' : \tau$. Fig. 6 shows the overview of the proof, which is adapted from Harper [15]. Several predicates are used in the figure. ER($\mathcal{R}$) states that $\mathcal{R}$ is an equivalence relation. CC($\mathcal{R}$) states that $\mathcal{R}$ is a consistent congruence. CERCC($\mathcal{R}$) states that $\mathcal{R}$ is an equivalence relation and $\mathcal{R}$ is the coarsest consistent congruence. The proof is divided into the "if" part, which depends on the closed version of the "if" lemma, and the "only if" part, which is done by first proving that CERCC($\Gamma \vdash e \cong e' : \tau$) and then proving that ER($\Gamma \vdash e \sim e' : \tau$) and CC($\Gamma \vdash e \sim e' : \tau$). The strong normalization theorem of STLC is exploited in the proof of the reflexivity and CC($\Gamma \vdash e \sim e' : \tau$).

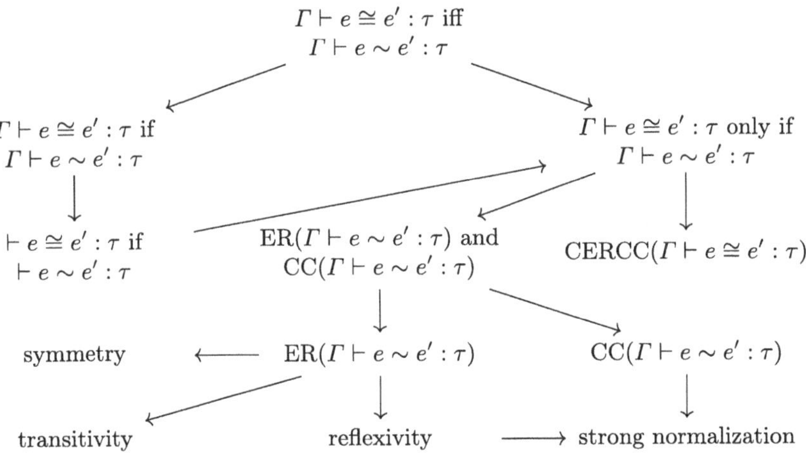

Fig. 6. Verification of Program Equivalence for STLC

We show the proof of the reflexivity property, which is one of the most complicated lemmas to prove in Fig. 6, as an example of formal reasoning with our generic library. The definitions of logical equivalence are stated as follows:

$$\begin{aligned}
\vdash e \sim e' : \tau &:= \exists \overline{n}, e \to^*_{cbv} \overline{n} \wedge e' \to^*_{cbv} \overline{n} && (\tau = nat)\\
& \forall \vdash e_2 \sim e_2' : \tau_1,\ \vdash (e\ e_2) \sim (e'\ e_2') : \tau_2 && (\tau = \tau_1 \to \tau_2)\\
\Gamma \vdash e \sim e' : \tau &:= \forall \gamma \sim_\Gamma \gamma',\ \vdash \widehat{\gamma}(e) \sim \widehat{\gamma'}(e') : \tau
\end{aligned}$$

where γ and γ' are substitutions for Γ, satisfying $\forall(x,\tau) \in \Gamma, \gamma(x) \sim \gamma'(x) : \tau$. The auxiliary lemma and reflexivity property are:

Lemma 2. *Suppose* $\vdash e \sim e' : \tau$. *If* $d \rightarrow_{cbv} e$ *and* $d' \rightarrow_{cbv} e'$, *then* $\vdash d \sim d' : \tau$.

Theorem 3 (Reflexivity). *If* $\Gamma \vdash e : \tau$, *then* $\Gamma \vdash e \sim e : \tau$.

The proof of Theorem 3 is by induction on $\Gamma \vdash e : \tau$ [15]. Consider the abstraction case where $e = \lambda x.e_2, \tau = \tau_1 \rightarrow \tau_2$. By the definition of $\Gamma \vdash e \sim e' : \tau$, assuming $\gamma \sim_\Gamma \gamma'$, we need to show $\vdash \widehat{\gamma}(\lambda x.e_2) \sim \widehat{\gamma'}(\lambda x.e_2) : \tau_1 \rightarrow \tau_2$. Assuming $\vdash e_1 \sim e_1' : \tau_1$, by Lemma 2, it is enough to show $[x \mapsto e_1]\widehat{\gamma}(e_2) \sim [x \mapsto e_1']\widehat{\gamma'}(e_2) : \tau_2$. Let $\gamma_2 = \gamma; (x \mapsto e_1)$ and $\gamma_2' = \gamma'; (x \mapsto e_1')$, we have $\gamma_2 \sim_{\Gamma;(x,\tau_1)} \gamma_2'$. By the induction hypothesis, we have $\widehat{\gamma_2}(e_2) \sim \widehat{\gamma_2'}(e_2) : \tau_2$. The goal is proved by unfolding γ_2 and γ_2'.

Compared with the proof on paper, the formal proof in LNR has additional goals to be proved. First, we need to prove $\widehat{\gamma}(\lambda.e) = \lambda.(\widehat{\gamma}(e))$, which states that multi-substitution commutes with the language construct λ. This statement is captured by the property *substmph_commutes_msubst* of substitution morphisms in §4.3. Second, by applying lemmas proved previously, we need to prove lots of subgoals about freshness and locally closedness, which are automated by our Ltac scripts. Third, Lemma 2 brings terms mixing the open-term operation with multi-substitution ($\vdash (\widehat{\gamma}(e_2))^v \sim (\widehat{\gamma'}(e_2'))^{v'} : \tau_2$) and the induction hypothesis brings terms mixing the opening operation with substitution ($\vdash \widehat{\gamma}([y \mapsto v]e_2^y) \sim \widehat{\gamma'}([y \mapsto v']e_2'^y) : \tau_2$). Lemmas *subst_open* and *subst_fresh* are exploited to prove the former and lemma *subst_intro* is used for the latter.

The proofs of the remaining lemmas in Fig. 6 follow the same pattern as the above example: the structure of the formal reasoning follows the proof on paper and the additional goals brought by LNR can be solved by combining Ltacs with the lemmas in our generic reasoning library. We observe that although the proof of program equivalence on paper is more complicated than the examples discussed in §3.1, the complexity brought by LNR does not increase much – the extra goals are still about freshness, locally closedness or manipulation of locally nameless operations, which can be solved by the corresponding locally nameless lemmas discussed in Table 2 (See also the evaluation in §8).

5.2 Compactness for PCF

PCF introduces general recursion, written $f^{(\omega)}$, which may cause the program to diverge. The compactness theorem states that the behavior of general recursion can be captured by its bounded recursion, written $f^{(m)}$, which first unfolds itself m times and then diverges.

Theorem 4 (Compactness). *Suppose that* $y : \tau \vdash e : nat$ *where* $y \notin f^{(\omega)}$. *If* $[y \mapsto f^{(\omega)}]e \rightarrow^*_{cbv} \overline{n}$, *then there exists* $m \geq 0$ *such that* $[y \mapsto f^{(m)}]e \rightarrow^*_{cbv} \overline{n}$.

The formal proof of the compactness theorem is similar to the proof on paper, which has three steps: first, we define the stack machine for PCF and prove its completeness and soundness; second, we prove another version of the compactness theorem which is described by transitions of the stack machine; third, the original compactness theorem can be proved by applying the completeness and soundness theorems to the completeness theorem in step two. When formalizing the definitions and theorems of the stack machine in step one, we discover that almost no locally nameless lemmas need to be manually applied in the reasoning. In step two, the structure of the formal proof follows the structure of proof on paper; a large part of the additional goals about locally closedness can be automated by Ltacs and the remaining goals about substitution can be solved by lemma *subst_open* (See also the evaluation in §8).

5.3 Discussion about Soundness and Completeness

Although the axioms about open-term, substitution and morphisms work well in STLC and PCF, whether they are valid in all languages (soundness) and capture all properties of LNR (completeness) is not investigated in this paper. Below we discuss these problems.

We conjecture that our approach is sound for functional languages that work on *well-formed* (or *well-typed*) programs. Our operations (open-terms, substitutions, morphisms) are designed for manipulating primitive binding structures that commonly occurs in λ-calculi. For instance, shift-morphisms are designed for handling λ-abstractions. Their axioms should hold for any type of λ-abstractions. Although we have only tested our approach on STLC and PCF, we do not see any obstacle to applying it to richer functional languages such as System F or even industrial ones like ML/OCaml. For instance, the `Fix` construct in ML is a shift-morphism and the `Catch` construct is a binary morphism.

As for completeness, the LNS paper proves that axioms $\mathbf{OC_1}$ to $\mathbf{OC_9}$ completely characterise the action of endofunctions of $\mathbf{N} \cup \mathbf{A}$ on finitely supported objects [21]. Meanwhile, we conjecture that we can get similar result about completeness of our approach by enriching our axioms about open-term, substitution and morphisms. Proving this conjecture is left for future work.

6 Evaluation

Our Coq development took 4 person-months. The entire artifact contains 7.9k lines of code (LOC) as shown in Table 3. The first column is about components in our development; the second column describes LOC in each component; the third column describes LOC relevant to LNR in each component; the last column is the percentage of LNR code in each component. It takes 1k LOC to formalize the basic data types and their properties (e.g., typing environments), and 1.1k LOC to develop the generic reasoning library. It takes 2.9k LOC to verify program equivalence for STLC and 2.9k LOC to prove the compactness theorem for PCF. In total, without the library the LOC about LNR is 483 (8.3% of 5.8k) and with it the LOC about LNR is 1.6k (20.2% of 7.9k). It shows that the overhead of reasoning about LNR is relatively low by using our library. We believe the low percentage of locally nameless code can be attributed to two factors. First, the locally nameless *lemmas* are proved only once in our library. Second, Ltac helps automate application of these lemmas and the proofs of locally nameless *axioms*.

Table 3. Statistics of Our Development

Components	LOC	LOC about LNR	Percentage
Base	1k	0	0
Generic Reasoning Library	1.1k	1.1k	100%
Program Equivalence for STLC	2.9k	176	6.1%
Compactness for PCF	2.9k	307	10.6%
Total (Without library)	5.8k	483	8.3%
Total	7.9k	1.6k	20.2%

7 Related Work

Locally Nameless Representation The vanilla LNR does not support generic reasoning or automation. We have compared with the two main approaches for automation in LNR in §3.1: LNS which we build upon and LNgen which depends on external tools.

De Bruijn indices The de Bruijn indices are nameless indices for representing variables which help reduce α-equivalence to syntactic equivalence [11,27]. However, shift operations are needed in substitution to make sure free variables are properly maintained [8]. Libraries for automating such operations have been developed and successfully applied to several projects (e.g., Autosubst [24,26]). However, the automation and manipulation of bindings is often not in the control of users. By contrast, the definitions, lemmas and their proofs in our generic library are modular and transparent to users, open to inspection and modification. Moreover, the fundamental problem with de Bruijn indices cannot be solved by automation: it is difficult to maintain relations between free variables in different terms which may be represented by different indices. In comparison, the same free variable in different terms is simply the same identifier in LNR.

Higher-Order Abstract Syntax In the higher-order abstract syntax [18] (HOAS, also known as λ-tree syntax [17]), the binders in meta-languages are used to encode binding structure of object languages. Syntactically equivalent terms in the object language correspond to definitionally equivalent terms in the meta-language. As a result, α-equivalence, β-conversion and substitutions are absorbed into the meta-language, making their properties easy to prove. Theorem provers supporting HOAS have been highly successful in formalizing meta-theory (e.g., Twelf [19], Beluga [20] and Abella [6]). However, HOAS cannot be directly supported in formalizing systems with rich function space (e.g., Coq and Agda), because meta-level terms may encode rich computation in those systems and not necessarily correspond to any well-formed terms in the object language [12]. Weaker forms of HOAS such as Parametric Higher-Order Abstract Syntax (PHOAS) has been proposed [10]. However, it relies on axioms about the object language which cannot be generally proved, which limits its application.

Second-Order Abstract Syntax The second-order abstract syntax translates the textual specification of a typed syntax with variable-binding operators into an intrinsically-encoded, inductive data type [1,13,14]. This type- and scope-safe syntax represents terms of a syntax as a type- and context- indexed family of sets. The advantage is that ill-typed and ill-scoped terms cannot be constructed since the typing rules are directly included in the term constructors. The system supports second-order equational/rewriting reasoning with parametrised metavariables and associated metasubstitution. Combined with the presheaf model [13] of the second-order abstract syntax, generic metatheory can be extracted and repetitive boilerplate can be minimized. In intrinsic encoding, terms are tightly coupled with their typing rules, while in extrinsic encoding they are defined separately. Further research is needed to investigate their relation.

8 Conclusion

We have proposed a generic reasoning approach of the locally nameless representation. With our approach, key lemmas about the locally nameless representation can be generically derived without any assumption on the language syntax. We have implemented a library for this kind of generic reasoning in Coq and applied it to prove the equivalence properties of STLC and the compactness theorem for PCF. Those efforts show that our generic reasoning approach can be effectively applied to non-trivial formalization of programming languages. In the future, we plan to investigate the theoretical underpinnings of our formalized theory by extending the theory of locally nameless sets.

Acknowledgements. We thank the anonymous referees for their feedback which improved this paper significantly. This work is supported by the National Natural Science Foundation of China (NSFC) under Grant No. 62372290 and 62002217.

References

1. Allais, G., Atkey, R., Chapman, J., McBride, C., McKinna, J.: A type and scope safe universe of syntaxes with binding: their semantics and proofs. In: Proceedings of the ACM on Programming Languages **2**(ICFP) (2018). https://doi.org/10.1145/3236785
2. Amin, N., Rompf, T.: Type soundness proofs with definitional interpreters. In: Proceedings of the 44th ACM SIGPLAN Symposium on Principles of Programming Languages, pp. 666–679. ACM, New York (2017). https://doi.org/10.1145/3009837.3009866
3. Aydemir, B., Charguéraud, A., Pierce, B.C., Pollack, R., Weirich, S.: Engineering formal metatheory. In: Proceedings of the 35th Annual ACM SIGPLAN-SIGACT Symposium on Principles of Programming Languages, pp. 3–15. ACM, New York (2008). https://doi.org/10.1145/1328438.1328443

4. Aydemir, B.E., Bohannon, A., Fairbairn, M., Foster, J.N., Pierce, B.C., Sewell, P., Vytiniotis, D., Washburn, G., Weirich, S., Zdancewic, S.: Mechanized metatheory for the masses: the POPLMARK challenge. In: Theorem Proving in Higher Order Logics, pp. 50–65. Springer, Heidelberg (2005). https://doi.org/10.1007/115418
5. Aydemir, B.E., Weirich, S.: Lngen: Tool support for locally nameless representations (2010). https://api.semanticscholar.org/CorpusID:2649490
6. Baelde, D., Chaudhuri, K., Gacek, A., Miller, D., Nadathur, G., Tiu, A., Wang, Y.: Abella: a system for reasoning about relational specifications. J. Formalized Reasoning **7**(2), 1–89 (2014). https://doi.org/10.6092/issn.1972-5787/4650
7. Bengtson, J., Bhargavan, K., Fournet, C., Gordon, A.D., Maffeis, S.: Refinement types for secure implementations. ACM Trans. Program. Lang. Syst. **33**(2) (2011). https://doi.org/10.1145/1890028.1890031
8. Berghofer, S., Urban, C.: A head-to-head comparison of de Bruijn indices and names. Electron. Notes Theor. Comput. Sci. **174**(5), 53–67 (2007). https://doi.org/10.1016/j.entcs.2007.01.018
9. Charguéraud, A.: The locally nameless representation. J. Autom. Reason. **49**, 363–408 (2012). https://doi.org/10.1007/s10817-011-9225-2
10. Chlipala, A.: Parametric higher-order abstract syntax for mechanized semantics. In: Proceedings of the 13th ACM SIGPLAN International Conference on Functional Programming, pp. 143–156. ACM, New York (2008). https://doi.org/10.1145/1411204.1411226
11. de Bruijn, N.: Lambda calculus notation with nameless dummies, a tool for automatic formula manipulation, with application to the Church-Rosser theorem. Indagationes Mathematicae (Proceedings) **75**(5), 381–392 (1972). https://doi.org/10.1016/1385-7258(72)90034-0
12. Despeyroux, J., Felty, A., Hirschowitz, A.: Higher-order abstract syntax in coq. In: International Conference on Typed Lambda Calculi and Applications, pp. 124–138. Springer, Heidelberg (1995). https://doi.org/10.1007/BFb0014049
13. Fiore, M.: Second-order and dependently-sorted abstract syntax. In: Proceedings of the 23rd Annual IEEE Symposium on Logic in Computer Science, pp. 57–68. IEEE, New York (2008). https://doi.org/10.1109/LICS.2008.38
14. Fiore, M., Szamozvancev, D.: Formal metatheory of second-order abstract syntax. Proc. ACM Program. Lang. **6**(POPL) (2022). https://doi.org/10.1145/3498715
15. Harper, R.: Practical Foundations for Programming Languages, pp. 455–474. Cambridge University Press (2016). http://www.cs.cmu.edu/~rwh/pfpl.html
16. McKinna, J., Pollack, R.: Pure type systems formalized. In: Typed Lambda Calculi and Applications: International Conference on Typed Lambda Calculi and Applications, pp. 289–305. Springer, Heidelberg (1993). https://doi.org/10.1007/BFb0037113
17. Miller, D.: Abstract syntax for variable binders: an overview. In: Proceedings of the First International Conference on Computational Logic, pp. 239–253. Springer, Heidelberg (2000). https://doi.org/10.1007/3-540-44957-4_16
18. Pfenning, F., Elliott, C.: Higher-order abstract syntax. In: Proceedings of the ACM SIGPLAN 1988 Conference on Programming Language Design and Implementation, pp. 199–208. ACM, New York (1988). https://doi.org/10.1145/53990.54010
19. Pfenning, F., Schürmann, C.: System description: Twelf—a meta-logical framework for deductive systems. In: Proceedings of the 16th International Conference on Automated Deduction: Automated Deduction, pp. 202–206. CADE-16, Springer, Heidelberg (1999). https://doi.org/10.1007/3-540-48660-7_14

20. Pientka, B., Dunfield, J.: Beluga: A framework for programming and reasoning with deductive systems (system description). In: Giesl, J., Hähnle, R. (eds.) Automated Reasoning, pp. 15–21. Springer, Heidelberg (2010). https://doi.org/10.1007/978-3-642-14203-1_2
21. Pitts, A.M.: Locally nameless sets. Proc. Program. Lang. **7**(POPL) (2023). https://doi.org/10.1145/3571210
22. Plotkin, G.: Lcf considered as a programming language. Theoret. Comput. Sci. **5**(3), 223–255 (1977). https://doi.org/10.1016/0304-3975(77)90044-5
23. Rossberg, A., Russo, C.V., Dreyer, D.: F-ing modules. In: Proceedings of the 5th ACM SIGPLAN Workshop on Types in Language Design and Implementation, pp. 89–102. ACM, New York (2010). https://doi.org/10.1145/1708016.1708028
24. Schäfer, S., Tebbi, T., Smolka, G.: Autosubst: reasoning with de Bruijn terms and parallel substitutions. In: Urban, C., Zhang, X. (eds.) Interactive Theorem Proving, pp. 359–374. Springer, Cham (2015). https://doi.org/10.1007/978-3-319-22102-1_24
25. Sewell, P., Nardelli, F.Z., Owens, S., Peskine, G., Ridge, T., Sarkar, S., et al.: Ott: effective tool support for the working semanticist. J. Funct. Program. **20**(1), 71–122 (2010). https://doi.org/10.1145/1291220.1291155
26. Stark, K., Schäfer, S., Kaiser, J.: Autosubst 2: reasoning with multi-sorted de bruijn terms and vector substitutions. In: Proceedings of the 8th ACM SIGPLAN International Conference on Certified Programs and Proofs, pp. 166–180. ACM, New York (2019). https://doi.org/10.1145/3293880.3294101
27. Vouillon, J.: A solution to the POPLMARK challenge based on de Bruijn indices. J. Autom. Reason. **49**(3), 327–362 (2012). https://doi.org/10.1007/s10817-011-9230-5
28. Weirich, S., Yorgey, B.A., Sheard, T.: Binders unbound. In: Proceedings of the 16th ACM SIGPLAN International Conference on Functional Programming, pp. 333–345. ACM, New York (2011). https://doi.org/10.1145/2034773.2034818

Building a Correct-by-Construction Type Checker for a Dependently Typed Core Language

Bohdan Liesnikov(✉) and Jesper Cockx

Delft University of Technology, Delft, The Netherlands
{b.liesnikov,j.g.h.cockx}@tudelft.nl

Abstract. Dependently typed languages allow us to state a program's expected properties and automatically check that they are satisfied at compile time. Yet the implementations of these languages are themselves just software, so can we really trust them? The goal of this paper is to develop a lightweight technique to improve their trustworthiness by giving a formal specification of the typing rules and intrinsically verifying the type checker with respect to these rules. Concretely, we apply this technique to a subset of Agda's internal language, implemented in Agda. Our development relies on erasure annotations to separate the specification from the runtime of the type checker. We provide guidelines for making design decisions for certified core type checkers and evaluate trade-offs.

Keywords: Dependent types · Agda · Correct-by-Construction Programming

1 Introduction

Developers use a variety of techniques to increase trust in the software projects they are working on, ranging from manual testing, to static type systems and formal specification and verification. The latter can guarantee adherence of the software to the specification - as demonstrated by projects such as CompCert [33], CakeML [31], sel4 [30], JSCert [13], and Verdi Raft [55]. The correctness of these formal verification efforts relies on the soundness of the tools used [8,41] - such as Coq [51], Agda [50], Idris [14,52], or Isabelle [37].

Being mere pieces of software, formal verification tools can also have bugs and are not inherently trustworthy. To mitigate this, a common countermeasure is to build them around a small and trusted kernel, as pioneered by LCF [28], Coq, and Twelf [39], and later adopted in Lean, Isabelle [32], Idris, and others. Andromeda developers [11] describe the kernel as "kept as simple as possible, and it only supports very straightforward type-theoretic constructions which directly correspond to applications of inference rules and admissible rules." While this does increase trust, they also note that "a careful code review of the nucleus will

O. Kiselyov (Ed.): APLAS 2024, LNCS 15194, pp. 63–83, 2024.
https://doi.org/10.1007/978-981-97-8943-6_4

probably unearth some bugs, and hopefully not very many." The same can be said about all other proof assistants, as witnessed by critical bugs that are still being discovered[1], even if these are hard to exploit accidentally [46].

Moving beyond a trusted core, MetaCoq [44,46] proposes to formally verify each part of the verification pipeline - from parsing to extraction. However, for dependently typed languages this can be a herculean task, taking teams many years to complete. MetaCoq itself began in 2014 with TemplateCoq [34] and is still ongoing in 2023 [46]. Thus existing approaches fail at either cost-effectiveness or strong verification assurances. We need techniques that provide a more rigorous verification process than pure code review, yet remain scalable and feasible for real-world sized systems.

In this paper we present a design that sits between these two extremes. We target a dependently typed core language modelled after a subset of Agda's internal syntax. Concretely, we contribute the following:

- We formally specify the syntax and typing rules for a dependently typed language with universes, dependent function types, simple datatypes, and case expressions.
- We implement a type checker for this language that produces evidence of well-typedness for each term it accepts.
- We demonstrate the use of erasure annotations [9,24,36,50] to ensure a clear separation between the parts of the type checker that are needed for computation, and those only needed for its verification.

The implementation consists of four parts: a well-scoped representation of the syntax for terms and signatures (Sect. 2, Sect. 4.1, and Sect. 5.1), a simple environment machine for reduction (Sect. 3.3, Sect. 4.2, and Sect. 5.2), a formal specification of the typing and conversion judgments (Sects. 3.1, 4.3, and 5.3), and a correct-by-construction type checker that outputs typing derivations (Sects. 3.2, 4.4, and 5.4).

While the language we present is far from novel [10,21], the focus of this paper is on how we formalize the syntax and typing rules, and how these choices influence the implementation of the type checker.

We introduce our implementation gradually, starting with the simply typed lambda calculus (STLC) in Sects. 2 and 3. In Sect. 4 we extend it to handle dependent function types and universes. Finally, in Sect. 5 we add simple inductive datatypes and defined symbols.

The source code for the paper is available at
github.com/jespercockx/agda-core/tree/aplas-2024.[2]

Limitations This paper is an experiment in language engineering rather than language theory. While we provide a formal specification of the syntax and typing rules, we refrain from proving any meta-theoretical properties. In particular, we are not formalising a variant of MLTT but take the typing rules as the source of truth. For the type checker we aim to strike a balance between formal guarantees

[1] github.com/coq/coq/blob/master/dev/doc/critical-bugs.md.

[2] archived at doi.org/10.4121/6f239149-2526-42a0-8d07-d0e9d6714f7f

and resources requried, in particular we prove soundness of our type checker but not completeness, as doing so would require inversion lemmas for our typing judgments. We also do not check termination or positivity, and hence do not ensure logical soundness.

2 Representing Well-Scoped Syntax

In this section, we present a well-scoped syntax for STLC, which relies on an abstract interface for representing scopes and names.

2.1 Well-Scoped Syntax for STLC

Well-scoped [3,12] syntax representations capture the variable names that can be used within a term. For STLC we define a type of terms parameterised by an abstract scope . Since the scope parameter is marked as erased (@0), at runtime the representation is equivalent to the plain Haskell datatype `Term` on the right.

```
data Term (@0 α : Scope name) : Set where       data Term where
  TVar :  (@0 x : name) → x ∈ α                   TVar  :: Int
       → Term α                                         -> Term
  TLam :  (@0 x : name) → (v : Term (x ◃ α))      TLam  :: Term
       → Term α                                         -> Term
  TApp :  (u : Term α) → (v : Term α)             TApp  :: Term -> Term
       → Term α                                         -> Term
```

Variables (TVar) consist of an erased name together with a proof of inclusion $x \in \alpha$, i.e. that x is in scope α. At runtime, this proof corresponds to a plain de Bruijn index of type `Int`. The TLam constructor binds x and ensures that the body of the lambda v is in a larger scope $x \triangleleft \alpha$, where α is the current ambient scope.

Types in STLC are defined as a simple datatype with a base type TyNat and a function type TyArr. Since there are no type variables, no scope is needed.

```
data Type : Set where
  TyNat : Type
  TyArr : (a b : Type) → Type
```

2.2 Scopes and Their Operations

To represent variables, language specifications have to choose between named variables - which are easy for humans to read but hard to reason about - and de Bruijn indices or other nameless representations - which are easier to formalize but notoriously confusing to humans. Our representation combines the best of both worlds by representing variables as an erased name together with a proof that it is in scope, which compiles to a de Bruijn index.

While scopes could be represented as a simple list of names, we choose to work with an abstract interface [29]. This allows us to switch to a more efficient representation if needed, and be explicit about which operations on scopes we require. This will prove to be useful later on, as we use scopes to model not just local variables but also global definitions, which can be much more numerous. Concretely, the interface we rely on is as follows:

- A type Scope : Set with constctors ∅ for empty scopes, [_] for singleton scopes, and <> for the disjoint union of two scopes.
- An operator ~ for reversing the order of the variables in a scope.
- A subscope predicate _⊆_ : @0 Scope → Scope → Set, with operations for deciding equality of subscope witnesses and computing the smaller scope's complement. A membership predicate _∈_ : @0 name → @0 Scope → Set is defined as $x \in \alpha = [\ x\ ] \subseteq \alpha$.
- A data structure All : (p : @0 name → Set) → @0 Scope → Set storing an element of type $p\ x$ for each name x in the scope, with a lookup operation.

The name argument to the singleton constructor [_] is erased, meaning that the names provide the extra convenience for writing Agda, but do not have any impact on the runtime representation of scopes. We do not enforce uniqueness of names, but the inclusions are unique and their equality is decidable.

As we will see later, certain definitions require a runtime representation of the scope. For this purpose, we use the type Rezz $a\ x$ of resurrections [24] of an erased variable @0 x : a, which contains a non-erased value that is propositionally equal to x. For example, we will later require a weakening function that converts Term β to Term β to Term (α <> β). In terms of de Bruijn indices it needs the size of α and Rezz Scope α is precisely that - a runtime representation of the spine, not to the names contained within it. Generally speaking, we can resurrect a value if we can recompute it - for example, we can resurrect the scope from the context - see rezzScope in Sect. 3.1 for usage. This is because the context is indexed by the scope, so the length of the context is precisely the size of the scope, which is Rezz Scope α.

Discussion Using well-scoped syntax helps us spot mistakes in the specification of our language - which matters since many bugs in type systems arise from incorrect handling of variables.

Our choice to use an abstract type of names rather than a simpler type of well-scoped de Bruijn indices is motivated by keeping our specification as readable as possible. It also gives more informative types to syntax operations, and rules out certain classes of errors that will be easier to miss with plain de Bruijn indices. For example, a function of type Term ($x \triangleleft y \triangleleft s$) → Term ($y \triangleleft x \triangleleft s$) makes it clear that the order of the variables x and y is swapped, while the type Term (2 + s) → Term (2 + s) does not tell us anything about the order.

Going beyond well-scoped syntax, one might also argue in favour of well-typed syntax, statically ruling out even more errors. However, defining well-typed syntax for languages with type-level computation is notoriously tricky [5,6,19], and would force us to define syntax and typing judgment in a mutually dependent way. In addition, it would not free us from also having to define untyped syntax, since we cannot assume the input to our type checker to be well-typed.

Finally, since the type checker expects the input to be well-scoped, we fundamentally rely on the parser to perform scope-checking. While in principle it is possible to perform scope and type checking in a single pass, we choose to keep them separate, thus gaining modularity but requiring the parser to be verified separately, which we defer to future work.

3 Type Checking STLC

Now that we have a syntax for STLC, let us take a look at three other big pieces: the specification of typing rules, the type checker, and the evaluator.

3.1 Typing Rules

To specify the typing rules of STLC, we need to define a type of contexts which will store the types of variables. The type of contexts is indexed by the scope of variables declared. We define Γ , $x : t$ as syntactic sugar for CtxExtend.

```
data Context : @0 Scope name → Set where
  CtxEmpty : Context ∅
  CtxExtend : Context α → (@0 x : name) → Type → Context (x ◃ α)
```

The typing judgment TyTerm (rendered as $\Gamma \vdash u : t$) is indexed by a context, a term, and its type. Each constructor of TyTerm corresponds to a typing rule.

```
data TyTerm (@0 Γ : Context α) : @0 Term α → @0 Type → Set where
  TyTVar :  (p : x ∈ α)
          → Γ ⊢ TVar x p : lookupVar Γ x p
  TyLam :   Γ , x : a ⊢ u : b
          → Γ ⊢ TLam x u : TyArr a b
  TyApp :   Γ ⊢ u : (TyArr a b)
          → Γ ⊢ v : a
          → Γ ⊢ TApp u v : b
```

For variables, the type is given by the context. A lambda has a function type, with the body living in an extended context. Finally, application asserts the type of the argument matches the domain of the head symbol and the result matches the codomain.

We choose to state the rules in a declarative way since they serve as part of the specification and should be easily understood. However, in the implementation of the type checker below, we follow a bidirectional discipline [26,40].

3.2 Type Checking

To implement a certified type checker, we first define a simple type checking monad with a failure capability (tcError):

```
TCM : Set → Set
TCM a = Either TCError a
```

Type checking function application requires *conversion checking*, that is - checking whether two types are equal. Since STLC has no type-level computation, conversion is just syntactic equality, so the conversion checker returns a proof of equality or throws an error.

```
    refl ← convert a1 a2
    refl ← convert b1 b2
    return refl
  convert _ _ = tcError "unequal types"
```

We use Agda's do-notation for the TCM monad, which includes the ability to pattern match on the result of a statement. Here we match the results of the recursive calls against refl, unifying the left- and right-hand sides of the equality for the remainder of the do-block.

The type checker itself follows a bidirectional style, with two functions checkType and inferType that are defined mutually. Both functions return a typing derivation, where inferType also returns the type of the given term, while checkType checks it against a specific type.

```
inferType  : ∀ (Γ : Context α) u → TCM (Σ[ ty ∈ Type ] (Γ ⊢ u : ty))
checkType : ∀ (Γ : Context α) u (ty : Type) → TCM (Γ ⊢ u : ty)

inferType ctx (TVar x p)   = return (lookupVar ctx x p , TyTVar p)
inferType ctx (TLam x te) = tcError "cannot infer type of lambda"
inferType ctx (TApp u v)   = do
  (TyArr a b) , gtu ← inferType ctx u
    where _ → tcError "application head should have a function type"
  gtv ← checkType ctx v a
  return (b , TyApp gtu gtv)
```

We infer types for all terms, except for a lambda. The `where` clause in the clause for `TApp` deals with any cases that are not on the 'happy path' where the result of the recursive call is a `TyArr`. In checking mode we type check only lambdas and for any other term we switch modes and perform a conversion check.

```
checkType ctx (TLam x v) (TyArr a b) = do
  gtv ← checkType (ctx , x : a) v b
  return (TyLam gtv)
checkType ctx (TLam x v) _ =
  tcError "lambda should have a function type"
checkType ctx u ty = do
  (gtu , dgty) ← inferType ctx u
  refl ← convert gtu ty
  return dgty
```

3.3 Reduction

While it is not yet necessary for the type checker, we also implement an evaluator for terms, as we will need it for checking dependent types. It is based on a call-by-value Krivine machine [22,43].

First, we define environments as lists of terms where each term can refer to the previous ones. They are indexed by an initial scope α and a final scope β.

```
EnvCons : Environment α β → (@0 x : name) → Term β
          → Environment α (x ◃ β)
```

The state of the evaluator consists of an environment, the current term it is focused on, and a stack of arguments it still needs to apply this term to. Both the focus and the stack can refer to values defined in the environment.

```
record State (@0 α : Scope name) : Set where
  constructor MkState
  field
    @0 {fullScope} : Scope name
    env   : Environment α fullScope
    focus : Term fullScope
    stack : List (Term fullScope)
```

The machine itself takes one step of reduction at a time, using the step function. Just means that another reduction step is possible and Nothing means that the evaluation is done.

```
step : (s : State α) → Maybe (State α)
step (MkState e (TVar x p) s) = case lookupEnvironment e p of λ where
  (Left _)  → Nothing
  (Right v) → Just (MkState e v s)
step (MkState e (TApp v w) s) = Just (MkState e v (w :: s))
step (MkState e (TLam x v) (w :: s)) =
  Just (MkState (e , x ↦ w) v (map weakenBind s))
step (MkState e (TLam x v) []) = Nothing
```

Variables are looked up in the context, application arguments are pushed to the stack, and lambdas move arguments from the stack to the environment before continuing to evaluate the body.

We start evaluation with an empty environment and an empty stack. When the machine halts we still have to extract the reduced term from the final state. For this, we convert the environment to a substitution to apply it to the focus.

Substitutions Subst α β (syntactic sugar $\alpha \Rightarrow \beta$ are a list-like data structure indexed over two scopes α and β.

```
data Subst : (@0 α β : Scope name) → Set where
  SNil  : Subst ∅ β
  SCons : Term β → Subst α β → Subst (x ◃ α) β
```

The function substTerm (not shown here) takes a substitution $\alpha \Rightarrow \beta$, and applies it to a term in Term α to get a term in Term β.

```
unState : Rezz _ α → State α → Term α
unState r (MkState e v s) = substTerm (envToSubst r e) (applys v s)
```

Since step can be applied to ill-typed terms, repeated application does not necessarily terminate. Hence to define a multi-step reduction, we use a fuel argument of type Nat that indicates a maximum number of reduction steps.

```
reduceState : Rezz _ α → (s : State α) → Nat → Maybe (Term α)
reduceState r s zero = Nothing
reduceState r s (suc fuel) = case (step s) of λ where
  (Just s') → reduceState r s' fuel
  Nothing  → Just (unState r s)

reduce : Rezz _ α → (v : Term α) → Nat → Maybe (Term α)
reduce {α = α} r v = reduceState r (makeState v)
```

Discussion Using substitution to extract a term from the final state duplicates the terms present in the environment if they occur more than once in the result. To avoid this, we could add let-expressions to our language and use them to maintain the environments generated by the machine. However, a naive implementation of this approach introduces let-bindings for unused terms (user-defined, as well as generated from the machine's state) which in practice renders it unusable. We could remove these spurious lets with a garbage-collection-like procedure, but such a procedure would add extra complexity, and with it extra opportunities for bugs. So while the duplication caused by substitution is an annoying downside, it leads to more manageable terms in the output.

An alternative to using fuel is the Delay monad [1,23]. In practice we ran into complications when trying to implement it: using Delay as part of a monad stack requires lifting other monads through it, which requires an altered definition to lift through later. To define Delay as a monad transformer we also need to ensure that m it transforms is strictly positive - either through a container encoding or implementing a new extension of Agda.

4 Dependent Function Types and Universes

In this section, we extend STLC defined in Sect. 2 and Sect. 3 with dependent function types (Π-types) and a universe hierarchy, thus getting a minimal dependently typed language.

The main change in the syntax is that types can now contain variables and hence also have to be scoped. Type conversion also becomes more complicated, as it needs to reduce terms.

4.1 Syntax

As types now contain terms, they are now also indexed over a scope. Concretely, we represent types as a pair of a term together with its sort. These sorts can be inserted by the elaborator if needed.

```
data Sort α where
  STyp : Nat → Sort α
```

```
record Type α where
  inductive; constructor El
  field typeSort : Sort α
        unType   : Term α
```

One further change is that we wrap the argument to function application in the Elim datatype, which will prove useful for future extensions (Sect. 5).

```
data Term α where
  TVar  : (@0 x : name) → x ∈ α → Term α
  TLam  : (@0 x : name) (v : Term (x ◃ α)) → Term α
  TApp  : (u : Term α) (es : Elim α) → Term α
  TPi   : (@0 x : name) (u : Type α) (v : Type (x ◃ α)) → Term α
  TSort : Sort α → Term α

data Elim α where
  EArg : Term α → Elim α
```

Contexts are the same as before, except with types now also being well-scoped.

```
data Context : @0 Scope name → Set where
  CtxEmpty : Context ∅
  CtxExtend : Context α → (@0 x : name) → Type α → Context (x ◃ α)
```

4.2 Reduction

Evaluation of functions is the same as for STLC. Π-types and sorts do not reduce.

4.3 Typing and Conversion Rules

In this section, we extend the typing judgment with rules for Π-types and sorts. We also add a rule to convert a derivation between two types, which in turn requires the definition of a conversion judgment.

Since the context can be considered an 'input' to the typing judgment, our typing rules do not enforce well-formedness of the types in the context but instead assume it. However, they do enforce well-formedness of the type – as well as the term itself.

Typing judgments The form of the typing judgment is the same as before, apart from the added scope argument to the type.

```
data TyTerm (@0 Γ : Context α) : @0 Term α → @0 Type α → Set where
```

We omit the rule for variables since it is precisely the same as in Sect. 3. In the rule for TLam, the name of the variable in u is x while the variable in b is named y, so we need to rename the latter using renameTopType, which maps Type $(x \triangleleft \alpha)$ to Type $(y \triangleleft \alpha)$.

```
TyLam : Γ , x : a ⊢ u : renameTopType r b      TyAppE : {b : Type α}
      → Γ ⊢ TLam x u : El k (TPi y a b)                → Γ ⊢ u : a
                                                       → TyElim Γ u e a b
                                                       → Γ ⊢ TApp u e : b
```

The application rule uses the auxiliary typing judgment TyElim, which checks that the head symbol is of Π-type and the argument type matches the domain. To get the type of the application it substitutes the argument into the codomain.

```
data TyElim (@0 Γ : Context α) :
  (@0 u : Term α) (@0 e : Elim α) (@0 t a : Type α) → Set where
    TyArg : (unType c) ≅ TPi x a b
          → Γ ⊢ v : a
          → TyElim Γ u (EArg v) c (substTopType r v b)
```

For computing the sort of Π-types and sorts, we rely on two functions piSort (maximum) and sucSort (successor).

```
TyPi   : Γ ⊢ u : sortType k
       → Γ , x : (El k u) ⊢ v : sortType l
       → Γ ⊢ TPi x (El k u) (El l v) : sortType (piSort k l)
TyType : Γ ⊢ TSort k : sortType (sucSort k)
```

Finally, the conversion rule maps a typing derivation between convertible types.

```
TyConv : Γ ⊢ u : a → (unType a) ≅ (unType b) → Γ ⊢ u : b
```

Conversion rules We use an untyped conversion judgment Conv (syntactic sugar ≅), since it allows us to define conversion separately from typing. Once again, the rules themselves closely follow the literature[20,38].

The two main conversion rules are CRedL and CRedR that allow us to reduce the left- and right-hand side respectively. These two rules use the predicate ReducesTo v w expressing that v reduces to w, when given sufficient fuel.

```
@0 ReducesTo : (v w : Term α) → Set
ReducesTo {α = α} v w = Σ[ (r , f) ∈ Rezz _ α × Nat ]
                           reduce r v f ≡ Just w
```

Aside from these two rules, conversion is reflexive and respects all term constructors.

```
data Conv where
  CRedL : @0 ReducesTo u u'        CApp : u ≅ u' → w ≃ w'
        → u' ≅ v → u ≅ v                → TApp u w ≅ TApp u' w'
```

For Π-types and lambdas, we need to rename the variable on one side in order to bring both terms to the same scope.

```
CPi : unType a ≅ unType a'                    CLam : u ≅ renameTop r v
    → unType b ≅ renameTop r (unType b')           → TLam y u ≅ TLam z v
    → TPi x a b ≅ TPi y a' b'
```

Discussion Untyped conversion allows us to simplify conversion rules, but prevents us from easily adding type-directed conversion rules such as eta-expansion and proof irrelevance. Theoretically, it would be possible to ask for a typing derivation locally when applying these rules, but that would require conversion to at least maintain a typing context. Moreover, implementing a type checker that can provide these derivations would require a proof of subject reduction, which we chose not to develop.

This problem could be circumvented by adding a typing rule that axiomatises subject reduction. Since reduction is already part of the trusted code base, this does not further compromise soundness. However, it would complicate any future attempts to do metatheory.

4.4 Type Checking and Conversion Checking

Conversion-checker The conversion checker has the following interface:

```
convert : ∀ Γ (t q : Term α) → TCM (t ≅ q)
```

Since checking conversion requires reduction, we extend the type checking monad TCM with a field storing a read-only fuel value. The top-level convert function gets this value and passes it to the auxiliary convertCheck, which recurses on it. The function reduceTo takes this fuel and a term v and returns the reduced term w together with a witness of type ReducesTo v w.

```
convertCheck : Nat → (r : Rezz _ α) → ∀ (t q : Term α) → TCM (t ≅ q)
convertCheck zero _ _ _ = tcError "need more fuel"
convertCheck (suc fl) r t q = do
  rgty ← reduceTo r t fl
  rcty ← reduceTo r q fl
```

To compare two variables, we use decidable equality of variable indices $x \in \alpha$. If the indices are equal, we match on refl to unify them so we can use CRefl.

```
(TVar x p ⟨ rpg ⟩ , TVar y q ⟨ rpc ⟩) →
  CRedL rpg <$> CRedR rpc <$>
    ifDec (decIn p q)
      (λ where {{refl}} → return CRefl)
      (tcError "two different variables aren't convertible")
```

Other terms are checked by a recursive descent. For example, for lambdas we check convertibility of the bodies, renaming variables as needed.

```
(TLam x u ⟨ rpg ⟩ , TLam y v ⟨ rpc ⟩) →
  CRedL rpg <$> CRedR rpc <$>
  CLam <$> convertCheck fl (rezzBind r) u (renameTop r v)
```

Type checker As before, we follow a bidirectional discipline, with only TyLam in checking mode again. When we encounter an inferrable term in a checkable position, we use the TyConv rule to switch modes.

```
checkCoerce : ∀ Γ (t : Term α) → Σ[ ty ∈ Type α ] Γ ⊢ t : ty
                → (cty : Type α) → TCM (Γ ⊢ t : cty)
checkCoerce ctx _ (ty , dty) cty =
  TyConv dty <$> convert ctx (unType ty) (unType cty)
```

We discuss two cases for illustrative purposes, the others are similar. To type check a lambda, we need to reduce the type before checking that it is a Π.

```
checkType ctx (TLam x u) (El s ty) = do
  let r = rezzScope ctx
  fuel ← tcmFuel
```

Type checking an application symbol relies on the auxiliary function inferElim.

```
inferType ctx (TApp u e) = do
  tu , gtu ← inferType ctx u
  a  , gte ← inferElim ctx u e tu
  return $ a , TyAppE gtu gte
```

The function inferElim itself again reduces the type to a Π-type and checks the argument against its domain.

```
inferElim ctx u (EArg v) tu = do
  let r = rezzScope ctx
  fuel ← tcmFuel
  (TPi x at rt) ⟨ rtp ⟩ ← reduceTo r (unType tu) fuel
    where _ → tcError "couldn't reduce head type to a pi type"
  gtv ← checkType ctx v at
  let tytype = substTopType r v rt
      gc     = CRedL rtp CRefl
  return $ tytype , TyArg gc gtv
```

5 Inductive Types

In this section, we expand the language with parameterised - but not indexed - inductive types and case-expressions. We also add globally defined symbols. From an infrastructure point of view the main addition are a set of global scopes - defScope for global definitions, conScope for constructor names, and fieldScope for the fields of each constructor - and signature of global definitions (datatypes and symbols).

5.1 Syntax

There are two new constructors added to the syntax. TDef represents a global symbol, where the name d has to be in the global scope of definitions defScope. TCon is a fully applied datatype constructor - it takes the name of the constructor, an inclusion proof in the global scope of constructors, and a list of arguments (represented as a substitution).

```
data Term α where
  TDef : ∀ (@0 d) →    d ∈ defScope  → Term α
  TCon : ∀ (@0 c) (cp : c ∈ conScope) → (fieldsOf cp) ⇒ α → Term α
```

We also have a new constructor ECase for Elim, representing a case expression with a list of branches and a return type or motive [35], which can depend on the scrutinee. As this is a constructor of Elim, the scrutinee itself is implicit.

```
data Elim α where
  ECase : (bs : Branches α cs) (m : Type (x ◃ α)) → Elim α
```

Each branch matches on a specific constructor c. The scopes ensure that the term on the right-hand side can access all the arguments to the constructor. Since scopes are extended to the left but argument lists grow to the right, the order of the scope has to be inverted (˜).

```
data Branch α where
  BBranch :  (@0 c : name) (c∈cons : c ∈ conScope)
             (let args = fieldsOf c∈cons)
          → Rezz _ args → Term (~ args <> α) → Branch α c
```

The type Branches α cs requires that there is one branch for each constructor in the scope cs, thus ensuring coverage.

```
data Branches α where
  BsNil  : Branches α ∅
  BsCons : Branch α c → Branches α cs → Branches α (c ◃ cs)
```

Signatures The scopes for defined symbols, constructors, and fields are collected in a type of Globals:

```
record Globals : Set where
  field defScope   : Scope name
        conScope   : Scope name
        fieldScope : All (λ _ → Scope name) conScope
```

The above provides only the *names* globally available, so we introduce another record Signature that associates a definition to each name in defScope: either a type and value for a global symbol, or a datatype declaration.

```
Signature : Set
Signature = All (λ _ → Type ∅ × Definition) defScope

data Definition where
  FunctionDef : (funBody : Term ∅) → Definition
  DatatypeDef : (datatypeDef : Datatype) → Definition
```

Datatype declarations DatatypeDef store a sort dataSort, telescopes for parameters dataParTel, and a list of constructors dataConstructors. Both the telescopes and the list of constructors are also given an (erased) scope of the names they declare.

```
field @0 dataPars        : Scope name
      @0 dataCons        : Scope name
      dataSort           : Sort dataPars
      dataParTel         : Telescope ∅ dataPars
      dataConstructors : All (λ c → Σ (c ∈ conScope)
                                        (Constructor dataPars c))
                                 dataCons
```

Each constructor definition stores a telescope for the types of its arguments. Since each part of the signature is guided by scopes, there is no risk of forgetting an argument when defining a datatype or its constructors.

```
record Constructor pars c cp where
  field conTelescope : Telescope pars (fieldsOf cp)
```

There are three well-formedness properties that we assume to hold:

1. From the information stored in the Datatype record we can compute its type, which should match the type given in the Signature.
2. The names of the constructors of each datatype should be distinct.
3. The types in each conTelescope should be no larger than dataSort.

5.2 Reduction

For the evaluator, we need new rules for unfolding defined symbols and for evaluating case expressions. For the latter, when the head symbol is reduced to a constructor, and the top element on the stack is a case elimination, we pick the appropriate branch, substituting the arguments into its body.

```
step sig (MkState e (TDef d q) s) = case getBody sig d q of λ where
  (Just v) → Just (MkState e (weakenGlobal v) s)
  Nothing → Nothing
step sig (MkState e (TCon c q vs) (ECase bs _ :: s)) =
  case lookupBranch bs c q of λ where
    (Just (r , v)) → Just $ MkState (extendEnvironment (revSubst vs) e)
                                    v
                                    (weakenRevEl r s)
    Nothing        → Nothing
```

5.3 Typing and Conversion Rules

Conversion We define three new conversion judgments for branches, lists of branches, and substitutions respectively.

```
data ConvBranch   {@0 α} : (@0 b₁  b₂  : Branch α cn)  → Set
data ConvBranches {@0 α} : (@0 bs₁ bs₂ : Branches α cs) → Set
data ConvSubst    {@0 α} : (@0 us₁ us₂ : β ⇒ α)         → Set
```

Constructors are convertible if they have the same name and convertible arguments.

```
data Conv {α} where
  CCon : (@0 cp : c ∈ conScope) {@0 us vs : fieldsOf cp ⇒ α}
         → ConvSubst us vs → TCon c cp us ≅ TCon c cp vs
```

Two case statements are convertible if their motives are convertible, and for each constructor the corresponding bodies are convertible.

```
CECase : (bs bp : Branches α cs)
         (ms : Type (x ◃ α)) (mp : Type (y ◃ α))

       → renameTop {y = z} r (unType ms) ≅ renameTop r (unType mp)
```

Global references TDef are convertible when the inclusions are equal, same as for TVar.

Typing A defined symbol has the type indicated in the signature sig.

```
data TyTerm {α} Γ where
  TyDef : (@0 p : f ∈ defScope)
          → Γ ⊢ TDef f p : weakenGlobalType (getType sig f p)
```

A constructor is well typed if its name c belongs to a datatype d and its arguments are typeable with respect to the telescope conTelescope of this constructor. The type of the constructor is computed by the constructorType function, which returns a type of the form TDef *d dp*.

```
TyCon :  ( @0 dp : d ∈ defScope) (@0 dt : Datatype)
      → ( @0 cq : c ∈ dataCons dt)
      →   @0 getDefinition sig d dp ≡ DatatypeDef dt
      → (let (cp , con) = lookupAll (dataConstructors dt) cq)
      → { @0 pars : dataPars dt ⇒ α}
      → { @0 us : fieldsOf cp ⇒ α}
      → (let ds = substSort pars (dataSort dt))
      → TySubst Γ us (substTelescope pars (conTelescope con))
      → Γ ⊢ TCon c cp us : constructorType d dp c cp con ds pars us
```

Substitutions are typed with respect to a telescope: each term in the substitution must be typeable with the corresponding type from the telescope.

A branch is well-typed if its body is well-typed with respect to a specialised motive. The motive is specialised to the constructor, which is applied to fresh variables from a context extended with the constructor arguments.

```
data TyBranch {α} Γ dt ps rt where
  TyBBranch : (c∈dcons : c ∈ dataCons dt)
    → (let (c∈cons , con ) = lookupAll (dataConstructors dt) c∈dcons
           ctel = ···; bsubst = ··· )
    → ∀ {rf} (rhs : Term (~ fieldsOf c∈cons <> α))
    → TyTerm (addContextTel ctel Γ) rhs (substType bsubst rt)
    → TyBranch Γ dt ps rt (BBranch c c∈cons rf rhs)
```

Finally, the TyBranches judgment simply checks well-typedness of each branch.

5.4 Type and Conversion Checker

Now that the typing rules are set, writing the type checker is mostly a mechanical task. Thus for brevity, we omit the actual definitions in this section and instead highlight the main challenges.

Representing type constructors Since we model type constructors as TDef we have to extract the parameters from it manually, via reduction to a TApp and a traversal of the eliminations in it. This is to ensure that the arguments to TDef are well-typed with respect to the declaration in the signature. Fundamentally, it is not a challenge, but in hindsight, having a dedicated constructor for type constructors would have made the implementation easier.

Coverage checking During the type checking of a TCase elimination we have to ensure that the Branches cover all constructors of the datatype. The type checker can tell us that the branches cover a certain scope β, we need to ensure that it matches dataCons dt, as required by the rule. To do this, we need to compare the run-time representation of both scopes, hence they need to be resurrected. We do it via the function allBranches : Branches α β $\rightarrow$ All (λ c $\rightarrow$ $c \in$ conScope) β, and the list of all constructors coming from the dataConstructors field of dt. Since both contain an inclusion proof $\in$ conScope associated with each c, we can establish their (in-)equality. In cases like this we find it helpful to think about the runtime representation of any decision taken, with a positive decision supported by an erased proof.

Well-scoped substitutions Since names ensure a lot of important correspondences, working with *well-scoped substitutions* makes it much easier to see when a substitution can be applied to a term - or how it should be lifted to do so. It also eliminates corner cases where we know statically that the sizes of two scopes are the same, which is helpful during development and reduces the number of potential bugs.

6 Related Work

Minimising the trusted computing base (TCB) of type checkers and proof checkers is not a new idea. It originated with de Bruijn [15], but only recently it has become possible to formalise the specification of a real-world core language and a few of those have been done. Below, we list related works in the order of decreasing topic proximity.

MetaCoq [44,45] is a formalization of Coq's core language in Coq. It originated from a formalisation by Barras [16] and a more recent metaprogramming development known as Template Coq [7,34]. The main difference with MetaCoq is that we aim to develop a certified type checker with minimal metatheory, while MetaCoq wants to be a full formalization of the Coq core. Aside from that, we also make a few different design decisions. First, we rely on Agda's erasure annotations instead of the `Prop` universe in Coq. Second, we use a well-scoped representation instead of plain de Bruijn indices. Third, while MetaCoq also uses a Krivine machine for reduction but it has a separate specification of the reduction rules, so the MetaCoq evaluator is not part of the TCB, while ours is. Fourth, our typing judgments assume well-formedness of contexts rather than requiring a proof of it for every rule. Fifth, we formalise only the declarative style of typing rules, but follow MetaCoq in using a bidirectional style for the type checker.

Adjedj et al. [4] formalise meta-theory for MLTT with Π, Σ , natural numbers, and an `Id` type. They also develop a simple complete and correct type checker for this language. There are four big differences between our works. On the surface, as MetaCoq, they use plain de Bruijn indices with Coq definitions derived using AutoSubst [42,47]. On a higher lever, the variant of MLTT they formalise uses recursors for the two induction types instead of pattern-matching. They also formalise typed reduction, with one of the main contributions being a reformulation of work by Abel et al.[2] to avoid induction-recursion. While we are interested in typed reduction, the complications they run into arise from meta-theoretical proofs. The techniques we develop are more light-weight since we do not do meta-theory. At last, their approach does not immediately allow extraction, while ours does, due to erasure.

Strub et al. [48] develop a self-certifying type checker for F*. This work requires a developed metatheory of the language in Coq, which we do not have. Many of the design decisions are similar to MetaCoq, so the differences mentioned there apply here too. They define reduction in terms of substitution, while we use a Krivine machine. Finally, we argue that due to focus on readability and simplicity, our design is overall less complicated and more compact.

Carneiro [17] develops a type checker ("external verifier") for Lean 4 in Lean. We believe the general direction of our works to be similar, but at the moment the typing judgement and the type checker are independent, thus providing no formal correctness or completeness guarantees. This aside, they make a novel choice of using single judgement for both typing and equality, while we pick a more conventional separate representations. Similar to Adjedj et al. [4] they implement MLTT with typed conversion and recursors.

Other related works fall in two camps. Stitch [27] and CakeML [49] are verified type checkers for simpler type systems, so they do not face many of the same challenges. Others formalise the specification and the metatheory - System DC [53] does this for Dependent Haskell, Abel et al. [2] focuses on decidability of conversion specifically, and Wieczorek and Biernacki [54] mechanise a normalisation-by-evaluation algorithm. These works are complementary to ours, they do meta-theory but do not develop a certified type checker, while we do the opposite.

7 Conclusion and Future Work

This paper presents a first step towards the goal of implementing a correct by construction type checker for a core language for Agda and moving from a trusted computing base to a trusted theory base.

In the process, we develop a set of techniques that can be useful for designing certified type checkers in general. We argue that using well-scoped syntax provides invaluable guidance, while not imposing too much of a proof burden on the developer. Using names rather than de Bruijn indices is useful for the same reason. Finally, we propose erasure annotations as an important tool to make the language developer more aware of the runtime behaviour of the code they are writing.

Future work There are many potential prospects to reach feature parity with Agda's internal language. Practically, we would like to add a pipeline to connect our existing development to Agda's compiler. We would also like to implement some core features of Agda, like indexed inductive datatypes, which would require a verified unification procedure, eta-equivalence, definitional irrelevance, and universe polymorphism. We plan to add termination and positivity checking, but we would like to procure certificates for these properties from Agda's compiler, which should simplify the implementation of the core checker.

Regarding applications, we would like to try using our embedded core language for type-safe metaprogramming [7,25,44] to automate tedious proofs, as well as for exchanging programs and proofs with other languages [18], enabling collaboration between different communities.

Acknowledgments. We would like to thank Lucas Escot for his contributions to the source code and valuable discussions. Jesper Cockx holds an NWO Veni grant on 'A trustworthy and extensible core language for Agda' (VI.Veni.202.216).

Disclosure of Interests. The authors have no competing interests to declare that are relevant to the content of this article.

References

1. Abel, A., Chapman, J.: Normalization by evaluation in the delay monad: a case study for conduction via copatterns and sized types (2014). https://doi.org/10.4204/EPTCS.153.4
2. Abel, A., Öhman, J., Vezzosi, A.: Decidability of conversion for type theory in type theory. In: Proceedings of the ACM on Programming Languages **2**(POPL), 23:1–23:29 (2017). https://doi.org/10.1145/3158111
3. Adams, R.: Formalized metatheory with terms represented by an indexed family of types. In: Filliâtre, J.C., Paulin-Mohring, C., Werner, B. (eds.) Types for Proofs and Programs. pp. 1–16. Springer, Berlin, Heidelberg (2006). https://doi.org/10.1007/11617990_1
4. Adjedj, A., Lennon-Bertrand, M., Maillard, K., Pédrot, P.M., Pujet, L.: Martin-Löf à la Coq. In: Proceedings of the 13th ACM SIGPLAN International Conference on Certified Programs and Proofs. pp. 230–245. CPP 2024, Association for Computing Machinery, New York, NY, USA (2024).https://doi.org/10.1145/3636501.3636951
5. Altenkirch, T., Kaposi, A.: Type theory in type theory using quotient inductive types. In: Proceedings of the 43rd Annual ACM SIGPLAN-SIGACT Symposium on Principles of Programming Languages. pp. 18–29. ACM, St. Petersburg FL USA (2016). https://doi.org/10.1145/2837614.2837638
6. Kaposi, A.: Towards quotient inductive-inductive-recursive types. In: 29th International Conference on Types for Proofs and Programs TYPES 2023 – Abstracts. pp. 124–126. Valencia (Spain) (2023). https://types2023.webs.upv.es/TYPES2023.pdf#section.11.4

7. Anand, A., Boulier, S., Cohen, C., Sozeau, M., Tabareau, N.: Towards certified meta-programming with typed template-Coq. In: Avigad, J., Mahboubi, A. (eds.) Interactive Theorem Proving, vol. 10895, pp. 20–39. Springer, Cham (2018). https://doi.org/10.1007/978-3-319-94821-8_2
8. Appel, A.W., Michael, N., Stump, A., Virga, R.: A Trustworthy proof checker. J. Autom. Reason. **31**(3), 231–260 (2003). https://doi.org/10.1023/B:JARS.0000021013.61329.58
9. Atkey, R.: Syntax and semantics of quantitative type theory. In: Proceedings of the 33rd Annual ACM/IEEE Symposium on Logic in Computer Science, pp. 56–65. LICS '18, Association for Computing Machinery, New York, NY, USA (2018). https://doi.org/10.1145/3209108.3209189
10. Barendregt, H.: Introduction to generalized type systems. J. Funct. Program. **1**(2), 125–154 (1991). https://doi.org/10.1017/S0956796800020025
11. Bauer, A., Gilbert, G., Haselwarter, P.G., Pretnar, M., Stone, C.A.: Design and implementation of the andromeda proof assistant. In: DROPS-IDN/v2/Document/10.4230/LIPIcs.TYPES.2016.5. Schloss Dagstuhl – Leibniz-Zentrum für Informatik (2018). https://doi.org/10.4230/LIPIcs.TYPES.2016.5
12. Bird, R.S., Paterson, R.: De Bruijn notation as a nested datatype. J. Funct. Program. **9**(1), 77–91 (1999). https://doi.org/10.1017/S0956796899003366
13. Bodin, M., Chargueraud, A., Filaretti, D., Gardner, P., Maffeis, S., Naudziuniene, D., Schmitt, A., Smith, G.: A trusted mechanised JavaScript specification. In: Proceedings of the 41st ACM SIGPLAN-SIGACT Symposium on Principles of Programming Languages, pp. 87–100. POPL '14, Association for Computing Machinery, New York, NY, USA (2014). https://doi.org/10.1145/2535838.2535876
14. Brady, E.: Idris, a general-purpose dependently typed programming language: design and implementation. J. Funct. Program. **23**(5), 552–593 (2013). https://doi.org/10.1017/S095679681300018X
15. Bruijnde Bruijn, N.G.: The mathematical language AUTOMATH, its usage, and some of its extensions. In: Laudet, M., Lacombe, D., Nolin, L., Schützenberger, M. (eds.) Symposium on Automatic Demonstration. pp. 29–61. Springer, Berlin, Heidelberg (1970). https://doi.org/10.1007/BFb0060623
16. Barras, B.: Coq en coq. Rapport de Recherche 3026, INRIA (1996)
17. Carneiro, M.: Lean4Lean: towards a formalized metatheory for the Lean theorem prover (2024). https://doi.org/10.48550/arXiv.2403.14064
18. Cauderlier, R., Dubois, C.: FoCaLiZe and dedukti to the rescue for proof interoperability. In: Itp, pp. 131–147 (2017). https://doi.org/10.1007/978-3-319-66107-0_9
19. Chapman, J.: Type Theory should eat itself. Electron. Notes Theor. Comput. Sci. **228**, 21–36 (2009). https://doi.org/10.1016/j.entcs.2008.12.114
20. Coquand, T.: An algorithm for testing conversion in type theory. In: Logical Frameworks, pp. 255–279. Cambridge University Press, USA (1991)
21. Coquand, T., Huet, G.: The calculus of constructions. Inf. Comput. **76**(2), 95–120 (1988). https://doi.org/10.1016/0890-5401(88)90005-3
22. Curien, P.L.: An abstract framework for environment machines. Theor. Comput. Sci. **82**(2), 389–402 (1991). https://doi.org/10.1016/0304-3975(91)90230-Y
23. Danielsson, N.A.: Operational semantics using the partiality monad. In: Proceedings of the 17th ACM SIGPLAN International Conference on Functional Programming. pp. 127–138. ICFP '12. Association for Computing Machinery, New York, NY, USA (2012). https://doi.org/10.1145/2364527.2364546
24. Danielsson, N.A.: Logical properties of a modality for erasure (2019). https://www.cse.chalmers.se/~nad/publications/danielsson-erased.pdf

25. Devriese, D., Piessens, F.: Typed syntactic meta-programming. In: Proceedings of the 18th ACM SIGPLAN International Conference on Functional Programming - ICFP '13, p. 73. ACM Press, Boston, Massachusetts, USA (2013). https://doi.org/10.1145/2500365.2500575
26. Dunfield, J., Krishnaswami, N.: Bidirectional typing. ACM Comput. Surveys **54**(5), 98:1–98:38 (2021). https://doi.org/10.1145/3450952
27. Eisenberg, R.A.: Stitch: The sound type-indexed type checker (functional pearl). In: Proceedings of the 13th ACM SIGPLAN International Symposium on Haskell, pp. 39–53. Haskell 2020. Association for Computing Machinery, New York, NY, USA (2020). https://doi.org/10.1145/3406088.3409015
28. Gordon, M.J., Milner, A.J., Wadsworth, C.P.: Edinburgh LCF. Lecture Notes in Computer Science, vol. 78. Springer, Berlin, Heidelberg (1979)
29. Jesper Cockx: Operations on syntax should not inspect the scope. In: Reyes, E.H., Villanueva, A. (eds.) TYPES 2023 – Abstracts, pp. 138–140. Valencia, Spain (2023). https://types2023.webs.upv.es/TYPES2023.pdf
30. Klein, G., Elphinstone, K., Heiser, G., Andronick, J., Cock, D., Derrin, P., Elkaduwe, D., Engelhardt, K., Kolanski, R., Norrish, M., Sewell, T., Tuch, H., Winwood, S.: seL4: formal verification of an OS kernel. In: Proceedings of the ACM SIGOPS 22nd Symposium on Operating Systems Principles, pp. 207–220. SOSP '09, Association for Computing Machinery, New York, NY, USA (2009). https://doi.org/10.1145/1629575.1629596
31. Kumar, R., Myreen, M.O., Norrish, M., Owens, S.: CakeML: A verified implementation of ML. In: Proceedings of the 41st ACM SIGPLAN-SIGACT Symposium on Principles of Programming Languages. pp. 179–191. POPL'14, Association for Computing Machinery, New York, NY, USA (Jan 2014) https://doi.org/10.1145/2535838.2535841
32. Paulson, L.C.: Isabelle: the next 700 theorem provers. In: P. Odifreddi (ed.) Logic and Computer Science, pp. 361–386. A.P.I.C. Studies in Data Processing, Academic Press (1990). https://www.cl.cam.ac.uk/~lp15/papers/Isabelle/chap700.pdf
33. Leroy, X.: Formal verification of a realistic compiler. Commun. ACM **52**(7), 107–115 (2009). https://doi.org/10.1145/1538788.1538814
34. Malecha, G.: Extensible proof engineering in intensional type theory. Ph.D. thesis, Harvard University, Graduate School of Arts & Sciences., Cambridge, Massachusetts (2014). http://nrs.harvard.edu/urn-3:HUL.InstRepos:17467172
35. McBride, C.: Elimination with a motive. In: Callaghan, P., Luo, Z., McKinna, J., Pollack, R., Pollack, R. (eds.) Types for Proofs and Programs, pp. 197–216. Springer, Berlin, Heidelberg (2002). https://doi.org/10.1007/3-540-45842-5_13
36. McBride, C.: I Got Plenty o' Nuttin'. In: Lindley, S., McBride, C., Trinder, P., Sannella, D. (eds.) A List of Successes That Can Change the World: Essays Dedicated to Philip Wadler on the Occasion of His 60th Birthday, pp. 207–233. Lecture Notes in Computer Science. Springer, Cham (2016). https://doi.org/10.1007/978-3-319-30936-1_12
37. Nipkow, T., Wenzel, M., Paulson, L.C., Goos, G., Hartmanis, J., Van Leeuwen, J. (eds.): Isabelle/HOL, Lecture Notes in Computer Science, vol. 2283. Springer, Berlin, Heidelberg (2002). https://doi.org/10.1007/3-540-45949-9
38. Norell, U.: Towards a practical programming language based on dependent type theory. Ph.D. thesis, Chalmers University of Technology and Göteborg University, Göteborg, Sweden (2007). https://www.cse.chalmers.se/~ulfn/papers/thesis.pdf
39. Pfenning, F., Schürmann, C.: System description: Twelf—A meta-logical framework for deductive systems, vol. 1632, pp. 202–206. Springer, Berlin, Heidelberg (1999). https://doi.org/10.1007/3-540-48660-7_14

40. Pierce, B.C., Turner, D.N.: Local type inference. ACM Trans. Program. Lang. Syst. **22**(1), 1–44 (2000). https://doi.org/10.1145/345099.345100
41. Pollack, R.: How to believe a machine-checked proof. In: Sambin, G., Smith, J.M. (eds.) Twenty Five Years of Constructive Type Theory, p. 0. Oxford University Press (Oct 1998). https://doi.org/10.1093/oso/9780198501275.003.0013
42. Schäfer, S., Tebbi, T., Smolka, G.: Autosubst: reasoning with de Bruijn terms and parallel substitutions. In: Urban, C., Zhang, X. (eds.) Interactive Theorem Proving. pp. 359–374. Springer, Cham (2015). https://doi.org/10.1007/978-3-319-22102-1_24
43. Sestoft, P.: Deriving a lazy abstract machine. J. Funct. Program. **7**(3), 231–264 (1997). https://doi.org/10.1017/S0956796897002712
44. Sozeau, M., Anand, A., Boulier, S., Cohen, C., Forster, Y., Kunze, F., Malecha, G., Tabareau, N., Winterhalter, T.: The MetaCoq Project. J. Autom. Reason. **64**(5), 947–999 (2020). https://doi.org/10.1007/s10817-019-09540-0
45. Sozeau, M., Boulier, S., Forster, Y., Tabareau, N., Winterhalter, T.: Coq Coq correct! verification of type checking and erasure for Coq, in Coq. Proceedings of the ACM on Programming Languages **4**(POPL), 1–28 (2020)https://doi.org/10.1145/3371076
46. Sozeau, M., Forster, Y., Lennon-Bertrand, M., Nielsen, J.B., Tabareau, N., Winterhalter, T.: Correct and Complete Type Checking and Certified Erasure for Coq, in Coq (2023). https://inria.hal.science/hal-04077552
47. Stark, K., Schäfer, S., Kaiser, J.: Autosubst 2: Reasoning with multi-sorted de Bruijn terms and vector substitutions. In: Proceedings of the 8th ACM SIGPLAN International Conference on Certified Programs and Proofs, pp. 166–180. CPP 2019. Association for Computing Machinery, New York, NY, USA (2019). https://doi.org/10.1145/3293880.3294101
48. Strub, P.Y., Swamy, N., Fournet, C., Chen, J.: Self-certification: Bootstrapping certified typecheckers in F* with Coq. ACM SIGPLAN Notices **47**(1), 571–584 (Jan2012). https://doi.org/10.1145/2103621.2103723
49. Tan, Y.K., Owens, S., Kumar, R.: A verified type system for CakeML. In: Proceedings of the 27th Symposium on the Implementation and Application of Functional Programming Languages. pp. 1–12. IFL '15, Association for Computing Machinery, New York, NY, USA (2015).https://doi.org/10.1145/2897336.2897344
50. The Agda Development Team: Agda 2.6.4 documentation (2023). https://agda.readthedocs.io/en/v2.6.4/
51. The Coq Development Team: The coq reference manual – release 8.18.0 (2023). https://coq.inria.fr/doc/V8.18.0/refman
52. The Idris Development Team: Documentation for the Idris language – version 1.3.4 (2020). http://docs.idris-lang.org/en/v1.3.4/
53. Weirich, S., Voizard, A., amorimde Amorim, P.H.A., Eisenberg, R.A.: A specification for dependent types in Haskell. PACMPL **1**(ICFP) (2017). https://doi.org/10.1145/3110275
54. Wieczorek, P., Biernacki, D.: A Coq formalization of normalization by evaluation for Martin-Löf type theory. In: Proceedings of the 7th ACM SIGPLAN International Conference on Certified Programs and Proofs, pp. 266–279. CPP 2018. Association for Computing Machinery, New York, NY, USA (2018). https://doi.org/10.1145/3167091
55. Wilcox, J.R., Woos, D., Panchekha, P., Tatlock, Z., Wang, X., Ernst, M.D., Anderson, T.: Verdi: A framework for implementing and formally verifying distributed systems. In: Proceedings of the 36th ACM SIGPLAN Conference on Programming Language Design and Implementation, pp. 357–368. PLDI '15, Association for Computing Machinery, New York, NY, USA (2015). https://doi.org/10.1145/2737924.2737958

Extending the Quantitative Pattern-Matching Paradigm

Sandra Alves[1,2], Delia Kesner[3], and Miguel Ramos[1,3,4(✉)]

[1] DCC/FCUP - Faculty of Sciences of the University of Porto, Porto, Portugal
jmiguelsramos@gmail.com
[2] CRACS/INESC-TEC - Center of Advanced Computing Systems, Porto, Portugal
[3] Université Paris Cité, IRIF, CNRS, Paris, France
[4] LIACC - Artificial Intelligence and Computer Science Laboratory, Porto, Portugal

Abstract. We show how (well-established) type systems based on non-idempotent intersection types can be extended to characterize termination properties of functional programming languages with pattern matching features. To model such programming languages, we use a (weak and closed) λ-calculus integrating a pattern matching mechanism on algebraic data types (ADTs). Remarkably, we also show that this language not only encodes Plotkin's CBV and CBN λ-calculus as well as other subsuming frameworks, such as the bang-calculus, but can also be used to interpret the semantics of effectful languages with exceptions. After a thorough study of the untyped language, we introduce a type system based on intersection types, and we show through purely logical methods that the set of terminating terms of the language corresponds exactly to that of well-typed terms. Moreover, by considering *non-idempotent* intersection types, this characterization turns out to be quantitative, *i.e.* the size of the type derivation of a term t gives an upper bound for the number of evaluation steps from t to its normal form.

1 Introduction

Pattern matching is a very useful and powerful mechanism in programming, as witnessed by functional programming languages. Indeed, Haskell and OCaml use pattern matching mechanisms to interact with *algebraic data types* (ADTs), notably by providing a mechanism to deconstruct complex data structures in a concise and readable manner. ADTs are types built by combining other types, such as *product types* and *sum types*. Product types are represented by tuples and sum types by tagged unions. Pattern matching also enhances expressiveness, making it easier to manipulate complex data structures intuitively. Due to the significant role that pattern matching plays in functional programming languages, it is not only important to study its standard semantics, but also its quantitative semantics. In particular, this work focuses on developing a

Supported by: FCT, within project LA/P/0063/2020, and grant 2021.04731.BD; Base Funding UIDB/00027/2020 for LIACC through FCT/MCTES (PIDDAC).

O. Kiselyov (Ed.): APLAS 2024, LNCS 15194, pp. 84–105, 2024.
https://doi.org/10.1007/978-981-97-8943-6_5

model that allows the study of *quantitative* properties of such languages. Semantics for pattern matching have been studied in the literature [1,3,5,6,9,11,16, 24,25], both for formalizing programming languages [1,3,16,24,25] and theorem provers [5,6,9,11]. However, they are either too simple (do not capture ADTs) [3,9,11], lack (quantitative) semantics [3,16,24,25], or do not deal with types [1].

Pattern Matching. (Purely) functional programming languages can be modeled by the λ-calculus. More specifically, they are modeled by the *weak* λ-calculus (*i.e.* no evaluation inside functions), and terms to be evaluated are *closed* (*i.e.* no occurrences of free variables). Therefore, it is natural to focus on pattern matching mechanisms in the framework of weak and closed λ-calculi. In this work, we consider an extension of the λ-calculus based on *generalized* λ *-abstractions* (see *e.g.* [26,27]), which are λ-abstractions of the form $\lambda p.t$, where t is a term and p is a pattern specifying the expected structure of its argument; and *case expressions* of the form $\text{case}\, u \,\text{of}\, (p_1.t_1, \ldots, p_n.t_n)$, where $t_1, \ldots, t_n, u$ are terms and $p_1, \ldots, p_n$ are patterns, further generalizing these λ-abstractions. These constructions can be encoded into more elementary syntax, but we prefer to work with a more expressive high-level language. Case expressions with a single branch could be understood as generalized λ-abstractions applied to an argument. For example, $\text{case}\, t \,\text{of}\, (\texttt{one}(x).\text{case}\, u \,\text{of}\, (\texttt{one}(y).xy))$ can be alternatively expressed as $(\lambda\texttt{one}(x).(\lambda\texttt{one}(y).xy))\; t\; u$. However, while in the former case u appears inside a branch, and thus can only be evaluated after t, in the latter case this order of evaluation is no longer imposed (at least) *a priori*. However, these two constructions do not behave in the exact same way. Indeed, while (generalized) λ-abstractions can in principle postpone the evaluation of their arguments (see Sect. 2), case expressions cannot, since they need to evaluate their arguments until a data matches some pattern in order to decide the branch to pick.

In this work, patterns are either variables (for which matching always succeeds) or *tagged products*, which are products tagged by a unique name. As an example, given a pair (binary product) of the form (x, y), we can build the *tagged* product $\texttt{pair}(x, y)$ by preceding (x, y) with the (unique) name $\texttt{pair}$. By requiring all patterns in case expressions to be unique tagged products, case expressions allow matching over tagged unions. Indeed, a function such as $\lambda x.\text{case}\, x \,\text{of}\, (\texttt{pair}(x, y).y, \texttt{triple}(x, y, z).x)$ is able to handle both data such as *pairs or triples* precisely because of the case expression inside its body. In sum, by adding generalized λ-abstractions and case expressions to the weak and closed λ-calculus, we obtain a simple, yet expressive formal language that can be used to study the semantics of programming languages with pattern matching.

Intersection Types. Type systems based on intersection types can not only guarantee termination (a typable term is terminating), but also characterize it (a terminating term is typable) [17]. *Intersection types* extend simple types with an intersection constructor $\cap$. Intuitively, a program t is typable with the intersection of types $\tau \cap \sigma$ if t is typable with both τ and σ independently [18]. Intersection types were first introduced as a model, for capturing computational properties of the λ-calculus in a broader sense. For example, termination of different evaluation strategies can be characterized by typability in some appropriate intersection type system [7,12], that is, a program t is terminating in a precise sense if and only if t is typable in an appropriate type system. Moreover, by considering non-idempotent intersections [29,36], none of the power of intersection types is lost, but there are substantial improvements. For example, typability in a type system using non-idempotent intersections does not only characterize a *qualitative* property such as termination, but also provides *quantitative* information about termination, such as *upper bounds* for the number of evaluation steps needed to reach a normal form [13,14,19,28]. Very roughly, for type systems based on non-idempotent intersection types, every evaluation step strictly decreases the size of the type derivation tree associated to a well-typed program [12]. This shift of perspective, from idempotent to non-idempotent intersection types, goes beyond lowering the logical complexity of the proof: the quantitative information provided by typing derivations in the non-idempotent setting unveils crucial quantitative relations between typing (statics) and evaluation (dynamics) of programs. For example, one particular consequence is that type inhabitation is undecidable for idempotent types, but becomes decidable for non-idempotent ones [10]. Moreover, there is a tight correspondence between non-idempotent intersection types and the multiplicative connective ! (read "of course") of linear logic [20]. Indeed, let A be a set of types. Then, $!A$ denotes a *multiset* of types of A. Since associativity, commutativity and idempotency are granted if intersections are denoted by sets, therefore, it is natural to represent non-idempotent intersections by multisets, as adopted in this work.

Related Work. Over the last couple of decades, a lot of work has been put towards studying extensions of the λ-calculus with pattern matching mechanisms, either from an operational point of view [16,23–25,30,38] or from a logical one [15,27,31,40]. More recently [9,11], a notion of observability for a calculus with pattern matching was introduced, in which the λ-calculus is extended with generalized λ-abstractions, but patterns are restricted to pairs. Inspired by the pioneering works of [13,14,19,28] and later [2], type systems providing upper-bounds and exact measures for the length of evaluation sequences and the size of normal forms were introduced in [5] for a language virtually identical to that in [9,11]. In [1], it was shown that matching steps can be assigned zero cost, as they are linear in the number of β-steps and the size of the initial term. The language considered in [1] extends the λ-calculus with case expressions and tagged products, but not with generalized λ-abstractions. Moreover, no type system is studied in that work, and no proper treatment of *stuck* case expressions is proposed. As a consequence, it is not possible to clearly distinguish programs that get stuck from those that halt because they have *successfully* finished computing. Another recent work involving the λ-calculus with pattern matching is [6], where non-idempotent intersection types are used to characterize weak normalization for a λ-calculus based on the Calculus of Inductive Construction, as introduced in [22]. Roughly, the latter is an extension of the λ-calculus with a fixpoint operator, case expressions, and tagged products. However, it is worth noting that their type system does *not* enforce *type safety*, *i.e.* many programs are syntactically well-formed but have no meaning at all. For instance, it is possible to write down a program applying data to an argument, which is clearly effectively meaningless. Type safety is then a desirable property that can be enforced by a type system in order to restrict the set of programs to those that do not evaluate to errors. This idea was explored by Milner in [33], which coined it with the slogan "well-typed programs cannot go wrong". Indeed, in [6], well-typed program *can* "go wrong". This does not mean that programs containing errors cannot be semantically sound. It simply means that, in order to ensure *type safety*, errors need to be introduced in a controlled manner, *e.g.* by using exceptions [35].

All the aforementioned works use *open* λ-calculi, where terms are allowed to have free occurrences of variables. However, as it is customary in λ-calculi modeling programming languages, programs are modeled by closed terms. Syntactically, the language considered in [1] is the closest to the one considered in this work. Still, there are two crucial differences. Besides case expressions, we also include generalized λ-abstractions, and we allow patterns to be nested.

- Including generalized λ-abstractions allows single-branched case expressions to be written as applications using generalized λ-abstractions. Currently, since we are going to adopt a weak call-by-name strategy and the calculus enjoys the one-step diamond property (Lemma 1), this redundant syntax is more expressive but completely inconsequential. However, if we consider a call-by-need (CBNeed) strategy with a garbage collecting step (which we leave as future work), it is possible to optimize single-branched case expressions by rewriting them as applications using generalized λ-abstractions. On one hand, case expressions must *always* reduce their arguments until a data matches some pattern in order to select *one* of its branches. On the other hand, applications may (potentially) postpone the evaluation of their arguments for longer, since evaluating the abstraction's body does not necessarily require the argument to be fully evaluated.
- Nested patterns, such as $\texttt{succ}(\texttt{succ}(x))$, do not result in any additional computational expressivity, but could be more convenient. Indeed, nested patterns can be encoded by generalized λ-abstractions. For instance, the term $\lambda\texttt{succ}(x).((\lambda\texttt{succ}(y).y)x)$ is an encoding of $\lambda\texttt{succ}(\texttt{succ}(x)).x$ that does *not* use nested patterns.

In contrast to previous contributions in the domain, here we also study *stuck case expressions*. These case expressions are those whose evaluation is stopped prematurely due to an inability to match any of the branches. Consider the following case expression:

$$t = \texttt{case}\,\texttt{pair}(r, u)\texttt{of}\ (\texttt{one}(x).x, \texttt{triple}(x, y, z).y)$$

Evaluation is *stuck* for t because $\texttt{pair}(r, u)$ neither matches $\texttt{one}(x)$ nor $\texttt{triple}(x, y, z)$. That is, t is a *stuck case expression*. It is also a normal form, but clearly meaningless. In practice, stuck case expressions like the previous one should be untypable, but we believe that they should also be studied and understood from a purely operationally (*i.e.* untyped) point-of-view *i.e.* by providing a characterization of normal forms. Finally, the crucial difference between [6] and this work is that our type system does *not* type errors: all typable programs terminate without errors (see Lemma 12, where *clash* is our notion of error). Indeed, our type system characterizes *error free* termination (see Theorem 1).

Contributions and Overview. This work extends the pattern calculi in [5,9, 11] with tagged products and case expressions, which capture ADT's. The calculus that is obtained, called the λ_c-calculus, models functional programming languages more closely. The main contributions of this work are threefold. First, we provide a detailed operational treatment of the λ_c-calculus in Sect. 2, for which we propose an evaluation strategy $\rightarrow_\mathrm{D}$ based on an extension of the well-known *weak head reduction* strategy. We also give a purely syntactical characterization of *clash-free* (*i.e.* error-free) normal forms. Then, we take a slight detour in Sect. 3 to show a surprising and unexpected consequence of our work: that the operational semantics of our calculus not only subsumes CBN and CBV [37], but can also encode another subsuming frameworks, such as the bang-calculus [8].

Finally, we define a non-idempotent intersection type system in Sect. 4 that naturally extends type system $\mathcal{U}$ from [5]. We provide a purely *logical* and *quantitative* characterization of termination, *i.e.* we show that a program t is typable if, and only if, its evaluation terminates (in a *clash-free* normal form). Moreover, the characterization result is *quantitative*: we show that the size of type derivations provide upper bounds for the number of evaluation steps. In Sect. 5 we conclude and suggest some future work.

2 The Pattern-Matching Calculus

Before introducing the syntax of the pattern-matching λ_c-calculus, we clarify some basic notation related to *tagged products*.

Tagged Products. Let c be a **tag** taken out of an enumerable set of tags C. A **constructor** c^n is built by assigning a unique *arity* $n \in \mathbb{N}$ to a *tag* c. Since each tag has a *unique* arity, constructors are identified uniquely by their tags. Constructors cannot be applied partially: a constructor c^n *must* be applied to n arguments. Accordingly, the application $\mathsf{c}^n\ a_1 \cdots\ a_n$ will be written $\mathsf{c}^n(a_1, \ldots, a_n)$ and called a **tagged product**, where the sequence of arguments $a_1 \cdots a_n$ is represented as a *tuple* (or *product* or *vector*) of arguments $(a_1, \ldots, a_n)$ of length n. It is possible to take advantage of the tuple notation and simply write $(a_1, \ldots, a_n)$ as $(a_i)_n$ (meaning that $1 \leq i \leq n$) in order to keep notation light. Tagged products represent **data** and will thus be referred to as such throughout the rest of this work. Moreover, the arity of constructors will always be left implicit, and all data is assumed to be well-formed (constructors are always applied to tuples of arguments of the appropriate length).

The Syntax of the λ_{c} ***-Calculus.*** Given an infinite but countable set of variables $x, y, z, \ldots \in V$, we introduce the following grammars:

$$\begin{array}{rl}
\textbf{(Patterns)} & p, q ::= x \mid \mathsf{c}(p_i)_n \\
\textbf{(Branches)} & b ::= \mathsf{c}(p_i)_n.t \\
\textbf{(Terms)} & t, u, r, v, s ::= x \mid \lambda p.t \mid tu \mid t[p\backslash u] \mid \mathsf{c}(t_i)_n \mid \mathrm{case}\, t \,\mathrm{of}\, (b_1, \ldots, b_n) \\
\textbf{(List Contexts)} & \mathtt{L} ::= \Box \mid \mathtt{L}[p\backslash t]
\end{array}$$

Let Λ_{c} denote the set of terms of the λ_{c}-calculus. In order to keep notation light, symbols P, B, and T are going to be used to denote **tuples of patterns**, **tuples of branches**, and **tuples of terms**, respectively. The pattern x is called a **variable pattern**, and $\mathsf{c}P$ is a **data pattern**. The term $\lambda p.t$ is a **generalized abstraction**, $t[p\backslash u]$ is a **matching closure** (where $[p\backslash u]$ is a called an **explicit matching operation**), $\mathsf{c}T$ is a **data term**, and $\mathrm{case}\, t \,\mathrm{of}\, B$ is a **case expression**. Remark in particular that the explicit matching operator is a new constructor in the language, and it is not on the meta-level. We write $\mathtt{I}$ as a special term representing the identity function $\lambda x.x$.

Free and Bound Variables. The **set of variables** of a pattern p is denoted by $\mathtt{vars}(p)$ and defined as expected. It will be useful to write $\hat{p}$ to denote *data patterns*, so that $\mathrm{case}\, t \,\mathrm{of}\, (\mathsf{c}_i P_i.u_i)_n$ can be written as $\mathrm{case}\, t \,\mathrm{of}\, (\hat{p}_i.u_i)_n$, where $\hat{p}_i = \mathsf{c}_i P_i$. The **sets of free and bound variables** of branches, terms and list contexts are also defined as expected. In particular:

$$\begin{aligned}
\mathtt{fv}(\lambda p.t) &\stackrel{\mathsf{def}}{=} \mathtt{fv}(t) \setminus \mathtt{vars}(p) \\
\mathtt{fv}(t[p\backslash u]) &\stackrel{\mathsf{def}}{=} (\mathtt{fv}(t) \setminus \mathtt{vars}(p)) \cup \mathtt{fv}(u) \\
\mathtt{fv}(\mathrm{case}\, t \,\mathrm{of}\, (\hat{p}_i.u_i)_n) &\stackrel{\mathsf{def}}{=} \mathtt{fv}(t) \textstyle\bigcup_{i \in [\![1,n]\!]} (\mathtt{fv}(u_i) \setminus \mathtt{vars}(\hat{p}_i)) \\
\mathtt{bv}(\mathtt{L}[p\backslash t]) &\stackrel{\mathsf{def}}{=} \mathtt{bv}(\mathtt{L}) \cup \mathtt{vars}(p)
\end{aligned}$$

Terms are α-equivalent if they only differ on the names of their bound variables. In this work, terms are going to be considered equal up-to α-equivalence. In particular, substitutions $t\{x\backslash u\}$ are capture avoiding, *i.e.* $x \notin \mathtt{bv}(t)$.

List Contexts. Terms can be surrounded by list contexts, which are sequences of explicit matching operations. Indeed, given a list context $\mathtt{L}$ and a term t, $\mathtt{L}(\!|t|\!)$ denotes the term obtained by **plugging the term** t **inside context** $\mathtt{L}$, *i.e.* by replacing the unique occurrence of $\Box$ in $\mathtt{L}$ with t (possibly allowing the capture of free variables of t). Thus, *e.g.* if $\mathtt{L} = \Box[x_1\backslash u_1][x_2\backslash u_2]$, then $\mathtt{L}(\!|x_1|\!)$ is the term $x_1[x_1\backslash u_1][x_2\backslash u_2]$. List contexts are important as they allow matching operations to be postponed, thus exposing redexes that might otherwise stay hidden due to premature normal forms (see Theorem 1). We use two special predicates to distinguish terms possibly affected by a list of explicit matching operators: $\mathtt{isabs}(t)$ iff $t = \mathtt{L}(\!|\lambda p.u|\!)$; $\mathtt{iscase}(t)$ iff $t = \mathtt{L}(\!|\mathrm{case}\, u \,\mathrm{of}\, B|\!)$; and $\mathtt{isdata}_{\mathsf{c}}(t)$ iff $t = \mathtt{L}(\!|\mathsf{c}T|\!)$, in which case we may also write $\mathtt{isdata}(t)$ whenever c is irrelevant.

Linear Patterns. Patterns are assumed to be **linear**, *i.e.* each variable occurs at most once, and so are tuples of patterns, *i.e.* no variable is shared between patterns in a tuple. Most modern programming languages with pattern matching implement linear patterns since this does not affect the expressivity the language, while avoiding to check for equality of terms.

Case Expressions. As mentioned in the introduction, case expressions capture the pattern-matching mechanism over tagged unions. Note that each branch of a case expression is built out of a tagged product and a term. Therefore, we require all tagged products to have a different top-level tag, thus branches are disjoint and matching is thus unambiguous. As such, case expressions can indeed be understood as *deconstructors* for **tagged unions**. As an example, the following case expression is a function whose behavior depends on whether its argument is a *pair* or a *triple*, like in $\lambda x.\text{case}\, x\, \text{of}\, (\texttt{pair}(x, y).y, \texttt{triple}(x, y, z).x)$.

2.1 Picking an Evaluation Strategy

We define our evaluation strategy as a having a lazy behavior. Indeed, with respect to generalized abstractions built from *variable patterns*, applications behave like in CBN, *i.e.* arguments are never evaluated before they are plugged into a term (see reduction rule ($\texttt{sub}$) bellow); however, generalized abstractions built from *data patterns* and case expressions behave differently: arguments need to be (partially) evaluated to some data in order to satisfy the matching conditions (see reduction rules ($\texttt{branch}$) and ($\texttt{match}$) bellow).

The **weak head reduction relation** $\rightarrow_{\texttt{WH}}$ is defined as the closure over **weak head contexts**

$$\texttt{WH} ::= \Box \mid \texttt{WH}\, t \mid \texttt{WH}[p\backslash u] \mid t[\hat{p}\backslash \texttt{WH}] \mid \text{case}\, \texttt{WH}\, \text{of}\, B$$

of the following four **reduction rules**:

$$\begin{array}{rcl} \texttt{L}(\!|\lambda p.t|\!)u & \mapsto_{\texttt{dB}} & \texttt{L}(\!|t[p\backslash u]|\!) \text{ if } \texttt{bv}(\texttt{L}) \cap \texttt{fv}(u) = \emptyset \\ \text{case } \texttt{L}(\!|\texttt{c}(u_i)_n|\!) \text{ of } (\ldots, \texttt{c}(p_i)_n.t, \ldots) & \mapsto_{\texttt{branch}} & \texttt{L}(\!|t[p_1\backslash u_1]\cdots[p_n\backslash u_n]|\!) \text{ if } \texttt{bv}(\texttt{L}) \cap \texttt{fv}(t) = \emptyset \\ t[\texttt{c}(p_i)_n\backslash\, \texttt{L}(\!|\texttt{c}(u_i)_n|\!)] & \mapsto_{\texttt{match}} & \texttt{L}(\!|t[p_1\backslash u_1]\cdots[p_n\backslash u_n]|\!) \text{ if } \texttt{bv}(\texttt{L}) \cap \texttt{fv}(t) = \emptyset \\ t[x\backslash u] & \mapsto_{\texttt{sub}} & t\{x\backslash u\} \end{array}$$

Rule ($\texttt{dB}$) is the usual starting rule of λ-calculi working *at a distance*. Indeed, since matchings and substitutions can be delayed, all terms are formally plugged into a (possibly empty) list of contexts. Thus, in applications, abstractions and arguments might be separated by a list context. Rules ($\texttt{branch}$) and ($\texttt{match}$) solve (top-level) matches between data patterns and data terms, respectively. It is worth noticing that the side conditions in these three rules are necessary in order to avoid the capture of free variables. And rule ($\texttt{sub}$) produces a *capture avoiding* substitution as a result of solving a matching between a variable pattern and a term. Also, note that it is safe to assume that all meta-level substitutions are capture avoiding due to α-conversion.

We write $t \rightarrow_{\texttt{WH}(s)} t'$ if $t \rightarrow_{\texttt{WH}} t'$ for $t = \texttt{WH}(\!|u|\!)$, $t' = \texttt{WH}(\!|u'|\!)$, and $u \mapsto_s u'$, where s is a reduction rule. Similarly, we write $t \rightarrow_{\texttt{WH}(\overline{s})} t'$ if $u \mapsto_{s'} u'$ and s' is some reduction rule different from s.

Let $\rightarrow_{\mathcal{R}}$ be some reduction relation. The **reflexive-transitive closure** of $\rightarrow_{\mathcal{R}}$ is written $\twoheadrightarrow_{\mathcal{R}}$. In particular, if $\rightarrow_{\mathcal{R}}=\rightarrow_{\mathtt{WH}}$, then $t \twoheadrightarrow_{\mathtt{WH}}^{(b,c,m,e)} u$ denotes that $t \twoheadrightarrow_{\mathtt{WH}} u$ using b dB-steps, c branch-steps, m match-steps, and e sub-steps.

Example 1. Let $\mathtt{c}_0, \mathtt{c}_1, \mathtt{c}_2 \in \mathtt{C}$. Going back to the last example of the previous section, we have the following:

$$\begin{array}{rl} & (\lambda x.\mathsf{case}\ x\ \mathsf{of}\ (\mathtt{pair}(x,y).y, \mathtt{triple}(x,y,z).x))\ \mathtt{triple}(\mathtt{c}_0,\mathtt{c}_1,\mathtt{c}_2) \\ \rightarrow_{\mathtt{WH(dB)}} & \mathsf{case}\ x\ \mathsf{of}\ (\mathtt{pair}(x,y).y, \mathtt{triple}(x,y,z).x)[x\backslash\mathtt{triple}(\mathtt{c}_0,\mathtt{c}_1,\mathtt{c}_2)] \\ \rightarrow_{\mathtt{WH(sub)}} & \mathsf{case}\ \mathtt{triple}(\mathtt{c}_0,\mathtt{c}_1,\mathtt{c}_2)\mathsf{of}\ (\mathtt{pair}(x,y).y, \mathtt{triple}(x,y,z).x) \\ \rightarrow_{\mathtt{WH(branch)}} & x[x\backslash\mathtt{c}_0][y\backslash\mathtt{c}_1][z\backslash\mathtt{c}_2] \rightarrow_{\mathtt{WH(sub)}} x[x\backslash\mathtt{c}_0][y\backslash\mathtt{c}_1] \rightarrow_{\mathtt{WH(sub)}} x[x\backslash\mathtt{c}_0] \rightarrow_{\mathtt{WH(sub)}} \mathtt{c}_0 \end{array}$$

The reduction relation $\rightarrow_{\mathtt{WH}}$ is not deterministic, *i.e.* given a term which is not in normal form, then it can be reduced in different ways. For example, going back to the previous example, after the branch-step, we could have chosen the following reduction sequence:

$$\begin{array}{rl} & (\lambda x.\mathsf{case}\ x\ \mathsf{of}\ (\mathtt{pair}(x,y).y, \mathtt{triple}(x,y,z).x))\ \mathtt{triple}(\mathtt{c}_0,\mathtt{c}_1,\mathtt{c}_2) \\ \twoheadrightarrow_{\mathtt{WH}}^{(1,1,0,1)} & x[x\backslash\mathtt{c}_0][y\backslash\mathtt{c}_1][z\backslash\mathtt{c}_2] \rightarrow_{\mathtt{WH(sub)}} \mathtt{c}_0[y\backslash\mathtt{c}_1][z\backslash\mathtt{c}_2] \rightarrow_{\mathtt{WH(sub)}} \mathtt{c}_0[z\backslash\mathtt{c}_2] \rightarrow_{\mathtt{WH(sub)}} \mathtt{c}_0 \end{array}$$

where instead of applying sub-steps from right-to-left, these are applied from left-to-right. However, it is possible to fix a particular evaluation strategy for $\rightarrow_{\mathtt{WH}}$ (see Lemma 1). Despite nondeterminism, as will be shown, $\rightarrow_{\mathtt{WH}}$ is not only confluent (Lemma 1), but all evaluation sequences leading to a normal form have the same size (Lemma 1).

Reduction relation $\rightarrow_{\mathcal{R}}$ is said to enjoy the **diamond property** if for every term t, if $u \leftarrow_{\mathcal{R}} t \rightarrow_{\mathcal{R}} r$, there exists a term v, such that $u \rightarrow_{\mathcal{R}} v \leftarrow_{\mathcal{R}} r$ (see Def.1.1.8.(v) of [39]). Note, however, that $\rightarrow_{\mathtt{WH}}$ is not reflexive. Still, by assuming that $u \neq r$, the following alternative version of the diamond property can be shown for $\rightarrow_{\mathtt{WH}}$. A reduction relation $\rightarrow_{\mathtt{WH}}$ is said to enjoy the **one-step diamond property** if for every term $t \in \Lambda_{\mathtt{c}}$, if $u \leftarrow_{\mathtt{WH}} t \rightarrow_{\mathtt{WH}} r$ with $u \neq r$, there exists a term $v \in \Lambda_{\mathtt{c}}$, such that $u \rightarrow_{\mathtt{WH}} v \leftarrow_{\mathtt{WH}} r$ (see Prop.1 of [32]).

Lemma 1. (One-Step Diamond) *Reduction relation $\rightarrow_{\mathtt{WH}}$ enjoys the one-step diamond property.*

As a corollary we obtain:

Corollary 1. (Confluence)

- *Reduction relation $\rightarrow_{\mathtt{WH}}$ is confluent.*
- *Any two different reduction paths to normal form have the same length.*

Weak Head Evaluation. One of the main distinguishing characteristics between reduction *relations* and evaluation *strategies* is that, while the former are (usually) *not* deterministic, the latter *are* (usually) deterministic, *i.e.* for any term t, if t is not a normal form, exactly one reduction rule applies. This is exactly the case for the **weak head evaluation strategy** $\rightarrow_{\mathtt{D}}$, which is defined by the set of reduction rules in Fig. 1.

$$\frac{\mathtt{bv}(\mathtt{L}) \cap \mathtt{fv}(u) = \emptyset}{\mathtt{L}(\!|\lambda p.t|\!)u \rightarrow_{\mathtt{D}} \mathtt{L}(\!|t[p\backslash u]|\!)}\ (\mathtt{dB}) \qquad \frac{\neg\mathtt{isabs}(t) \quad t \rightarrow_{\mathtt{D}} t'}{tu \rightarrow_{\mathtt{D}} t'u}\ (\mathtt{appL})$$

$$\frac{\mathtt{bv}(\mathtt{L}) \cap \mathtt{fv}(t) = \emptyset}{t[\mathtt{c}(p_i)_n\backslash\mathtt{L}(\!|\mathtt{c}(u_i)_n|\!)] \rightarrow_{\mathtt{D}} \mathtt{L}(\!|t[p_1\backslash u_1]\cdots[p_n\backslash u_n]|\!)}\ (\mathtt{match}) \qquad \frac{}{t[x\backslash u] \rightarrow_{\mathtt{D}} t\{x\backslash u\}}\ (\mathtt{sub})$$

$$\frac{\neg\mathtt{isdata}_{\mathtt{c}}(u) \quad t \rightarrow_{\mathtt{D}} t'}{t[\mathtt{c}P\backslash u] \rightarrow_{\mathtt{D}} t'[\mathtt{c}P\backslash u]}\ (\mathtt{esL}) \qquad \frac{\neg\mathtt{isdata}_{\mathtt{c}}(u) \quad t \not\rightarrow_{\mathtt{D}} \quad u \rightarrow_{\mathtt{D}} u'}{t[\mathtt{c}P\backslash u] \rightarrow_{\mathtt{D}} t[\mathtt{c}P\backslash u']}\ (\mathtt{esR})$$

$$\frac{\mathtt{bv}(\mathtt{L}) \cap \mathtt{fv}(t) = \emptyset}{\mathtt{case}\ \mathtt{L}(\!|\mathtt{c}(u_i)_n|\!)\ \mathtt{of}\ (\ldots, \mathtt{c}(p_i)_n.t, \ldots) \rightarrow_{\mathtt{D}} \mathtt{L}(\!|t[p_1\backslash u_1]\cdots[p_n\backslash u_n]|\!)}\ (\mathtt{branch})$$

$$\frac{t \rightarrow_{\mathtt{D}} t' \quad \neg\mathtt{isdata}_{\mathtt{c}_i}(t) \text{ for all } i \in [\![1, n]\!]}{\mathtt{case}\ t\ \mathtt{of}\ (\mathtt{c}_i P_i.u_i)_n \rightarrow_{\mathtt{D}} \mathtt{case}\ t'\ \mathtt{of}\ (\mathtt{c}_i P_i.u_i)_n}\ (\mathtt{caseArg})$$

Fig. 1. The weak head evaluation strategy $\rightarrow_{\mathtt{D}}$

As expected, $\rightarrow_{\mathtt{D}}$ can be taken as an evaluation strategy:

Proposition 1. (Determinism) *The reduction relation* $\rightarrow_{\mathtt{D}}$ *is deterministic.*

Note that the evaluation sequence in Example 1 follows, in particular, the weak head evaluation strategy defined above. Moreover, it is not difficult to show that $\rightarrow_{\mathtt{D}}$ has the same set of normal forms as $\rightarrow_{\mathtt{WH}}$. Thus, since every reduction path in $\rightarrow_{\mathtt{WH}}$ has the same length, it is safe to work with $\rightarrow_{\mathtt{D}}$ instead of $\rightarrow_{\mathtt{WH}}$.

Encoding Exceptions. Here, we portray the expressive power of the $\lambda_{\mathtt{C}}$-calculus, by giving a concrete example. Indeed, the following fragment of the $\lambda_{\mathtt{C}}$-calculus is enough to encode exceptions' la Moggi [34,35]:

$$\begin{aligned} v, w &::= x \mid \lambda x.t \\ t, u &::= \mathsf{v}(v) \mid \mathsf{e}(t) \mid vw \mid t[x\backslash u] \mid \mathrm{case}\, t\, \mathrm{of}\, (\mathsf{v}(x).u, \mathsf{e}(y).y) \\ &\mid\ \mathrm{case}\, t\, \mathrm{of}\, (\mathsf{v}(x).u, \mathsf{e}(y).\mathsf{e}(y)) \end{aligned}$$

where v and e are unary constructors used to tag values and exceptions, respectively. Terms $\mathsf{v}(v)$ and $\mathsf{e}(t)$ distinguish between values and exceptions. Case expressions of the form $\mathrm{case}\, t\, \mathrm{of}\, (\mathsf{v}(x).u, \mathsf{e}(y).y)$ compose terms sequentially (*i.e.* they force t to be evaluated before u), to deal with the fact that terms either reduce to a value or to an exception with a continuation. Note that in the latter case, the continuation must be returned. Moreover, an application of the form tu can be encoded as

$$\mathrm{case}\, t\, \mathrm{of}\, (\mathsf{v}(x).\mathrm{case}\, t\, \mathrm{of}\, (\mathsf{v}(y).xy, \mathsf{e}(z).\mathsf{e}(z)), \mathsf{e}(z).\mathsf{e}(z))$$

The following examples illustrate three terms encoding the expected behavior of a term of the form $(\lambda x.u)t$ in the presence of exceptions, depending on whether t evaluates (successfully) to $\mathtt{v}(v)$ or (exceptionally) to $\mathtt{e}(r)$:

$$\begin{aligned} t_1 &= \mathtt{case}\,\mathtt{v}(v)\mathtt{of}\ (\mathtt{v}(x).u, \mathtt{e}(y).y) \twoheadrightarrow_{\mathtt{D}} u\{x\backslash v\} \\ t_2 &= \mathtt{case}\,\mathtt{e}(r)\mathtt{of}\ (\mathtt{v}(x).u, \mathtt{e}(y).y) \twoheadrightarrow_{\mathtt{D}} r \\ t_3 &= \mathtt{case}\,\mathtt{e}(r)\mathtt{of}\ (\mathtt{v}(x).u, \mathtt{e}(y).\mathtt{e}(y)) \twoheadrightarrow_{\mathtt{D}} \mathtt{e}(r) \end{aligned}$$

The first term t_1 encodes a successful application $(\lambda x.u)(\mathtt{v}(v)) \twoheadrightarrow_{\mathtt{D}} u\{x\backslash v\}$; t_2 encodes a short-circuited application $(\lambda x.u)(\mathtt{e}(r)) \rightsquigarrow r$ that handles the exception $\mathtt{e}$; and t_3 encodes a short-circuited application $(\lambda x.u)(\mathtt{e}(r)) \rightsquigarrow \mathtt{e}(r)$ that simply propagates exception $\mathtt{e}$ outwards.

Normal Forms and Match Operations. In order to syntactically describe the set of irreducible forms for $\rightarrow_{\mathtt{D}}$ (and thus for $\rightarrow_{\mathtt{WH}}$), it is necessary to place special care in the treatment of **stuck matchings**. The latter can arise in two ways: (1) from rule $(\mathtt{dB})$ whenever the abstraction is built from a data pattern; and (2) from rule $(\mathtt{branch})$. Consider the two following examples:

$$(\lambda\mathtt{pair}(x,y).y)(\mathtt{duo}(t,u)) \rightarrow_{\mathtt{dB}} y[\mathtt{pair}(x,y)\backslash\mathtt{duo}(t,u)] \not\rightarrow_{\mathtt{match}} \quad (1)$$

$$\mathtt{case}\,\mathtt{duo}(t,u)\mathtt{of}\ (\mathtt{one}(x).x, \mathtt{pair}(x,y).y) \not\rightarrow_{\mathtt{branch}} \quad (2)$$

In both cases, evaluation is *stuck* due to a stuck matching. Clearly, these irreducible terms are not the desired results of computations. Moreover, the same is true if $\mathtt{duo}(t,u)$ is replaced with an abstraction. These kinds of situations will be dealt with later by introducing the notion of **clash** and the set of **clash-free** normal forms (see Lemma 3). Still, to provide a syntactical description of irreducible terms, these situations need to be considered. Note that stuck matchings that result from matching a data pattern with a different constructor (in the examples above, data $\mathtt{duo}(t,u)$ is matched against patterns $\mathtt{pair}(x,y)$ and $\mathtt{one}(x)$) can be described by: (1) inspecting the matching operation $[\hat{p}\backslash t]$ in a matching closure $u[\hat{p}\backslash t]$, and checking that whenever t is data, it has the same constructor as $\hat{p}$; (2) inspecting t in a case expression $\mathtt{case}\,t\,\mathtt{of}\,(b_1,\ldots,b_n)$, and checking that whenever t is data, it has the same constructor as the data pattern of one of the branches $b_1,\ldots,b_n$. Naturally, different data patterns in closure matchings and sets of data patterns in vectors of branches generate different sets of stuck matching. Thus, the set of irreducible of the λ_{c}-calculus is the union over the sets of normal forms with respect to a particular constructor $\mathtt{c} \in \mathtt{C}$. To capture that, we define three categories of terms: **neutral**, **neutral data**, and **normal**. The set of **neutral forms** is written $\mathtt{ne}$ and does not depend on any constructor. The **set of normal (resp. neutral data) forms** is written $\mathtt{no}$ (resp. $\mathtt{na}$) and defined as $\mathtt{no} \stackrel{\mathtt{def}}{=} \bigcup_{\mathtt{c}\in\mathtt{C}} \mathtt{no}^{\mathtt{c}}$ (resp. $\mathtt{na} \stackrel{\mathtt{def}}{=} \bigcup_{\mathtt{c}\in\mathtt{C}} \mathtt{na}^{\mathtt{c}}$), where $\mathtt{no}^{\mathtt{c}}$ (resp. $\mathtt{na}^{\mathtt{c}}$) is the **set of normal (resp. neutral data) forms with respect to** $\mathtt{c} \in \mathtt{C}$.

Let $\mathtt{C}' \subseteq \mathtt{C}$. Then, $\mathtt{no}^{\neg \mathtt{C}'} \stackrel{\text{def}}{=} \{t \in \mathtt{no}^{\mathtt{c}} \mid \mathtt{c} \in \mathtt{C} \setminus \mathtt{C}'\}$, and $\mathtt{WH}(\!|\mathtt{no}^{\neg \mathtt{C}'}|\!) \stackrel{\text{def}}{=} \{\mathtt{WH}(\!|t|\!) \mid t \in \mathtt{no}^{\neg \mathtt{C}'}\}$. Then, $\mathtt{no}^{\mathtt{c}}$ is generated by the following grammars:

$$\begin{array}{rrl} \textbf{(Neutral)} & \mathtt{ne} ::= & x \mid \mathtt{na}\ t \mid \mathtt{ne}[\mathtt{c}'P \backslash \mathtt{no}^{\neg \mathtt{c}'}] \mid \mathtt{case}\ \mathtt{no}^{\neg \{\mathtt{c}_1, \ldots, \mathtt{c}_n\}} \mathtt{of}\ (\mathtt{c}_i P_i . u_i)_n \\ \textbf{(Neutral Data)} & \mathtt{na}^{\mathtt{c}} ::= & \mathtt{ne} \mid \mathtt{c}T \mid \mathtt{na}^{\mathtt{c}}[\mathtt{c}'P \backslash \mathtt{no}^{\neg \mathtt{c}'}] \\ \textbf{(Normal)} & \mathtt{no}^{\mathtt{c}} ::= & \mathtt{na}^{\mathtt{c}} \mid \lambda p.t \mid \mathtt{no}^{\mathtt{c}}[\mathtt{c}'P \backslash \mathtt{no}^{\neg \mathtt{c}'}] \end{array}$$

and $\mathtt{no}^{\neg \mathtt{c}'}$ is written for $\mathtt{no}^{\neg \{\mathtt{c}'\}}$. Intuitively, $t \in \mathtt{no}^{\mathtt{c}}$ if and only if t is an irreducible term, and either $\neg\mathtt{isdata}(t)$ or $\mathtt{isdata}_{\mathtt{c}}(t)$. The set of neutral forms $\mathtt{ne}$ corresponds to irreducible terms that do not produce any redexes whenever plugged into any context $\mathtt{WH}$, *i.e.* the set of terms $t \in \mathtt{no}^{\mathtt{c}}$, such that $\neg\mathtt{isabs}(t)$ and $\neg\mathtt{isdata}(t)$ hold. The set $\mathtt{na}^{\mathtt{c}}$ is the set of irreducible terms (with respect to $\mathtt{c}$) that do not produce any redexes whenever plugged into a context of the form $\mathtt{WH}\ t$, *i.e.* the set of terms $t \in \mathtt{no}^{\mathtt{c}}$, such that $\neg\mathtt{isabs}(t)$ holds.

Example 2. The following terms are normal forms:

$$\mathtt{case}\,\mathtt{duo}(\mathtt{I},\mathtt{I})\mathtt{of}\ (\mathtt{pair}(x,y).y) \in \mathtt{ne} \qquad \mathtt{case}\,\mathtt{I}\,\mathtt{of}\ (\mathtt{pair}(x,y).y) \in \mathtt{ne}$$
$$\mathtt{pair}(\mathtt{II},\mathtt{I}) \in \mathtt{no}^{\mathtt{pair}} \subseteq \mathtt{no}\mathtt{pair}(\mathtt{II},\mathtt{I})\ \mathtt{I} \in \mathtt{no}$$

In particular, note that $\mathtt{duo}(\mathtt{I},\mathtt{I}) \in \mathtt{no}^{\mathtt{duo}} \subseteq \mathtt{no}^{\neg\mathtt{pair}}$ and $\mathtt{I} \in \mathtt{no}^{\neg\mathtt{pair}}$.

Set $\mathtt{no}$ precisely captures the notion of irreducible term as follows.

Lemma 2. (Normal Forms) *Let $t \in \Lambda_{\mathtt{c}}$. Then, $t \in \mathtt{no}$ iff $t \not\to_{\mathtt{D}}$.*

Note that the set of normal forms was defined for *open* terms. This is a technical detail that allows induction to go through smoothly in the proofs. The set of normal forms for *closed* term (programs) is obtained by removing x from the definition of normal forms and assuming every term to be closed.

Clashes. As was discussed in the introduction and also mentioned at the beginning of this section, not all normal forms are the desired results of a computation. Indeed, some normal forms are semantically meaningless. Of course, programs containing meaningless subprograms are also meaningless. Such programs are called *clashes* and are generated by the following grammars:

$$\begin{array}{rrl} \textbf{(Base Clashes)} & \mathtt{SH}^0 ::= & \mathtt{L}(\!|\mathtt{c}T|\!)\ u \mid t[\mathtt{c}P \backslash\ \mathtt{L}(\!|\lambda q.u|\!)] \mid t[\mathtt{c}P \backslash\ \mathtt{L}(\!|\mathtt{c}'T|\!)] \text{ where } \mathtt{c} \neq \mathtt{c}' \\ & \mid & \mathtt{case}\ \mathtt{L}(\!|\lambda p.t|\!)\mathtt{of}\ B \\ & \mid & \mathtt{case}\ \mathtt{L}(\!|\mathtt{c}T|\!)\mathtt{of}\ (\mathtt{c}_i P_i . u_i)_n \text{ where } \mathtt{c} \notin \{\mathtt{c}_1, \ldots, \mathtt{c}_n\} \\ \textbf{(Clashes)} & \mathtt{SH} ::= & \mathtt{SH}^0 \mid \mathtt{SH}\ t \mid \mathtt{SH}[p \backslash u] \mid t[p \backslash \mathtt{SH}] \mid \mathtt{case}\ \mathtt{SH}\mathtt{of}\ B \end{array}$$

Example 3. Going back to Example 2, term $\mathtt{pair}(\mathtt{II},\mathtt{I}) \notin \mathtt{SH}$ is *not* a clash. But the three following terms are clashes:

$$\mathtt{case}\,\mathtt{duo}(\mathtt{I},\mathtt{I})\mathtt{of}\ (\mathtt{pair}(x,y).y) \in \mathtt{SH}$$
$$\mathtt{case}\,\mathtt{I}\,\mathtt{of}\ (\mathtt{pair}(x,y).y) \in \mathtt{SH} \qquad \mathtt{pair}(\mathtt{II},\mathtt{I})\ \mathtt{I} \in \mathtt{SH}$$

Clearly, it is easy to refine the set of normal forms by excluding clashes. The resulting set is called the **set of clash-free normal forms** and is generated by the following grammars:

$$\begin{array}{ll}\textbf{(Clash-Free Ne. Forms)}\ \mathtt{ne}_{\mathtt{SHF}} ::= x \mid \mathtt{ne}_{\mathtt{SHF}}\ t \mid \mathtt{ne}_{\mathtt{SHF}}[\mathtt{c}P\backslash \mathtt{ne}_{\mathtt{SHF}}] \mid \mathtt{case}\ \mathtt{ne}_{\mathtt{SHF}}\ \mathtt{of}\ B \\ \textbf{(Clash-Free No. Forms)}\ \mathtt{no}_{\mathtt{SHF}} ::= \mathtt{ne}_{\mathtt{SHF}} \mid \lambda p.t \mid \mathtt{c}T \mid \mathtt{no}_{\mathtt{SHF}}[\mathtt{c}P\backslash \mathtt{ne}_{\mathtt{SHF}}]\end{array}$$

Set $\mathtt{no}_{\mathtt{SHF}}$ precisely captures the notion of clash-free normal form as follows.

Lemma 3. (Clash-Free Normal Forms) *Let $t \in \Lambda_{\mathsf{c}}$. Then, $t \in \mathtt{no}_{\mathtt{SHF}}$ iff $t \not\to_{\mathtt{D}}$ and $t \notin \mathtt{SH}$*

Again, note that the set of clash-free normal forms was defined for *open* terms. Unsurprisingly, by restricting this set to *closed* terms, the set of clash-free normal forms collapses as follows.

Lemma 4. (Closed Clash-Free Normal Forms) *Let $t \in \Lambda_{\mathsf{c}}$ be a closed term. Then, $t \not\to_{\mathtt{D}}$ and $t \notin \mathtt{SH}$ iff $t = \lambda p.u$ or $t = \mathtt{c}T$ for $\mathtt{c} \in \mathtt{C}$.*

Programs that are neither clashes nor in normal form can still *evaluate* to clashes. As an example, term $((\lambda x.\mathtt{pair}(\mathtt{I},\mathtt{I}))\mathtt{I})\mathtt{I} \notin \mathtt{SH}$, but evaluates to the *clash* $\mathtt{pair}(\mathtt{I},\mathtt{I})\ \mathtt{I} \in \mathtt{SH}$ from Example 3.

Formally, a program t is a **clash-free program** iff there is no $u \in \mathtt{SH}$ such that $t \twoheadrightarrow_{\mathtt{D}} u$. It is clearly not possible to provide a syntactical characterization of clash-freeness. However, as mentioned in the introduction, type systems can be used in order to provide a *logical* one. Indeed, a term t is **weak head terminating** if weak head evaluation terminates for t with a clash-free normal form. In Sect. 4, we purpose such a type system, which can be seen as a natural extension of type system $\mathcal{U}$ from [5] to data (patterns) and case expressions, thus characterizing the set of weak head terminating terms of the λ_{c}-calculus.

3 The λ_{c}-Calculus as a Subsuming Framework

In this section, we take a slight detour in order to explore some of the encoding capabilities of the λ_{c}-calculus. In particular, it is shown that our language encodes Plotkin's CBV and CBN λ-calculus [37], and also the bang-calculus, written $\lambda^{!}$, that was proposed in [8] as a subsuming framework for CBN and CBV λ-calculus based on Girard's encodings [21]. While the λ_{c}-calculus is clearly capturing expressive pattern matching programs, it is neither natural nor intuitive that is also able to subsume two different calling paradigms such as CBN and CBV. This is an interesting observation of this work.

Plotkin's CBN. It is easy to see that Plotkin's CBN λ-calculus is a strict subset of our language. The set of **terms** and **CBN contexts** of Plotkin's CBN λ-calculus are generated by the following grammars:

$$\textbf{(Terms)}\ t, u ::= x \mid \lambda x.t \mid tu \qquad \textbf{(CBN Contexts)}\ \mathtt{N} ::= \Box \mid \mathtt{N}t$$

The CBN reduction relation $\rightarrow_{\mathtt{n}}$ is defined as the closure by (pure) CBN contexts $\mathtt{N}$ of the β-rule:

$$(\lambda x.t)u \rightarrow_{\beta} t\{x\backslash u\}$$

Plotkin's CBN λ-calculus can be fully embedded into the $\lambda_{\mathtt{c}}$-calculus through the identity translation. Let $\Lambda_{\mathtt{n}}$ denote the set of terms of Plotkin's CBN λ-calculus, respectively and $\lambda_{\mathtt{c}}^{\mathtt{n}}$ be the image of the aforementioned (trivial) translation, extended with matching closures restricted to variable patterns and terms $t[x\backslash u]$. The set of **terms** of the $\lambda_{\mathtt{c}}^{\mathtt{n}}$-calculus is generated by the grammar:

$$\textbf{(Terms)}\ t, u ::= x \mid tu \mid t[x\backslash u]$$

The operational semantics of Plotkin's CBN is captured as follows.

Lemma 5 (CBN Simulation). *For $t, u \in \Lambda_{\mathtt{n}}$, $t \twoheadrightarrow_{\mathtt{n}} u$ implies $t \twoheadrightarrow_{\mathtt{WH}} u$.*

Plotkin's CBV. More interestingly, Plotkin's CBV λ-calculus can also be encoded into the $\lambda_{\mathtt{c}}$-calculus. The sets of **values**, **terms**, and **CBV contexts** of Plotkin's CBV λ-calculus are generated by the following grammars:

$$\textbf{(Values)}\ v ::= x \mid \lambda x.t \quad \textbf{(Terms)}\ t, u ::= v \mid tu \quad \textbf{(CBV Contexts)}\ \mathtt{V} ::= \Box \mid \mathtt{V}t \mid v\mathtt{V}$$

The CBV reduction relation $\rightarrow_{\mathtt{v}}$ is defined as the closure by CBV contexts $\mathtt{V}$ of the usual β-rule restricted to values:

$$(\lambda x.t)v \rightarrow_{\beta_{\mathtt{v}}} t\{x\backslash v\}$$

Plotkin's CBV λ-calculus can be fully embedded into the $\lambda_{\mathtt{c}}$-calculus through translation $(\_)^{\bullet}$. Let $\Lambda_{\mathtt{v}}$ and $\mathcal{V}$ denote the sets of terms and values of Plotkin's CBV λ-calculus, respectively. Translation $(\_)^{\bullet}$ is defined as follows in 2 columns:

$$\begin{array}{ll} (\_)^{\bullet} : \Lambda_{\mathtt{v}} \mapsto \Lambda_{\mathtt{c}} & (\_)^{\circ} : \mathcal{V} \mapsto \Lambda_{\mathtt{c}} \\ (v)^{\bullet} = \mathtt{v}((v)^{\circ}) & (x)^{\circ} = x \\ (tu)^{\bullet} = (xy)[\mathtt{v}(y)\backslash(u)^{\bullet}][\mathtt{v}(x)\backslash(t)^{\bullet}] & (\lambda x.t)^{\circ} = \lambda x.(t)^{\bullet} \end{array}$$

where $\mathtt{v}$ is a unary constructor used to tag values. This allows us to capture the operational semantics of Plotkin's CBV:

Lemma 6 (CBV Simulation). *For $t, u \in \Lambda_{\mathtt{v}}$, $t \twoheadrightarrow_{\mathtt{v}} u$ implies $(t)^{\bullet} \twoheadrightarrow_{\mathtt{WH}} (u)^{\bullet}$.*

Note that the use of the explicit matching operation in the translation of an application is crucial in order to obtain the simulation result above. Since in Plotkin's CBV, an application of the form tu can (in general) be evaluated by first evaluating either t or u, thus translation $(\_)^{\bullet}$ must allow this as well. Let $t \rightarrow_{\mathtt{v}} t'$.

Consider an alternative translation $(tu)^\bullet = (\lambda \mathtt{v}(x).\lambda \mathtt{v}(y).xy)(t)^\bullet(u)^\bullet$. Then, it is not difficult to see that Lemma 6 does not hold anymore. Now, consider another alternative translation $(tu)^\bullet = \text{case}\, u \,\text{of}\, (\mathtt{v}(y).\text{case}\, t \,\text{of}\, (\mathtt{v}(x).xy))$. Then, $\rightarrow_{\mathtt{WH}}$ reduction forces u to be evaluated first. Alternatively, we could have considered another alternative translation $(tu)^\bullet = \text{case}\, u \,\text{of}\, (\mathtt{v}(y).\text{case}\, t \,\text{of}\, (\mathtt{v}(x).xy))$. However, the same problem arises if one simply realizes that the translations must also take into account the case where $u \rightarrow_{\mathtt{v}} u'$ happens first.

The Bang-Calculus. The **terms, list contexts**, and **weak head surface contexts** of the $\lambda^!$-calculus are generated by the grammars[1]:

$$\begin{array}{rl} \textbf{(Terms)} & t, u ::= x \mid \lambda x.t \mid tu \mid !t \mid t[x\backslash u] \\ \textbf{(List Contexts)} & \mathtt{J} ::= \Box \mid \mathtt{J}[x\backslash t] \\ \textbf{(Weak Head Surface Contexts)} & \mathtt{S} ::= \Box \mid \mathtt{S}t \mid \mathtt{S}[x\backslash u] \mid t[x\backslash \mathtt{S}] \end{array}$$

The reduction relation $\rightarrow_!$ is defined as the closure by weak head surface contexts of the following rules:

$$\begin{array}{rl} \mathtt{J}\langle\lambda x.t\rangle\, u \rightarrow_{\mathtt{dB}} \mathtt{J}\langle t[x\backslash u]\rangle & \text{if } \mathtt{bv}(\mathtt{J}) \cap \mathtt{fv}(u) = \emptyset \\ t[x\backslash \mathtt{J}\langle !u\rangle] \rightarrow_{\mathtt{s}} \mathtt{J}\langle t\{x\backslash u\}\rangle & \text{if } \mathtt{bv}(\mathtt{J}) \cap \mathtt{fv}(t) = \emptyset \end{array}$$

The $\lambda^!$-calculus can be fully embedded into the $\lambda_{\mathtt{c}}$-calculus through translation $(\_)^\star$. Let $\Lambda^!$ denote the set of terms of the $\lambda^!$-calculus. Translation $(\_)^\star : \Lambda^! \mapsto \Lambda_{\mathtt{c}}$ is defined as follows:

$$\begin{array}{rlrl} (x)^\star &= x & (!t)^\star &= \mathtt{b}((t)^\star) \\ (\lambda x.t)^\star &= \lambda \mathtt{b}(x).(t)^\star & (t[x\backslash u])^\star &= (t)^\star[\mathtt{b}(x)\backslash(u)^\star] \\ (tu)^\star &= (t)^\star(u)^\star & & \end{array}$$

where $\mathtt{b}$ is a unary constructor used to tag banged terms. This allows us to capture the operational semantics of the $\lambda^!$-calculus:

Lemma 7. (Bang Simulation) *For* $t, u \in \Lambda^!$, $t \twoheadrightarrow_! u$ *implies* $(t)^\star \twoheadrightarrow_{\mathtt{WH}} (u)^\star$.

4 Type System

The type system for the $\lambda_{\mathtt{c}}$-calculus is inspired by the non-idempotent type system in [5]. We consider the following grammars:

$$\begin{array}{rl} \textbf{(Data Types)} & \mathtt{D} ::= \mathtt{c}(\ \mathtt{M}_i)_n \\ \textbf{(Multiset Types)} & \mathtt{M} ::= [\sigma_i]_{i\in I} \text{ where } I \text{ is a finite set} \\ \textbf{(Term Types)} & \sigma ::= \mathtt{D} \mid \mathtt{abs} \mid \mathtt{M} \rightarrow \sigma \\ \textbf{(Types)} & \mathtt{t} ::= \sigma \mid \mathtt{M} \end{array}$$

[1] Some formulations of the bang-calculus also use a *dereliction* constructor, but this can be encoded using the identity.

Notice that we distinguish between **multiset types** and **term types**. As will be evident once we introduce the type system, every term can be typed with the empty multiset type, so we will only consider a term to be typable if it can be assigned a term type. This is made more precise once we discuss typing derivations. The size of multiset type $\mathtt{M}$ (*i.e.* its length) is denoted by $|\ \mathtt{M}|$. The empty multiset type is denoted by $[\,]$. Multiset union is denoted by $\sqcup$. Data types are tagged products of multiset types. Type $\mathtt{abs}$ is a special constant type that is used to type abstractions for which no arguments are provided.

Typing contexts. Capital Greek letters Γ and Δ are used to denote **typing contexts**, which are defined as total functions from variables to multiset types that map finitely many variables to the non-empty multiset type. The **domain of a typing context** Γ is denoted by $\mathtt{dom}(\Gamma)$ and defined as $\mathtt{dom}(\Gamma) = \{x \mid \Gamma(x) \neq [\,]\}$. The **union of two typing contexts** Γ and Δ is denoted by $\Gamma + \Delta$ and defined as $(\Gamma+\Delta)(x) = \Gamma(x) \sqcup \Delta(x)$. This notation can be naturally extended to an arbitrary number of typing contexts. Whenever $\mathtt{dom}(\Gamma) \cap \mathtt{dom}(\Delta) = \emptyset$, the union is written as $\Gamma; \Delta$. In particular, $\Gamma; x : [\,]$ is identified as Γ. The restriction of a typing context Γ to a set of variables $X \subseteq V$ is denoted by $\Gamma|_X$, the complementary is denoted by $\Gamma \backslash\backslash X$, and they are defined as follows:

$$(\Gamma|_x(x)) \begin{cases} \Gamma(x) \; if\, x \in X \\ [] \quad\;\; otherwise \end{cases} \qquad (\Gamma\backslash\backslash X)(x) = \begin{cases} [] \qquad\; if\, x \in X \\ \Gamma(x) \; otherwise \end{cases}$$

The **type system** for the λ_{c}-calculus is denoted by $\mathcal{T}$ and defined by the typing rules in Fig. 2, where $[\![1, n]\!]$ is used as shorthand for $\{1, \ldots, n\}$.

Typing derivations. Capital Greek letters Φ, Ψ, Σ, and Π are used to denoted **typing derivations**. Term type derivations ending with the sequent $\Gamma \vdash t : \sigma$ (resp. $\Gamma \vdash t :\ \mathtt{M}$) are denoted by $\Phi \triangleright \Gamma \vdash t : \sigma$ (resp. $\Phi \triangleright \Gamma \vdash t :\ \mathtt{M}$), and pattern type derivations ending with the sequent $\Gamma \Vdash p :\ \mathtt{M}$ are denoted by $\Pi \triangleright \Delta \Vdash p :\ \mathtt{M}$. The **size of a type derivation** Φ **(resp.** Π) is denoted by $\mathtt{sz}(\Phi)$ (resp. $\mathtt{sz}(\Pi)$) and defined as the number of rules in Φ (resp. Π) except rules $(\mathtt{many})$ and $(\mathtt{match})$. Indeed, rule $(\mathtt{many})$ is more like a meta-rule (it could be removed, but it makes proofs simpler); rule $(\mathtt{match})$ types a term $t[p\backslash u]$, where the real information about the number of steps comes from t, p and u, but not from the explicit matching operator itself. A term t (resp. pattern p) is **typable** if there exists a derivation $\Phi \triangleright \Gamma \vdash t : \sigma$ (respectively, $\Pi \triangleright \Gamma \Vdash p :\ \mathtt{M}$).

The Typing Rules. Most of the rules are straightforward. Rules $((\mathtt{var}))$ and $((\mathtt{data}))$ are used to type variable patterns and data patterns, respectively. The remaining rules are used to type terms. Rule $(\mathtt{abs}^\star)$ is necessary due to evaluation being weak *i.e.* not occurring in the body of λ-abstractions. Rule $(\mathtt{case})$ is very similar to $(\mathtt{match})$. However, the former appears to have a non-deterministic flavor, but it is not. As we show (see Theorem 1), all typable programs terminate in either a generalized λ-abstraction or a data. More specifically, programs typed with arrow types terminate in generalized λ-abstractions, and programs typed with data pattern types terminate in data with the same top-level tag. Consider a typable case expression $t = \mathsf{case}\, u\, \mathsf{of}\; (\hat{p}_i.s_i)_n$. Then, t must be typed using rule

$$\frac{}{x : \mathtt{M} \Vdash x : \mathtt{M}} \;(\!(\mathtt{var})\!) \qquad \frac{(\Gamma_i \Vdash p_i : \mathtt{M}_i)_{i \in [\![1,n]\!]}}{+_{i\in[\![1,n]\!]}\Gamma_i \Vdash \mathtt{c}(p_1, \ldots, p_n) : [\mathtt{c}(\mathtt{M}_1, \ldots, \mathtt{M}_n)]} \;(\!(\mathtt{data})\!)$$

$$\frac{}{x : [\sigma] \vdash x : \sigma} \;(\mathtt{var}) \qquad \frac{(\Gamma_i \vdash t : \sigma_i)_{i\in I}}{+_{i\in I}\Gamma_i \vdash t : [\sigma_i]_{i\in I}} \;(\mathtt{many})$$

$$\frac{\Gamma \vdash t : \sigma \qquad \Gamma|_{\mathtt{vars}(p)} \Vdash p : \mathtt{M}}{\Gamma \setminus\!\!\setminus \mathtt{vars}(p) \vdash \lambda p.t : \mathtt{M} \to \sigma} \;(\mathtt{abs}) \qquad \frac{}{\vdash \lambda p.t : \mathtt{abs}} \;(\mathtt{abs}^*)$$

$$\frac{\Gamma \vdash t : \mathtt{M} \to \sigma \qquad \Delta \vdash u : \mathtt{M}}{\Gamma + \Delta \vdash tu : \sigma} \;(\mathtt{app})$$

$$\frac{(\Gamma_i \vdash t_i : \mathtt{M}_i)_{i\in[\![1,n]\!]}}{+_{i\in[\![1,n]\!]}\Gamma_i \vdash \mathtt{c}(t_1, \ldots, t_n) : \mathtt{c}(\mathtt{M}_1, \ldots, \mathtt{M}_n)} \;(\mathtt{data})$$

$$\frac{\Gamma \vdash t : \sigma \qquad \Gamma|_{\mathtt{vars}(p)} \Vdash p : \mathtt{M} \qquad \Delta \vdash u : \mathtt{M}}{(\Gamma \setminus\!\!\setminus \mathtt{vars}(p)) + \Delta \vdash t[p\backslash u] : \sigma} \;(\mathtt{match})$$

$$\frac{\Delta \vdash t : \mathtt{M} \qquad \Gamma|_{\mathtt{vars}(\hat{p}_k)} \Vdash \hat{p}_k : \mathtt{M} \qquad \Gamma \vdash u_k : \sigma \qquad \text{for some } k \in [\![1,n]\!]}{(\Gamma \setminus\!\!\setminus \mathtt{vars}(\hat{p}_i)) + \Delta \vdash \mathtt{case}\ t\ \mathtt{of}\ (\hat{p}_i.u_i)_n : \sigma} \;(\mathtt{case})$$

Fig. 2. Type system for the λ_{c}-calculus

$(\mathtt{case})$, and u must be typable as well. The type assigned to u must match the type assigned to one of the data patterns in the tuple of branches $(\hat{p}_i.s_i)_n$. Recall that all $\hat{p}_i$ are distinct by construction. Therefore, their types are all different and the type of t can only match the type of the data pattern of *exactly* one of the branches. In sum, rule $(\mathtt{case})$, *is* deterministic.

Let us recall the following term from Example 1, that we call here t_0:

$$t_0 = (\lambda x.\mathtt{case}\, x\, \mathtt{of}\ (\mathtt{pair}(x, y).y, \mathtt{triple}(x, y, z).x))\ \mathtt{triple}(\mathtt{c}_0, \mathtt{c}_1, \mathtt{c}_2)$$

We can build a type derivation for t_0, by first considering the following type derivations for the subterms of t_0:

Φ_1:

$$\dfrac{\dfrac{}{x : [\mathtt{triple}([\mathtt{c}_0], [\,], [\,])] \vdash x : \mathtt{triple}([\mathtt{c}_0], [\,], [\,])} \;(\mathtt{var})}{x : [\mathtt{triple}([\mathtt{c}_0], [\,], [\,])] \vdash x : [\mathtt{triple}([\mathtt{c}_0], [\,], [\,])]} \;(\mathtt{many})$$

Φ_2:

$$\dfrac{\dfrac{}{x : [\mathtt{c}_0] \Vdash x : [\mathtt{c}_0]} \;(\!(\mathtt{var})\!) \qquad \dfrac{}{\Vdash y : [\,]} \;(\!(\mathtt{var})\!) \qquad \dfrac{}{\Vdash z : [\,]} \;(\!(\mathtt{var})\!)}{x : [\mathtt{c}_0] \Vdash \mathtt{triple}(x, y, z) : [\mathtt{triple}([\mathtt{c}_0], [\,], [\,])]} \;(\!(\mathtt{data})\!)$$

Ψ_1:

$$\dfrac{\Phi_1 \quad \Phi_2 \quad \dfrac{}{x : [\mathtt{c}_0] \vdash x : \mathtt{c}_0}\ (\mathtt{var})}{\dfrac{x : [\mathtt{triple}([\mathtt{c}_0], [\,], [\,])] \vdash \mathtt{case}\ x\ \mathtt{of}\ (\mathtt{pair}(x, y).y, \mathtt{triple}(x, y, z).x) : \mathtt{c}_0}{\vdash \lambda x.\mathtt{case}\ x\ \mathtt{of}\ (\mathtt{pair}(x, y).y, \mathtt{triple}(x, y, z).x) : [\mathtt{triple}([\mathtt{c}_0], [\,], [\,])] \to \mathtt{c}_0}\ (\mathtt{abs})}\ (\mathtt{case})$$

Ψ_2:

$$\dfrac{\dfrac{\dfrac{\dfrac{}{\vdash \mathtt{c}_0 : \mathtt{c}_0}\ (\mathtt{data})}{\vdash \mathtt{c}_0 : [\mathtt{c}_0]}\ (\mathtt{many}) \quad \dfrac{}{\vdash \mathtt{c}_1 : [\,]}\ (\mathtt{many}) \quad \dfrac{}{\vdash \mathtt{c}_2 : [\,]}\ (\mathtt{many})}{\vdash \mathtt{triple}(\mathtt{c}_0, \mathtt{c}_1, \mathtt{c}_2) : \mathtt{triple}([\mathtt{c}_0], [\,], [\,])}\ (\mathtt{data})}{\vdash \mathtt{triple}(\mathtt{c}_0, \mathtt{c}_1, \mathtt{c}_2) : [\mathtt{triple}([\mathtt{c}_0], [\,], [\,])]}\ (\mathtt{many})$$

The following derivation is a type derivation for t_0: Σ :

$$\dfrac{\Psi_1 \quad \Psi_2}{\vdash (\lambda x.\mathtt{case}\ x\ \mathtt{of}\ (\mathtt{pair}(x, y).y, \mathtt{triple}(x, y, z).x))\ \mathtt{triple}(\mathtt{c}_0, \mathtt{c}_1, \mathtt{c}_2) : \mathtt{c}_0}\ (\mathtt{app})$$

Note that $\mathtt{sz}(\Sigma) = 11$, which is bigger than that number of evaluation steps taking t_0 to normal form, which is 6.

We now proceed to show our main result, which is the characterization of termination with respect to clash-free normal forms.

4.1 Characterizing Termination

Preliminary Properties. Relevance holds whenever typing contexts have complete information about free variables.

Lemma 8. *Let* $t \in \lambda_\mathtt{c}$ *and* $\Phi \triangleright \Gamma \vdash t : \sigma$. *Then,* $\mathtt{dom}(\Gamma) \subseteq \mathtt{fv}(t)$. *Moreover, if* t *is closed, then* $\Gamma = \emptyset$.

The following property tells us that terms are typable with a multiset type $\mathtt{M}$ if and only if, they can be typed with any sub(multi)set of $\mathtt{M}$ without losing any information.

Lemma 9. (Split and Merge for Multiset Types) *Let* $t \in \lambda_\mathtt{c}$ *and* $\mathtt{M} = \sqcup_{i \in I} \mathtt{M}_i$. *Then, there exists* $\Phi \triangleright \Gamma \vdash t : \mathtt{M}$ *iff there exist* $(\Phi_i \triangleright \Gamma_i \vdash t : \mathtt{M}_i)_{i \in I}$, *s.t.* $\Gamma = +_{i \in I} \Gamma_i$. *Moreover,* $\mathtt{sz}(\Phi) = +_{i \in I} \mathtt{sz}(\Phi_i)$.

Soundness. We start by proving the correctness of type system $\mathcal{T}$. In particular, we prove that typability implies clash-freedom (Lemma 12). We start by proving that clashes (errors) cannot be typed.

Lemma 10. (Clashes are not Typable) *If* $t \in \mathtt{SH}$, *there is no* $\Phi \triangleright \Gamma \vdash t : \sigma$.

Now, we can use a *quantitative* version of the subject reduction property in order to show that all typable terms are clash-free.

Lemma 11. (Weighted Subject Reduction) *Let* $t, t' \in \lambda_\mathtt{c}$ *and there exists* $\Phi_t \triangleright \Gamma \vdash t : \sigma$. *If* $t \to_\mathtt{D} t'$, *then there exists* $\Phi_{t'} \triangleright \Gamma \vdash t' : \sigma$, *s.t.* $\mathtt{sz}(\Phi_t) > \mathtt{sz}(\Phi_{t'})$.

Proof. The proof is by induction on $\rightarrow_{\mathtt{D}}$. The most interesting case is $t \rightarrow_{\mathtt{D(sub)}} t'$, which needs a weighted version of the usual substitution lemma (see the technical details in [4]). □

The quantitative flavor of Lemma 11 gives us a good measure that ensures termination. Together with Lemma 10, the preservation of typings allows usto prove that typable terms cannot terminate in a clash.

Lemma 12. (Typability Implies Clash-Freedom) *Let* $t \in \lambda_{\mathtt{c}}$. *If* $\Gamma \vdash t : \sigma$, *then* t *is clash-free.*

Proof. We reason by contraposition. Assume t is *not* clash-free. Then, there exists $t' \in \mathtt{SH}$, such that $t \twoheadrightarrow_{\mathtt{D}} t'$. Therefore, either $t = t'$, in which case $\Phi \rhd \Gamma \vdash t' : \sigma$ by hypothesis, or $t \rightarrow_{\mathtt{D}} t'$ and by Lemma 11, we can conclude that there exists $\Phi \rhd \Gamma \vdash t' : \sigma$. However, this cannot be the case according to Lemma 10. Therefore, there is no such t' and thus t is clash-free. □

Completeness. To show the completeness of type system $\mathcal{T}$ we need to show that all (closed) clash-free normal forms are typable.

Lemma 13. (Typability of Closed Clash-Free Normal Forms) *Let* $t \in \lambda_{\mathtt{c}}$ *be a closed term. If* $t \in \mathtt{NO}_{\mathtt{SHF}}$, *then there exists* $\Phi \rhd \vdash t : \sigma$.

Then, we can use a *quantitative* version of the subject expansion property in order to show that all typable terms are clash-free.

Lemma 14. (Weighted Subject Expansion) *Let* $t, t' \in \lambda_{\mathtt{c}}$ *and there exist* $\Phi_{t'} \rhd \Gamma \vdash t' : \sigma$. *If* $t \rightarrow_{\mathtt{D}} t'$, *then there exists* $\Phi_t \rhd \Gamma \vdash t : \sigma$, *s.t.* $\mathtt{sz}(\Phi_t) > \mathtt{sz}(\Phi_{t'})$.

Proof. The proof is by induction on $\rightarrow_{\mathtt{D}}$. The most interesting case is $t \rightarrow_{\mathtt{D(sub)}} t'$, which needs a weighted version of the usual anti-substitution lemma (see the technical details in [4]). □

4.2 Characterization of Weak Head-Termination for Closed Terms

We are finally able to state and prove the main results of this work.

Theorem 1. *Let* $t \in \lambda_{\mathtt{c}}$ *be a closed term. Then,* t *is typable iff* t *is weak head terminating. Moreover, if* $\Phi \rhd \Gamma \vdash t : \sigma$, *then* t *weak head evaluation terminates in at most* $\mathtt{sz}(\Phi)$ *steps.*

Proof. The left-to-right implication follows from the weighted subject reduction property (Lemma 11). The right-to-left implication follows by the typability of all closed terms in clash-free normal form (Lemma 13) and weighted subject expansion (Lemma 14). In particular, the "moreover" part of the statement follows from the quantitative nature of Lemma 11 and Lemma 14. □

An interesting corollary of this theorem is that typability also implies termination of the weak head reduction $\rightarrow_{\mathtt{WH}}$, since it is not difficult to prove that $t \not\rightarrow_{\mathtt{D}}$ implies $t \not\rightarrow_{\mathtt{WH}}$. Moreover, if t terminates for the weak head reduction $\rightarrow_{\mathtt{WH}}$, then t terminates for the weak head evaluation $\rightarrow_{\mathtt{D}}$, so that we can conclude:

Corollary 2. *Let* $t \in \lambda_{\mathtt{c}}$ *be a closed term. Then,* t *is typable iff* t *terminates for the weak head relation* $\rightarrow_{\mathtt{WH}}$.

5 Conclusion and Future Work

This work provides a quantitative insight into the semantics of programming languages with pattern matching. In particular, we define a quantitative type system $\mathcal{T}$ that characterizes weak head termination for the λ_c-calculus and provides upper-bounds for the number of steps needed to fully evaluate a term to normal form. Crucially, we also prove that system $\mathcal{T}$ ensures that "well-typed programs do not go wrong" or, equivalently, by using the terminology adopted in this work, that typable programs are clash-free.

Future work includes adopting call-by-need (CBNeed) in order to fully capture the operational semantics of lazy functional programming languages such as Haskell. Indeed, in [1] it is shown that pattern matching steps are negligible for CBN only when using a CBNeed strategy, so it would be fruitful to develop a CBNeed version of our calculus. We also believe that type system $\mathcal{E}$ from [5] can be naturally extended to the λ_c-calculus. This would allow us to obtain exact measures (instead of upper-bounds) for evaluation. The calculus in [6] includes a fixpoint, we would like to consider such an extension as well. Something that looks challenging is to consider an open version of λ_c-calculus. This would allow us to extend the results in [11] to generalized λ-abstractions and case expressions. Last, but not least, it would be interesting, and challenging, to explore *nondeterministic* versions of case expressions. These could be used to simulate logic programming languages (which usually have nondeterministic evaluation strategies) within a functional setting.

References

1. Accattoli, B., Barras, B.: The negligible and yet subtle cost of pattern matching. In: Chang, B.E. (ed.) Programming Languages and Systems - 15th Asian Symposium, APLAS 2017, Suzhou, China, November 27-29, 2017, Proceedings. Lecture Notes in Computer Science, vol. 10695, pp. 426–447. Springer (2017). https://doi.org/10.1007/978-3-319-71237-6_21
2. Accattoli, B., Graham-Lengrand, S., Kesner, D.: Tight typings and split bounds, fully developed. J. Funct. Program. **30**, e14 (2020). https://doi.org/10.1017/S095679682000012X
3. Alves, S., Dundua, B., Florido, M., Kutsia, T.: Pattern-based calculi with finitary matching. Log. J. IGPL **26**(2), 203–243 (2018). https://doi.org/10.1093/JIGPAL/JZX059
4. Alves, S., Kesner, D., Ramos, M.: Extending the quantitative pattern-matching paradigm (full version) (2024). https://arxiv.org/abs/2408.11007
5. Alves, S., Kesner, D., Ventura, D.: A quantitative understanding of pattern matching. In: Bezem, M., Mahboubi, A. (eds.) 25th International Conference on Types for Proofs and Programs (TYPES 2019). Leibniz International Proceedings in Informatics (LIPIcs), vol. 175, pp. 3:1–3:36. Schloss Dagstuhl–Leibniz-Zentrum für Informatik, Dagstuhl, Germany (2020).https://doi.org/10.4230/LIPIcs.TYPES.2019.3
6. Barenbaum, P., Bonelli, E., Mohamed, K.: Pattern matching and fixed points: resource types and strong call-by-need: extended abstract. In: Proceedings of the

20th International Symposium on Principles and Practice of Declarative Programming, pp. 1–12. ACM, Frankfurt am Main Germany (2018). https://doi.org/10.1145/3236950.3236972
7. Bono, V., Dezani-Ciancaglini, M.: A tale of intersection types. In: Hermanns, H., Zhang, L., Kobayashi, N., Miller, D. (eds.) LICS '20: 35th Annual ACM/IEEE Symposium on Logic in Computer Science, Saarbrücken, Germany, 8–11 July 2020, pp. 7–20. ACM (2020).https://doi.org/10.1145/3373718.3394733
8. Bucciarelli, A., Kesner, D., Ríos, A., Viso, A.: The bang calculus revisited. Inf. Comput. **293**, 105047 (2023). https://doi.org/10.1016/J.IC.2023.105047
9. Bucciarelli, A., Kesner, D., Rocca, S.R.D.: Observability for pair pattern calculi. In: Altenkirch, T. (ed.) 13th International Conference on Typed Lambda Calculi and Applications, TLCA 2015, 1–3 July 2015, Warsaw, Poland. LIPIcs, vol. 38, pp. 123–137. Schloss Dagstuhl - Leibniz-Zentrum für Informatik (2015https://doi.org/10.4230/LIPICS.TLCA.2015.123
10. Bucciarelli, A., Kesner, D., Rocca, S.R.D.: Inhabitation for non-idempotent intersection types. Log. Methods Comput. Sci. **14**(3) (2018).https://doi.org/10.23638/LMCS-14(3:7)2018
11. Bucciarelli, A., Kesner, D., Rocca, S.R.D.: Solvability = typability + inhabitation. Log. Methods Comput. Sci. **17**(1) (2021), https://lmcs.episciences.org/7141
12. Bucciarelli, A., Kesner, D., Ventura, D.: Non-idempotent intersection types for the lambda-calculus. Log. J. IGPL **25**(4), 431–464 (2017). https://doi.org/10.1093/JIGPAL/JZX018
13. de Carvalho, D.: Sémantiques de la logique linéaire et temps de calcul. Université Aix-Marseille II, These de doctorat (2007)
14. de Carvalho, D.: Execution time of λ-terms via denotational semantics and intersection types. Math. Struct. Comput. Sci. **28**(7), 1169–1203 (2018). https://doi.org/10.1017/S0960129516000396
15. Cerrito, S., Kesner, D.: Pattern matching as cut elimination. In: 14th Annual IEEE Symposium on Logic in Computer Science, Trento, Italy, 2–5 July 1999, pp. 98–108. IEEE Computer Society (1999). https://doi.org/10.1109/LICS.1999.782596
16. Cirstea, H., Kirchner, C.: The rewriting calculus - part I. Log. J. IGPL **9**(3), 339–375 (2001). https://doi.org/10.1093/JIGPAL/9.3.339
17. Coppo, M., Dezani-Ciancaglini, M.: A new type assignment for λ-terms. Arch. Math. Log. **19**(1), 139–156 (1978). https://doi.org/10.1007/BF02011875
18. Coppo, M., Dezani-Ciancaglini, M.: A new type assignment for lambda-terms. Archiv für Math. Logik **19**, 139–156 (1978)
19. Gardner, P.: Discovering needed reductions using type theory. In: Hagiya, M., Mitchell, J.C. (eds.) Theoretical Aspects of Computer Software, International Conference TACS '94, Sendai, Japan, 19–22 April 1994, Proceedings. Lecture Notes in Computer Science, vol. 789, pp. 555–574. Springer (1994).https://doi.org/10.1007/3-540-57887-0_115
20. Girard, J.: Linear logic. Theor. Comput. Sci. **50**, 1–102 (1987). https://doi.org/10.1016/0304-3975(87)90045-4
21. Girard, J.Y.: Linear logic. Theoret. Comput. Sci. **50**(1), 1–101 (1987). https://doi.org/10.1016/0304-3975(87)90045-4
22. Grégoire, B., Leroy, X.: A compiled implementation of strong reduction. In: Wand, M., Jones, S.L.P. (eds.) Proceedings of the Seventh ACM SIGPLAN International Conference on Functional Programming (ICFP '02), Pittsburgh, Pennsylvania, USA, 4–6 Oct 2002, pp. 235–246. ACM (2002).https://doi.org/10.1145/581478.581501

23. Huet, G., Lévy, J.J.: Computations in orthogonal rewriting systems - Part I and Part II. In: Lassez, J.L., Plotkin, G. (eds.) Computational Logic, Essays in Honor of Alan Robinson, pp. 395–443. MIT Press (1991)
24. Jay, C.B., Kesner, D.: First-class patterns. J. Funct. Program. **19**(2), 191–225 (2009). https://doi.org/10.1017/S0956796808007144
25. Kahl, W.: Basic pattern matching calculi: a fresh view on matching failure. In: Kameyama, Y., Stuckey, P.J. (eds.) Functional and Logic Programming, 7th International Symposium, FLOPS 2004, Nara, Japan, 7–9 Apr 2004, Proceedings. Lecture Notes in Computer Science, vol. 2998, pp. 276–290. Springer (2004). https://doi.org/10.1007/978-3-540-24754-8_20
26. Kesner, D.: Reasoning about redundant patterns. J. Funct. Log. Program. **1997**(4) (1997). http://danae.uni-muenster.de/lehre/kuchen/JFLP/articles/1997/A97-04/A97-04.html
27. Kesner, D., Puel, L., Tannen, V.: A typed pattern calculus. Inf. Comput. **124**(1), 32–61 (1996). https://doi.org/10.1006/INCO.1996.0004
28. Kfoury, A.J.: A linearization of the lambda-calculus and consequences. J. Log. Comput. **10**(3), 411–436 (2000). https://doi.org/10.1093/LOGCOM/10.3.411
29. Kfoury, A.J., Wells, J.B.: Principality and decidable type inference for finite-rank intersection types. In: Appel, A.W., Aiken, A. (eds.) POPL '99, Proceedings of the 26th ACM SIGPLAN-SIGACT Symposium on Principles of Programming Languages, San Antonio, TX, USA, 20–22 Jan 1999, pp. 161–174. ACM (1999). https://doi.org/10.1145/292540.292556
30. Khasidashvili, Z.: Expression reduction systems. In: Proceedings of IN Vekua Institute of Applied Mathematics. vol. 36. Tbilisi (1990)
31. Krishnaswami, N.R.: Focusing on pattern matching. In: Shao, Z., Pierce, B.C. (eds.) Proceedings of the 36th ACM SIGPLAN-SIGACT Symposium on Principles of Programming Languages, POPL 2009, Savannah, GA, USA, 21–23 Jan 2009, pp. 366–378. ACM (2009). https://doi.org/10.1145/1480881.1480927
32. Lago, U.D., Martini, S.: The weak lambda calculus as a reasonable machine. Theor. Comput. Sci. **398**(1–3), 32–50 (2008). https://doi.org/10.1016/J.TCS.2008.01.044
33. Milner, R.: A theory of type polymorphism in programming. J. Comput. Syst. Sci. **17**(3), 348–375 (1978). https://doi.org/10.1016/0022-0000(78)90014-4
34. Moggi, E.: Computational lambda-calculus and monads. In: Proceedings of the Fourth Annual Symposium on Logic in Computer Science (LICS '89), Pacific Grove, California, USA, 5–8 June 1989, pp. 14–23. IEEE Computer Society (1989). https://doi.org/10.1109/LICS.1989.39155
35. Moggi, E.: Notions of computation and monads. Inf. Comput. **93**(1), 55–92 (1991). https://doi.org/10.1016/0890-5401(91)90052-4
36. Neergaard, P.M., Mairson, H.G.: Types, potency, and idempotency: why nonlinearity and amnesia make a type system work. In: Okasaki, C., Fisher, K. (eds.) Proceedings of the Ninth ACM SIGPLAN International Conference on Functional Programming, ICFP 2004, Snow Bird, UT, USA, 19–21 Sept 2004, pp. 138–149. ACM (2004). https://doi.org/10.1145/1016850.1016871
37. Plotkin, G.D.: Call-by-name, call-by-value and the lambda-calculus. Theor. Comput. Sci. **1**(2), 125–159 (1975). https://doi.org/10.1016/0304-3975(75)90017-1
38. Sekar, R.C., Ramakrishnan, I.V.: Programming in equational logic: Beyond strong sequentiality. Inf. Comput. **104**(1), 78–109 (1993). https://doi.org/10.1006/INCO.1993.1026
39. Terese: Term Rewriting Systems, Cambridge tracts in Theoretical Computer Science, vol. 55. Cambridge University Press (2003)

40. Zeilberger, N.: Focusing and higher-order abstract syntax. In: Necula, G.C., Wadler, P. (eds.) Proceedings of the 35th ACM SIGPLAN-SIGACT Symposium on Principles of Programming Languages, POPL 2008, San Francisco, California, USA, 7–12 Jan 2008, pp. 359–369. ACM (2008). https://doi.org/10.1145/1328438.1328482

Probabilistic and Declarative Programming

Hybrid Verification of Declarative Programs with Arithmetic Non-fail Conditions

Michael Hanus(✉)

Institut für Informatik, Kiel University, Kiel, Germany
mh@informatik.uni-kiel.de

Abstract. Functions containing arithmetic operations have often restrictions not expressible by standard type systems of programming languages. The division operation requires that the divisor is non-zero and the factorial function should not be applied to negative numbers. Such partial operations might lead to program crashes if they are applied to unintended arguments. Checking the arguments before each call is tedious and decreases the run-time efficiency. To avoid these disadvantages and support the safe use of partially defined operations, we present an approach to verify the correct use of operations at compile time. To simplify its use, our approach automatically infers non-fail conditions of operations from their definitions and checks whether these conditions are satisfied for all uses of the operations. Arithmetic conditions can be verified by SMT solvers, whereas conditions in operations defined on algebraic data types can be inferred and verified by appropriate type abstractions. Therefore, we present a hybrid method which is applicable to larger programs since only a few arithmetic non-fail conditions need to be checked by an external SMT solver. This approach is implemented for functional logic Curry programs so that it is also usable for purely functional or logic programs.

1 Introduction

Programs often contain partially defined operations that do not yield meaningful results for particular argument values. A typical example is the division operation which is not defined if the divisor is zero. User-defined operations might also have restrictions on argument values. For instance, consider the following definition of the factorial function in the functional language Haskell [31]:

```
fac :: Int → Int
fac n | n == 0 = 1
      | n > 0  = n * fac (n - 1)
```

Due to the conditions "`n == 0`" and "`n > 0`", a run-time error occurs if `fac` is applied to a negative number since there is no branch for this case. Such an error might be avoided at compile time by restricting the argument type of `fac` to natural numbers and checking whether each call satisfy this restriction. Unfortunately, this restriction is not expressible in type systems of current strongly

O. Kiselyov (Ed.): APLAS 2024, LNCS 15194, pp. 109–129, 2024.
https://doi.org/10.1007/978-981-97-8943-6_6

typed declarative programming languages, such as Haskell. This is also due to the fact that a call like `fac (m-n)` must be considered as ill-typed if `m` is smaller than `n`, i.e., the correct typing depends on values available at run time.

In order to avoid program crashes due to such errors, one could transform the factorial function into a total function that returns a specific value indicating a meaningless result. In Haskell, this could be expressed by using the predefined type of partial values

```
data Maybe a = Nothing | Just a
```

`Nothing` represents "no value" and `Just` x the value x. Using this type, we could define a "totalized" version of `fac` as follows:

```
facT :: Int  →  Maybe Int
facT n | n < 0  = Nothing
       | n == 0 = Just 1
       | n > 0  = case facT (n - 1) of Nothing  →  Nothing
                                       Just m   →  Just (n * m)
```

This total programming style yields ugly and less comprehensible code (note that also each client of `facT` has to check and transform the computed result). Moreover, the code is less efficient due to the additional case distinction in each recursive call.

In order to use the partially defined function `fac` without the risk of run-time errors, one can check the value of the argument before the actual call. For instance, the following code snippet defines an operation to read a number and, if it is non-negative, prints its factorial (`readInt` reads a string from the user input until it is an integer):

```
printFac = do putStr "Factorial computation for: "
              n <- readInt
              if n<0 then putStrLn "Negative number!" >> printFac
                     else print (fac n)
```

By checking the value of `n` before evaluating `(fac n)`, `printFac` never fails.

In this paper we present a fully automatic tool which can verify the non-failure of this program. For this purpose, our tool infers the *non-fail condition*

```
fac'nonfail :: Int  →  Bool
fac'nonfail n = (n == 0) || (n > 0)
```

from the definition of `fac`. Then it checks whether this condition is satisfied at all call sites of `fac`. For instance, it is satisfied for the recursive call `fac (n-1)` since `n > 0`. This property is automatically checked by an SMT solver [29]. The entire process is iterative since a non-fail condition for some operation f might require new non-fail conditions for operations that use f. For the operation

```
fac2 n = n * fac (n + 2)
```

the non-fail condition of `fac` requires `fac2'nonfail n = (n+2 == 0) || (n+2 > 0)`.

Non-fail conditions [16] are predicates which restrict the standard types of operations so that run-time failures are excluded. This idea is also present in *dependent types*, as in Agda [30], Coq [9], or Idris [10], or *refinement types* [32], as used in LiquidHaskell [36,37]. Since the development of programs w.r.t. such advanced type systems requires more work [34], we intend to support the traditional programming style with automated verification support where non-fail conditions are inferred. If they are not precise enough, the programmer can provide explicit non-fail conditions.

We specify and implement our approach in the declarative multi-paradigm language Curry [19] which extends Haskell by logic programming features. Thus, our approach can also be applied to purely functional or logic programs [17]. In this context, it is important to distinguish non-fail conditions and preconditions [7]: a precondition *must* be satisfied for any call of an operation, whereas a satisfied non-fail condition assures that a computation does not fail. Hence, it is an error if a precondition is not satisfied for some call, whereas in a logic computation, where one searches for values or solutions, one could also invoke operations with unsatisfied non-fail conditions. Hence, non-fail conditions as well as preconditions are meaningful concepts in functional logic programming (computing with failures is a feature enabling new design patterns [4]). Since top-level computations should not fail, subcomputations with possible failures must be encapsulated by specific search handlers. This provides also an opportunity to deal with complex non-fail conditions which cannot be inferred or checked automatically: encapsulate calls to such operations and check whether such a subcomputation has no result. This view is different from approaches where constraints or dependent types are generated [20,32,35] to ensure that no failures occur.

This paper is structured as follows. After reviewing the basics of Curry in the next section, we discuss non-fail conditions in Sect. 3. Section 4 defines our method to check and infer valid non-fail conditions for all operations in a program. Section 5 reviews call types which can be considered as abstract non-fail conditions for algebraic data types. Both kinds of non-fail conditions are combined and implemented in our hybrid verification tool which we describe and evaluate in Sect. 6 before we conclude with a discussion of related work.

2 Functional Logic Programming with Curry

We develop and implement our method in Curry so that it is also applicable to purely functional or logic programs. The declarative programming language Curry [19] amalgamates features from functional programming (demand-driven evaluation, strong typing, higher-order functions) and logic programming (computing with partial information, unification, constraints), see [6,15] for surveys. The syntax of Curry is close to Haskell[1] [31]. In addition to Haskell, Curry applies rules with overlapping left-hand sides in a (don't know) non-deterministic manner (where Haskell always selects the first matching rule) and allows *free (logic) variables* in conditions and right-hand sides of defining rules. The operational semantics combines lazy and non-deterministic evaluation [3].

[1] Variables and function names start with lowercase letters and the names of type and data constructors start with an uppercase letter. The application of f to e is denoted by juxtaposition ("f e").

A Curry program consists of data type definitions introducing *constructors* for data types (as shown with the type Maybe in Sect. 1) and *functions* or *operations* on these types. As an example, we show the definition of two operations on lists: the list concatenation "++" and an operation aPos which returns some positive number occurring in a list of integers[2]:

```
(++) :: [a] → [a] → [a]            aPos :: [Int] → Int
[]     ++ ys = ys                  aPos xs | xs == ys++[z]++zs && z>0
(x:xs) ++ ys = x : (xs ++ ys)              = z    where ys,z,zs free
```

The equation "xs == ys ++ [z] ++ zs" in the condition of aPos is solved by searching for appropriate lists such that they concatenate to xs and contain some element z. aPos is also called a *non-deterministic operation*, because it might deliver more than one value for a given argument, e.g., aPos [0,-1,2,-3,4] yields 2 and 4. Such operations, interpreted as mappings from values into sets of values [14], are an important feature of contemporary functional logic languages.

To collect the results of non-deterministic operations and use them in purely deterministic computations (e.g., to print them), Curry offers *search handlers*, i.e., operations to encapsulate non-deterministic computations and return their results in some data structure (e.g., [5,11,22,23]). For instance, allValues returns all values of its argument expression in a list. The handler oneValue returns a single value in a Maybe structure and Nothing in case of a failure. These operations can be used to avoid program crashes with partially defined operations. For instance, the total operation facT shown in Sect. 1 can be defined as

```
facT n = oneValue (fac n)
```

Since Curry has many more features than described so far, language processing tools for Curry (compilers, analyzers,...) often use an intermediate language, called FlatCurry [1,15], where the syntactic sugar of the source language has been eliminated and the pattern matching strategy is explicit. Since our inference method is based on FlatCurry, we sketch the structure of FlatCurry programs.

The abstract syntax of FlatCurry is summarized in Fig. 1. A FlatCurry program consists of a sequence of function definitions (for the sake of simplicity, data type definitions are omitted), where each function is defined by a single rule. Patterns in source programs are compiled into case expressions, overlapping rules are joined by explicit disjunctions, and arguments of constructor and function calls are variables (introduced in left-hand sides, let expressions, or patterns). We assume that FlatCurry programs satisfy the following properties:

- All variables introduced in a rule (parameters, free variables, let bindings, pattern variables) have unique identifiers.
- Let bindings are non-recursive, i.e., all recursion is introduced by functions.

[2] Curry requires the explicit declaration of free variables, as ys,z,zs in the rule of aPos, to ensure checkable redundancy.

$P ::= D_1 \ldots D_m$	(program)
$D ::= f(x_1, \ldots, x_n) = e$	(function definition)
$e ::= x$	(variable)
$\mid c(x_1, \ldots, x_n)$	(constructor application)
$\mid f(x_1, \ldots, x_n)$	(function call)
$\mid e_1 \textit{ or } e_2$	(disjunction)
$\mid \textit{let } x_1, \ldots, x_n \textit{ free in } e$	(free variables)
$\mid \textit{let } x = e \textit{ in } e'$	(let binding)
$\mid \textit{case } x \textit{ of } \{p_1 \to e_1; \ldots; p_n \to e_n\}$	(case expression)
$p ::= c(x_1, \ldots, x_n)$	(pattern)

Fig. 1. Syntax of the intermediate language FlatCurry

- The patterns in case expressions are non-overlapping and cover all data constructors of the type of the discriminating variable. Hence, if this type contains n constructors, there are n branches without overlapping patterns. This can be ensured by adding missing branches with failure expressions, e.g., the predefined Curry operation `failed` which has no value.

For instance, the operation `fac` is transformed into the following FlatCurry program (which contains infix operators and some non-variable arguments for the sake of readability):

```
fac(n) = let n0 = n==0 in
         case n0 of { True  → 1
                    ; False → let n1 = n>0 in
                              case n1 of { True  → n * fac(n-1)
                                         ; False → failed } }
```

Note that conditional rules are translated into nested case distinctions. The final `failed` branch is included to ensure that each case expression branches over all data constructors of a type. Usually, the front end of a Curry compiler transforms source programs into such a simplified form for easier compilation [2,8].

3 Non-fail Conditions

A *non-fail condition*, as introduced in [16], is a predicate to specify when an operation can be used without running into a failure. A satisfied non-fail condition does not ensure that some value is eventually computed—an infinite computation has no run-time failure. A *non-fail condition* of an n-ary operation f of type $\tau_1 \to \cdots \to \tau_n \to \tau$ is specified as an operation f`'nonfail` of type $\tau_1 \to \cdots \to \tau_n \to$ `Bool`. For instance, a non-fail condition for the factorial function `fac` as defined above can be specified as

```
fac'nonfail :: Int  → Bool
fac'nonfail n = n >= 0
```

As a further example, the integer division operation `div` has the non-fail condition

```
div'nonfail :: Int → Int → Bool
div'nonfail x y = y /= 0
```

Although non-fail conditions can be defined by the user, our objective is to provide a tool which frees the programmer from this task, i.e., non-fail conditions are inferred for all user-defined operations. This is useful especially for local and auxiliary operations.

The *trivial non-fail condition* for an n-ary operation f has the form

```
f'nonfail :: τ1 → ··· → τn → Bool
f'nonfail x1 ... xn = True
```

and is the default if there is no explicitly defined non-fail condition. The *unsatisfiable non-fail condition*

```
f'nonfail :: τ1 → ··· → τn → Bool
f'nonfail x1 ... xn = False
```

expresses that there is no known condition under which the operation does not fail. For instance, the predefined operation `failed` mentioned above has the non-fail condition

```
failed'nonfail :: Bool
failed'nonfail = False
```

An unsatisfiable non-fail condition might be used for non-trivial logic-oriented operations, like `aPos` defined in Sect. 2:

```
aPos'nonfail :: [Int] → Bool
aPos'nonfail xs = False
```

Due to the logic-oriented non-deterministic definition of `aPos`, there are no argument values ensuring a computation without failures, e.g., the evaluation of `aPos` [1] contains, apart from the successful computation, also non-deterministic failing branches. This means that an application of `aPos` should be encapsulated by a search handler like `allValues`.

4 Checking and Inferring Non-fail Conditions

In this section we present our first method to infer and check non-fail conditions without considering algebraic data types in a specific manner. In a first step (Sect. 4.1), we present a method to check non-fail conditions if they are provided for all operations. In a second step (Sect. 4.2), we modify this method to infer non-fail conditions such that they can be successfully checked.

4.1 Checking Non-fail Conditions

In order to check non-fail conditions, we assume that, for each defined operation f of arity n, a non-fail condition f`'nonfail` is defined as an n-ary predicate. This predicate can be predefined by some formula, which is usually the case for externally defined operations, or it might be defined by a Boolean Curry operation.[3]

The checking of non-fail conditions is defined by the rules shown in Fig. 2. This inference system derives judgements of the form "$\Gamma, C \vdash e$" where Γ is a mapping from variables into expressions, also called *heap* in operational descriptions like [1], C is the current assertion, i.e., a Boolean expression satisfied in the current branch under consideration, and e is a (FlatCurry) expression. The heap Γ contains the bindings of variables introduced by let expressions. We denote by $\Gamma[x \mapsto e]$ the heap Γ' with $\Gamma'(x) = e$ and $\Gamma'(y) = \Gamma(y)$ for all $x \neq y$. σ^Γ denotes the substitution, i.e., a mapping from expressions into expressions, represented by the heap Γ. σ^Γ satisfies $\sigma^\Gamma(x) = x$ if $\Gamma(x) = x$ (i.e., there is no binding for x) and $\sigma^\Gamma(x) = \sigma^\Gamma(e)$ if $\Gamma(x) = e$ with $x \neq e$. This recursive definition is well defined since there are no cyclic bindings in Γ, which is ensured by our restrictions on FlatCurry programs (non-recursive let bindings). σ^Γ can also be interpreted as *dereferencing* w.r.t. Γ.

Intuitively, $\Gamma, C \vdash e$ means that, if σ is a substitution such that $\sigma(C)$ holds, the expression $\sigma(\sigma^\Gamma(e))$ evaluates without a failure, i.e., the non-fail conditions of all operations occurring during this evaluation are satisfied. To check the non-fail condition of an operation f defined by $f(x_1, \ldots, x_n) = e$, we try to derive the judgement $\{\}, f\texttt{'nonfail}(x_1, \ldots, x_n) \vdash e$. Thus, we analyze the right-hand side of the rule under the assumption that the non-fail condition is satisfied. Now we discuss the rules in Fig. 2 in more detail.

$$
\begin{array}{ll}
\mathsf{Var}_{nf} & \Gamma, C \vdash x \\[1ex]
\mathsf{Cons}_{nf} & \Gamma, C \vdash c(x_1, \ldots, x_n) \\[1ex]
\mathsf{Func}_{nf} & \Gamma, C \vdash f(x_1, \ldots, x_n) \quad \text{if } C \text{ implies } f\texttt{'nonfail}(\sigma^\Gamma(x_1), \ldots, \sigma^\Gamma(x_n)) \\[1ex]
\mathsf{Or}_{nf} & \dfrac{\Gamma, C \vdash e_1 \quad \Gamma, C \vdash e_2}{\Gamma, C \vdash e_1 \; \mathit{or} \; e_2} \\[2ex]
\mathsf{Free}_{nf} & \dfrac{\Gamma, C \vdash e}{\Gamma, C \vdash \mathit{let} \; x_1, \ldots, x_n \; \mathit{free} \; \mathit{in} \; e} \\[2ex]
\mathsf{Let}_{nf} & \dfrac{\Gamma, C \vdash e \quad \Gamma[x \mapsto e], C \vdash e'}{\Gamma, C \vdash \mathit{let} \; x = e \; \mathit{in} \; e'} \\[2ex]
\mathsf{Case}_{nf} & \dfrac{\Gamma, C \vdash x \quad \Gamma, C_1 \vdash e_1 \quad \ldots \quad \Gamma, C_n \vdash e_n}{\Gamma, C \vdash \mathit{case} \; x \; \mathit{of} \; \{p_1 \to e_1; \ldots; p_n \to e_n\}} \quad \text{where } C_i = C \wedge \sigma^\Gamma(x) = p_i
\end{array}
$$

Fig. 2. Checking non-fail conditions

[3] The precise structure of non-fail conditions is not relevant. In the implementation it is only necessary to decide whether an implication w.r.t. a non-fail condition holds, which is done by an SMT solver by axiomatizing the semantics of operations defined in Curry, see Sect. 6.2. If it cannot be decided, e.g., due to a timeout, it is assumed that the implication does not hold.

Rule Var_{nf} states that the evaluation of a variable cannot cause a failure. This is justified because the variable is either free or it is bound to some expression which cannot fail because rule Let_{nf} checks each bound expression (even if it is not required in a lazy evaluation). Similarly, the evaluation of a constructor-rooted expression cannot fail, as expressed by rule Cons_{nf}. Rule Func_{nf} requires that the current assertion C implies the non-fail condition of the operation to be evaluated. Since the argument variables $x_1, \ldots, x_n$ might be bound to expressions introduced by let expressions, they have to be dereferenced by σ^Γ.

Rule Or_{nf} states that both expressions of a choice must be evaluable without a failure. It could be relaxed by requiring that at least one of the choices is free of failures, but we put this stronger condition since completely fail-free computations could support simpler and more efficient implementations.

Rule Free_{nf} checks the expression without a binding for the free variables in the heap so that they are universally quantified when testing the implication in rule Func_{nf}. This is different in rule Let_{nf} where the binding $x \mapsto e$ is put into the heap before the main expression is checked. The bound expression is also checked but without a binding for x because we assume that bindings are non-recursive. Since the property whether x is actually evaluated in e' is undecidable in general, we safely approximate it by assuming that x might be evaluated, i.e., we require that the evaluation of e yields no failure.

Rule Case_{nf} is the most important rule to ensure that a potentially failing operation does not cause a problem if its application is wrapped by an appropriate condition. Each branch of a case expression is checked with an extended assertion which takes into account that the discriminating variable must be equal to the corresponding branch pattern.[4] This extended assertion is used to check further function calls occurring in this branch by rule Func_{nf} so that it is important to collect the condition about the discriminating variable in the current assertion. For instance, consider an extended definition of the factorial function:

```
facInt x = if x < 0 then 0 else fac x
```

This is translated into the FlatCurry definition

```
facInt(x) = let y = x < 0 in
            case y of { True → 0 ; False → fac(x) }
```

Assume that `facInt'nonfail`(x) = *true* and `fac'nonfail`$(x) = x \geq 0$. When checking the case expression of `facInt`, we have $\Gamma = \{y \mapsto x < 0\}$ and $C = \mathit{true}$. Then the expression `fac(x)` of the `False`-branch is checked with the extended assertion $C_2 = \mathit{true} \wedge (x < 0) = \mathit{false}$ which is equivalent to $x \geq 0$. Hence, C_2 implies the non-fail condition of `fac`.

Checking non-fail conditions can also be used to ensure that operations defined by rules with several guards are completely defined. For instance, consider the operation to compute the absolute value of an integer:

```
abs n | n >= 0 = n
```

[4] In principle, we could omit the premise $\Gamma, C \vdash x$ since it is always satisfiable by rule Var_{nf}, but we included it to make it explicit that the discriminating argument must be also non-failing.

```
  | n <  0 = 0 - n
```

Similarly to the FlatCurry representation of `fac` shown in Sect. 2, `abs` has the FlatCurry representation

```
abs(n) = let c1 = n>=0 in
         case c1 of { True  → n
                    ; False → let c2 = n<0 in
                              case c2 of { True  → 0 - n
                                         ; False → failed } }
```

When checking this definition with the trivial non-fail condition of `abs`, the assertion in the final `failed` branch is $(n \geq 0) = \mathit{false} \wedge (n < 0) = \mathit{false}$. Since this can be shown as unsatisfiable by an SMT solver, this branch is unreachable so that the operation `failed` will never be called, i.e., `abs` is totally defined. Hence, a compiler could use this information to transform the code into the following slightly more efficient code:

```
abs(n) = let c1 = n>=0 in case c1 of { True  → n
                                     ; False → 0 - n }
```

We can state the correctness of the inference rules in Fig. 2 as follows.

Theorem 1. *Assume that the non-fail conditions of all defined operations are successfully checked by the rules in Fig. 2. Let f be defined by $f(x_1, \ldots, x_n) = e$, $C = f$'nonfail$(x_1, \ldots, x_n)$ and $\{\}, C \vdash e$ be derivable by these inference rules, and σ be a substitution such that $\sigma(C)$ holds. If $g(t_1, \ldots, t_m)$ is reduced in any reduction of $\sigma(e)$, g'nonfail$(t_1, \ldots, t_m)$ holds.*

Hence, if all non-fail conditions are successfully checked and we evaluate an operation with a satisfied non-fail condition, the non-fail conditions of all operations reduced during this evaluation hold. The proof, which is omitted due to lack of space, is by induction on the number evaluation steps and a nested induction on the height of the inference tree.

4.2 Inferring Non-fail Conditions

In order to infer non-fail conditions for user-defined operations, we start with trivial non-fail conditions for all operations, except for externally defined operations with non-trivial non-fail conditions, like division operators or `failed`. As can be seen in the rules of Fig. 2, the only situation where a rule might not be applicable is rule Func_{nf} due to its side condition. Hence, if this condition does not hold, we enforce it by adding the implication, i.e., the formula

$\neg C \vee f$'`nonfail`$(\sigma^\Gamma(x_1), \ldots, \sigma^\Gamma(x_n))$

is added as a conjunct to the non-fail condition of the operation currently checked. If the extended non-fail condition is unsatisfiable, we set it to *false*.

As an example, consider the operation `fac` where its FlatCurry definition is shown in Sect. 2 When checking the occurrence of `failed`, the current assertion is $(n = 0) = \mathit{false} \wedge (n > 0) = \mathit{false}$. Obviously, this does not imply the non-fail condition *false* of `failed`. Therefore, we add the conjunct

$\neg\,((n = 0) = \mathit{false} \wedge (n > 0) = \mathit{false}) \vee \mathit{false}$

which is equivalent to $(n = 0) \vee (n > 0)$, to the existing trivial non-fail condition of `fac`. When we re-check the definition of `fac` with this modified non-fail condition, the current assertion when checking `failed` is

$((n = 0) \vee (n > 0)) \wedge (n = 0) = \mathit{false} \wedge (n > 0) = \mathit{false}$

This is equivalent to *false* (i.e., the current branch is not reachable) so that the non-fail condition of `failed` holds. Similarly, the new non-fail condition holds for the recursive call to `fac`. Thus, the inferred non-fail condition of `fac` is valid.

Note that the inference of non-fail conditions is an iterative process. For instance, if our program contains the definition of `fac` as well as the operation

```
facMult n = n * fac n
```

then checking `facMult` is successful w.r.t. the initial trivial non-fail conditions. After refining the non-fail condition of `fac`, we have to check `facMult` again and infer a refined non-fail condition also for `facMult`, which is identical to the non-fail condition of `fac`. Checking `facMult` w.r.t. the refined non-fail condition is successful so that no further iteration is necessary.

The iterative refinement of non-fail conditions has the risk of non-termination. For instance, consider the operation

```
infpos n | n > 0 = infpos (n - 1)
```

When checking it with the trivial non-fail condition, we obtain the refined non-fail condition $n > 0$. Using this condition in the next iteration, we obtain the refined non-fail condition $n > 0 \;\wedge\; (n-1) > 0$ which is equivalent to $n > 1$. Further iterations yields the non-fail conditions $n > 2$, $n > 3$, and so on. To avoid such infinite loops, one has to stop the refinements at some point and set the non-fail condition to *false*. In our implementation, we stop it after the second refinement. Although this heuristic seems limited, the manual inspection of the few cases where unsatisfiable non-fail conditions are inferred in existing programs (see Sect. 6.3) showed that better results would not be computable by increasing this limit.

4.3 External Operations and User-defined Non-fail Conditions

The inference of non-fail conditions is based on the analysis of the rules defining operations. In particular, the inferred non-fail conditions are determined by the structure of case expressions. This has the consequence that externally defined operations, i.e., predefined operations defined by the run-time system, cannot be analyzed. Therefore, we assume that predefined operations have a trivial non-fail condition except for a few operations where a non-fail condition is explicitly defined, like the always failing operation `failed`, division operations (`mod`, `div`,

"/",...) where the divisor must be non-zero, the square root operation where the argument must be non-negative, among others.[5]

Based on the non-fail conditions of external operations, one can infer non-fail conditions for all user-defined operations as described in the previous section. In the worst case, unsatisfiable non-fail conditions might be derived, as for the operation `infpos` shown above, but our evaluation in Sect. 6.3 shows that meaningful non-fail conditions are inferred in most practical cases. However, there are also cases where an inferred non-fail condition is not precise enough. For instance, consider the operation `nth` which selects the n-th element of a given list:

```
nth :: [a]  →  Int  →  a
nth (x:xs) n | n == 0 = x
             | n > 0  = nth xs (n - 1)
```

The inferred non-fail condition, in a simplified form, is

```
nth'nonfail xs n = not (null xs) && n <= 0 && n >= 0
```

(the predicate `null` is satisfied if the argument is an empty list). This is equivalent to

```
nth'nonfail xs n = not (null xs) && n == 0
```

Although this condition is satisfiable and ensures that `nth` does not fail for arguments satisfying this condition, it is obviously too strong. A reasonable and more relaxed non-fail condition has to ensure that the index is not negative and the argument list has enough elements for the selection. This can be specified by the following condition:

```
nth'nonfail xs n = n >= 0 && length xs > n
```

This non-fail condition can be successfully checked with our method. The potentially failing branches for an empty list xs or a negative number n are not reachable due to the condition that n is non-negative and the length of the list is positive. Furthermore, the non-fail condition of the recursive call to `nth` holds. For this purpose, one has to verify that the current assertion at this call

$$n \geq 0 \ \wedge \ \texttt{length}(xs) > n \ \wedge \ xs = (y{:}ys) \ \wedge \ n \neq 0 \ \wedge \ n > 0$$

implies the non-fail condition

$$(n-1) \geq 0 \ \wedge \ \texttt{length}(ys) > (n-1)$$

of the recursive call. The proof of the first conjunct uses reasoning on integer arithmetic, as supported by SMT solvers, and the second conjunct can also be proved by SMT solvers when the rules of the operation `length` are axiomatized as logic formulas (see Sect. 6.2).

Due to these considerations, our tool takes into account explicit user-defined non-fail conditions. If they do not hold, i.e., they are refined as described in Sect. 4.2, then they are replaced by an unsatisfiable non-fail condition so that the resulting conditions are always correct.

[5] Search handlers are treated differently: their arguments are not transformed into let expressions so that the arguments are not checked, because their failures are encapsulated.

5 Combining Non-fail Conditions and Call Types

So far, we discussed the verification of arithmetic non-fail conditions, although our method can also be applied to conditions involving algebraic data types, as shown by the list index operation `nth` above. However, operations on algebraic data types might require more complex reasoning about input/output dependencies. For instance, consider the following operation which splits a list into sublists of ascending elements [27]:

```
risers []         = []
risers [x]        = [[x]]
risers (x:y:etc) = let (s:ss) = risers (y:etc)
                    in if x <= y then (x:s):ss else [x]:(s:ss)
```

In order to show the non-failure of this operation on all lists, one has to verify that the recursive call to `risers` always returns a non-empty list (so that the pattern matching in the let expression does not fail). Though this is not true in general, an analysis of `risers` shows that it returns an empty list for an empty input list and, for a non-empty input list, it returns a non-empty result list. Hence, the pattern matching on the result of the recursive call is non-failing.

Such a type-based reasoning is proposed in [18] where input/output type relations (also called *in/out types*) are approximated for operations. These are used to approximate *call types*, i.e., under-approximations of sets of argument values which ensure the non-failing execution of operations. For this purpose, a domain of *abstract types* is used where each element in the domain approximates a set of concrete values. For instance, the domain of top constructors (also called depth-1 abstraction in [33]) contains sets of data constructors as abstract elements or the specific constraint $\top$ denoting any value. Sets of data constructors denote terms having one of the constructors at the root. In this case, the in/out type of `risers` is

$$\{\{\texttt{[]}\} \hookrightarrow \{\texttt{[]}\}, \{\texttt{:}\} \hookrightarrow \{\texttt{:}\}\}$$

This can be read as: if the argument is an empty list ($\{\texttt{[]}\}$), the result is an empty list, and if the argument is a non-empty list ($\{\texttt{:}\}$), the result is a non-empty list. Hence, the in/out type of `risers` ensures that the recursive call always returns a non-empty list, which is used to verify `risers` as non-failing. Therefore, $\{\texttt{[]}, \texttt{:}\}$ is a valid call type of `risers`. This verification does not demand any user annotation. In contrast, LiquidHaskell requires an explicit specification of the input/output behavior of `risers` to verify it as a total operation [36].

As another example, consider the definition of an operation to return the last element of a list:

```
last [x]      = x
last (_:x:xs) = last (x:xs)
```

A valid call type of `last` is $\{\texttt{:}\}$ since it fails on the empty list.

If the domain of abstract types is finite (as the top constructor domain sketched above), fixpoint iterations with such types terminate (when monotonic operations are used). This can yield more precise results compared to our method which might stop iterations too early (as discussed in Sect. 4.2). On the other hand, our method can deal with more precise information on arithmetic domains but requires an external verifier to check implications. Thus, it is reasonable to use a hybrid approach where both methods are combined. An implementation of this idea is sketched in the next section.

6 Implementation and Evaluation

We implemented the hybrid verification method, based on the ideas discussed above, in a fully automatic tool written in Curry[6] and exploiting the SMT solver Z3 [29]. In the following, we sketch its implementation and show the result of applying it to various libraries.

6.1 Basic Implementation Scheme

In order to enable the verification of larger programs, the verification is performed in an incremental modular manner: when a Curry module M has been checked, the analysis results of M (non-fail conditions and call types) are stored so that they are available for other modules importing M. Thus, our tool performs the following steps to check a single Curry module:

- The module is translated into a corresponding FlatCurry program by the standard front end of Curry.
- For all imported modules, their non-fail conditions and call types are loaded (after they have been checked). This is necessary since imported operations might be used in the right-hand sides of operations defined in the current module.
- For each operation defined in the current module, in/out types and call types are inferred, as described in [18]. If an inferred call type is empty, i.e., there is no condition on the arguments, expressible as a call type, to ensure that the operation does not fail, a non-fail condition is inferred and checked as described in Sect. 4.
- If a non-fail condition or call type of some operation is refined (as discussed in Sect. 4.2), the current module is checked again w.r.t. the new condition. This fixpoint computation terminates when all conditions are stabilized. For an efficient computation, a call dependency graph is computed so that one has to re-check only operations with refined conditions and the operations that use them.

Thus, non-fail conditions are not computed (i.e., they are trivial) and checked if the set of non-failing arguments can be expressed by a call type, as in the operation `last` above. This hybrid method is useful since the satisfaction of non-trivial non-fail conditions (see rule Func_{nf} in Fig. 2) is checked by invoking an SMT solver: this might be costly since the formulas to be checked may contain operations defined in Curry that have to be translated into SMT formulas, as described next.

[6] Available as package https://cpm.curry-lang.org/pkgs/verify-non-fail.html.

6.2 Axiomatization of Defined Operations

As discussed for the list index operator `nth` (Section 4.3), it might be necessary to use some information about user-defined operations during verification. Thus, their semantics must be known to the verifier. For this purpose, user-defined operations are translated into SMT formulas which axiomatize their intended semantics. Each rule defining a Curry operation is translated into an SMT formula stating an equality[7] between a function call and the right-hand side. For instance, consider the operation to compute the length of a list in its FlatCurry representation:

```
length(zs) = case zs of { []       → 0
                        ; (x:xs)  → 1 + length(xs) }
```

This definition is transformed into an SMT formula by using a `match` binder:

```
(assert
  (forall ((x1 (List TVar)))
    (= (length x1)
       (match x1 ((nil 0)
                  ((insert x2 x3) (+ 1 (length x3))))))))
```

Our tool generates these axiomatizations by collecting all user-defined operations occurring in non-fail conditions, loading the FlatCurry code of these operations, and then translating this code into SMT formulas. If polymorphic operations occur in contexts with different type instances, their axiomatizations are duplicated for each type instance.

6.3 Evaluation

In the following we evaluate our approach by discussing some examples and applying it to various libraries.

Compared to a previous tool to verify non-failing Curry programs [16] which also used an SMT solver to verify non-fail conditions, our tool is fully automatic. The tool in [16] requires that the programmer annotates all partially defined operations with non-fail conditions. These are translated into proof obligations to be checked by an SMT solver. In contrast, our tool can be used without explicit non-fail conditions and, thanks to our hybrid approach, an SMT solver is required only in the cases where an unsatisfiable call type is inferred, e.g., when arithmetic conditions are involved. All non-fail conditions provided in [16] for the libraries shown below are automatically derived by our tool, except for the prelude operation "`!!`", which is identical to `nth` shown in Sect. 4.3, where our tool infers a less precise non-fail condition. If we explicitly define the same non-fail condition as in [16], our tool verifies it. This also demonstrates the intended use of our tool. Since it reports all inferred non-trivial non-fail conditions and call types, the user can examine them and decide to either accept them, provide other non-fail conditions, or modify the program code to handle possible failures (by using search handlers, like `oneValue`) so that trivial non-fail conditions suffice.

[7] The semantics of non-deterministic operations is axiomatized by disjunctions.

Table 1. Inference of non-fail conditions for some standard libraries

Module	Operations Pub/all	Call types Pub/all	Non-fail conditions Pub/all	Failing Pub/all	Checked calls All/SMT	iterations	verify time
Prelude	214/1263	20/69	2/9	9/51	66/14	5	6474
Data.Char	9/9	0/0	0/0	0/0	0/0	1	64
Data.Either	7/11	2/2	0/0	0/0	0/0	1	4
Data.List	49/87	8/16	0/0	1/1	18/2	3	2287
Data.Maybe	8/9	0/0	0/0	0/0	0/0	1	3
Numeric	5/7	0/0	0/0	0/0	0/0	1	15
System.IO	23/51	0/0	0/0	0/0	0/0	1	26
Text.Show	4/4	0/0	0/0	0/0	0/0	1	2
Examples	11/15	1/3	4/4	0/0	17/13	3	382

Table 1 contains the results of checking various Curry libraries and the module `Examples` containing most of the examples discussed in this paper. Non-fail conditions were not explicitly provided (except for external operations, see Sect. 4.3). The "operations" column contains the number of public (exported) user-defined operations and the number of all operations (defined or generated) in the module. Similarly, the following three columns show the information for public and all operations:

- *call types*: This column shows the numbers of inferred non-trivial call types. Thus, this is the number of operations which might fail but the set of arguments to avoid a failing computation can be described by a non-empty call type (so that an SMT solver is not required to check it).
- *non-fail conditions*: These are the numbers of operations where a non-trivial but satisfiable non-fail conditions is inferred (so that an SMT solver is invoked to check their correct usage).
- *failing*: These are the numbers of operations where an unsatisfiable non-fail condition is inferred. Thus, there is no precise information about the arguments required to ensure a non-failing evaluation (e.g., `failed` or operations involving unification).

Thus, all operations not counted in these columns have trivial non-fail conditions, i.e., they do not fail when applied to any argument. The column *checked calls* contains the number of function calls in right-hand sides of program rules where the called operation has a non-trivial call type so that it needs to be checked. The first number is the total number of such calls (in all iterations) and the second number is the number of such calls where an external SMT solver is used to check the satisfaction of the non-fail condition (according to rule Func_{nf} in Fig. 2), i.e., without the SMT-component of our hybrid approach, these calls are classified as failing. The difference between these numbers is the number of calls where the consideration of call types is sufficient for the verification, thanks to our hybrid approach.

To show how many iterations are required to infer this information (this is only relevant for the inference of call types), their number is shown in the next to last column. The last column shows the verification time in milliseconds.[8]

This evaluation indicates that even quite complex modules, like the prelude, have only a few operations with non-trivial non-fail conditions or call types that need to be checked. The low numbers in the column *non-fail conditions* indicate that the standard libraries contain only a few operations with non-trivial arithmetic conditions. This might be different in application programs using more arithmetic operations. The higher numbers in the column *call types* indicate an advantage of our hybrid approach. In a purely SMT-based approach, all these operations need to be checked by SMT scripts, as in [16], and it is not obvious how to infer these conditions for polymorphic operations on recursive data structures, as relevant in the `Data.List` module.

A manual inspection of the functions appearing in the *failing* column shows that the reason is not a weakness of our method: precise non-fail conditions for these functions are demanding. For instance, non-fail conditions of prelude operations involving unification have to consider the unifiability of arguments. The single failing operation of the module `Data.List` is the matrix operation `transpose`: since the input matrix is represented by a list of lists, all input lists must have the same length to avoid a failure when transposing the matrix. Although such a non-fail condition can be expressed by some Curry code using auxiliary operations, the automatic inference of such a complex condition fails so that it is approximated by the unsatisfiable non-fail condition.

7 Related Work

We have shown in the introduction that operations which are not totally defined on their statically declared input type domain are useful, because programming a "totalized" version yields less comprehensible code. Our practical evaluation of various system libraries in the previous section indicated that partial operations are the exception. However, a single occurrence and wrong use can crash an entire application. Although this could be avoided by exception handlers, these handlers are often used to catch environment (input/output) errors rather than controlling partial operations, like division operators. Therefore, the exclusion of such run-time failures is a practically relevant but also challenging issue.

Contracts, as introduced in the context of imperative and object-oriented programming languages [24], are a method to specify intended invocations of operations. Our non-fail conditions can also be considered as contracts on input arguments to ensure the non-failing evaluation of operations. Contracts can be tested at run time to obtain better error messages. However, they can also be checked at compile time. For instance, the Eiffel compiler ensures by appropriate type declarations and static analysis that pointer dereferencing failures ("null pointer exceptions") cannot occur in a program accepted by the compiler [25].

[8] We measured the verification time on a Linux machine running Ubuntu 22.04 with an Intel Core i7-1165G7 (2.80GHz) processor with eight cores.

In the following, we review approaches for functional and logic programming related to our work.

In logic programming, there is no common definition of "non-failing" due to different interpretations of non-determinism. We are interested to exclude any failure in a top-level computation, i.e., also in branches of some non-deterministic computation. Other approaches, like [12,13], consider a predicate in a logic program as non-failing if at least one answer is produced. Similarly to our approach, non-failure properties are approximated, but the concrete methods are different due to the different meaning of a non-failed computation.

Another notion of failing programs in a dynamically typed programming language is based on success types, e.g., as used in Erlang [21]. Success types over-approximate possible uses of an operation: if a success type is empty, it indicates that an operation never evaluates to a value. Success types can show definite failures, whereas we are interested in definite non-failures.

Strongly typed programming languages are a reasonable basis to check run-time failures at compile time, since the type system already ensures that some failures cannot occur ("well-typed programs do not go wrong" [26]). As discussed above, failures due to definitions with partial patterns are not covered by a standard type system. Therefore, Mitchell and Runciman developed a checker for Haskell to verify the absence of pattern-match errors due to incomplete patterns [27,28]. Their checker extracts and solves specific constraints from pattern-based definitions. In contrast to our approach, only pattern failures are considered there. As a result, programs where the completeness depends on complete case distinctions on numbers cannot be handled by these tools.

An approach to handle more complex non-fail conditions is described in [20]. Their HMC algorithm is based on generating (arithmetic) constraints which have to be satisfied by a safe functional program, i.e., a program which does not fail, e.g., due to an incorrect array index access. These constraints are translated into an imperative program such that the constraints are satisfiable iff the translated program is safe. Similarly to our approach, HMC supports a fully automatic verification of functional programs but it is not applicable to logic-oriented subcomputations. Furthermore, it is not clear whether HMC scales for larger programs.

Another approach to ensure the absence of failures is to make the type system more expressive in order to encode non-failing conditions on the type level. For instance, dependently typed programming languages, such as Coq [9], Agda [30], or Idris [10], require that operations are total functions, i.e., they must be terminating and non-failing. These languages have termination checkers but non-fail conditions need to be explicitly encoded in the types. Therefore, each use of an operation with a non-trivial non-fail condition must be accompanied with an explicit proof for the satisfaction of the non-fail condition w.r.t. the actual arguments. Although these proofs are checked by the type checker, programming in a dependently typed language is more challenging since the programmer has to construct such non-failure proofs.

Refinement or liquid types [32], as used in LiquidHaskell [36,37], are another approach to encode non-failing conditions or more general contracts on the type level. Refinement types extend standard types by a predicate that restricts the set of allowed values. In contrast to our approach, where non-fail conditions can contain arbitrary user-defined operations, refinement types use a specific set of primitive functions and predicates (arithmetic operators and comparisons, length operation, etc). This allows the inference of refinement types based on generating and solving constraints w.r.t. these functions [32] provided that the expected refinement types can be described with the given entities. The latter restriction is relaxed in [35], where dependent types are inferred by generating constraints and solving and refining them by finding interpolants. These approaches could infer in many cases precise type refinements to verify specific properties of programs, e.g., safe array access or sorted result lists. However, if such properties cannot be inferred, the program is not valid. In contrast, our approach always infers non-fail conditions. Since we do not require a type language with fixed entities but possibly generate non-fail conditions with arbitrary user-defined predicates, the inferred non-fail conditions of some operations might not be precise enough, e.g., unsatisfiable in the worst case. However, this does not mean that we cannot use such operations. Instead, we can wrap their application with appropriate search handlers in order to control possible failures at run time. Moreover, our hybrid approach allows to verify operations defined on algebraic data types without an external (SMT) solver, as discussed in the `risers` example in Sect. 5

As already mentioned, potentially failing operations can be encapsulated with search handlers, which is relevant to the application of logic programming techniques. This aspect is also the motivation for the non-failure checking tool proposed in [16]. As already discussed in Sect. 6.3, the advantage of our new approach is the automatic inference of non-failing conditions which supports aneasier application to larger programs. Although this aspect is covered in [18], our hybrid approach extends non-failure checking to a larger class of programs, in particular, operations with arithmetic constraints.

8 Conclusions

In this paper we proposed a new technique and a fully automatic tool to check declarative programs for the absence of failing computations, involving arithmetic conditions as well as conditions on algebraic data types. In contrast to other approaches, our approach does not require the explicit specification of non-fail conditions but is able to infer them—even for larger programs in a reasonable amount of time. Since we developed our approach for Curry, it is also applicable to purely functional and logic programs. We do not intend to abandon all potentially failing operations because partially defined operations and failing evaluations are reasonable in logic-oriented subcomputations provided that they are encapsulated in order to control possible failures. This distinguishes non-fail conditions from traditional preconditions, since preconditions have to be satisfied before invoking the operation.

The inference of non-fail conditions is based on a fixpoint iteration and might yield, in the worst case, unsatisfiable non-fail conditions. However, our practical evaluation showed that even larger programs contain only a few operations with non-trivial non-fail conditions which are inferred after a small number of iterations. When a non-trivial non-fail condition is inferred for some operation, the programmer can either modify the definition of this operation (e.g., by adding results for missing cases) or control the invocation of this operation by checking its outcome with some search handler.

Acknowledgments. The author is grateful to the anonymous reviewers for their helpful comments to improve the paper.

References

1. Albert, E., Hanus, M., Huch, F., Oliver, J., Vidal, G.: Operational semantics for declarative multi-paradigm languages. J. Symb. Comput. **40**(1), 795–829 (2005). https://doi.org/10.1016/j.jsc.2004.01.001
2. Antoy, S.: Constructor-based conditional narrowing. In: Proceedings of the 3rd International ACM SIGPLAN Conference on Principles and Practice of Declarative Programming (PPDP 2001), pp. 199–206. ACM Press (2001).https://doi.org/10.1145/773184.773205
3. Antoy, S., Echahed, R., Hanus, M.: A needed narrowing strategy. J. ACM **47**(4), 776–822 (2000). https://doi.org/10.1145/347476.347484
4. Antoy, S., Hanus, M.: Functional logic design patterns. In: Proceedings of the 6th International Symposium on Functional and Logic Programming (FLOPS 2002), pp. 67–87. Springer LNCS 2441 (2002)https://doi.org/10.1007/3-540-45788-7_4
5. Antoy, S., Hanus, M.: Set functions for functional logic programming. In: Proceedings of the 11th ACM SIGPLAN International Conference on Principles and Practice of Declarative Programming (PPDP'09), pp. 73–82. ACM Press (2009). https://doi.org/10.1145/1599410.1599420
6. Antoy, S., Hanus, M.: Functional logic programming. Commun. ACM **53**(4), 74–85 (2010). https://doi.org/10.1145/1721654.1721675
7. Antoy, S., Hanus, M.: Contracts and specifications for functional logic programming. In: Proceedings of the 14th International Symposium on Practical Aspects of Declarative Languages (PADL 2012), pp. 33–47. Springer LNCS 7149 (2012). https://doi.org/10.1007/978-3-642-27694-1_4
8. Antoy, S., Hanus, M., Jost, A., Libby, S.: ICurry. In: Declarative Programming and Knowledge Management—Conference on Declarative Programming (DECLARE 2019), pp. 286–307. Springer LNCS 12057 (2020). https://doi.org/10.1007/978-3-030-46714-2_18
9. Bertot, Y., Castéran, P.: Interactive Theorem Proving and Program Development - Coq'Art: The Calculus of Inductive Constructions. Texts in Theoretical Computer Science. An EATCS Series, Springer (2004). https://doi.org/10.1007/978-3-662-07964-5
10. Brady, E.: Idris, a general-purpose dependently typed programming language: Design and implementation. J. Funct. Program. **23**(5), 552–593 (2013). https://doi.org/10.1017/S095679681300018X
11. Braßel, B., Hanus, M., Huch, F.: Encapsulating non-determinism in functional logic computations. J. Funct. Logic Program. **2004**(6) (2004)

12. Bueno, F., López-García, P., Hermenegildo, M.: Multivariant non-failure analysis via standard abstract interpretation. In: 7th International Symposium on Functional and Logic Programming (FLOPS 2004). pp. 100–116. Springer LNCS 2998 (2004). https://doi.org/10.1007/978-3-540-24754-8_9
13. Debray, S., López-García, P., Hermenegildo, M.: Non-failure analysis for logic programs. In: 14th International Conference on Logic Programming (ICLP'97), pp. 48–62. MIT Press (1997)
14. González-Moreno, J., Hortalá-González, M., López-Fraguas, F., Rodríguez-Artalejo, M.: An approach to declarative programming based on a rewriting logic. J. Log. Program. **40**, 47–87 (1999). https://doi.org/10.1016/S0743-1066(98)10029-8
15. Hanus, M.: Functional logic programming: from theory to Curry. In: Programming Logics - Essays in Memory of Harald Ganzinger, pp. 123–168. Springer LNCS 7797 (2013). https://doi.org/10.1007/978-3-642-37651-1_6
16. Hanus, M.: Verifying fail-free declarative programs. In: Proceedings of the 20th International Symposium on Principles and Practice of Declarative Programming (PPDP 2018), pp. 12:1–12:13. ACM Press (2018). https://doi.org/10.1145/3236950.3236957
17. Hanus, M.: From logic to functional logic programs. Theory Pract. Logic Program. **22**(4), 538–554 (2022). https://doi.org/10.1017/S1471068422000187
18. Hanus, M.: Inferring non-failure conditions for declarative programs. In: Proceedings of the 17th International Symposium on Functional and Logic Programming (FLOPS 2024), pp. 167–187. Springer LNCS 14659 (2024). https://doi.org/10.1007/978-981-97-2300-3_10
19. Hanus, M. (ed.): Curry: an integrated functional logic language (vers. 0.9.0). Available at http://www.curry-lang.org (2016)
20. Jhala, R., Majumdar, R., Rybalchenko, A.: HMC: verifying functional programs using abstract interpreters. In: 23rd International Conference on Computer Aided Verification (CAV 2011). pp. 470–485. Springer LNCS 6806 (2011).https://doi.org/10.1007/978-3-642-22110-1_38
21. Lindahl, T., Sagonas, K.: Practical type inference based on success typings. In: Proceedings of the 8th International ACM SIGPLAN Conference on Principles and Practice of Declarative Programming (PPDP 2006). pp. 167–178. ACM Press (2006). https://doi.org/10.1145/1140335.1140356
22. López-Fraguas, F., Sánchez-Hernández, J.: A proof theoretic approach to failure in functional logic programming. Theory Pract. Logic Program. **4**(1), 41–74 (2004). https://doi.org/10.1017/S1471068403001728
23. Lux, W.: Implementing encapsulated search for a lazy functional logic language. In: Proceedings of 4th Fuji International Symposium on Functional and Logic Programming (FLOPS'99), pp. 100–113. Springer LNCS 1722 (1999). https://doi.org/10.1007/10705424_7
24. Meyer, B.: Object-oriented Software Construction, 2nd edn. Prentice Hall (1997)
25. Meyer, B.: Ending null pointer crashes. Commun. ACM **60**(5), 8–9 (2017). https://doi.org/10.1145/3057284
26. Milner, R.: A theory of type polymorphism in programming. J. Comput. Syst. Sci. **17**, 348–375 (1978)
27. Mitchell, N., Runciman, C.: A static checker for safe pattern matching in Haskell. In: Trends in Functional Programming, vol. 6, pp. 15–30. Intellect (2007)
28. Mitchell, N., Runciman, C.: Not all patterns, but enough: an automatic verifier for partial but sufficient pattern matching. In: Proceedings of the 1st ACM SIGPLAN

Symposium on Haskell (Haskell 2008), pp. 49–60. ACM (2008). https://doi.org/10.1145/1411286.1411293
29. de Moura, L., Bjørner, N.: Z3: an efficient SMT solver. In: Proceedings of the 14th International Conference on Tools and Algorithms for the Construction and Analysis of Systems (TACAS 2008). pp. 337–340. Springer LNCS 4963 (2008). https://doi.org/10.1007/978-3-540-78800-3
30. Norell, U.: Dependently typed programming in Agda. In: Proceedings of the 6th International School on Advanced Functional Programming (AFP'08). pp. 230–266. Springer LNCS 5832 (2008). https://doi.org/10.1007/978-3-642-04652-0_5
31. Peyton Jones, S. (ed.): Haskell 98 Language and Libraries—The Revised Report. Cambridge University Press (2003)
32. Rondon, P., Kawaguchi, M., Jhala, R.: Liquid types. In: Proceedings of the ACM SIGPLAN 2008 Conference on Programming Language Design and Implementation (PLDI'08). pp. 159–169. ACM Press (2008). https://doi.org/10.1145/1375581.1375602
33. Sato, T., Tamaki, H.: Enumeration of success patterns in logic programs. Theoret. Comput. Sci. **34**, 227–240 (1984). https://doi.org/10.1016/0304-3975(84)90119-1
34. Stump, A.: Verified Functional Programming in Agda. ACM and Morgan & Claypool (2016). https://doi.org/10.1145/2841316
35. Unno, H., Kobayashi, N.: Dependent type inference with interpolants. In: Proceedings of the 11th ACM SIGPLAN International Conference on Principles and Practice of Declarative Programming (PPDP'09). pp. 277–288. ACM Press (2009). https://doi.org/10.1145/1599410.1599445
36. Vazou, N., Seidel, E., Jhala, R.: LiquidHaskell: experience with refinement types in the real world. In: Proceedings of the 2014 ACM SIGPLAN Symposium on Haskell, pp. 39–51. ACM Press (2014).https://doi.org/10.1145/2633357.2633366
37. Vazou, N., Seidel, E., Jhala, R., Vytiniotis, D., Peyton Jones, S.: Refinement types for Haskell. In: Proceedings of the 19th ACM SIGPLAN International Conference on Functional Programming (ICFP). pp. 269–282. ACM Press (2014). https://doi.org/10.1145/2628136.2628161

Explaining Explanations in Probabilistic Logic Programming

German Vidal[(✉)]

VRAIN, Universitat Politècnica de València, Valencia, Spain
gvidal@dsic.upv.es

Abstract. The emergence of tools based on artificial intelligence has also led to the need of producing explanations which are understandable by a human being. In most approaches, the system is considered a *black box*, making it difficult to generate appropriate explanations. In this work, though, we consider a setting where models are *transparent*: probabilistic logic programming (PLP), a paradigm that combines logic programming for knowledge representation and probability to model uncertainty. However, given a query, the usual notion of *explanation* is associated with a set of choices, one for each random variable of the model. Unfortunately, such a set does not explain *why* the query is true and, in fact, it may contain choices that are actually irrelevant for the considered query. To improve this situation, we present in this paper an approach to explaining explanations which is based on defining a new query-driven inference mechanism for PLP where proofs are labeled with *choice expressions*, a compact and easy to manipulate representation for sets of choices. The combination of proof trees and choice expressions allows us to produce comprehensible query justifications with a causal structure.

1 Introduction

Explainable AI (XAI) [5] is an active area of research that includes many different approaches. Explainability is especially important in the context of decision support systems, where the user often demands to know the reasons for a decision. Furthermore, the last regulation on data protection in the European Union [12] has introduced a "right to explanation" for algorithmic decisions.

The last decades have witnessed the emergence of a good number of proposals to combine logic programming and probability, e.g., Logic Programs with Annotated Disjunctions (LPADs) [40], CP-logic [39], ProbLog [27], Probabilistic Horn Abduction [24], Independent Choice Logic [25], PRISM [37], Stochastic Logic Programs [20], and Bayesian Logic Programs [16], to name a few (see, e.g., the survey [34] and references therein). Most of these approaches are based

This work has been partially supported by grant PID2019-104735RB-C41 funded by MICIU/AEI/ 10.13039/501100011033, by the *Generalitat Valenciana* under grant CIPROM/2022/6 (FassLow), and by TAILOR, a project funded by EU Horizon 2020 research and innovation programme under GA No 952215.

O. Kiselyov (Ed.): APLAS 2024, LNCS 15194, pp. 130–152, 2024.
https://doi.org/10.1007/978-981-97-8943-6_7

on the so-called *distribution* semantics introduced by Sato [36]. In this work, we mainly follow the LPAD [40] approach to probabilistic logic programming (PLP), which has an expressive power similar to, for example, Bayesian networks [32]. For instance, the following probabilistic clause:

$$heads(X){:}0.5;\ tails(X){:}0.5 \leftarrow toss(X), \neg biased(X).$$

specifies that every time a coin X which is not biased is tossed, it lands on heads with probability 0.5 and on tails with probability 0.5. Note that only one choice can be true for a given X (thus ";" should not be interpreted as logical disjunction). One can say that each instance of the clause above represents a *random variable* with as many values as head disjuncts (two, in this case).

Given a program, a *selection* is basically a choice of values for *all* the random variables represented in a probabilistic logic program. Every selection induces a possible *world*, a normal logic program which is obtained by choosing the head determined by the selection in each grounding of each probabilistic clause (and removing its probability). For example, given an instance of the clause above for $X = coin1$, a selection that chooses $heads(coin1)$ will include the normal clause

$$heads(coin1) \leftarrow toss(coin1), \neg biased(coin1).$$

In this context, an *explanation* often refers to a selection or, equivalently, to the world induced from it. For instance, the MPE task [38], which stands for *Most Probable Explanation*, basically consists in finding the world with the highest probability given a query (typically denoting a set of observed *evidences*).

A world can be seen indeed as an interpretable model in which a given query holds. However, this kind of explanations also presents several drawbacks. First, a world might include clauses which are irrelevant for the query, thus adding noise to the explanation. Second, the chain of inferences that proved the query is far from obvious from the explanation (i.e., from the given world). In fact, there can be several different chains of inferences that explain why the query is true, each with an associated probability. Finally, a world (a set of clauses) might be too technical an explanation for non-experts.

Alternatively, some work considers that an explanation for a query is given by a set of choices: those that are *necessary* to prove the query (see, e.g., [30]). Although in this case there is no irrelevant information, it still does not have a causal structure. Furthermore, a set of choices does not provide an intuitive explanation about why the query holds. In order to *explain* explanations, we propose in this work a combination of proof trees—that show the chain of inferences used to prove a query—and a new representation for choices that gives rise to a more compact notation. For this purpose, we make the following contributions:

- First, we introduce an algebra of *choice expressions*, a new notation for representing sets of choices that can be easily manipulated using standard rules like distributivity, double negation elimination, De Morgan's laws, etc.

- Then, we present SLPDNF-resolution, a query-driven top-down inference mechanism that extends SLDNF-resolution to deal with LPADs. We prove its soundness and completeness regarding the computation of explanations.
- Finally, we show how the proofs of SLPDNF-resolution can be used to produce comprehensible representations of the explanations of a query, which might help the user to understand why this query is indeed true.

We note that a practical evaluation of the proposed techniques will require the design and implementation of a software tool for generating explanations, which is left as future work.

Proofs of technical results can be found in the companion report [42].

2 Some Concepts of Logic Programming and PLP

In this section, we introduce some basic notions of logic programming [1,18] and probabilistic logic programming [34].

2.1 Logic Programming

We consider a *function-free* first-order language with a fixed vocabulary of predicate symbols, constants, and variables denoted by Π, $\mathcal{C}$ and $\mathcal{V}$, respectively. An *atom* has the form $f(t_1, \ldots, t_n)$ with $f/n \in \Pi$ and $t_i \in (\mathcal{C} \cup \mathcal{V})$ for $i = 1, \ldots, n$. A *literal* l is an atom a or its negation $\neg a$. A *query* Q is a conjunction of literals,[1]

where the empty query is denoted by $\Box$. We use capital letters to denote (possibly atomic) queries. A *clause* has the form $h \leftarrow B$, where h (the *head*) is a positive literal (an atom) and B (the *body*) is a query; when the body is empty, the clause is called a *fact* and denoted just by h; otherwise, it is called a *rule*. A (normal) logic *program* P is a finite set of clauses.

We let $\mathsf{var}(s)$ denote the set of variables in the syntactic object s, where s can be a literal, a query or a clause. A syntactic object s is *ground* if $\mathsf{var}(s) = \emptyset$. Substitutions and their operations are defined as usual, where $\mathcal{D}om(\sigma) = \{x \in \mathcal{V} \mid \sigma(x) \neq x\}$ is called the *domain* of a substitution σ. We let *id* denote the empty substitution. The application of a substitution θ to a syntactic object s is usually denoted by juxtaposition, i.e., we write $s\theta$ rather than $\theta(s)$. A syntactic object s_1 is *more general* than a syntactic object s_2, denoted $s_1 \leqslant s_2$, if there exists a substitution θ such that $s_1\theta = s_2$. A *variable renaming* is a substitution that is a bijection on $\mathcal{V}$. A substitution θ is a *unifier* of two syntactic objects s_1 and s_2 iff $s_1\theta = s_2\theta$; furthermore, θ is the *most general unifier* of s_1 and s_2, denoted by $\mathsf{mgu}(s_1, s_2)$ if, for every other unifier σ of s_1 and s_2, we have that $\theta \leqslant \sigma$,[2] i.e., there exists a substitution γ such that $\theta\gamma = \sigma$ when the domains are restricted to the variables of $\mathsf{var}(s_1) \cup \mathsf{var}(s_2)$.

In this work, we consider *negation as failure* [11] and SLDNF-resolution [3]. We say that a query $Q = l_1, \ldots, l_n$ *resolves* to Q' via σ with respect to literal l_i

[1] As is common in logic programming, we write a query $l_1 \wedge l_2 \wedge \ldots \wedge l_n$ as $l_1, l_2, \ldots, l_n$.

[2] Here, we assume that $\mathcal{D}om(\theta) \subseteq \mathsf{var}(s_1) \cup \mathsf{var}(s_2)$ if $\mathsf{mgu}(s_1, s_2) = \theta$.

and clause c, in symbols $Q \leadsto_\sigma Q'$, if either i) $h \leftarrow B$ is a renamed apart variant of c, $\sigma = \mathsf{mgu}(l_i, h)$, and $Q' = (l_1, \ldots, l_{i-1}, B, l_{i+1}, \ldots, l_n)\sigma$, or ii) l_i is a negative literal, $\sigma = id$, and $Q' = l_1, \ldots, l_{i-1}, l_{i+1}, \ldots, l_n$. A (finite or infinite) sequence of resolution steps of the form $Q_0 \leadsto_{\sigma_1} Q_1 \leadsto_{\sigma_2} \ldots$ is called a *pseudoderivation*. As we will see below, an SLDNF-derivation is a pseudoderivation where the deletion of negative (ground) literals is justified by a finitely failed SLDNF-tree.

An SLDNF-tree Γ is given by a triple $(\mathcal{T}, T, \mathsf{subs})$, where $\mathcal{T}$ is a set of trees, $T \in \mathcal{T}$ is called the main tree, and subs is a function assigning to some nodes of trees in $\mathcal{T}$ a (subsidiary) tree from $\mathcal{T}$. Intuitively speaking, an SLDNF-tree is a directed graph with two types of edges, the usual ones (associated to resolution steps) and the ones connecting a node with the root of a subsidiary tree. A node can be marked with *failed*, *sucess*, and *floundered*. A tree is *successful* if it contains at least a leaf marked as success, and *finitely failed* if it is finite and all leaves are marked as *failed*.

Given a query Q_0, an SLDNF-tree for Q_0 starts with a single node labeled with Q_0. The tree can then be *extended* by selecting a query $Q = l_1, \ldots, l_n$ which is not yet marked (as failed, success or floundered) and a literal l_i and then proceeding as follows:

- If l_i is an atom, we add a child labeled with Q' for each resolution step $Q \leadsto_\sigma Q'$. The query is marked as *failed* if no such resolution steps exist.
- If l_i is a negative literal, $\neg a$, we have the following possibilities:
  - if a is nonground, the query Q is marked as *floundered*;
  - if $\mathsf{subs}(Q)$ is undefined, a new tree T' with a single node labeled with a is added to $\mathcal{T}$ and $\mathsf{subs}(Q)$ is set to the root of T';
  - if $\mathsf{subs}(Q)$ is defined and the corresponding tree is successful, then Q is marked as *failed*.
  - if $\mathsf{subs}(Q)$ is defined and the corresponding tree is finitely failed, then we have $Q \leadsto_{id} Q'$, where Q' is obtained from Q by removing literal l_i.

Empty leaves are marked as success. The extension of an SLDNF-tree continues until all leaves of the trees in $\mathcal{T}$ are marked.[3] An SLDNF-tree for a query Q is an SLDNF-tree in which the root of the main tree is labeled with Q. An SLDNF-tree is called *successful* (resp. finitely failed) if the main tree is successful (resp. finitely failed). An SLDNF-derivation for a query Q is a branch in the main tree of an SLDNF-tree Γ for Q, together with the set of all trees in Γ whose roots can be reached from the nodes of this branch. Given a successful SLDNF-derivation, $Q_0 \leadsto_{\sigma_1} Q_1 \leadsto_{\sigma_2} \ldots \leadsto_{\sigma_n} Q_n$, the composition $\sigma_1\sigma_2\ldots\sigma_n$ (restricted to the variables of Q_0) is called a *computed answer substitution* of Q_0.

A normal logic program is *range-restricted* if all the variables occurring in the head of a clause also occur in the positive literals of its body. For range-restricted programs, every successful SLDNF-derivation completely grounds the initial query [21].

[3] In [3] only the limit of the sequence of trees is called an SLDNF-tree, while the previous ones are called pre-SLDNF-trees. We ignore this distinction here for simplicity.

2.2 Logic Programs with Annotated Disjunctions

We assume that $\Pi = \Pi_p \uplus \Pi_d$, the set of predicate symbols, is partitioned into a set Π_p of *probabilistic predicates* and a set Π_d of *derived predicates*, which are disjoint. An atom $f(t_1, \ldots, t_n)$ is called a *probabilistic atom* if $f \in \Pi_p$ and a *derived atom* if $f \in \Pi_d$. An LPAD $\mathcal{P} = \mathcal{P}_p \uplus \mathcal{P}_d$—or just *program* when no confusion can arise—consists of a set of probabilistic clauses $\mathcal{P}_p$ and a set of normal clauses $\mathcal{P}_d$ defining derived predicates. A *probabilistic clause* has the form $h_1 : p_1; \ldots; h_n : p_n \leftarrow B$, where $h_1, \ldots, h_n$ are probabilistic atoms, $p_1, \ldots, p_n$ are real numbers in the interval $[0, 1]$ (their respective probabilities) such that $\sum_{i=1}^{n} p_i \leqslant 1$, and B is a query. When $\sum_{i=1}^{n} p_i < 1$, we implicitly assume that a special atom none is added to the head of the clause, where $\mathsf{none}/0$ is a fresh predicate which does not occur in the original program, with associated probability $1 - \sum_{i=1}^{n} p_i$. Thus, in the following, we assume w.l.o.g. that $\sum_{i=1}^{n} p_i = 1$ for all clauses.

Example 1. Consider the following clause[4]

$$covid(X){:}0.4; flu(X){:}0.3 \leftarrow contact(X, Y), covid(Y).$$

It states that, if X is a contact of Y and Y has covid, then either X has covid too (probability 0.4) or X has the flu (probability 0.3). Moreover, X has neither covid nor the flu (i.e., none holds) with probability 0.3 $(1 - 0.4 - 0.3)$.

Now we consider the semantics of programs. Given a probabilistic clause $c = (h_1 : p_1; \ldots; h_n : p_n \leftarrow B)$, each ground instance $c\theta$ represents a choice between n (normal) clauses: $(h_1 \leftarrow B)\theta, \ldots (h_n \leftarrow B)\theta$. A particular choice is denoted by a triple (c, θ, i), $i \in \{1, \ldots, n\}$, which is called an *atomic choice*, and has as associated probability $\pi(c, i)$, i.e., p_i in the clause above. We say that a set κ of atomic choices is *consistent*, in symbols, *consistent*(κ), if it does not contain two atomic choices for the same grounding of a probabilistic clause, i.e., it cannot contain (c, θ, i) and (c, θ, j) with $i \neq j$. A set of consistent atomic choices is called a *composite choice*. It is called a *selection* when the composite choice includes an atomic choice for each grounding of each probabilistic clause of the program. We let $\mathcal{S}_\mathcal{P}$ denote the set of all possible selections for a given program (which is finite since we consider function-free programs). Each selection $s \in \mathcal{S}_\mathcal{P}$ identifies a *world* ω_s which contains a (ground) normal clause $(h_i \leftarrow B)\theta$ for each atomic choice $(c, \theta, i) \in s$, together with the clauses for derived predicates:

$$\omega_s = \{(h_i \leftarrow B)\theta \mid c = (h_1 {:} p_1; \ldots; h_n {:} p_n \leftarrow B) \in \mathcal{P}_p \wedge (c, \theta, i) \in s\} \cup \mathcal{P}_d$$

We assume in this work that programs are *sound*, i.e., each world has a unique two-valued well-founded model [14] which coincides with its stable model [15], and SLDNF-resolution is sound and complete. We write $\omega_s \models Q$ to denote that

[4] Here and in the remaining examples we do not show the ocurrences of none.

the (ground) query Q is true in the unique model of the program. Soundness can be ensured, e.g., by requiring logic programs to be stratified [17], acyclic [2] or modularly acyclic [35]. These characterizations can be extended to LPADs in a natural way, e.g., an LPAD is stratified if each possible world is stratified.

Given a selection s, the probability of world ω_s is then defined as follows: $P(\omega_s) = P(s) = \prod_{(c,\theta,i)\in s} \pi(c,i)$. Given a program $\mathcal{P}$, we let $\mathcal{W}_\mathcal{P}$ denote the (finite) set of possible worlds, i.e., $\mathcal{W}_\mathcal{P} = \{\omega_s \mid s \in \mathcal{S}_\mathcal{P}\}$. Here, $P(\omega)$ defines a probability distribution over $\mathcal{W}_\mathcal{P}$. By definition, the sum of the probabilities of all possible worlds is equal to 1. The probability of a (ground) query Q in a program $\mathcal{P}$, called the *success probability* of Q in $\mathcal{P}$, in symbols $P(Q)$, is obtained by marginalization from the joint distribution $P(Q,\omega)$ as follows:

$$P(Q) = \sum_{\omega\in\mathcal{W}_\mathcal{P}} P(Q,\omega) = \sum_{\omega\in\mathcal{W}_\mathcal{P}} P(Q|\omega)\cdot P(\omega)$$

where $P(Q|\omega) = 1$ if $\omega \models Q$ and $P(Q|\omega) = 0$ otherwise. Intuitively speaking, the success probability of a query is the sum of the probabilities of all the worlds where this query is provable (equivalently, has a successful SLDNF-derivation).

3 Query-Driven Inference in PLP

In this section, we present our approach to query-driven inference for probabilistic logic programs. In order to ease the understanding, let us first consider the case of programs *without negation*. In this case, it suffices to redefine queries to also include an associated composite choice κ. Intuitively speaking, κ denotes a restriction on the worlds where the computation performed so far can be proved.

An initial query has thus the form $\langle Q, \emptyset\rangle$, where Q is a standard query and $\emptyset$ is an empty composite choice. Resolution steps with probabilistic clauses should update the current composite choice accordingly. For this operation to be well-defined, computations must be performed w.r.t. the grounding $\mathcal{G}(\mathcal{P})$ of program $\mathcal{P}$ (which is finite since the considered language is function-free).[5] Given a query $\langle Q,\kappa\rangle$, resolution is then defined as follows:[6]

- If the selected atom is a derived atom and $Q \leadsto_\sigma Q'$, then $\langle Q,\kappa\rangle \leadsto_\sigma \langle Q',\kappa\rangle$.
- If the selected atom is a probabilistic atom, a, then we have a resolution step $\langle Q,\kappa\rangle \leadsto_\sigma \langle Q', \kappa\cup\{(c,\theta,i)\}\rangle$ for each (ground) clause $c\theta = (h_1 : p_1; \ldots; h_n : p_n \leftarrow B)\theta \in \mathcal{G}(\mathcal{P})$ such that $Q \leadsto_\sigma Q'$ is a resolution step with respect to atom a and clause $h_i\theta \leftarrow B\theta$ and, moreover, $\kappa\cup\{(c,\theta,i)\}$ is consistent.

Example 2. Consider the following program $\mathcal{P}$:

5 In practice, given a query, it suffices to compute the *relevant* groundings of $\mathcal{P}_p$ for this query (see [13, Section 5.1] for a discussion on this topic).

6 For simplicity, we use the same arrow $\leadsto$ for both standard resolution and its extended version for probabilistic logic programs.

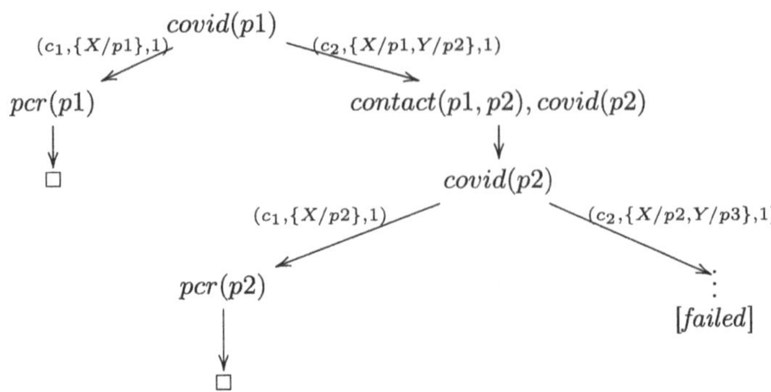

Fig. 1. Tree for the query *covid*(*p*1)

(c_1) $covid(X){:}0.9 \leftarrow pcr(X).$
(c_2) $covid(X){:}0.4; flu(X){:}0.3 \leftarrow contact(X,Y), covid(Y).$
$pcr(p1).\ \ pcr(p2).\ \ contact(p1,p2).\ \ person(p1).\ \ person(p2).\ \ person(p3).$

Here, the grounding $\mathcal{G}(\mathcal{P})$ will contain an instance of c_1 and c_2 for each person $p1$, $p2$, and $p3$. Figure 1 shows the resolution tree for the query *covid*($p1$). For simplicity, we only considered two groundings for c_2: $\{X/p1, Y/p2\}$ and $\{X/p2, Y/p3\}$; moreover, we always select the leftmost literal in a query. In the tree, for clarity, we show ordinary queries as nodes and label the edges with the atomic choices computed in the step (if any).

Here, we have two successful derivations for *covid*($p1$) that compute the composite choices $\{(c_1, \{X/p1\}, 1)\}$ and $\{(c_2, \{X/p1, Y/p2\}, 1), (c_1, \{X/p2\}, 1)\}$, i.e., the union of the atomic choices labeling the steps of each root-to-leaf successful derivation. Their probabilities are $\pi(c_1, 1) = 0.9$ and $\pi(c_2, 1) \times \pi(c_1, 1) = 0.4 * 0.9 = 0.36$, respectively. The computation of the marginal probability of a query is not generally the sum of the probabilities of its proofs since the associated worlds may overlap (as in this case). Computing the probability of a query is an orthogonal issue which is out of the scope of this paper (in this case, the marginal probability is 0.936); see Section 4 for further details on this topic.

3.1 Introducing Negation

Now, we consider the general case. In the following, we say that a selection s *extends* a composite choice κ if $\kappa \subseteq s$. Moreover, a composite choice κ identifies the set of worlds ω_κ that can be obtained by extending κ to a selection in all possible ways. Formally, $\omega_\kappa = \{\omega_s \mid s \in \mathcal{S}_\mathcal{P} \wedge \kappa \subseteq s\}$. Given a set of composite choices K, we let $\omega_K = \cup_{\kappa \in K}\, \omega_\kappa$.

In principle, we could adapt Riguzzi's strategy in [30] for ICL (*Independent Choice Logic* [25]) to the case of LPAD. Basically, a resolution step for a query where a negated (ground) literal $\neg a$ is selected could proceed as follows:

- First, as in SLDNF, a tree for query a is built. Assume that the successful branches of this tree compute the composite choices $\kappa_1, \ldots, \kappa_n$, $n > 0$.
- Then, we know that a succeeds—equivalently, $\neg a$ fails—in all the worlds that extend the composite choices $\kappa_1, \ldots, \kappa_n$. Hence, we calculate a set of composite choices K that are *complementary* to those in $\kappa_1, \ldots, \kappa_n$.
- If K is not empty, the query where $\neg a$ was selected will have as many children as composite choices in K. For each child, the negated literal is removed from the query and the corresponding composite choice is added to the current one (assuming their union is consistent).

In order to formalize these ideas, we first recall the notion of *complement* [26]: If K is a set of composite choices, then a *complement* of K is a set K' of composite choices such that for all world $\omega \in \mathcal{W}_\mathcal{P}$, we have $\omega \in \omega_K$ iff $\omega \notin \omega_{K'}$. The notion of *dual* [26,30] is introduced to have an operational definition:

Definition 1. (dual). *If K is a set of composite choices, then composite choice κ' is a* dual *of K if for all $\kappa \in K$ there exist atomic choices $(c, \theta, i) \in \kappa$ and $(c, \theta, j) \in \kappa'$ such that $i \neq j$. A dual is* minimal *if no proper subset is also a dual. Let $\mathsf{duals}(K)$ be the set of minimal duals of K.*

The set of duals is indeed a complement of a set of composite choices (cf. Lemma 4.8 in [26]). The computation of $\mathsf{duals}(K)$ can be carried out using the notion of *hitting set* [28]. Let C be a collection of sets. Then, set H is a *hitting set* for C if $H \subseteq \bigcup_{S \in C} S$ and $H \cap S \neq \emptyset$ for each $S \in C$. In particular, we only consider hitting sets where exactly one element of each set $S \in C$ is selected Formally, $\mathsf{hits}(\{S_1, \ldots, S_n\}) = \{\{s_1, \ldots, s_n\} \mid s_1 \in S_1, \ldots, s_n \in S_n\}$.

In the following, given an atomic choice α, we let $\overline{\alpha}$ denote the relative complement (the standard notion from set theory) of $\{\alpha\}$ w.r.t. the domain of possible atomic choices for the same (ground) clause, i.e.,

$$\overline{(c, \theta, i)} = \{(c, \theta, j) \mid c = (h_1 \!:\! p_1; \ldots; h_n \!:\! p_n \leftarrow B),\ i \neq j,\ j \in \{1, \ldots, n\}\}$$

We use $\alpha, \alpha', \ldots$ to denote atomic choices and $\beta, \beta', \ldots$ for either standard atomic choices or their complements. Furthermore, we let $\overline{K} = \{\overline{\kappa_1}, \ldots, \overline{\kappa_n}\}$ if $K = \{\kappa_1, \ldots, \kappa_n\}$, and $\overline{\kappa} = \overline{\alpha_1} \cup \ldots \cup \overline{\alpha_m}$ if $\kappa = \{\alpha_1, \ldots, \alpha_m\}$. The duals of a set of composite choices K can then be obtained from the hitting sets of $\overline{K}$:

Definition 2. (duals). *Let K be a set of composite choices. Then, $\mathsf{duals}(K) = \mathsf{mins}(\mathsf{hits}(\overline{K}))$, where function mins removes inconsistent and redundant composite choices, i.e., $\mathsf{mins}(K) = \{\kappa \in K \mid consistent(\kappa)$ and $\kappa' \not\subset \kappa$ for all $\kappa' \in K\}$.*

It is easy to see that the above definition is more declarative but equivalent to similar functions in [26,30].

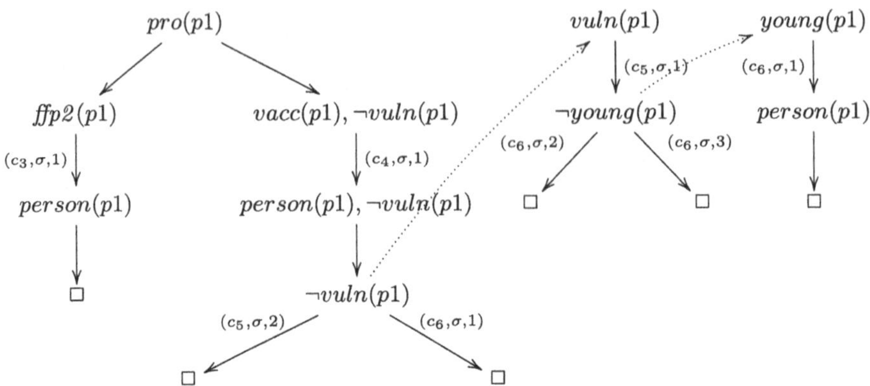

Fig. 2. Trees for the query *protected*(p1), where predicates *protected*, *vaccinated*, and *vulnerable* are abbreviated as *pro*, *vacc*, and *vuln*, respectively

Example 3. Consider the following LPAD program $\mathcal{P}$:

$(c_1)\ covid(X){:}0.9 \leftarrow pcr(X).$
$(c_2)\ covid(X){:}0.4; flu(X){:}0.3 \leftarrow contact(X,Y), covid(Y), \neg protected(X).$
$(c_3)\ ffp2(X){:}0.3; surgical{:}0.4; cloth{:}0.1 \leftarrow person(X).$
$(c_4)\ vaccinated(X){:}0.8 \leftarrow person(X).$
$(c_5)\ vulnerable(X){:}0.6 \leftarrow \neg young(X).$
$(c_6)\ young(X){:}0.2; adult(X){:}0.5 \leftarrow person(X).$

$\quad protected(X) \leftarrow ffp2(X).$
$\quad protected(X) \leftarrow vaccinated(X), \neg vulnerable(X).$
$\quad pcr(p1).\ \ pcr(p2).\ \ contact(p1,p2).\ \ person(p1).\ \ person(p2).\ \ person(p3).$

The grounding $\mathcal{G}(\mathcal{P})$ will contain an instance of clauses $c_1, \ldots, c_6$ for each person $p1$, $p2$, and $p3$. As in the previous example, we show ordinary queries as nodes and label the edges with the new atomic choices of the step (if any). Figure 2 shows the trees for the query *protected*(p1). Here, *young*(p1) has only one successful derivation with composite choice $\{(c_6, \sigma, 1)\}$, where $\sigma = \{X/p1\}$. Let $K_1 = \{\{(c_6, \sigma, 1)\}\}$. In order to resolve $\neg young(p1)$, we compute the duals of K_1:

$$\begin{aligned}\mathsf{duals}(K_1) &= \mathsf{mins}(\mathsf{hits}(\overline{K_1})) = \mathsf{mins}(\mathsf{hits}(\{\overline{\{(c_6,\sigma,1)\}}\})) \\ &= \mathsf{mins}(\mathsf{hits}(\{\{(c_6,\sigma,2),(c_6,\sigma,3)\}\})) = \{\{(c_6,\sigma,2)\},\{(c_6,\sigma,3)\}\}\end{aligned}$$

Hence, $\neg young(p1)$ has two children with atomic choices $(c_6, \sigma, 2)$ and $(c_6, \sigma, 3)$. Consider now *vulnerable*(p1). The tree includes two successful branches that compute composite choices $\{(c_5, \sigma, 1), (c_6, \sigma, 2)\}$ and $\{(c_5, \sigma, 1), (c_6, \sigma, 3)\}$. Let K_2 be a set with these two composite choices. In order to resolve

$\neg vulnerable(p1)$ in the tree for $protected(p1)$, we first need the duals of K_2:

$$\begin{aligned}
&\mathsf{duals}(K_2) = \mathsf{mins}(\mathsf{hits}(\overline{K_2}))\\
&= \mathsf{mins}(\mathsf{hits}(\{\overline{\{(c_5,\sigma,1),(c_6,\sigma,2)\}},\overline{\{(c_5,\sigma,1),(c_6,\sigma,3)\}}\}))\\
&= \mathsf{mins}(\mathsf{hits}(\{\{(c_5,\sigma,2),(c_6,\sigma,1),(c_6,\sigma,3)\},\{(c_5,\sigma,2),(c_6,\sigma,1),(c_6,\sigma,2)\}\}))\\
&= \mathsf{mins}(\{\{(c_5,\sigma,2)\},\{(c_5,\sigma,2),(c_6,\sigma,1)\},\{(c_5,\sigma,2),(c_6,\sigma,2)\},\{(c_6,\sigma,1)\},\\
&\qquad \{(c_6,\sigma,1),(c_6,\sigma,2)\},\{(c_6,\sigma,3),(c_5,\sigma,2)\},\{(c_6,\sigma,3),(c_6,\sigma,1)\},\\
&\qquad \{(c_6,\sigma,3),(c_6,\sigma,2)\}\}) = \{\{(c_5,\sigma,2)\},\{(c_6,\sigma,1)\}\}
\end{aligned}$$

Note that function mins removes redundant composite choices (e.g., all strict supersets of $\{(c_5,\sigma,2)\}$ and $\{(c_6,\sigma,1)\}$) as well as inconsistent composite choices like $\{(c_6,\sigma,3),(c_6,\sigma,2)\}$. Hence, $\neg vulnerable(p1)$ has two children with associated atomic choices $(c_5,\sigma,2)$ and $(c_6,\sigma,1)$.

We do not show the details here but, given the computed composite choices $\{(c_3,\sigma,1)\}$, $\{(c_4,\sigma,1),(c_5,\sigma,2)\}$, and $\{(c_4,\sigma,1),(c_6,\sigma,1)\}$ for $protected(p1)$, a call of the form $\neg protected(p1)$ would have twelve children.

3.2 An Algebra of Choice Expressions

The main drawback of the previous approach is that it usually produces a large number of proofs (i.e., successful branches), most of them identical except for the computed composite choice. For instance, as mentioned in Example 3, a call to $\neg protected(p1)$ will have twelve children. Likewise, a query of the form $\neg protected(p1), \neg protected(p2)$ will end up with a total of 144 children, all of them with a copy of the same query.

Our focus in this work is explainability. Hence, we aim at producing proofs that are as simple and easy to understand and manipulate as possible. An obvious first step into this direction could consist in associating *a set of composite choices* to each query rather than a single composite choice. In this way, the resolution of a query with a negative literal would produce a single child with the composition of the current set of composite choices and those returned by function duals.

For example, the query $\neg vulnerable(p1)$ in the first tree of Fig. 2 would now have the form $\langle \neg vulnerable(p1),\ \{\{(c_4,\sigma,1)\}\}\rangle$. Given the duals of K_2 computed above, $\mathsf{duals}(K_2) = \{\{(c_5,\sigma,2)\},\{(c_6,\sigma,1)\}\}$, the child of $\neg vulnerable(p1)$ would have the following associated set of composite choices:

$$\{\{(c_4,\sigma,1)\}\} \otimes \left\{ \begin{array}{l} \{(c_5,\sigma,2)\}, \\ \{(c_6,\sigma,1)\} \end{array} \right\} = \left\{ \begin{array}{l} \{(c_4,\sigma,1),(c_5,\sigma,2)\}, \\ \{(c_4,\sigma,1),(c_6,\sigma,1)\} \end{array} \right\}$$

where the operation "$\otimes$" is defined as follows:

$$K_1 \otimes K_2 = \mathsf{mins}(\{\kappa_1 \cup \kappa_2 \mid \kappa_1 \in K_1, \kappa_2 \in K_2\}) \tag{1}$$

However, this approach would only reduce the number of identical nodes in the tree, but the computed composite choices would be the same as before.

As an alternative, we introduce an algebra of *choice expressions*, a representation for sets of composite choices which enjoy several good properties: they are more compact and can be easily manipulated using well-known logical rules (distributive laws, double negation elimination, De Morgan's laws, etc.).

Definition 3. *A choice expression is defined inductively as follows:*

- $\bot$ *and* $\top$ *are choice expressions;*
- *an atomic choice* α *is a choice expression;*
- *if* C, C' *are choice expressions then* $\neg\mathsf{C}$, $\mathsf{C}\wedge\mathsf{C}'$, *and* $\mathsf{C}\vee\mathsf{C}'$ *are choice expressions too, where* $\neg$ *has higher precedence than* $\wedge$, *and* $\wedge$ *higher than* $\vee$.

Given a program $\mathcal{P}$, *we let* $\mathbb{C}_\mathcal{P}$ *denote the associated domain of choice expressions that can be built using the atomic choices of* $\mathcal{P}$. *We will omit the subscript* $\mathcal{P}$ *in* $\mathbb{C}_\mathcal{P}$ *when the program is clear from the context or irrelevant.*

A choice expression essentially represents a set of composite choices. E.g., the expression $(\alpha_1 \wedge \alpha_2) \vee \alpha_3 \vee (\alpha_4 \wedge \alpha_5)$ represents the set $\{\{\alpha_1, \alpha_2\}, \{\alpha_3\}, \{\alpha_4, \alpha_5\}\}$. In particular, negation allows us to represent sets of composite choices in a more compact way. For example, $\neg(c_3, \sigma, 1) \wedge \neg(c_6, \sigma, 1)$ represents a set with 6 composite choices, i.e., all combinations of pairs from $\{(c_3, \sigma, 2), (c_3, \sigma, 3), (c_3, \sigma, 4)\}$ and $\{(c_6, \sigma, 2), (c_6, \sigma, 3)\}$. The following function γ formalizes this equivalence:

Definition 4. *Given a choice expression* $\mathsf{C} \in \mathbb{C}$, *we let* $\gamma(\mathsf{C})$ *denote the associated set of composite choices, where function* γ *is defined inductively as follows:*

- $\gamma(\bot) = \{\}$, *i.e.,* $\bot$ *denotes an inconsistent set of atomic choices.*
- $\gamma(\top) = \{\{\}\}$, *i.e.,* $\top$ *represents a composite choice,* $\{\}$, *that can be extended in order to produce all possible selections.*
- $\gamma(\alpha) = \{\{\alpha\}\}$.
- $\gamma(\neg\mathsf{C}) = \mathsf{duals}(\gamma(\mathsf{C}))$, *i.e.,* $\neg\mathsf{C}$ *represents a complement of* C.
- $\gamma(\mathsf{C}_1 \wedge \mathsf{C}_2) = \mathsf{mins}(\gamma(\mathsf{C}_1) \otimes \gamma(\mathsf{C}_2))$, *where "*$\otimes$*" is defined in (1) above.*
- $\gamma(\mathsf{C}_1 \vee \mathsf{C}_2) = \mathsf{mins}(\gamma(\mathsf{C}_1) \cup \gamma(\mathsf{C}_2))$.

In practice, a set of composite choices K is just a device to represent a set of worlds ω_K. Therefore, we will not distinguish two choice expressions, C_1 and C_2, as long as the worlds identified by $\gamma(\mathsf{C}_1)$ and $\gamma(\mathsf{C}_2)$ are the same. For example, the choice expressions α_1 and $(\alpha_1 \wedge \alpha_2) \vee (\alpha_1 \wedge \neg\alpha_2)$ are equivalent, since both represent the same set of selections (those including atomic choice α_1).

Formally, we introduce the following equivalence relation on choice expressions: $\mathsf{C}_1 \sim \mathsf{C}_2$ if $\omega_{\gamma(\mathsf{C}_1)} = \omega_{\gamma(\mathsf{C}_2)}$. Roughly speaking, C_1 and C_2 are equivalent if the sets of composite choices in $\gamma(\mathsf{C}_1)$ and $\gamma(\mathsf{C}_2)$ can be extended to produce the same set of selections.

Let $\widetilde{\mathbb{C}}$ denote the quotient set of $\mathbb{C}$ by "$\sim$". Moreover, we let $\mathsf{C} \in \widetilde{\mathbb{C}}$ denote the equivalence class $[\mathsf{C}]$ when no confusion can arise. Then, $\langle \widetilde{\mathbb{C}}, \wedge, \vee, \neg, \top, \bot \rangle$ is a Boolean algebra and the following axioms hold:
Associativity $\mathsf{C}_1 \vee (\mathsf{C}_2 \vee \mathsf{C}_3) = (\mathsf{C}_1 \vee \mathsf{C}_2) \vee \mathsf{C}_3$ and $\mathsf{C}_1 \wedge (\mathsf{C}_2 \wedge \mathsf{C}_3) = (\mathsf{C}_1 \wedge \mathsf{C}_2) \wedge \mathsf{C}_3$.
Commutativity $\mathsf{C}_1 \vee \mathsf{C}_2 = \mathsf{C}_2 \vee \mathsf{C}_1$ and $\mathsf{C}_1 \wedge \mathsf{C}_2 = \mathsf{C}_2 \wedge \mathsf{C}_1$.
Absorption $\mathsf{C}_1 \vee (\mathsf{C}_1 \wedge \mathsf{C}_2) = \mathsf{C}_1$ and $\mathsf{C}_1 \wedge (\mathsf{C}_1 \vee \mathsf{C}_2) = \mathsf{C}_1$.
Identity $\mathsf{C} \vee \bot = \mathsf{C}$ and $\mathsf{C} \wedge \top = \mathsf{C}$.

Distributivity $\mathsf{C}_1 \vee (\mathsf{C}_2 \wedge \mathsf{C}_3) = (\mathsf{C}_1 \vee \mathsf{C}_2) \wedge (\mathsf{C}_1 \vee \mathsf{C}_3)$ and $\mathsf{C}_1 \wedge (\mathsf{C}_2 \vee \mathsf{C}_3) = (\mathsf{C}_1 \wedge \mathsf{C}_2) \vee (\mathsf{C}_1 \wedge \mathsf{C}_3)$.
Complements $\mathsf{C} \vee \neg\mathsf{C} = \top$ and $\mathsf{C} \wedge \neg\mathsf{C} = \bot$.
Furthermore, double negation elimination and De Morgan's laws also hold:
Double negation elimination $\neg\neg\mathsf{C} = \mathsf{C}$.
De Morgan $\neg(\mathsf{C}_1 \vee \mathsf{C}_2) = \neg\mathsf{C}_1 \wedge \neg\mathsf{C}_2$ and $\neg(\mathsf{C}_1 \wedge \mathsf{C}_2) = \neg\mathsf{C}_1 \vee \neg\mathsf{C}_2$.

In the following, function "mins" is redefined in terms of the following rewrite rules which are applied modulo associativity and commutativity of $\wedge$ and $\vee$:

$$
\begin{array}{lll}
\alpha_1 \wedge \alpha_2 \to \bot \;\; \text{if } \alpha_1 \in \overline{\alpha_2} & \mathsf{C} \wedge \neg\mathsf{C} \to \bot & \mathsf{C} \vee \neg\mathsf{C} \to \top \\
\alpha_1 \wedge \neg\alpha_2 \to \alpha_1 \;\; \text{if } \alpha_1 \in \overline{\alpha_2} & \mathsf{C} \wedge \top \to \mathsf{C} & \mathsf{C} \wedge \bot \to \bot \\
 & \mathsf{C} \vee \top \to \top & \mathsf{C} \vee \bot \to \mathsf{C} \\
 & \mathsf{C}_1 \vee (\mathsf{C}_1 \wedge \mathsf{C}_2) \to \mathsf{C}_1 & \mathsf{C} \wedge \mathsf{C} \to \mathsf{C}
\end{array}
$$

The first rule introduces an inconsistency when a conjunction includes two different atomic choices for the same clause $c\theta$. The second rule simplifies a conjunction since $\neg\alpha_2$ denotes any atomic choice in $\overline{\alpha_2}$ but $\alpha_1 \in \overline{\alpha_2}$ is more specific. The remaining rules are just oriented axioms or an obvious simplification.

It is often useful to compute the DNF (Disjunctive Normal Form) of a choice expression in order to have a canonical representation:

Definition 5. *Let* C *be a choice expression. Then,* $\mathsf{dnf}(\mathsf{C})$ *is defined as follows:* $\mathsf{dnf}(\mathsf{C}) = \mathsf{mins}(\mathsf{C}')$, *where* $\mathsf{C} \to^* \mathsf{C}' \not\to$ *and the relation* $\to$ *is defined by the following canonical term rewrite system:*

$$
\begin{array}{lll}
\neg\neg\mathsf{C} \to \mathsf{C} & \neg(\mathsf{C}_1 \vee \mathsf{C}_2) \to \neg\mathsf{C}_1 \wedge \neg\mathsf{C}_2 & \mathsf{C}_1 \wedge (\mathsf{C}_2 \vee \mathsf{C}_3) \to (\mathsf{C}_1 \wedge \mathsf{C}_2) \vee (\mathsf{C}_1 \wedge \mathsf{C}_3) \\
 & \neg(\mathsf{C}_1 \wedge \mathsf{C}_2) \to \neg\mathsf{C}_1 \vee \neg\mathsf{C}_2 & (\mathsf{C}_1 \vee \mathsf{C}_2) \wedge \mathsf{C}_3 \to (\mathsf{C}_1 \wedge \mathsf{C}_3) \vee (\mathsf{C}_2 \wedge \mathsf{C}_3)
\end{array}
$$

In the following, if a tree for atom a has n successful derivations computing choice expressions $\mathsf{C}_1, \ldots, \mathsf{C}_n$, we let $\mathsf{dnf}(\neg(\mathsf{C}_1 \vee \ldots \vee \mathsf{C}_n))$ denote its duals.

3.3 SLPDNF-Resolution

Finally, we can formalize the construction of SLPDNF-trees.[7] In principle, they have the same structure of SLDNF-trees. The main difference is that nodes are now labeled with pairs $\langle Q, \mathsf{C}\rangle$ and that the edges are labeled with both an mgu (as before) and a choice expression (when a probabilistic atom is selected). Given a query Q_0, the construction of an SLPDNF-tree for Q_0 starts with a single node labeled with $\langle Q_0, \top\rangle$. An SLPDNF-tree can then be *extended* by selecting a query $\langle Q, \mathsf{C}\rangle$ with $Q = l_1, \ldots, l_n$ which is not yet marked (as failed, success or floundered) and a literal l_i of Q and then proceeding as follows:

- If l_i is a derived atom and $Q \leadsto_\sigma Q'$, then $\langle Q, \mathsf{C}\rangle \leadsto_\sigma \langle Q', \mathsf{C}\rangle$.

[7] SLPDNF stands for Selection rule driven Linear resolution for Probabilistic Definite clauses augmented by the Negation as Failure rule.

- If l_i is a probabilistic atom, then we have a resolution step $\langle Q, \mathsf{C}\rangle \leadsto_{\sigma,(c,\theta,i)} \langle Q', \mathsf{C}'\rangle$ for each clause $c\theta = (h_1 : p_1; \ldots ; h_n : p_n \leftarrow B)\theta \in \mathcal{G}(\mathcal{P})$ such that $Q \leadsto_\sigma Q'$ is a resolution step with respect to atom l_i and clause $h_i\theta \leftarrow B\theta$ and, moreover, $\mathsf{C}' = \mathsf{dnf}(\mathsf{C} \wedge (c, \theta, i)) \neq \bot$.
- If l_i is a negative literal $\neg a$ we have the following possibilities:
  - if a is nonground, the query $\langle Q, \mathsf{C}\rangle$ is marked as *floundered*;
  - if $\mathsf{subs}(Q)$ is undefined, a new tree T' with a single node labeled with $\langle a, \top\rangle$ is added to $\mathcal{T}$ and $\mathsf{subs}(Q)$ is set to the root of T';
  - if $\mathsf{subs}(Q)$ is defined, the corresponding tree cannot be further extended, and it has n leaves marked as success with associated choice expressions $\mathsf{C}_1, \ldots, \mathsf{C}_n$, $n \geq 0$, then we have $\langle Q, \mathsf{C}\rangle \leadsto_{id,\mathsf{C}_a} \langle Q', \mathsf{C}'\rangle$, where Q' is obtained from Q by removing literal l_i, $\mathsf{C}_a = \mathsf{dnf}(\neg(\mathsf{C}_1 \vee \ldots \vee \mathsf{C}_n))$, and $\mathsf{C}' = \mathsf{dnf}(\mathsf{C} \wedge \mathsf{C}_a) \neq \bot$. If $\mathsf{C}' = \bot$ or $n = 0$, the node is marked as failed.

Leaves with empty queries are marked as success. An SLPDNF-tree for a query Q is an SLPDNF-tree in which the root of the main tree is labeled with $\langle Q, \top\rangle$. An SLPDNF-tree is called *successful* (resp. finitely failed) if the main tree is successful (resp. finitely failed). An SLPDNF-derivation for a query Q is a branch in the main tree of an SLPDNF-tree Γ for Q, together with the set of all trees in Γ whose roots can be reached from the nodes of this branch.

Given a successful SLPDNF-derivation for Q—also called a *proof*—of the form $\langle Q, \top\rangle = \langle Q_0, \mathsf{C}_0\rangle \leadsto_{\sigma_1} \langle Q_1, \mathsf{C}_1\rangle \leadsto_{\sigma_2} \cdots \leadsto_{\sigma_n} \langle Q_n, \mathsf{C}_n\rangle = \langle \Box, \mathsf{C}\rangle$, the composition $\sigma_1\sigma_2\ldots\sigma_n$ (restricted to $\mathsf{var}(Q)$) is called a *computed answer substitution* of Q and C represents the worlds where this derivation can be proved.

Example 4. Consider again the LPAD from Example 3 and the same grounding for $p1$, $p2$, and $p3$. As in Example 2, we only consider two groundings for c_2 for simplicity: $\{X/p1, Y/p2\}$ and $\{X/p2, Y/p3\}$. Figure 3 shows the SLPDNF-tree for the query $covid(p1)$. Here, we have two proofs for $covid(p1)$. The choice expression C_1 of the first proof is just $(c_1, \sigma, 1)$, where $\sigma = \{X/p1\}$. The choice expression C_2 of the second proof is given by

$$\begin{array}{l} (c_2, \{X/p1, Y/p2\}, 1) \wedge (c_1, \{X/p2\}, 1) \wedge \neg(c_3, \sigma, 1) \wedge \neg(c_4, \sigma, 1) \\ \vee\, (c_2, \{X/p1, Y/p2\}, 1) \wedge (c_1, \{X/p2\}, 1) \wedge \neg(c_3, \sigma, 1) \wedge (c_5, \sigma, 1) \wedge \neg(c_6, \sigma, 1) \end{array}$$

Here, C_2 represents a total of 9 composite choices which are obtained by replacing negated atomic choices by their corresponding atomic choices (i.e., $\gamma(\mathsf{C}_2)$).

Traditionally, an explanation for a ground query Q is defined as a selection s such that Q is true in the world ω_s associated to this selection. As in [26], we consider in this work a more relaxed notion and say that a composite choice κ is an explanation for ground query Q if Q is true in *all* worlds associated to every selection that extends κ. Formally, κ is an *explanation* for Q if $\omega_s \models Q$ for all selection $s \supseteq \kappa$. We also say that a set of composite choices K is *covering* w.r.t. (ground) query Q if for all $\omega \in \mathcal{W}_\mathcal{P}$ such that $\omega \models Q$ we have $\omega \in \omega_K$ [26].

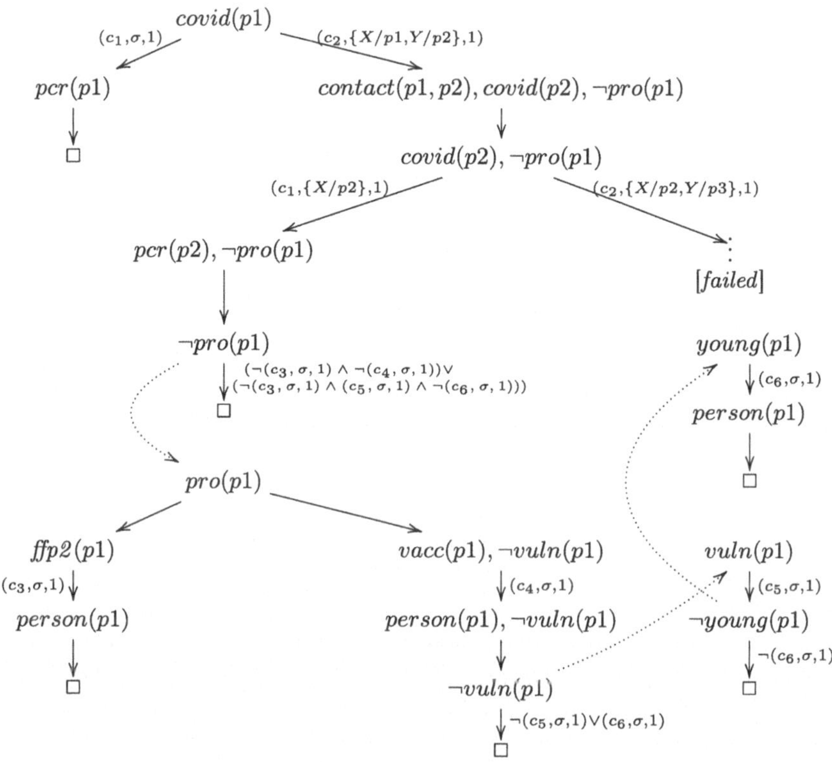

Fig. 3. SLPDNF-tree for query *covid(p1)*, where $\sigma = \{X/p1\}$ and predicates *protected*, *vaccinated*, and *vulnerable* are abbreviated as *pro*, *vacc*, and *vuln*, respectively

Finding the most likely explanation of a query attracted considerable interest in the probabilistic logic programming field (where it is also called *Viterbi proof* [23]). Note that, although it may seem counterintuitive, the selection with the highest probability cannot always be obtained by extending the most likely proof of a query (see [38, Example 6]). Let $\mathsf{expl}_{\mathcal{P}}(Q)$ denote the set of composite choices represented by the choice expressions in the successful leaves of the SLPDNF-tree for Q w.r.t. $\mathcal{G}(\mathcal{P})$, i.e., $\mathsf{expl}_{\mathcal{P}}(Q) = \bigcup_{\mathsf{C} \in L} \gamma(\mathsf{C})$, where L is the set of leaves marked as success in the main SLPDNF-tree. The following result assumes that the query Q is ground, but could be extended to non-ground queries by considering each proof separately and backpropagating the computed answer substitution (which grounds the query since the program is range-restricted [21]).

Theorem 1. *Let $\mathcal{P}$ be a sound program and Q a ground query. Then, $\omega_s \models Q$ iff there exists a composite choice $\kappa \in \mathsf{expl}_{\mathcal{P}}(Q)$ such that $\kappa \subseteq s$.*

Therefore, $\mathsf{expl}(Q)$ is indeed a finite set of explanations which is covering for Q.

4 Proofs as Explanations

In this section, we focus on the representation of the explanations of a query. In principle, we propose to show the proofs of a query (its successful SLPDNF-derivations) as its explanations, from highest to lowest probability. Previous approaches only considered the probability of a standard derivation D computing a composite choice κ so that $P(D) = \prod_{(c,\theta,i)\in\kappa} \pi(c,i)$. Unfortunately, this is not applicable to SLPDNF-derivations computing a choice expression (equivalently, computing a set of composite choices). Therefore, we define the probability of an SLPDNF-derivation as follows:

Definition 6. *Let $\mathcal{P}$ be a program. Given a successful SLPDNF-derivation D for a query Q computing the choice expression C, its associated probability is $P(D) = \sum_{\omega\in\omega_{\gamma(\mathsf{C})}} P(\omega)$, i.e., the sum of the probabilities of all the worlds where the successful derivation can be proved.*

Computing $P(D)$ resembles the problem of computing the probability of a query: summing up the probabilities of the composite choices in $\gamma(\mathsf{C})$ for a computed choice expression C would not be correct since their associated worlds may overlap (i.e., there might be $\kappa, \kappa' \in \gamma(\mathsf{C})$ with $\kappa \neq \kappa'$ such that $\omega_\kappa \cap \omega_{\kappa'} \neq \emptyset$).

There is ample literature on computing the probability of a query, e.g., by combining inference and a conversion to some kind of Boolean formula [13]. We consider this problem an orthogonal topic which is outside of the scope of this paper. Nevertheless, we present a transformational approach that converts the problem of computing the probability of an SLPDNF-derivation into the problem of computing the probability of a query in an LPAD program.

Definition 7. *The first transformation takes an LPAD and returns a new LPAD:*

$$\begin{aligned}\mathsf{trp}(\mathcal{P}) = \{ch_1\!:\!p_1;\ldots;ch_n\!:\!p_n \mid c\theta = (h_1\!:\!p_1;\ldots;h_n\!:\!p_n \leftarrow B)\theta \in \mathcal{G}(\mathcal{P})\\ \textit{and } ch_i = ch(c,\overline{\mathsf{var}}(c)\theta,i),\ i\in\{1,\ldots,n\}\}\end{aligned}$$

where $\overline{\mathsf{var}}(c)$ returns a list *with the clause variables. Our second transformation takes a choice expression and returns a (ground) query as follows:*

$$\begin{array}{ll}\mathsf{trc}(\top) = \mathit{true} & \mathsf{trc}(\bot) = \mathit{false}\\ \mathsf{trc}((c,\theta,i)) = ch(c,\overline{\mathsf{var}}(c)\theta,i) & \mathsf{trc}(\neg\mathsf{C}) = \neg\mathsf{trc}(\mathsf{C})\\ \mathsf{trc}(\mathsf{C}_1\wedge\mathsf{C}_2) = \mathsf{trc}(\mathsf{C}_1),\mathsf{trc}(\mathsf{C}_2) & \mathsf{trc}(\mathsf{C}_1\vee\mathsf{C}_2) = \mathsf{trc}(\mathsf{C}_1);\mathsf{trc}(\mathsf{C}_2)\end{array}$$

Now, given an LPAD $\mathcal{P}$, the probability of an SLPDNF-derivation D computing choice expression C can be obtained from the probability of query $\mathsf{trc}(\mathsf{C})$ in LPAD $\mathsf{trp}(\mathcal{P})$. The correctness of the transformation is an easy consequence of the fact that the probability distribution of $\mathcal{P}$ and $\mathsf{trp}(\mathcal{P})$ is the same and that the query $\mathsf{trc}(\mathsf{C})$ computes an equivalent choice expression in $\mathsf{trp}(\mathcal{P})$; namely, an atomic choice (c,θ,i) has now the form $(c\theta,\{\},i)$ but the structure of the computed choice expression is the same.

Example 5. Consider again LPAD $\mathcal{P}$ from Example 3 and its grounding for $p1$, $p2$, and $p3$. $\mathsf{trp}(\mathcal{P})$ is as follows (for clarity, only the clauses of interest are shown):

$$\begin{array}{l} ch(c_1,[p1],1){:}0.9. \quad ch(c_1,[p2],1){:}0.9. \\ ch(c_2,[p1,p2],1){:}0.4; ch(c_2,[p1,p2],2){:}0.3. \\ ch(c_3,[p1],1){:}0.3; ch(c_3,[p1],2){:}0.4; ch(c_3,[p1],3){:}0.1. \\ ch(c_4,[p1],1){:}0.8. \quad ch(c_5,[p1],1){:}0.6. \quad ch(c_6,[p1],1){:}0.2; ch(c_6,[p1],2){:}0.5. \end{array}$$

The query $covid(p1)$ computes two choice expressions: $\mathsf{C}_1 = (c_1, \sigma, 1)$, where $\sigma = \{X/p1\}$, and $\mathsf{C}_2 =$

$$\begin{array}{l} (c_2,\{X/p1,Y/p2\},1) \wedge (c_1,\{X/p2\},1) \wedge \neg(c_3,\sigma,1) \wedge \neg(c_4,\sigma,1) \\ \vee\ (c_2,\{X/p1,Y/p2\},1) \wedge (c_1,\{X/p2\},1) \wedge \neg(c_3,\sigma,1) \wedge (c_5,\sigma,1) \wedge \neg(c_6,\sigma,1) \end{array} \quad (2)$$

Here, we have $\mathsf{trc}(\mathsf{C}_1) = ch(c_1,[p1],1)$ and $\mathsf{trc}(\mathsf{C}_2) =$

$$\begin{array}{l} ch(c_2,[p1,p2],1), ch(c_1,[p2],1), \neg ch(c_3,[p1],1), \neg ch(c_4,[p1],1) \\ ; ch(c_2,[p1,p2],1), ch(c_1,[p2],1), \neg ch(c_3,[p1],1), ch(c_5,[p1],1), \neg ch(c_6,[p1],1) \end{array}$$

The probability of $\mathsf{trc}(\mathsf{C}_1)$ in $\mathsf{trp}(\mathcal{P})$ using a system like PITA [33] or ProbLog [13] is 0.9, while that of $\mathsf{trc}(\mathsf{C}_2)$ is 0.147168. The probability of the query $covid(p1)$ can be obtained from the probability of the disjunction $\mathsf{trc}(\mathsf{C}_1); \mathsf{trc}(\mathsf{C}_2)$, which gives 0.9147168.

As mentioned before, we propose to show the proofs of a query as explanations, each one with its associated probability. However, instead of using SLPDNF-derivations, each proof will be represented by an AND-tree [7], whose structure is more intuitive. Roughly speaking, while an SLPDNF-derivation is a sequence of queries, in an AND-tree each node is labeled with a literal; when it is resolved with a (possibly probabilistic) clause with body literals $b_1, \ldots, b_n$, we add n nodes as children labeled with $b_1, \ldots, b_n$ (no children if $n = 0$, i.e., the clause is a fact). W.l.o.g., we assume in the following that the initial query is atomic.[8]

In order to represent the AND-trees of the proofs of a query (i.e., its successful SLPDNF-derivations), we follow these guidelines:

- First, we backpropagate the computed mgu's to all queries in the considered derivation, so that all of them become ground (a consequence of the program being range-restricted [21]). Formally, if D has the form $\langle Q_0, \mathsf{C}_0\rangle \leadsto_{\sigma_1} \cdots \leadsto_{\sigma_n} \langle Q_n, \mathsf{C}_n\rangle$, we consider $\langle Q_0\sigma, \mathsf{C}_0\rangle \leadsto_{\sigma'_1} \cdots \leadsto_{\sigma'_n} \langle Q_n\sigma, \mathsf{C}_n\rangle$ instead, where $\sigma = \sigma_1\sigma_1 \ldots \sigma_n$.
- As for the choice expressions labeling the edges of the original derivation, we only show those associated to the resolution of negative literals. The case of (probabilistic) positive atoms is considered redundant since the information given by an atomic choice is somehow implicit in the tree.

[8] Nevertheless, one could consider an arbitrary query Q by adding a clause of the form $main(X_1, \ldots, X_n) \leftarrow Q$ for some fresh predicate $main/n$, where $\mathsf{var}(Q) = \{X_1, \ldots, X_n\}$, and then consider query $main(X_1, \ldots, X_n)$ instead.

– Negative literals $\neg a$ have only one child, $\Box$, and the edge is labeled with the same choice expression as in the SLPDNF-derivation, since this information cannot be extracted from the AND-tree. However, in order to improve its readability, we choose a more intuitive representation for choice expressions, which is inductively defined as follows:

$$\mathsf{chq}(\mathsf{C}) = \begin{cases} h_i\theta & \text{if } \mathsf{C} = (c,\theta,i),\ c = (h_1\!:\!p_1;\ldots;h_n\!:\!p_n \leftarrow B) \\ \neg\mathsf{chq}(\mathsf{C}') & \text{if } \mathsf{C} = \neg\mathsf{C}' \\ \mathsf{chq}(\mathsf{C}_1) \wedge \mathsf{chq}(\mathsf{C}_2) & \text{if } \mathsf{C} = \mathsf{C}_1 \wedge \mathsf{C}_2 \\ \mathsf{chq}(\mathsf{C}_1) \vee \mathsf{chq}(\mathsf{C}_2) & \text{if } \mathsf{C} = \mathsf{C}_1 \vee \mathsf{C}_2 \end{cases}$$

E.g., given the following choice expression from Example 4:

$$\mathsf{C} = (\neg(c_3,\sigma,1) \wedge \neg(c_4,\sigma,1)) \vee (\neg(c_3,\sigma,1) \wedge (c_5,\sigma,1) \wedge \neg(c_6,\sigma,1))$$

we have $\mathsf{chq}(\mathsf{C}) =$

$$(\neg \mathit{ffp2}(p1) \wedge \neg \mathit{vaccinated}(p1)) \vee (\neg \mathit{ffp2}(p1) \wedge \mathit{vulnerable}(p1) \wedge \neg \mathit{young}(p1))$$

Let $\mathsf{chq}(\mathsf{C})$ be the expression labeling the edge from $\neg a$. We further remove the occurrences of $\neg a$ in $\mathsf{chq}(\mathsf{C})$ (if any) since they are clearly redundant.

Consider, for instance, the two proofs of query $\mathit{covid}(p1)$ shown in Fig. 3. The corresponding AND-trees are shown in Fig. 4, each one with its associated probability (see Example 5 above), where the only edge issuing from a negative literal, $\neg \mathit{protected}(p1)$, is labeled with $\mathsf{chq}(\mathsf{C}) = (\neg \mathit{ffp2}(p1) \wedge \neg \mathit{vacc}(p1)) \vee (\neg \mathit{ffp2}(p1) \wedge \mathit{vuln}(p1) \wedge \neg \mathit{young}(p1))$ as computed above (here, *vacc* and *vuln* stands for *vaccinated* and *vulnerable*, as usual).

AND-trees can also be represented in textual form, as shown in Fig. 5 (a), where *protected*, *vaccinated*, and *vulnerable* are abbreviated as *pro*, *vacc*, and *vuln*, respectively. Alternatively, one can easily rewrite the textual representation using natural language. For this purpose, the user should provide appropriate program annotations. For instance, given the following annotation:

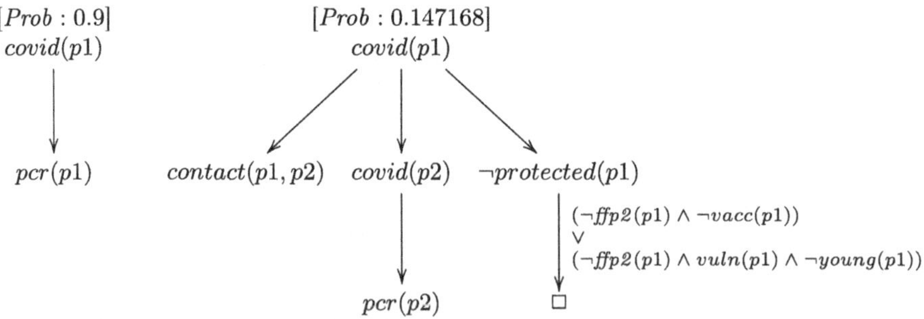

Fig. 4. Representing explanations with AND-trees

Explanations for query $covid(p1)$:

	(a)	(b)
$[Prob : 0.9]$	$covid(p1)$	$p1$ has covid-19 because
	$\quad pcr(p1)$	the pcr test of $p1$ was positive
$[Prob : 0.147168]$	$covid(p1)$	$p1$ has covid-19 because
	$\quad contact(p1, p2)$	$p1$ had contact with $p2$
	$\quad covid(p2)$	and $p2$ has covid-19 because
	$\quad\quad pcr(p2)$	the pcr test of $p2$ was positive
	$\quad \neg pro(p1)$	and $p1$ was not protected because
	$\quad\quad \neg ffp2(p1)$	$p1$ didn't wear an ffp2 mask
	$\quad\quad \neg vacc(p1)$	and $p1$ was not vaccinated
	$\quad\quad ;$	or because
	$\quad\quad \neg ffp2(p1)$	$p1$ didn't wear an ffp2 mask
	$\quad\quad vuln(p1)$	and $p1$ is vulnerable
	$\quad\quad \neg young(p1)$	and $p1$ is not young

Fig. 5. Textual representation for explanations

```
%!read covid(A) as:"A has covid-19"
```

we could replace $covid(p1)$ by the sentence "p1 has covid-19". Given appropriate annotations, the AND-trees in Fig. 4 could also be represented as shown in Fig. 5 (b).

Furthermore, one can easily design an appropriate interface where initially all elements are *folded* and one can click on each fact in order to unfold the list of reasons. In this way, the user could more easily navigate through the explanation and focus on her particular interests. Another improvement could consist in showing the concrete alternatives to negative literals. For example, one can show $\{surgical(p1), cloth(p1), none\}$ when hovering over $\neg ffp2(p1)$.

5 Related Work

We found very few works in which a query-driven inference mechanism for some form of probabilistic logic programs with negation is formalized. Among them, the closest are the works of Riguzzi [29–31], although the aim is different to ours (efficiently computing the marginal probability of a query rather than producing comprehensible explanations). Specifically, [29] proposes an algorithm for performing inference with LPADs where a modification of SLDNF-resolution is used for computing explanations in combination with BDDs. Later on, [31] presents an algorithm for performing inference on non-modularly acyclic LPADs. For this purpose, SLGAD (SLG for Annotated Disjunctions) is introduced, an extension of SLG-resolution for LPAD. Here, the inference mechanism uses tabling to avoid redundant computations and to avoid infinite loops. A distinctive feature of this approach is that the SLGAD-tree computes a set of composite choices which are *mutually incompatible.* This is achieved by performing a sort of *linearization* in the computation of atomic choices, so that every time a choice is done, a new branch where this choice is not selected is also added. This is appropriate for computing the marginal probability of a query but makes the (typically huge) trees much less useful from the point of view of explainability.

The closest work is [30], which presents an extension of SLDNF-resolution for ICL (*Independent Choice Logic* [25]). There are, however, some significant differences to our work. First, the considered language is different (ICL vs LPAD). Second, [30] aims at defining a technique to compute the marginal probability of a query while our work is concerned with the generation of comprehensible explanations. Finally, the shape of the resolution trees are different since we deal with sets of composite choices (represented by choice expressions) so that queries where a negated literal is selected have (at most) one child. Indeed, the introduction of an algebra of choice expressions, together with negated atomic choices for a more compact representation, are significant differences w.r.t. [30], and they are essential for producing appropriate explanations. We also note that [30] does not require grounding the program, although in return it imposes some very strong conditions in order to guarantee that every time a literal is selected, it is ground and, morever, the computed mgu completely grounds the considered clause in the resolution step.

A different approach to computing explanations is introduced in [41]. The aim of this work is similar to ours, but there are significant differences too. On the one hand, the language considered is ProbLog without negation nor annotated disjunctions, so it is a much simpler setting (it can be seen as a particular case of the language considered in this work). On the other hand, the generated explanations are *programs* (a set of ground probabilistic clauses), which are obtained through different unfolding transformations. In fact, [41] can be seen as a complementary approach to the one presented here.

Finally, let us mention several approaches to improve the generation of explanations in some closely related but non-probabilistic fields: logic programming and *answer set programming* (ASP) [6]. First, [9] presents a tool, `xclingo`, for generating explanations from annotated ASP programs. Annotations are then used to construct derivation trees containing textual explanations. Moreover, the language allows the user to select *which* atoms or rules should be included in the explanations. On the other hand, [4] presents so-called *justifications* for ASP programs with constraints, now based on a goal-directed semantics. As in the previous work, the user can decide the level of detail required in a justification tree, as well as add annotations to produce justifications using natural language. Some of the ideas presented in Sect. 4 follow an approach which is similar to that of [4]. Other related approaches are the *off-line and on-line justifications* of [22], which provide a graph-based explanation of the truth value of a literal, and the *causal graph justifications* of [8], which explains why a literal is contained in an answer set (though negative literals are not represented). Obviously, our work shares the aim of these papers regarding the generation of comprehensible explanations in a logic setting. However, the considered language and the applied techniques are different. Nevertheless, we believe that our approach could be enriched with some of the ideas in these works.

6 Concluding Remarks and Future Work

In this work, we have presented a new approach for query-driven inference in a probabilistic logic language, thus defining an extension of the SLDNF-resolution principle, called SLPDNF-resolution, that keeps the structure of the original SLDNF-trees. Here, each proof of a query is now accompanied by a so-called *choice expression* that succinctly represents the possible worlds where this proof holds. We have also shown that choice expressions form a Boolean algebra, which allows us to manipulate them in a very flexible way. Furthermore, the generated proofs are especially appropriate to produce comprehensible explanations for a given query. In particular, we represent each proof in a way that its causal structure becomes evident, using either AND-trees or an equivalent textual representation using natural language.

As future work, we consider several extensions. On the one hand, we plan to deal with a broader class of programs. For this purpose, we will explore the definition of an extension of SLG-resolution [10] and/or some of the approaches for goal-directed execution of ASP programs (e.g., [19]). On the other hand, we would also like to extend the inference mechanism in order to include *evidences* (that is, ground facts whose true/false value is known). Finally, on the practical side, we plan to develop a robust tool for generating explanations that can be used with ProbLog and LPAD programs. Such a tool will allow us to evaluate in practice the usefulness of the techniques presented in this work.

Acknowledgements. I would like to thank the anonymous reviewers for their suggestions to improve this paper.

References

1. Apt, K.R.: From Logic Programming to Prolog. Prentice Hall (1997)
2. Apt, K.R., Bezem, M.: Acyclic programs. New Gener. Comput. **9**(3–4), 335–64 (1991). https://doi.org/10.1007/BF03037168
3. Apt, K.R., Doets, K.: A new definition of SNDNF-resolution. J. Log. Program. **18**(2), 177–190 (1994). https://doi.org/10.1016/0743-1066(94)90051-5
4. Arias, J., Carro, M., Chen, Z., Gupta, G.: Justifications for goal-directed constraint answer set programming. In: Ricca, F., Russo, A., Greco, S., Leone, N., Artikis, A., Friedrich, G., Fodor, P., Kimmig, A., Lisi, F.A., Maratea, M., Mileo, A., Riguzzi, F. (eds.) Proceedings of the 36th International Conference on Logic Programming (ICLP Technical Communications 2020). EPTCS, vol. 325, pp. 59–72 (2020). https://doi.org/10.4204/EPTCS.325.12
5. Arrieta, A.B., Rodríguez, N.D., Ser, J.D., Bennetot, A., Tabik, S., Barbado, A., García, S., Gil-Lopez, S., Molina, D., Benjamins, R., Chatila, R., Herrera, F.: Explainable artificial intelligence (XAI): concepts, taxonomies, opportunities and

challenges toward responsible AI. Inf. Fusion **58**, 82–115 (2020). https://doi.org/10.1016/j.inffus.2019.12.012
6. Brewka, G., Eiter, T., Truszczynski, M.: Answer set programming at a glance. Commun. ACM **54**(12), 92–103 (2011). https://doi.org/10.1145/2043174.2043195
7. Bruynooghe, M.: A practical framework for the abstract interpretation of logic programs. J. Log. Program. **10**(2), 91–124 (1991)
8. Cabalar, P., Fandinno, J., Fink, M.: Causal graph justifications of logic programs. Theory Pract. Log. Program. **14**(4–5), 603–618 (2014). https://doi.org/10.1017/S1471068414000234
9. Cabalar, P., Fandinno, J., Muñiz, B.: A system for explainable answer set programming. In: Ricca, F., Russo, A., Greco, S., Leone, N., Artikis, A., Friedrich, G., Fodor, P., Kimmig, A., Lisi, F.A., Maratea, M., Mileo, A., Riguzzi, F. (eds.) Proceedings of the 36th International Conference on Logic Programming (ICLP Technical Communications 2020). EPTCS, vol. 325, pp. 124–136 (2020). https://doi.org/10.4204/EPTCS.325.19
10. Chen, W., Warren, D.S.: Tabled evaluation with delaying for general logic programs. J. ACM **43**(1), 20–74 (1996). https://doi.org/10.1145/227595.227597
11. Clark, K.L.: Negation as failure. In: Gallaire, H., Minker, J. (eds.) Proceedings of the Symposium on Logic and Data Bases, pp. 293–322. Advances in Data Base Theory. Plemum Press, New York (1977). https://doi.org/10.1007/978-1-4684-3384-5_11
12. EU, EEA: Regulation (EU) 2016/679 on the protection of natural persons with regard to the processing of personal data and on the free movement of such data. Available from: https://eur-lex.europa.eu/eli/reg/2016/679/oj
13. Fierens, D., den Broeck, G.V., Renkens, J., Shterionov, D.S., Gutmann, B., Thon, I., Janssens, G., Raedt, L.D.: Inference and learning in probabilistic logic programs using weighted Boolean formulas. Theory Pract. Log. Program. **15**(3), 358–401 (2015). https://doi.org/10.1017/S1471068414000076
14. Gelder, A.V., Ross, K.A., Schlipf, J.S.: The well-founded semantics for general logic programs. J. ACM **38**(3), 620–650 (1991). https://doi.org/10.1145/116825.116838
15. Gelfond, M., Lifschitz, V.: The stable model semantics for logic programming. In: Kowalski, R.A., Bowen, K.A. (eds.) Proceedings of the 5th International Conference on Logic Programming (ICLP'88), pp. 1070–1080. MIT Press (1988)
16. Kersting, K., Raedt, L.D.: Towards combining inductive logic programming with Bayesian networks. In: Rouveirol, C., Sebag, M. (eds.) Proceedings of the 11th International Conference on Inductive Logic Programming (ILP 2001). Lecture Notes in Computer Science, vol. 2157, pp. 118–131. Springer (2001). https://doi.org/10.1007/3-540-44797-0_10
17. Lifschitz, V.: On the declarative semantics of logic programs with negation. In: Minker, J. (ed.) Foundations of Deductive Databases and Logic Programming, pp. 177–192. Morgan Kaufmann (1988). https://doi.org/10.1016/B978-0-934613-40-8.50008-7
18. Lloyd, J.W.: Foundations of Logic Programming, 2nd edn. Springer (1987). https://doi.org/10.1007/978-3-642-83189-8
19. Marple, K., Bansal, A., Min, R., Gupta, G.: Goal-directed execution of answer set programs. In: Schreye, D.D., Janssens, G., King, A. (eds.) Principles and Practice of Declarative Programming (PPDP'12), pp. 35–44. ACM (2012). https://doi.org/10.1145/2370776.2370782
20. Muggleton, S.: Stochastic logic programs. In: de Raedt, L. (ed.) Advances in Inductive Logic Programming, pp. 254–264. IOS Press (1996)

21. Muggleton, S.H.: Learning stochastic logic programs. Electron. Trans. Artif. Intell. **4**(B), 141–153 (2000). http://www.ep.liu.se/ej/etai/2000/015/
22. Pontelli, E., Son, T.C., El-Khatib, O.: Justifications for logic programs under answer set semantics. Theory Pract. Log. Program. **9**(1), 1–56 (2009). https://doi.org/10.1017/S1471068408003633
23. Poole, D.: Logic programming, abduction and probability—a top-down anytime algorithm for estimating prior and posterior probabilities. New Gener. Comput. **11**(3), 377–400 (1993). https://doi.org/10.1007/BF03037184
24. Poole, D.: Probabilistic horn abduction and Bayesian networks. Artif. Intell. **64**(1), 81–129 (1993). https://doi.org/10.1016/0004-3702(93)90061-F
25. Poole, D.: The independent choice logic for modelling multiple agents under uncertainty. Artif. Intell. **94**(1–2), 7–56 (1997). https://doi.org/10.1016/S0004-3702(97)00027-1
26. Poole, D.: Abducing through negation as failure: stable models within the independent choice logic. J. Log. Program. **44**(1–3), 5–35 (2000). https://doi.org/10.1016/S0743-1066(99)00071-0
27. Raedt, L.D., Kimmig, A., Toivonen, H.: ProbLog: A probabilistic Prolog and its application in link discovery. In: Veloso, M.M. (ed.) Proceedings of the 20th International Joint Conference on Artificial Intelligence (IJCAI 2007), pp. 2462–2467 (2007). http://ijcai.org/Proceedings/07/Papers/396.pdf
28. Reiter, R.: A theory of diagnosis from first principles. Artif. Intell. **32**(1), 57–95 (1987). https://doi.org/10.1016/0004-3702(87)90062-2
29. Riguzzi, F.: A top down interpreter for LPAD and CP-logic. In: Basili, R., Pazienza, M.T. (eds.) AI*IA 2007: Artificial Intelligence and Human-Oriented Computing, 10th Congress of the Italian Association for Artificial Intelligence, Rome, Italy, September 10-13, 2007, Proceedings. Lecture Notes in Computer Science, vol. 4733, pp. 109–120. Springer (2007). https://doi.org/10.1007/978-3-540-74782-6_11, https://doi.org/10.1007/978-3-540-74782-6_11
30. Riguzzi, F.: Extended semantics and inference for the independent choice logic. Log. J. IGPL **17**(6), 589–629 (2009). https://doi.org/10.1093/JIGPAL/JZP025
31. Riguzzi, F.: SLGAD resolution for inference on logic programs with annotated disjunctions. Fundam. Informaticae **102**(3–4), 429–466 (2010). https://doi.org/10.3233/FI-2010-313
32. Riguzzi, F.: Foundations of Probabilistic Logic Programming: Languages, Semantics. River Publishers, Inference and Learning (2018)
33. Riguzzi, F., Swift, T.: Well-definedness and efficient inference for probabilistic logic programming under the distribution semantics. Theory Pract. Log. Program. **13**(2), 279–302 (2013). https://doi.org/10.1017/S1471068411000664
34. Riguzzi, F., Swift, T.: A survey of probabilistic logic programming. In: Kifer, M., Liu, Y.A. (eds.) Declarative Logic Programming: Theory, Systems, and Applications, ACM Books, vol. 20, pp. 185–228. ACM/Morgan & Claypool (2018). https://doi.org/10.1145/3191315.3191319
35. Ross, K.A.: Modular acyclicity and tail recursion in logic programs. In: Rosenkrantz, D.J. (ed.) Proceedings of the Tenth ACM SIGACT-SIGMOD-SIGART Symposium on Principles of Database Systems, pp. 92–101. ACM Press (1991). https://doi.org/10.1145/113413.113422
36. Sato, T.: A statistical learning method for logic programs with distribution semantics. In: Sterling, L. (ed.) Logic Programming, Proceedings of the Twelfth International Conference on Logic Programming, pp. 715–729, Tokyo, Japan, June 13–16, 1995. MIT Press (1995)

37. Sato, T., Kameya, Y.: PRISM: a language for symbolic-statistical modeling. In: Proceedings of the Fifteenth International Joint Conference on Artificial Intelligence, IJCAI 97, Nagoya, Japan, August 23–29, 1997, 2 Volumes, pp. 1330–1339. Morgan Kaufmann (1997). http://ijcai.org/Proceedings/97-2/Papers/078.pdf
38. Shterionov, D.S., Renkens, J., Vlasselaer, J., Kimmig, A., Meert, W., Janssens, G.: The most probable explanation for probabilistic logic programs with annotated disjunctions. In: Davis, J., Ramon, J. (eds.) Proceedings of the 24th International Conference on Inductive Logic Programming (ILP 2014). Lecture Notes in Computer Science, vol. 9046, pp. 139–153. Springer (2014). https://doi.org/10.1007/978-3-319-23708-4_10
39. Vennekens, J., Denecker, M., Bruynooghe, M.: CP-logic: a language of causal probabilistic events and its relation to logic programming. Theory Pract. Log. Program. **9**(3), 245–308 (2009). https://doi.org/10.1017/S1471068409003767https://doi.org/10.1017/S1471068409003767
40. Vennekens, J., Verbaeten, S., Bruynooghe, M.: Logic programs with annotated disjunctions. In: Demoen, B., Lifschitz, V. (eds.) Logic Programming, 20th International Conference, ICLP 2004, Saint-Malo, France, September 6–10, 2004, Proceedings. Lecture Notes in Computer Science, vol. 3132, pp. 431–445. Springer (2004). https://doi.org/10.1007/978-3-540-27775-0_30
41. Vidal, G.: Explanations as programs in probabilistic logic programming. In: Hanus, M., Igarashi, A. (eds.) Proceedings of the 16th International Symposium on Functional and Logic Programming (FLOPS 2022). Lecture Notes in Computer Science, vol. 13215, pp. 205–223. Springer (2022). https://doi.org/10.1007/978-3-030-99461-7_12
42. Vidal, G.: Explaining explanations in probabilistic logic programming. CoRR **abs/2401.17045** (2024). https://doi.org/10.48550/ARXIV.2401.17045

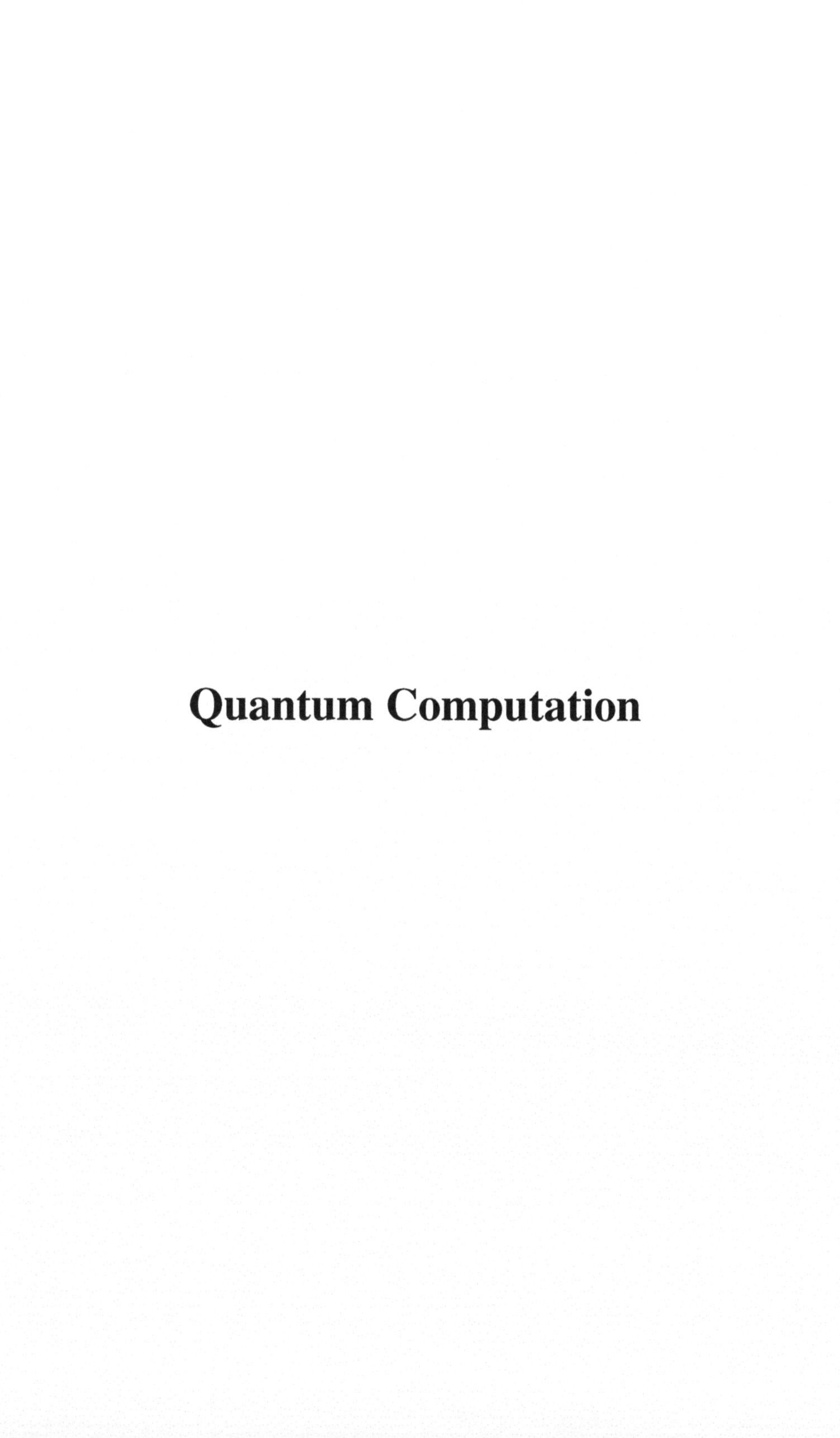

Quantum Computation

Quantum Programming Without the Quantum Physics

Jun Inoue(✉)

National Institute of Advanced Industrial Science and Technology, 1-8-31 Midorigaoka Ikeda, Osaka, Japan
jun.inoue@aist.go.jp

Abstract. We propose a quantum programming paradigm where all data are familiar classical data, and the only non-classical element is a random number generator that can return results with negative probability. Currently, the vast majority of quantum programming languages instead work with quantum data types made up of qubits. The description of their behavior relies on heavy linear algebra and many interdependent concepts and intuitions from quantum physics, which takes dedicated study to understand. We demonstrate that the proposed view of quantum programming explains its central concepts and constraints in more accessible, computationally relevant terms. This is achieved by systematically reducing everything to the existence of that negative-probability random generator, avoiding mention of advanced physics. This makes quantum programming more accessible to programmers without a deep background in physics or linear algebra. The bulk of this paper is written with such an audience in mind. As a working vehicle, we lay out a simple quantum programming language under this paradigm, showing that not only can it express all quantum algorithms, it also naturally captures the semantics of measurement without ever mentioning qubits or collapse.

Keywords: Quantum programming · Probabilistic programming · Programming model

1 Introduction

In this article, we reconstruct quantum programming in terms that are readily intelligible to programmers with only a passing knowledge of linear algebra or quantum theory. The key idea, inspired by Aaronson [2] and Mu and Bird [17], is that *quantum programming is probabilistic programming with negative probabilities*, where "probabilistic programming" just means "the writing of programs that call random number generators".[1]

[1] In the literature, "probabilistic programming" has come to mean a related but broader set of activities, which is discussed in the related works section.

O. Kiselyov (Ed.): APLAS 2024, LNCS 15194, pp. 155–175, 2024.
https://doi.org/10.1007/978-981-97-8943-6_8

We show that universal quantum computation (in the sense of computational universality [4]) can be achieved by leveraging nothing but a random number generator that returns certain results with negative probability. A negative-probability outcome is like a normal outcome, except that it can cancel with a positive-probability outcome that leads to the same machine state; canceled outcomes are then never observed. What emerges is a new programming model, quantum probabilistic programming (QPP), which dispenses entirely with the notion of qubit, working with familiar classical data. Quantum weirdness is instead pushed into the computational effect of quantum non-determinism.

Of course, probability in the usual sense cannot be negative. Negative probabilities are probabilities in only a generalized sense, but by drawing parallels with ordinary probabilities, this concept helps to foster intuitions about the behavior of quantum programs. Constraints on quantum computation like reversibility are derived from commonsense assumptions as to what characterizes probabilistic programming, rather than imposed on an ad-hoc basis. Even measurements can be understood without qubits as effective loss of signs on probabilities, again allowing constraints to be explained rather than imposed.

Why do this? The point of the exercise is to rectify the current situation in which quantum programming is very difficult to get into. A dizzying array of quantum programming languages exist [5,7,11,14,16,21,23–25,27,29,30], but they invariably define a qubit type, which denotes a 2-dimensional Hilbert space, arrays of which denote tensor products, which are operated on by unitaries. This is already enough non-computer-related jargon to give the novice a run for Wikipedia, but it is only the beginning. There follows a journey of confusion through intuition-free abstractions and unexpected constraints, with many of the latter coming out of seemingly random physics facts. To wit:

- Qubits' distinguishing feature is their ability to be in superposition, but the meaning of this is already murky. Many sources say it means being "0 and 1 simultaneously", enabling massive parallelization, but prominent experts warn against this intuition [3], offering no good alternatives.
- Qubits can't be copied due to no-cloning, a result which holds because cloning would violate Heisenberg's uncertainty principle.
- All operations must be reversible because it must be unitary, which in turn is because of the general form of solutions to Schrödinger's equation.
- Qubits can't be discarded willy-nilly because discarding somehow involves measurement. Can't we just throw away qubits without looking at them?
- Measurement of one qubit modifies other entangled qubits, but this can't be used to send information because of special relativity.
- Entanglement seems to mean correlation between qubits' values, but initializing qubits to all 0's, giving perfect correlation, somehow doesn't count.
- Entanglement underlies many counter-intuitive behaviors: for instance, merely referencing qubit A to decide whether to flip qubit B can affect the value of qubit A later on (see [20, Sect. 3] for an example).

While trying to internalize all of this, one must wade through heaps of complex-number linear algebra, which is alien to most other kinds of programming.

The root of the problem is that quantum computing has been framed in terms familiar to physicists and not to computer scientists, let alone ordinary programmers. As such, one has to navigate a sea of concepts and facts that offer rich physical meanings but little intuition on how they help or constrain program construction. It is quite telling how textbooks in this field generally start with expositions of quantum physics rather than programming models or primitives [8,12,18]. Existing quantum programming languages have inherited this physics-centric, linear algebra-heavy view, starting with the concept of qubits. As such, until programmers grok a nontrivial amount of quantum physics, they can barely have a sense that they've understood the principles behind a quantum programming language's design, making it seem arbitrary and unpredictable.

In this article, we show that negative probabilities provide a simpler, more computationally appealing metaphor for explaining quantum programming concepts, facts, and constraints than qubits. For example:

- Data inside quantum computers are familiar classical data. They do not entangle, and they can be copied.
- Superposition is just a list of possible outcomes of a randomized trial, weighted by probability. It's just that, unlike with classical randomness, the outcomes can interact—they can later meet and cancel if they occur with opposite-sign probabilities.
- Unitarity is just the law that probabilities always add to 1, in the presence of negative probabilities.
- Measurement is the loss of signs from some of the probabilities. Its irreversibility is helpful in only limited contexts because it merely succeeds in being irreversible at throwing away the advantages of quantum computing.
- Discarding behaves like measurement because both are about information leakage that ruins the programmer's control over cancellation.

In this way, negative probabilities tie together all the concepts that a programmer needs to digest in order to get a feel for quantum programming.

Though some authors have written on the idea of negative probabilities before, it was for different purposes. Aaronson [1,2] quipped that quantum *theory* (not programming) is what one gets by incorporating negative numbers to probability theory. Mu and Bird, in an apparently unpublished draft [17], explored qubit-less programming with negative probabilities, trying to understand quantum non-determinism as a monad-like structure. But neither tried to systematically reduce concepts to negative probabilities, putting together a comprehensive narrative of how quantum programming works, embodied in a concrete programming language. This usage, to our knowledge, is novel.

Our treatment of measurement is especially noteworthy. We split uncertainty in a quantum program into two layers, a quantum layer with signed probabilities and a classical layer with ordinary, unsigned probabilities. We then explain measurement as a movement of uncertainty from the quantum to the classical layer--effectively, a loss of signs. While mathematically just a rehash of ensembles and density matrices, this view again offers great simplifying power. Not only does it avoid discussions of qubits and their intricate behavior under measurement,

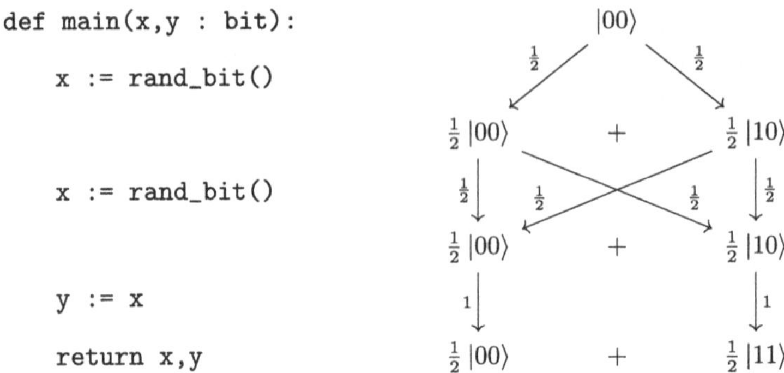

Fig. 1. Example of a classical probabilistic program and its transition diagram. Each row of nodes in the diagram shows which worlds (i.e. states) the program can be in at the source line aligned with that row, as a sum weighted by probabilities. Arrows show which worlds transition to which given the source lines next to them, labeled with transition probabilities.

it also clarifies the relationship between measurement, discarding, output, and information leakage, all while relying on just one difference between quantum and classical randomness---signed probabilities.

The contributions of this paper are as follows.

- We define what it means for classical probabilistic programming (reviewed in Sect. 2) to be fitted with negative probabilities, giving a simple quantum programming language QPPL. We show how the other features of quantum programming arise from that one modification (Sect. 3).
- Through a simple programming example, we show how negative probabilities help to understand and motivate quantum algorithms (Sect. 4).
- We show how QPP offers an understanding of measurement and discarding that does not depend on the concept of qubits. By splitting uncertainty into quantum and classical layers, we can formulate them as losses of control over cancellation due to information leakage (Sect. 5).
- We define a formal semantics for QPPL and show that it is both implementable and computationally universal (Sect. 6).

Sections 2 to 5 should be accessible to readers without a background in quantum computing or programming language theory. A modicum of basic linear algebra over the real numbers is required: the concept of linearity, conditions for injectivity of linear maps, dot products, and orthogonality.

2 Background: Classical Probabilistic Programming

In this section, we review how classical probabilistic programming and its semantics can be conceptualized, setting up notation and vocabulary.

Figure 1 shows an example of a (contrived) classical probabilistic program in a toy language, CPPL. On the left is a program that declares two inputs `x,y` of type `bit`, both implicitly initialized to 0. It generates a random bit twice, storing the result in `x` each time, overwriting the first result by the second. The second result is copied to `y`, and the two copies are returned as the final program result. For simplicity, CPPL only allows `return` at the end of the program.

The program's source lines are spaced apart to align with the state transition diagram on the right. The diagram's node labels $|xy\rangle$ show the memory contents of a machine executing the program. The arrows show possible transitions, weighted by the probabilities by which those transitions happen. Randomized operations like `rand_bit()` make multiple outgoing transitions from each node and are said to be *non-deterministic*. Non-randomized operations like `y := x` create one transition out of every node and are said to be *deterministic*.

The nodes are called *worlds* because they represent different potential states of the world: for example, the $|00\rangle$ on the second row of the diagram represents a world in which the first `rand_bit()` returned `0`, while the $|10\rangle$ on its right represents an alternate reality in which the `rand_bit()` gave `1`. A path in the transition diagram is called a *world line*. The probability that a world line is realized (i.e. that execution follows that path) is given by the product of the weights on the arrows along that path.

After executing each line in the program, the program can be in one of several worlds. This uncertainty is captured by a *superposition*, written as a sum of worlds weighted by their likelihoods. For instance, the program state $\frac{1}{2}|00\rangle + \frac{1}{2}|10\rangle$ means $x, y = 0, 0$ or $x, y = 1, 0$ with equal probability at that point in the program. In Fig. 1, the transition diagram's nodes are arranged into rows of such sums. These sums are just a notation for vectors over $\mathbb{R}$, called *state vectors*, which list the weights of all worlds. For example, $\frac{1}{2}|00\rangle + \frac{1}{2}|10\rangle$ denotes the vector $[\frac{1}{2}, 0, \frac{1}{2}, 0]^T$, where we listed coefficients for $|00\rangle, |01\rangle, |10\rangle, |11\rangle$ in that order. The operations in the language denote mappings between state vectors. A single-world state vector like $|xy\rangle$ is called a *basis state*. In matrix notation, a basis state has 1 in exactly one place, with 0 everywhere else.

Not all vectors and mappings between them are implementable, however. For the weights to make sense as probabilities, we need two commonsense properties:

- Law of total probability: probabilities appearing in a program state must sum to 1, and operations must preserve this total.
- Linearity: the state vector after any operation should be a linear function of the state vector before the operation. Equivalently, the probability of landing in a given world should equal the sum of the probabilities of realization of all world lines leading up to that world.

Linearity means that operations form matrices. By convention, its j-th *column* lists the probabilities of transitions going out of the j-th basis sate.

3 Quantum Programming as Probabilistic Programming

In this section, we derive quantum programming as a modification to classical probabilistic programming by allowing for negative transition weights, turning CPPL into a quantum programming language QPPL. We explain how this modification leads to such concepts as destructive interference, unitarity, and reversibility, as well as the changes it mandates on programming languages.

In QPPL, a state vector $\sum_x q_x|x\rangle$ has real but possibly negative weights $q_x \in [-1..1]$ with $\sum_x |q_x|^2 = 1$, i.e. it has vector length 1 instead of total 1. Each q_x is called a *probability amplitude*, or *amplitude* for short. Amplitudes are related to (classical) probabilities as follows: like in CPPL, a QPPL program ending in state vector $\sum_x q_x|x\rangle$ produces output by choosing a world randomly from that sum and having that world dictate the output, but in QPPL, world $|x\rangle$ is chosen with probability $|q_x|^2$. Thus, amplitudes still measure likelihoods, just on a different scale than probabilities, and with sign.

The addition of sign with the square relationship with probabilities is the *only* modification we impose on probabilistic programming in this section; all other changes fall out as byproducts. For instance, the vector length being 1 is just the law of total probability, accounting for the square relationship. Operations must preserve these lengths instead of totals. Operations remain linear, though note that they are linear in q_x, not $|q_x|^2$.

Remark 1. The reader might find the square relationship between amplitudes and probabilities rather arbitrary, but it's more or less mathematically forced. Aaronson [1] gives an elementary proof that other exponents lead either to classical probabilistic programming or to a trivial programming model where all operations are deterministic. Gleason's theorem gives an even more general argument, though its assumptions need physical intuitions to justify.

Figure 2 illustrates the resulting changes to programming. The quantum cointoss `qrand_bit(x)` takes a variable as argument, and its effect depends on the variable's value: if `x` is 0, then it sets `x` to 0 or 1 with equal probability amplitudes; if `x` is 1, then it sets `x` to 0 or 1 with equal but opposite-sign amplitudes.[2] Whereas splitting into two equal probabilities meant splitting into $\frac{1}{2}$ and $\frac{1}{2}$, with amplitudes it means splitting into $\frac{1}{\sqrt{2}}$ and $\frac{1}{\sqrt{2}}$, due to the scale difference. Instead of assignment `y := x`, QPPL uses XOR-assignment `y ^= x`, which sets `y` to the bitwise XOR of `y` and `x`. This is because of reversibility, discussed below.

An `if` statement works just like in classical probabilistic programming: each world independently evaluates the condition to decide whether or not to execute the body. In this case, the body `qnegate()` does nothing with probability amplitude -1, i.e. with certainty but with negative amplitude. The effect is to flip the sign of the probability amplitude of being in the current world. Put together, `if x == 1: qnegate()` flips the amplitude's sign in those worlds where `x` is `1`.[3]

---

[2] Conventional quantum programming calls this the Hadamard gate.

[3] Conventional quantum programming calls this the Z gate.

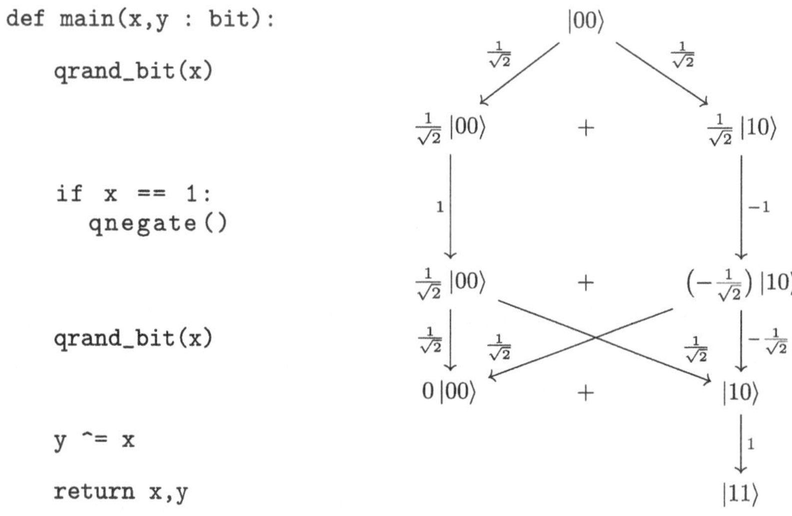

Fig. 2. Example of a quantum probabilistic program and its transition diagram.

The main difference made by negative weights is the possibility of cancellation, known as *destructive interference*. As before, we land in a world with probability amplitude given by the sum of products of amplitudes on all incoming world lines. But since amplitudes can be negative, they can sum to zero, like in the bottom-left node of the diagram in Fig. 2. Thus, after the second call to `qrand_bit(x)`, the example program has *zero* chances of landing in world $|00\rangle$.

Destructive interference causes a subtle change in the relationship between the worlds. Before, the worlds were completely independent trials that never interact, as only one of them could really happen at a time. With destructive interference, we must think that all worlds are simultaneously real, interacting to decide which possibilities live and which ones die. But this interaction happens only when worlds evolve to identical states, which is tricky to control under reversibility constraints discussed below. Using it to consolidate information from multiple worlds is the central challenge in quantum programming [3].

The law of total probability on amplitudes has two interrelated consequences.

- Preservation of orthogonality: because the dot product can be expressed by vector lengths,[4] preserving lengths means preserving dot products, hence preserving orthogonality. Basis states are orthogonal, so all operations must map them to orthogonal states, i.e. the corresponding matrix's columns must be orthogonal. This property is called *isometricity* or, in the absence of memory allocation, *unitarity*.
- Reversibility: as linear maps are non-injective precisely when they collapse several dimensions into one (or to the trivial space $\{0\}$), every orthogonality-preserving matrix is injective. Thus, a quantum program must be built up

[4] Known as the polarization identity: for real vectors, $u \cdot v = \frac{1}{2}(|u+v|^2 - |u|^2 - |v|^2)$.

from only injective operations. Such a program is said to be *reversible*, as it can be executed in reverse, undoing its operations one by one [10].

These are prices to be paid for negative amplitudes and destructive interference.

Preservation of orthogonality explains the design of `qrand_bit(x)`, characterized as the simplest non-deterministic operation, an analogue of the classical coin toss. To have orthogonal (hence disinct) columns, it must change its behavior depending on the world, i.e. on preexisting memory contents. Thus, it must read a variable `x` before deciding how to generate the random bit. As the simplest non-deterministic operation, it shouldn't read any other variables if possible; but that forces it to write to `x` as well, for the only alternative is to write to some `y` without reading it, failing to behave differently on worlds differing only in the preexisting value of `y`. If we want the operation to give `0` and `1` with equal amplitudes (as a coin toss should) at least when the preexisting value of `x` is `0`, the transition matrix (in the simple case where `x` is the only program variable) must have the form $\frac{1}{\sqrt{2}}\begin{bmatrix}1 & a\\ 1 & b\end{bmatrix}$. Column orthogonality and normalization force $a = -b = \pm 1$, which gives `qrand_bit(x)` up to a choice of sign.

Reversibility induces a more pervasive change, which has been studied extensively in classical languages [10]. An assignment like `y := x` is quintessentially irreversible, as it erases information about the value previously held by `y`. A standard trick is to use XOR-assignment `y ^= x` instead, which can be undone by executing `y ^= x` once more. But for this reversal to work, the value of `x` must remain undisturbed by the modification to `y`. QPPL ensures this by requiring that the right-hand side `x` (which in general can be an expression referencing multiple variables) does not mention the assigned-to variable `y`.

A similar provision is needed for conditionals. To undo a conditional like `if COND: BODY`, it is necessary to know whether the `BODY` was executed and therefore needs to be undone. For this, it is necessary to preserve the value of `COND` across the execution of `BODY`. QPPL ensures this by requiring that `BODY` does not assign to variables mentioned in `COND`.

Note that QPPL requires reversibility only at the level of statements—things that can appear on lines of their own, like XOR-assignments, `if` blocks, `qrand_bit(x)`, or `qnegate()`. The parts of statements that calculate values (called expressions), like `COND` above or the right-hand side of an XOR-assignment, need not be reversible. They can use non-injective functions like logical AND or arithmetic, but in exchange, they cannot contain statements like XOR-assignment.

Remark 2. Readers familiar with conventional, qubit-based quantum programming may have noticed that QPP is really "just" a change in perspective:

- QPP views a computation from an observer inside the computer, running along a particular world-line and describing how each step evolves the current world into one or more futures.
- Conventional quantum programming views the computation from an observer external to the worlds who can see all the branching structure.

For readers familiar with the list monad, the former is analogous to coding in monadic style in that monad, while the latter is like direct manipulation of lists. Quantum non-determinism is not quite a monad but has return and bind that satisfy the monad laws [17,28]. The point of this paper is to show what a conceptual difference this change in perspective makes.

Remark 3. Quantum theory famously requires complex numbers to describe, so the reader may wonder why we only mention real numbers, and whether that constitutes a limitation. QPP can in fact be formulated equally well with complex numbers. Just change "negative probabilities" to "complex probabilities", $q_x \in [0..1]$ to $q_x \in \mathbb{C} \wedge |q_x| \leq 1$, and "square" to "square-absolute value", and most of this paper stands, verbatim. We nonetheless left out complex numbers because:

- They are not necessary. A complex-amplitude state vector $\sum_x (a_x + ib_x)|x\rangle$ with $a_x, b_x \in \mathbb{R}$ can be encoded by real amplitudes as $\sum_x a_x|x0\rangle + \sum_x b_x|x1\rangle$ with just 1 bit of overhead. This simple encoding can implement any complex-amplitude computation with only constant slowdown [4,6].
- They are less intuitive. What they add is the ability to cancel along axes other than the real line. While this extra freedom is handy in algorithms like Shor's, introducing complex linear algebra with its lesser known inner product seems ill-motivated until one gets to such algorithms. Complex or real, in QPP it is the ability to have outcomes occur with opposite signs and cancel that defines quantum programming, and we feel the extra freedom obscures this idea.

Whether generalizing to complex numbers is worth the conceptual complication is an interesting open question. Because complex amplitudes can be so simply encoded by real ones, we suspect one can comfortably program all the way with real numbers, but whether that works in practice remains to be seen.

4 Programming Example

In this section, we show an example that illustrates what it is like to program in QPPL. This shows how the QPP point of view can be a useful device for explaining or motivating quantum algorithms, at least in simple cases.

Figure 3 shows Deutsch's algorithm in QPPL. The task it performs is: given a black-box mapping `f` from a single bit to a single bit, determine if `f` is a constant mapping (returning 1 if non-constant). The displayed algorithm does so in time taken to call `f` only once (with constant overhead), no matter how long `f` takes, which is evidently impossible in classical computing. For simplicity, `f` is treated as a macro that can be used in the condition expression of an `if` statement. There are several techniques to represent it with a user-defined function instead (such as injectivization [10] or irreversible functions [19]), but user-defined functions are out of scope for this paper.

The crux of the algorithm is the dotted box in Fig. 3. Prior to that box, we set up two worlds, one evaluating `f(0)` and the other evaluating `f(1)`. We do this because judging constancy of `f` requires checking the values of both `f(0)`

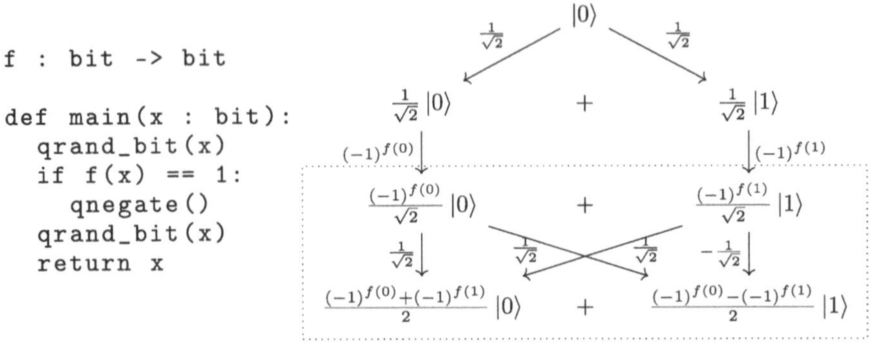

Fig. 3. Deutsch's algorithm in QPPL. Source lines are not aligned with the transition diagram to conserve space.

and `f(1)`, but to do that in time taken for one call to `f`, we have no choice but to split the work between different worlds. Now, in classical probabilistic programming, we'd be stuck, for there is no way to consolidate information from these worlds, which are independent trials and therefore never interact. However, in quantum programming, worlds can interact via destructive interference. Conversely, destructive interference is our only hope of performing this classically impossible feat, for as explained in Sect. 3, destructive interference is the only essential difference between quantum and classical computing.

For two worlds to destructively interfere, we need to steer them towards identical states, or memory contents. The two worlds so far have memory $|0\rangle$ and $|1\rangle$, so they meet by having either the 0 rewritten to 1 or vice versa. Which should it be? Well, both: reversible, deterministic operations can only permute worlds, so worlds can only meet during a non-deterministic operation like `qrand_bit(x)`, which performs both rewrites.

As seen from the arrows in the dotted box, `qrand_bit(x)` makes two equal-amplitude transitions into $|0\rangle$ and two opposite-signed transitions into $|1\rangle$. Thus, weights from the two worlds add on the $|0\rangle$ side whereas they subtract on the $|1\rangle$ side. Hence, to get cancellation on the desired side, it suffices to steer the worlds' weights before `qrand_bit(x)` to be equal when $f(0) = f(1)$, but equal and opposite-signed when $f(0) \neq f(1)$. The program achieves that by calling `qnegate()` in just those worlds with `f(x) == 1`.

Motivating the algorithm through QPP like this is not only useful for understanding the algorithm but also gives lessons on the benefits and challenges of quantum computing in general. Namely, negative amplitudes let us consolidate information from many worlds, but reversibility makes that tricky, which is why experts warn against naïvely thinking of the worlds as parallel processors [3]. It remains to be seen if QPP aids in developing general intuitions that help construct more advanced algorithms.

5 Measurements

In this section, we add a layer of classical probability on top of the model from Sect. 3, which gives us a *two-layer probability model*. This model lets us explain measurements, along with why it is involved in storage deallocation or output.

Most existing quantum programming languages have a `measure` operation, whose behavior is explained as irreversibly collapsing qubits into classical states. Concretely, it maps a qubit in superposition $q_0|0\rangle + q_1|1\rangle$ to a state with definite classical value, either $|0\rangle$ or $|1\rangle$ with classical probabilities $|q_0|^2$ and $|q_1|^2$, respectively. Measurement can also be done on a subset of qubits in the program.

Measurement also happens implicitly at the end of every program, when we read the program's output. The output is determined by collapsing the final superposition to a single world, just like how a classical probabilistic program executes by deciding on a single outcome. Measurement also happens implicitly when discarding data: reversibility requires that no data is ever thrown away, so measurement is needed to convert it to classical data first.

How can we understand measurements in QPP, which has no notion of qubits? In QPP, output, discarding, and measurement can all be understood uniformly as losses of chance for destructive interference. We've mentioned that interference happens when multiple worlds converge on the same program state, but to be completely accurate, they must converge on the same state for everything in the entire universe. We can get away with focusing exclusively on the machine state because a quantum computer is sufficiently isolated from its surroundings that its state is decoupled from the rest of the universe. Output and discarding break this isolation.

Ink on paper, electrical state of classical RAM, memory stored in a human brain---whatever the form, output affects a part of "the rest of the universe" in a way that depends on parts of program memory. If a world wants to interfere with another world that had different data in those parts of memory, it not only has to merge the memory contents but also hunt down and modify all traces of the output so that they match as well, an impossibility. Likewise, deallocation is a vow not to touch a part of the storage anymore, effectively turning it into a part of "the rest of the universe" that cannot be brought to cooperate with interference. Explicit measurement is similar: conceptually, `measure` is an operation that reads out the values of the measured bits into a classical medium, where "classical" means "does not cooperate with interference".

Mathematically, loss of interference can be modeled as conversion of amplitudes to probabilities. Recall that in QPP, negative amplitudes and the destructive interference they enable are *the* defining feature of quantum. Taking for simplicity the case where all bits in the program are measured, all future destructive interference is eliminated, so the superposition resulting at that point may as well be classical. In effect, the measurement has converted amplitudes to probabilities. To capture this idea, we enrich program states from state vectors to classical probability distributions over them.[5]

[5] These distributions are known as *ensembles* in quantum theory [18, Chap. 2].

A *two-layer state* is a list of pairs $[(p_j, \sum_{x\in 2^n} q_{j,x}|x\rangle)]_{j=1}^m$ where:

- The p_j's are classical probabilities, i.e. real numbers in $[0..1]$ that add to 1.
- For each j, the $\sum_{x\in 2^n} q_{j,x}|x\rangle$ is a valid (i.e. length-1) state vector called the j-th *branch*. World $|x\rangle$ in the j-th branch is called the j, x-th *world* of the two-layer state.

If a program is in two-layer state $[(p_j, \sum_x q_{j,x}|x\rangle)]_j$, then the machine is actually in a single branch, the j-th one with probability p_j. The p's thus reflect our ignorance of which branch the machine is in. If the machine is in the j-th branch, then it's also in the j, x-th world with probability amplitude $q_{j,x}$, which can destructively interfere with other worlds in the j-th branch. The q's reflect the quantum non-determinism explained in Sect. 3.

Measuring the m rightmost bits in an n-bit program ($m \le n$) evolves the two-layer state by the following function:

$$\text{measure}_m^n\left[\left(p_j, \sum_{x\in 2^{n-m}, y\in 2^m} q_{j,x,y}|xy\rangle\right)\right]_j = \left[\left(p_j Q_{j,y}^2, \sum_x \frac{q_{j,x,y}}{Q_{j,y}}|xy\rangle\right)\right]_{j,y} \quad (1)$$

where $Q_{j,y} := \sqrt{\sum_x |q_{j,x,y}|^2}$. In each branch, the worlds with a common y value are collected into a new branch, moving the y index from the $\sum$ to the brackets marking the list of branches. The probability amplitude of being in those worlds (the $Q_{j,y}$) gets squared and turned into probability. Effectively, the q's capture quantum non-determinism introduced by `qrand_bit`, which can produce destructive interference, and the p's are the mass of amplitudes that has lost that capability to measurement.

Example 1. Fig. 4 shows a simplified example of quantum error correction. A logical bit is triplicated into physical bits `x`, `y`, `z`. An unwanted rogue particle that enters the quantum computer and causes an error is modeled as a bit `r`. (Though the particle is not a part of the device's memory, we can model it as if it is.) The error caused by the rogue particle is a bit-flip error in `z`, whose effect is modeled by `z ^= r`. The error correction code tests for mismatches among `x`, `y`, `z` using XOR (`^`), stores the results to ancillary (i.e. temporary) storage `a`, `b`, and measures them. The rogue particle also exits the device around this time, causing an information leak also modeled as measurement. The sequence of `if`'s then corrects for the error, making `x`, `y`, `z` equal again.

Let us trace this code in the two-layer probability model. Assume `x`, `y`, `z` are initialized to $q_0|000\rangle + q_1|111\rangle$, representing the logical bit $q_0|0\rangle + q_1|1\rangle$, while the rogue particle starts out in state $r_0|0\rangle + r_1|1\rangle$ (where $|q_0|^2 + |q_1|^2 = |r_0|^2 + |r_1|^2 = 1$). Ancillary bits `a` and `b` are initialized to 0. Coming from different sources, the rogue particle's value is independent of the program variables `x`, `y`, `z`, `a`, `b`, so just like in classical probability theory, the probability amplitude of $xyzab = 00000 \wedge r = 0$ is the product of the amplitudes of $xyzab = 00000$ and $r = 0$. Thus, writing worlds in the format $|xyz, abr\rangle$, the probability amplitude of being in world $|000, 000\rangle$ is $q_0 r_0$. Analyzing all combinations of values for xyz, abr in the same way,[6] we get the first two-layer state shown in the figure.

[6] This is known in conventional quantum programming as taking the *tensor product*.

```
... # init x,y,z,a,b,r
z ^= r # bit-flip error
a ^= (x ^ y)
b ^= (y ^ z)
measure (a,b,r)
if a,b == 0,1: z ^= 1
if a,b == 1,0: x ^= 1
if a,b == 1,1: y ^= 1
```

$$\left[\left(1, \left(\begin{array}{l} q_0 r_0 |000,000\rangle + q_1 r_0 |111,000\rangle \\ +q_0 r_1 |000,001\rangle + q_1 r_1 |111,001\rangle \end{array}\right)\right)\right]$$

$$\left[\left(1, \left(\begin{array}{l} q_0 r_0 |000,000\rangle + q_1 r_0 |111,000\rangle \\ +q_0 r_1 |001,011\rangle + q_1 r_1 |110,011\rangle \end{array}\right)\right)\right]$$

$$\left[\begin{array}{l} (|r_0|^2, q_0 |000,000\rangle + q_1 |111,000\rangle) \\ , (|r_1|^2, q_0 |001,011\rangle + q_1 |110,011\rangle) \end{array}\right]$$

$$\left[\begin{array}{l} (|r_0|^2, q_0 |000,000\rangle + q_1 |111,000\rangle) \\ , (|r_1|^2, q_0 |000,011\rangle + q_1 |111,011\rangle) \end{array}\right]$$

Fig. 4. A model of quantum error correction, omitting `def main` and initialization. On the right are the intermediate two-layer states at select points in the code indicated by line segments. Worlds are written in $|xyz, abr\rangle$ format.

All operations before `measure` are deterministic, so they simply act independently on each world, giving the second two-layer state in the figure. We want to restore triplication, getting a state of the form $q_0|000, abr\rangle + q_1|111, abr\rangle$, but no reversible operation can do that: abr differs across worlds, carrying information about which world saw what kind of error, and eliminating the error requires erasing this information, which reversible operations cannot do.

Measuring `a`, `b`, `r` splits the state into branches according to those variables' values. Two worlds have $abr = 000$, with amplitudes $q_0 r_0$ and $q_1 r_0$, so the likelihood of transitioning to a branch with $abr = 000$ is $|q_0 r_0|^2 + |q_1 r_0|^2 = |r_0|^2$. Those worlds thus form a branch realized by probability $|r_0|^2$, with amplitudes rescaled so that the branch has vector length 1. Worlds with $abr = 011$ are treated likewise, giving the third two-layer state in the figure.

Then the `if`'s correct the bit-flip error. At a high level, this is made possible because *in each branch*, the value of abr is now uniform across worlds and no longer carries information that needs to be erased. The abr now identifies the branch instead, so the information it contains has effectively moved from the amplitude to the classical layer.

QPP's understanding of measurement also suggests how we can avoid the crippling effects of information leakage. The trouble was that leaked values preserve differences in the worlds, preventing destructive interference. It follows that if the leaked bits happen to have the same value in all worlds, then no interference is lost. This leads to the idea of *uncomputation*: setting temporary bits to the same value (usually 0) in all worlds (in each branch) before discarding them.

QPPL allows storage allocation by a `new` statement:

```
def main (x : bit):
  new y := ¬x # y initialized to complement of x
  new z := y
  return y # x,z are discarded
```

$$
\begin{aligned}
x, y &\in \mathit{Vars} \\
P \in \mathit{Prog} &::= \texttt{def main}\,(\overline{x})(\overline{S}) \\
S \in \mathit{Stmt} &::= \texttt{new}\,(\overline{x}) \mid \texttt{measure}\,(\overline{x}) \mid C \\
C \in \mathit{Comp} &::= \texttt{if}\, E\,(\overline{C})\ [\mathrm{FV}(E) \cap \mathrm{AV}(\overline{C}) = \varnothing] \mid x \texttt{ \^{}= } E\ [x \notin \mathrm{FV}(E)] \\
&\quad \mid \texttt{qrand}\,(x) \mid \texttt{qneg}\,() \\
E \in \mathit{Expr} &::= x \mid 0 \mid 1 \mid \neg E \mid E \wedge E \mid E \vee E
\end{aligned}
$$

$$
\mathrm{AV}(C, \overline{C'}) = \mathrm{AV}(C) \cup \mathrm{AV}(\overline{C'}) \qquad \mathrm{AV}(\texttt{if}\, E\,(\overline{C})) = \mathrm{AV}(\overline{C}) \qquad \mathrm{AV}(x \texttt{ \^{}= } E) = \{x\}
$$

$$
\mathrm{AV}(\texttt{qrand}\,(x)) = \{x\} \qquad \mathrm{AV}(\texttt{qneg}\,()) = \varnothing
$$

Fig. 5. Syntax of core QPPL. Production rules marked $[\phi]$ apply only if ϕ is true; for example, $x \texttt{ \^{}= } E$ is a valid expression only if $x \notin \mathrm{FV}(E)$.

Though user-defined functions are beyond the scope of this paper, if they are added, then it is most natural that storage allocated inside them are discarded when the function returns, except for those returned as part of the function's return value. In that case, it is the programmer's responsibility to ensure proper uncomputation if destructive interference is desired thereafter.

Measurement cannot be used inside conditionals because that's unimplementable: it would involve leaking information in some worlds and not others, requiring a measurement that cooperates with quantum non-determinism, an oxymoron. QPPL also forbids conditional allocation (useful in dynamic allocation scenarios), though this is just for simplicity.

Automatic verification and generation of uncompute code have been studied extensively [7,20,22], and a programming language that deals with iteration and dynamic allocation is also known [21]. Growing QPPL into a full-fledged programming language offering such conveniences is left for future work.

6 Formal Semantics

In this section, we give a formal semantics to a core subset of QPPL. We prove that its operations are both implementable (i.e. definable by unitaries, measurements, and initialization of new qubits) and computationally universal (i.e. it can efficiently approximate all possible quantum programs, provided data is encoded in a certain way). This section assumes familiarity with quantum computing and programming language theory.

The syntax of core QPPL is formalized in Fig. 5. We write sequences of length n like $\overline{S}^n$ or simply $\overline{S}$ if the length is unimportant or understood from context. *Comp* is the subset of statements usable inside conditionals, called *computational statements*. $\mathrm{FV}(E)$ stands for the free variables in an expression E (definition omitted). $\mathrm{AV}(\overline{C})$ stands for the variables assigned to in $\overline{C}$.

The syntax is mostly as presented before, with the following simplifications:

- All variables are implicitly of type `bit`, and expressions are built from standard Boolean operators.
- `new` omits initialization expressions. All variables are initialized to zero, and the programmer can set them to any desired value with XOR-assignment.
- There is no explicit `return` statement. All live variables are returned implicitly as quantum data at the end of the program. An alternative semantics where all bits are implicitly measured at the end can be simulated by explicitly calling `measure`.
- Some names are slightly abbreviated (e.g. `qrand_bit` $\rightarrow$ `qrand`).

The reference semantics for QPPL is defined in terms of the two-layer probability model, as that model is an integral part of how semantics is explained to the programmer. We will later show that the two-layer model translates to a more standard density matrix semantics.

A two-layer state is a probability distribution on an amplitude distribution. An *amplitude distribution* is like a probability distribution, except it assigns probability amplitudes to outcomes, whose squares add to 1. Continuing from preceding sections, we write $\sum_x q_x|x\rangle$ for the amplitude distribution assigning amplitude q_x to outcome $|x\rangle$, while writing $[(p_j, a_j)]_j$ for the probability distribution assigning probability p_j to outcome a_j. The two-layer state notation from before is a combination of these notations.

Definition 1. *For any finite set X, let PX be the set of all probability distributions over X. For functions $f : X \to Y$, define the linear map $Pf : PX \to PY$ by $Pf[(1, x)] := [(1, f(x))]$. Similarly, let QX be the set of all amplitude distributions and set $Qf|x\rangle := |f(x)\rangle$.*[7]

The reference two-layer probability semantics is summarized in Fig. 6, using the following auxiliary definitions.

- I_n is the $n \times n$ identity matrix and I_m^n with $m \leq n$ is I_n cut short to m columns (i.e. an inclusion map $\mathbb{R}^m \to \mathbb{R}^n$).
- H is the 2×2 Hadamard matrix.
- $\text{if}(e, c, a)$ is c if $e = 1$ and a otherwise.
- measure_m^n is as defined in (1) of Sect. 5.
- $[f(j, j', k, k')]_{k\in n, k'\in n'}^{j\in m, j'\in m'}$ denotes the $mm' \times nn'$ matrix A whose $(j, j'), (k, k')$-entry is $f(j, j', k, k')$.

When a sequence of statements $\overline{S}$ that allocates k new variables appears in a context that defines the variables $\overline{x}^n$, its semantics is a function $[\![\overline{x} \vdash \overline{S}]\!] : P(Q(2^n)) \to P(Q(2^{n+k}))$. The semantics of a program is the semantics of its statements with the inputs as the defined variables.

The semantics of each statement is as described in previous sections. For the handling of `if`, we note that by straightforward induction, $[\![\overline{x} \vdash \overline{C}]\!]$ is always of the form PU with linear U. Moreover, P is faithful (i.e. injective on functions), so $PU = [\![\overline{x}, \overline{y} \vdash \overline{C}]\!]$ uniquely defines U. Intuitively, this extracts the semantics

$$
\begin{aligned}
[\![\texttt{def main}\,(\overline{x})(\overline{S})]\!] &= [\![\overline{x} \vdash \overline{S}]\!] \\
[\![\overline{x}^n \vdash \texttt{new}\,(\overline{y}^m), \overline{S}]\!] &= P(Q(I_{2^n}^{2^{n+m}})); [\![\overline{x}, \overline{y} \vdash \overline{S}]\!] \\
[\![\overline{x}^n, \overline{y}^m \vdash \texttt{measure}\,(\overline{y}), \overline{S}]\!] &= \mathrm{measure}_m^{n+m}; [\![\overline{x}, \overline{y} \vdash \overline{S}]\!] \\
[\![\overline{x}^n, \overline{y}^m \vdash \texttt{if}\, E\,(\overline{C}), \overline{S}]\!] &= P\left([\langle \xi'\eta' | \mathrm{if}(e(\xi), U, I_{2^{n+m}}) | \xi\eta\rangle]_{\xi \in 2^n, \eta \in 2^m}^{\xi' \in 2^n, \eta \in 2^m} \right); [\![\overline{x}, \overline{y} \vdash \overline{S}]\!] \\
& \quad \text{where} \quad \mathrm{FV}(E) \subseteq \overline{x} \quad \mathrm{AV}(\overline{C}) \subseteq \overline{y} \\
& \qquad\qquad\quad e = [\![\overline{x} \vdash E]\!] \quad PU = [\![\overline{x}, \overline{y} \vdash \overline{C}]\!] \\
[\![x, \overline{y}^n \vdash x \mathbin{\texttt{\^{}=}} E, \overline{S}]\!] &= P\left([\mathrm{if}(\xi' = \xi \oplus e(\eta), 1, 0)]_{\xi \in 2, \eta \in 2^n}^{\xi' \in 2, \eta \in 2^n} \right); [\![x, \overline{y} \vdash \overline{S}]\!] \\
& \quad \text{where} \quad \mathrm{FV}(E) \subseteq \overline{y} \quad e = [\![\overline{x} \vdash E]\!] \\
[\![\overline{x}^n, y \vdash \texttt{qrand}\,(y), \overline{S}]\!] &= P(I_n \otimes H); [\![\overline{x}, y \vdash \overline{S}]\!] \\
[\![\overline{x}^n \vdash \texttt{qneg}\,(), \overline{S}]\!] &= P(-I_n); [\![\overline{x} \vdash \overline{S}]\!] \\
[\![\overline{x}^n \vdash E]\!] &= (\text{the obvious interpretation as a function } 2^n \to 2)
\end{aligned}
$$

Fig. 6. Two-layer probability semantics for core QPPL. We implicitly coerce matrices to linear maps: e.g. $P(-I_n)$ is P applied to the negation map $v \mapsto -v$. Semicolons denote composition of maps. We omit the permutation matrices needed to reorder the variables so that statements match the left-hand sides of these definitions.

of $\overline{C}$ restricted to the amplitude layer. The semantics of `if` $E(\overline{C})$ is then $[\![\overline{C}]\!]$ in worlds where E is true, but the identity (i.e. no-op) in other worlds.

Lemma 1. $[\![\overline{x} \vdash \overline{C}]\!]$ *is unitary.*

Proof. Induction with the inductive hypothesis strengthened with: if $\overline{x}$ has length $n + m$, the last m of which equals $\mathrm{AV}(\overline{C})$, then $\langle \xi\eta | U | \xi'\eta' \rangle = 0$ for any $\xi, \xi' \in 2^n$ and $\eta, \eta' \in 2^m$ with $\xi \neq \xi'$. With this strengthening, it is easily seen that the interpretation of `if` is retracted by its Hermitian conjugate. Since the interpretation is a square matrix, it must be unitary. The other cases are straightforward.

Now, let us connect this two-layer probability semantics to the more established density matrix representation (for which see [18]). A two-layer state is just an ensemble, so there is a unique density matrix reproducing its measurement statistics: $\sum_j p_j \sum_k \sum_{k'} q_{j,k} q_{j,k'} |k\rangle\langle k'|$.[8] The only difference is that the two-layer state remembers which ensemble it arose from, whereas the density matrix conflates observationally indistinguishable ensembles, similar to the relationship between $\beta\eta\delta$ equality and observational equivalence in PCF.

By Theorem 1, the two-layer probability semantics for computational statements are of the form $[(p_j, \sum_k q_{j,k}|k\rangle)]_j \mapsto [(p_j, \sum_k q_{j,k} U|k\rangle)]_j$ for a unitary U,

[7] In other words, P, Q are probability/amplitude distribution functors **FinSet** $\to$ **Set**.

[8] The $q_{j,k'}$ needs to be conjugated when generalizing to complex amplitudes. The trick of swapping indices like $q_{j,k'} \mapsto q_{k',j}$ to express conjugation common in superficially similar sums does not work, since the q's are not entries of a unitary matrix but a coefficient indexed by indices with different ranges.

which is simulated by the completely positive map $\rho \mapsto U\rho U^\dagger$ in the density matrix representation. Allocation by `new` can be understood along similar lines using the isometry $I_{2^n}^{2^{n+k}}$ in place of U. One can check that the formula for measurement from Sect. 5 is simulated by projective measurements, which map $\rho \mapsto \sum_{r \in 2^n} P_r \rho P_r^\dagger$ where P_r is a projector that projects to the subspace where the measured n bits have value r. Thus, we get:

Theorem 1. *Core QPPL semantics is implementable by unitaries, initialization, and measurement. More precisely, the translation to density matrices is computationally adequate (in the sense of reproducing measurement statistics), and the translated semantics is implementable by those operations.*

Conversely, core QPPL can implement computationally universal sets of quantum gates. An easy choice is Toffoli (z `^=` $x \wedge y$) and Hadamard (`qrand`(x)) [4]. Therefore:

Theorem 2. *Core QPPL is computationally universal.*

Remark 4. There are several notions of universality of quantum gate sets. Strict universality means that any unitary matrix can be approximated. Computational universality [4] is similar but allows quantum states to be encoded in a non-standard way. Since we chose to present QPPL as a real-only formalism, we established computational universality over the encoding of complex amplitudes by real ones. If strict universality is desired, one can generalize to complex amplitudes and add a variant of `qnegate()` that multiplies i to the current world's amplitude, allowing to implement the strictly universal gate set of Hadamard, CNOT, and S.

7 Related Works

Apart from Aaronson [1,2] and Mu and Bird [17] mentioned in the introduction, the view of quantum computation as non-deterministic transitions weighted by possibly-negative probabilities features prominently in the textbook proof of BQP $\subseteq$ PSPACE. The idea that negative probabilities is the essence of quantum computing goes all the way back to the foundation of the field: Feynman identifies them as the primary feature of quantum processes that cannot be efficiently simulated on classical computers [9]. The computational universality of real-amplitude gates [4] can be seen as another vindication of the primacy of negative probabilities. So the idea that quantum computing is characterized by negative probability is quite pervasive, but few have tried to distill a programming paradigm based on it.

The pseudocode conventions by Knill [15] often gets credit as the first precursor to quantum programming languages. Van Tonder [27] was among the first to investigate functional quantum programming, a key feature of which was the use of linear types to rule out replication of variables, motivated by the no-cloning theorem. It was Altenkirch and Grattage [5] who pointed out that one could rather control discarding instead of copying, as the latter could be understood as sharing. This idea was a part of the inspiration for QPP, which makes it obvious that data can be copied world-by-world. A plethora of other quantum programming languages have been proposed [7,11,14,16,19,21,23–25,29,30], but all rest on the assumption that quantum programs should manipulate quantum data, whose finicky properties the programmer should know from studies elsewhere.

In classical computing, "probabilistic programming" has come to mean writing code that samples from infinite or even continuous distributions, possibly employing a post-selection construct that filters the samples for desired features [26]. The resulting artifact is often not readily executable with reasonable resources and may have subtle semantics due to singularities [13]. It is used more like a formal model of a stochastic process supporting statistical inference than an executable program. QPP can perhaps be adapted for similar modeling and analysis of quantum processes, though whether that can be useful is unknown.

8 Conclusion

We proposed a new quantum programming paradigm, QPP. It views quantum programming as probabilistic programming with negative probabilities, doing away with the concept of qubits and putting all the quantum weirdness into the quantum non-determinism effect. This makes quantum programming more accessible by systematically providing computationally intuitive metaphors not involving advanced physics. Throughout the paper, we talk only of computationally relevant concepts like the desire to control destructive interference for speed gains, instead of physical concepts like limitations on ripple-effects from measurements due to relativistic no-signaling principles, or intuition-free linear algebraic concepts like eigenvalues of Hermitian operators.

This paper only fleshed out the core ideas of QPP and its conceptual advantages over qubit-based programming. Much work remains on growing this into a full-fledged, practical programming language, adding such things to QPPL as: more advanced data types like numbers and inductive data types, user-defined functions, iteration, and more sophisticated handling of allocation. Higher-level intuitions that aid algorithm design are also wanted.

Another topic of future research is communication. QPP views a single lump of qubits as one quantum non-deterministic computation. Independent quantum computers, or mutually unentangled chunks of a single quantum computer's memory, can be naturally understood as multiple such computations. Formalizing communication between such lumps as a merger of multiple non-deterministic computations would not only help to model communication protocols but also reconstruct the concept of qubits and quantum data, equipped with a perspective for better understanding and manipulating what's inside.

Acknowledgments. We thank Hideaki Nishihara and Akira Mori for insightful comments on early drafts of this paper.

Disclosure of Interests. The author has no competing interests to declare that are relevant to the content of this article.

References

1. Aaronson, S.: Is Quantum Mechanics an Island in Theoryspace? (2004). http://arxiv.org/abs/quant-ph/0401062
2. Aaronson, S.: Quantum Computing Since Democritus, 1st edn. Cambridge University Press, Cambridge (2013)
3. Aaronson, S.: What Makes Quantum Computing So Hard to Explain? Quanta Magazine (2021). https://www.quantamagazine.org/why-is-quantum-computing-so-hard-to-explain-20210608/
4. Aharonov, D.: A Simple Proof that Toffoli and Hadamard are Quantum Universal (2003). https://doi.org/10.48550/arXiv.quant-ph/0301040
5. Altenkirch, T., Grattage, J.: A functional quantum programming language. In: 20th Annual IEEE Symposium on Logic in Computer Science (LICS' 05), pp. 249–258 (2005). https://doi.org/10.1109/LICS.2005.1
6. Bernstein, E., Vazirani, U.: Quantum complexity theory. In: Proceedings of the Twenty-Fifth Annual ACM Symposium on Theory of Computing, pp. 11–20. STOC '93, Association for Computing Machinery, New York, NY, USA (1993). https://doi.org/10.1145/167088.167097, https://doi.org/10.1145/167088.167097
7. Bichsel, B., Baader, M., Gehr, T., Vechev, M.: Silq: a high-level quantum language with safe uncomputation and intuitive semantics. In: Proceedings of the 41st ACM SIGPLAN Conference on Programming Language Design and Implementation, pp. 286–300. ACM, London UK (2020). https://doi.org/10.1145/3385412.3386007
8. Coecke, B., Kissinger, A.: Picturing Quantum Processes: A First Course in Quantum Theory and Diagrammatic Reasoning, 1st edn. Cambridge University Press, Cambridge, United Kingdom New York, NY Melbourne, VIC Delhi Singapore (2017)
9. Feynman, R.P.: Simulating physics with computers. Int. J. Theor. Phys. **21**(6), 467–488 (1982). https://doi.org/10.1007/BF02650179
10. Glück, R., Yokoyama, T.: Reversible computing from a programming language perspective. Theoret. Comput. Sci. **953**, 113429 (2023). https://doi.org/10.1016/j.tcs.2022.06.010
11. Green, A.S., Lumsdaine, P.L., Ross, N.J., Selinger, P., Valiron, B.: Quipper: a scalable quantum programming language. In: Proceedings of the 34th ACM SIGPLAN Conference on Programming Language Design and Implementation, pp. 333–342. PLDI '13, Association for Computing Machinery, New York, NY, USA (2013). https://doi.org/10.1145/2491956.2462177
12. Quantum Computing: An Applied Approach. Springer, Cham (2021). https://doi.org/10.1007/978-3-030-83274-2_15
13. Jacobs, J.: Paradoxes of probabilistic programming: and how to condition on events of measure zero with infinitesimal probabilities. Proc. ACM Program. Lang. **5**(POPL), 58:1–58:26 (2021). https://doi.org/10.1145/3434339
14. Jorrand, P., Lalire, M.: From quantum physics to programming languages: a process algebraic approach. In: Banâtre, J.-P., Fradet, P., Giavitto, J.-L., Michel, O. (eds.) UPP 2004. LNCS, vol. 3566, pp. 1–16. Springer, Heidelberg (2005). https://doi.org/10.1007/11527800_1

15. Knill, E.: Conventions for quantum pseudocode. Tech. Rep. LA-UR-96-2724, Los Alamos National Lab. (LANL), Los Alamos, NM (United States) (1996). https://doi.org/10.2172/366453
16. Lampis, M., Ginis, K.G., Papakyriakou, M.A., Papaspyrou, N.S.: Quantum data and control made easier. Electron. Notes Theor. Comput. Sci. **210**, 85–105 (2008). https://doi.org/10.1016/j.entcs.2008.04.020
17. Mu, S.C., Bird, R.: Functional Quantum Programming (2001). https://www.cs.ox.ac.uk/people/richard.bird/online/MuBird2001Functional.pdf
18. Nielsen, M.A., Chuang, I.L.: Quantum Computation and Quantum Information, anniversary edn. 10th, Anniversary Cambridge University Press, Cambridge, New York (2011)
19. Ömer, B.: Structured Quantum Programming. Ph.D. thesis, Vienna University of Technology, Vienna (2003)
20. Paradis, A., Bichsel, B., Steffen, S., Vechev, M.: Unqomp: synthesizing uncomputation in Quantum circuits. In: Proceedings of the 42nd ACM SIGPLAN International Conference on Programming Language Design and Implementation, pp. 222–236. PLDI 2021, Association for Computing Machinery, New York, NY, USA (2021). https://doi.org/10.1145/3453483.3454040
21. Péchoux, R., Perdrix, S., Rennela, M., Zamdzhiev, V.: Quantum programming with inductive datatypes: causality and affine type theory. In: UPP 2004. LNCS, vol. 3566, pp. 562–581. Springer, Cham (2020). https://doi.org/10.1007/978-3-030-45231-5_29
22. Rand, R., Paykin, J., Lee, D.H., Zdancewic, S.: ReQWIRE: reasoning about reversible quantum circuits. Electron. Proc. Theor. Comput. Sci. **287**, 299–312 (2019). https://doi.org/10.4204/EPTCS.287.17
23. Sanders, J.W., Zuliani, P.: Quantum programming. In: Backhouse, R., Oliveira, J.N. (eds.) MPC 2000. LNCS, vol. 1837, pp. 80–99. Springer, Heidelberg (2000). https://doi.org/10.1007/10722010_6
24. Selinger, P., Valiron, B.: Quantum lambda calculus. In: Mackie, I., Gay, S. (eds.) Semantic Techniques in Quantum Computation, pp. 135–172. Cambridge University Press, Cambridge (2009).https://doi.org/10.1017/CBO9781139193313.005
25. Svore, K.M., Geller, A., Troyer, M., Azariah, J., Granade, C., Heim, B., Kliuchnikov, V., Mykhailova, M., Paz, A., Roetteler, M.: Q#: enabling scalable quantum computing and development with a high-level domain-specific language. In: Proceedings of the Real World Domain Specific Languages Workshop 2018, pp. 1–10 (2018). https://doi.org/10.1145/3183895.3183901
26. van de Meent, J.W., Paige, B., Yang, H., Wood, F.: An Introduction to Probabilistic Programming (2021). https://doi.org/10.48550/arXiv.1809.10756
27. van Tonder, A.: A Lambda Calculus for Quantum Computation (2003)
28. Vizzotto, J., Altenkirch, T., Sabry, A.: Structuring quantum effects: superoperators as arrows. Math. Struct. Comput. Sci. **16**, 453–468 (2006). https://doi.org/10.1017/S0960129506005287
29. Wecker, D., Svore, K.M.: LIQUi| >: A Software Design Architecture and Domain-Specific Language for Quantum Computing (2014). https://doi.org/10.48550/arXiv.1402.4467
30. Ying, M., Feng, Y., Duan, R., Ji, Z.: An algebra of quantum processes. ACM Trans. Comput. Log. **10**(3), 19:1–19:36 (2009). https://doi.org/10.1145/1507244.1507249

Quantum Bisimilarity Is a Congruence Under Physically Admissible Schedulers

Lorenzo Ceragioli[1(✉)], Fabio Gadducci[2], Giuseppe Lomurno[2], and Gabriele Tedeschi[2]

[1] IMT School for Advanced Studies, Lucca, Italy
lorenzo.ceragioli@imtlucca.it
[2] University of Pisa, Pisa, Italy
fabio.gadducci@unipi.it,
{giuseppe.lomurno,gabriele.tedeschi}@phd.unipi.it

Abstract. The development of quantum algorithms and protocols calls for adequate modelling and verification techniques, which requires abstracting and focusing on the basic features of quantum concurrent systems, like CCS and CSP have done for their classical counterparts. So far, an equivalence relation is still missing that is a congruence for parallel composition and adheres to the limited discriminating power implied by quantum theory. In fact, defining an adequate bisimilarity for quantum-capable, concurrent systems proved a difficult task, because unconstrained non-determinism allows to spuriously discriminate indistinguishable quantum systems. We investigate this problem by enriching a linear quantum extension of CCS with simple physically admissible schedulers. We show that our approach suffices for deriving a well-behaved bisimilarity that satisfies the aforementioned desiderata.

Keywords: Quantum process calculi · bisimulation congruences

1 Introduction

Recent years have seen a flourishing development of *quantum computation* and *quantum communication* technologies. Both of them exploit quantum phenomena like superposition and entanglement to achieve quantitative advantages with respect to their classical counterparts. The former focuses on the (supposedly) higher computational power of quantum computers, while the latter on security and reliability properties of communication, featuring solutions for key distribution [26], cryptographic coin tossing [2], direct communication [24], and private information retrieval [18]. Quantum communication also promises to allow linking multiple computers via the *Quantum Internet* [6,29], therefore providing quantum algorithms with large enough memories for practical applications.

Research carried out within the National Centre on HPC, Big Data and Quantum Computing - SPOKE 10 (Quantum Computing) and partly funded from the European Union Next-GenerationEU - National Recovery and Resilience Plan (NRRP) - MISSION 4 COMPONENT 2, INVESTMENT N. 1.4 - CUP N. I53C22000690001.

O. Kiselyov (Ed.): APLAS 2024, LNCS 15194, pp. 176–195, 2024.
https://doi.org/10.1007/978-981-97-8943-6_9

With these advances, the need emerged for modelling and verification techniques applicable to quantum distributed algorithms and protocols, but an accepted standard is still missing. Numerous works [10,16,19,23] rely on *quantum process calculi*, an algebraic formalism successfully applied to classical protocols and concurrent systems. While the features of these calculi are mostly comparable, the bisimilarities greatly vary. The desiderata for a bisimilarity relation are that it is a congruence for parallel composition and that it adheres to the limited discriminating power implied by quantum theory. Furthermore, it should make the atomic observable properties explicit through a labelled approach, thus making the verification simpler and more efficient to implement. However, none of the previous proposals yields a relation satisfying all these criteria.

Concerning the discriminating power, quantum theory prescribes that the state of a quantum system cannot be observed directly, but only through *measurements*, which have a probabilistic outcome and cannot avoid altering the state they are measuring. Moreover, there are different kinds of measurements, each capable of discriminating only some of the different states, while equating others. This constraint limits the capability of discerning the behaviour of quantum systems. Even though quantum process calculi only allow measurements to inspect the quantum state, [13,20] showed that some of the proposed bisimilarities behave as if they can implicitly compare quantum values, and highlighted some non-bisimilar processes that should be indistinguishable. In [10], the authors prove that this discrepancy with respect to quantum theory is due to the discriminating power of non-deterministic choices. If not constrained to be based on classical information, non-determinism allows processes to act according to unknown quantum values, implicitly revealing them.

Consider e.g. a family of processes $P_{|0\rangle}, P_{|1\rangle}, P_{|+\rangle}$, and $P_{|-\rangle}$, with $P_{|\psi\rangle}$ sending a qubit in state $|\psi\rangle$. Take two qubit sources: the first sends a qubit either in state $|0\rangle$ or $|1\rangle$ with equal probability, the second sends a qubit either in $|+\rangle$ or $|-\rangle$. Quantum theory deems the values of the received qubits indistinguishable, as they yield the same result under any possible measurement. Nonetheless, consider an observer O that receives the qubit and chooses non-deterministically which measurement to perform between $\mathbb{M}_A$ and $\mathbb{M}_B$: the former telling apart $|0\rangle$ from $|1\rangle$ and equating $|+\rangle$ and $|-\rangle$, the latter equating $|0\rangle$, $|1\rangle$, $|+\rangle$ and $|-\rangle$. Figure 1 presents the evolution of the two sources paired with the observer, where $O_{|\psi\rangle}$ is the observer after receiving a qubit in state $|\psi\rangle$, and the immediately distinguishable states S and F are chosen according to the result of the measurement.

Straight arrows models actions, while the squiggly ones represent the elements of a distribution, labelled by the probability (we omit 1). Take the system on the left. If the measurement is chosen according to the value of the received qubit, the observer can perform $\mathbb{M}_A$ when receiving $|0\rangle$ and $\mathbb{M}_B$ otherwise, therefore obtaining the state S with probability $3/4$. The system on the right cannot replicate this behaviour, thus O distinguishes the two sources. This contradicts the prescriptions of quantum theory. However, it should be impossible to know

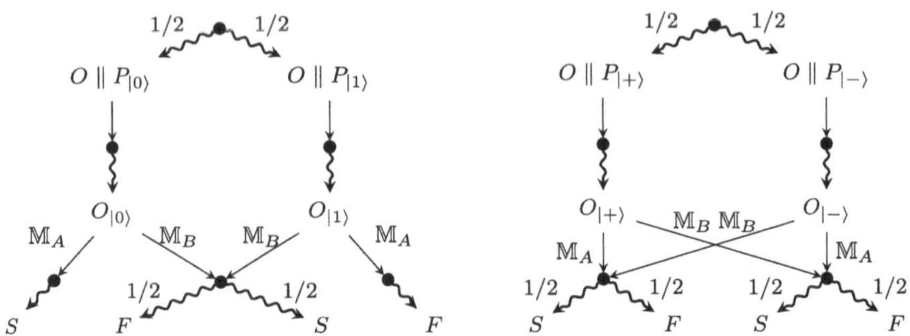

Fig. 1. Observer in parallel with indistinguishable qubit sources.

the quantum state without first performing a measurement, hence such a combination of non-deterministic choices is not physically plausible.

In this paper, we introduce a labelled version of the operational semantics of lqCCS [10], a linearly typed quantum extension of CCS, and we investigate schedulers and scheduled bisimilarity [11]. Schedulers are usually employed to characterize "admissible" or "realistic" choices, e.g. the ones agnostic with respect to private data. We use them to make non-deterministic choices of lqCCS compliant with quantum theory.

Our main result is that simple syntactic schedulers suffice for recovering a notion of bisimilarity that satisfies all our desiderata. More in detail, we mark the available choices of processes with tags that do not depend on quantum values, and we force schedulers to choose based on tags only. We define a scheduled version of (probabilistic) saturated bisimilarity $\sim_s$, pairing processes that are indistinguishable under any context and scheduler. Our proposed $\sim_s$ is a congruence for parallel composition, and satisfies the indistinguishability property introduced by [10], which lifts the known equivalence of quantum values to lqCCS processes. Finally, we derive a labelled bisimilarity $\sim_l$, and we prove it equivalent to $\sim_s$. This characterizes the atomic observable properties of quantum capable processes, and paves the way for automated verification.

Related Works. Our work proposes a saturated and a labelled bisimilarity, both based on schedulers, and proves them equivalent. The choice of saturated bisimilarity as the milestone behavioural equivalence is introduced in [10], where it is shown that unconstrained non-deterministic contexts do not comply with the observational limitations of quantum theory. That paper presents a different semantics for processes and contexts, constraining non-determinism only of the latter. Here we instead treat them uniformly by adding tags to and constraining non-determinism in both of them, obtaining a congruence with respect to parallel composition. Moreover, we additionally propose an equivalent labelled semantics, explicitly representing the observable properties of concurrent quantum systems.

Tagged processes have been introduced in [12], and are vastly used in probabilistic systems for characterizing which choices are "admissible" or "realistic" [1,7,28]. Our tags are reminiscent of the ones used by [11,12] to prevent schedulers from choosing a move based on private data. In the same works, the authors show that different tagging policies correspond to different classes of schedulers. Our usage of tags is somehow similar, as we use them to impose limitations on what can affect the choice of schedulers, but our constraints are motivated by the physical limitations prescribed by quantum theory instead of secrecy assumptions. The schedulers of [11,12] are *deterministic*, meaning that they choose a transition in a deterministic manner. We extend them to randomized schedulers, which may choose how to reduce probabilistically [27]. However, our schedulers lack conditionals, which are present in [12]. This is intended as we focus on simple, constrained schedulers and not general ones. We use schedulers as subscripts of the transition relation, as is Sect. 5 of [11].

An equivalence between saturated and labelled bisimilarity for quantum protocols was introduced in [15], but their bisimilarity was later found too strict to adhere to the prescriptions of quantum theory [17,21]. The most recent labelled bisimilarity for their calculus has been presented in [14], which proposes a semantics made of sub-distributions, and compares the visible qubits of sub-distributions as a whole, instead of comparing single configurations. However, no general property is proved about the adherence with quantum theory, and the proposed bisimilarity is not a congruence with respect to the parallel operator, as shown in [10]. We employ the same sub-distribution approach of [14] for our labelled bisimilarity, making it a congruence thanks to the adequate treatment of constrained schedulers, and we prove that our version correctly relates processes acting on indistinguishable quantum states.

Synopsis. In Sect. 2 we give some background about probability distributions and quantum computing. In Sect. 3 we present our scheduled semantics for lqCCS. In Sect. 4 we propose our behavioural equivalence and we investigate its properties, also providing an equivalent labelled characterization. Finally, we wrap-up the paper in Sect. 5. The article presents proof sketches of its main results. The full proofs are available in its extended version [9].

2 Background

We recall some background on probability distributions and quantum computing, referring to [25] for further reading.

2.1 Probability Distributions

A *sub-probability distribution* over a set S is a function $\Delta : S \to [0,1]$ such that $\sum_{s \in S} \Delta(s) \leq 1$. When a distribution Δ satisfies $\sum_{s \in S} \Delta(s) = 1$ we say it is a *probability distribution.* We call the *support* of a distribution Δ the set $\lceil \Delta \rceil = \{s \in S \mid \Delta(s) > 0\}$. We denote with $\mathcal{D}^{\leq}(S)$ the set of sub-probability distributions with finite support, and with $\mathcal{D}(S) \subsetneq \mathcal{D}^{\leq}(S)$ the probability ones.

For each $s \in S$, we let $\overline{s}$ be the *point distribution* $\overline{s}(s) = 1$. Given a finite set of non-negatives reals $\{p_i\}_{i \in I}$ such that $\sum_{i \in I} p_i = 1$, we write $\sum_{i \in I} p_i \bullet \Delta_i$ for the distribution determined by $(\sum_{i \in I} p_i \bullet \Delta_i)(s) = \sum_{i \in I} p_i \Delta_i(s)$. The notation $\Delta_1 \,{}_p\!\oplus \Delta_2$ is a shorthand for $p \bullet \Delta_1 + (1-p) \bullet \Delta_2$.

A relation $\mathcal{R} \subseteq \mathcal{D}(S) \times \mathcal{D}(S)$ is said to be *linear* if $(\Delta_1 \,{}_p\!\oplus \Delta_2) \mathrel{\mathcal{R}} (\Theta_1 \,{}_p\!\oplus \Theta_2)$ for any $p \in [0,1]$ whenever $\Delta_i \mathrel{\mathcal{R}} \Theta_i$ for $i = 1, 2$. Moreover, $\mathcal{R}$ is *left-decomposable* if $(\Delta_1 \,{}_p\!\oplus \Delta_2) \mathrel{\mathcal{R}} \Theta$ implies $\Theta = (\Theta_1 \,{}_p\!\oplus \Theta_2)$ for some Θ_1, Θ_2 with $\Delta_i \mathrel{\mathcal{R}} \Theta_i$ for $i = 1, 2$ and for any $p \in [0,1]$. Right-decomposability is defined symmetrically, and a relation is *decomposable* when it is both left- and right-decomposable.

Given $\mathcal{R} \subseteq A \times \mathcal{D}(B)$, its *lifting* $\text{lift}(\mathcal{R}) \subseteq \mathcal{D}(A) \times \mathcal{D}(B)$ is the smallest linear relation such that $\overline{s} \text{ lift}(\mathcal{R}) \Theta$ when $s \mathrel{\mathcal{R}} \Theta$. We generalize this to $\text{lift}_{A_i}(\mathcal{R}) \subseteq (A_1 \times \cdots \times \mathcal{D}(A_i) \times \cdots \times A_n) \times \mathcal{D}(B)$ for the lifting on the i-th component of an n-ary relation $\mathcal{R} \subseteq (A_1 \times \cdots \times A_i \times \cdots \times A_n) \times \mathcal{D}(B)$, obtained by fixing the other arguments. For example, $\text{lift}_{A_n}(\mathcal{R})$ is defined as

$$\{(a_1, \ldots, a_{n-1}, \Delta, \Theta) \mid (\Delta, \Theta) \in \text{lift}(\{(a_n, \Theta) | (a_1, \ldots a_{n-1}, a_n, \Theta) \in R\})\}.$$

2.2 Quantum Computing

An isolated physical system is associated to a *Hilbert space* $\mathcal{H}$, i.e. a complex vector space equipped with an inner product $\langle \cdot | \cdot \rangle$. We indicate column vectors as $|\psi\rangle$ and their conjugate transpose as $\langle \psi| = |\psi\rangle^\dagger$. The states of a system are *unit vectors* in $\mathcal{H}$, i.e. vectors $|\psi\rangle$ such that $\langle \psi | \psi \rangle = 1$. A two-dimensional physical system is known as a *qubit*, and we denote its Hilbert space as $\widehat{\mathcal{H}} = \mathbb{C}^2$. The vectors $|0\rangle = (1,0)^T$ and $|1\rangle = (0,1)^T$ form the *computational basis* of $\widehat{\mathcal{H}}$. Other important states are $|+\rangle = \frac{1}{\sqrt{2}}(|0\rangle + |1\rangle)$ and $|-\rangle = \frac{1}{\sqrt{2}}(|0\rangle - |1\rangle)$, which form the *Hadamard basis*. In the quantum jargon, the states in the Hadamard basis are *superpositions* with respect to the computational basis, as they are a linear combination of $|0\rangle$ and $|1\rangle$. A third basis of $\widehat{\mathcal{H}}$ contains $|i\rangle = \frac{1}{\sqrt{2}}(|0\rangle + i\,|1\rangle)$ and $|-i\rangle = \frac{1}{\sqrt{2}}(|0\rangle - i\,|1\rangle)$. Both $|+\rangle, |-\rangle$ and $|i\rangle, |-i\rangle$ are uniform superpositions of $|0\rangle, |1\rangle$, but they differ in the *phase* of the $|1\rangle$ coefficient.

We represent the state space of a composite physical system as the *tensor product* of the state spaces of its components. Consider the Hilbert spaces $\mathcal{H}_A$ with $\{|\psi_i\rangle\}_{i \in I}$ one of its bases, and $\mathcal{H}_B$ with $\{|\phi_j\rangle\}_{j \in I}$ one of its bases. We let their tensor product $\mathcal{H}_A \otimes \mathcal{H}_B$ be the Hilbert space with bases $\{|\psi_i\rangle \otimes |\phi_j\rangle\}_{(i,j) \in I \times J}$, where $|\psi\rangle \otimes |\phi\rangle$ is the Kronecker product. We often omit the tensor product and write $|\psi\phi\rangle$ for $|\psi\rangle \otimes |\phi\rangle$. We write $\widehat{\mathcal{H}}^{\otimes n}$ for the 2^n-dimensional Hilbert space defined as the tensor product of n copies of $\widehat{\mathcal{H}}$ (i.e. the possible states of n qubits). A quantum state in $\mathcal{H}_A \otimes \mathcal{H}_B$ is *separable* when it can be expressed as the Kronecker product of two vectors of $\mathcal{H}_A$ and $\mathcal{H}_B$. Otherwise, it is *entangled*, like the Bell state $|\Phi^+\rangle = \frac{1}{\sqrt{2}}(|00\rangle + |11\rangle)$.

In quantum physics, the evolution of an isolated system is described by a unitary transformation. For each linear operator A on $\mathcal{H}$, its *adjoint* $A^\dagger$ is the unique linear operator such that $\langle \psi | A | \phi \rangle = \langle A^\dagger \psi | \phi \rangle$. A linear operator U is *unitary* when $UU^\dagger = U^\dagger U = \mathbb{I}$, with $\mathbb{I}$ the identity matrix. Quantum computers allow the programmer to manipulate registers via unitaries like H, X, Z and $CNOT$, satisfying $H|0\rangle = |+\rangle$ and $H|1\rangle = |-\rangle$; $X|0\rangle = |1\rangle$ and $X|1\rangle = |0\rangle$; $Z|+\rangle = |-\rangle$ and $Z|-\rangle = |+\rangle$; $CNOT|10\rangle = |11\rangle$, $CNOT|11\rangle = |10\rangle$ and $CNOT|0\psi\rangle = |0\psi\rangle$ (all the other cases are defined by linearity).

2.3 Density Operator Formalism

The density operator formalism puts together quantum systems and probability distributions by considering mixed states, i.e. *sub-probability distributions of quantum states*. A point distribution $\overline{|\psi\rangle}$ (called a pure state) is represented by the matrix $|\psi\rangle\langle\psi|$. In general, a mixed state $\Delta \in \mathcal{D}^{\leq}(\widehat{\mathcal{H}}^{\otimes n})$ for n qubits is represented as the matrix $\rho_\Delta \in \mathbb{C}^{2^n \times 2^n}$, known as its *density operator*, with $\rho_\Delta = \sum_{|\psi\rangle} \Delta(|\psi\rangle)\,|\psi\rangle\langle\psi|$. We write $\mathcal{DO}^{\leq}(\mathcal{H})$ for the set of density operators of $\mathcal{H}$ and $\mathcal{DO}(\mathcal{H})$ for the set $\{\rho \in \mathcal{DO}^{\leq}(\mathcal{H}) \mid tr(\rho) = 1\}$, corresponding to probability distributions of quantum states. For example, the mixed state $\overline{|0\rangle}\ {}_{1/3}\!\oplus \overline{|+\rangle}$ is represented as the density operator $\frac{1}{3}|0\rangle\langle 0| + \frac{2}{3}|+\rangle\langle +|$.

Note that the encoding of probabilistic mixtures of quantum states as density operators is not injective. For example, $\frac{1}{2}\mathbb{I}$ is called the *maximally mixed state* and represents both distributions $\Delta_C = \overline{|0\rangle}\ {}_{1/2}\!\oplus \overline{|1\rangle}$ and $\Delta_H = \overline{|+\rangle}\ {}_{1/2}\!\oplus \overline{|-\rangle}$. This is a desired feature, as the laws of quantum mechanics deem indistinguishable all the distributions that result in the same density operator.

Fact 2.1. *Two distributions of pure quantum states $\Delta, \Theta \in \mathcal{D}(\mathcal{H})$ are indistinguishable for any physical observer whenever*

$$\rho_\Delta = \sum\nolimits_{|\psi\rangle} \Delta(|\psi\rangle)\,|\psi\rangle\langle\psi| = \sum\nolimits_{|\psi\rangle} \Theta(|\psi\rangle)\,|\psi\rangle\langle\psi| = \rho_\Theta.$$

Since density operators are just distributions of pure states, the same result is easily extended to indistinguishable distributions of mixed states.

When modelling composite systems, density operators are composed with the Kronecker product as well. Differently from pure states, they can also describe local information about subsystems. Let $\mathcal{H}_{AB} = \mathcal{H}_A \otimes \mathcal{H}_B$ represent a composite system, with subsystems A and B. Given a (not necessarily separable) $\rho^{AB} \in \mathcal{H}_{AB}$, the state of the subsystem A is described as the *reduced density operator* $\rho^A = \mathrm{tr}_B(\rho^{AB})$, with tr_B the *partial trace over* B, defined as the linear transformation such that $\mathrm{tr}_B(|\psi\rangle\langle\psi|\,\psi' \otimes |\phi\rangle\langle\phi|\,\phi') = |\psi\rangle\langle\psi|\,\psi'\mathrm{tr}(|\phi\rangle\langle\phi|\,\phi')$.

When applied to pure separable states, the partial trace returns the actual state of the subsystem. When applied to an entangled state, instead, it produces a mixed state, because "forgetting" the information on the subsystem B leaves us with only partial information on subsystem A. For example, the partial trace over the first qubit of $|\Phi^+\rangle\langle\Phi^+|$ is the maximally mixed state.

The dynamics of mixed states is given by *trace non-increasing superoperators*, i.e. functions on density operators. A superoperator $\mathcal{E} : \mathcal{DO}^{\leq}(\mathcal{H}) \to \mathcal{DO}^{\leq}(\mathcal{H})$ on a d-dimensional Hilbert space $\mathcal{H}$ is a function defined by its *Kraus operator sum decomposition* $\{E_i\}_{i=1,\dots,d^2}$, satisfying that $\mathcal{E}(\rho) = \sum_i E_i \rho E_i^\dagger$ and $\sum_i E_i^\dagger E_i \sqsubseteq \mathbb{I}$, where $A \sqsubseteq B$ means that $B - A$ is a positive semidefinite matrix. We call $\mathcal{SO}^{\leq}(\mathcal{H})$ the set of trace non-increasing superoperators on $\mathcal{H}$, and $\mathcal{SO}(\mathcal{H}) \subseteq \mathcal{SO}^{\leq}(\mathcal{H})$ the set of all *trace-preserving* superoperators, i.e. such that $\sum_i E_i^\dagger E_i = \mathbb{I}$. Roughly, trace-preserving superoperators map distributions of quantum states to distributions of quantum states, while the result of applying a trace non-increasing superoperator to a distribution may be a *sub*-probability distribution.

Noticeably, the tensor product of superoperators is obtained by tensoring their Kraus decompositions, and any unitary transformation U can be seen as a superoperator, that we still denote as U, having $\{U\}$ as its Kraus decomposition.

Quantum measurements describe how to extract information from a physical system. Performing a measurement on a quantum state returns a probabilistic classical result and causes the quantum state to change (i.e. to *decay*). A measurement with k different outcomes is a set $\mathbb{M} = \{M_m\}_{m=0}^{k-1}$ of k linear operators, satisfying the *completeness* equation $\sum_{m=0}^{k-1} M_m^\dagger M_m = \mathbb{I}$. If the state of the system is ρ before the measurement, then the probability of m-th outcome occurring is $p_m = tr(M_m \rho M_m^\dagger)$. If m is the outcome, then the state after the measurement will be $M_m \rho M_m^\dagger / p_m$. Note that each operator M_m defines a trace non-increasing superoperator $\mathcal{M}_m$, with $\mathcal{M}_m(\rho) = M_m \rho M_m^\dagger$, and the resulting state after the m-th outcome is the normalization of $\mathcal{M}_m(\rho)$.

The simplest measurements project a state into the elements of a basis, e.g. $\mathbb{M}_{01} = \{|0\rangle\langle 0|, |1\rangle\langle 1|\}$ and $\mathbb{M}_{\pm} = \{|+\rangle\langle +|, |-\rangle\langle -|\}$ for the computational and Hadamard basis of $\widehat{\mathcal{H}}$. As expected, applying $\mathbb{M}_{01}$ to $|0\rangle$ always returns the classical outcome 0 and the state $|0\rangle$. When applying the same measurement on $|+\rangle$, instead, the result is 0 and $|0\rangle$, or 1 and $|1\rangle$ with equal probability. Symmetrically, measuring $|0\rangle$ with $\mathbb{M}_{\pm}$ leads to either 0 and $|+\rangle$, or 1 and $|-\rangle$, with equal probability. Finally, applying the measurement $\mathbb{M}_{\pm i} = \{|i\rangle\langle i|, |-i\rangle\langle -i|\}$ to each of $|0\rangle$, $|1\rangle$, $|+\rangle$ and $|-\rangle$ returns 0 and $|i\rangle$, or 1 and $|-i\rangle$ with equal probability.

3 A Quantum Process Algebra

In the following sections we describe the syntax and the type system of lqCCS processes, as well as a semantics decorated with schedulers. Our process calculus is enriched with a linear type system, reflecting the *no-cloning theorem* of quantum mechanics, which forbids quantum values to be copied or broadcast. Moreover, we introduce tags in the syntax, naming all the possible non-deterministic choices, and schedulers in the semantics, choosing among the available tags.

3.1 Syntax and Type System

The syntax of tagged lqCCS processes is defined by the productions

$$
\begin{aligned}
P &::= t\!:\!\tau.P \mid (t,t)\!:\!\tau.P \mid t\!:\!\mathcal{E}(\tilde{e}).P \mid t\!:\!\mathbb{M}(\tilde{e} \rhd x).P \mid t\!:\!c?x.P \mid \mathbf{0}_{\tilde{e}} \\
&\quad \mid t\!:\!c!e.P \mid \textbf{if } e \textbf{ then } P \textbf{ else } P \mid P + P \mid P \parallel P \mid P \setminus c \\
e &::= x \mid b \mid n \mid q \mid \neg e \mid e \vee e \mid e \leq e \mid e = e
\end{aligned}
$$

where $b \in \mathbb{B}$, $n \in \mathbb{N}$, $q \in \mathcal{Q}$, $x \in \mathrm{Var}$, $c \in \mathrm{Chan}$ with $\mathcal{Q}$, Var, Chan denumerable sets of respectively qubit names, variables and channels, each typed. The types for channels are $\widehat{\mathbb{N}}, \widehat{\mathbb{B}}$ and $\widehat{\mathcal{Q}}$. We use $\tilde{e}$ to denote a (possibly empty) tuple $e_1, \ldots, e_n$ of expressions.

We assume a denumerable set $Tag = \{t_1, t_2, \ldots\}$ of tags, and the actions are tagged with a tag $t \in Tag$. For the silent action τ we consider two possibilities, either a single tag or a pair of tags. This is useful for using τ actions to write an abstract specification of a concrete protocol: $t : \tau$ models an action with tag t, $(t, t') : \tau$ models a synchronization. The process $\mathbf{0}_{\tilde{e}}$ *discards* the qubits in $\tilde{e}$. It behaves as a deadlock process that maintains ownership of the qubits in $\tilde{e}$ and makes them inaccessible to other processes. Discard processes will be shown semantically equivalent to any deadlock process using the same qubits. The process $\mathbf{0}_{q_1,q_2}$ is, e.g., equivalent to $\mathbf{0}_{q_2,q_1}$ and to $(c!q_1.c!q_2.\mathbf{0}) \setminus c$, since q_1 and q_2 will never be available. When $\tilde{e}$ is the empty sequence, we write $\mathbf{0}$ to stress the equivalence with the nil process of standard CCS. This feature of lqCCS allows marking which qubits are hidden to the environment, thus relieving bisimilar processes to agree on them. A symbol $\mathcal{E}$ denotes a trace-preserving superoperator on $\widehat{\mathcal{H}}^{\otimes n}$ for some $n > 0$, and we write $\mathcal{E} : \mathrm{Op}(n)$ to indicate that $\mathcal{E}$ is a superoperator of arity n. A symbol $\mathbb{M}$ denotes a measurement $\{M_0, \ldots, M_{k-1}\}$ with k different outcomes; we write $\mathbb{M} : \mathrm{Meas}(n)$ to indicate that each M_i acts on n qubits, and denote $|\mathbb{M}|$ the cardinality k of $\mathbb{M}$. Recall that $\mathbb{M}_{01}, \mathbb{M}_{\pm}$ and $\mathbb{M}_{\pm i}$ are the projective measurements in the bases $\{|0\rangle, |1\rangle\}$, $\{|+\rangle, |-\rangle\}$ and $\{|i\rangle, |-i\rangle\}$. Parallel composition, non-deterministic sum and restriction are the standard CCS ones.

As for lqCCS, the visibility of qubits is enforced explicitly through a linear type system. The typing system of [10] is applicable also to tagged processes, since the tags are annotations that do not change the ownership of qubits. The typing judgment $\Sigma \vdash P$ indicate that the process P is well-typed under the usage of the set of qubits $\Sigma \subseteq \mathcal{Q}$. The typing for processes is unique [10], i.e. whenever $\Sigma \vdash P$ and $\Sigma' \vdash P$ then $\Sigma = \Sigma'$. For this reason we will call Σ_P the only context which types P. The type system for tagged processes appears in [9].

Example 3.1. Consider a quantum lottery $\mathbf{QL} = \mathbf{Pr} \parallel \mathbf{An}$ formed by processes $\mathbf{Pr}$, which prepares a qubit used as a source of randomness, and $\mathbf{An}$, which receives it, measures it, and announces the winner between Alice and Bob.

$$\mathbf{Pr} = (t_1 : X(q).t_3 : c!q.\mathbf{0}) + (t_2 : H(q).t_3 : c!q.\mathbf{0})$$
$$\mathbf{An} = t_4 : c?x.t_4 : \mathbb{M}_{01}(x \rhd y).\mathbf{if}\ y = 0\ \mathbf{then}\ t_5 : a!1.\mathbf{0}_x\ \mathbf{else}\ t_6 : b!1.\mathbf{0}_x$$

Intuitively, $\mathbf{Pr}$ can prepare and send a qubit by applying either X or H to its qubit q, and $\mathbf{An}$ announces that Alice wins with $a!1$ if the qubit is found in state $|0\rangle$, or that Bob wins with $b!1$ if the received qubit is found in state $|1\rangle$. The unique typing of $\mathbf{QL}$ is $\{q\} \vdash \mathbf{QL}$, with $a, b : \widehat{\mathbb{N}}$, $c : \widehat{\mathcal{Q}}$, $y : \mathbb{N}$, and $q, x : \mathcal{Q}$.

3.2 Operational Semantics

We describe a labelled semantics for lqCCS in terms of *configurations* $\langle \rho, P \rangle \in Conf$, each composed by a global quantum state and a tagged lqCCS process.

Given a set $\Sigma = \{q_1, \dots, q_n\} \subseteq \mathcal{Q}$ and its associated Hilbert space $\mathcal{H}_\Sigma = \widehat{\mathcal{H}}^{\otimes n}$, a global quantum state ρ is a density operator in $\mathcal{DO}(\mathcal{H}_\Sigma)$. The type system is extended to configurations by considering the qubits of the underlying quantum state. Let Σ_ρ be the set of qubits appearing in ρ.

Definition 3.1. *Let $\langle \rho, P \rangle \in Conf$ and $\Delta \in \mathcal{D}(Conf)$. We let $(\Sigma_\rho, \Sigma_P) \vdash \langle \rho, P \rangle$ if $\Sigma_P \subseteq \Sigma_\rho$, and $(\Sigma, \Sigma') \vdash \Delta$ if $(\Sigma, \Sigma') \vdash \mathcal{C}$ for any $\mathcal{C} \in \lceil \Delta \rceil$.*

Hereafter, we restrict ourselves to well-typed distributions, and denote with $\Sigma_{\overline{P}}$ the set $\Sigma_\rho \setminus \Sigma_P$, i.e. the qubits only available to the environment.

Our semantics is decorated with *syntactic schedulers*, which resolve non-determinism by choosing a tag. The syntax of schedulers $s \in Sched$ for tagged lqCCS distributions is defined as follows

$$s ::= h \mid t \mid (t,\ t)$$

A scheduler can stop the execution with the symbol h, select an action with a tag t, and select a synchronization with a pair (t_1, t_2). Intuitively, tags represent available visible options, upon which the scheduler can choose (possibly using a pair of them for synchronization).

Assume a set Act of actions, containing τ, $c!v$ and $c?v$ for any channel c and value v. The semantics of lqCCS is a probabilistic LTS (pLTS), i.e. a triple $(Conf, Act, \longrightarrow)$, with $\longrightarrow\ \subseteq Conf \times Act \times Sched \times \mathcal{D}(Conf)$. A transition $(\langle \rho, P \rangle, \mu, s, \Delta) \in\ \longrightarrow$ is also denoted as $\langle \rho, P \rangle \xrightarrow{\mu}_s \Delta$.

The transition relation $\longrightarrow$ is the smallest relation over configurations with closed processes that satisfies the rules in Fig. 2. As expected, tagged actions require a matching tag on the transition. Expressions e are evaluated through a big step semantics $e \Downarrow v$ with v a value, i.e. either $n \in \mathbb{N}$, $b \in \mathbb{B}$, or $q \in \mathcal{Q}$. We restrict to arithmetic and logical operations, and therefore omit the rules and assume that free variables are not evaluated. Note that the value of the qubits can only be observed through measurements, which alter such value and have a probabilistic outcome. In particular, the expression $q = q'$ just compares two qubit names, and not their values. In rule QOP, the superoperator $\mathcal{E}$ is applied to the qubits in $\tilde{q}$. Since $\tilde{q}$ can be smaller than the whole Σ_ρ, we define $\mathcal{E}^{\tilde{q}}$ as the superoperator that acts on the whole ρ but "ignores" the qubits outside $\tilde{q}$. More precisely, $\mathcal{E}^{\tilde{q}}$ is obtained by composing (i) a suitable set of SWAP unitaries to bring the qubits $\tilde{q}$ in the first positions; (ii) the tensor product of the superoperator $\mathcal{E}$ with the identity on untouched qubits on the right; and (iii) the inverse of the SWAP operators of point (i) to recover the original order of qubits [22]. In rule QMEAS, given a measurement $\mathbb{M} = \{M_m\}$, for each m, $\mathcal{M}_m$ stands for the trace non-increasing superoperator such that $\mathcal{M}_m(\sigma) = M_m \sigma M_m^\dagger$, and $\mathcal{M}_m^{\tilde{q}}$ is defined as before. In the rules PARL and PARR the parallel composition of a distribution $\Delta = \sum_{i \in I} p_i \bullet \overline{\langle \rho_i, P_i \rangle}$ and a process Q is defined as $\sum_{i \in I} p_i \bullet \overline{\langle \rho_i, P_i \parallel Q \rangle}$, and similarly for the restriction $\Delta \setminus c$. Notice that in PARL we require that P does not receive a qubit that is already owned by Q, and symmetrically in PARR.

$$\frac{\langle \rho, P\rangle \xrightarrow{\mu}_s \Delta \quad e \Downarrow tt}{\langle \rho, \textbf{if } e \textbf{ then } P \textbf{ else } Q\rangle \xrightarrow{\mu}_s \Delta}\ \textsc{IteT} \qquad \frac{\langle \rho, Q\rangle \xrightarrow{\mu}_s \Delta \quad e \Downarrow f\!f}{\langle \rho, \textbf{if } e \textbf{ then } P \textbf{ else } Q\rangle \xrightarrow{\mu}_s \Delta}\ \textsc{IteF}$$

$$\frac{}{\langle \rho, t\colon\tau.P\rangle \xrightarrow{\tau}_t \overline{\langle \rho, P\rangle}}\ \textsc{Tau} \qquad \frac{}{\langle \rho, (t,t')\colon\tau.P\rangle \xrightarrow{\tau}_{(t,t')} \overline{\langle \rho, P\rangle}}\ \textsc{TauPair}$$

$$\frac{e \Downarrow v}{\langle \rho, t\colon c!e.P\rangle \xrightarrow{c!v}_t \overline{\langle \rho, P\rangle}}\ \textsc{Send} \qquad \frac{c : \widehat{\mathcal{Q}} \Rightarrow v \in \Sigma_\rho}{\langle \rho, t\colon c?x.P\rangle \xrightarrow{c?v}_t \overline{\langle \rho, P[^v/_x]\rangle}}\ \textsc{Receive}$$

$$\frac{\langle \rho, P\rangle \xrightarrow{\mu}_s \Delta \quad \mu \notin \{c!v, c?v\}}{\langle \rho, P\setminus c\rangle \xrightarrow{\mu}_s \Delta\setminus c}\ \textsc{Restrict} \qquad \frac{}{\langle \rho, t\colon\mathcal{E}(\tilde{q}).P\rangle \xrightarrow{\tau}_t \overline{\langle \mathcal{E}^{\tilde{q}}(\rho), P\rangle}}\ \textsc{QOp}$$

$$\frac{p_m = \mathrm{tr}\big(\mathcal{M}^{\tilde{q}}_m(\rho)\big)}{\langle \rho, t\colon\mathbb{M}(\tilde{q} \rhd y).P\rangle \xrightarrow{\tau}_t \sum_{m=0}^{|\mathbb{M}|-1} p_m \bullet \overline{\langle \frac{1}{p_m}\mathcal{M}^{\tilde{q}}_m(\rho), P[^m/_y]\rangle}}\ \textsc{QMeas}$$

$$\frac{\langle \rho, P\rangle \xrightarrow{\mu}_s \Delta \quad \mu \notin \{c?v \mid v \in \Sigma_Q\}}{\langle \rho, P \parallel Q\rangle \xrightarrow{\mu}_s \Delta \parallel Q}\ \textsc{ParL} \qquad \frac{\langle \rho, Q\rangle \xrightarrow{\mu}_s \Delta \quad \mu \notin \{c?v \mid v \in \Sigma_P\}}{\langle \rho, P \parallel Q\rangle \xrightarrow{\mu}_s P \parallel \Delta}\ \textsc{ParR}$$

$$\frac{\langle \rho, P\rangle \xrightarrow{\mu}_s \Delta}{\langle \rho, P + Q\rangle \xrightarrow{\mu}_s \Delta}\ \textsc{SumL} \qquad \frac{\langle \rho, P\rangle \xrightarrow{c!v}_t \overline{\langle \rho, P'\rangle} \quad \langle \rho, Q\rangle \xrightarrow{c?v}_{t'} \overline{\langle \rho, Q'\rangle}}{\langle \rho, P \parallel Q\rangle \xrightarrow{\tau}_{(t,t')} \overline{\langle \rho, P' \parallel Q'\rangle}}\ \textsc{SynchL}$$

$$\frac{\langle \rho, Q\rangle \xrightarrow{\mu}_s \Delta}{\langle \rho, P + Q\rangle \xrightarrow{\mu}_s \Delta}\ \textsc{SumR} \qquad \frac{\langle \rho, Q\rangle \xrightarrow{c!v}_t \overline{\langle \rho, Q'\rangle} \quad \langle \rho, P\rangle \xrightarrow{c?v}_{t'} \overline{\langle \rho, P'\rangle}}{\langle \rho, P \parallel Q\rangle \xrightarrow{\tau}_{(t,t')} \overline{\langle \rho, P' \parallel Q'\rangle}}\ \textsc{SynchR}$$

Fig. 2. Rules of lqCCS semantics.

Example 3.2. The pLTS semantics of the quantum lottery **QL** from Example 3.1 on quantum state $|0\rangle\langle 0|$ is in Figure 3, where $\mathbf{An}'$ stands for $t_4 : \mathbb{M}_{01}(x \rhd y).\mathbf{An}''$, and $\mathbf{An}''$ is **if** $y = 0$ **then** $t_5 : a!1.\mathbf{0}_x$ **else** $t_6 : b!1.\mathbf{0}_x$. To simplify the presentation, we draw $\xrightarrow{s:\mu}$ instead of $\xrightarrow{\mu}_s$. A scheduler for **QL** must decide (i) which unitary **Pr** applies to the qubit q, either X (i.e. $s = t_1$) or H (i.e. $s = t_2$); and (ii) if the qubit is sent to **An** or to the external environment (notice that the channel is not restricted), i.e. the available moves are with label τ and scheduler (t_3, t_4), or with label $c!q$ and $s = t_3$. Intuitively, if **Pr** chooses X, then Bob will win, otherwise either Alice or Bob will win with the same probability. Note that at the beginning, in configuration $\langle |0\rangle\langle 0|, \mathbf{QL}\rangle$, the choice t_4 cannot be taken because the quantum state has no qubit apart from those in $\Sigma_{\mathbf{QL}}$.

It is useful to consider a pLTS as a simple LTS between (sub-)distributions. First, we add a "deadlock" configuration $\bot$, allowing distributions to evolve in sub-distributions if a move is not legal for some elements of the support of the distribution [14]. Formally, we let $\mathit{Conf}_\bot = \mathit{Conf} \cup \{\bot\}$ and define $\mathit{bot}(\longrightarrow) \in \mathit{Conf}_\bot \times \mathit{Act} \times \mathit{Sched} \times \mathcal{D}(\mathit{Conf}_\bot)$ as the least relation such that $\mathit{bot}(\longrightarrow) \supseteq \longrightarrow$ and $\mathcal{C}\ \mathit{bot}(\xrightarrow{\mu}_s)\ \overline{\bot}$ if there is no Δ such that $\mathcal{C} \xrightarrow{\mu}_s \Delta$. We extend typing

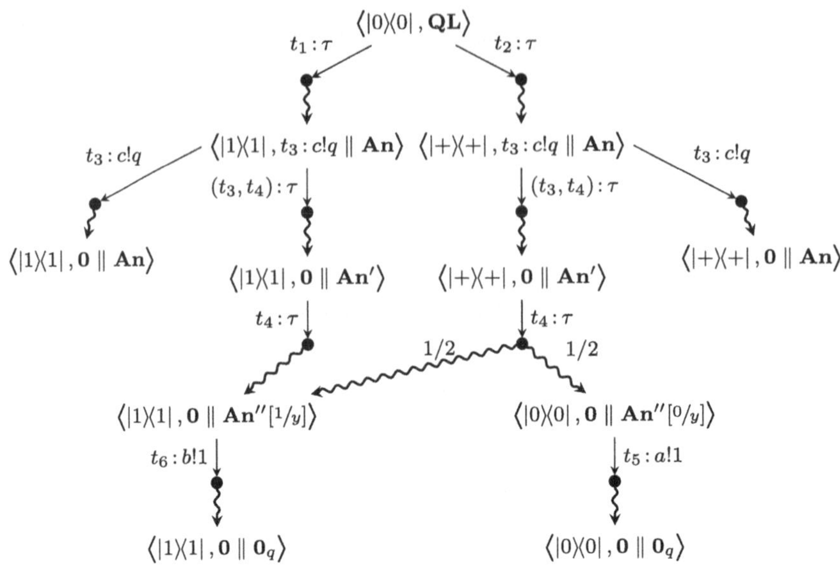

Fig. 3. Semantics of the quantum lottery process.

to $Conf_\perp$ by imposing $(\Sigma, \Sigma') \vdash \perp$ for any Σ and Σ'. Since an element Δ of $D(Conf_\perp)$ represents a sub-distribution, we call *mass* the probability of all the configurations in Δ different from $\perp$: $|\Delta| = 1 - \Delta(\perp)$.

Then, we lift the semantics to deal with distributions of schedulers and distributions of configurations. Consider $\mathrm{lift}_{Conf_\perp}(\mathrm{lift}_{Sched}(bot(\longrightarrow))) : \mathcal{D}(Conf_\perp) \times Act \times \mathcal{D}(Sched) \times \mathcal{D}(Conf_\perp)$, where we first lift the transition relation to distributions of schedulers, hence allowing for randomized schedulers [27], and then lift over the input configurations. When clear from the context, we will adopt $\longrightarrow$ also as the symbol for the lifting of the semantics to distributions, and we will write $\longrightarrow_s$ for $\longrightarrow_{\overline{s}}$ with $\overline{s}$ the randomized scheduler that behaves as s with probability 1. To avoid clashing notation, we will use δ instead of Δ for distributions of schedulers, e.g. in the transition $\mathcal{C} \xrightarrow{\tau}_\delta \Delta$.

Example 3.3. Recall Example 3.2. In the lifted semantics, it is possible to define a randomized scheduler choosing the unitary by tossing a fair coin, i.e. obtaining the following sequence of reductions

$$\begin{aligned}
&\overline{\langle |0\rangle\langle 0| \,, \mathbf{QL}\rangle} \xrightarrow{\tau}_{\overline{t_1}\,_{1/2}\oplus \overline{t_2}} \overline{\langle |1\rangle\langle 1| \,, c!q \parallel \mathbf{An}\rangle} \,_{\frac{1}{2}}\oplus \overline{\langle |+\rangle\langle +| \,, c!q \parallel \mathbf{An}\rangle} \\
&\xrightarrow{\tau}_{\overline{(t_3,t_4)}} \overline{\langle |1\rangle\langle 1| \,, \mathbf{0} \parallel \mathbf{An}'\rangle} \,_{\frac{1}{2}}\oplus \overline{\langle |+\rangle\langle +| \,, \mathbf{0} \parallel \mathbf{An}'\rangle} \\
&\xrightarrow{\tau}_{\overline{t_4}} \overline{\langle |1\rangle\langle 1| \,, \mathbf{0} \parallel \mathbf{An}''[1/y]\rangle} \,_{\frac{3}{4}}\oplus \overline{\langle |0\rangle\langle 0| \,, \mathbf{0} \parallel \mathbf{An}''[0/y]\rangle} \xrightarrow{a!1}_{\overline{t_5}} \overline{\perp} \,_{\frac{3}{4}}\oplus \overline{\langle |0\rangle\langle 0| \,, \mathbf{0} \parallel \mathbf{0}_q\rangle}
\end{aligned}$$

Note that in the last step we end up in a sub-distribution, since the choice t_5 with action $a!1$ is not available for $\overline{\langle |1\rangle\langle 1| \,, \mathbf{0} \parallel \mathbf{An}''[1/y]\rangle}$, which transitions to $\overline{\perp}$.

It is worth noting that the typing is preserved by τ-transitions.

Theorem 3.1. (Typing Preservation) *If* $(\Sigma_\rho, \Sigma_P) \vdash \langle \rho, P \rangle$ *and* $\langle \rho, P \rangle \xrightarrow{\tau}_s \Delta$ *then* $(\Sigma_\rho, \Sigma_P) \vdash \Delta$.

As hinted by the previous theorem, type preservation does not hold in general. However, the updated typing context is uniquely determined by the transition label, and it is still a subset of the qubits available in the quantum state.

Theorem 3.2. (Typing Quasi-Preservation) *Let* $\Sigma \subseteq \mathcal{Q}$ *and* $\mu \in Act$. *Then there exists* Σ' *such that for all* $(\Sigma'', \Sigma) \vdash \mathcal{C}$ *and* $\Delta \in \mathcal{D}(Conf)$ *with* $\mathcal{C} \xrightarrow{\mu}_s \Delta$ *it holds* $(\Sigma'', \Sigma') \vdash \Delta$.

Hereafter, we make the standard assumption that processes are tagged in a deterministic way, meaning that the evolution of distributions is uniquely determined by the scheduler [11,12].

Assumption 1. *For any distribution* $\Delta \in \mathcal{D}(Conf_\perp)$, *scheduler distribution* δ *and action* μ, *if* $\Delta \xrightarrow{\mu}_\delta \Delta'$ *and* $\Delta \xrightarrow{\mu}_\delta \Delta''$, *then* $\Delta' = \Delta''$.

4 Behavioural Equivalence

We start by defining a saturated bisimilarity *à la* [5], a natural notion of behavioural equivalence that pairs systems when they are indistinguishable for any observer. We show that schedulers guarantee adherence with the prescriptions of quantum theory, as contexts cannot choose their move based on the unknown states of unmeasured qubits, a problem previously highlighted in [10]. Finally, we give an equivalent characterization in terms of labelled bisimulations.

4.1 Saturated Bisimilarity

In saturated bisimilarities, contexts $B[\cdot]$ are processes with a typed hole that play the role of process-discriminating observers.

Definition 4.1. *A context* $B[\cdot]_\Sigma$ *is generated by the production* $B[\cdot]_\Sigma ::= [\cdot]_\Sigma \parallel P$, *typed according to the rules in [9], and to the following one*

$$\frac{\Sigma' \setminus \Sigma \vdash P \quad \Sigma \subseteq \Sigma'}{\Sigma' \vdash [\cdot]_\Sigma \parallel P} \text{ HOLE}$$

A process P is applied to contexts by replacing the hole with P. Intuitively, a context $\Sigma' \vdash B[\cdot]_\Sigma$ is a function that given a process P returns a process $B[P]$ obtained by replacing P for $[\cdot]$, where Σ is the typing context of the valid inputs and Σ' the one of the outputs. Note that a context can own some qubits and each qubit cannot be referred to in both P and $B[\cdot]$. We apply $\Sigma' \vdash B[\cdot]_\Sigma$ to configurations $(\Sigma_\rho, \Sigma_P) \vdash \langle \rho, P \rangle$ obtaining $(\Sigma_\rho, \Sigma') \vdash \langle \rho, B[P] \rangle$ when $\Sigma' \subseteq \Sigma_\rho$ and $\Sigma = \Sigma_P$, i.e. when the qubits referred by $B[\cdot]$ are defined in ρ and the process P is as prescribed by $B[\cdot]$. We write $B[\langle \rho, P \rangle]$ for $\langle \rho, B[P] \rangle$, $B[\perp]$ for

$\perp$, and $B[\Delta]$ for the distribution obtained by applying $B[\cdot]$ to the support of Δ. It is trivial to show that if Δ and Θ are typed by the same typing context, then $B[\Delta]$ is defined if and only if $B[\Theta]$ is defined.

A saturated bisimulation is a relation over distributions where related pairs must have the same type and mass, and must reduce in related distributions under every possible context.

Definition 4.2. (Saturated Bisimilarity) *A relation $\mathcal{R} \subseteq \mathcal{D}(Conf_\perp) \times \mathcal{D}(Conf_\perp)$ is a* saturated bisimulation *if $\Delta \mathcal{R} \Theta$ implies $(\Sigma, \Sigma') \vdash \Delta$ and $(\Sigma, \Sigma') \vdash \Theta$ for some Σ, Σ', $|\Delta| = |\Theta|$ and for any context $B[\cdot]_{\Sigma'}$ it holds that*

- *whenever $B[\Delta] \xrightarrow{\tau}_\delta \Delta'$, there exists Θ' such that $B[\Theta] \xrightarrow{\tau}_\delta \Theta'$ and $\Delta' \mathcal{R} \Theta'$;*
- *whenever $B[\Theta] \xrightarrow{\tau}_\delta \Theta'$, there exists Δ' such that $B[\Delta] \xrightarrow{\tau}_\delta \Delta'$ and $\Delta' \mathcal{R} \Theta'$.*

Let saturated bisimilarity, *denoted $\sim_s$, be the largest saturated bisimulation.*

Notice that $\sim_s$ is a congruence with respect to $\|$ by definition. We now compare our proposed bisimilarity with the prescriptions of quantum theory.

4.2 Assessment of Saturated Bisimilarity

As a first result, we notice that $\sim_s$ is a linear relation, meaning that the convex combination of bisimilar distributions yields bisimilar distributions.

Theorem 4.1. *If $\Delta_i \sim_s \Theta_i$ for $i=1,2$ and $p \in [0,1]$ then $\Delta_1 {}_p\!\oplus \Delta_2 \sim_s \Theta_1 {}_p\!\oplus \Theta_2$.*

The second property we address is purely quantum, and lifts to lqCCS the indistinguishability relations between quantum states of Fact 2.1.

This property has been originally defined in [10], and states that the same process, acting on two different but indistinguishable mixed quantum states, exhibits a behaviour that cannot be distinguished by any observer, therefore yielding bisimilar distributions.

Theorem 4.2. *If $\sum_i p_i \cdot \rho_i = \sum_j q_j \cdot \rho_j$ then $\sum_i p_i \bullet \overline{\langle \rho_i, P \rangle} \sim_s \sum_j q_j \bullet \overline{\langle \sigma_j, P \rangle}$.*

Proof (sketch). We prove by induction $\Delta = \overline{\langle \rho, P \rangle} {}_p\!\oplus \overline{\langle \sigma, P \rangle} \sim_s \overline{\langle \rho \, {}_p\!\oplus \sigma, P \rangle} = \Theta$, and the theorem follows by transitivity. First, we show that Δ replicates the moves of Θ by the linearity of superoperators, i.e. $\mathcal{E}(\rho) \, {}_p\!\oplus \mathcal{E}(\sigma) = \mathcal{E}(\rho \, {}_p\!\oplus \sigma)$, and similarly for measurements. Then, we show that Θ simulates Δ. Here, the presence of schedulers is key: it forbids Δ from combining different non-deterministic choices to perform a move that would not be available to Θ (see Example 4.1).

This result directly derives from the use of schedulers, and it is not common in quantum versions of CCS: it holds only for specific distributions in [10] and in [14]. To see the role of schedulers, consider the following example about indistinguishable qubit sources, formalizing the intuition of Fig. 1.

Example 4.1. Consider a pair of non-biased random qubit sources, the first sending a qubit in state $|0\rangle$ or $|1\rangle$, the second in state $|+\rangle$ or $|-\rangle$. Quantum theory prescribes that these two sources cannot be distinguished by any observer, as the received qubit behaves the same [25]. Indeed, the (mixed) states of the qubits sent by both sources are represented by the density operator $\frac{1}{2}\mathbb{I}$. Fittingly, the lqCCS encodings of these sources are bisimilar by Theorem 4.2: $\Delta_{01} \sim_s \Delta_{\pm}$, for

$$\Delta_{01} = \overline{\langle |0\rangle\langle 0|, t_0 : c!q\rangle}\ {}_{1/2}\!\oplus \overline{\langle |1\rangle\langle 1|, t_0 : c!q\rangle} \sim_s \overline{\left\langle \frac{1}{2}\mathbb{I}, t_0 : c!q\right\rangle}$$

$$\Delta_{\pm} = \overline{\langle |+\rangle\langle +|, t_0 : c!q\rangle}\ {}_{1/2}\!\oplus \overline{\langle |-\rangle\langle -|, t_0 : c!q\rangle} \sim_s \overline{\left\langle \frac{1}{2}\mathbb{I}, t_0 : c!q\right\rangle}$$

By contrast, assume the *unscheduled semantics* that ignores tags, defined as $\xrightarrow{\mu}_u = \mathrm{lift}_{Conf_\perp}(\bigcup_s bot(\xrightarrow{\mu}_s)) : \mathcal{D}(Conf_\perp) \times Act \times \mathcal{D}(Conf_\perp)$, and let the *unscheduled bisimilarity* $\sim_{us}$ be the saturated bisimilarity for this transition relation. The unscheduled bisimilarity erroneously discriminates the two sources. To see that $\Delta_{01} \not\sim_{us} \Delta_{\pm}$, take $B[\cdot] = [\cdot] \parallel t_1 : c?x.(P + Q)$ where

$$P = t_2 : \mathbb{M}_{01}(x \rhd y).R\ , \text{ and } \ Q = t_3 : \mathbb{M}_{\pm i}(x \rhd y).R, \text{ with}$$
$$R = (\textbf{if } y = 0 \textbf{ then } t_4 : \tau \textbf{ else } \mathbf{0}) \parallel \mathbf{0}_x$$

Notice that P and Q perform different measurements and make the outcome observable by enabling a τ-transition only when $y = 0$.

Let $\mathcal{C}_\psi$ be $\langle |\psi\rangle\langle\psi|, P + Q\rangle[q/x]$, then $B[\Delta_{01}]$ reduces to $\Delta'_{01} = \overline{\mathcal{C}_0}\ {}_{1/2}\!\oplus \overline{\mathcal{C}_1}$, and $B[\Delta_{\pm}]$ can only reduce to $\Delta'_{\pm} = \overline{\mathcal{C}_+}\ {}_{1/2}\!\oplus \overline{\mathcal{C}_-}$ to match this move. The following moves are available for $\mathcal{C}_0$ and $\mathcal{C}_1$

$$\mathcal{C}_0 \xrightarrow{\tau}_{\overline{t_2}} \overline{\langle |0\rangle\langle 0|, R[0/y]\rangle} = \Delta_0,$$
$$\mathcal{C}_1 \xrightarrow{\tau}_{\overline{t_3}} \overline{\langle |i\rangle\langle i|, R[0/y]\rangle}\ {}_{1/2}\!\oplus \overline{\langle |-i\rangle\langle -i|, R[1/y]\rangle} = \Delta_1$$

Consider now the convex combination of the two distributions above, $\Delta''_{01} = \Delta_0\ {}_{1/2}\!\oplus \Delta_1$, and notice that $\mathcal{C}_0 \xrightarrow{\tau}_u \Delta_0$ and $\mathcal{C}_1 \xrightarrow{\tau}_u \Delta_1$. In the unscheduled semantics, Δ'_{01} can mix the two choices and reduce $\mathcal{C}_0$ with t_2 and $\mathcal{C}_1$ with t_3, formally, $\Delta'_{01} \xrightarrow{\tau}_u \Delta''_{01}$.

Finally, note that $\Delta''_{01} \longrightarrow_{\overline{t_4}} \Theta_{01}$ with $|\Theta_{01}| = 3/4$.

Consider now $\Delta'_{\pm}$, all the available moves for $\mathcal{C}_+$ and $\mathcal{C}_-$ follow

$$\mathcal{C}_+/\mathcal{C}_- \xrightarrow{\tau}_{\overline{t_2}} \overline{\langle |0\rangle\langle 0|, R[0/y]\rangle}\ {}_{1/2}\!\oplus \overline{\langle |1\rangle\langle 1|, R[1/y]\rangle},$$
$$\mathcal{C}_+/\mathcal{C}_- \xrightarrow{\tau}_{\overline{t_3}} \overline{\langle |i\rangle\langle i|, R[0/y]\rangle}\ {}_{1/2}\!\oplus \overline{\langle |-i\rangle\langle -i|, R[1/y]\rangle}.$$

It is easy to check that $\Delta'_{\pm}$ cannot replicate the behaviour of Δ'_{01}: for any choice of t_2 and t_3 it will reduce to a distribution $\Theta_{\pm}$ with $|\Theta_{\pm}| = 1/2$.

Schedulers solve this issue by forbidding to combine moves labelled by different choices: Δ'_{01} cannot mix the two choices in our scheduled semantics, and this allows us to prove Theorem 4.2.

Example 4.1 is paradigmatic, where different mixtures of quantum states are discriminated because the moves are chosen according to the value of some received qubit, which in theory should be unknown. Our schedulers do not allow processes to replicate this behaviour, forcing distributions to make a reasonable choice based on classically determined tags.

4.3 Labelled Bisimilarity

In this section we give an equivalent labelled characterization of our saturated bisimilarity, thus making explicit the observable properties of lqCCS processes.

We need some auxiliary definitions. First, given a distribution Δ of lqCCS processes, we let $qs(\Delta)$ be its quantum state $\sum_{\langle\rho,P\rangle\in\lceil\Delta\rceil}\Delta(\langle\rho,P\rangle)\cdot\rho$. Notice that $qs(\Delta)$ is a density operator in $\mathcal{DO}^{\leq}(\mathcal{H})$, with $\mathrm{tr}(qs(\Delta)) = |\Delta|$.

As a second ingredient, we allow applying superoperators to configurations and distributions. Given $\mathcal{E}\in\mathcal{SO}^{\leq}(\mathcal{H})$, we define $\dot{\mathcal{E}}:\mathcal{D}(Conf)\to\mathcal{D}(Conf)$ as

$$\dot{\mathcal{E}}\left(\sum_i p_i\bullet\langle\rho_i,P_i\rangle\right)=\sum_i\frac{p_i\cdot tr(\mathcal{E}(\rho_i))}{p_{\mathcal{E}}}\bullet\overline{\left\langle\frac{\mathcal{E}(\rho_i)}{\mathrm{tr}(\mathcal{E}(\rho_i))},P_i\right\rangle}$$

where $p_{\mathcal{E}}=\sum_i p_i\cdot tr(\mathcal{E}(\rho_i))$. Roughly, if $\mathcal{E}$ is trace-preserving, $\dot{\mathcal{E}}$ just applies $\mathcal{E}$ in the configurations. If $\mathcal{E}$ is trace non-increasing, $\dot{\mathcal{E}}$ applies $\mathcal{E}$ to each ρ_i and normalizes the resulting matrix; the new weight of the i-th configuration is the conditioned probability of being in i knowing that $\mathcal{E}$ happened. We extend $\dot{\mathcal{E}}$ to $\mathcal{D}(Conf_\perp)$ imposing that $\dot{\mathcal{E}}(\Delta\ {}_p\!\oplus\perp)=\dot{\mathcal{E}}(\Delta)\ {}_p\!\oplus\perp$ if $|\Delta|=1$. Given $\Sigma,\Sigma'\vdash\Delta$, if $\mathcal{E}$ is defined on $\tilde{q}$, which are only some of the qubits in Σ, we write $\dot{\mathcal{E}}(\Delta)$ for $\dot{\mathcal{E}}^{\tilde{q}}(\Delta)$ (recall that $\dot{\mathcal{E}}^{\tilde{q}}$ extends $\dot{\mathcal{E}}$ by tensoring it with the identity).

We can now define our labelled bisimilarity. In addition to the usual conditions about labelled transitions, labelled bisimulations are required to satisfy two additional conditions: paired distributions must share the same *environment*, i.e., the portion of the quantum state that is immediately visible to the context; and the relation must be closed for the application of normalized superoperators over the qubits of the environment. This superoperator-closure is needed for proving that labelled bisimilarity has the same observing power of saturated bisimilarity, as a context $B[\cdot]=[\cdot]\parallel Q$ can read and modify the qubits of the environment.

Definition 4.3. (Labelled Bisimilarity) *A relation* $\mathcal{R}\subseteq\mathcal{D}(Conf_\perp)\times\mathcal{D}(Conf_\perp)$ *is a* labelled bisimulation *if* $\Delta\,\mathcal{R}\,\Theta$ *implies* $(\Sigma,\Sigma')\vdash\Delta$ *and* $(\Sigma,\Sigma')\vdash\Theta$ *for some* Σ,Σ', *and it holds that*

- $tr_{\Sigma'}(qs(\Delta))=tr_{\Sigma'}(qs(\Theta))$;
- $\dot{\mathcal{E}}(\Delta)\ \mathcal{R}\ \dot{\mathcal{E}}(\Theta)$ *for any superoperator* $\mathcal{E}\in\mathcal{SO}^{\leq}(\mathcal{H}_{\Sigma\setminus\Sigma'})$;
- *whenever* $\Delta\xrightarrow{\mu}_\delta\Delta'$, *there exists* Θ' *such that* $\Theta\xrightarrow{\mu}_\delta\Theta'$ *and* $\Delta'\,\mathcal{R}\,\Theta'$;
- *whenever* $\Theta\xrightarrow{\mu}_\delta\Theta'$, *there exists* Δ' *such that* $\Delta\xrightarrow{\mu}_\delta\Delta'$ *and* $\Delta'\,\mathcal{R}\,\Theta'$.

Let labelled bisimilarity, *denoted* $\sim_l$, *be the largest labelled bisimulation.*

Note that superoperators acting over qubits that are not in the process may affect some of the qubits of the process too, due to entanglement.

Example 4.2. Let $\mathcal{C} = \langle |\Phi^+\rangle\langle\Phi^+|, \mathbb{M}_{01}(q_2 \rhd x).c!x.\mathbf{0}_{q_2}\rangle$ for $(\{q_1, q_2\}, \{q_2\}) \vdash \mathcal{C}$. Consider the trace non-increasing superoperator $\mathcal{E}^{q_1} = \{|0\rangle\langle 0|\}$ projecting the state of the first qubit (in the environment) to the value $|0\rangle\langle 0|$. The result of applying $\dot{\mathcal{E}}^{q_1}$ to $\mathcal{C}$ is $\langle |00\rangle\langle 00|, \mathbb{M}_{01}(q_2 \rhd x).c!x.\mathbf{0}_{q_2}\rangle$, where also the second qubit held by the process is updated.

Since the additional requirements of $\sim_l$ are inspired by discriminating contexts, it is to be expected that $\sim_s \subseteq \sim_l$. Indeed, the converse is also true.

Theorem 4.3. *For any Δ and Θ, $\Delta \sim_l \Theta$ if and only if $\Delta \sim_s \Theta$.*

Proof (sketch). First, we prove that $\sim_s$ is a labelled bisimulation: we assume $\Delta \sim_s \Theta$ and show that if the conditions of Definition 4.3 do not hold, then there exists a distinguishing context $B[\cdot]$ contradicting our assumption. If the visible quantum states differ, then $B[\cdot]$ just performs a measurement. If $\dot{\mathcal{E}}(\Delta) \not\sim \dot{\mathcal{E}}(\Theta)$, then $B[\cdot]$ applies a trace non-increasing superoperator on visible qubits. Finally, if Δ performs a labelled transition (e.g. an input action) that cannot be matched by Θ, then $B[\cdot]$ perform the "dual" transition (e.g. an output action).

Then, we prove that $\sim_l$ is a saturated bisimulation. Given $\Delta \sim_l \Theta$, and a generic context $B[\cdot]$, we consider all the three possible transitions for $B[\Delta]$: i) Δ moves with a τ action, thus also Θ does; ii) $B[\cdot]$ and Δ synchronize, meaning that Δ moves with a visible action, and so does Θ; iii) $B[\cdot]$ moves, possibly measuring or modifying the visible qubits, but thanks to the first two bullet points of Definition 4.3, $B[\Delta]$ and $B[\Theta]$ express the same behaviour.

We conclude with two real-world examples, quantum teleportation [3] and superdense coding [4].

Example 4.3. The objective of quantum teleportation is to allow Alice to send quantum information to Bob without a quantum channel. Alice and Bob must have each one of the qubits of an entangled pair $|\Phi^+\rangle$. The protocol works as follows: Alice performs a fixed set of unitaries to the qubit to transfer and to her part of the entangled pair; then, she measures the qubits and sends the classical outcome to Bob, which applies different unitaries to his own qubit according to the received information. In the end, the qubit of Bob will be in the state of Alice's one, and the entangled pair is discarded.

Consider the following encoding of the protocol $\mathbf{Tel} = (\mathbf{A} \parallel \mathbf{B}) \setminus c$, where we assume that Alice ($\mathbf{A}$) and Bob ($\mathbf{B}$) already share an entangled pair (q_1, q_2) (we write $(n)_2$ to stress that n is in binary representation)

$$\begin{aligned}
\mathbf{A} &= t\!:\!\mathrm{CNOT}(q_0, q_1).t\!:\!\mathrm{H}(q_0).t\!:\!\mathbb{M}^{01}_{23}(q_0, q_1 \rhd x).(t\!:\!c!x \parallel \mathbf{0}_{q_0,q_1}) \\
\mathbf{B} &= t'\!:\!c?y.\ \mathbf{if}\ y = (00)_2\ \mathbf{then}\ t'\!:\!\mathbb{I}(q_2).t'\!:\!\mathit{out}!q_2 \\
&\qquad \mathbf{else}\ (\mathbf{if}\ y = (01)_2\ \mathbf{then}\ t'\!:\!\mathrm{X}(q_2).t'\!:\!\mathit{out}!q_2 \\
&\qquad \mathbf{else}\ (\mathbf{if}\ y = (10)_2\ \mathbf{then}\ t'\!:\!\mathrm{Z}(q_2).t'\!:\!\mathit{out}!q_2 \\
&\qquad \mathbf{else}\ t'\!:\!\mathrm{ZX}(q_2).t'\!:\!\mathit{out}!q_2)) \\
\mathbf{Spec} &= t\!:\!\mathrm{SWAP}(q_0, q_2).t\!:\!\tau.t\!:\!\tau.(t, t')\!:\!\tau.t'\!:\!\tau.(t'\!:\!\mathrm{out}!q_2 \parallel \mathbf{0}_{q_0,q_1})
\end{aligned}$$

where $\mathbb{M}_{23}^{01}$ is the two-qubit measurement in the basis $\{|00\rangle, |01\rangle, |10\rangle, |11\rangle\}$. We let $\Delta = \overline{\langle|\psi\rangle\langle\psi| \otimes |\Phi^+\rangle\langle\Phi^+|, \mathbf{Tel}\rangle}$, with $\Theta = \overline{\langle|\psi\rangle\langle\psi| \otimes |\Phi^+\rangle\langle\Phi^+|, \mathbf{Spec}\rangle}$ its specification, for $|\psi\rangle = \alpha|0\rangle + \beta|1\rangle$, and sketch the proof for $\Delta \sim_l \Theta$ below. Note that **Spec** simply states that, after the tagged operations, the state of qubits is swapped and the correct state is communicated over the expected channel.

Since there is no qubit in $|\psi\Phi^+\rangle\langle\psi\Phi^+|$ apart from the ones in $\Sigma_{\mathbf{Tel}}$, the environment of the two distributions is trivially the same, and no superoperator is to be considered. The evolution of Δ and Θ is exactly the same until a send over the unrestricted channel *out* is reached. The relevant steps are

$$\Delta \xrightarrow{\tau}_t^3 \sum_{n=0}^{3} \frac{1}{4} \bullet \overline{\langle|n\rangle\langle n| \otimes |\psi_n\rangle\langle\psi_n|, (t\colon m!n \parallel \mathbf{0}_{q_0,q_1} \parallel \mathbf{B}) \setminus c\rangle}$$
$$\xrightarrow{\tau}_{(t,t')} \xrightarrow{\tau}_{t'} \Delta' = \sum_{n=0}^{3} \frac{1}{4} \bullet \overline{\langle|n\rangle\langle n| \otimes |\psi\rangle\langle\psi|, (\mathbf{0}_{q_0,q_1} \parallel t'\colon out!q_2) \setminus c\rangle}$$
$$\Theta \xrightarrow{\tau}_t^3 \xrightarrow{\tau}_{(t,t')} \xrightarrow{\tau}_{t'} \Theta' = \overline{\langle|\Phi^+\rangle\langle\Phi^+| \otimes |\psi\rangle\langle\psi|, t'\colon out!q_2 \parallel \mathbf{0}_{q_0,q_1}\rangle}$$

where $|\psi_0\rangle = |\psi\rangle$, $|\psi_1\rangle = \beta|0\rangle + \alpha|1\rangle$, $|\psi_2\rangle = \alpha|0\rangle - \beta|1\rangle$, $|\psi_3\rangle = \beta|0\rangle - \alpha|1\rangle$, and where, abusing notation, we use $|0\rangle = |00\rangle, |1\rangle = |01\rangle, |2\rangle = |10\rangle$ and $|3\rangle = |11\rangle$ when speaking of pairs of qubits. The last move is then a send on the channel *out* for both distributions

$$\Delta' \xrightarrow{out!q_2}_{t'} \Delta'' = \sum_{n=0}^{3} \frac{1}{4} \bullet \overline{\langle|n\rangle\langle n| \otimes |\psi\rangle\langle\psi|, (\mathbf{0}_{q_0,q_1})\rangle}$$
$$\Theta' \xrightarrow{out!q_2}_{t'} \Theta'' = \overline{\langle|\Phi^+\rangle\langle\Phi^+| \otimes |\psi\rangle\langle\psi|, \mathbf{0}_{q_0,q_1}\rangle}$$

The bisimilarity then is easily checked as Δ'' and Θ'' are in deadlock, and $\mathrm{tr}_{q_0,q_1}(qs(\Delta'')) = |\psi\rangle\langle\psi| = \mathrm{tr}_{q_0,q_1}(qs(\Theta''))$.

Example 4.4. Assume Alice and Bob have each a qubit of $|\Phi^+\rangle$. The protocol allows Alice to communicate a two-bit integer to Bob by sending her single qubit.

The protocol is as follows: Alice chooses an integer in $[0,3]$ and encodes it by applying suitable transformations to her qubit, which is then sent to Bob; Bob receives the qubit and decodes it by performing CNOT and $\mathrm{H} \otimes \mathbb{I}$ on the pair of qubits (the received qubit and his original one). Finally, he measures the qubits in the standard basis, recovering the integer chosen by Alice.

We consider the following encoding of the protocol $\mathbf{SDC} = (\mathbf{A} \parallel \mathbf{B}) \setminus c$.

$$\begin{aligned}
\mathbf{A} &= (t_0\colon \mathbb{I}(q_0).t\colon c!q_0) + (t_1\colon X(q_0).t\colon c!q_0) \\
&\quad + (t_2\colon Z(q_0).t\colon c!q_0) + (t_3\colon ZX(q_0).t\colon c!q_0) \\
\mathbf{B} &= t'\colon c?x.t'\colon \mathrm{CNOT}(x,q_1).t'\colon \mathrm{H}(x).t'\colon \mathbb{M}_{23}^{01}(x,q_1 \rhd y).t'\colon out!y.\mathbf{0}_{x,q_1} \\
\mathbf{Spec} &= t_0\colon \tau.(t,t')\colon \tau.t'\colon \tau.t'\colon \tau.t'\colon \tau.t'\colon out!0.\mathbf{0}_{q_0,q_1} + \\
&\quad t_1\colon \tau.(t,t')\colon \tau.t'\colon \tau.t'\colon \tau.t'\colon \tau.t'\colon out!1.\mathbf{0}_{q_0,q_1} + \\
&\quad t_2\colon \tau.(t,t')\colon \tau.t'\colon \tau.t'\colon \tau.t'\colon \tau.t'\colon out!2.\mathbf{0}_{q_0,q_1} + \\
&\quad t_3\colon \tau.(t,t')\colon \tau.t'\colon \tau.t'\colon \tau.t'\colon \tau.t'\colon out!3.\mathbf{0}_{q_0,q_1}
\end{aligned}$$

We let $\Delta = \overline{\langle |\Phi^+\rangle \langle \Phi^+| , \mathbf{SDC}\rangle}$, with $\Theta = \overline{\langle |\Phi^+\rangle \langle \Phi^+| , \mathbf{Spec}\rangle}$ its specification. Note that **Spec** states that the choice of the initial unitary determines the final value to be communicated.

Since there is no qubit in $|\Phi^+\rangle \langle \Phi^+|$ apart from the ones in $\Sigma_{\mathbf{SDC}}$, the environment of the two distributions is trivially the same, and no superoperator is to be considered. The evolutions of Δ and Θ are as follows, for $n = 0, 1, 2, 3$

$$\begin{aligned}
\Delta \xrightarrow{\tau}_{t_n} \xrightarrow{\tau}_{(t,t')} \xrightarrow{\tau}{}^{2}_{t'} & \overline{\langle |n\rangle \langle n| , \mathrm{M}^{01}_{23}(q_0, q_1 \rhd y).t' : out!y.\mathbf{0}_{q_0,q_1} \setminus c\rangle} \\
\xrightarrow{\tau}_{t'} & \Delta_n = \overline{\langle |n\rangle \langle n| , t' : out!n.\mathbf{0}_{q_0,q_1} \setminus c\rangle} \\
\Theta \xrightarrow{\tau}_{t_n} \xrightarrow{\tau}_{(t,t')} \xrightarrow{\tau}{}^{3}_{t'} & \Theta_n = \overline{\langle |\Phi^+\rangle \langle \Phi^+| , t' : out!n.\mathbf{0}_{q_0,q_1} \setminus c\rangle}
\end{aligned}$$

where we use $|n\rangle$ for the two qubits binary representation of the natural number $n \in \{0, 1, 2, 3\}$, namely $|0\rangle = |00\rangle , |1\rangle = |01\rangle , |2\rangle = |10\rangle$ and $|3\rangle = |11\rangle$.

Finally, note that $\Delta_n \sim_l \Theta_n$ for any n, because both distributions Δ_n and Θ_n sends the number n on the channel *out*, and reduce to deadlock distributions with empty quantum environment.

5 Conclusions and Future Work

We introduced a labelled version of lqCCS [10] enriched by tag-based schedulers. Resorting to simple schedulers allowed us to constrain processes so that they perform physically admissible choices only, i.e. independent of the quantum states. This suffices for making our proposed saturated bisimilarity $\sim_s$ compliant with the limited observational power prescribed by quantum theory (Theorem 4.2). Moreover, $\sim_s$ is by definition a congruence with respect to parallel composition. Finally, we characterized the atomic observable properties of lqCCS by deriving a labelled bisimilarity $\sim_l$, provably equivalent to $\sim_s$ (Theorem 4.3).

To the best of our knowledge, our work is the first behavioural equivalence for distributed, non-deterministic quantum systems that (*i*) is a congruence for the parallel operator, (*ii*) abides the prescriptions of quantum theory, and (*iii*) makes explicit the observables through labels.

Future Work. A fourth desideratum of a behavioural equivalence is being decidable. Our labelled bisimilarity goes in this direction, saving us from comparing processes under every possible context. However, the prescribed closure for superoperators still requires considering an infinite number of cases. As future work we will investigate if this condition can be safely removed from the definition of $\sim_l$, possibly in some specific cases. This would allow the bisimilarity of distributions of configurations to be decided. Moreover, we will investigate symbolic approaches for comparing lqCCS processes directly, i.e. for guaranteeing that they are bisimilar for all "ground" systems obtained by instantiating the quantum input. These approaches all maintain the same semantic model, that of probability distributions of configurations. We are investigating an alternative model, made of "quantum distributions", which generalize probability distributions by pairing a process with a single (partial) density operator, encoding both the quantum state and the probability, in the style of [8]. Such semantics would satisfy Theorem 4.2 by construction, and seems more adequate to model quantum protocols. Finally, a different line of research is to compare our tag-based approach with those of semantic schedulers, and to extend the capability of schedulers while preserving our results.

References

1. Andrés, M.E., Palamidessi, C., van Rossum, P., Sokolova, A.: Information hiding in probabilistic concurrent systems. Theoret. Comput. Sci. **412**(28), 3072–3089 (2011)
2. Bennett, C.H., Brassard, G.: Quantum cryptography: public key distribution and coin tossing. Theoret. Comput. Sci. **560**, 7–11 (2014)
3. Bennett, C.H., Brassard, G., Crépeau, C., Jozsa, R., Peres, A., Wootters, W.K.: Teleporting an unknown quantum state via dual classical and Einstein-Podolsky-Rosen channels. Phys. Rev. Lett. **70**, 1895–1899 (1993)
4. Bennett, C.H., Wiesner, S.J.: Communication via one- and two-particle operators on Einstein-Podolsky-Rosen states. Phys. Rev. Lett. **69**, 2881–2884 (1992)
5. Bonchi, F., Gadducci, F., Monreale, G.V.: A general theory of barbs, contexts, and labels. ACM Trans. Comput. Log. **15**(4), 1–27 (2014)
6. Caleffi, M., Cacciapuoti, A.S., Bianchi, G.: Quantum internet: from communication to distributed computing! In: Benediktsson, J.A., Dressler, F. (eds.) NANOCOM 2018, pp. 3:1–3:4. ACM (2018)
7. Canetti, R., Cheung, L., Kaynar, D.K., Liskov, M.D., Lynch, N.A., Pereira, O., Segala, R.: Time-bounded task-PIOAs: a framework for analyzing security protocols. In: Dolev, S. (ed.) DISC 2006. LNCS, vol. 4167, pp. 238–253. Springer (2006)
8. Ceragioli, L., Gadducci, F., Lomurno, G., Tedeschi, G.: Effect semantics for quantum process calculi. In: Majumdar, R., Silva, A. (eds.) CONCUR 2024. LIPIcs, vol. 311, pp. 16:1–16:22. Schloss Dagstuhl - Leibniz-Zentrum für Informatik (2024)
9. Ceragioli, L., Gadducci, F., Lomurno, G., Tedeschi, G.: Quantum bisimilarity is a congruence under physically admissible schedulers. CoRR **abs/2408.15087** (2024)
10. Ceragioli, L., Gadducci, F., Lomurno, G., Tedeschi, G.: Quantum bisimilarity via barbs and contexts: curbing the power of non-deterministic observers. Proc ACM Prog Lang **8**(POPL), 43:1269–43:1297 (2024)
11. Chatzikokolakis, K., Norman, G., Parker, D.: Bisimulation for demonic schedulers. In: de Alfaro, L. (ed.) FOSSACS 2009. LNCS, vol. 5504, pp. 318–332. Springer (2009)
12. Chatzikokolakis, K., Palamidessi, C.: Making random choices invisible to the scheduler. In: Caires, L., Vasconcelos, V.T. (eds.) CONCUR 2007. LNCS, vol. 4703, pp. 42–58. Springer (2007)
13. Davidson, T.A.S.: Formal Verification Techniques Using Quantum Process Calculus. Ph.D. thesis, University of Warwick (2012)
14. Deng, Y.: Bisimulations for probabilistic and quantum processes. In: Schewe, S., Zhang, L. (eds.) CONCUR 2018. LIPIcs, vol. 118, pp. 2:1–2:14. Schloss Dagstuhl - Leibniz-Zentrum für Informatik (2018)
15. Deng, Y., Feng, Y.: Open bisimulation for quantum processes. In: Baeten, J.C.M., Ball, T., de Boer, F.S. (eds.) TCS 2012. LNCS, vol. 7604, pp. 119–133. Springer (2012)

16. Feng, Y., Duan, R., Ying, M.: Bisimulation for quantum processes. ACM Trans. Program. Lang. Syst. **34**(4), 17:1–17:43 (2012)
17. Feng, Y., Ying, M.: Toward automatic verification of quantum cryptographic protocols. In: Aceto, L., de Frutos-Escrig, D. (eds.) CONCUR 2015. LIPIcs, vol. 42, pp. 441–455. Schloss Dagstuhl - Leibniz-Zentrum für Informatik (2015)
18. Gao, F., Qin, S., Huang, W., Wen, Q.: Quantum private query: a new kind of practical quantum cryptographic protocol. Sci. China Phys. Mech. Astron. **62**(7), 70301 (2019)
19. Gay, S.J., Nagarajan, R.: Communicating quantum processes. In: Palsberg, J., Abadi, M. (eds.) POPL 2005, pp. 145–157. ACM (2005)
20. Kubota, T., Kakutani, Y., Kato, G., Kawano, Y., Sakurada, H.: Application of a process calculus to security proofs of quantum protocols. In: Arabnia, H.R., Gravvanis, G.A., Solo, A.M.G. (eds.) FCS 2012, pp. 141–147. CSREA Press (2012)
21. Kubota, T., Kakutani, Y., Kato, G., Kawano, Y., Sakurada, H.: Semi-automated verification of security proofs of quantum cryptographic protocols. J. Symb. Comput. **73**, 192–220 (2016)
22. Lalire, M.: Relations among quantum processes: bisimilarity and congruence. Math. Struct. Comput. Sci. **16**(3), 407–428 (2006)
23. Lalire, M., Jorrand, P.: A process algebraic approach to concurrent and distributed quantum computation: operational semantics. CoRR **quant-ph/0407005** (2004)
24. Long, G.l., Deng, F.g., Wang, C., Li, X.H., Wen, K., Wang, W.Y.: Quantum secure direct communication and deterministic secure quantum communication. Front. Phys. China **2**(3), 251–272 (2007)
25. Nielsen, M.A., Chuang, I.L.: Quantum Computation and Quantum Information: 10th Anniversary Edition. Cambridge University Press (2010)
26. Nurhadi, A.I., Syambas, N.R.: Quantum key distribution (QKD) protocols: a survey. In: ICWT 2018, pp. 1–5. IEEE (2018)
27. Segala, R.: Modeling and Verification of Randomized Distributed Real-time Systems. Ph.D. thesis, Massachusetts Institute of Technology (1995)
28. Song, L., Feng, Y., Zhang, L.: Decentralized bisimulation for multiagent systems. In: Weiss, G., Yolum, P., Bordini, R.H., Elkind, E. (eds.) AAMAS 2015, pp. 209–217. ACM (2015)
29. Zhang, P., Chen, N., Shen, S., Yu, S., Wu, S., Kumar, N.: Future quantum communications and networking: a review and vision. IEEE Wirel. Commun. **31**(1), 141–148 (2024)

Non-deterministic, Probabilistic, and Quantum Effects Through the Lens of Event Structures

Vítor Fernandes[1](✉), Marc de Visme[2], and Benoît Valiron[2]

[1] University of Minho and INESC-TEC, Braga, Portugal
vitor.e.fernandes@inesctec.pt

[2] Université Paris-Saclay, CentraleSupélec, CNRS, ENS Paris-Saclay, Inria, Laboratoire Méthodes Formelles, 91190 Gif-sur-Yvette, France

Abstract. In this paper, we consider event structures and their probabilistic and quantum extensions as originally defined by Winskel. If these structures have already been part of sophisticated computational models, they have rarely been directly studied as an immediate model of execution traces of programs. This paper offers such an analysis. We propose a simple imperative operational framework and show how to derive soundness and adequacy results with event structures considered as a semantics. We show how event structures naturally handle non-deterministic, probabilistic and quantum effects.

1 Introduction

Concurrency is pervasive in modern computer architecture. Starting in the early 1960s, the study of its semantics, both operational and denotational, and within different paradigms (from interleaving to the so-called true concurrency) became a highly active research area with concrete implications in language design.

In the interleaving paradigm, saying that two atomic actions a and b are in parallel is interpreted as a then b or b then a. On the other hand, from a true concurrent point of view, the same command is interpreted as a and b, which are causally unrelated. We focus on the latter interpretation for which event structures [17,18] are a known model.

An event structure is a partial order with a conflict relation on events. If a and b are in conflict, then they are incompatible events, *i.e.* they cannot be performed in the same computation. Furthermore, event structures are very flexible, and proof of that is the fact that they have been used to study several computational effects: parallelism [18], probabilities [13,15,16], quantum effects [5,19], shared weak memory [3], etc.

Despite all the work around event structures on different computational effects, when the goal is to provide denotational semantics to a programming language, they seem to play a secondary role. More often than not, they serve as the backbone of some much more complex models, such as games and strategies [4,5,9]. Some exceptions are the works of Winskel [17,18], in which he

O. Kiselyov (Ed.): APLAS 2024, LNCS 15194, pp. 196–215, 2024.
https://doi.org/10.1007/978-981-97-8943-6_10

used event structures to give denotational semantics to CCS [7], and Marc de Visme [16], in which two notions of conflict are used in order to accommodate both probabilistic and non-deterministic choices in a probabilistic extension of CCS [2], who have used event structures as the primary model.

Contribution. In this paper, we aim at giving event structures the leading role as a computational model. Our work combines parallelism with three different algebraic effects: non-determinism, probabilities, and quantum. For each algebraic effect, we propose a small imperative-style programming language together with suitable operational semantics, wherein for the non-deterministic and quantum cases, we used a simple labeled transition system – or, in the probabilistic case, a labeled Segala automaton [11,12].

We rely on different flavors of event structures. For the non-deterministic case, we use the event structures defined by Winskel [18] as a base model. For the probabilistic case, we use probabilistic event structures [19]. For the quantum case, we consider a restriction of the definition in [19], which we call Unitary event structures. This modification allows us to extend [19, Theorem 3], which states that quantum event structures without events in conflict are probabilistic event structures when given an initial state, by dropping the necessity of having an empty conflict relation.

We also show that the operational and denotational semantics are sound and adequate for the three different algebraic effects considered. We do it by checking that the words created by the operational semantics and the covering chains in event structures, which are essentially finite sequences of events, coincide.

Plan of the paper. Section 2 presents the definition of the event structures used. Our contributions begin in Sect. 3 when we deal with the case of non-determinism, followed by the probabilistic case in Sect. 4, and finish in Sect. 5 where we deal with the quantum case, including the extension of [19, Theorem 3]. In Sect. 6 we give an overview of the related work.

Link to the Technical Report. The complete development, with proofs and extended discussions, can be found here [6]

2 Event Structures

An event structure [18] is a framework for representing events, their causal relation and their potential incompatibility. The latter is called *conflict*, and typically serve as a model of non-determinism.

Formally, an *event structure* is a structure $\mathrm{E} = (E, \leq, \#)$ consisting of a set E of events, which are partially ordered by $\leq$[1], the *causal dependency relation*, and a binary, symmetric, irreflexive relation $\# \subseteq E \times E$, the *conflict relation*, such that (1) for all $e \in E$ the set $\{e' \mid e' \leq e\}$ is finite, and (2) for all $e, e', e'' \in E$,

[1] for any two events $e_1, e_2 \in E$, $e_1 \leq e_2$ is read: e_2 depends on e_1.

if $e \# e' \leq e''$[2] then $e \# e''$. Events that are not causally related nor in conflict are said concurrent: e co e' is defined by $\neg(e \leq e')$, $\neg(e' \leq e)$, and $\neg(e \# e')$.

Configuration. To capture computations within event structures, we use the notion of *configuration*: subsets of the set of events for which events are not in conflict and are either concurrent or causally related. Formally: $x \subseteq E$ is a configuration if

- $\forall e, e' \in x \,.\, \neg(e \# e')$ (conflict-freeness);
- $\forall e, e' \,.\, e' \leq e \wedge e \in x \Rightarrow e' \in x$ (downward-closedness).

We write $\mathcal{C}(\mathrm{E})$ for the set of finite configurations of an event structure E, and $\mathcal{C}_{\max}(\mathrm{E})$ for the set of maximal configurations for the inclusion[3].

We say that the configuration x enables the event e, denoted $x \xrightarrow{e}\!\!\subset x \cup \{e\}$, when x is a configuration, $e \notin x$ and $x \cup \{e\}$ is a configuration. This allow us to softly introduce the notion of a *covering chain* of a configuration x, which will play an important role when showing the equivalence of the different semantics developed for the different languages. We define a covering chain over a configuration x as being a finite sequence of events $e_0, e_1, \ldots, e_n$ such that $\emptyset \xrightarrow{e_1}\!\!\subset x_1 \xrightarrow{e_2}\!\!\subset x_2 \xrightarrow{e_3}\!\!\subset \cdots \xrightarrow{e_n}\!\!\subset x_n$, with $x_n = x$. Note that for a configuration x, there may exist more than one covering chain, as shown in Example 2.1. Furthermore we may write $\emptyset \xrightarrow{\omega}\!\!\subset x$ instead of $\emptyset \xrightarrow{e_1}\!\!\subset x_1 \xrightarrow{e_2}\!\!\subset x_2 \xrightarrow{e_3}\!\!\subset \cdots \xrightarrow{e_n}\!\!\subset x_n$, where $\omega = e_1 e_2 \ldots e_n$ and $x_n = x$.

The causal relation is transitive and the conflict relation is hereditary over events. Combining these two relations, when drawing an event structure, would lead to redundant information, making the event structure harder to understand. To ease such task, we find it useful to use the notions of *immediate causality*, pictured by $\rightarrowtriangle$, and *minimal conflict*, represented by $\sim$. Let E be an event structure such that $e_1, e_2 \in E$. We say $e_1 \rightarrowtriangle e_2$ iff $e_1 < e_2$ and $\nexists e_3 \in E \,.\, e_1 < e_3 < e_2$. We say $e_1 \sim e_2$ iff $e_1 \# e_2$ and whenever $e_1' \leq e_1$, $e_1' \# e_2'$, and $e_2' \leq e_2$ we have $e_1 = e_1'$ and $e_2 = e_2'$. Note that it is possible to deduce the causal and conflict relations from the immediate causality and minimal conflict relations.

Example 2.1. To get the reader familiarized with event structures we show in Fig. 1a an event structure with four events, a, b, c, and d, where: b causally depends on a, c and d are concurrent events which are in conflict with a, and consequently also with b. Furthermore, note that a is in minimal conflict with c and d. The set of configurations, *i.e.* the set of possible computations, is $\{\emptyset, \{a\}, \{c\}, \{d\}, \{a, b\}, \{c, d\}\}$. The configuration $\{c, d\}$, which is composed of two concurrent events, has two possible covering chains: $\emptyset \xrightarrow{d}\!\!\subset \{d\} \xrightarrow{c}\!\!\subset \{c, d\}$ and $\emptyset \xrightarrow{c}\!\!\subset \{c\} \xrightarrow{d}\!\!\subset \{c, d\}$. Moreover, $\{b\}$ is not a configuration because it is not down-closed, *i.e.* b causally depends on a but $a \notin \{b\}$.

[2] $e \# e' \leq e''$ is to be understood as $(e \# e')$ and $(e' \leq e'')$.
[3] *i.e.* a configuration x is maximal iff $\nexists y \in \mathcal{C}(\mathrm{E})$ such that $x \subset y$.

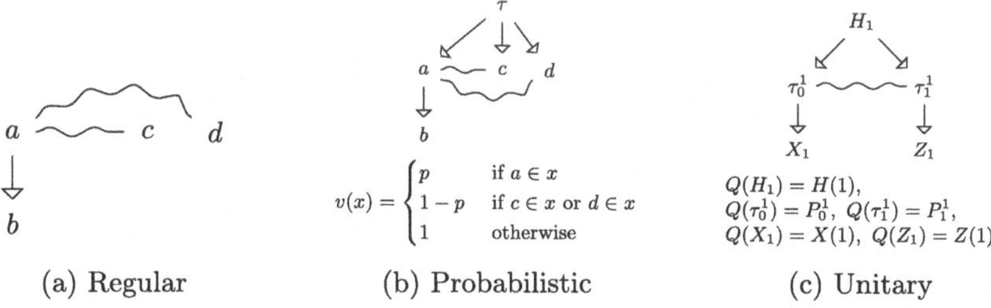

Fig. 1. Examples of event structures

2.1 Probabilistic Event Structures

Event structures are versatile enough to support effects. In this section, we describe how to endow event structures with a probabilistic effect, while Sect. 2.2 will be devoted to the quantum case.

Probabilistic event structures [19] are event structures together with a valuation on configurations $v : \mathcal{C}(\mathrm{E}) \to [0,1]$, which given a configuration x gives us the probability of reaching at least that configuration, such that $v(\emptyset) = 1$ and a condition that assures the non-existence of negative probabilities.

Definition 2.2. (Probabilistic event structure) Let $\mathrm{E} = (E, \leq, \#)$ be an event structure. A configuration-valuation on E is a function $v : \mathcal{C}(\mathrm{E}) \to [0,1]$ such that $v(\emptyset) = 1$ and $\forall y, x_1, \ldots x_n \in \mathcal{C}(\mathrm{E})$ such that $y \subseteq x_1, \ldots, x_n$, we have

$$v(y) - \sum_{\emptyset \neq I \subseteq \{1,\ldots,n\}} (-1)^{|I|+1} v\left(\bigcup_{i \in I} x_i\right) \geq 0 \tag{1}$$

where $v(x) = 0$ whenever $x \notin \mathcal{C}(\mathrm{E})$. A *probabilistic event structure* $\mathrm{P} = (\mathrm{E}, v)$ is defined as the data consisting of an event structure $\mathrm{E} = (E, \leq, \#)$ together with a configuration-valuation $v : \mathcal{C}(\mathrm{E}) \to [0,1]$.

From Eq. 1 we can conclude that the valuation on configurations is decreasing, *i.e.* $y \subseteq x \Rightarrow v(y) \geq v(x)$. Furthermore, the sum of the probability of events in conflict is less than or equal to one: $\forall 1 \leq i \leq n$, $x \xrightarrow{e_i}\!\!\subset x_i$ and $\forall 1 \leq i < j \leq n$, $e_i \# e_j \Rightarrow \sum_{i=1}^{n} \dfrac{v(x \cup \{e_i\})}{v(x)} \leq 1$.

Remark 2.3. The definition of probabilistic event structures in [19] makes use of a *drop condition* function, which is intuitively seen as the probability of reaching at least a configuration y without reaching any of the $x_1, \ldots, x_n$ with $y \subseteq x_1, \ldots, x_n$. The formulation of the drop condition we use in Definition 2.2 follows from [19, Proposition 1].

Example 2.4. Fig. 1b shows a probabilistic event structure very similar to the event structure in Fig. 1a, the only difference being the addition of a new event τ, for which the events a, c, and d are causally dependent. The event τ is used to indicate that the events that are causally immediate to it, *i.e.* $\tau \rightarrow a$, $\tau \rightarrow c$, and $\tau \rightarrow d$ arose from a probabilistic choice and consequently they have probabilities associated, as can be seen by the configuration-valuation. The set of configurations is composed of $\{\emptyset, \{\tau\}, \{\tau, a\}, \{\tau, c\}\{\tau, d\}, \{\tau, a, b\}, \{\tau, c, d\}\}$, where $\{\tau, a, b\}$ and $\{\tau, c, d\}$ are maximal configurations with probability p and $1-p$, respectively.

2.2 Unitary Event Structures

The basic unit in quantum information is the qubit, a unit vector in the Hilbert space $\mathbb{C}^2$. Using Dirac notation, we can write the state of a qubit as a linear combination $\alpha|0\rangle + \beta|1\rangle$, where $|0\rangle$ and $|1\rangle$ are the basis vectors of $\mathbb{C}^2$ and $\alpha, \beta \in \mathbb{C}$ such that $|\alpha|^2 + |\beta|^2 = 1$. For a system of n qubits, the tensor product of each qubit gives its associated space, *i.e.* $\mathbb{C}^{2^{\otimes n}}$.

To manipulate qubit states, we use unitary operations and measurements. A unitary operation U is an invertible linear function that preserves the norm of a quantum state. A measurement projects a quantum state onto one of the basis vectors, which results in probabilistic outcomes. For example, a one-qubit system in the state $\alpha|0\rangle + \beta|1\rangle$ is projected to $|0\rangle$ with probability $|\alpha|^2$ or to $|1\rangle$ with probability $|\beta|^2$.

For our purposes, we also need a partial density operator, which is a positive operator whose trace is less or equal to one. The general form of a partial density operator is $\rho = \sum_i p_i |\psi_i\rangle\langle\psi_i|$, where p_i is a probability and ψ_i are quantum states, with $\langle\psi_i|$ being the conjugate transpose of $|\psi_i\rangle$. We denote by $\mathcal{H}$ the associated space of the partial density operators. We let $\mathcal{D}_{\leq 1}(\mathcal{H})$ be the set of partial density operators, and we use ρ to represent a partial density operator. More details about these topics can be found in [8].

A quantum event structure [19] is an event structure together with a function that maps events to unitary operators or projections on a finite-dimensional Hilbert space $\mathcal{H}$, stating that operators of concurrent events must commute.

For reasons that shall be detailed in Sect. 5.2, we add two new conditions to Winskel's definition and we call the resultant structure *unitary event structures.* We impose the minimal conflict to be transitive and the sum of the operators from events in minimal conflict should be a unitary operator. The intuition behind the restrictions is to consider events in minimal conflict as measurements. To define unitary event structures we make use of the equivalence class of an event e, which is composed by itself or by the events in which e is in minimal conflict, *i.e.* $[e] = \{e' \mid e = e' \text{ or } e \sim e'\}$.

Definition 2.5. (Unitary Event Structure) A unitary event structure over a finite-dimensional Hilbert space $\mathcal{H}$, is a pair $(\mathrm{E},\ Q : E \rightarrow Op(\mathcal{H}))$ comprised of an event structure $\mathrm{E} = (E, \leq, \#)$, where Q maps events $e \in E$ to projection/unitary operators on $\mathcal{H}$ such that:

- $\forall e_1, e_2 \in E$, e_1 co $e_2 \Rightarrow Q(e_1)Q(e_2) = Q(e_2)Q(e_1)$
- $\sim$ is transitive
- $\forall e \in E$, $\sum_{e' \in [e]} Q(e')$ is unitary

Given a finite configuration, $x \in \mathcal{C}(\mathrm{E})$, define the operator A_x to be the composition $Q_{e_n}Q_{e_{n-1}} \cdots Q_{e_2}Q_{e_1}$ for some covering chain $\emptyset \overset{e_1}{-\!\!\subset} x_1 \overset{e_2}{-\!\!\subset} x_2 \cdots \overset{e_n}{-\!\!\subset} x_n$ in $\mathcal{C}(\mathrm{E})$, with $x_n = x$. We additionally set $A_\emptyset = \mathsf{id} : \mathcal{H} \rightarrow \mathcal{H}$ for the initial configuration. An *initial state* is given by a density operator ρ on $\mathcal{H}$.

As discussed in [19], A_x is well-defined because for any two coverings chains of x, the corresponding sequences of events are Mazurkiewicz trace equivalent, *i.e.* one is obtainable from the other by successively interchanging concurrent events.

Despite knowing that measurements are the cause of probabilities, from Definition 2.5 we note that no probabilities are associated with unitary event structures, unlike what happens with probabilistic event structures. However, according to [19, Theorem 3], there is a way to transform quantum event structures without conflicting events, also known as elementary quantum event structures, into probabilistic event structures. In Sect. 5.2, we explore how this is done and how the additional restrictions allow us to remove the elementary condition.

Example 2.6. In Fig. 1c, we have depicted a unitary event structure composed of the events H_1, τ_0^1, τ_1^1, X_1, and Z_1. H_1 is the initial event, followed by τ_0^1, which leads to X_1, and τ_1^1, which leads to Z_1. Note that τ_0^1 and τ_1^1 are in conflict (specifically, in minimal conflict). Furthermore, since the conflict relation is hereditary, X_1 and Z_1 are also in conflict.

Following the definition, the set of configurations is $\{\emptyset$, $\{H_1\}$, $\{H_1, \tau_0^1\}$, $\{H_1, \tau_1^1\}$, $\{H_1, \tau_0^1, X_1\}$, $\{H_1, \tau_1^1, Z_1\}\}$. As said in Definition 2.5, from a configuration x we can define the operator A_x. For example, if we consider the maximal configurations $\{H_1, \tau_0^1, X_1\}$ and $\{H_1, \tau_1^1, Z_1\}$, the respective operators are $X(1)P_0^1\, H(1)$ and $Z(1)P_1^1\, H(1)$. The former applies the Hadamard gate to qubit 1, projects it to $|0\rangle$, and then applies the X gate. The latter, after applying the Hadamard gate, projects the qubit to $|1\rangle$ and then applies the Z gate.

3 Non-deterministic Effects

3.1 Language

We present a language with non-deterministic and recursion operators, which is similar to the one in [1]. It is described by the following grammar,

$$C ::= \mathit{skip} \mid a \in \mathit{Act} \mid C\,;\,C \mid C \,||\, C \mid C \,\Box\, C \mid \mu X.C \mid \; \mathrm{X}$$

where *skip* is a command that does nothing; a is an atomic action from a predetermined set of atomic actions, denoted as *Act*; $C\,;\,C$ is the usual sequential composition of programs; $C \,||\, C$ is the parallel composition of commands; $C \,\Box\, C$ represents the non-deterministic choice; $\mu X.C$ is the recursive command; and

$$skip \xrightarrow{sk} \checkmark \qquad a \xrightarrow{a} \checkmark \qquad \frac{C_1 \xrightarrow{l} \checkmark}{C_1\,;C_2 \xrightarrow{l} C_2} \qquad \frac{C_1 \xrightarrow{l} C_1'}{C_1\,;C_2 \xrightarrow{l} C_1'\,;C_2} \qquad \frac{C_1 \xrightarrow{l} \checkmark}{C_1 \square C_2 \xrightarrow{l} \checkmark}$$

$$\frac{C_1 \xrightarrow{l} C_1'}{C_1 \square C_2 \xrightarrow{l} C_1'} \qquad \frac{C_1 \xrightarrow{l} \checkmark}{C_1 \,||\, C_2 \xrightarrow{l} C_2} \qquad \frac{C_1 \xrightarrow{l} C_1'}{C_1 \,||\, C_2 \xrightarrow{l} C_1' \,||\, C_2} \qquad \frac{C \xrightarrow{l} C'}{\mu X.C \xrightarrow{l} C'[X \leftarrow \mu X.C]}$$

(and the symmetric rules for $\square$ and $||$)

$$\frac{C \xrightarrow{l} C'}{C \overset{l}{\twoheadrightarrow} C'} \qquad \frac{C \xrightarrow{l} C'' \quad C'' \overset{\omega'}{\twoheadrightarrow} C'}{C \overset{l:\omega'}{\twoheadrightarrow} C'}$$

Fig. 2. Rules of the operational semantics

$X \in Var$ with Var a set of command variables. Furthermore, we only consider closed commands, *i.e.* commands in which every variable X is bound by a recursion μX and in sequential composition we only allow recursion to occur on the right-hand-side.

We denote by $L = Act \cup \{sk\}$[4] the set of labels, which is ranged by l, and we consider a *terminal command*, denoted by $\checkmark$, representing the end of a computation. The small-step semantics is then defined as the smallest relation $\xrightarrow{l} \subseteq C \times L \times (C \cup \{\checkmark\})$ obeying the rules in Fig. 2.

The rules depicted in Fig. 2 are strongly influenced by CCS [7, Sect. 2], where commands lack associated states and transitions are labeled by triggering actions, and an imperative language [10, Chaps. 6 and 8], where both of the actions *skip* and a lead to the terminal command (or, as in [10, Chaps. 6 and 8], to a final state). Furthermore, we keep implicit the rules for the right command for the non-deterministic and parallel operators (for the languages in Sects. 4 and 5 we proceed in a similar way).

We now introduce an n-step semantics based on the small-step semantics. We begin by defining $\omega ::= l \mid l : \omega$ as being a *word*, where $l : \omega$ appends l to the beginning of ω. Intuitively, a word is a sequence of labels, hence it can also be seen as an element of L^+, *i.e.* a non-empty finite sequence. The n-step transition is defined by the relation $\overset{\omega}{\twoheadrightarrow} \subseteq C \times L^+ \times (C \cup \{\checkmark\})$ obeying the two bottom rules in Fig. 2. The relation $\overset{\omega}{\twoheadrightarrow}$ can be seen as the transitive closure of $\xrightarrow{l}$, where the left rule represents the base case and the right rule represents the transitive part.

Example 3.1. The initial program is $(a\,; b) \square (c \,||\, d)$, from which we have three possible transitions: by a, c or d. If we transit by a, we reach the command b, which we execute to finish the computation. Otherwise, we could either transit via c and then execute d, or transit via d and then execute c, in order to finish the computation. With the support of Fig. 3a together with the above explanation, we can straightforwardly deduce the words that can be formed by the n-step semantics: a, c, d, ab, cd, and dc.

[4] *sk* is the label for the command *skip*.

Example 3.2. Fig. 3d illustrates the behavior of a non-deterministic toss coin, which produces a possibly empty sequence of a's that finishes with sk. To understand this we observe that the initial program has two possible transitions: (1) we execute sk that terminates the computation; (2) we execute a, and we transit to a command equal to the initial one with the same two possible transitions.

3.2 Constructions on Event Structures

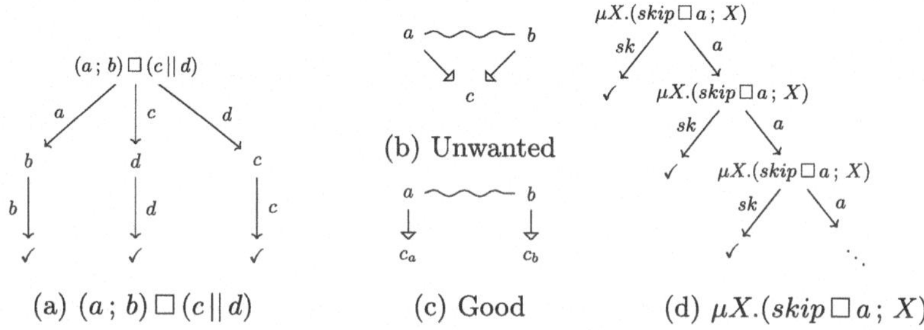

(a) $(a\,;\,b)\,\Box\,(c\,||\,d)$ (b) Unwanted (c) Good (d) $\mu X.(skip\,\Box\,a\,;\,X)$

Fig. 3. Examples of executions

To capture the behavior of the language's operators, we need to define them in terms of event structures.

Let us begin with sequential composition. Consider $a\,;\,b$ to be the sequential combination of two actions, a and b. According to the rules in Fig. 2, we execute b after a has been executed, which with an event structure view means that b causally depends on a. As a first attempt to define the sequential composition of two event structures, $\mathrm{E}_1\,;\,\mathrm{E}_2$, one might try to connect every event of E_1 with every event of E_2. However, this approach fails to interpret programs like $(a\,\Box\,b)\,;\,c$, as show in Fig. 3b. This failure arises because there are two ways to reach event c, which come from conflicting events. According to the definition of event structures, the conflict relation is hereditary and an event is not in conflict with itself. Thus, we would end up with an invalid event structure. To address this issue, we introduce a 'copy' for each event of E_2 regarding the different ways it can be reached. For example, in the program mentioned above, we create two copies of c: one indicating it was reached by executing event a, and another indicating it was reached by executing event b, as can be seen in Fig. 3c.

Definition 3.3. (Sequential Composition) Let $\mathrm{E}_1 = (E_1, \leq_1, \#_1)$ and $\mathrm{E}_2 = (E_2, \leq_2, \#_2)$ be event structures. Define $\mathrm{E}_1\,;\,\mathrm{E}_2 = (E, \leq, \#)$ as:

$$
\begin{aligned}
E &= E_1 \uplus (E_2 \times \mathcal{C}_{\max}(\mathrm{E}_1))\\
\leq &= \{e_1 \leq e_1' \mid e \leq_1 e'\} \cup \{(e_2, x) \leq (e_2', x) \mid\ e_2 \leq_2 e_2'\} \cup \{e_1 \leq (e_2, x) \mid e_1 \in x\}\\
\# &= \{e\#e' \mid \exists (e_1 \leq e, e_1' \leq e')\,.\, e_1\#_1 e_1'\} \cup \{(e_2, x)\#(e_2', x) \mid e_2\#_2 e_2'\}
\end{aligned}
$$

where $E_2 \times \mathcal{C}_{\max}(\mathrm{E}_1) = \{(e, x) \mid e \in E_2,\ x \in \mathcal{C}_{\max}(\mathrm{E}_1)\}$ and $\uplus$ denotes the disjoint union[5].

Note that we multiply E_2 with the maximal configurations of E_1, since maximal configurations represent finished computations.

The absence of communication in the language considered simplifies the definition of the parallel composition in event structures compared to [18] since we do not need a synchronization mechanism. In our case, we place the two event structures 'side-by-side'.

Definition 3.4. (**Parallel Composition**) Let $\mathrm{E}_1 = (E_1, \leq_1, \#_1)$ and $\mathrm{E}_2 = (E_2, \leq_2, \#_2)$ be event structures. Define $\mathrm{E}_1 \,||\, \mathrm{E}_2$ as $(E_1 \uplus E_2,\ \leq_1 \uplus \leq_2,\ \#_1 \uplus \#_2)$.

In Definition 3.4 we use the disjoint union to ensure that whenever we interpret the same command in parallel, *i.e.* $C \,||\, C$, we have two copies of C within the event structure, as each action of C can occur twice.

At last we have the non-deterministic composition of event structures. Let us use the rules in Fig. 2 to give the intuition behind the definition. Consider the command $a \,\Box\, b$. According to the operational semantics, if we execute a then we cannot execute b and if we execute b we cannot execute a. If we abstract ourselves and instead of $a \,\Box\, b$ we consider $C_1 \,\Box\, C_2$, we notice that if we execute an action from C_1, then it is no longer possible to execute any action of C_2 and vice-versa. To capture this behavior in event structures, we need to put all the events corresponding to C_1 in conflict with all the events corresponding to C_2. Formally:

Definition 3.5. (**Non-deterministic Sum**) Let $\mathrm{E}_1 = (E_1, \leq_1, \#_1)$ and $\mathrm{E}_2 = (E_2, \leq_2, \#_2)$ be event structures. Define $\mathrm{E}_1 \,\Box\, \mathrm{E}_2$ by

$$(E_1 \uplus E_2, \quad \leq_1 \uplus \leq_2, \quad \#_1 \uplus \#_2 \cup \{e_1 \# e_2 \mid e_1 \in E_1,\ e_2 \in E_2\})$$

To define the interpretation of $\mu X.C$ we use the least-fixed point. We begin by defining an ordering of event structures that does not ignore the copies created by the sequential composition of event structures.

Definition 3.6. (**Partial Order**) Let $\mathrm{E}_1 = (E_1, \leq_1, \#_1)$ and $\mathrm{E}_2 = (E_2, \leq_2, \#_2)$ be event structures. We write $\mathrm{E}_1 \trianglelefteq \mathrm{E}_2$ whenever $E_1 \subseteq E_2$ and $\forall e, e' \,.\, e \leq_1 e' \Leftrightarrow e, e' \in E_1 \wedge e \leq_2 e'$ and $\forall e, e' \,.\, e \#_1 e' \Leftrightarrow e, e' \in E_1 \wedge e \#_2 e'$.

The relation $\trianglelefteq$ in Definition 3.6 is a cpo with bottom and with least upper bounds for every ω-chain, denoted with $\bigsqcup_n \mathrm{E}_n$. We also write $fix(\Gamma)$ for the least upper bound of the chain $\bot \trianglelefteq \Gamma(\bot) \trianglelefteq \cdots \trianglelefteq \Gamma^n(\bot) \trianglelefteq \ldots$. We can prove that the operators of the language are continuous, with sequential composition being only right-continuous (consequence of only allowing recursive commands on the right-hand-side).

Having defined all the constructors of the language in terms of event structures, we can now interpret commands as event structures as follows.

---

[5] The proper definition of the disjoint union is $A \uplus B = \{(0, a) | a \in A\} \cup \{(1, b) | b \in B\}$. For $R, S \in A \times B$, the disjoint union extends to a relation as $(i, e) R \uplus S (i', e')$ whenever $i = 0 = i'$ and eRe' or $i = 1 = i'$ and eSe'. For the sake of keeping the notations readable, we will keep the 0s and 1s implicit.

Definition 3.7. Let an *environment* be a function $\gamma : Var \to \mathrm{E}$ from variables to event structures. For a command C and an environment γ define $[\![C]\!]_\gamma$ as follows: $[\![skip]\!]_\gamma = (\{sk\}, \{sk \leq sk\}, \emptyset)$, $[\![a]\!]_\gamma = (\{a\}, \{a \leq a\}, \emptyset)$, $[\![X]\!]_\gamma = \gamma(X)$. The binary operators are $[\![C_1 \,;\, C_2]\!]_\gamma = [\![C_1]\!]_\gamma \,;\, [\![C_2]\!]_\gamma$, $[\![C_1 \,\square\, C_2]\!]_\gamma = [\![C_1]\!]_\gamma \,\square\, [\![C_2]\!]_\gamma$, $[\![C_1 \,||\, C_2]\!]_\gamma = [\![C_1]\!]_\gamma \,||\, [\![C_2]\!]_\gamma$. The fixpoint is $[\![\mu X.C]\!]_\gamma = fix(\Gamma^{C,\gamma})$, where $\Gamma^{C,\gamma} : \mathrm{E} \to \mathrm{E}$ is given by $\Gamma^{C,\gamma}(\mathrm{E}) = [\![C]\!]_{\gamma(X \leftarrow \mathrm{E})}$. Note how $\Gamma^{C,\gamma}$ is continuous.

3.3 Semantics Equivalence

To relate the operational semantics with the denotational semantics, we need to consider the relationship between the event structure of a program C and the program C' to which it reduces. C' is typically C minus its initial command. From the denotational semantics point of view, this amounts to remove the initial event of the corresponding event structure.

When removing an initial event from an event structure, not only the event itself but also all conflicting events are eliminated. This decision aims to mimic, within event structures, what happens in a transition using the small-step semantics. In small-step semantics, once an action triggers a transition, that same action cannot be executed again. Furthermore, if the transition occurs within a non-deterministic program, only the program associated with the triggering action continues, while the others are discarded.

Definition 3.8. (**Remove initial event**) Let $\mathrm{E} = (E, \leq, \#)$ be an event structure and $a \in \mathcal{I}(\mathrm{E}) = \{e' \mid \nexists e \in E \,.\, e \leq e' \wedge e \neq e'\}$, with $\mathcal{I}(\mathrm{E})$ being the set of initial events of E. Define $\mathrm{E}\backslash a$ as

$$(\{e \in E \mid \neg(e\#a),\, e \neq a\},\quad \{e \leq e' \mid e, e' \in E'\},\quad \{e\#e' \mid e, e' \in E'\})$$

The removal of the initial event is compatible with the various constructions of event structures that we defined above. For instance, $(\mathrm{E}_1 \,;\, \mathrm{E}_2)\backslash l \equiv (\mathrm{E}_1\backslash l) \,;\, \mathrm{E}_2$ and $(\mathrm{E}_1 \,||\, \mathrm{E}_2)\backslash l \equiv (\mathrm{E}_1\backslash l) \,||\, (\mathrm{E}_2\backslash l)$. From this we can derive a local soundness result, stating that if $C \xrightarrow{l} C'$ then $[\![C']\!]_\gamma \equiv [\![C]\!]_\gamma\backslash l$, and a local adequacy result, stating that if $l \in \mathcal{I}([\![C]\!]_\gamma)$, then $\exists C' \in (C \cup \{\checkmark\})$ s.t $C \xrightarrow{l} C'$ and $[\![C]\!]_\gamma\backslash l \equiv [\![C']\!]_\gamma$.

This makes it possible to show the main result of this section.

Theorem 3.9. *(**Soundness**) If $C \overset{\omega}{\twoheadrightarrow} C'$, then there exists $x \in \mathcal{C}([\![C]\!]_\gamma)$ such that $\emptyset \overset{\omega}{-\!\!\subset} x$.* □

Theorem 3.10. *(**Adequacy**) If $\emptyset \neq x \in \mathcal{C}([\![C]\!]_\gamma)$ with $\emptyset \overset{\omega}{-\!\!\subset} x$ then there exists C' s.t. $C \overset{\omega}{\twoheadrightarrow} C'$.* □

Theorem 3.9 states that every word ω derived from the n-step semantics corresponds to a covering chain, and consequently to a configuration. Conversely, Theorem 3.10 indicates that if we have a non-empty covering chain ω, then there exists a command C' reachable from C by executing ω.

Example 3.11. The event structure in Example 2.1 corresponds to the command in Example 3.1. To see how the semantics relate, recall the configurations in Example 2.1 and the words in Example 3.1. Let us select the words cd and dc. It is straightforward to see that each word corresponds to a covering chain, $\emptyset \stackrel{d}{-\!\!\subset} \{d\} \stackrel{c}{-\!\!\subset} \{d,c\}$ and $\emptyset \stackrel{c}{-\!\!\subset} \{c\} \stackrel{d}{-\!\!\subset} \{d,c\}$, respectively. Both covering chains correspond to the configuration $\{d,c\}$. Conversely, the configuration $\{d,c\}$ is obtained by two covering chains: $\emptyset \stackrel{d}{-\!\!\subset} \{d\} \stackrel{c}{-\!\!\subset} \{d,c\}$ and $\emptyset \stackrel{c}{-\!\!\subset} \{c\} \stackrel{d}{-\!\!\subset} \{d,c\}$. It is straightforward to see that each covering chain corresponds to the words dc and cd, respectively.

$$skip \to 1 \cdot (sk, \checkmark) \qquad a \to 1 \cdot (a, \checkmark) \qquad C_1 +_p C_2 \to p \cdot (\tau, C_1) + (1-p) \cdot (\tau, C_2)$$

$$\frac{C_1 \to 1 \cdot (l, \checkmark)}{C_1 \,;\, C_2 \to 1 \cdot (l, C_2)} \quad \frac{C_1 \to \sum_i p_i \cdot (l', C_i)}{C_1 \,;\, C_2 \to \sum_i p_i \cdot (l', C_i \,;\, C_2)} \quad \frac{C_1 \to 1 \cdot (l, \checkmark)}{C_1 \,||\, C_2 \to 1 \cdot (l, C_2)} \quad \frac{C_1 \to \sum_i p_i \cdot (l', C_i)}{C_1 \,||\, C_2 \to \sum_i p_i \cdot (l', C_i \,||\, C_2)}$$

$$\frac{C \to 1 \cdot (l, C')}{\mu X.C \to 1 \cdot (l, C'[X \leftarrow \mu X.C])} \quad \frac{C \to \sum_i p_i \cdot (\tau, C_i)}{\mu X.C \to \sum_i p_i \cdot (\tau, C_i[X \leftarrow \mu X.C])}$$

$$\frac{C \to \sum_i p_i \cdot (l', C_i)}{C \twoheadrightarrow \sum_i p_i \cdot (l', C_i)} \qquad \frac{C \to \sum_i p_i (l', C_i) \qquad \forall i\, C_i \twoheadrightarrow \sum_j p_j \cdot (\omega_{ij}, C_{ij})}{C \twoheadrightarrow \sum_i p_i \left(\sum_j p_j \cdot (l' : \omega_{ij}, C_{ij})\right)}$$

Fig. 4. Rules of the probabilistic operational semantics

4 Probabilistic Effects

In this section, we show how the probabilistic event structure presented in Sect. 2.1 can be seen as a model of probabilistic computation. To this end, we take as basis the previous language and substitute the non-deterministic choice by a probabilistic choice, as shown in the following grammar,

$$C ::= skip \mid a \in Act \mid C \,;\, C \mid C \,||\, C \mid C +_p C \mid \mu X.C \mid \mathrm{X}$$

where $C +_p C$ is the probabilistic choice operator in which $p \in]0,1[$.

In the design of this language we made two choices: the first was to substitute the non-deterministic operator by the probabilistic operator and the second concerns the intervals for which p ranges. The justification for the former is related with the chosen probabilistic event structure. In sum, Winskel probabilistic event structures are not suitable to model a language that posses both non-deterministic and probabilistic operators as explained in [16]. Regarding the latter, the intervals chosen are influenced by Definition 4.7, since it is not reasonable to remove an initial event when its probability is zero.

We extend the set of labels with a new label τ, *i.e.* $L' = L \cup \{\tau\}$ and let it be ranged by l'. Similarly to process algebra, τ will denote an invisible transition.

We fix $\mathrm{D}(X) = \{\psi : X \to [0,1] \mid sup(\psi) \text{ finite}, \sum_{x \in X} \psi(x) = 1\}$ as being the probabilistic finite support functor and we define the small-step transition step (labeled Segala automaton [11,12]), $\rightarrow\subseteq C \times \mathrm{D}(L' \times (C \cup \{\checkmark\}))$, as the smallest relation obeying the rules in Fig. 4.

The rules in Fig. 4 are a probabilistic extension of the ones in Fig. 2, being the probabilistic transition the new one. Similarly to what was done with the small-step semantics, the n-step semantics for the probabilistic part is a probabilistic extension of the rules in Fig. 2. Consequently words are now elements of $(L')^+$. The n-step transition is then defined by the relation $\twoheadrightarrow\subseteq C \times \mathrm{D}((L')^+ \times (C \cup \{\checkmark\}))$, obeying the two bottom rules in Fig. 4. The left rule represents the execution of a single step in a computation, while the right rule represents multiple computation steps.

Example 4.1. In Fig. 5a we use straight arrows to denote a transition from a command to a distribution, which we denote by $\bullet$, labeled by the triggering action and wiggly arrows to represent a transition from a distribution to a command labeled by the associated probability. From $(a\,;\,b) +_p (c\,||\,d)$ we transit with τ to the distribution $p \cdot a\,;\,b + (1-p) \cdot c\,||\,d$, which transits with probability p to $a\,;\,b$ and with probability $1-p$ to $c\,||\,d$. For the former, we reach the end of the computation by executing first a and then b. For the latter, since it is a concurrent program, to finish the computation we can either execute first c and then d or we can execute first d and then c. Based on Fig. 5a and following the rules in Fig. 4, we can deduce that with probability p the word τab leads to a final computation and the same behavior is captured with probability $1-p$ with the words τcd and τdc.

Example 4.2. Fig. 5b illustrates a probabilistic toss coin scenario where each time we toss the coin, it executes with probability p the command *skip* or continues the tossing with probability $1-p$. To understand this behavior, focus on the initial command. From there, we transit to a distribution formed by the commands *skip* and $\mu X.(X +_p \mathit{skip})$, which is the same as the initial command. From this distribution we transit to *skip* with probability p or to $\mu X.(X +_p \mathit{skip})$ with probability $1-p$, enabling us to repeat the process.

4.1 Constructions on Probabilistic Event Structures

The constructions on probabilistic event structures are an extension of the ones in Sect. 3.2. Hence, the explanation of the sequential and parallel composition will be focused on the valuation and we detail more the probabilistic choice.

Let P_1 and P_2 be two probabilistic event structures. For the valuation of the sequential composition we note the following: either the configuration belongs to $\mathcal{C}(\mathrm{P}_1)$ and in that case the valuation of the sequential composition equals the valuation of P_1, or the configuration has elements of both probabilistic event structures. In that case, we multiply the valuation of a maximal configuration in P_1 with the valuation of a configuration in P_2 whose events are reached by the maximal configuration of P_1.

Definition 4.3. (Sequential Composition) Let $\mathrm{P}_1 = (E_1, \leq_1, \#_1, v_1)$ and $\mathrm{P}_2 = (E_2, \leq_2, \#_2, v_2)$ be probabilistic event structures. Define $\mathrm{P}_1\,;\,\mathrm{P}_2$ as in

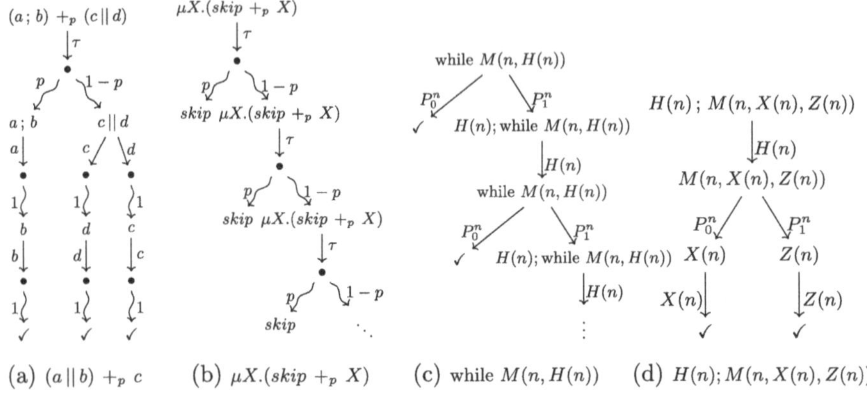

(a) $(a \| b) +_p c$ (b) $\mu X.(skip +_p X)$ (c) while $M(n, H(n))$ (d) $H(n); M(n, X(n), Z(n))$

Fig. 5. Figures for Examples 4.1, 4.2, 5.2 and 5.7.

Definition 3.3, with $(E_1, \leq_1, \#_1) ; (E_2, \leq_2, \#_2)$ together with $v(x)$ defined for $x \in \mathcal{C}(\mathrm{P}_1 ; \mathrm{P}_2)$ as $v_1(x)$ if $x \in \mathcal{C}(\mathrm{P}_1)$, and if $x = x_1 \cup (x_2 \times \{x_1\}) = x_1 \cup \{(e_2, x_1) \mid e_2 \in x_2\}$ with $x_1 \in \mathcal{C}_{\max}(\mathrm{P}_1)$ and $x_2 \in \mathcal{C}(\mathrm{P}_2)$, $v(x) = v_1(x_1) \cdot v_2(x_2)$.

For the parallel composition, and by taking advantage of the intuition that the parallel composition is just putting 'side-by-side' the two event structures, the valuation is the multiplication of the valuations resulting from projecting the configuration in $\mathrm{P}_1 \,||\, \mathrm{P}_2$ into the respective configurations of P_1 and P_2.

Definition 4.4. **(Parallel Composition)** Let $\mathrm{P}_1 = (E_1, \leq_1, \#_1, v_1)$ and $\mathrm{P}_2 = (E_2, \leq_2, \#_2, v_2)$ be probabilistic event structures. Define $\mathrm{P}_1 \,||\, \mathrm{P}_2$ as the probabilistic event structure $(E_1 \uplus E_2, \leq_1 \uplus \leq_2, \#_1 \uplus \#_2, v)$ with v defined by $v(x) = v_1(x \cap E_1) \cdot v_2(x \cap E_2)$.

For the probabilistic choice, $\mathrm{P}_1 +_p \mathrm{P}_2$, we note that the invisible action τ should be the initial event to comply with the operational semantics. Furthermore, the behavior of the probabilistic choice is very similar to that of the non-deterministic choice, in which if we choose a side we cannot execute the other. In terms of event structures, this means that the events of both sides should be in conflict. Regarding the valuations, if the configuration obtained by removing τ belongs to $\mathcal{C}(\mathrm{P}_1)$, then we multiply by p the valuation in P_1, otherwise we multiply by $(1 - p)$.

Definition 4.5. **(Probabilistic Sum)**Let $\mathrm{P}_1 = (E_1, \leq_1, \#_1, v_1)$ and $\mathrm{P}_2 = (E_2, \leq_2, \#_2, v_2)$ be probabilistic event structures. Define $\mathrm{P}_1 +_p \mathrm{P}_2$ as $(\{\tau\} \uplus E, \{\tau \leq e \mid e \in \{\tau\} \uplus E\} \cup \leq, \#)$ (with $(E, \leq, \#)$ as in Definition 3.5), together with v defined as $p \cdot v_1(x \backslash \tau)$ if $x \backslash \tau \in \mathcal{C}(\mathrm{P}_1)$, $(1 - p) \cdot v_2(x \backslash \tau)$ if $x \backslash \tau \in \mathcal{C}(\mathrm{P}_2)$ and 1 otherwise.

Similarly to what was done in Sect. 3.2, we can interpret the recursive command using the least-fixed point of an ordering relation: the relation $\trianglelefteq$ of Definition 3.6 can be extended to probabilistic event structures: $(\mathrm{E}_1, v_1) \trianglelefteq (\mathrm{E}_2, v_2)$ if

$E_1 \trianglelefteq E_2$ and $\forall x \in \mathcal{C}(P_1) \,.\, v_1(x) = v_2(x)$. The discussion of the non-deterministic case in Sect. 3.2 can be carried here: The relation gives a cpo with similar properties, making it possible to define $fix(\Gamma)$ as the least upper-bound of the sequence $\bot \trianglelefteq \Gamma(\bot) \trianglelefteq \cdots \trianglelefteq \Gamma^n(\bot) \trianglelefteq \ldots$.

We interpret commands as probabilistic event structures as follows:

Definition 4.6. Define an environment to be a function $\gamma : Var \rightarrow P$ from variables to probabilistic event structures. For a command C and an environment γ define $[\![C]\!]_\gamma$ as follows: $[\![skip]\!]_\gamma = (\{sk\}, \{sk \leq sk\}, \emptyset, v(\{sk\}) = 1)$, $[\![a]\!]_\gamma = (\{a\}, \{a \leq a\}, \emptyset, v(\{a\}) = 1)$, $[\![C_1 \,;\, C_2]\!]_\gamma = [\![C_1]\!]_\gamma \,;\, [\![C_2]\!]_\gamma$, $[\![C_1 +_p C_2]\!]_\gamma = [\![C_1]\!]_\gamma +_p [\![C_2]\!]_\gamma$, $[\![C_1 \,||\, C_2]\!]_\gamma = [\![C_1]\!]_\gamma \,||\, [\![C_2]\!]_\gamma$, $[\![X]\!]_\gamma = \gamma(X)$, $[\![\mu X.C]\!]_\gamma = fix(\Gamma^{C,\gamma})$, where $\Gamma^{C,\gamma} : P \rightarrow P$ is given by $\Gamma^{C,\gamma}(P) = [\![C]\!]_{\gamma(X \leftarrow P)}$.

Following the same strategy developed in Sect. 3.3, we can define what it means to remove the initial event of a probabilistic event structure. However, we need to guarantee that the probability of said event is not zero, as removing an event with zero probability would lead to a division by zero. Furthermore, this is the reason why $p \in]0, 1[$ in the probabilistic operator.

Definition 4.7. (**Remove initial event**)Let $P = (E, v)$ be a probabilistic event structure and $a \in \mathcal{I}(E)$, s.t $v(\{a\}) \neq 0$. Define $P \backslash a$ as $E \backslash a$ (as in Def. 3.8) together with v' defined as $v'(x) = v(x \cup \{a\}) / v(\{a\})$.

We can then derive a local soundness result stating that if $C \rightarrow 1 \cdot (l, C')$ then $[\![C']\!]_\gamma \equiv [\![C]\!]_\gamma \backslash l$ and that if $C \rightarrow \sum_i p_i(\tau, C_i)$ then $[\![C]\!]_\gamma \subseteq \sum_i p_i [\![C_i]\!]_\gamma$, and a local adequacy result stating that whenever, if $l' \neq \tau$ then $\exists C' \in (C \cup \{\checkmark\}) \,.\, C \rightarrow 1 \cdot (l', C')$ and $[\![C]\!]_\gamma \backslash l' \equiv [\![C']\!]_\gamma$, and if $l' = \tau$, then $\exists C', C'' \,.\, \exists e' \in \mathcal{I}([\![C']\!]_\gamma) \,.\, C \rightarrow p \cdot C' + (1-p) \cdot C''$ and $[\![C]\!]_\gamma \subseteq p \cdot [\![C']\!]_\gamma + (1-p) \cdot [\![C'']\!]_\gamma$, with $p = v(\{\tau, e'\})$. As a side-note, we see the usefulness of introducing the label τ. It helps us identifying the situations where a transition occurred due to the probabilistic command.

From these local results we can derive the desired results.

Theorem 4.8. *(**Soundness**) If $C \twoheadrightarrow p_0(\omega_0, \checkmark) + \sum_k p_k(\omega_k, C_k)$ then exists $x_0 \in \mathcal{C}_{max}([\![C]\!]_\gamma)$ such that $\emptyset \xrightarrow{\omega_0}\!\!\!\!\subset x_0$ and $p_0 = v(x_0)$.* □

Theorem 4.9. *(**Adequacy**) For all $x_0 \in \mathcal{C}_{max}([\![C]\!]_\gamma)$, if $\emptyset \xrightarrow{\omega_{x_0}}\!\!\!\!\subset x_0$ then we have $C \twoheadrightarrow v(x_0)(\omega_0, \checkmark) + \sum_k p_k(\omega_k, C_k)$, for some ω_k, p_k, C_k.* □

Theorem 4.8 assures us that whenever any execution of the program leads to a terminal command, we have a maximal configuration that matches the word and the respective probability. Theorem 4.9 tells us that for every maximal configuration of a command C and for every covering chain of that configuration, there is an execution of the program leading to a terminal command that matches the covering chain and the respective probability.

Example 4.10. The probabilistic event structure in Example 2.4 corresponds to the command in Example 4.1. To see how both semantics relate to each other, recall the maximal configurations in Example 2.4 and the words that lead to the end of a computation in Example 4.1. Similarly to what was shown in Example 3.11, it is straightforward to see that each word corresponds to a covering chain and vice-versa. What is left to verify is the probability. From Example 4.1, we know that the word τab has probability p, which is the same probability of the corresponding covering chain. Similarly, the words τcd and τdc have probability $1-p$, which equals the probability of the respective covering chains. Conversely, if we pick a covering chain of a maximal configuration, we quickly notice that its probability and the probability of the respective word are the same.

$$skip \xrightarrow{sk} \checkmark \quad U(\mathbf{n}) \xrightarrow{U(\mathbf{n})} \checkmark \quad M(n, C_1, C_2) \xrightarrow{P_0^n} C_1 \quad M(n, C_1, C_2) \xrightarrow{P_1^n} C_2$$

$$\frac{C_1 \xrightarrow{l} \checkmark}{C_1\,;\,C_2 \xrightarrow{l} C_2} \quad \frac{C_1 \xrightarrow{l'} C_1'}{C_1\,;\,C_2 \xrightarrow{l'} C_1'\,;\,C_2} \quad \frac{C_1 \xrightarrow{l} \checkmark}{C_1 \,||\, C_2 \xrightarrow{l} C_2} \quad \frac{C_1 \xrightarrow{l'} C_1'}{C_1 \,||\, C_2 \xrightarrow{l'} C_1' \,||\, C_2}$$

$$\text{while } M(n, C) \xrightarrow{P_0^n} \checkmark \quad \text{while } M(n, C) \xrightarrow{P_1^n} C\,;\,\text{while } M(n, C)$$

Fig. 6. Rules of the small-step operational semantics

5 Quantum Effects

We adapt the language shown in Sect. 3.1 to the quantum setting. For that, we need some preliminaries. We consider at our disposal a finite number of qubits N, whose associated space is $\mathbb{C}^{2^{\otimes N}}$. Each qubit is identified by a natural number n and we let $\mathbf{n} \subseteq N$ be a subset of the set of qubits. The set of actions is now composed of a set of unitary gates $\mathcal{U}$ together with a set of projections $\{P_0^n, P_1^n\}$ in which P_0^n and P_1^n represent the projection of qubit n into $|0\rangle$ and $|1\rangle$, respectively. The set of labels is now $L' = L \cup \{P_0^n,\, P_1^n\}$, with $L = Act \cup \{sk\}$.

The language is described by the following grammar,

$$C ::= skip \mid U(\mathbf{n}) \mid C\,;\,C \mid M(n, C_1, C_2) \mid C \,||\, C \mid \text{while } M(n, C)$$

where $U(\mathbf{n})$ applies the unitary gate U to the qubits in $\mathbf{n}$, the parallel composition is disjoint[6] (as a consequence of Definition 5.4), $M(n, C_1, C_2)$ represents the measurement of a qubit n such that if the measurement is made by P_0^n then we execute C_1, else if the measurement is made by P_1^n then we execute C_2, and while $M(n, C)$ is a while loop that stops the computation if the measurement is made by P_0^n. Note that the behavior of $M(n, C_1, C_2)$ is similar to that of a classical if clause.

The small-step semantics, in Fig. 6, is similar to the one in Fig. 2, in which we adapt the rules to the respective commands. In the quantum setting probabilities arise when performing a measurement. However, if we treat a measurement as being a non-deterministic operator, we can 'hide' the probabilities on the label that triggered the measurement, *i.e.* in P_0^n and P_1^n. The n-step transition is the same as the one in Fig. 2.

[6] $C_1 \,||\, C_2$ being disjoint means that C_1 and C_2 do not share any qubit.

Remark 5.1. In this section, we use a while loop instead of a recursive command for cyclic behavior, unlike Sects. 3.1 and 4. The reason to opt by a while loop in this section comes from the behavior of a measurement resembling an if-then-else command. Furthermore projections decide if the computation stops or continues, allowing us to implement the while loop without needing a notion of state. On the other hand, implementing the while loop in Sects. 3.1 and 4 would require a notion of state associated with the command, which would obliged us to change the operational semantics we have designed without loops.

Example 5.2. Fig. 5c illustrates the behavior of a quantum toss coin, which, similarly to Example 3.2, produces a possibly empty sequence of $H(n)P_1^n$ that finishes with P_0^n. To understand this we observe that the initial program has two possible transitions: (1) transits through P_0^n and the computation finishes; (2) transits through P_1^n to $H(n)$; while $M(n, H(n))$, which executes $H(n)$ to transit to while $M(n, H(n))$, which is the same command as the initial one.

5.1 Constructions on Unitary Event Structures

To define the constructions on unitary event structures, we extend the definitions of sequential and parallel composition from Sect. 3.2 to include the corresponding mapping of events to unitary or projection operators. Additionally, we define the measurement composition by slightly adjusting the definition of the non-deterministic composition provided in Sect. 3.2.

Definition 5.3. (Sequential Composition) Let $\mathrm{U}_1 = (\mathrm{E}_1, Q_1)$ and $\mathrm{U}_2 = (\mathrm{E}_2, Q_2)$ be unitary event structures. Define $\mathrm{U}_1 \,;\, \mathrm{U}_2$ as $\mathrm{E}_1 \,;\, \mathrm{E}_2$ together with Q defined by $Q(e) = Q_1(e)$ if $e \in E_1$ and $Q_2(e_2)$ if $e = (e_2, x) \in E_2 \times \mathcal{C}_{\max}(\mathrm{U}_1)$.

When defining the parallel composition we must consider the restriction in Definition 2.5 requiring that the operators associated with concurrent events must commute. In Definition 3.4 every event in E_1 is concurrent with every event of E_2. It then follows that the associated operators must commute.

Definition 5.4. (Parallel Composition) Consider the unitary event structures $\mathrm{U}_1 = (\mathrm{E}_1, Q_1)$ and $\mathrm{U}_2 = (\mathrm{E}_2, Q_2)$. We define $\mathrm{U}_1 \,||\, \mathrm{U}_2$ similarly to Definitin 5.3: the parallel composition of Definition 3.4 together with Q defined by $Q(e) = Q_1(e)$ if $e \in E_1$ and $Q_2(e)$ if $e \in E_2$ where $\forall e_1 \in E_1, e_2 \in E_2.\ [Q_1(e_1), Q_2(e_2)] = 0$.

Similarly to the previous definition, we need to take into account the restriction in Definition 2.5 that requires that the sum of operators associated with events in minimal conflict must be the identity, which is a unitary.

Definition 5.5. (Measurement) Let $\mathrm{U}_1 = (\mathrm{E}_1, Q_1)$ and $\mathrm{U}_2 = (\mathrm{E}_2, Q_2)$ be unitary event structures. Similarly to the probabilistic sum, define $M(n, \mathrm{U}_1, \mathrm{U}_2)$ based on the non-deterministic sum, together with Q defined by $Q(e) = P_0^n$ if $e = \tau_0^n$, P_1^n if $e = \tau_1^n$, $Q_1(e)$ is $e \in E_1$ and $Q_2(e)$ if $e \in E_2$, where $Q(\tau_0^n) + Q(\tau_1^n) = Id$.

We can then extend the ordering relation to the quantum setting by saying that $(\mathrm{E}_1, Q_1) \trianglelefteq (\mathrm{E}_2, Q_2)$ whenever $E_1 \trianglelefteq E_2$ and if $\forall e \in E_1 \,.\, Q_1(e) = Q_2(e)$. As for the previous cases this order yields a cpo with a least upper bound. The denotation ($[\![-]\!] : C \to \mathrm{U}$) is then defined similarly as before, as $[\![skip]\!] = (\{sk\}, \{sk \leq sk\}, \emptyset, Q(sk) = Id)$, $[\![U_\mathbf{n}]\!] = (\{U_\mathbf{n}\}, \{U_\mathbf{n} \leq U_\mathbf{n}\}, \emptyset, Q(U_\mathbf{n}) = U(\mathbf{n}))$, $[\![M(n, C_1, C_2)]\!] = \mathrm{P}_0^n \,;\, [\![C_1]\!] + \mathrm{P}_1^n \,;\, [\![C_2]\!]$, $[\![C_1 \,;\, C_2]\!] = [\![C_1]\!] \,;\, [\![C_2]\!]$, $[\![C_1 \,||\, C_2]\!] = [\![C_1]\!] \,||\, [\![C_2]\!]$, $[\![\text{while } M(n, C)]\!] = fix(\Gamma^n)$, where $\Gamma^n : \mathrm{U} \to \mathrm{U}$ is given by $\Gamma^n(\mathrm{U}) = \mathrm{P}_0^n + \mathrm{P}_1^n \,;\, \mathrm{U}$.

5.2 Semantics Equivalence

According to [19, Theorem 3], an elementary quantum event structure paired with an initial state ρ, along with a valuation function $v(x) = \mathrm{Tr}(A_x^\dagger A_x \rho)$ corresponds to a probabilistic event structure, where $A_x^\dagger$ is the conjugate transpose of A_x. The following proposition formally states the result in our restricted setting.

Proposition 5.6. *Let* $\mathrm{U} = (E, \leq, \#, Q)$ *be a unitary event structure with initial state* ρ*. For each* $x \in \mathcal{C}(\mathrm{U})$ *let* $v(x) = Tr(\rho_x) = Tr(A_x^\dagger A_x \rho)$*. Then* $\mathrm{U} = (\mathrm{U}, \rho, v)$ *is a probabilistic event structure.* □

We can also associate an initial state in the context of the operational semantics. The idea is to use the word ω generated by the n-step and apply it to a given initial state ρ. If the size of ω is one, then we do $\omega\rho\omega^\dagger$. Otherwise, we apply the head of ω to ρ, giving ρ', and repeat the procedure with the tail of ω applied to ρ'. We then define $\omega(\rho)$ as the probability $Tr(\omega\rho\omega^\dagger)$.

Example 5.7. Fig. 5d shows the labeled transition system of the command $H(n) \,;\, M(n, X(n), Z(n))$. This program applies first the Hadamard gate to qubit n and then measures it. If the measurement was made by P_0^n then we apply the X gate to qubit n and we are done. On the other side, if the measurement was performed by P_1^n we apply the Z gate to qubit n finishing the computation. With the help of Fig. 5d, it is straightforward to see that the words that lead to a terminal command are: $H(n)P_0^n X(n)$ and $H(n)P_1^n Z(n)$. By applying each word to the state $\rho = |0\rangle\langle 0|$, we obtain the following possible final states: $(H(n)P_0^n X(n))(|0\rangle\langle 0|) = \dfrac{1}{2}|1\rangle\langle 1|$ and $(H(n)P_1^n Z(n))(|0\rangle\langle 0|) = \dfrac{1}{2}|1\rangle\langle 1|$.

The results obtained in Sect. 3.3 can be adapted to the quantum setting. It is worth to emphasize that removing an initial element from $M(n, \mathrm{U}_1, \mathrm{U}_2)$ is equal to U_1 or to U_2 if the event removed is τ_0^n or τ_1^n, respectively.

Theorem 5.8. *(**Soundness**) Let* ρ *be an initial state. If* $C \overset{\omega}{\twoheadrightarrow} C'$ *then* $\exists x \in \mathcal{C}([\![C]\!]\rho)$ *such that* $\emptyset \overset{\omega}{\longrightarrow}\!\!\subset x$ *and the probability* $\omega(\rho)$ *equals* $v(x)$*.* □

Theorem 5.9. *(**Adequacy**) Let* ρ *be an initial state. If* $\emptyset \neq x \in \mathcal{C}([\![C]\!]\rho)$ *s.t.* $\emptyset \overset{\omega}{\longrightarrow}\!\!\subset x$ *then* $\exists C'$ *s.t.* $C \overset{\omega}{\twoheadrightarrow} C'$ *and the probability* $\omega(\rho)$ *equals* $v(x)$*.* □

Theorem 5.8 differs from Theorem 3.9 with the addition of the probability clause. The same reasoning is also applied to Theorem 5.9 and Theorem 3.10.

Example 5.10. The quantum event structure in Example 2.6 corresponds to the interpretation of the command in Example 5.7. To see the equivalence between both semantics, recall the maximal configurations in Example 2.6 and the words used in Example 5.7. It is trivial to see that for each word we have a corresponding covering chain, and vice-versa. It lacks to verify the probability when an initial state is given. Consider that the initial state is $\rho = |0\rangle\langle 0|$. Applying the word $H(n)P_0^n X(n)$ to ρ yields a probability of 0.5, which matches the probability of the respective covering chain. Similarly, when we apply the word $H(n)P_1^n Z(n)$ to ρ, we obtain a probability of 0.5, once again matching the probability of the respective covering chain. Conversely, if we obtained the probability from the trace of $A_x \rho A_x^\dagger$, where x is a configuration from a covering chain, we observe that applying the respective word to ρ gives the same probability. Concretely, the covering chain of $\{H_1, \tau_0^1, X_1\}$ is $\emptyset \overset{H_1}{\longrightarrow\!\!\!\!\subset} \{H_1\} \overset{\tau_0^1}{\longrightarrow\!\!\!\!\subset} \{H_1, \tau_0^1\} \overset{X_1}{\longrightarrow\!\!\!\!\subset} \{H_1, \tau_0^1, X_1\}$. The associated operator A_x is $X(1)P_0^1 H(1)$. By applying A_x and $A_x^\dagger$ to ρ we obtain the state $|1\rangle\langle 1|$ with probability 0.5, which corresponds to the probability of applying the respective word to ρ.

6 Related Work

Most work on event structures extend them to different computational effects and when they give denotational semantics for a language, most of the languages include notions of communication, which are absent in the languages we consider.

In the classical setting, Winskel used event structures to give denotational semantics to CCS [17,18]. In the probabilistic setting, Varacca and Yoshida used a probabilistic version of event structures [14] to interpret a probabilistic π-calculus [13]. Marc de Visme later adapted Winskel's probabilistic event structures [19], equivalent to Varacca's definition, to furnish a probabilistic CCS [2] with a denotational semantics. In the quantum setting event structures have only been used as the backbone for game semantics [5].

A closer approach to ours is found in Castellan's work [3], where event structures interpret a simple imperative and concurrent language in the context of weak memory models. His goal was to capture execution paths generated by compilers during code optimization, missed by interleaving semantics. Interestingly, his definition of sequential and parallel composition are similar to ours.

7 Conclusion

In this paper, we discussed how Winskel's event structures can be tamed as a model of computation for representing sequences of actions, with causal and conflicting relationships, and even refined Winskel's notion of quantum event structure to better match the probabilistic ones. We show how Winskel's event structures support non-deterministic, probabilistic and quantum effects.

Acknowledgments. This work has been partially funded by the French National Research Agency (ANR) by the project RECIPROG ANR-21-CE48-0019, PPS ANR-19-CE48-0014, TaQC ANR-22-CE47-0012 and within the framework of "Plan France 2030", under the research projects EPIQ ANR-22-PETQ-0007, OQULUS ANR-23-PETQ-0013, HQI-Acquisition ANR-22-PNCQ-0001 and HQI-R&D ANR-22-PNCQ-0002. This work is partially financed by National Funds through the Portuguese funding agency, FCT— Fundação para a Ciência e a Tecnologia, within project UIDB/50014/2020. DOI 10.54499/UIDB/50014/2020—https://doi.org/10.54499/uidb/50014/2020.
Disclosure of Interests. The authors have no competing interests to declare.

References

1. Andersen, J., Elsborg, E., Henglein, F., Simonsen, J.G., Stefansen, C.: Compositional specification of commercial contracts. Int. J. Softw. Tools Technol. Transf. **8**(6), 485–516 (2006). https://doi.org/10.1007/S10009-006-0010-1
2. Baier, C., Kwiatkowska, M.: Domain equations for probabilistic processes (extended abstract). Electron. Notes Theor. Comput. Sci. **7**, 34–54 (1997). https://doi.org/10.1016/S1571-0661(05)80465-7. https://www.sciencedirect.com/science/article/pii/S1571066105804657
3. Castellan, S.: Weak memory models using event structures. In: Vingt-septièmes Journées Francophones des Langages Applicatifs (JFLA 2016) (2016)
4. Castellan, S.: Concurrent structures in game semantics. Bull. EATCS **123** (2017), http://eatcs.org/beatcs/index.php/beatcs/article/view/501
5. Clairambault, P., de Visme, M., Winskel, G.: Game semantics for quantum programming. Proc. ACM Program. Lang. **3**(POPL), 32:1–32:29 (2019). https://doi.org/10.1145/3290345
6. Fernandes, V., de Visme, M., Valiron, B.: Non-deterministic, probabilistic, and quantum effects through the lens of event structures (technical report) (2024). https://arxiv.org/abs/2408.14563
7. Milner, R.: Communication and Concurrency, vol. 84. Prentice Hall, New York (1989)
8. Nielsen, M.A., Chuang, I.L.: Quantum Computation and Quantum Information. Cambridge University Press, Cambridge (2000)
9. Paquet, H.: Probabilistic concurrent game semantics. Ph.D. thesis, University of Cambridge, UK (2020). https://doi.org/10.17863/CAM.61919, https://ethos.bl.uk/OrderDetails.do?uin=uk.bl.ethos.821543
10. Reynolds, J.C.: Theories of Programming Languages. Cambridge University Press, Cambridge (1998)
11. Segala, R.: Modeling and verification of randomized distributed real-time systems. Ph.D. thesis, Massachusetts Institute of Technology (1995)
12. Sokolova, A., De Vink, E.P.: Probabilistic automata: system types, parallel composition and comparison. In: Validation of Stochastic Systems: A Guide to Current Research, pp. 1–43 (2004)
13. Varacca, D., Völzer, H., Winskel, G.: Probabilistic event structures and domains. Theor. Comput. Sci. **358**(2–3), 173–199 (2006). https://doi.org/10.1016/J.TCS.2006.01.015
14. Varacca, D., Winskel, G.: Distributing probability over non-determinism. Math. Struct. Comput. Sci. **16**(1), 87–113 (2006)

15. Varacca, D., Yoshida, N.: Probabilistic pi-calculus and event structures. In: Aldini, A., van Breugel, F. (eds.) Proceedings of the Fifth Workshop on Quantitative Aspects of Programming Languages, QAPL 2007, Braga, Portugal, March 24-25, 2007. Electronic Notes in Theoretical Computer Science, vol. 190, pp. 147–166. Elsevier, Amsterdam (2007). https://doi.org/10.1016/J.ENTCS.2007.07.009
16. de Visme, M.: Event structures for mixed choice. In: The 30th International Conference on Concurrency Theory (CONCUR 2019) (2019)
17. Winskel, G.: Event structure semantics for ccs and related languages. In: International Colloquium on Automata, Languages, and Programming, pp. 561–576. Springer, Berlin (1982)
18. Winskel, G.: An introduction to event structures. In: Workshop/School/Symposium of the REX Project (Research and Education in Concurrent Systems), pp. 364–397. Springer, Berlin (1988)
19. Winskel, G.: Probabilistic and quantum event structures. In: Horizons of the Mind. A Tribute to Prakash Panangaden, pp. 476–497. Springer, Berlin (2014)

Type-Based Verification of Connectivity Constraints in Lattice Surgery

Ryo Wakizaka[1(✉)], Yasunari Suzuki[2], and Atsushi Igarashi[1]

[1] Graduate School of Informatics, Kyoto University, Kyoto, Japan
wakizaka@fos.kuis.kyoto-u.ac.jp, igarashi@kuis.kyoto-u.ac.jp
[2] NTT Computer and Data Science Laboratories, Musashino 180-8585, Japan
yasunari.suzuki@ntt.com

Abstract. Fault-tolerant quantum computation using lattice surgery can be abstracted as operations on graphs, wherein each logical qubit corresponds to a vertex of the graph, and multi-qubit measurements are accomplished by connecting the vertices with paths between them. Operations attempting to connect vertices without a valid path will result in abnormal termination. As the permissible paths may evolve during execution, it is necessary to statically verify that the execution of a quantum program can be completed. This paper introduces a type-based method to statically verify that well-typed programs can be executed without encountering halts induced by surgery operations. Alongside, we present $\mathcal{Q}_{LS}$, a first-order quantum programming language to formalize the execution model of surgery operations. Furthermore, we provide a type checking algorithm by reducing the type checking problem to the offline dynamic connectivity problem.

Keywords: fault-tolerant quantum computation · lattice surgery · program verification · type systems

1 Introduction

Fault-tolerant quantum computation is a method that enables the large-scale quantum computation required for applications, for example, in quantum chemistry [3,29] and cryptanalysis [5,18,34], by addressing quantum errors that occur on quantum hardware. In recent years, small-scale fault-tolerant quantum computation has begun to be realized on actual hardware [1,6,12,14,28], leading to an urgent need to develop quantum software such as quantum compilers to generate quantum programs executable on fault-tolerant quantum computers.

The primary technology to realize fault-tolerant quantum computation is quantum error-correcting codes, which build a logical qubit from multiple physical qubits. However, since physical qubits can only interact (i.e., perform multi-qubit operations) with neighboring qubits, error-correcting codes can be implemented in a way that satisfies such locality conditions. Numerous quantum error-correcting codes have been proposed, with topological codes [26] such as surface

O. Kiselyov (Ed.): APLAS 2024, LNCS 15194, pp. 216-237, 2024.
https://doi.org/10.1007/978-981-97-8943-6_11

codes [17] and color codes [7] standing out as promising candidates because they exhibit robust performance and are relatively straightforward to implement in quantum computers with locally connected physical qubits.

To achieve fault-tolerant quantum computation, it is imperative not only to construct logical qubits but also to execute logical operations on them. Several methods [17,23] have been proposed to realize logical operations on topological codes, and lattice surgery [23] in particular has attracted attention as a method that can efficiently implement multi-qubit logical operations. Roughly speaking, lattice surgery involves allocating a logical qubit on a vertex of a graph determined by a target architecture, with each logical operation depicted as an operation on the graph. It is established that lattice surgery with several simple operations can execute a universal gate set, thereby enabling universal fault-tolerant quantum computation.

An essential operation in lattice surgery is the *merge* operation, facilitating logical operations on two or more logical qubits. The merge operation establishes a connection along a path between the target qubits positioned on the vertices. The point here is that no other logical qubit must be assigned to any vertex (except endpoints) included in the merge path. If no path meeting this condition exists during a merge operation, the execution of a quantum program will halt. Therefore, the compiler must schedule instructions to prevent situations where no merge paths exist during execution.

Quantum compilers typically involve multiple optimization passes, and the improper combination of these passes may lead to compiled programs that no longer adhere to connectivity constraints. Therefore, it is essential to statically verify that the compilation result indeed satisfies these constraints. Additionally, such verification tools should be capable of addressing quantum programs with high-level features, such as function calls and branches, as fault-tolerant quantum computation programs often tend to be large, making circuit-based methods impractical for scaling. However, to the best of our knowledge, there is currently no formal verification framework specifically tailored for lattice surgery.

To tackle this challenge, we present a type-based verification approach to ensuring the satisfaction of connectivity constraints between logical qubits in lattice surgery. Our contributions primarily encompass the following components: (1) the introduction of $\mathcal{Q}_{LS}$, a first-order quantum programming language whose operational semantics reflects graph operations in lattice surgery, (2) a type system ensuring that well-typed $\mathcal{Q}_{LS}$ programs inherently adhere to the connectivity constraints during execution, and (3) a type checking algorithm grounded in the offline dynamic connectivity problem. Although the details are not covered in this paper, we have also implemented our approach in Rust and applied it to several examples.[1]

This paper is organized as follows: Sect. 2 explains the background of this work, including the basics of quantum computing and fault-tolerant quantum computation by lattice surgery. Section 3 gives a motivating example. Section 4

[1] The source code is available at https://github.com/SoftwareFoundationGroupAtKyotoU/tysurgery.

introduces $\mathcal{Q}_{LS}$ to describe lattice surgery's operations and semantics. Section 5 formalizes a type system for the verification of connectivity constraints. Section 6 discusses how to extend our language. Section 7 provides the related work, and finally, Sect. 8 concludes this paper with future directions. For full definitions and proofs, readers are referred to a full version available at https://www.fos.kuis.kyoto-u.ac.jp/wakizaka/papers/aplas24-tysurgery.pdf.

2 Background

2.1 The Basics of Quantum Computation

In quantum computation, a *qubit* is the unit of information. A *quantum state* of a qubit is a normalized vector of the 2-dimensional Hilbert space $\mathcal{H} \cong \mathbb{C}^2$. Each state is represented by $\alpha |0\rangle + \beta |1\rangle$, where $\alpha, \beta \in \mathbb{C}$ satisfying $|\alpha|^2 + |\beta|^2 = 1$ and $\{|0\rangle, |1\rangle\}$ denotes the standard basis vectors of $\mathbb{C}^2$. Here, we use *Dirac notation*, which encloses integers or variables with $|$ and $\rangle$, to denote quantum states. The state of n qubits is a normalized vector of the tensor product $\bigotimes_{i=1}^{n} \mathbb{C}^2 \cong \mathbb{C}^{2^n}$. For example, if $|\psi\rangle = |0\rangle$ and $|\phi\rangle = \frac{1}{\sqrt{2}}(|0\rangle + |1\rangle)$, then $|\psi\rangle \otimes |\phi\rangle = |\psi\rangle |\phi\rangle = \frac{1}{\sqrt{2}}(|00\rangle + |01\rangle)$. We call a quantum state $|\psi\rangle \in \mathbb{C}^{2^n}$ a *pure state*. On the other hand, when we have one of the quantum states $\{|\psi_i\rangle\}$ generated randomly with probabilities p_i and do not know which state was generated, we call the state $\{(p_i, |\psi_i\rangle)\}$ *mixed state*. A mixed state can be described by a *density operator* $\rho = \sum_i p_i |\psi_i\rangle \langle\psi_i|$, where $\langle\psi_i|$ is the adjoint of $|\psi_i\rangle$ and $\sum_i p_i = 1$. We often use density operators to describe quantum states because they can uniformly express both pure and mixed states. We write $\mathcal{S}(\mathcal{H})$ for the set of density operators.

A quantum state can be manipulated by unitary operators called *quantum gates*. For example, the Hadamard gate and the CX (controlled X) gate are defined by $H|x\rangle = \frac{1}{\sqrt{2}}(|0\rangle + (-1)^x |1\rangle)$, $CX|x\rangle|y\rangle = |x\rangle|x \oplus y\rangle$, where $x, y \in \{0, 1\}$ and $\oplus$ denotes the Boolean XOR operation. The *Pauli operators* defined by $\mathcal{P}_n = \{I, X, Y, Z\}^{\otimes n}$ for a n qubits system are also important quantum operations. The operator on density operators corresponding to U is described as a super operator $U[\cdot]U^\dagger : \mathcal{S}(\mathcal{H}) \to \mathcal{S}(\mathcal{H})$, where $U^\dagger$ is the adjoint of U.

An instruction set architecture generally provides a *universal* gate set, a subset of quantum gates that realizes (approximate) universal quantum computation. For example, $\{H, T, CX\}$ is a well-known universal quantum gate set.

To get the result of quantum computation, we have to perform *quantum measurements* which consist of measurement operators $M_1, M_2, \ldots, M_n$ acting on the state space and satisfying $\sum_i M_i^\dagger M_i = I$. When performing measurements to a quantum state ρ, we get an outcome corresponding to one of M_i with probability $p_i = (M_i^\dagger M_i \rho)$, and then the quantum state is changed to $\frac{M_i \rho M_i^\dagger}{p_i}$. The measurements defined by $\mathcal{M}_P = \{(I + (-1)^s P)/2\}_{s=0,1}$ for a Pauli operator $P \in \mathcal{P}_n$ is called Pauli measurements, which plays an important role in fault-tolerant quantum computation.

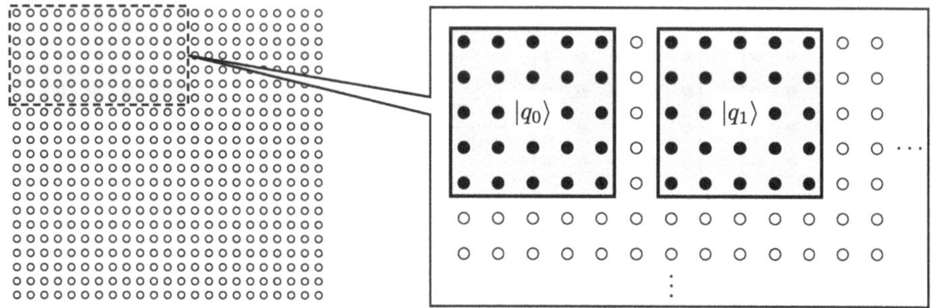

Fig. 1. (Left) A 2D layout of physical qubits on a quantum computer. (Right) Two logical qubits constructed with the surface code.

2.2 Fault-Tolerant Quantum Computation with Lattice Surgery

This section explains fault-tolerant quantum computation employing lattice surgery. We utilize surface codes as an illustrative example, although analogous principles apply to other topological codes. We note that the error correction procedure is omitted in this paper as it is unnecessary for comprehending this study.

Quantum error-correcting codes serve to protect quantum data against quantum noises by constructing a logical qubit from noisy physical qubits. However, for these codes to be implemented on real quantum devices, they must satisfy various architectural constraints, particularly connectivity constraints. These constraints dictate that two-qubit gates, such as the CX gate, can only be applied to pairs of directly connected qubits. Therefore, the error correction process itself must also satisfy these locality conditions. For example, the left-hand side of Fig. 1 represents an architecture in which physical qubits (white circles) are arranged in two dimensions, with only nearest-neighbor interactions allowed, and such configuration is standard in quantum computers [5,10,29].

The surface code [17] is a topological code that satisfies locality conditions and holds promise for future implementation. A logical qubit encoded by surface codes is represented by a rectangle of physical qubits, as depicted on the right-hand side of Fig. 1. In Fig. 1, there are two logical qubits, q_0 and q_1, where filled circles represent physical qubits used to construct a logical qubit. In this way, multiple logical qubits can be created using some of the regions of the physical qubits on a quantum computer. Logical qubits can be arranged freely as long as they do not overlap each other's proprietary areas, but in practice, it is customary to arrange them so that their relative positions are simple to facilitate hardware control and compiler optimization. Additionally, physical qubits represented by unfilled circles can be used as auxiliary qubits to implement logical operations on logical qubits, as explained later.

To achieve fault-tolerant quantum computation, logical operations on logical qubits must also be accomplished. In this paper, we briefly describe logical operations that can be performed with low latency and, when combined,

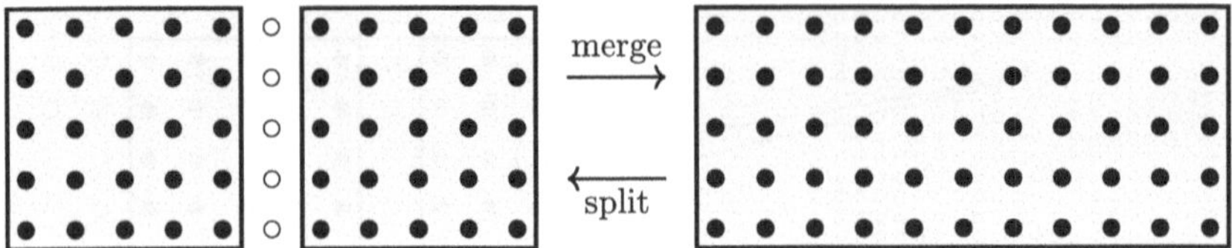

Fig. 2. The merge and split operation for the surface code.

enable universal quantum computation. These logical operations will later serve as the instruction set of $\mathcal{Q}_{LS}$. For more details, readers are referred to literatures [16,30].

Qubit allocation/deallocation. The qubit initialization to the logical $|0\rangle$ state can be achieved by occupying an unused area of the physical qubits and initializing the state. Initialization can also be done to a state $|m\rangle = (|0\rangle + e^{i\pi/4}|1\rangle)/\sqrt{2}$, known as the magic state, which is necessary for implementing the logical T gate required for universal quantum computation[2]. In contrast, qubit deallocation is achieved by making the allocated area unused after performing the single qubit Pauli measurement described below.

Single qubit operations. The Pauli gates X, Z, the Hadamard gate H and the phase gate S are logical operations that can be easily realized on topological codes. Additionally, the logical Pauli measurements M_Z and M_X for a single logical qubit can be performed.

Multi-qubit operations. Multi-qubit operations can be realized by lattice surgery in a manner that satisfies the locality condition of physical qubits. Specifically, in lattice surgery, Pauli measurements $\mathcal{M}_P$ are achieved through operations known as *merge* and *split* operations. As shown in Fig. 2, the merge operation connects the target logical qubits using auxiliary physical qubits in between, while the split operation disconnects them via an appropriate physical measurement operation. It is important to note that sufficient free space between the target qubits is required to perform the merge operation. Such space is released by the split operation immediately after the merge operation. Multi-qubit Pauli measurements can be used, for example, to implement the logical CX gate (Fig. 3) and the logical T gate, which enable universal quantum computation.

Remark 1. Strictly speaking, which boundaries of the logical qubits (e.g., the four sides of each rectangle in Fig. 2) can be used for a merge operation depends on the basis of measurement. For simplicity, we will ignore this constraint in this paper. However, it is straightforward to extend our proposed method to account for this constraint.

[2] This process is called magic state injection and does not actually initialize the qubit in the exact $|m\rangle$ state. To generate $|m\rangle$ states with negligible approximation errors, it is necessary to use a protocol called magic state distillation [8,27].

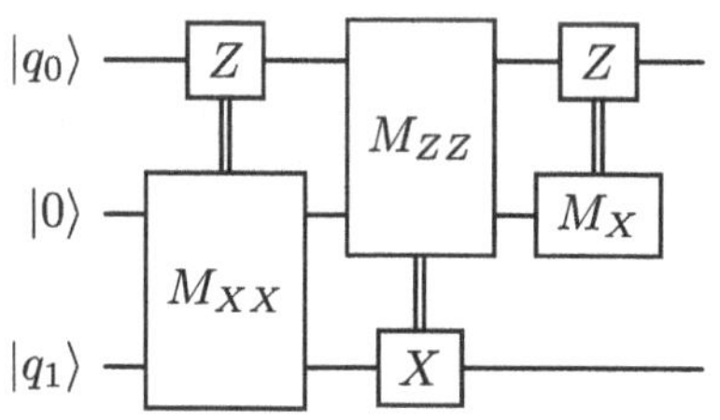

Fig. 3. The implementation of the CX gate.

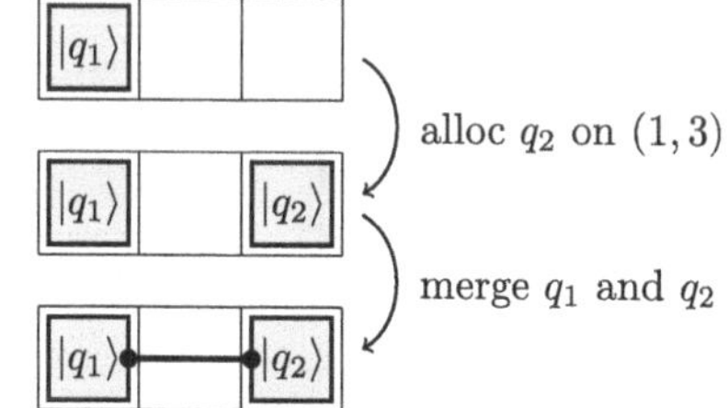

Fig. 4. The abstracted surgery operations.

To summarize this section, we provide an example of how surgery operations on surface codes proceed in Fig. 4. In the case of surface codes, the physical qubits are divided into compartments on the grid, and logical qubits are allocated so that they just fit into their respective cells. This abstracts the merge operation to the process of connecting target cells on the graph using free paths between them. Note that we can merge two adjacent cells because there is a thin gap between them as shown in Fig. 1. The $\mathcal{Q}_{LS}$ language is formalized using this abstracted execution model. From now on, abstracted graphs (e.g., grid graphs) will be referred to as architecture graphs.

3 Motivating Example

We illustrate instances where a quantum program utilizing surgery operations gets stuck by presenting examples depicted in Fig. 5. In these scenarios, quantum programs attempt to manipulate qubits, represented as squares on a 2D grid graph. For example, in the first scenario (Fig. 5a), the program tries to merge q_1 and q_4. This operation succeeds as an accessible path between q_1 and q_4 exists, as indicated by the black line.

Conversely, in the remaining examples, their merge operations fail. The second example (Fig. 5b) attempts to merge q_1 and q_4 but fails because qubit q_2 interrupts their connectivity, unlike the first scenario. The third example (Fig. 5c) is more intricate than the others. In Figure 5c, $CX(q_1, q_4)$ and $CX(q_2, q_3)$ are depicted midway through execution. In reality, a situation akin to Fig. 5c unfolds through the following steps: (1) we express $CX(q_1, q_4)$ and $CX(q_2, q_3)$ in a source language in this sequence, (2) a compiler transpiles them into surgery operations, decomposing the CX gate (Fig. 3), (3) and a transpiler pass erroneously reorders the instruction allocating an ancilla $|0\rangle$ for $CX(q_2, q_3)$ before completing $CX(q_1, q_4)$. Ultimately, in both examples, the programs fail to execute the merge operation, leading to abnormal termination.

As discussed above, the execution of a quantum program utilizing lattice surgery may halt for various reasons, notably inappropriate compiler strategies in qubit allocation and merge path scheduling. Regrettably, such issues are likely to persist because the availability of nodes for logical qubits and merge paths

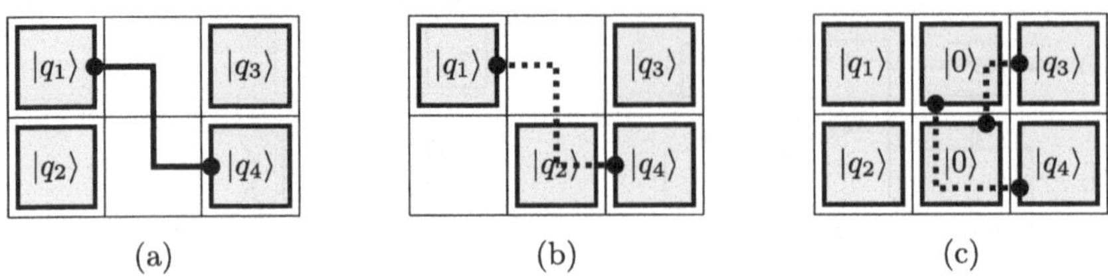

Fig. 5. Making attempts to merge qubits in several situations.

Location variables	$l \in \mathit{Locations}$
Function declarations	$d := f \mapsto [\bar{l}](x_1, .., x_n)e$
Expressions	$e := x \mid \textbf{let } x = \textbf{init } (l) \textbf{ in } e \mid \textbf{let } x = \textbf{minit } (l) \textbf{ in } e \mid$
	$\textbf{free } x; e \mid \textbf{let } y = M_{B_1,..,B_n}(x_1, .., x_n) \textbf{ in } e \mid U(x) \mid$
	$\textbf{let } x = \textbf{mkref } e \textbf{ in } e \mid *e \mid x := e \mid e_1; e_2 \mid$
	$\textbf{if } e_1 \textbf{ then } e_2 \textbf{ else } e_3 \mid \textbf{while } e_1 \textbf{ do } e_2 \mid f[\bar{l}](x_1, .., x_n)$
Values	$v := x \mid l \mid \textbf{unit} \mid \texttt{true} \mid \texttt{false}$
Program	$P := \langle \{d_1, .., d_n\}, e \rangle$
Measurement basis	$B := X \mid Z$
Gates	$U := X \mid Z \mid H \mid S$

Fig. 6. The grammar of $\mathcal{Q}_{LS}$.

will remain limited even in the future. Hence, we advocate for the necessity of a framework to statically verify whether a given program can complete its execution without getting stuck at any point.

4 $\mathcal{Q}_{LS}$: Quantum PL for Lattice Surgery

Before presenting our verification methodology, we introduce $\mathcal{Q}_{LS}$, an imperative quantum programming language encompassing lattice surgery operations, mutable references, and first-order functions. $\mathcal{Q}_{LS}$ is primarily designed to serve as a target language for quantum compilers.

4.1 Syntax

The grammar of $\mathcal{Q}_{LS}$ is given in Fig. 6. We assume that an architecture configuration is represented as a graph $G = (V, E)$, where $V \subseteq \mathit{Locations}$, and a location variable, denoted by l, signifies a location where qubits can be allocated. We use $l \in \mathit{Locations} \setminus V$ to denote a function parameter that is substituted with a specific location upon function invocation. We write $\bar{l}$ for a sequence of location variables $l_1, .., l_n$. We also use L to denote a set of location variables.

There are four primitives for quantum operations in $\mathcal{Q}_{LS}$: qubit allocation, deallocation, unitary operations, and quantum measurements. Qubit allocating

```
1 [l0,l1,l2]
2 cx(q0:qbit(l0), q1:qbit(l1)) {
3   let aux = init(l2) in
4   let a = meas[X,X](aux, q1) in
5   (if a then Z(q0));
6   let b = meas[Z,Z](q0, aux) in
7   (if b then X(q1));
8   let c = meas[X](aux) in
9   (if c then Z(q0));
10  free(aux)
11 }
```

Fig. 7. An implementation of CX

operations **init** (l) and **minit** (l) initialize a location l with a logical state $|0\rangle$ and a magic state $|m\rangle$, respectively. In $\mathcal{Q}_{LS}$, all locations of qubits in a program are statically determined at compile time. A unitary operation $U(x)$ applies a unitary gate U to x, where U must be one of H, X, Z, and S gate. Note that the T gate for universal quantum computation can be realized through a combination of if expressions, basic gates, and measurements with a magic state.

Our language supports quantum measurements with one or two qubits. We can measure qubits with different bases per each qubit; for example, $M_{X,Z}(x_1, x_2)$ measures x_1, x_2 with X, Z bases, respectively. Although a two-qubit measurement is implemented through merge and split operations, as explained in n Secti 2.2, our language does not explicitly specify a path for a merge operation between the target qubits. Instead, we leave the pathfinding problem to the runtime. It is straightforward to extend the language with measurements specifying paths.

A program is represented as a pair $\langle D, e\rangle$, where $D = \{d_1, \dots, d_n\}$ constitutes a set of first-order and non-recursive function definitions, and e denotes the program entry point. A function declaration $d = f \mapsto [\bar{l}](x_1, .., x_n)e$ maps a function name f to a tuple of location variables $\bar{l}$ and argument names $x_1, \dots, x_n$ bound within the function body e. The parameters $\bar{l}$ in a function declaration allow us to call a function in various scenarios where the topology of qubits used within its body varies.

For example, an implementation of the CX gate in $\mathcal{Q}_{LS}$ is provided in Fig. 7. The function cx features location parameters l_0, l_1, l_2 and accepts two qubits as arguments. The location variable l_2 is employed for internal qubit allocation (see line 3). The ancilla qubit aux is deallocated at the end of cx (see line 10), allowing for the reuse of l_2 after the function call. Notably, we use an if-expression without an else clause, which is a syntax sugar representing an if-expression where the else clause is a unit expression.

4.2 Semantics

We design operational semantics of our language to model the execution of quantum programs with lattice surgery. The complete definition is given in Fig. 8. We define the operational semantics as a transition relation on *runtime states* denoted by a triple $[H, \rho, e]$; H is a partial function from *Variables* to *Values*, ρ is a quantum state, and e is a reducing expression. Then we write the transition relation as $\rightarrow_{D,G}$, where D contains function definitions and G is an architecture graph. From here, we explain briefly each transition rule.

A qubit allocation $\mathbf{let}\, x = \mathbf{init}\,(l)\,\mathbf{in}\, e$ allocates a qubit at l and binds a qubit variable x to l. The semantics of $\mathbf{minit}\,(l)$ is defined similarly. Both expressions require that the location l is empty. On the other hand, an expression $\mathbf{free}\, x$ deallocates a qubit x on a location $l = H(x)$ and removes x from a current heap H. The quantum state after deallocating a qubit at l is the partial trace over the qubit corresponding to l. For example, deallocating a qubit at l_1, which is one of the Bell pair $|\Phi_+\rangle_{l_1,l_2}\langle\Phi_+|$ where $|\Phi_+\rangle = (|00\rangle + |11\rangle)/\sqrt{2}$, produces a mixed state $\frac{1}{2}|0\rangle_{l_1}\langle 0| + \frac{1}{2}|1\rangle_{l_1}\langle 1|$.

An expression $\mathbf{let}\, x = M_{B_1,..,B_n}(x_1, .., x_n)\,\mathbf{in}\, e$ performs quantum measurements to $x_1, .., x_n$ with basis $B_1, .., B_n$ ($n = 1$ or 2). The variable x is bound to $v \in \{0, 1\}$, the result of the measurement, and the quantum state ρ changes to $M_v \rho M_v^\dagger / p_v$. The point is that two qubit measurements require that there exists a free path between the target locations l_1 and l_2. This requirement is formalized as $G \mid L \vDash l_1 \sim l_2$, indicating that there is a path between l_1 and l_2 on a graph G, where L represents a set of locations where any qubits are allocated. If such a path does not exist, the program gets stuck. On the other hand, single-qubit measurements always succeed.

We omit other expressions in this paper, as their semantics are similar to those in common programming languages.

5 Typing

This section presents the definition of a type system for $\mathcal{Q}_{LS}$. The aim of our type system is to ensure that well-typed programs do not halt execution due to surgery operations. We proved this property as type soundness.

5.1 Types, Environments and Commands

The syntax of types, environments, and commands is provided in Fig. 9. The type $\mathtt{qbit}(l)$ denotes the type of a qubit, where l represents the location of the qubit. Our type system distinguishes each qubit from others to analyze how qubits are manipulated within a given graph. The qubit type can be considered a kind of singleton type [19]. The other types are consistent with those commonly used in many programming languages: **unit**, `bool` and $\mathbf{ref}\,\tau$ denote the type of the unit value, Boolean values, and references to a value of type τ, respectively.

A type environment Γ maps variables to types and also manages a set of qubit locations. The symbol $\bullet$ denotes the empty environment. We use $\Gamma, x : \tau$

$$\boxed{[H, \rho, e] \rightarrow_{D,G} [H', \rho', e']}$$

$$\frac{x' \notin \text{dom}(H) \qquad l \notin \text{cod}(H) \qquad l \in G}{[H, \rho, \textbf{let } x = \textbf{init}\,(l) \textbf{ in } e] \rightarrow_{D,G} \left[H\{x' \mapsto l\}, \rho \otimes |0\rangle_l \langle 0|, [x'/x]\, e\right]} \text{(E-INIT)}$$

$$\frac{x' \notin \text{dom}(H) \qquad l \notin \text{cod}(H) \qquad l \in G}{[H, \rho, \textbf{let } x = \textbf{minit}\,(l) \textbf{ in } e] \rightarrow_{D,G} \left[H\{x' \mapsto l\}, \rho \otimes |T\rangle_l \langle T|, [x'/x]\, e\right]} \text{(E-MINIT)}$$

$$\frac{H(x) = l}{[H, \rho, \textbf{free}\, x; e] \rightarrow_{D,G} [H \setminus x, \text{Tr}_l(\rho), e]} \text{(E-FREE)} \qquad \frac{H(x) = l}{[H, \rho, U(x)] \rightarrow_{D,G} \left[H, U_l \rho U_l^\dagger, ()\right]} \text{(E-GATE)}$$

$$\frac{\begin{array}{c} H(x_1) = l_1 \qquad H(x_2) = l_2 \qquad M_s := (I + (-1)^s B_1 B_2)/2 \ (s = 0, 1) \\ x' \notin \text{dom}(H) \qquad v \in \{0, 1\} \qquad p_v := \text{Tr}\left(M_v^\dagger M_v \rho\right) \neq 0 \qquad G \mid V(G) \setminus \text{Used}(H) \vDash l_1 \sim l_2 \end{array}}{[H, \rho, \textbf{let } x = M_{B_1, B_2}(x_1, x_2) \textbf{ in } e] \rightarrow_{D,G} \left[H\{x' \mapsto v\}, M_v \rho M_v^\dagger / p_v, [x'/x]\, e\right]} \text{(E-MEAS2)}$$

$$\frac{f \mapsto [\overline{l'}](x_1', .., x_n')e' \in D}{\left[H, \rho, f[\overline{l}](x_1, .., x_n)\right] \rightarrow_{D,G} \left[H, \rho, [\overline{l}/\overline{l'}]\, [x_1/x_1'] .. [x_n/x_n']\, e'\right]} \text{(E-CALL)}$$

Fig. 8. Operational semantics (excerpt).

Types	$\tau := \texttt{qbit}(l) \mid \textbf{unit} \mid \texttt{bool} \mid \textbf{ref}\,\tau \mid \ldots$
Function Types	$\theta := \Pi \bar{l}.\, \langle x_1 : \tau_1, .., x_n : \tau_n \rangle \xrightarrow{\overline{C}} \langle \Gamma \mid \tau \rangle$
Typing Environment	$\Gamma := \bullet \mid \Gamma, x : \tau \mid \Gamma, l$
Function Type Environment	$\Theta := \bullet \mid \Theta, f : \theta$
Commands	$C := l_1 \sim l_2 \mid \textbf{alloc}\,(l) \mid \textbf{free}\,(l) \mid \overline{C_1}^* \mid \overline{C_1} \vee \overline{C_2}$

Fig. 9. Types, environments and commands

to denote the extension of environment Γ with a type binding $x : \tau$, and Γ, l to represent the extension of Γ with a location l. If $l \in \Gamma$, it means that no qubit is allocated at l. We assume that all variable names and locations in Γ are distinct. A function type environment Θ maps function names f to function types θ.

A command C denotes an operation on locations, which can be perceived as a form of computational effects. We write $\overline{C}$ for a sequence of commands and ϵ for the empty command sequence, indicating that an expression does not manipulate any locations. The concatenation of command sequences $\overline{C}_1$ and $\overline{C}_2$ is denoted by $\overline{C}_1 + \overline{C}_2$. Commands **alloc** (l) and **free** (l) signify qubit allocation and deallocation, respectively, which are generated by expressions **init** (l) and **free** (l). A merge command $l_1 \sim l_2$ signifies an occurrence of a merge operation between l_1 and l_2, which is generated by measurements. Additionally, our language supports loops and branches, thus commands have constructors for them. A command $\overline{C}^*$ represents zero or more repetitions of $\overline{C}$, and $\overline{C_1} \vee \overline{C_2}$ denotes a branch that chooses either $\overline{C_1}$ or $\overline{C_2}$ at runtime.

We denote function types as $\Pi \bar{l}.\, \langle x_1 : \tau_1, .., x_n : \tau_n \rangle \xrightarrow{\overline{C}} \langle \Gamma | \tau \rangle$, where $\bar{l}$ represents a sequence of location parameters, $x_1 : \tau_1, .., x_n : \tau_n$ denote the types of arguments, Γ represents a new typing environment, τ signifies the type of a return value, and $\overline{C}$ is a command sequence generated upon function invocation. Here, the environment Γ is utilized to monitor which locations and variables remain valid after the function call. The parameter $\bar{l}$ enables function invocation in diverse contexts wherein the locations of qubits passed as arguments vary.

5.2 Type System

The typing rules are provided in Figs. 10 and 11. A typing judgment has the form $\Theta \mid \Gamma \vdash e : \tau \Rightarrow \Gamma' \mid \overline{C}$, indicating that e is well-typed under a function type environment Θ and typing environment Γ, evaluates to a value of type τ, leading to a change in the type environment to Γ', and generating a command sequence $\overline{C}$. Throughout the description of our type system, we use $\mathrm{flv}(\Gamma)$ and $\mathrm{flv}(\tau)$ to denote all free location variables in Γ and τ, respectively.

The typing rules for quantum expressions, which may generate several commands, are provided in Fig. 10. In T-Init and T-MInit for qubit allocation, a location $l \in \Gamma$ removed to create a type $\texttt{qbit}(l)$. Conversely, the rule T-Free removes a qubit variable x from the typing environment and returns the location variable l associated with the type of x, allowing it to be reused for another qubit allocation. These two rules ensure that at most only one variable can have ownership over a location, and in this sense they are related to linear types [38]. The rule T-Meas2 requires that the arguments are qubits and adds a command $l_1 \sim l_2$. It is noteworthy that it does not validate whether l_1 and l_2 are connected at this time. The T-Gate and T-Meas1 rules do not generate any commands because single qubit measurements and applications of basic gates do not entail changes to qubit locations or connections between qubits.

The typing rules for classical expressions are outlined in Fig. 11. The rules for creating references, dereferencing, and assigning a value to reference cells closely resemble those of ordinary ML-like languages and are thus omitted here due to space constraints.

The rule T-Seq checks the type of e_1 and then proceeds to the subsequent expression e_2 with Γ_1, which is obtained from e_1, and concatenates two command sequences $\overline{C_1}$ and $\overline{C_2}$, which are obtained from e_1 and e_2, respectively.

In rule T-If, we ensure that each subexpression returns the same type environment Γ'. This stipulation ensures that regardless of which expression is chosen, the allocation state of the qubits after the if expression is the same. This property facilitates the implementation of an efficient type-checking algorithm, as explained in Sect. 5.3.

In rule T-While, we guarantee that the guard expression e_1 and the body expression e_2 return the typing environment Γ unchanged. This is imperative because the sequential execution of e_1 and e_2 must not alter the allocation state of qubits before and after the loop, as the number of loop iterations is unknown.

$$\frac{\Theta \mid \Gamma, x : \texttt{qbit}(l) \vdash e : \tau \Rightarrow \Gamma' \mid \overline{C}}{\Theta \mid \Gamma, l \vdash \textbf{let}\ x = \textbf{init}\ (l)\ \textbf{in}\ e : \tau \Rightarrow \Gamma' \mid \textbf{alloc}\ (l) + \overline{C}} \quad \text{(T-INIT)}$$

$$\frac{\Theta \mid \Gamma, l \vdash e : \tau \Rightarrow \Gamma' \mid \overline{C}}{\Theta \mid \Gamma, x : \texttt{qbit}(l) \vdash \textbf{free}\ x; e : \tau \Rightarrow \Gamma' \mid \textbf{free}\ (l) + \overline{C}} \quad \text{(T-FREE)}$$

$$\frac{y : \texttt{qbit}(l) \in \Gamma \qquad \Theta \mid \Gamma, x : \texttt{bool} \vdash e : \tau \Rightarrow \Gamma' \mid \overline{C}}{\Theta \mid \Gamma \vdash \textbf{let}\ x = M_B(y)\ \textbf{in}\ e : \tau \Rightarrow \Gamma' \mid \overline{C}} \quad \text{(T-MEAS1)}$$

$$\frac{x_1 : \texttt{qbit}(l_1), x_2 : \texttt{qbit}(l_2) \in \Gamma \qquad \Theta \mid \Gamma, x : \texttt{bool} \vdash e : \tau \Rightarrow \Gamma' \mid \overline{C}}{\Theta \mid \Gamma \vdash \textbf{let}\ x = M_{B_1, B_2}(x_1, x_2)\ \textbf{in}\ e : \tau \Rightarrow \Gamma' \mid l_1 \sim l_2 + \overline{C}} \quad \text{(T-MEAS2)}$$

$$\frac{x : \texttt{qbit}(l) \in \Gamma}{\Theta \mid \Gamma \vdash U(x) : \textbf{unit} \Rightarrow \Gamma \mid \epsilon} \quad \text{(T-GATE)}$$

Fig. 10. Typing rules for quantum expressions.

In rule T-CALL, we use a substitution map σ_l to instantiate occurrences of location variables l in the argument type $\tau_1, \ldots, \tau_n$, return type τ, command sequence $\overline{C}$, and typing environment Γ'. Prior to calling a function, the caller must ensure that all locations $\overline{l''}$ are free, where qubits will be allocated in the function body. After the function call, the portion of the typing environment used within the function transitions to $\sigma_l \Gamma'$. Consequently, the rule returns this modified environment along with the unused environment Γ. Additionally, it returns a command sequence $\sigma_l \overline{C}$ generated by the function call.

In rule T-FUNDECL, akin to let-polymorphism in ML, all free location variables are universally quantified. This enables us to call functions in diverse contexts. Here, location variables $\overline{l'}$, which directly appear in the typing environment within the assumption, will be used to allocate new qubits during the execution of the function body. Subsequently, we append the function type, along with the resulting typing environment and command sequence, to a function type environment Θ. We remark that the type of a function is not included in Θ in the current type checking, as $\mathcal{Q}_{LS}$ does not support recursive function calls.

The T-PROG rule requires that the function definitions in Θ are well-typed and that the main expression e is also well-typed under Θ and an initial typing environment $V(G)$, where G represents an architecture graph since all locations are initially unused.

In T-PROG, we also check whether $\overline{C}$ obtained through the type checking of the main expression is valid under the architecture graph G. The judgment form for the validity of a command sequence is $G \mid L \vdash \overline{C} \Rightarrow L'$, indicating that the process specified by $\overline{C}$ can be safely completed, starting with free locations L under a graph G, and that L' are free after executing $\overline{C}$. Formally, we define the rules for the validity of command sequences in Fig. 12.

We prove that any well-typed program under our type system will never encounter a halt in its execution. This assertion is formalized as type soundness, as shown in the following theorem.

$$\frac{x : \tau \in \Gamma}{\Theta \mid \Gamma \vdash x : \tau \Rightarrow \Gamma \mid \epsilon} \quad \text{(T-VAR)}$$

$$\frac{\Theta \mid \Gamma \vdash e_1 : \textbf{unit} \Rightarrow \Gamma_1 \mid \overline{C_1} \qquad \Theta \mid \Gamma_1 \vdash e_2 : \tau \Rightarrow \Gamma_2 \mid \overline{C_2}}{\Theta \mid \Gamma \vdash e_1; e_2 : \tau \Rightarrow \Gamma_2 \mid \overline{C_1} + \overline{C_2}} \quad \text{(T-SEQ)}$$

$$\frac{\begin{array}{c}\Theta \mid \Gamma \vdash e_1 : \texttt{bool} \Rightarrow \Gamma' \mid \overline{C_1} \\ \Theta \mid \Gamma' \vdash e_2 : \tau \Rightarrow \Gamma'' \mid \overline{C_2} \qquad \Theta \mid \Gamma' \vdash e_3 : \tau \Rightarrow \Gamma'' \mid \overline{C_3}\end{array}}{\Theta \mid \Gamma \vdash \textbf{if } e_1 \textbf{ then } e_2 \textbf{ else } e_3 : \tau \Rightarrow \Gamma'' \mid \overline{C_1} + (\overline{C_2} \vee \overline{C_3})} \quad \text{(T-IF)}$$

$$\frac{\Theta \mid \Gamma \vdash e_1 : \texttt{bool} \Rightarrow \Gamma \mid \overline{C_1} \qquad \Theta \mid \Gamma \vdash e_2 : \textbf{unit} \Rightarrow \Gamma \mid \overline{C_2}}{\Theta \mid \Gamma \vdash \textbf{while } e_1 \textbf{ do } e_2 : \textbf{unit} \Rightarrow \Gamma \mid (\overline{C_1} + \overline{C_2})^* + \overline{C_1}} \quad \text{(T-WHILE)}$$

$$\frac{\Theta(f) = \Pi \overline{l'}. \langle x_1 : \tau_1, .., x_n : \tau_n \rangle \xrightarrow{\overline{C}} \langle \Gamma' | \tau \rangle \qquad \sigma_l = [\overline{l}/\overline{l'}] \qquad \overline{l''} = \overline{l} \setminus (\bigcup_{i=1}^n \mathrm{flv}(\sigma_l \tau_i))}{\Theta \mid \Gamma, \overline{l''}, x_1 : \sigma_l \tau_1, .., x_n : \sigma_l \tau_n \vdash f[\overline{l}](x_1, .., x_n) : \sigma_l \tau \Rightarrow \Gamma, \sigma_l \Gamma' \mid \sigma_l \overline{C}} \quad \text{(T-CALL)}$$

$$\frac{\Theta \vdash D \qquad \Theta \mid \overline{l'}, x_1 : \tau_1, .., x_n : \tau_n \vdash e : \tau \Rightarrow \Gamma \mid \overline{C} \qquad \overline{l} = \overline{l'} \uplus (\bigcup_{i=1}^n \mathrm{flv}(\tau_i))}{\Theta, f : \Pi \overline{l}. \langle x_1 : \tau_1, .., x_n : \tau_n \rangle \xrightarrow{\overline{C}} \langle \Gamma | \tau \rangle \vdash D, f \mapsto [\overline{l}](x_1, .., x_n) e} \quad \text{(T-FUNDECL)}$$

$$\frac{\Theta \vdash D \qquad \Theta \mid V(G) \vdash e : \tau \Rightarrow \Gamma \mid \overline{C} \qquad G \mid V(G) \vdash \overline{C} \Rightarrow L}{G \vdash \langle D, e \rangle} \quad \text{(T-PROG)}$$

Fig. 11. Typing rules for classical expressions (excerpt).

$$\frac{l \in L}{G \mid L \vdash \textbf{alloc}\,(l) \Rightarrow L \setminus l} \text{(C-ALLOC)} \qquad G \mid L \vdash \textbf{free}\,(l) \Rightarrow L, l \text{ (C-FREE)}$$

$$\frac{G \mid L \vDash l_1 \sim l_2}{G \mid L \vdash l_1 \sim l_2 \Rightarrow L} \text{(C-MERGE)} \qquad \frac{G \mid L \vdash \overline{C}_1 \Rightarrow L' \qquad G \mid L \vdash \overline{C}_2 \Rightarrow L'}{G \mid L \vdash \overline{C}_1 \vee \overline{C}_2 \Rightarrow L'} \text{(C-IF)}$$

$$\frac{G \mid L \vdash \overline{C} \Rightarrow L}{G \mid L \vdash \overline{C}^* \Rightarrow L} \text{(C-LOOP)} \qquad \frac{G \mid L \vdash \overline{C}_1 \Rightarrow L' \qquad G \mid L' \vdash \overline{C}_2 \Rightarrow L''}{G \mid L \vdash \overline{C}_1 + \overline{C}_2 \Rightarrow L''} \text{(C-CONCAT)}$$

Fig. 12. The rules for connectivity checking.

Theorem 1. *(Soundness) If* $G \vdash \langle D, e \rangle$*, then* $[\emptyset, 1, e]$ *does not get stuck.*

5.3 Type Checking Algorithm

Assuming that $\overline{C}$ is derived from a well-typed expression by type inference, the remaining task involves connectivity checking $G \mid V(G) \vdash \overline{C} \Rightarrow L$ for some L. In this section, we first give a naive algorithm for solving it and then speed it up by reducing the problem to the offline dynamic connectivity problem.

Basically, the problem can be solved by simulating the command sequence from the front to the back. In the simulation, we use the constraints imposed on command sequences in the type system to process the loop and branching commands. In the case of loops, we can straightforwardly consider $\overline{C}^*$ as $\overline{C}$ because the T-While rule requires that the locations where qubits are allocated remain unchanged after $\overline{C}$. In other words, the state of locations remains consistent regardless of the number of iterations.

In the case of branches, while we can indeed check both $\overline{C_1} + \overline{C}$ and $\overline{C_2} + \overline{C}$ for $(\overline{C_1} \vee \overline{C_2}) + \overline{C}$ naively, this approach leads to an exponential increase in verification costs for the number of occurrences of non-nested branches. To address this issue, we leverage the fact that the allocation states immediately following $\overline{C_1}$ and $\overline{C_2}$ are identical due to the T-If rule. Consequently, it suffices to check $\overline{C_1}$ and $\overline{C_2} + \overline{C}$ for $(\overline{C_1} \vee \overline{C_2}) + \overline{C}$, as shown in Fig. 1.

Lemma 1. *Suppose that $(\overline{C_1} \vee \overline{C_2}) + \overline{C}$ is obtained from a well-typed expression. $G \mid L \vdash (\overline{C_1} \vee \overline{C_2}) + \overline{C} \Rightarrow L'$ if and only if $G \mid L \vdash \overline{C_1} \Rightarrow L''$ and $G \mid L \vdash \overline{C_2} + \overline{C} \Rightarrow L'$ for some L''.*

The discussion so far gives a type checking algorithm that processes a command sequence in order from the front in a depth-first manner while managing the current allocation state. The time complexity of this approach is $O(E+V)$ for finding a path in a merge command, so the overall operation takes $O(|\overline{C}|(E+V))$ time.

This algorithm, however, does not scale for large architecture graphs. To address this issue, we reduce the type checking problem to the *offline dynamic connectivity* problem described as follows:

Definition 1. *(Offline dynamic connectivity) Given a set of vertices V and Q queries $q_1, \ldots, q_Q$. Each query is one of the following:*

- `add`(u, v) *: Add an edge $\{u, v\}$ to G.*
- `remove`(u, v) *: Remove the edge $\{u, v\}$ from G.*
- `connected`(u, v) *: Answer whether u and v are connected in G.*

Dynamic connectivity is known to be efficiently solved [20, 22, 37], particularly for offline dynamic connectivity, where each query can be processed in $\mathcal{O}(\log V)$ time with a link-cut tree [35] maintaining a maximum spanning forest. The rest of this section concentrates on showing how to reduce our connectivity checking problem to the offline dynamic connectivity problem.

The reduction to offline dynamic connectivity is accomplished by converting a command sequence into a single command sequence without branches. Specifically, we transform $\overline{C_1} \vee \overline{C_2}$ to $\overline{C_1} + (\overline{C_1})^{-1} + \overline{C_2}$, where $\overline{C_1}^{-1}$ is the inverse of $\overline{C_1}$, an operation that undoes the change in the allocation state made by $\overline{C_1}$. Roughly speaking, $\overline{C}^{-1}$ can be obtained by reversing the meaning of **alloc** (l) and **free** (l) in $\overline{C}$ and then reversing the order of $\overline{C}$. We can verify $\overline{C_1}$ and $\overline{C_2}$ simultaneously by verifying the single command sequence obtained through this conversion. We define this process as the serialization of a command sequence.

Definition 2. *For a command sequence $\overline{C}$, the serialized command sequence* $\mathrm{ser}(\overline{C})$ *is defined by:*

$$\mathrm{ser}(\epsilon) = \epsilon \qquad \mathrm{ser}(l_1 \sim l_2 +\!\!+ \overline{C}) = l_1 \sim l_2 +\!\!+ \mathrm{ser}(\overline{C})$$
$$\mathrm{ser}(\mathbf{alloc}\,(l) +\!\!+ \overline{C}) = \mathbf{alloc}\,(l) +\!\!+ \mathrm{ser}(\overline{C}) +\!\!+ \mathbf{free}\,(l)$$
$$\mathrm{ser}(\mathbf{free}\,(l) +\!\!+ \overline{C}) = \mathbf{free}\,(l) +\!\!+ \mathrm{ser}(\overline{C}) +\!\!+ \mathbf{alloc}\,(l)$$
$$\mathrm{ser}((\overline{C}_1 \vee \overline{C}_2) +\!\!+ \overline{C}_3) = \mathrm{ser}(\overline{C}_1) +\!\!+ \mathrm{ser}(\overline{C}_2 +\!\!+ \overline{C}_3) \qquad \mathrm{ser}(\overline{C}^* +\!\!+ \overline{C}') = \mathrm{ser}(\overline{C} +\!\!+ \overline{C}')$$

Example 1. Consider the following program and $\overline{C}$ obtained from the program:

```
let q1 = init(l1) in
let w = mkref
  if true then
    let q2 = init(l2) in
    H(q2);
    let w = meas[Z](q2) in w
  else
    let q2 = init(l2) in
    let w = meas[X, X](q1, q2) in w
in ()
```

$$\overline{C} = \mathbf{alloc}\,(l_1),\ \mathbf{alloc}\,(l_2) \vee (\mathbf{alloc}\,(l_2), l_1 \sim l_2)$$
$$\mathrm{ser}(\overline{C}) = \mathbf{alloc}\,(l_1),\ \mathbf{alloc}\,(l_2), \underline{\mathbf{free}\,(l_2)},\ \mathbf{alloc}\,(l_2), l_1 \sim l_2, \underline{\mathbf{free}\,(l_2)},\ \underline{\mathbf{free}\,(l_1)}$$

The branch command in $\overline{C}$ is serialized as follows:

1. The **then** clause: **free** (l_2) is inserted after **alloc** (l_2) to restore the allocation state to one immediately before entering the then clause. As a result, we obtain **alloc** (l_2), $\underline{\mathbf{free}\,(l_2)}$.
2. The **else** clause and the subsequent commands: **free** (l_2) is inserted after these commands because the subsequent expression does not change the allocation state. The merge command $l_1 \sim l_2$ is ignored during inversion. As a result, we obtain $\mathbf{alloc}\,(l_2), l_1 \sim l_2, \underline{\mathbf{free}\,(l_2)}$.
3. Concatenate the results of steps 1 and 2.

Finally, the underlined commands in $\mathrm{ser}(\overline{C})$ are inserted as an inverse operation.

Indeed, we can employ $\mathrm{ser}(\overline{C})$ for connectivity checking in place of $\overline{C}$. Moreover, the length of $\mathrm{ser}(\overline{C})$ is less than twice the length of $\overline{C}$, namely $\mathcal{O}(|\overline{C}|)$. We show these properties in the following propositions.

Proposition 1. *Suppose that $\overline{C}$ is obtained from a well-typed expression. Then $G \mid L \vdash \mathrm{ser}(\overline{C}) \Rightarrow L$ if and only if $G \mid L \vdash \overline{C} \Rightarrow L'$ for some L'.*

Proposition 2. *For any $\overline{C}$, $|\mathrm{ser}(\overline{C})| \leq 2|\overline{C}|$.*

The final task is to convert **alloc** (l) and **free** (l), which are operations on vertices, into edge operations in the dynamic connectivity problem. This can be done as follows: when encountering **alloc** (l), we remove all edges incident to vertex l, and conversely, when encountering **free** (l), we restore them. Subsequently, we can determine whether $l_1 \sim l_2$ is valid by checking if they are adjacent to each other or there exist $l_1' \in \mathrm{adj}(l_1)$ and $l_2' \in \mathrm{adj}(l_2)$ such that l_1' and l_2' are connected. Here, $\mathrm{adj}(l)$ denotes the set of adjacent vertices of l in the initial graph. In fact, if such a path exists, we can use the path $l_1 \to l_1' \to l_2' \to l_2$ to merge l_1 and l_2.

Example 2. Consider a path graph G where $V(G) = \{l_1, l_2, l_3, l_4\}$ and $E(G) = \{\{l_1, l_2\}, \{l_2, l_3\}, \{l_3, l_4\}\}$. If **alloc** (l_1), **alloc** (l_3), $l_1 \sim l_3$ are obtained, then it is converted into the following queries: $\mathtt{remove}(l_1, l_2)$, $\mathtt{remove}(l_2, l_3)$, $\mathtt{remove}(l_3, l_4)$, $\underline{\mathtt{connected}(l_2, l_2), \mathtt{connected}(l_2, l_4)}$. This sequence is safe if either underlined query is true. In this case, $\mathtt{connected}(l_2, l_2)$ returns true and thus it is safe.

The computational complexity of our type checking algorithm for general architecture graphs is $\mathcal{O}(|\overline{C}|V^2 \log V)$. This is because the length of $\mathrm{ser}(\overline{C})$ is $\mathcal{O}(|\overline{C}|)$, as indicated by proposition 2. Additionally, up to $|\mathrm{adj}(l)|^2 = \mathcal{O}(V^2)$ queries are generated for each command.[3] However, in practice, architecture graphs are often sparse, meaning the size of $\mathrm{adj}(l)$ remains at most constant (e.g., 4 in a grid graph). In such cases, the algorithm works in $\mathcal{O}(|\overline{C}| \log V)$.

It is important to note that the size of $\overline{C}$ can grow exponentially with respect to the size of a given program, as command sequences are copied in function calls. However, this problem does not occur with loops. Roughly speaking, the size of $\overline{C}$ corresponds to the number of surgery operations performed at runtime, assuming that all loops are expanded exactly once.

6 Extensions

6.1 Recursive Functions

Currently, $\mathcal{Q}_{LS}$ lacks support for recursive functions. However, we can introduce support for recursive functions while disregarding the cost of type checking. This section outlines the extension of $\mathcal{Q}_{LS}$ with recursive functions.

We introduce command variables $\alpha, \beta, \ldots$ into $\overline{C}$ and assign them to functions for type inference. Through type inference, we derive production rules on command sequences denoted as $\alpha \to \overline{C_\alpha}$, where $\overline{C_\alpha}$ may recursively include α itself. For instance, if a function f has $e_1; f[\overline{l}](x_1, .., x_n); e_2$ as its body and e_1, e_2 generate command sequences $\overline{C}_1, \overline{C}_2$ respectively, then we obtain $\alpha \to \overline{C}_1 +\!\!+ \alpha +\!\!+ \overline{C}_2$. Consequently, we establish a language $\mathcal{L}$ where each word $\overline{C} \in \mathcal{L}$ corresponds to a potential execution trace of a given program. Our objective is to ascertain whether $\mathcal{L}$ is *safe*, meaning $\forall \overline{C} \in \mathcal{L}.\ \exists L.\ G \mid V(G) \vdash \overline{C} \Rightarrow L$.

We can address this decision problem by constructing the safe language $\mathcal{L}_{\mathsf{safe}} = \mathcal{L}(\mathcal{A})$ from an architecture graph, where $\mathcal{A}$ is a nondeterministic finite automaton created by the following steps:

1. Prepare $2^{|V(G)|}$ vertices with empty edges. Each state represents a graph state with cells allocated in different patterns. All states are accepting states.

[3] There is an implementation trick to improve the complexity to $\mathcal{O}(|\overline{C}|V \log V)$.

2. For each state $u, v \in \mathcal{A}$, add an edge $u \to v$ if a transition from u to v can occur via **alloc** (l) or **free** (l) for some l.
3. Add self-loops $u \to u$ labeled with $l_1 \sim l_2$ if there is a path from l_1 to l_2 in the state u.

The language $\mathcal{L}_{\text{safe}} = \mathcal{L}(\mathcal{A})$ contains all safe command sequences, and thus we can reduce the decision problem to the model checking problem: $\mathcal{L} \cap \overline{\mathcal{L}_{\text{safe}}} = \emptyset$? However, two primary issues arise. Firstly, efficiently solving this emptiness problem is challenging because $\mathcal{L}$ is generally a context-free language. Secondly, the number of states of $\mathcal{A}$ grows exponentially concerning the number of cells n.

One solution to tackle the first issue is constraining recursive function calls. For example, this can be achieved by restricting recursive calls so that the production rules are left-normal or right-normal form and the language $\mathcal{L}$ is normal.

As for the second issue, we currently need a fundamental solution. However, if $|V(G)|$ is not excessively large, this may not present a problem in practice. In fact, it is challenging to increase the number of logical qubits per core significantly.

6.2 Multi-qubit Quantum Measurements

The merge operation in lattice surgery can accept three or more qubits, enabling the implementation of multi-body measurements $M_{B_1,\ldots,B_n}$ for $n > 2$. Extending $\mathcal{Q}_{LS}$ with multi-qubit measurements is straightforward by generalizing the binary relation $l_1 \sim l_2$ in our system to an n-ary relation $\mathrm{c}(l_1, .., l_n)$. In this scenario, $\mathrm{c}(l_1, .., l_n)$ indicates that a program aims to merge $l_1, .., l_n$ on a Steiner tree with $l_1, .., l_n$ as endpoints, rather than on a path.

Supporting multi-qubit measurements does incur higher costs in type checking due to the increased complexity of the Steiner tree problem compared to pathfinding. For instance, the Dreyfus–Wagner algorithm [13], a widely-known method for finding a minimum Steiner tree, operates in exponential time. However, the Steiner tree for merging qubits does not necessarily need to be minimum, and thus we can employ simpler algorithms to address this task.

7 Related Work

Verified Quantum Compilation One of the most widely studied verifications of quantum compilers is the equivalence checking of quantum circuits, which ensures that the compiler preserves the semantics of the program. Amy developed a framework for reasoning about quantum circuits based on Feynman path integral formalism [2]. Additionally, several approaches based on decision diagrams have been proposed [9,31,39]. Another technique is ZX-calculus [11], a graphical language with a small set of rewrite rules on string diagrams called ZX diagrams. The completeness of the ZX-calculus [24] allows for the transformation of a ZX diagram into any equivalent diagram, making it useful for equivalence checking [33] and verified optimization [15,25] of quantum circuits.

While these studies aim to verify the equivalence of quantum programs before and after compilation, our study focuses on verifying whether quantum programs can be executed without runtime errors on quantum devices, considering various hardware constraints.

Our work is not the only framework aimed at verifying if a quantum program satisfies hardware constraints. Smith and Thornton [36] provided a software tool based on Quantum Multiple Decision Diagrams (QMDDs), which synthesizes a logical quantum circuit and maps it to a physical one on a specified architecture. Hietala et al. [21] developed VOQC, a verified optimizer for quantum circuits implemented using the Coq proof assistant, which can verify the correctness of their mapping algorithm that maps qubit variables to physical qubits to handle connectivity constraints. In contrast to these studies, our work is the first to address the connectivity problem between logical qubits in lattice surgery.

Quantum Compilers for Lattice Surgery OpenSurgery [32], presented by Paler and Fowler, compiles Clifford+T circuits naively using the Solovay–Kitaev algorithm. Watkins [40] has recently extended this work, developing a toolchain targeting surface codes and lattice surgery. This extension allows large quantum programs to be compiled efficiently, addressing scalability and performance in fault-tolerant quantum computation. Litinski [30] presented a Pauli-based approach, which translates a quantum circuit to a sequence of Pauli product measurements of $\pi/8$ and $\pi/4$ rotations and results in removing all Clifford gates from the circuit. Beverland et al. [4] developed an efficient algorithm called Edge-Disjoint Paths Compilation (EDPC) to optimize the depth of quantum circuits by parallelizing merge operations. Since our method does not rely on a specific compilation algorithm, we can readily apply our framework to verify the programs produced by these advanced compilers.

8 Conclusion

We presented a type-based verification method based on $\mathcal{Q}_{LS}$, which formalizes the execution model of surgery operations. The type system of $\mathcal{Q}_{LS}$ allows us to extract a command sequence representing the graph operations performed by tracking the positions of individual qubits at the type level. We proved the type soundness by stating that if the resulting command sequence on the architecture graph is safe, the target program will not terminate illegally during execution. Furthermore, we developed an algorithm in this study that efficiently inspects whether the resulting command sequence is safe. Our algorithm achieves this by reducing the type checking problem to the offline dynamic connectivity problem.

Several future challenges remain in this research. Firstly, we intend to extend the methodology of this study to concurrent programs. Optimizing high-level quantum programs and transforming them into $\mathcal{Q}_{LS}$ programs is also an important task.

Acknowledgments. This work was supported by JST SPRING, Grant Number JPMJSP2110. This work is also supported by JST CREST Grant Number

JPMJCR23I4, JST Moonshot R&D Grant Number JPMJMS2061, MEXT Q-LEAP Grant No. JPMXS0120319794, and No. JPMXS0118068682.

References

1. Acharya, R., Aleiner, I., Allen, R., Andersen, T.I., Ansmann, M., Arute, F., Arya, K., Asfaw, A., Atalaya, J., Babbush, R., Bacon, D., Bardin, J.C., Basso, J., Bengtsson, A., Boixo, S., Bortoli, G., Bourassa, A., Bovaird, J., Brill, L., Broughton, M., Buckley, B.B., Buell, D.A., Burger, T., Burkett, B., Bushnell, N., Chen, Y., Chen, Z., Chiaro, B., Cogan, J., Collins, R., Conner, P., Courtney, W., Crook, A.L., Curtin, B., Debroy, D.M., Del Toro Barba, A., Demura, S., Dunsworth, A., Eppens, D., Erickson, C., Faoro, L., Farhi, E., Fatemi, R., Flores Burgos, L., Forati, E., Fowler, A.G., Foxen, B., Giang, W., Gidney, C., Gilboa, D., Giustina, M., Grajales Dau, A., Gross, J.A., Habegger, S., Hamilton, M.C., Harrigan, M.P., Harrington, S.D., Higgott, O., Hilton, J., Hoffmann, M., Hong, S., Huang, T., Huff, A., Huggins, W.J., Ioffe, L.B., Isakov, S.V., Iveland, J., Jeffrey, E., Jiang, Z., Jones, C., Juhas, P., Kafri, D., Kechedzhi, K., Kelly, J., Khattar, T., Khezri, M., Kieferová, M., Kim, S., Kitaev, A., Klimov, P.V., Klots, A.R., Korotkov, A.N., Kostritsa, F., Kreikebaum, J.M., Landhuis, D., Laptev, P., Lau, K.M., Laws, L., Lee, J., Lee, K., Lester, B.J., Lill, A., Liu, W., Locharla, A., Lucero, E., Malone, F.D., Marshall, J., Martin, O., McClean, J.R., McCourt, T., McEwen, M., Megrant, A., Meurer Costa, B., Mi, X., Miao, K.C., Mohseni, M., Montazeri, S., Morvan, A., Mount, E., Mruczkiewicz, W., Naaman, O., Neeley, M., Neill, C., Nersisyan, A., Neven, H., Newman, M., Ng, J.H., Nguyen, A., Nguyen, M., Niu, M.Y., O'Brien, T.E., Opremcak, A., Platt, J., Petukhov, A., Potter, R., Pryadko, L.P., Quintana, C., Roushan, P., Rubin, N.C., Saei, N., Sank, D., Sankaragomathi, K., Satzinger, K.J., Schurkus, H.F., Schuster, C., Shearn, M.J., Shorter, A., Shvarts, V., Skruzny, J., Smelyanskiy, V., Smith, W.C., Sterling, G., Strain, D., Szalay, M., Torres, A., Vidal, G., Villalonga, B., Vollgraff Heidweiller, C., White, T., Xing, C., Yao, Z.J., Yeh, P., Yoo, J., Young, G., Zalcman, A., Zhang, Y., Zhu, N., Google Quantum, A.I.: Suppressing quantum errors by scaling a surface code logical qubit. Nature **614**(7949), 676–681 (2023). https://doi.org/10.1038/s41586-022-05434-1
2. Amy, M.: Towards large-scale functional verification of universal quantum circuits. Electron. Proc. Theor. Comput. Sci. **287**, 1–21 (2019). https://doi.org/10.4204/EPTCS.287.1
3. Babbush, R., Gidney, C., Berry, D.W., Wiebe, N., McClean, J., Paler, A., Fowler, A., Neven, H.: Encoding electronic spectra in quantum circuits with linear T complexity. Phys. Rev. X **8**(4), 041015 (2018). https://doi.org/10.1103/PhysRevX.8.041015
4. Beverland, M., Kliuchnikov, V., Schoute, E.: Surface code compilation via edge-disjoint paths. PRX Quant. **3**(2), 020342 (May2022). https://doi.org/10.1103/PRXQuantum.3.020342
5. Beverland, M.E., Murali, P., Troyer, M., Svore, K.M., Hoefler, T., Kliuchnikov, V., Low, G.H., Soeken, M., Sundaram, A., Vaschillo, A.: Assessing requirements to scale to practical quantum advantage (2022).https://doi.org/10.48550/arXiv.2211.07629
6. Bluvstein, D., Evered, S.J., Geim, A.A., Li, S.H., Zhou, H., Manovitz, T., Ebadi, S., Cain, M., Kalinowski, M., Hangleiter, D., Bonilla Ataides, J.P., Maskara, N., Cong, I., Gao, X., Sales Rodriguez, P., Karolyshyn, T., Semeghini, G., Gullans,

M.J., Greiner, M., Vuletić, V., Lukin, M.D.: Logical quantum processor based on reconfigurable atom arrays. Nature **626**(7997), 58–65 (2024). https://doi.org/10.1038/s41586-023-06927-3
7. Bombin, H., Martin-Delgado, M.A.: Topological quantum distillation. Phys. Rev. Lett. **97**(18), 180501 (2006). https://doi.org/10.1103/PhysRevLett.97.180501
8. Bravyi, S., Kitaev, A.: Universal Quantum Computation with ideal Clifford gates and noisy ancillas. Phys. Rev. A **71**(2), 022316 (2005). https://doi.org/10.1103/PhysRevA.71.022316
9. Burgholzer, L., Wille, R.: Improved DD-based equivalence checking of quantum circuits. In: 2020 25th Asia and South Pacific Design Automation Conference (ASP-DAC), pp. 127–132 (2020).https://doi.org/10.1109/ASP-DAC47756.2020.9045153
10. Chamberland, C., Campbell, E.T.: Universal quantum computing with twist-free and temporally encoded lattice surgery. arXiv:2109.02746 [quant-ph] (2021)
11. Coecke, B., Duncan, R.: Interacting Quantum Observables. In: Aceto, L., Damgård, I., Goldberg, L.A., Halldórsson, M.M., Ingólfsdóttir, A., Walukiewicz, I. (eds.) Automata, Languages and Programming, pp. 298–310. Lecture Notes in Computer Science. Springer, Berlin (2008). https://doi.org/10.1007/978-3-540-70583-3_25
12. da Silva, M.P., Ryan-Anderson, C., Bello-Rivas, J.M., Chernoguzov, A., Dreiling, J.M., Foltz, C., Frachon, F., Gaebler, J.P., Gatterman, T.M., Grans-Samuelsson, L., Hayes, D., Hewitt, N., Johansen, J., Lucchetti, D., Mills, M., Moses, S.A., Neyenhuis, B., Paz, A., Pino, J., Siegfried, P., Strabley, J., Sundaram, A., Tom, D., Wernli, S.J., Zanner, M., Stutz, R.P., Svore, K.M.: Demonstration of logical qubits and repeated error correction with better-than-physical error rates (2024). https://doi.org/10.48550/arXiv.2404.02280
13. Dreyfus, S.E., Wagner, R.A.: The steiner problem in graphs. Networks **1**(3), 195–207 (1971). https://doi.org/10.1002/net.3230010302
14. Erhard, A., Poulsen Nautrup, H., Meth, M., Postler, L., Stricker, R., Stadler, M., Negnevitsky, V., Ringbauer, M., Schindler, P., Briegel, H.J., Blatt, R., Friis, N., Monz, T.: Entangling logical qubits with lattice surgery. Nature **589**(7841), 220–224 (2021). https://doi.org/10.1038/s41586-020-03079-6
15. Fagan, A., Duncan, R.: Optimising clifford circuits with quantomatic. https://arxiv.org/abs/1901.10114v1 (2019). https://doi.org/10.4204/EPTCS.287.5
16. Fowler, A.G., Gidney, C.: Low overhead quantum computation using lattice surgery. arXiv:1808.06709 [quant-ph] (2019)
17. Fowler, A.G., Mariantoni, M., Martinis, J.M., Cleland, A.N.: Surface codes: towards practical large-scale quantum computation. Phys. Rev. A **86**(3), 032324 (2012). https://doi.org/10.1103/PhysRevA.86.032324
18. Gidney, C., Ekerå, M.: How to factor 2048 bit RSA integers in 8 hours using 20 million noisy qubits. Quantum **5**, 433 (2021).https://doi.org/10.22331/q-2021-04-15-433
19. Hayashi, S.: Singleton, union and intersection types for program extraction. In: Proceedings of the International Conference on Theoretical Aspects of Computer Software (TACS '91), pp. 701–730. Springer, Berlin (1991)
20. Henzinger, M.R., King, V.: Maintaining minimum spanning trees in dynamic graphs. In: Degano, P., Gorrieri, R., Marchetti-Spaccamela, A. (eds.) Automata, Languages and Programming, pp. 594–604. Springer, Berlin (1997). https://doi.org/10.1007/3-540-63165-8_214
21. Hietala, K., Rand, R., Hung, S.H., Wu, X., Hicks, M.: A Verified optimizer for quantum circuits. Proc. ACM Program. Lang. **5**(POPL), 37:1–37:29 (2021). https://doi.org/10.1145/3434318

22. Holm, J., de Lichtenberg, K., Thorup, M.: Poly-logarithmic deterministic fully-dynamic algorithms for connectivity, minimum spanning tree, 2-edge, and biconnectivity. In: Proceedings of the Thirtieth Annual ACM Symposium on Theory of Computing (STOC '98), pp. 79–89. Association for Computing Machinery, New York, NY, USA (1998). https://doi.org/10.1145/276698.276715
23. Horsman, C., Fowler, A.G., Devitt, S., Meter, R.V.: Surface code quantum computing by lattice surgery. New J. Phys. **14**(12), 123011 (2012). https://doi.org/10.1088/1367-2630/14/12/123011
24. Jeandel, E., Perdrix, S., Vilmart, R.: A complete axiomatisation of the ZX-calculus for clifford+T quantum mechanics. In: Proceedings of the 33rd Annual ACM/IEEE Symposium on Logic in Computer Science (LICS '18), pp. 559–568. Association for Computing Machinery, New York, NY, USA (2018). https://doi.org/10.1145/3209108.3209131
25. Kissinger, A., van de Wetering, J.: PyZX: Large scale automated diagrammatic reasoning. Electron. Proc. Theor. Compu. Sci. **318**, 229–241 (2020). https://doi.org/10.4204/EPTCS.318.14
26. Kitaev, A.Y.: Fault-tolerant quantum computation by anyons. Ann. Phys. **303**(1), 2–30 (2003). https://doi.org/10.1016/S0003-4916(02)00018-0
27. Knill, E.: Fault-Tolerant postselected quantum computation: schemes. arXiv:quant-ph/0402171 (2004)
28. Krinner, S., Lacroix, N., Remm, A., Di Paolo, A., Genois, E., Leroux, C., Hellings, C., Lazar, S., Swiadek, F., Herrmann, J., Norris, G.J., Andersen, C.K., Müller, M., Blais, A., Eichler, C., Wallraff, A.: Realizing repeated quantum error correction in a distance-three surface code. Nature **605**(7911), 669–674 (2022). https://doi.org/10.1038/s41586-022-04566-8
29. Lee, J., Berry, D.W., Gidney, C., Huggins, W.J., McClean, J.R., Wiebe, N., Babbush, R.: Even more efficient quantum computations of chemistry through tensor hypercontraction. PRX Quant. **2**(3), 030305 (2021). https://doi.org/10.1103/PRXQuantum.2.030305
30. Litinski, D.: A game of surface codes: large-scale quantum computing with lattice surgery. Quantum **3**, 128 (2019).https://doi.org/10.22331/q-2019-03-05-128
31. Miller, D., Thornton, M.: QMDD: A decision diagram structure for reversible and quantum circuits. In: 36th International Symposium on Multiple-Valued Logic (ISMVL'06), pp. 30–30 (2006).https://doi.org/10.1109/ISMVL.2006.35
32. Paler, A., Fowler, A.G.: OpenSurgery for topological assemblies. arXiv:1906.07994 [quant-ph] (2020)
33. Peham, T., Burgholzer, L., Wille, R.: Equivalence checking of quantum circuits with the ZX-calculus. IEEE J. Emerg. Sel. Topics Circ. Syst. **12**(3), 662–675 (2022). https://doi.org/10.1109/JETCAS.2022.3202204
34. Shor, P.W.: Polynomial-time algorithms for prime factorization and discrete logarithms on a quantum computer. SIAM J. Comput. **26**(5), 1484–1509 (1997). https://doi.org/10.1137/S0097539795293172
35. Sleator, D.D., Tarjan, R.E.: A data structure for dynamic trees. In: Proceedings of the Thirteenth Annual ACM Symposium on Theory of Computing (STOC '81), pp. 114–122. Association for Computing Machinery, New York, NY, USA (1981). https://doi.org/10.1145/800076.802464
36. Smith, K.N., Thornton, M.A.: A quantum computational compiler and design tool for technology-specific targets. In: Proceedings of the 46th International Symposium on Computer Architecture (ISCA '19), pp. 579–588. Association for Computing Machinery, New York, NY, USA (2019).https://doi.org/10.1145/3307650.3322262

37. Thorup, M.: Near-optimal fully-dynamic graph connectivity. In: Proceedings of the Thirty-Second Annual ACM Symposium on Theory of Computing (STOC '00), pp. 343–350. Association for Computing Machinery, New York, NY, USA (2000). https://doi.org/10.1145/335305.335345
38. Turner, D.N., Wadler, P., Mossin, C.: Once upon a type. In: Proceedings of the Seventh International Conference on Functional Programming Languages and Computer Architecture (FPCA '95), pp. 1–11. Association for Computing Machinery, New York, NY, USA (1995). https://doi.org/10.1145/224164.224168
39. Wang, S.A., Lu, C.Y., Tsai, I.M., Kuo, S.Y.: An XQDD-based verification method for quantum circuits. IEICE Trans. Fundam. Electron. Commun. Comput. Sci. **E91-A**(2), 584–594 (2008). https://doi.org/10.1093/ietfec/e91-a.2.584
40. Watkins, G., Nguyen, H.M., Watkins, K., Pearce, S., Lau, H.K., Paler, A.: A High Performance Compiler for Very Large Scale Surface Code Computations (2024). https://doi.org/10.48550/arXiv.2302.02459

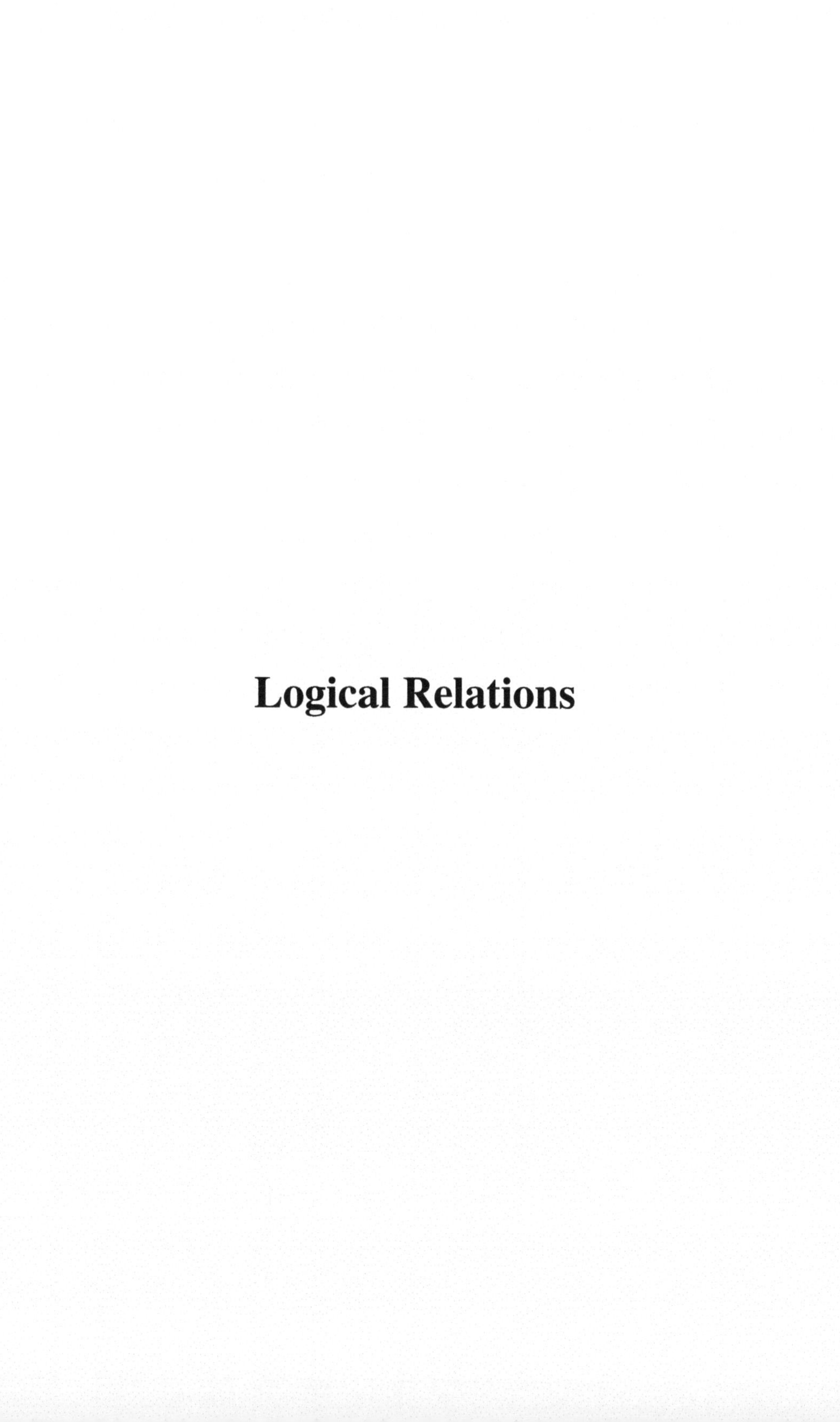

Logical Relations

On Computational Indistinguishability and Logical Relations

Ugo Dal Lago[1,2], Zeinab Galal[1,2(✉)], and Giulia Giusti[3]

[1] University of Bologna, Bologna, Italy
zeinab.galal@unibo.it
[2] INRIA Sophia Antipolis, Valbonne, France
[3] ENS Lyon, Lyon, France

Abstract. A λ-calculus is introduced in which all programs can be evaluated in probabilistic polynomial time and in which there is sufficient structure to represent sequential cryptographic constructions and adversaries for them, even when the latter are oracle-based. A notion of observational equivalence capturing computational indistinguishability and a class of approximate logical relations are then presented, showing that the latter represent a sound proof technique for the former. The work concludes with the presentation of an example of a security proof in which the encryption scheme induced by a pseudorandom function is proven secure against active adversaries in a purely equational style.

Keywords: Computational indistinguishability · Probabilistic effects · Metrics · Logical relations

Introduction

The two predominant models in cryptography, namely the computational [28] and the symbolic [20] models, have had very different fates with respect to the application of language-based verification techniques to them. In the symbolic model, which does not account for complexity nor for probability, the application of classic verification methodologies (e.g. model checking [22], rewriting [43] and abstract interpretation [1]) is natural and has been extensively done. In the computational model, instead, all this is notoriously more problematic.

An interesting line of work, which has given rise to an increasing number of contributions in the last 25 years (see, e.g., [16,31,34,41]), consists in the application of classical program equivalence theories to programming languages specifically designed to capture the reference notion of complexity in the computational model, namely that of a probabilistic polynomial time algorithm (PPT below). Once this is done, the gold standard notion of equivalence in cryptography, namely *computational indistinguishability* [27,36], becomes a form of observational equivalence, thus paving the way towards the study of computational indistinguishability via standard tools from programming language theory, like logical relations [50,51] and applicative bisimilarity [2,48], which are sound by construction (although not necessarily complete) for observational equivalence.

O. Kiselyov (Ed.): APLAS 2024, LNCS 15194, pp. 241–263, 2024.
https://doi.org/10.1007/978-981-97-8943-6_12

This is precisely the direction we explore in this work; our objective is to define a typed λ-calculus with references and probabilistic choice able to naturally capture the complexity constraints mentioned above through a form of graded modality, at the same time allowing to easily express primitives, experiments and reductions, which are the building blocks on which game-based proofs are based. The language we introduce, called λ**BLL**, can be seen as derived from Bounded Linear Logic [26]. Its syntax and operational properties are analyzed in detail in Sect. 1.

In Sect. 2, we then move on to define a notion of logical relation for λ**BLL** and demonstrate that it is *sound* for an approximate observational equivalence precisely capturing computational indistinguishability. A crucial aspect is that the proposed logical relation, in fact based on a logical *metric*, is *approximate* and therefore manages to capture programs that do not behave *exactly* the same way.

Section 3 is devoted to showing how a set of equations all justifiable through the introduced logical relations allows us to prove the security of an intrinsically second-order cryptographic construction, i.e. the proof that the encryption scheme induced by a pseudorandom function is CPA-secure, a classic result in cryptography. Notably, this proof intrinsically relies on approximate notions of equivalence. Moreover, parts of it make essential use of references.

For more details and proofs, we refer the reader to [14].

1 λBLL: A Calculus Capturing PPT

We define a language λ**BLL**, inspired by graded λ-calculi [46] and CBPV [21,39], and expressive enough to model complex cryptographic experiments requiring to keep track of the messages on which the oracle is queried by the adversary.

Types At the level of types, λ**BLL** has a linear type system (Fig. 1) with a correspondence to Bounded Linear Logic (**BLL**) [26] and graded-calculi [46] with indexed comonadic types. In our case, the grades are polynomials and serve to keep the complexity of the attackers under control. They are built from positive natural numbers ($\mathbb{N}_{\geq 1}$), addition and multiplication, but also contain a polynomial variable i (corresponding to the security parameter), allowing us to reason on indexed families of types and terms as in **BLL** [26]. Ground types are generated from unit $\mathbb{U}$, booleans $\mathbb{B}$ and binary strings $\mathbb{S}[p]$ of length p for some polynomial p. We distinguish between positive types and general types in the CBPV style [21,39] to restrict the argument of an application to be of positive type. To model references, we use effect typing [25] and annotate the bang and arrow types with reference contexts providing information on which memory cells are used during program execution. We also consider two types of contexts to distinguish between term variables x and memory references r.

Terms Grammars for values and computations are in Fig. 1. Memory references can only store values of ground type, and are handled in a simple way via reading and writing operators on locations. The term $\texttt{set}\,r\,V$ corresponds to updating

Ground types	$G ::= \mathbb{U} \mid \mathbb{B} \mid \mathbb{S}[p]$	**Ground values**	$W ::= \star \mid \mathbf{t} \mid \mathbf{f} \mid s$
Positive types	$P ::= G \mid P \otimes P \mid !^{\Theta}_{p} A$	**Positive values**	$Z ::= x \mid W \mid \langle Z, Z\rangle \mid !M$
Types	$A ::= P \mid P \overset{\Theta}{\multimap} A$	**Values**	$\mathcal{V} \ni V ::= Z \mid \lambda x.M$
		Computations	$\Lambda \ni M ::= \mathtt{return}\, V \mid \mathtt{der}(Z) \mid MZ$
Variable contexts	$\Gamma ::= \varnothing \mid x : P, \Gamma$		$\mid \mathtt{let}\, x = N \,\mathtt{in}\, M \mid f_p(Z_1, \dots, Z_m)$
Reference contexts	$\Theta ::= \varnothing \mid r : G, \Theta$		$\mid \mathtt{loop}\, V\, p\, \mathtt{times\, from}\, M \mid \mathtt{set}\, r\, Z$
			$\mid \mathtt{if}\, Z\, \mathtt{then}\, M\, \mathtt{else}\, N \mid \mathtt{get}\, r$
Polynomials	$p ::= 1 \mid i \mid p + p \mid p \times p$		$\mid \mathtt{let}\, \langle x, y\rangle = Z\, \mathtt{in}\, M$

Fig. 1. Syntax of λ**BLL**

the memory location referenced by r with the value V and $\mathtt{get}\, r$ returns the value under the reference r.

We enrich the grammar of λ-calculus with function symbols computing probabilistic polytime functions, which are the basic building blocks of any cryptographic protocol. We fix a set of function symbols $\mathcal{F}$ and each function symbol f in $\mathcal{F}$ comes equipped with:

- a type denoted $\mathsf{typeof}(f)$ of the form $G_1 \times \cdots \times G_m \to G$ where $G_1, \dots, G_m$ and G are ground types;
- for every polynomial p in $\mathbb{N}_{\geq 1}[i]$, a term constructor f_p of arity m.

For example, we will consider the function symbol $\mathtt{random}$ with $\mathsf{typeof}(\mathtt{random}) = \mathbb{S}[i]$ and arity 0 interpreted as a map randomly generating a string in $\{0,1\}^i$, and the function symbol $\mathtt{xor}$ with $\mathsf{typeof}(\mathtt{xor}) = \mathbb{S}[i] \times \mathbb{S}[i] \to \mathbb{S}[i]$ and arity 2 interpreted as a map computing the *bitwise exclusive-or* of binary strings.

Furthermore, in order to make λ**BLL** expressive enough to model experiments involving an adversary that can access an oracle a polynomial number of times, the grammar of computations includes an iterator $\mathtt{loop}$.

Typing Rules The typing rules for λ**BLL** are given in Fig. 2. We have two kinds of typing judgements:

$$\Gamma \vdash V : A \quad \text{and} \quad \Gamma; \Theta \vdash M : A$$

for values and computations respectively, where $\Gamma = x_1 : P_1, \dots, x_n : P_n$ is a context assigning positive types to term variables and $\Theta = r_1 : G_1, \dots, r_n : G_n$ is a reference context assigning ground types to reference variables. The operation of polynomial addition induces a binary partial operation $\boxplus$ on positive types defined by induction below:

$$G \boxplus G := G$$
$$(P \otimes Q) \boxplus (R \otimes S) := (P \boxplus R) \otimes (Q \boxplus S)$$
$$(!^{\Theta}_{p} A) \boxplus (!^{\Theta}_{q} A) := !^{\Theta}_{p+q} A.$$

$$\frac{}{\Gamma, x : P \vdash x : P}\ \text{VAR} \qquad \frac{}{\Gamma \vdash \mathbf{t} : \mathbb{B}}\ \text{TRUE} \qquad \frac{}{\Gamma \vdash \mathbf{f} : \mathbb{B}}\ \text{FALSE}$$

$$\frac{\text{typeof}(f) = G_1 \times \cdots \times G_m \to G \quad (\Gamma_k p \vdash Z_k : G_k p)_{1 \le k \le m} \quad p \in \mathbb{N}_{\geq 1}[i]}{\boxplus_k \Gamma_k p; \Theta \vdash f_p(Z_1, \ldots, Z_m) : Gp}\ \text{FUN}$$

$$\frac{s \in \{0,1\}^c \quad p : i \mapsto c \text{ is a constant polynomial}}{\Gamma \vdash s : \mathbb{S}[p]}\ \text{STRING} \qquad \frac{\Gamma \vdash Z_1 : P \quad \Delta \vdash Z_2 : Q}{\Gamma \boxplus \Delta \vdash \langle Z_1, Z_2 \rangle : P \otimes Q}\ \text{TENSOR}$$

$$\frac{\Gamma \vdash Z : P \otimes Q \quad x : P, y : Q, \Delta; \Theta \vdash M : A}{\Gamma \boxplus \Delta; \Theta \vdash \texttt{let}\ \langle x, y \rangle = Z\ \texttt{in}\ M : A}\ \text{LET} \qquad \frac{}{\Gamma \vdash \star : \mathbb{U}}\ \text{UNIT} \qquad \frac{\Gamma; \Theta \vdash M : A}{p * \Gamma \vdash !M : !_p^{\Theta} A}\ \text{BANG}$$

$$\frac{\Gamma \vdash Z : !_1^{\Theta} A}{\Gamma; \Theta \vdash \texttt{der}(Z) : A}\ \text{DER} \qquad \frac{\Gamma; \Theta \vdash M : P \overset{\Theta}{\multimap} A \quad \Delta \vdash Z : P}{\Gamma \boxplus \Delta; \Theta \vdash MZ : A}\ \text{APP} \qquad \frac{\Gamma, x : P; \Theta \vdash M : A}{\Gamma \vdash \lambda x.M : P \overset{\Theta}{\multimap} A}\ \text{LAM}$$

$$\frac{\Gamma \vdash V : A}{\Gamma; \Theta \vdash \texttt{return}\ V : A}\ \text{ETA} \qquad \frac{\Gamma; \Theta \vdash N : P \quad x : P, \Delta; \Theta \vdash M : A}{\Gamma \boxplus \Delta; \Theta \vdash \texttt{let}\ x = N\ \texttt{in}\ M : A}\ \text{LET}$$

$$\frac{\Gamma \vdash V : P \overset{\Theta}{\multimap} P \quad \Delta; \Theta \vdash M : P}{(p * \Gamma) \boxplus \Delta; \Theta \vdash \texttt{loop}\ V\ p\ \texttt{times from}\ M : P}\ \text{LOOP} \qquad \frac{\Gamma \vdash Z : G}{\Gamma; \Theta, r : G \vdash \texttt{set}\ r\ Z : \mathbf{U}}\ \text{SET}$$

$$\frac{}{\Gamma; \Theta, r : G \vdash \texttt{get}\ r : G}\ \text{GET} \qquad \frac{\Gamma; \Theta \vdash Z : \mathbb{B} \quad \Delta; \Theta \vdash M : A \quad \Delta; \Theta \vdash N : A}{\Gamma \boxplus \Delta; \Theta \vdash \texttt{if}\ Z\ \texttt{then}\ M\ \texttt{else}\ N : A}\ \text{CASE}$$

Fig. 2. **λBLL** typing rules

To account for polynomial multiplication, we also define for every polynomial $p \in \mathbb{N}_{\geq 1}[i]$, a total unary operation on positive types by induction:

$$\begin{aligned} p * G &:= G \\ p * (P \otimes Q) &:= (p * P) \otimes (p * Q) \\ p * (!_q^{\Theta} A) &:= !_{p \times q}^{\Theta} A. \end{aligned}$$

It is important to note that on ground types, the identities $G \boxplus G = G$ and $p * G = G$ mean that ground values (unit $\star$, booleans $\mathbf{t}, \mathbf{f}$ and binary strings $s \in \{0,1\}^*$) are duplicable whereas we keep track of the polytime complexity for higher-order applications and effects similarly to [18].

The partial operation $\boxplus$ on positive types can be extended to a total operation on variable contexts:

$$\varnothing \boxplus \varnothing := \varnothing$$

$$(x : P, \Gamma) \boxplus \Delta := \begin{cases} x : P, \Gamma \boxplus \Delta & \text{if } x \text{ does not occur in } \Delta \\ x : P \boxplus Q, \Gamma \boxplus \Sigma & \text{if } \Delta = x : Q, \Sigma \end{cases}$$

We also extend the operation $p * (-)$ on positive types to a total operation on term variables contexts:

$$\begin{aligned} p * \varnothing &:= \varnothing \\ p * (x : P, \Gamma) &:= (x : p * P), p * \Gamma \end{aligned}$$

For a polynomial p in $\mathbb{N}_{\geq 1}[i]$ and a type A, we write Ap for the type $A[p/i]$ where we substitute all the occurrences of the security parameter i by p. Similarly, for a term M, we write Mp for the term $M[p/i]$.

Probability Distributions Our calculus incorporates probabilistic effects with references by combining the distribution monad and the state monad. Recall that for a set X, a *(finite) probability distribution* is a function $\mu : X \to [0,1]$ with finite support, *i.e.* the set $\mathbf{supp}(\mu) := \{x \in X \mid \mu(x) > 0\}$ is finite, and such that $\sum_{x\in X} \mu(x) = 1$. We denote by $\delta_x : X \to [0,1]$ the *Dirac distribution* mapping an element y in X to 1 if $y = x$ and to 0 otherwise. Any probability distribution μ is then equal to

$$\sum_{1\leq k\leq m} a_k \cdot \delta_{x_k} \quad \text{where } \{x_1, \ldots, x_m\} = \mathbf{supp}(\mu) \quad \text{and} \quad a_k = \mu(x_k)$$

for $1 \leq k \leq m$. We denote by $\mathbf{D}(X)$ the set of all probability distributions over X. It induces a monad $(\mathbf{D}, \eta_{\mathbf{D}}, \gg\!=_{\mathbf{D}})$ on the category **Set** of sets and functions (we will omit the subscripts if there is no ambiguity). The unit has components $\eta_X : x \mapsto \delta_x$ given by Dirac distributions and the bind operator

$$\gg\!= : \mathbf{D}(X) \times \mathbf{Set}(X, \mathbf{D}(Y)) \to \mathbf{D}(Y)$$

maps a distribution $\mu = \sum_k a_k \delta_{x_k} \in \mathbf{D}(X)$ and a function $f : X \to \mathbf{D}(Y)$ to the pushforward distribution $\mu \gg\!= f := \sum_k a_k \delta_{f(a_k)}$.

Combining Probability with References The general idea is that a *store* is a map from memory reference variables to values that preserves typing. More precisely, for a fixed closed reference context $\Theta = r_1 : G_1, \ldots, r_m : G_m$ (meaning that the security parameter variable i does not occur in the types $G_1, \ldots G_m$), we denote by St_Θ the set of functions $e : \{r_1, \ldots, r_m\} \to \mathcal{V}$ such that $e(r_j) \in \{V \in \mathcal{V} \mid \cdot \vdash V : G_j\}$ for all $1 \leq j \leq m$.

We associate to every closed Θ a corresponding monad $(\mathbf{T}_\Theta, \eta_\Theta, \gg\!=_\Theta)$ on **Set** given by the tensor product [33] of the distribution monad with the state monad $\mathbf{T}_\Theta := (\mathbf{D}(- \times \mathrm{St}_\Theta))^{\mathrm{St}_\Theta}$, similarly to [4]. The unit of $\mathbf{T}_\Theta$ has components $X \to \mathbf{D}(X \times \mathrm{St}_\Theta)^{\mathrm{St}_\Theta}$ mapping $x \in X$ and $e \in \mathrm{St}_\Theta$ to the Dirac distribution $\delta_{(x,e)}$. The bind operator

$$\gg\!=_\Theta : \mathbf{T}_\Theta X \times \mathbf{Set}(X, \mathbf{T}_\Theta Y) \to \mathbf{T}_\Theta Y$$

takes $\varphi \in \mathbf{T}_\Theta X$ and $f : X \to \mathbf{T}_\Theta Y$ to the map $\boldsymbol{\lambda} e.(\varphi(e) \gg\!=_{\mathbf{D}} \mathbf{eval} \circ (f \times \mathrm{id}_{\mathrm{St}_\Theta}))$ where $\boldsymbol{\lambda}$ and **eval** are respectively the Currying operator and the evaluation map induced by the Cartesian closed structure of **Set**.

From Sets to Indexed Families To work with general term sequents where the security parameter i *may occur freely*, we generalize the discussion above from sets to families of sets. Let **ISet** be the category whose objects are families $X = \{X_n\}_{n\geq 1}$ of sets indexed by $\mathbb{N}_{\geq 1}$ and a morphism from $X = \{X_n\}_{n\geq 1}$ to $Y = \{Y_n\}_{n\geq 1}$ is a family of functions $\{f_n : X_n \to Y_n\}_{n\geq 1}$.

In our calculus, probabilistic effects are generated via the function symbols in $\mathcal{F}$. For each $f \in \mathcal{F}$ with $\mathsf{typeof}(f) = G_1 \times \cdots \times G_m \to G$, we assume that:

- there is a family $[\![f]\!] = \{[\![f]\!]_n\}_{n\geq 1}$ of set-functions $[\![f]\!]_n : [\![G_1]\!]_n \times \cdots \times [\![G_m]\!]_n \rightarrow \mathbf{D}([\![G]\!]_n)$ indexed over the security parameter $n \geq 1$ where $[\![\mathbb{S}[p]]\!]_n := \{0,1\}^{p(n)}$, $[\![\mathbb{B}]\!]_n := \{\mathbf{t},\mathbf{f}\}$ and $[\![\mathbb{U}]\!]_n := \{\star\}$.
- these functions can be evaluated in probabilistic polynomial time: there exists a PPT algorithm $\mathsf{alg}(f)$ such that for every $n \geq 1$, if $\mathsf{alg}(f)$ is fed with input 1^n and a tuple $t \in [\![G_1]\!]_n \times \cdots \times [\![G_m]\!]_n$, it returns $x \in [\![G]\!]_n$ with probability $[\![f]\!]_n(t)(x)$. This can be achieved by taking function symbols from a language guaranteeing the aforementioned complexity bounds [19,41]. A very small amount of these would however be sufficient for completeness.

Now, for a general reference context Θ (whose types may contain i), we define a monad on **ISet** mapping an indexed family $X = \{X_n\}_{n\geq 1}$ to the family

$$\{\mathbf{T}_{\Theta n}(X_n)\}_{n\geq 1} = \{(\mathbf{D}(X_n \times \mathrm{St}_{\Theta n}))^{\mathrm{St}_{\Theta n}}\}_{n\geq 1}$$

which we will use for the operational semantics of λ**BLL**.

Operational Semantics For every variable context Γ, reference context Θ and type A, we define indexed families $\Lambda^{\Theta}(\Gamma;A) = \{\Lambda^{\Theta}_n(\Gamma;A)\}_{n\geq 1}$ and $\mathcal{V}(\Gamma;A) = \{\mathcal{V}_n(\Gamma;A)\}_{n\geq 1}$ of typable terms and values respectively as

$$\Lambda^{\Theta}_n(\Gamma;A) := \{M \in \Lambda \mid \Gamma n; \Theta n \vdash M : An\} \quad \text{and}$$
$$\mathcal{V}_n(\Gamma;A) := \{V \in \mathcal{V} \mid \Gamma n \vdash V : An\}.$$

If the variable context Γ is empty, we write $\Lambda^{\Theta}_n(A)$ and $\mathcal{V}_n(A)$ for $\Lambda^{\Theta}_n(\varnothing;A)$ and $\mathcal{V}_n(\varnothing;A)$ respectively.

For a fixed reference context Θ, the small step operational semantics (Fig. 3) is an indexed relation $\longrightarrow = \{\longrightarrow_n\}_{n\geq 1}$ with

$$\longrightarrow_n \subseteq (\Lambda^{\Theta}_n \times \mathrm{St}_{\Theta n}) \times \mathbf{D}(\Lambda^{\Theta}_n \times \mathrm{St}_{\Theta n})$$

where $\Lambda^{\Theta}_n := \{M \in \Lambda \mid \Gamma n; \Theta n \vdash M : An \text{ for some } \Gamma, A\}$. For a triple $(M, e, \mathscr{D})$ in $\longrightarrow_n$, we write $(M,e) \longrightarrow_n \mathscr{D}$ and for ease of readability, we denote a probability distribution $\sum_{1\leq k\leq m} a_k \delta_{x_k}$ in set theoretic fashion $\{x_1^{a_1}, \ldots, x_m^{a_m}\}$.

For the case $\mathtt{set}\, r\, V$, $e[V/r]$ denotes the store mapping a reference r' to $e(r')$ if $r' \neq r$ and to V if $r' = r$.

Our calculus is strongly normalizing and in addition to the small step operational semantics for one step reductions, we also provide a final or big step semantics for the convergence behavior of terms. For a fixed reference context Θ and a type A, the final semantics $(\!| - |\!)^{\Theta,A}$ for closed λ**BLL**-terms is a map in **ISet** corresponding to the indexed family of functions

$$\{(\!| - |\!)^{\Theta,A}_n : \Lambda^{\Theta}_n(A) \rightarrow \mathbf{D}(\mathcal{V}_n(A) \times \mathrm{St}_{\Theta n}))^{\mathrm{St}_{\Theta n}}\}_{n\geq 1}$$

obtained in two steps:

1. We first use the fact that the monad $\mathbf{T}_{\Theta}$ on **Set** extends to the category of ω-complete partial orders with a bottom element (ω-cppo) and Scott-continuous morphisms (it follows easily from the fact that both the distribution and the

$$\frac{}{(\texttt{let}\, x = \texttt{return}\, V \,\texttt{in}\, M, e) \longrightarrow_n \{(M[V/x], e)^1\}}$$

$$\frac{(N, e) \longrightarrow_n \{(N_k, e_k)^{a_k}\}}{(\texttt{let}\, x = N \,\texttt{in}\, M, e) \longrightarrow_n \{(\texttt{let}\, x = N_k \,\texttt{in}\, M, e_k)^{a_k}\}}$$

$$\frac{}{(\texttt{let}\, \langle x, y\rangle = \texttt{return}\, \langle V, W\rangle \,\texttt{in}\, M, e) \longrightarrow_n \{(M[V/x, W/y], e)^1\}}$$

$$\frac{}{(\texttt{der}(!M), e) \longrightarrow_n \{(M, e)^1\}} \qquad \frac{(M, e) \longrightarrow_n \{(M_k, e_k)^{a_k}\}}{(MV, e) \longrightarrow_n \{(M_k V, e_k)^{a_k}\}}$$

$$\frac{}{(\texttt{if}\,\texttt{t}\,\texttt{then}\, M \,\texttt{else}\, N, e) \longrightarrow_n \{(M, e)^1\}} \qquad \frac{}{(\texttt{if}\,\texttt{f}\,\texttt{then}\, M \,\texttt{else}\, N, e) \longrightarrow_n \{(N, e)^1\}}$$

$$\frac{}{(\texttt{set}\, r\, V, e) \longrightarrow_n \{(\star, e[V/r])^1\}} \qquad \frac{}{(\texttt{get}\, r, e) \longrightarrow_n \{(e(r), e)^1\}}$$

$$\frac{}{(\texttt{loop}\, \lambda x.M\; 1\, \texttt{times}\,\texttt{from}\, N, e) \longrightarrow_n \{(\texttt{let}\, x = N \,\texttt{in}\, M, e)^1\}}$$

$$\frac{}{(f_p(W_1, \ldots, W_m), e) \longrightarrow_n \{([\![f]\!]_{p(n)}(W_1, \ldots, W_m), e)^1\}}$$

$$\frac{}{(\texttt{loop}\, \lambda x.M\; k+1\, \texttt{times}\,\texttt{from}\, N, e) \longrightarrow_n \{(\texttt{let}\, x = (\texttt{loop}\,(\lambda x.M)\; k\,\texttt{times}\,\texttt{from}\, N) \,\texttt{in}\, M, e)^1\}}$$

Fig. 3. Small step semantics of λ**BLL**

state monads extend to ω-cppo's). It allows us to define inductively a family $(\!| - |\!)_n^{\Theta,A} : \Lambda_n(A) \to \mathbf{T}^{\perp}_{\Theta n}(\mathcal{V}_n(A))$ where for a set X, $\mathbf{T}^{\perp}_{\Theta n} := \mathbf{T}_{\Theta n}(X \uplus \{\perp\}, \leq)$ is the image of the flat ordering ($\perp \leq x$ for all $x \in X$) under $\mathbf{T}_{\Theta n}$ (the bottom element $\perp$ is added to account for computations which are possibly non-terminating). Similarly to [38], each map $(\!| - |\!)_n^{\Theta,A}$ is obtained as the supremum $\bigvee_{k\in\omega} (\!| - |\!)_{n,k}^{\Theta,A}$ where $(\!| - |\!)_{n,k}^{\Theta,A}$ is defined inductively below:

$$(\!| M |\!)_{n,0}^{\Theta,A} := \perp \qquad (\!| \texttt{return}\, V |\!)_{n,k+1}^{\Theta,A} := \eta_{\mathcal{V}_n(A)}(V)$$
$$(\!| \texttt{if}\,\texttt{t}\,\texttt{then}\, M \,\texttt{else}\, N |\!)_{n,k+1}^{\Theta,A} := (\!| M |\!)_{n,k}^{\Theta,A} \quad (\!| \texttt{if}\,\texttt{f}\,\texttt{then}\, M \,\texttt{else}\, N |\!)_{n,k+1}^{\Theta,A} := (\!| N |\!)_{n,k}^{\Theta,A}$$
$$(\!| \texttt{der}(!M) |\!)_{n,k+1}^{\Theta,A} := (\!| M |\!)_{n,k}^{\Theta,A} \qquad (\!| \texttt{set}\, r\, Z |\!)_{n,k+1}^{\Theta,A}(e) := \delta_{(\star, e[Z/r])}$$
$$(\!| \texttt{get}\, r |\!)_{n,k+1}^{\Theta,A}(e) := \delta_{(e(r), e)}$$

$$(\!| MZ |\!)_{n,k+1}^{\Theta,A} := (\!| M |\!)_{n,k}^{\Theta, P \multimap A} \gg\!= (\lambda x.N \mapsto (\!| N[Z/x] |\!)_{n,k}^{\Theta,A})$$
$$(\!| \texttt{let}\, x = N \,\texttt{in}\, M |\!)_{n,k+1}^{\Theta,A} := (\!| N |\!)_{n,k}^{\Theta,P} \gg\!= (U \mapsto (\!| M[U/x] |\!)_{n,k}^{\Theta,A})$$
$$(\!| \texttt{let}\, \langle x, y\rangle = \langle Z, Z'\rangle \,\texttt{in}\, M |\!)_{n,k+1}^{\Theta,A} := (\!| M[Z/x, Z'/y] |\!)_{n,k}^{\Theta,A}$$

For the case $(\!| \texttt{loop}\, \lambda x.M\; m\, \texttt{times}\,\texttt{from}\, N |\!)_{n,k+1}^{\Theta,A}$, if $m = 1$, we define it to be $(\!| N |\!)_{n,k}^{\Theta,A} \gg\!= (U \mapsto (\!| M[U/x] |\!)_{n,k}^{\Theta,A})$ and if $m > 1$, we take

$$(\!| \texttt{loop}\, \lambda x.M\; (m-1)\, \texttt{times}\,\texttt{from}\, N |\!)_{n,k}^{\Theta,A} \gg\!= (U \mapsto (\!| M[U/x] |\!)_{n,k}^{\Theta,A}).$$

For a function symbol f with $\mathsf{typeof}(f) = G_1 \times \cdots \times G_m \to G$ and a polynomial p, $(\!| f_p(W_1, \ldots, W_m) |\!)^{\Theta,A}_{n,k+1}(e)$ is the mapping

$$(V, e') \mapsto \delta_e(e')[\![f]\!]_{p(n)}(W_1, \ldots, W_m)(V).$$

2. We prove that for any $M \in \Lambda^{\Theta}_n(A)$ and $e \in \mathrm{St}_{\Theta n}$, (M, e) reduces to some distribution $\mathscr{D}$ in polynomial time. As a corollary, we obtain that the final semantics map $(\!| - |\!)^{\Theta,A}_n$ can in fact be restricted to $\Lambda^{\Theta}_n(A) \to \mathbf{T}_{\Theta n}(\mathcal{V}_n(A))$ since $\lambda\mathbf{BLL}$ is strongly normalizing.

To express the standard correspondence between the final (big step) semantics and the transitive closure of the small step semantics, we define an indexed relation

$$\Downarrow = \{\Downarrow^m_n \subseteq (\Lambda^{\Theta}_n \times \mathrm{St}_{\Theta n}) \times \mathbf{D}(\Lambda^{\Theta}_n \times \mathrm{St}_{\Theta n})\}_{n \geq 1, m \geq 0}$$

where the additional natural number m models the number of steps in the small step semantics:

$$\frac{}{(\mathtt{return}\,V, e) \Downarrow^0_n \{(\mathtt{return}\,V, e)^1\}} \qquad \frac{(M, e) \longrightarrow_n \mathscr{D} \qquad \{E \Downarrow^{m_k}_n \mathscr{E}_E\}_{E \in \mathbf{supp}(\mathscr{D})}}{(M, e) \Downarrow^{1+\max_k m_k}_n \sum_E \mathscr{D}(E) \cdot \mathscr{E}_E}$$

and formulate the result as follows:

Lemma 1. *For a fixed reference context Θ, type A and security parameter n, the following are equivalent for any term $M \in \Lambda^{\Theta}_n(A)$, store $e \in \mathrm{St}_{\Theta n}$ and distribution $\mathscr{D} \in \mathbf{D}(\mathcal{V}_n(A) \times \mathrm{St}_{\Theta n})$:*

$$(\!| M |\!)^{\Theta,A}_n(e) = \mathscr{D} \Leftrightarrow \exists k \in \mathbb{N}, \quad (\!| M |\!)^{\Theta,A}_{n,k}(e) = \mathscr{D} \Leftrightarrow \exists m \in \mathbb{N}, (M, e) \Downarrow^m_n \mathscr{D}$$

Soundness and Completeness for Polynomial Time A calculus like $\lambda\mathbf{BLL}$ makes sense, particularly in view of the cryptographic applications that we will present in the last part of this article, if there is a correspondence with the concept of probabilistic polynomial time. This section is dedicated to giving evidence that such a correspondence indeed holds.

Before moving on to the description of soundness and completeness, however, it is worth outlining what is meant in this context by probabilistic polynomial time. In fact, what we mean by a PPT function can be deduced from how we defined function symbols in $\mathcal{F}$: these are families of functions, indexed on natural numbers, which possibly return a distribution and are computable by a probabilistic Turing machine working in polynomial time on the value of the underlying parameter. That basic functions are PPT holds by hypothesis, but that the same remains true for any term definable in the calculus needs to be proved. Moreover, the fact that any such function can be represented in $\lambda\mathbf{BLL}$ has to be proved as well.

Soundness for PPT The goal is to show that there exists a polynomial bound on the length of reduction sequences for any term of $\lambda\mathbf{BLL}$:

Theorem 1. (Polytime Soundness) *For every type derivation π of a term M in $\lambda\mathbf{BLL}$, there exists a polynomial q_π such that for every natural numbers $n \geq 1, m \geq 0$ and store e, if $(Mn, e) \Downarrow^m_n \mathscr{D}$, then $m \leq q_\pi(n)$.*

Similarly to Sect. 4.2 in [16], the proof of Theorem 1 is structured into three steps:

- We assign a polynomial q_π to every type derivation π defined by induction on the structure of π.
- We prove that $q_{(\cdot)}$ is stable under polynomial substitution: for every type derivation π with conclusion $\Gamma; \Theta \vdash M : A$ and for every polynomial p, there is a type derivation ζ with conclusion $\Gamma p; \Theta p \vdash Mp : Ap$ such that $q_\zeta(n) = q_\pi(p(n))$ for all $n \geq 1$.
- Finally, we prove that $q_{(\cdot)}$ strictly decreases along term reduction: if π derives N and $(N, e) \longrightarrow_n \mathscr{D}$, then for all (N', e') in $\mathbf{supp}(\mathscr{D})$, there exists a type derivation ζ for N' such that $q_\pi > q_\zeta$.

Completeness for PPT Theorem 1 implicitly tells us that algorithms formulated as typable λ**BLL** terms are PPT, since the number of reduction steps performed is polynomially bounded and reduction can be simulated by a Turing machine [3,17]. One can further prove that all PPT functions can be represented by λ**BLL** terms. Given the freedom we have about picking more and more basic function symbols, this does not seem surprising: we are anyway allowed to throw in new basic function symbols whenever needed. However, one can prove that completeness for PPT can be achieved with a very minimal set of basic functions symbols only including cyclic shift functions on strings and functions testing the value of the first bit in a string. Noticeably, soundness and completeness as presented above scale to *second-order* PPT, namely a notion of probabilistic polynomial time function accessing an oracle. This is quite relevant in our setting, given our emphasis on cryptographic constructions, and the fact that adversaries for some of those have oracle access to the underlying primitive.

2 Computational Indistinguishability

In this section, we define logical relations which we show to be sound for computational indistinguishability and which we will use in Sect. 3 to prove security of the private key encryption scheme induced by a pseudorandom function. Our approach is to first define a *logical metric* on terms from which we derive the indistinguishability logical relation containing terms whose distance is negligible with respect to this metric.

Term Relations In Sect. 1, we have considered indexed families $\Lambda^\Theta(\Gamma; A)$ and $\mathcal{V}(\Gamma; A)$ of sets containing terms that are closed for the security parameter variable i. On the other hand, computational indistinguishability, which is the main focus of this paper, is a relation between terms where the security parameter is a free variable and can be instantiated for every positive natural number n.

For a variable context Γ, a location context Θ and a type A, we let $\Lambda^\Theta_o(\Gamma; A)$ and $\mathcal{V}_o(\Gamma; A)$ be the sets of derivable computation terms and values respectively which are open for the security parameter variable i:

$$\Lambda^\Theta_o(\Gamma; A) := \{M \in \Lambda \mid \Gamma; \Theta \vdash M : A\} \quad \mathcal{V}_o(\Gamma; A) := \{V \in \mathcal{V} \mid \Gamma \vdash V : A\}.$$

Lemma 2. *The following rules are derivable for all $n \geq 1$:*

$$\frac{\Gamma; \Theta \vdash M : A}{\Gamma n; \Theta n \vdash Mn : An} \qquad \frac{\Gamma \vdash V : A}{\Gamma n \vdash Vn : An}$$

It implies that if M is in $\Lambda_o^{\Theta}(\Gamma; A)$, then Mn is in $\Lambda_n^{\Theta}(\Gamma; A)$ for all $n \geq 1$ and a similar statement holds for values in $\mathcal{V}_o(\Gamma; A)$.

Definition 1. *An* open term relation $\mathcal{R}$ *is an indexed family of pairs of relations* $\{(\mathcal{RC}^{\Theta}(\Gamma; A), \mathcal{RV}(\Gamma; A))\}_{\Gamma,\Theta,A}$ *with*

$$\mathcal{RC}^{\Theta}(\Gamma; A) \subseteq \Lambda_o^{\Theta}(\Gamma; A) \times \Lambda_o^{\Theta}(\Gamma; A) \qquad \mathcal{RV}(\Gamma; A) \subseteq \mathcal{V}_o(\Gamma; A) \times \mathcal{V}_o(\Gamma; A).$$

A closed *(for term variables)* term relation $\mathcal{R}$ *is an indexed family of pairs of relations* $\{(\mathcal{RC}^{\Theta}(A), \mathcal{RV}(A))\}_{\Theta,A}$ *with* $\mathcal{RC}^{\Theta}(A) \subseteq \Lambda_o^{\Theta}(A) \times \Lambda_o^{\Theta}(A)$ *and* $\mathcal{RV}(A) \subseteq \mathcal{V}_o(A) \times \mathcal{V}_o(A)$.

Every open term relation induces a closed term relation by restricting to empty term variable contexts. For the other direction, we use the standard notion of *open extension* of a closed relation via substitutions with positive values.

Contextual Indistinguishability The notion of behavioral equivalence we consider here is *computational indistinguishability* with respect to a polytime adversary represented as a λ**BLL**-context. Recall that a function which grows asymptotically slower than the inverse of any polynomial is called negligible [10]:

Definition 2. *A function $\varepsilon : \mathbb{N} \to \mathbb{R}_+$ is* negligible *if for all $k \in \mathbb{N}$, there exists $N \in \mathbb{N}$ such that for all $n \geq N$, $\varepsilon(n) < \frac{1}{n^k}$.*

Definition 3. *For terms M, N in $\Lambda_o^{\Theta}(\Gamma; A)$, we say that M and N are* contextually indistinguishable *if for every closing context C such that $C[M]$ and $C[N]$ are in $\Lambda_o^{\Xi}(\mathbb{B})$ for some reference context Ξ, there exists a negligible function $\varepsilon : \mathbb{N} \to \mathbb{R}_+$ such that for every $n \geq 1$, $e \in \mathrm{St}_{\Xi n}$ and subset $X \subseteq \{\mathbf{t}, \mathbf{f}\} \times \mathrm{St}_{\Xi n}$,*

$$||(\!|C[M]n|\!)_n^{\Xi,\mathbb{B}}(e)(X) - (\!|C[N]n|\!)_n^{\Xi,\mathbb{B}}(e)(X) \leq \varepsilon(n).$$

We adopt a coinductive characterization of contextual indistinguishability following the approach in [29,37] in the case of contextual equivalence for applicative bisimilarity. The contextual indistinguishability relation can indeed be alternatively defined as the largest open λ**BLL**-term relation that is both *compatible* and *adequate*. Compatibility means that the relation is closed under contexts: if (M, N) is in $\mathcal{R}$ and C is a context, then $(C[M], C[N])$ is also in $\mathcal{R}$. Adequacy on the other hand depends on the observational behavior we consider, it is typically termination for contextual equivalence or probability of convergence for non-deterministic calculi. In our case, the notion of interest in computational indistinguishability:

Definition 4. *We define an indexed relation* $\approx = \{\approx_\Theta \subseteq \Lambda_o^\Theta(\mathbb{B}) \times \Lambda_o^\Theta(\mathbb{B})\}_\Theta$ *on closed (for term variables) terms of Boolean type which are indistinguishable: a pair* (M, N) *is in the relation* $\approx_\Theta$ *if and only if there exists a negligible function* $\varepsilon : \mathbb{N} \to \mathbb{R}_+$ *such that for every* $n \geq 1$, $e \in \mathrm{St}_{\Theta n}$ *and subset* $X \subseteq \{\mathbf{t}, \mathbf{f}\} \times \mathrm{St}_{\Theta n}$,

$$||(\!|Mn|\!)_n^{\Theta,\mathbb{B}}(e)(X) - (\!|Nn|\!)_n^{\Theta,\mathbb{B}}(e)(X) \leq \varepsilon(n).$$

We call an open λ**BLL**-term relation $\mathcal{R}$ *adequate* if it is included in $\approx$ for closed Boolean terms, *i.e.* $\mathcal{R}^\Theta(\mathbb{B}) \subseteq \approx_\Theta$ for all reference contexts Θ and we obtain that the predicate of adequacy on open λ**BLL**-term relations is closed under countable unions and relational composition.

Lemma 3. *Contextual indistinguishability is the largest adequate compatible open* λ**BLL***-relation and we denote it by* $\sim$.

This coinductive characterization provides a useful proof principle to show soundness: any open relation $\mathcal{R}$ that is both compatible and adequate must be included in $\sim$ and is therefore *sound* for contextual indistinguishability (*i.e.* any pair of terms (M, N) in $\mathcal{R}$ are contextually indistinguishable).

Background on Metrics

Weighted Relations For metric reasoning on λ**BLL**, we consider distances valued in the unit real interval $[0, 1]$ equipped with the operation of *truncated addition* $x \oplus y := \min\{1, x + y\}$ for $x, y \in [0, 1]$. We have in particular that $1 = 1 \oplus 1$ which has a direct correspondence with the fact that values of ground type are arbitrarily duplicable in λ**BLL** (see Remark 1).

Recall that a (unital) *quantale* is a tuple $(\mathcal{Q}, \leq, \otimes, 1)$ where $(\mathcal{Q}, \leq)$ is a complete lattice, $(\mathcal{Q}, \otimes, 1)$ is a monoid and $\otimes$ distributes over arbitrary joins [47]. The unit interval with the opposite of the natural order (the natural order is defined as: $x \leq y$ if and only if there exists z such that $x \oplus z = y$) can be equipped with a quantale structure $\mathcal{L} = ([0, 1], \geq, \oplus, 0)$, called the *Łukasiewicz quantale*.

For sets X and Y, an *$\mathcal{L}$-weighted relation* $R : X \nrightarrow Y$ from X to Y consists of a function $X \times Y \to [0, 1]$. They form a category, which we denote by $\mathbf{Rel}_\mathcal{L}$, where the identity $\mathrm{id}_X : X \nrightarrow X$ maps a pair (x, y) to 0 if $x = y$ and 1 otherwise. The composite of two relations $R : X \nrightarrow Y$ and $S : Y \nrightarrow Z$ is the relation $S \circ R : X \nrightarrow Z$ mapping a pair (x, z) to $\inf_{y \in Y} R(x, y) \oplus S(y, z)$. The category $\mathbf{Rel}_\mathcal{L}$ can be equipped with a *dual* (transpose) operation mapping a relation $R : X \nrightarrow Y$ to the relation $R^{\mathrm{op}} : Y \nrightarrow X$ which simply maps (y, x) to $R(x, y)$. Any function $f : X \to Y$, induces a $\mathcal{L}$-relation via its graph $\mathbf{gr}(f) : X \nrightarrow Y$ mapping a pair (x, y) to 0 if $f(x) = y$ and 1 otherwise.

Pseudo-metric Spaces If we restrict to the special case of weighted endo-relations $R : X \nrightarrow X$ that are reflexive ($R \leq \mathrm{id}_X$), symmetric ($R = R^{\mathrm{op}}$) and transitive ($R \leq R \circ R$), we obtain the notion of pseudo-metric space:

Definition 5. *A* pseudo-metric space *consists of a pair* (X, d_X) *where* X *is a set and* d_X *is a function from* $X \times X \to [0, 1]$ *satisfying the following axioms:*

- *reflexivity: for all x in X, $d_X(x,x) = 0$;*
- *symmetry: for all x, y in X, $d_X(x,y) = d(y,x)$;*
- *triangular inequality: for all x, y, z in X, $d_X(x,z) \leq d_X(x,y) \oplus d_X(y,z)$*

If d_X further satisfies the separation axiom (for all x, y, $d_X(x,y) = 0$ implies $x = y$), then (X, d_X) is a metric space.

For the rest of the paper, even if we do not assume that the separation axiom holds, we will just say metric space instead of pseudo-metric space. Note that metric space with the *discrete metric* $\mathrm{disc} : X \times X \to [0,1]$ mapping a pair (x,y) to 0 if $x = y$ and 1 otherwise corresponds exactly to the identity weighted relation defined above.

Definition 6. *For two metric spaces (X, d_X) and (Y, d_Y), a function $f : X \to Y$ is said to be* non-expansive *if for all x, x' in X, $d_Y(f(x), f(x')) \leq d_X(x, x')$. We denote by* **PMet** *the category of pseudo-metric spaces and non-expansive maps.*

The category **PMet** is equivalent to the category of $\mathcal{L}$-enriched categories and $\mathcal{L}$-enriched functors between them [32]. We recall below some properties of **PMet** which we will use to define the logical metric in the following section, they are all instances of more general statements on quantale-enriched categories and we refer the reader to [32] for a complete account. **PMet** is symmetric monoidal closed with tensor product $(X, d_X) \otimes (Y d_Y)$ given by $(X \times Y, d_{X \otimes Y})$ where for all $x, x' \in X$ and $y, y' \in Y$,

$$d_{X \otimes Y}((x,y),(x',y')) := d_X(x,x') \oplus d_Y(y,y').$$

The unit is given by $\mathbf{1} = (\{\star\}, \mathrm{disc})$ and the linear hom $X \multimap Y$ has underlying set $\mathbf{PMet}(X,Y)$ (the set of non-expansive maps from X to Y) and distance $d_{X \multimap Y}(f,g) := \sup_{x \in X} d_Y(f(x), g(x))$. For any $k \geq 1$ and $x \in [0,1]$, we define inductively $k \cdot x$ as $1 \cdot x := x$ and $(k+1) \cdot x := (k \cdot x) \oplus x$. This operation induces a *scaling* operation $k \cdot (X, d_X) := (X, k \cdot d_X)$ on **PMet** which we use to model the graded bang of λ**BLL**. Note that if $f : (X, d_X) \to (Y, d_Y)$ is non-expansive, then $f : (X, k \cdot d_X) \to (Y, k \cdot d_Y)$ is also non-expansive for all $k \in \mathbb{N}$.

Extending Monadic Effects from Sets to Metric Spaces In order to define the logical metric on computation terms, we need to extend the effect monad $\mathbf{T}_\Theta$ defined in Sect. 1 from sets to metric spaces. To do so, we follow the standard approach of monad extensions from sets to quantale weighted relations [7,32]. It is well-known that the distribution monad $\mathbf{D}$ (and therefore the monads $\mathbf{T}_\Theta$ as well) on sets only *laxly* extends to weighted relations via *Kantorovich lifting* [8,12,35]. The Kantorovich lifting for distributions fits into the more general framework of *Barr extensions* for monads from sets to quantale relations [32].

In this section, we only give the explicit definition of how the Barr lax extension $\overline{\mathbf{T}}_\Theta$ of the effect monad acts on metric spaces and we refer the reader to [23,52] for more background on lax extensions for weighted relations. The Kantorovich lifting can be formulated in terms of couplings for probability distributions:

Definition 7. *For sets X, Y and distributions $\mu \in \mathbf{D}(X)$, $\psi \in \mathbf{D}(Y)$, a* coupling *over μ and ν is a distribution $\gamma \in \mathbf{D}(X \times Y)$ such that*

$$\forall x \in X, \mu(x) = \sum_{y \in Y} \gamma(x, y) \quad \textit{and} \quad \forall y \in Y, \nu(y) = \sum_{x \in X} \gamma(x, y).$$

We denote by $\Omega(\mu, \nu)$ the set of all couplings over μ and ν.

For a metric space (X, d_X), the Kantorovich lifting of the distance d_X is the distance $\mathbf{K}(d_X)$ on $\mathbf{D}(X)$ mapping distributions $\mu, \nu \in \mathbf{D}(X)$ to

$$\mathbf{K}(d_X)(\mu, \nu) := \inf_{\gamma \in \Omega(\mu,\nu)} \sum_{x_1, x_2 \in X} \gamma(x_1, x_2) \cdot d_X(\mu(x_1), \nu(x_2)).$$

While there are many other possible choices of metrics on distribution spaces besides the Kantorovich distance $\mathbf{K}(d_X)$ [24], it is the smallest among the ones which laxly extends to weighted relations and it also coincides with the *statistical distance* (or *total variation distance*) when d_X is the discrete metric.

Definition 8. *For a set X, the* statistical distance $d_{\text{stat}} : \mathbf{D}(X) \times \mathbf{D}(X) \to [0, 1]$ *maps two distributions $\mu, \nu \in \mathbf{D}(X)$ to*

$$d_{\text{stat}}(\mu, \nu) := \frac{1}{2} \cdot \sum_{x \in X} ||\mu(x) - \nu(x) = \sup_{A \subseteq X} ||\mu(A) - \nu(A).$$

For a closed (for the security parameter variable) location context Θ, the action of the lax extension $\overline{\mathbf{T}}_\Theta$ on a metric space (X, d_X) is the metric space with underlying set $\mathbf{T}_\Theta(X)$ and distance $\overline{\mathbf{T}}_\Theta(d_X)$ mapping functions $\varphi, \psi : \mathrm{St}_\Theta \to \mathbf{D}(X \times \mathrm{St}_\Theta)$ to

$$\overline{\mathbf{T}}_\Theta(d_X)(\varphi, \psi) := \sup_{e \in \mathrm{St}_\Theta} \mathbf{K}(d_{X \otimes \mathrm{St}})(\varphi(e), \psi(e)). \tag{1}$$

Logical Metric We now have all the ingredients to define a logical metric for λ**BLL**-terms using the lax extension of the monad $\mathbf{T}_\Theta$ to metric spaces.

Definition 9. *We define a family of metrics on closed computations and values indexed by the security parameter:*

$$\mathbf{dV}_n^A : \mathcal{V}_n(A) \times \mathcal{V}_n(A) \to [0, 1] \quad \textit{and} \quad \mathbf{dC}_n^{\Theta,A} : \Lambda_n^\Theta(A) \times \Lambda_n^\Theta(A) \to [0, 1]$$

by mutual induction on the type A:

$$\mathbf{dV}_n^{\mathbb{S}[p]}(s, s') := \mathrm{disc}_{\mathbb{S}[p(n)]}(s, s') \quad \mathbf{dV}_n^{\mathbb{B}}(W, W') := \mathrm{disc}_{\mathbb{B}}(W, W')$$

$$\mathbf{dV}_n^{\mathbb{U}}(\star, \star) := \mathrm{disc}_{\mathbb{U}}(\star, \star) = 0 \quad \mathbf{dV}_n^{!_p^\Theta A}(!M, !N) := \oplus_{p(n)} \mathbf{dC}_n^{\Theta,A}(M, N)$$

$$\mathbf{dV}_n^{P \otimes Q}(\langle U, V \rangle, \langle U', V' \rangle) := \mathbf{dV}_n^P(U, U') \oplus \mathbf{dV}_n^Q(V, V')$$

$$\mathbf{dV}_n^{P \multimap_\Theta A}(\lambda x.M, \lambda y.N) := \sup_{V \in \mathcal{V}_n(P)} \mathbf{dC}_n^{\Theta,A}(M[V/x], N[V/y])$$

$$\mathbf{dC}_n^{\Theta,A}(M, N) := \bar{\mathbf{T}}_\Theta(\mathbf{dV}_n^A)((\!|M|\!)_n^{\Theta,A}, (\!|N|\!)_n^{\Theta,A})$$

where disc *denotes the discrete metric and $\bar{\mathbf{T}}_\Theta$ is the lax extension of the functor $\mathbf{T}_\Theta : \mathbf{Set} \to \mathbf{Set}$ defined in (1).*

In our setting, the metric version of the fundamental lemma states that substitution by positive value terms is a non-expansive operation:

Lemma 4. (Fundamental Lemma for Logical Metrics) *For a context $\Gamma = x_1 : P_1, \ldots, x_m : P_m$ and a term M in $\Lambda_n^{\Theta}(\Gamma; A)$ with $n \geq 1$, for every closed positive values $Z_j, Z_j' \in \mathcal{V}_n(P_j)$ with $1 \leq j \leq m$, we have*

$$\mathbf{dC}_n^{\Theta,A}(M\rho, M\rho') \leq \bigoplus_{1 \leq j \leq m} \mathbf{dV}_n^{P_j}(Z_j, Z_j')$$

where $\rho := [Z_1/x_1, \ldots, Z_m/x_m]$ and $\rho' := [Z_1'/x_1, \ldots, Z_m'/x_m]$. A similar statement holds for open value terms in $\mathcal{V}_n(\Gamma; A)$.

Remark 1. A key ingredient in the proof of the fundamental lemma is the equality $\mathbf{dV}_n^{P \boxplus Q}(V, W) = \mathbf{dV}_n^{P}(V, W) \oplus \mathbf{dV}_n^{Q}(V, W)$ for closed values V, W, it allows to keep a precise track of how distances are amplified when contexts are added $\Gamma \boxplus \Delta$ in rules such as `let` or $\otimes$ for example. We can see here that the main motivation behind using truncated addition $\oplus$ in our setting is that it allows for the additional flexibility of having ground types being duplicable without loosing the ability to measure distances for higher types: if P and Q are equal to some ground type G, and $V \neq W$, then the equality above indeed rewrites to $1 = 1 \oplus 1$ which would not be possible if we had considered for example the Lawvere quantale with regular addition instead of the Łukasiewicz quantale with truncated addition.

Indistinguishability Logical Relation We now define a closed (for term variables) λ**BLL**-relation $\mathbf{Ind} = (\mathbf{IndC}, \mathbf{IndV})$ with

$$\mathbf{IndC}^{\Theta}(A) \subseteq \Lambda_o^{\Theta}(A) \times \Lambda_o^{\Theta}(A) \quad \text{and} \quad \mathbf{IndV}(A) \subseteq \mathcal{V}_o(A) \times \mathcal{V}_o(A).$$

For terms M, N in $\Lambda_o^{\Theta}(A)$, the pair (M, N) is in $\mathbf{IndC}^{\Theta}(A)$ if there exists a negligible function $\varepsilon : \mathbb{N} \to \mathbb{R}_+$ such that for all $n \geq 1$,

$$\mathbf{dC}_n^{\Theta,A}(Mn, Nn) \leq \varepsilon(n).$$

The relation on values $\mathbf{IndV}(A)$ is defined similarly via the logical metric on values $\mathbf{dV}^A$.

The fundamental lemma for the indistinguishability logical relation can now be directly derivable from the non-expansiveness of the logical metric (Lemma 4) and basic closure properties of negligible functions:

Lemma 5. *For a variable context $\Gamma = x_1 : P_1, \ldots, x_m : P_m$ and closed positive values (Z_k, Z_k') in $\mathbf{IndV}(P_k)$ with $1 \leq k \leq m$, we have for all $M \in \Lambda_o^{\Theta}(\Gamma; A)$ and $U \in \mathcal{V}_o(\Gamma; A)$,*

$$(M\rho, M\rho') \in \mathbf{IndC}^{\Theta}(A) \quad \textit{and} \quad (U\rho, U\rho') \in \mathbf{IndV}(A)$$

where $\rho := [Z_1/x_1, \ldots, Z_m/x_m]$ and $\rho' := [Z_1'/x_1, \ldots, Z_m'/x_m]$. In particular, for a closed term $M \in \Lambda^{\Theta}(A)$, we have $(M, M) \in \mathbf{IndC}^{\Theta}(A)$.

Theorem 2. *The open extension of* **Ind** *is adequate and compatible.*

Since the contextual indistinguishability relation $\sim$ is the largest compatible adequate relation, it contains **Ind** by Lemma 3, which implies that **Ind** is *sound* for contextual indistinguishability. Full abstraction on the other hand is not possible within our framework: since base types are equipped with the discrete metric whose Kantorovich lifting coincides with statistical distance, we cannot hope to capture the whole contextual indistinguishability relation as it is well-known that statistical closeness is strictly included in computational indistinguishability (*e.g.* Proposition 3.2.3 in [27]).

3 Proving Encryption Scheme Secure Equationally

This section is devoted to the presentation of a game-based proof [49] of security against active attacks for the encryption scheme Π_F induced by any pseudorandom function F. The proof is rather standard and a less formal version of it can be found in many cryptography textbooks (see, *e.g.*, [36]). Following the advice of the anonymous reviewers, we are keeping the presentation as self-contained as possible.

Pseudorandom Functions and Private-Key Encryption Schemes A *pseudorandom function* [36] is a function computed by any deterministic polytime algorithm taking two strings in input, and producing a string as output, in such a way that when the first of the two parameters is picked at random, the unary function obtained through currying is indistinguishable from a random one, all this to the eyes of adversaries working in probabilistic polynomial time. The notion of a pseudorandom function is closely related to that of a secure block-cipher.

Private key encryption schemes [36], instead, are triples of algorithms in the form (Gen, Enc, Dnc), where Gen is responsible for generating a private key at random, Enc is responsible for turning a message into a ciphertext and Dec is responsible for turning a ciphertext into a message. Both Enc and Dec make essential use of a private shared key. One way to construct private key encryption schemes is by way of pseudorandom functions: given one such function F, the scheme Π_F is such that Enc encrypts a message m as the pair $(r, F_k(r) \oplus m)$, where r is a random string generated on the fly and $\oplus$ is the bitwise exclusive-or operator. The algorithm Gen, instead, simply returns a string picked uniformly at random between those whose length is equal to that of the input. When written down as λ**BLL** terms, the algorithms Enc for encryption and Gen for key generation have the types in Fig. 4.

Defining Security The security of any encryption scheme, and of Π_F in particular, is defined on the basis of a so-called *cryptographic experiment*, which following [36] we call $PrivKCPA^F$. Such an experiment allows the scheme Π_F and a generic adversary Adv to interact. The experiment proceeds by first allowing Adv the possibility of generating two distinct messages m_0 and m_1, then encoding m_b (where b is picked at random) with a fresh key k, passing the obtained ciphertext c to *Adv*, and asking it to determine which one between m_0 and m_1 the ciphertext c corresponds to. The experiment $PrivKCPA^F$ then returns 1 if and only if *Adv* succeeds in this task. In doing all this, the adversary is *active*, i.e. it has the possibility of accessing an oracle for $Enc_k(\cdot)$. Consequently, the adversary is naturally modeled as a second-order term, see again Fig. 4. Obviously, how *Adv* works internally is not known, but the considerations in Sect. 1 allow us to conclude that all PPT functions of that type can be encoded in λ**BLL**. The security of Π_F can be expressed as the fact that for every such *Adv*, the probability that $PrivKCPA^F$ returns 1 is at most $\frac{1}{2}+\varepsilon(n)$, where ε is a negligible function. This depends, in an essential way, on the fact that the function F is indeed pseudorandom.

$$\vdash Gen : \mathbb{U} \multimap \mathbb{S}[p_k]$$
$$\vdash Enc : \mathbb{S}[p_k] \otimes \mathbb{S}[p_m] \multimap \mathbb{S}[p_c]$$
$$\vdash Oracle : \mathbb{S}[p_k] \multimap \mathbb{S}[p_m] \multimap \mathbb{S}[p_c]$$
$$\vdash Adv : !_q(\mathbb{S}[p_m] \multimap \mathbb{S}[p_c]) \multimap \mathbb{S}[p_m] \otimes \mathbb{S}[p_m] \otimes !_1(\mathbb{S}[p_c] \multimap \mathbb{B})$$
$$\vdash PrivKCPA^F : \mathbb{B}$$
$$\vdash D : !_q(\mathbb{S}[p_m] \multimap \mathbb{S}[p_c]) \multimap \mathbb{B}$$

Fig. 4. Types for terms in the CPA-security proof

Proving Security How is the security of Π_F actually *proved*? In fact, the proof is, like most cryptographic proofs, done *by reduction*. In other words, it proceeds contrapositively, turning any hypothetical adversary *Adv* for Π_F into a *distinguisher* D for F (namely an algorithm designed to distinguish F from a truly random function). If D can be proved successful whenever *Adv* is successful, we can conclude that Π_F is secure whenever F is pseudorandom, both notions being spelled out as the *non-existence* of adversaries of the appropriate kind.

The aforementioned reduction can actually be organized as follows. First of all, we have to define how a distinguisher D can be defined with *Adv* as a subroutine. The idea is to design D in such a way as to create the right environment around *Adv*, letting it believe that it is interacting with the experiment *PrivKCPA*, and exploiting its capabilities for the sake of distinguishing F from a random function. In the context of λ**BLL**, the distinguisher D becomes an ordinary term having the type in Fig. 4.

Then, we have to form two instances on D namely that interacting with the pseudorandom function F, which we indicate as D^F, and that interacting with a genuinely random function f, indicated as D^f. Both F and f can be assumed to be terms of λ**BLL**, but while the former can be taken as a term which does not use any reference, the latter can only be captured by a stateful computation—one cannot hope to pick uniformly at random a function on n-bit strings in polynomial time in n without the help of some bookkeeping mechanism. The latter will actually be implemented as a reference, call it *ledger*, whose purpose is to keep track of the previous strings on which the function has been queried, so that randomness can be generated *only when needed*. Since the type of f reflects the presence of *ledger*, the type of D is to be updated accordingly, as we are going to describe in the next paragraph.

For an arbitrary type A and a location context Ξ whose variables do not occur in A, we define $A \cdot \Xi$ inductively as follows:

$$G \cdot \Xi := G \qquad (P \otimes Q) \cdot \Xi := (P \cdot \Xi) \otimes (Q \cdot \Xi)$$
$$(!_p^{\Theta} A) \cdot \Xi := !_p^{\Theta,\Xi}(A \cdot \Xi) \quad (P \overset{\Theta}{\multimap} A) \cdot \Xi := (P \cdot \Xi) \overset{\Theta,\Xi}{\multimap} (A \cdot \Xi)$$

This operation can be easily extended to term variable contexts as follows:

$$\varnothing \cdot \Xi := \varnothing \quad (\Gamma, x : P) \cdot \Xi := \Gamma \cdot \Xi, x : P \cdot \Xi$$

Lemma 6. *For every derivable judgments $\Gamma; \Theta \vdash M : A$ and $\Gamma \vdash V : A$ and every location context Ξ whose variables do not occur in Γ, Θ and A, we obtain that the jugdments $\Gamma \cdot \Xi; \Theta, \Xi \vdash M : A \cdot \Xi$ and $\Gamma \cdot \Xi \vdash V : A \cdot \Xi$ are also derivable.*

We also have to define an encryption scheme Π_f which is structurally identical to Π_F, but which works with truly random functions (as opposed to *pseudorandom* ones) as keys. Accordingly, one can form a variation $PrivKCPA^f$ on $PrivKCPA^F$.

Now, the security of Π^F becomes the equation $PrivKCPA^F \asymp$ `flipcoin`, whereas `flipcoin` is the term, of boolean type, returning each possible result with probability $\frac{1}{2}$, while $\asymp$ is a relation coarser than $\approx$ defined by observing, through marginals, only the actual boolean value returned by the computation, without looking at the underlying store. The aforementioned equation can be proved under the hypothesis that F is pseudorandom, and this last condition also becomes an equation. This time, however, the terms to be compared are D^F and D^f.

The security proof then proceeds by contraposition, as explained schematically in Fig. 5: from the negation of the thesis, the negation of the hypothesis is derived and this is done by proving that both on the right and on the left sides of the diagram it is possible to *link* the terms through the relation $\approx$. In this context, it is clear that the use of observational indistinguishability and logical relations becomes useful. In particular, a number of equations can be used, as discussed in the following section. Noticeably, all of them can be proved sound for observational indistinguishability through logical relations.

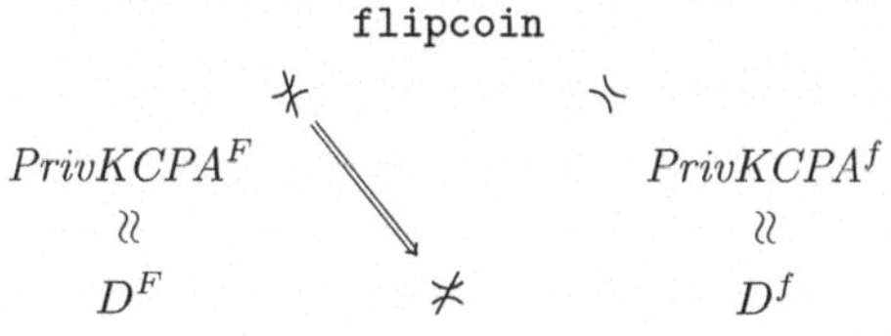

Fig. 5. Outline proof of security

Examples of Indistinguishability Equivalences Term equations and behavioral equivalences have been generalized to the setting of metric spaces via quantitative (in)equations $M =_{\varepsilon} N$ [40] and behavioral metrics [8,23]. In our case, terms $M = \{M_n\}_n$ are families indexed by the security parameter and compared to the previous approaches, the contextual indistinguishability relation $M \sim N$ intuitively means that for every n, $M_n =_{\varepsilon(n)} N_n$ for some negligible function ε.

We present below two typical examples of pairs of terms which are in the contextual indistinguishability relation and are used for proving security properties. A first example is the pair

$$\texttt{return}\,\mathbf{f} \sim \texttt{let}\, y = M \,\texttt{in}\,\texttt{let}\, x = \texttt{random}\,\texttt{in}\,\texttt{equal}(x, y) \quad \text{(randF)}$$

where M is any computation term $\vdash M : \mathbb{S}[i]$. Intuitively, it means that for a given binary string represented here by M, testing equality with a randomly generated string returns true with a negligible probability.

The function symbol $\texttt{random}$ is interpreted as the *uniform* distribution in $\mathbf{D}(\{0,1\}^n)$ given by $[\![\texttt{random}]\!]_n : s \mapsto \frac{1}{2^n}$ for $n \geq 1$. The function symbol $\texttt{equal}$ is interpreted as the function mapping a pair of strings $(s_1, s_2) \in \{0,1\}^n$ to $\delta_{\mathbf{t}}$ if $s_1 = s_2$ and to $\delta_{\mathbf{f}}$ otherwise for all $n \geq 1$. Therefore, we obtain that for all $n \geq 1$, the final (big step) semantics of $\texttt{return}\,\mathbf{f}$ is given by $(\!|\texttt{return}\,\mathbf{f}|\!)_n = \delta_{\mathbf{f}} \in \mathbf{D}(\{\mathbf{t}, \mathbf{f}\})$ and for $N := \texttt{let}\, y = M \,\texttt{in}\,\texttt{let}\, x = \texttt{random}\,\texttt{in}\,\texttt{equal}(x, y)$, we have:

$$(\!|N|\!)_n = \sum_{s \in \{0,1\}^n} (\!|M|\!)_n(s) \cdot \left(\frac{1}{2^n}\delta_{\mathbf{t}} + \left(1 - \frac{1}{2^n}\right)\delta_{\mathbf{f}}\right) = \frac{1}{2^n}\delta_{\mathbf{t}} + \left(1 - \frac{1}{2^n}\right)\delta_{\mathbf{f}}$$

We can easily see that $\texttt{return}\,\mathbf{f}$ and N are *not* contextually equivalent since they reduce to different distributions. They are however contextually indistinguishable which would be quite difficult to prove directly since it requires to quantify over all closing contexts which can possibly copy their argument.

Instead, we use the logical metric defined in Sect. 2, which here coincides with statistical distance (Definition 8) and obtain that for all $n \geq 1$, $\mathbf{dC}_n^{\mathbb{B}}(\texttt{return}\,\mathbf{f}, N) = \frac{1}{2^n}$. Since the function $\varepsilon : n \mapsto \frac{1}{2^n}$ is negligible, the pair $(\texttt{return}\,\mathbf{f}, N)$ is in $\mathbf{IndC}(\mathbb{B})$ and we obtain $\texttt{return}\,\mathbf{f} \sim N$ by soundness (Theorem 2).

Another required equation states that sampling a random string is equivalent to random sampling followed by a performing a $\texttt{xor}$ operation by a fixed string (represented by a computation term $\vdash M : \mathbb{S}[i]$):

$$\texttt{random} \sim \texttt{let}\, y = M \,\texttt{in}\,\texttt{let}\, x = \texttt{random}\,\texttt{in}\,\texttt{xor}(x, y) \quad \text{(randXOR)}$$

The equation above is an example of *Kleene equivalence* as the two terms $\texttt{random}$ and $P := \texttt{let}\, y = M \,\texttt{in}\,\texttt{let}\, x = \texttt{random}\,\texttt{in}\,\texttt{xor}(x, y)$ have the same final (big step) semantics. The function symbol $\texttt{xor}$ is interpreted by the standard *exclusive-or* function on binary strings mapping a pair (s_1, s_2) to $\delta_{\texttt{xor}(s_1,s_2)}$. The final semantics of $(\!|P|\!)_n$ for $n \geq 1$ is therefore given by:

$$(\!|P|\!)_n(s) = \sum_{s_2} (\!|M|\!)_n(s_2) \cdot \left(\sum_{s_1} \frac{1}{2^n} \delta_{\mathtt{xor}(s_1,s_2)}(s) \right)$$
$$= \sum_{s_2} (\!|M|\!)_n(s_2) \cdot \frac{1}{2^n} = \frac{1}{2^n}$$

where the penultimate equality holds since $\delta_{\mathtt{xor}(s_1,s_2)}(s) = 1$ if $s = \mathtt{xor}(s_1, s_2)$ (or equivalently $s_1 = \mathtt{xor}(s, s_2)$) and $\delta_{\mathtt{xor}(s_1,s_2)}(s) = 0$ otherwise. Since $(\!|P|\!)_n = (\!|\mathtt{random}|\!)_n$, the distance between the two terms is therefore equal to 0 for the logical metric and we can conclude immediately that they are in particular contextually indistinguishable. We can prove more generally that if two closed terms are Kleene equivalent, then they are contextually indistinguishable.

Related Work

Although the literature regarding formal methods for the security analysis of protocols and primitives is much more abundant in the symbolic model than in the computational one, it certainly cannot be said that the latter has not been the subject of attention by the research community. The work on probabilistic relational Hoare logic which gave rise to the `EasyCrypt` tool [13], must certainly be mentioned. The result of Bana and Comon Lundt on inconsistency proofs as security proofs [9], which in turn gave rise to the `Squirrel` tool [6], is another pertinent example. In both cases, the model provides for the possibility of higher-order constructions, which however are not fully-fledged. In particular, managing complexity aspects and higher-order functions at the same time turns out to be hard.

This last direction is the one followed by the work on CSLR and its formalization [45]. In this case we find ourselves faced with a λ-calculus for polynomial time and its application to the study of cryptographic primitives. There are two differences with this work. First of all, the greater expressiveness of λ**BLL** allows to capture PPT even for second-order constructions. Furthermore, the logical relations introduced here effectively give rise to a notion of metric, while in CSLR the underlying equational theories are exact, even though a notion of observational equivalence similar to ours has been introduced.

Another attempt that goes in the same direction as ours is the work by Mitchell et al. [42], who introduced a process algebra in the style of Milner's CCS capable of modeling cryptographic protocols. Unlike ours, the resulting calculus is concurrent and this gives rise to a series of complications. Once again, despite the underlying notion of observational equivalence being approximate and therefore adhering to computational indistinguishability, the proposed notion of bisimulation is exact and as such much finer.

Logical relations [44,51] are a powerful tool for relational reasoning about higher-order terms. They are known to work well in calculi with effects and in particular in presence of probabilistic choice effects [5,11,30]. It is also known that metric versions of logical relations can be given, and that they are useful for sensitivity analysis [15,46]. The possibility of applying logical relations to calculi such as the cryptographic λ-calculus is well-known [31], but the underlying calculus turns out to be fundamentally different from ours, being in the tradition of the symbolic model and abstracting away from probabilistic effects and complexity constraints.

Conclusion

This work shows how an approximate form of logical relation can be defined and proved sound for computational indistinguishability in a higher order λ-calculus with probabilistic effects and references. This allows cryptographic proofs to be carried out in a purely equational way by justifying the equations used.

Possible topics for future work include the transition to a logic in the style of higher-order logic, this way enabling the combination of relational and logical reasoning, in the sense of the work of Aguirre and co-authors [4].

Acknowledgments. The first two authors are partially supported by the MUR FARE project CAFFEINE, and by the ANR PRC project PPS (ANR-19-CE48-0014). The third author is partially supported by Fondation CFM.

References

1. Abadi, M.: Security protocols: principles and calculi. In: Aldini, A., Gorrieri, R. (eds.) Foundations of Security Analysis and Design IV, pp. 1–23 (2006). https://doi.org/10.1007/978-3-540-74810-6_1
2. Abramsky, S.: The lazy lambda calculus. In: Research Topics in Functional Programming, pp. 65-116. Addison-Wesley Longman Publishing Co., Inc. (1990)
3. Accattoli, B., Dal Lago, U.: (Leftmost-outermost) beta reduction is invariant, indeed. Log. Methods Comput. Sci. **12**(1) (2016). https://doi.org/10.2168/LMCS-12(1:4)2016
4. Aguirre, A., Barthe, G., Gaboardi, M., Garg, D., Katsumata, S.Y., Sato, T.: Higher-order probabilistic adversarial computations: categorical semantics and program logics. In: Proceedings of the ICFP 2021, pp. 1–30. ACM (2021). https://doi.org/10.1145/3473598
5. Aguirre, A., Birkedal, L.: Step-indexed logical relations for countable nondeterminism and probabilistic choice. In: Proceedings of POPL 2023, vol. 7, pp. 33–60. ACM (2023). https://doi.org/10.1145/3571195
6. Baelde, D., Jacomme, C.: The squirrel prover and its logic. ACM SIGLOG News **11**(2), 62–83 (2024). https://doi.org/10.1145/3665453.3665461
7. Balan, A., Kurz, A., Velebil, J.: Extending set functors to generalised metric spaces. Log. Methods Comput. Sci. **15**(1) (2019). https://doi.org/10.23638/LMCS-15(1:5)2019
8. Baldan, P., Bonchi, F., Kerstan, H., König, B.: Coalgebraic behavioral metrics. Log. Methods Comput. Sci. **14**(3) (2018). https://doi.org/10.23638/LMCS-14(3:20)2018
9. Bana, G., Comon-Lundh, H.: A computationally complete symbolic attacker for equivalence properties. In: Proceedings of the CCS 2014, pp. 609–620 (2014). https://doi.org/10.1145/2660267.2660276
10. Bellare, M.: A note on negligible functions. J. Cryptol. **15**(4), 271–284 (2002). https://doi.org/10.1007/s00145-002-0116-x
11. Bizjak, A., Birkedal, L.: Step-indexed logical relations for probability. In: Proceedings of FoSSaCS 2015, pp. 279–294. Springer (2015). https://doi.org/10.1007/978-3-662-46678-0_18

12. van Breugel, F.: The metric monad for probabilistic nondeterminism. Draft available at http://www.cse.yorku.ca/franck/research/drafts/monad.pdf (2005)
13. Canetti, R., Stoughton, A., Varia, M.: EasyUC: using EasyCrypt to mechanize proofs of universally composable security. In: Proceedings of the CSF 2019, pp. 167–183. IEEE (2019). https://doi.org/10.1109/CSF.2019.00019
14. Dal Lago, U., Galal, Z., Giusti, G.: On Computational Indistinguishability and Logical Relations (2024). http://arxiv.org/abs/2408.17340
15. Dal Lago, U., Gavazzo, F.: A relational theory of effects and coeffects. In: Proceedings of the POPL 2022, vol. 6, pp. 1–28. ACM (2022). https://doi.org/10.1145/3498692
16. Dal Lago, U., Giusti, G.: On session typing, probabilistic polynomial time, and cryptographic experiments. In: Proceedings of the CONCUR 2022, vol. 243, pp. 37:1–37:18 (2022). https://doi.org/10.4230/LIPICS.CONCUR.2022.37
17. Dal Lago, U., Martini, S.: On constructor rewrite systems and the lambda calculus. Log. Methods Comput. Sci. (2012). https://doi.org/10.1007/978-3-642-02930-1_14
18. Dal Lago, U., Petit, B.: Linear dependent types in a call-by-value scenario. In: Proceedings of the PPDP 2012, pp. 115–126. ACM (2012). https://doi.org/10.1145/2370776.2370792
19. Dal Lago, U., Zuppiroli, S., Gabbrielli, M.: Probabilistic recursion theory and implicit computational complexity. Sci. Ann. Comput. Sci. 177–216 (2014). https://doi.org/10.7561/SACS.2014.2.177
20. Dolev, D., Yao, A.: On the security of public key protocols. IEEE Trans. Inf. Theory **29**(2), 198–207 (1983). https://doi.org/10.1109/TIT.1983.1056650
21. Ehrhard, T., Tasson, C.: Probabilistic call by push value. Log. Methods Comput. Sci. **15**(1) (2019). https://doi.org/10.23638/LMCS-15(1:3)2019
22. Fiore, M., Abadi, M.: Computing symbolic models for verifying cryptographic protocols. In: Proceedings of the CSFW 2001, pp. 160–173. IEEE (2001). https://doi.org/10.1109/CSFW.2001.930144
23. Gavazzo, F.: Quantitative behavioural reasoning for higher-order effectful programs: applicative distances. In: Proceedings of the LICS 2018, pp. 452–461. ACM (2018). https://doi.org/10.1145/3209108.3209149
24. Gibbs, A.L., Su, F.E.: On choosing and bounding probability metrics. Int. Stat. Rev. **70**(3), 419–435 (2002). https://doi.org/10.2307/1403865
25. Gifford, D.K., Lucassen, J.M.: Integrating functional and imperative programming. In: Proceedings of the 1986 ACM Conference on LISP and Functional Programming, pp. 28–38. ACM (1986). https://doi.org/10.1145/319838.319848
26. Girard, J.Y., Scedrov, A., Scott, P.J.: Bounded linear logic: a modular approach to polynomial-time computability. Theoret. Comput. Sci. **97**(1), 1–66 (1992). https://doi.org/10.1016/0304-3975(92)90386-T
27. Goldreich, O.: Foundations of Cryptography. Vol. 1: Basic Tools. Cambridge University Press, Cambridge (2007)
28. Goldwasser, S., Micali, S.: Probabilistic encryption. J. Comput. Syst. Sci. **28**(2), 270–299 (1984). https://doi.org/10.1016/0022-0000(84)90070-9
29. Gordon, A.D.: Operational equivalences for untyped and polymorphic object calculi. In: Higher-Order Operational Techniques in Semantics, Publications of the Newton Institute, pp. 9–54. Cambridge University Press (1998)
30. Goubault-Larrecq, J., Lasota, S., Nowak, D.: Logical relations for monadic types. Math. Struct. Comput. Sci. 1169–1217 (2008). https://doi.org/10.1007/3-540-45793-3_37

31. Goubault-Larrecq, J., Lasota, S., Nowak, D., Zhang, Y.: Complete lax logical relations for cryptographic lambda-calculi. In: Proceedings of the CSL 2004, pp. 400–414. Springer (2004).https://doi.org/10.1007/978-3-540-30124-0_31
32. Hofmann, D., Seal, G.J., Tholen, W.: Monoidal Topology: A Categorical Approach to Order, Metric, and Topology. Cambridge University Press (2014)
33. Hyland, M., Plotkin, G., Power, J.: Combining effects: sum and tensor. Theoret. Comput. Sci. **357**(1), 70–99 (2006). https://doi.org/10.1016/j.tcs.2006.03.013
34. Impagliazzo, R., Kapron, B.M.: Logics for reasoning about cryptographic constructions. J. Comput. Syst. Sci. **72**(2), 286–320 (2006). https://doi.org/10.1016/j.jcss.2005.06.008
35. Kantorovich, L.V.: On the translocation of masses. J. Math. Sci. **133**(4), 1381–1382 (2006). https://doi.org/10.1007/s10958-006-0049-2
36. Katz, J., Lindell, Y.: Introduction to Modern Cryptography. CRC Press (2020)
37. Lassen, S.B.: Relational reasoning about contexts. In: Higher-Order Operational Techniques in Semantics, Publications of the Newton Institute, vol. 91, pp. 91–136. Cambridge University Press (1998)
38. Leroy, X., Grall, H.: Coinductive big-step operational semantics. Inf. Comput. **207**(2), 284–304 (2009). https://doi.org/10.1016/j.ic.2007.12.004
39. Levy, P.B.: Call-by-Push-Value: A Functional/Imperative Synthesis, vol. 2. Springer Science & Business Media (2012)
40. Mardare, R., Panangaden, P., Plotkin, G.: Quantitative algebraic reasoning. In: Proceedings of the LICS 2016, pp. 700–709. ACM (2016). https://doi.org/10.1145/2933575.2934518
41. Mitchell, J., Mitchell, M., Scedrov, A.: A linguistic characterization of bounded oracle computation and probabilistic polynomial time. In: Proceedings of the SFCS 1998, pp. 725–733. IEEE (1998). https://doi.org/10.1109/SFCS.1998.743523
42. Mitchell, J.C., Ramanathan, A., Scedrov, A., Teague, V.: A probabilistic polynomial-time process calculus for the analysis of cryptographic protocols. Theoret. Comput. Sci. **353**(1–3) (2006). https://doi.org/10.1016/j.tcs.2005.10.044
43. Mitchell, J.C.: Multiset rewriting and security protocol analysis. In: Proceedings of the RTA 2002, pp. 19–22. Springer (2002). https://doi.org/10.1007/3-540-45610-4_2
44. Mitchell, J.C., Scedrov, A.: Notes on sconing and relators. In: Proceedings of the CSL 1992, pp. 352–378. Springer (1992). https://doi.org/10.1007/3-540-56992-8_21
45. Nowak, D., Zhang, Y.: A calculus for game-based security proofs. In: Proceedings of the ProvSec 2010. Springer (2010). https://doi.org/10.1007/978-3-642-16280-0_3
46. Reed, J., Pierce, B.C.: Distance makes the types grow stronger: a calculus for differential privacy. In: Proceedings of the ICFP 2010, pp. 157–168. ACM (2010). https://doi.org/10.1145/1863543.1863568
47. Rosenthal, K.I.: Quantales and Their Applications. Wiley (1990)
48. Sangiorgi, D., Rutten, J.: Advanced Topics in Bisimulation and Coinduction. Cambridge University Press (2011)
49. Shoup, V.: Sequences of games: a tool for taming complexity in security proofs. IACR Cryptol. ePrint Arch., p. 332 (2004). http://eprint.iacr.org/2004/332
50. Statman, R.: Logical relations and the typed λ-calculus. Inf. Control **65**(2–3), 85–97 (1985). https://doi.org/10.1016/S0019-9958(85)80001-2

51. Tait, W.W.: Intensional interpretations of functionals of finite type I. J. Symbol. Log. **32**(2), 198–212 (1967). https://doi.org/10.2307/2271658
52. Wild, P., Schröder, L.: Characteristic logics for behavioural hemimetrics via fuzzy lax extensions. Log. Methods Comput. Sci. (2022). https://doi.org/10.46298/lmcs-18(2:19)2022

Relative Completeness of Incorrectness Separation Logic

Yeonseok Lee[(✉)] and Koji Nakazawa

Nagoya University, Nagoya, Japan
lee.yeonseok.x2@s.mail.nagoya-u.ac.jp

Abstract. Incorrectness Separation Logic (ISL) is a proof system that is tailored specifically to resolve problems of under-approximation in programs that manipulate heaps, and it primarily focuses on bug detection. This approach is different from the over-approximation methods that are used in traditional logics such as Hoare Logic or Separation Logic. Although the soundness of ISL has been established, its completeness remains unproven. In this study, we establish relative completeness by leveraging the expressiveness of the weakest postconditions; expressiveness is a factor that is critical to demonstrating relative completeness in Reverse Hoare Logic. In our ISL framework, we allow for infinite disjunctions in disjunctive normal forms, where each clause comprises finite symbolic heaps with existential quantifiers. To compute the weakest postconditions in ISL, we introduce a canonicalization that includes variable aliasing.

Keywords: Separation logic · Incorrectness logic · Completeness

1 Introduction

1.1 Background

Software verification is a crucial aspect of software engineering, as it ensures that software systems are reliable, safe, and secure. To verify software, we rely on formal methods, which are essentially a set of guidelines and tools for checking software.

One of the most important tools is Hoare Logic (HL) [11] which checks *correctness* of programs. Hoare Triples in the form of $\{P\}\ \mathbb{C}\ \{Q\}$ mean that for all states s in precondition P, if running $\mathbb{C}$ on s terminates in s', then s' is in postcondition Q. Let us say that $\mathsf{post}(\mathbb{C}, P)$ describes the set of states obtained by executing $\mathbb{C}$ from a state in P. Then the Hoare triple $\{P\}\ \mathbb{C}\ \{Q\}$ means that Q *over-approximates* $\mathsf{post}(\mathbb{C}, P)$ that is, $\mathsf{post}(\mathbb{C}, P) \subseteq Q$.

O. Kiselyov (Ed.): APLAS 2024, LNCS 15194, pp. 216-237, 2024.
https://doi.org/10.1007/978-981-97-8943-6_13

Recently, there have been some interesting logics for checking *incorrectness*, meaning the presence of bugs, which are different from HL. Reverse Hoare Logic (RHL) [8] is one of these logics. The triples of RHL take the form $[P]\ \mathbb{C}\ [Q]$[1], which means that for all states s' in Q, s' can be reached by running $\mathbb{C}$ on some s in P. Here, Q *under-approximates* $\mathsf{post}(\mathbb{C}, P)$, meaning that $\mathsf{post}(\mathbb{C}, P) \supseteq Q$. It is important to note that the direction of inclusion is *reversed*. Let us explore the differences between HL and RHL using some simple examples.

- $\{\top\}\, x := y\, \{\top\}$ is valid, but $[\top]\, x := y\, [\top]$ is not.
  In RHL, $x = 1 \wedge y = 2$ satisfying $\top$ (postcondition) is unreachable from states satisfying $\top$ (precondition) after executing $x := y$.
- $\{\top\}\ x := y\ \{0 < x < 10 \wedge x = y\}$ is invalid, but $[\top]\ x := y\ [0 < x < 10 \wedge x = y]$ is not.
  In HL, after $x := y$ is executed, $x = 10 \wedge y = 10$ can be reached from $\top$. However, this state does not satisfy $0 < x < 10 \wedge x = y$.

Additionally, Incorrectness Logic (IL), which also uses under-approximation, has been proposed [16]. Triples in IL are similar to those in RHL, but IL includes an exit condition within postconditions: $[P]\ \mathbb{C}\ [\epsilon : Q]$, where ϵ is either *ok* for normal termination or *er* for erroneous termination.

Separation Logic (SL), which was built upon HL and introduced by Reynolds [20], offers a framework for the modular proofs of programs that manipulate pointers. It achieves this by allowing us to reason about disjoint parts of a heap using the *separating conjunction* operator denoted as "$*$". For example, $P * R$ asserts that the heap can be split into two disjoint parts where P and R respectively hold. A crucial aspect of SL is its (Frame) rule, which supports local reasoning. (Frame) rule states the following.

$$\frac{\{P\}\ \mathbb{C}\ \{Q\}}{\{P * R\}\ \mathbb{C}\ \{Q * R\}}$$

This rule states that if the program $\mathbb{C}$ does not affect the portion of memory described by R, then R can coexist with the conditions P and Q. This feature improves the scalability of verification, especially the verification of complex programs. Numerous verification tools have been built with SL as the foundation, with one of the most renowned being Infer by Meta [5,6].

Raad et al. [19] proposed Incorrectness Separation Logic (ISL), which includes heap manipulation like SL in the IL system. They demonstrate that the Frame rule is not sound in the IL setting without the inclusion of a *negative heap assertion* $x \not\mapsto$, which indicates that x exists in the heap domain

[1] Note that in some literature, the notation $[P]\ \mathbb{C}\ [Q]$ is used for the Hoare triple, representing total correctness. This notation asserts that if $\mathbb{C}$ is executed in a state that satisfies P, it always terminates, and the final state satisfies Q. However, in this paper, we use square brackets in triples to signify that the triple is an Incorrectness logic triple [16].

and has been deallocated. The following is an example from [19], where $x \mapsto -$ denotes that the location x is allocated.

$$\frac{[x \mapsto -]\ \texttt{free}(x)\ [\mathsf{emp}]}{[x \mapsto - * x \mapsto -]\ \texttt{free}(x)\ [\mathsf{emp} * x \mapsto -]}$$

The premise is valid, but the conclusion is not. Since these are ISL triples, the conclusion means that every state satisfying the postcondition can be reached from some state satisfying the precondition $x \mapsto - * x \mapsto -$, which is unsatisfiable. Hence, the inference is unsound.

However, this case can be corrected by adding $x \not\mapsto$, as was demonstrated in [19].

$$\frac{[x \mapsto -]\ \texttt{free}(x)\ [x \not\mapsto]}{[x \mapsto - * x \mapsto -]\ \texttt{free}(x)\ [x \not\mapsto * x \mapsto -]}$$

In this case, both triples are valid. The precondition and postcondition of the conclusion are false, which makes the triple trivially valid. The semantics of $x \not\mapsto$ are similar to $x \uparrow$ in [13,14], but they differ in whether x is in the heap domain ($x \not\mapsto$) or not ($x \uparrow$).

1.2 Relative Completeness of Under-Approximation Systems

In the context of proof systems, it is crucial to establish both soundness and completeness. Soundness ensures that all provable statements are true, while completeness ensures that all true statements can be proven. Hoare logic is known to be incomplete. Consider the Hoare triple $\{\top\}$ `skip` $\{A\}$, where `skip` is a command that does nothing. This triple is logically equivalent to the assertion A because the triple implies $\top \rightarrow A$, which is equivalent to A. Hence, if the assertion theory includes arithmetic, a complete proof system for Hoare logic would contradict Gödel's incompleteness theorems [10]. Similarly, we can demonstrate the incompleteness of ISL, since the ISL triple $[A]$ `skip` $[\top]$ is equivalent to A.

Cook suggests a concept called *relative completeness* [7]. Relative completeness of Hoare logic means that if we had an oracle capable of checking the validity of entailment, then Hoare logic could prove all valid Hoare triples. Relative completeness has also been proven in IL [16] and RHL [8]. In IL, semantic predicates are utilized. In RHL, calculating the weakest postcondition is crucial to proving relative completeness. De Vries et al. demonstrated that their weakest postcondition could be expressed using formulas with infinite disjunctions [8]. This property is referred to as *expressiveness*. They then used this result to prove relative completeness. However, in ISL [19], only soundness has been proven.

1.3 Our Contribution: Proving the Relative Completeness of ISL by Weakest Postcondition Calculus

This study establishes the relative completeness of ISL. This endeavor aims to preserve the relative completeness of RHL while expanding it to incorporate exit conditions and heap manipulation within ISL. Unlike IL [16] and the original ISL [19], our proof does not rely on semantic predicates and allows for infinite disjunctions, similar to those used in RHL [8]. It is known that entailment checking for symbolic heaps with restricted predicates, and without arithmetic, is decidable [1,17,22]. Consequently, we can develop an ISL proof system that is complete, rather than relatively complete, because our system employs symbolic heaps with restricted predicates and no arithmetic.

We follow the proof method of de Vries et al. [8] to demonstrate the expressiveness of the weakest postconditions (Proposition 2). To calculate the weakest postconditions, we introduce a process called *canonicalization*, where we perform case analysis on variables and use the disjunctive normal form as our syntax. Even if our system includes arithmetic, canonicalization for finite formulas remains feasible because we are only dealing with a finite number of cases. However, for simplicity, we omit arithmetic in this paper.

Case Analysis. The function $\mathsf{wpo}(P, \mathbb{C}, \epsilon)$, which stands for Weakest POstcondition, calculates the weakest postcondition given the input precondition P, program $\mathbb{C}$, and exit condition ϵ. Consider the following example.

$$\mathsf{wpo}(y \mapsto e, \mathtt{free}(x), ok) = ???$$

In the above situation, we cannot determine the weakest postcondition because we do not know whether x is aliasing with y or not. Consequently, we perform a case analysis to determine whether x is aliasing with y or not. For the case $x = y$, we have

$$\mathsf{wpo}(x = y \wedge y \mapsto e, \mathtt{free}(x), ok) = y \not\mapsto \wedge\, x = y.$$

This case illustrates that if y aliases with x and a location mapped by y is allocated, then the $\mathtt{free}$(x) attempts to deallocate a heap mapped by the location pointed to by x. As a result, this program safely terminates, freeing the heap denoted by x which aliases with y. On the other hand, if $x \neq y$, we have

$$\mathsf{wpo}(x \neq y \wedge y \mapsto e, \mathtt{free}(x), er) = y \mapsto e \wedge x \neq y.$$

In this case, $\mathtt{free}(x)$ terminates with an error because there is no heap denoted by x; that is, there is no heap to be freed. To address these situation, we conduct a case analysis that considers all the possibilities of aliasing. Further details are discussed in Sect. 3.

Disjunctive Normal Form (DNF). As the syntax of the assertions, we adopt DNFs that is, (infinite) disjunctions of symbolic heaps, which are restricted formulas that are widely studied in the literature [1,2,21]. Using the equivalence

$$(P_1 \vee P_2) * P' \equiv (P_1 * P') \vee (P_2 * P')$$

in [20], we can convert general formulas with $*$ and $\vee$ into DNF whose clauses are symbolic heaps [9,15]. The case analysis discussed in the previous part works well on such DNFs. The weakest postcondition wpo can be calculated as

$$\mathsf{wpo}(P \vee Q, \mathbb{C}, \epsilon) = \mathsf{wpo}(P, \mathbb{C}, \epsilon) \vee \mathsf{wpo}(Q, \mathbb{C}, \epsilon),$$

and we can then focus on the wpo for symbolic heaps.

The remainder of this paper is organized as follows: Sect. 2 introduces the syntax and semantics of ISL. Section 3 presents the calculation of wpo with canonicalization. We demonstrate the relative completeness of our ISL by using an approach similar to that of RHL, in Sect. 4. Finally, in Sect. 5, we discuss related work, and we conclude in Sect. 6.

2 Incorrectness Separation Logic

We define the ISL, which is slightly changed from the original one [19].

2.1 Assertions

First, we introduce assertions in ISL, which are (infinite) disjunctions of existentially quantified symbolic heaps. The quantifier-free symbolic heaps consist of equalities ($x \approx y$) and inequalities ($x \not\approx y$) between variables and heap predicates ($x \mapsto t$ or $x \not\mapsto$) connected by the separating conjunction $*$. The operators $\vee$, $\wedge$, and $\neg$ are not permitted in symbolic heaps.

We assume countably infinite set of variables $\textsc{Var}$, and we use the metavariables $x, y, z, \ldots$ for variables.

Definition 1. (Assertions of ISL). *An assertion P is defined as follows, where I is finite or countably infinite index set. A term t is either a variable or the constant* `null`.

$$
\begin{aligned}
P &::= \bigvee_{i \in I} \exists \overrightarrow{x_i}.\psi_i && \textit{Top-level} \\
\psi &::= \psi * \psi && \textit{Quantifier-free Symbolic Heaps} \\
&\quad \mid \mathsf{emp} \mid x \mapsto t \mid x \not\mapsto && \textit{Atomic Spatial Formulas} \\
&\quad \mid t \approx t' \mid t \not\approx t' && \textit{Atomic Pure Formulas} \\
t &::= x \mid \texttt{null} && \textit{Terms}
\end{aligned}
$$

Here, we employ vector notation to represent a sequence, for instance, $\overrightarrow{x_i}$ denotes the sequence $x_{i1}, \ldots, x_{in}$. The notation $\mathsf{fv}(P)$ represents the set of free variables in P. We consider only assertions P such that $\mathsf{fv}(P)$ is finite. For $I = \emptyset$, $\bigvee_{i \in I} \exists \overrightarrow{x_i}.\psi_i$ is denoted by false. *We ignore the order of disjuncts in assertions and atomic formulas in symbolic heaps. Specifically, we identify the formulas $\psi_1 * \psi_2$ and $\psi_2 * \psi_1$ as being equivalent. Additionally, we refer to a formula connected by $*$ with only atomic pure formulas as a* pure formula.

Our language draws primarily from the conventions of traditional SL [20], IL [16], RHL [8], and ISL [19].

For the semantics of the assertions, we assume the set $\textsc{Val}$ of values and the set $\textsc{Loc}$ of locations such that $\textsc{Loc} \subseteq \textsc{Val}$. We also assume $\mathit{null} \in \textsc{Val} \setminus \textsc{Loc}$ for the denotation of the constant `null`. Additionally, $\perp \notin \textsc{Val}$ is employed to keep track of deallocated locations. The concept of using $\perp$ to signify deallocated locations was introduced by Raad et al. [19], specifically for negative heaps, expressed as $x \not\mapsto$. Please note that $\perp$ does not refer to the undefined case of partial functions, as in some literature.

Definition 2. (States, Stores, and Heaps). *A* state, *denoted by* $\sigma \in \text{STATE}$, *is defined as a pair* (s, h)*, consisting of a store* $s \in \text{STORE}$ *and a heap* $h \in \text{HEAP}$.

A store *is a total function from* VAR *to* VAL. *A store* s *is straightforwardly extended to a function on terms by* $s(\texttt{null}) = null$. *For a store* s, $s[x \mapsto v]$ *denotes the store defined as* $s[x \mapsto v](x) = v$ *and* $s[x \mapsto v](y) = s(y)$ *for* $y \neq x$.

A heap *is a finite partial function from* LOC *to* $\text{VAL} \cup \{\perp\}$. $h[l \mapsto v]$ *is defined in a similar way to* $s[x \mapsto v]$. *Two heaps* h_1 *and* h_2 *are disjoint iff* $\mathsf{dom}(h_1) \cap \mathsf{dom}(h_2) = \emptyset$. $h_1 \circ h_2$ *is the operation combining two disjoint heaps* h_1 *and* h_2*, which is defined as follows:*

$$(h_1 \circ h_2)(l) = \begin{cases} h_1(l) & \text{if } l \in \mathsf{dom}(h_1) \\ h_2(l) & \text{if } l \in \mathsf{dom}(h_2) \\ \text{undefined} & \text{if } l \notin \mathsf{dom}(h_1) \cup \mathsf{dom}(h_2) \end{cases}$$

$h_1 \circ h_2$ *is undefined when* h_1 *and* h_2 *are not disjoint.*

The semantics of the assertions of ISL is defined as follows.

Definition 3. (Assertion Semantics of ISL). We define the relation $(s, h) \models P$ as

$$\begin{aligned}
(s,h) \models \bigvee_{i \in I} \exists \overrightarrow{x_i}.\psi_i &\Leftrightarrow (s,h) \models \exists \overrightarrow{x_i}.\psi_i \text{ for some } i \in I, \\
(s,h) \models \exists \overrightarrow{x_i}.\psi_i &\Leftrightarrow \exists \overrightarrow{v_i} \in \text{VAL}.(s[\overrightarrow{x_i} \mapsto \overrightarrow{v_i}], h) \models \psi_i, \\
(s,h) \models \psi_1 * \psi_2 &\Leftrightarrow \exists h_1, h_2.h = h_1 \circ h_2 \text{ and } (s,h_1) \models \psi_1 \text{ and } (s,h_2) \models \psi_2, \\
(s,h) \models \mathsf{emp} &\Leftrightarrow \mathsf{dom}(h) = \emptyset, \\
(s,h) \models x \mapsto t &\Leftrightarrow \mathsf{dom}(h) = \{s(x)\} \text{ and } h(s(x)) = s(t), \\
(s,h) \models x \not\mapsto &\Leftrightarrow \mathsf{dom}(h) = \{s(x)\} \text{ and } h(s(x)) = \perp, \\
(s,h) \models t \approx t' &\Leftrightarrow s(t) = s(t') \text{ and } \mathsf{dom}(h) = \emptyset, \\
(s,h) \models t \not\approx t' &\Leftrightarrow s(t) \neq s(t') \text{ and } \mathsf{dom}(h) = \emptyset,
\end{aligned}$$

where $s[\overrightarrow{x_i} \mapsto \overrightarrow{v_i}]$ means $s[x_{i1} \mapsto v_{i1}] \dots [x_{in} \mapsto v_{in}]$. For a pure formula B, $s \models B$ means that $(s, \emptyset) \models B$ for the empty heap $\emptyset$.

2.2 Program Language

We recall the program language for ISL in [19].

Definition 4. (Program Language $\mathbb{C} \in$ COMM).

$$\begin{aligned}\mathbb{C} ::= &\ \texttt{skip} \mid x := t \mid x := * \mid \texttt{assume}(B) \mid \texttt{local}\, x \,\texttt{in}\, \mathbb{C} \\ &\mid \mathbb{C}_1; \mathbb{C}_2 \mid \mathbb{C}_1 + \mathbb{C}_2 \mid \mathbb{C}^\star ? \\ &\mid x := \texttt{alloc()} \mid \texttt{free}(x) \mid x := [y] \mid [x] := t \mid \texttt{error}\end{aligned}$$

Here, B is a pure formula.

The program language includes standard constructs such as `skip`, assignment $x := t$, nondeterministic assignment $x := *$ (where $*$ represents a nondeterministically selected value), assume statements $\texttt{assume}(B)$, local variable declarations $\texttt{local}\ x\ \texttt{in}\ \mathbb{C}$, sequential composition $\mathbb{C}_1; \mathbb{C}_2$, nondeterministic choice $\mathbb{C}_1 + \mathbb{C}_2$, and loops $\mathbb{C}^\star$. Additionally, it includes error statements `error` and instructions for heap manipulation.

Instructions for heap manipulation encompass operations such as allocation, deallocation, lookup, and mutation. For instance, the instruction $x := \texttt{alloc()}$ reserves a new unused location on the heap and assigns it to the variable x. Conversely, $\texttt{free}(x)$ deallocates the memory location referred to by x. To read the contents of a heap location, $x := [y]$ is used, where the value stored at the location specified by y is retrieved and assigned to x. In contrast, the heap mutation $[x] := t$ involves replacing the data stored at the location indicated by x with the value of t.

Note that deterministic choices (`if`) and loops (`while`) can be encoded using nondeterministic choices (+) and `assume` statements [16,19].

$$\texttt{if}\ B\ \texttt{then}\ \mathbb{C}_1\ \texttt{else}\ \mathbb{C}_2 \stackrel{\text{def}}{=} (\texttt{assume}(B); \mathbb{C}_1) + (\texttt{assume}(!B); \mathbb{C}_2)$$

$$\texttt{while}(B)\mathbb{C} \stackrel{\text{def}}{=} (\texttt{assume}(B); \mathbb{C})^\star; \texttt{assume}(!B)$$

$$\texttt{assert}(B) \stackrel{\text{def}}{=} (\texttt{assume}(!B); \texttt{error}) + \texttt{assume}(B)$$

$$x := \texttt{malloc()} \stackrel{\text{def}}{=} x := \texttt{alloc()} + x := \texttt{null}$$

Here, we define $\texttt{assume}(!B)$ for a pure formula $B = b_1 * \ldots * b_n$, where each b_i is an atomic pure formula. The definition is as follows:

$$\texttt{assume}(!B) = \texttt{assume}(\neg b_1) + \ldots + \texttt{assume}(\neg b_n),$$

where $\neg b_i$ is defined as $\neg(t_i \approx t_i') = t_i \not\approx t_i'$ and $\neg(t_i \not\approx t_i') = t_i \approx t_i'$.

We provide the denotational semantics of our programming languages.

Definition 5. (Denotational Semantics of ISL) *We define* $[\![\mathbb{C}]\!]_\epsilon$ *for a program* $\mathbb{C}$ *and an exit condition* $\epsilon \in \{ok, er\}$ *as a binary relation on* STATE. *We use the composition of binary relations: for binary relations* R_1 and R_2, $R_1; R_2$ *is the relation* $\{(a, c) \mid \exists b.(a, b) \in R_1$ *and* $(b, c) \in R_2\}$.

$$[\![\texttt{skip}]\!]_\epsilon = \begin{cases} \{(\sigma,\sigma) \mid \sigma \in \textsc{State}\} & \epsilon = ok \\ \emptyset & \epsilon = er \end{cases}$$

$$[\![x := t]\!]_\epsilon = \begin{cases} \{((s,h),(s[x \mapsto s(t)],h))\} & \epsilon = ok \\ \emptyset & \epsilon = er \end{cases}$$

$$[\![x := *]\!]_\epsilon = \begin{cases} \{((s,h),(s[x \mapsto v],h)) \mid v \in \textsc{Val}\} & \epsilon = ok \\ \emptyset & \epsilon = er \end{cases}$$

$$[\![\texttt{assume}(B)]\!]_\epsilon = \begin{cases} \{(\sigma,\sigma) \mid \sigma = (s,h) \wedge s \models B\} & \epsilon = ok \\ \emptyset & \epsilon = er \end{cases}$$

$$[\![\texttt{error}]\!]_\epsilon = \begin{cases} \emptyset & \epsilon = ok \\ \{(\sigma,\sigma) \mid \sigma \in \textsc{State}\} & \epsilon = er \end{cases}$$

$$[\![\mathbb{C}_1;\mathbb{C}_2]\!]_\epsilon = \begin{cases} [\![\mathbb{C}_1]\!]_{ok};[\![\mathbb{C}_2]\!]_{ok} & \epsilon = ok \\ [\![\mathbb{C}_1]\!]_{er} \cup [\![\mathbb{C}_1]\!]_{ok};[\![\mathbb{C}_2]\!]_{er} & \epsilon = er \end{cases}$$

$$[\![\texttt{local}\, x \,\mathrm{in}\, \mathbb{C}]\!]_\epsilon = \{((s,h),(s',h')) \mid \exists v,v' \in \textsc{Val}.((s[x \mapsto v],h),(s'[x \mapsto v'],h')) \in [\![\mathbb{C}]\!]_\epsilon \wedge s(x) = s'(x)\}$$

$$[\![\mathbb{C}_1 + \mathbb{C}_2]\!]_\epsilon = [\![\mathbb{C}_1]\!]_\epsilon \cup [\![\mathbb{C}_2]\!]_\epsilon$$

$$[\![\mathbb{C}^\star]\!]_\epsilon = \bigcup_{m \subset \mathbb{N}} [\![\mathbb{C}^m]\!]_\epsilon$$

$$[\![x := \texttt{alloc()}]\!]_\epsilon = \begin{cases} \{((s,h),(s[x \mapsto l],h[l \mapsto v])) \mid v \in \textsc{Val} \wedge (l \notin \mathsf{dom}(h) \vee h(l) = \bot)\} & \epsilon = ok \\ \emptyset & \epsilon = er \end{cases}$$

$$[\![\texttt{free}(x)]\!]_\epsilon = \begin{cases} \{(\sigma,(s,h[s(x) \mapsto \bot])) \mid \sigma = (s,h) \wedge h(s(x)) \in \textsc{Val}\} & \epsilon = ok \\ \{(\sigma,\sigma) \mid \sigma = (s,h) \wedge (s(x) = null \vee h(s(x)) = \bot)\} & \epsilon = er \end{cases}$$

$$[\![x := [y]]\!]_\epsilon = \begin{cases} \{(\sigma,(s[x \mapsto h(s(y))],h)) \mid \sigma = (s,h) \wedge h(s(y)) \in \textsc{Val}\} & \epsilon = ok \\ \{(\sigma,\sigma) \mid \sigma = (s,h) \wedge (s(y) = null \vee h(s(y)) = \bot)\} & \epsilon = er \end{cases}$$

$$[\![[x] := t]\!]_\epsilon = \begin{cases} \{(\sigma,(s,h[s(x) \mapsto s(t)])) \mid \sigma = (s,h) \wedge h(s(x)) \in \textsc{Val}\} & \epsilon = ok \\ \{(\sigma,\sigma) \mid \sigma = (s,h) \wedge (s(x) = null \vee h(s(x)) = \bot)\} & \epsilon = er \end{cases}$$

Here, $\mathbb{C}^0 = \texttt{skip}$ and $\mathbb{C}^{m+1} = \mathbb{C};\mathbb{C}^m$.

2.3 ISL Triples and Proof Rules

The ISL triples are of the form $[P]\ \mathbb{C}\ [\epsilon : Q]$, and their validity is defined as follows.

Definition 6. (Validity of ISL Triples).

$$\models [P]\ \mathbb{C}\ [\epsilon : Q] \overset{def}{\iff} \forall \sigma' \models Q, \exists \sigma \models P.(\sigma,\sigma') \in [\![\mathbb{C}]\!]_\epsilon$$

Before presenting our ISL proof rules, we provide some additional definitions. $\mathsf{mod}(\mathbb{C})$ denotes the set of free variables modified by a program $\mathbb{C}$.

Definition 7. (The Set of Variables Modified by $\mathbb{C}$, $\mathsf{mod}(\mathbb{C})$).

$$\begin{array}{rr}
\mathsf{mod}(\mathtt{skip}) = \emptyset & \mathsf{mod}(x := t) = \{x\} \\
\mathsf{mod}(x := *) = \{x\} & \mathsf{mod}(\mathtt{assume}(B)) = \emptyset \\
\mathsf{mod}(\mathtt{error}) = \emptyset & \mathsf{mod}(x := \mathtt{alloc()}) = \{x\} \\
\mathsf{mod}(\mathtt{free}(x)) = \emptyset & \mathsf{mod}(x := [y]) = \{x\} \\
\mathsf{mod}([x] := t) = \emptyset & \mathsf{mod}(\mathtt{local}\ x\ \mathtt{in}\ \mathbb{C}) = \mathsf{mod}(\mathbb{C}) \setminus \{x\}
\end{array}$$

$$\begin{aligned}
\mathsf{mod}(\mathbb{C}_1; \mathbb{C}_2) &= \mathsf{mod}(\mathbb{C}_1) \cup \mathsf{mod}(\mathbb{C}_2) \\
\mathsf{mod}(\mathbb{C}_1 + \mathbb{C}_2) &= \mathsf{mod}(\mathbb{C}_1) \cup \mathsf{mod}(\mathbb{C}_2) \\
\mathsf{mod}(\mathbb{C}^\star) &= \mathsf{mod}(\mathbb{C})
\end{aligned}$$

The canonical forms of quantifier-free symbolic heaps with respect to a set of variables V are defined. In a canonical form, the case analysis for all combinations of terms in $V \cup \{\mathtt{null}\}$ is done. As we will see in the next section, any symbolic heap can be transformed to a disjunction of canonical forms.

Definition 8. (Canonical Forms).

$$\begin{aligned}
\mathsf{CF}_{\mathrm{sh}}(V) = \{\psi \mid\ & \psi \text{ is a quantifier free symbolic heap} \\
& \wedge \forall t, u \in V \cup \{\mathtt{null}\}.\psi \text{ contains either } t \approx u \text{ or } t \not\approx u\}
\end{aligned}$$

If $\psi \in \mathsf{CF}_{\mathrm{sh}}(V)$ for $V = \mathsf{fv}(\psi) \cup \mathsf{fv}(\mathbb{C})$, then ψ is called canonical for $\mathbb{C}$. We also say that $\bigvee_{i \in I} \exists \overrightarrow{x_i}.\psi_i$ is canonical for $\mathbb{C}$ if, for all i, ψ_i is canonical for $\mathbb{C}$.

Definition 9. (ISL Proof Rules). *In Figs. 1 and 2, we present our ISL proof rules, where the axioms of the form $[P]\ \mathbb{C}\ [ok : Q_1][er : Q_2]$ means that both $[P]\ \mathbb{C}\ [ok : Q_1]$ and $[P]\ \mathbb{C}\ [er : Q_2]$ can be deduced.*

Noted that certain heap manipulation rules, such as FREE, LOAD, and STORE, require that symbolic heaps are in canonical form as a premise. We employ infinitary syntax and incorporate an infinitary version of the DISJ rule following a similar approach used in RHL [8].

3 Weakest Postcondition

In this section, we describe the definition of the weakest postcondition and introduce a function $\mathsf{wpo}(P, \mathbb{C}, \epsilon)$ that computes weakest postconditions. Prior to defining wpo, we introduce the canonicalization, which transforms a formula into a canonical formula.

3.1 Canonicalization

In canonicalization, the function CA (abbreviation for case analysis), which connects all possible equalities and inequalities within assertions, is applied to each disjunct. For a quantifier-free symbolic heap ψ and a program $\mathbb{C}$, $\mathsf{CA}(\psi, \mathbb{C})$ returns the result of case analysis for ψ with respect to the free variables in ψ and $\mathbb{C}$.

Definition 10. (Case Analysis CA). *The function* CA*, taking a symbolic heap* ψ *and a command* $\mathbb{C}$ *as inputs, is defined as follows.*

$$\mathsf{CA}(\psi, \mathbb{C}) = \{\pi * \psi \mid \pi \in \Pi(\mathsf{fv}(\psi) \cup \mathsf{fv}(\mathbb{C})) \wedge (\pi * \psi) \textit{ is satisfiable}\},$$

where Π *is defined as*

$$\Pi(V) = \{(\mathop{\ast}_{(t,s)\in S} t \approx s) * (\mathop{\ast}_{(t,s)\notin S} t \not\approx s) \mid S \subseteq (V \cup \{\mathtt{null}\})^2 \wedge S \textit{ is reflexive and symmetric}\}$$

$$\textsc{Skip}\quad \frac{}{[P]\ \mathtt{skip}\ [ok: P]\ [er: \mathsf{false}]}$$

$$\textsc{Error}\quad \frac{}{[P]\ \mathtt{error()}\ [ok: \mathsf{false}]\ [er: P]}$$

$$\textsc{Seq1}\quad \frac{[P]\ \mathbb{C}_1\ [er: Q]}{[P]\ \mathbb{C}_1; \mathbb{C}_2\ [er: Q]}$$

$$\textsc{Seq2}\quad \frac{[P]\ \mathbb{C}_1\ [ok: R] \quad [R]\ \mathbb{C}_2\ [\epsilon: Q]}{[P]\ \mathbb{C}_1; \mathbb{C}_2\ [\epsilon: Q]}$$

$$\textsc{Loop zero (equal to Skip)}\quad \frac{}{[P]\ \mathbb{C}^\star\ [ok: P]\ [er: \mathsf{false}]}$$

$$\textsc{Loop non-zero}\quad \frac{[P]\ \mathbb{C}^\star; \mathbb{C}\ [\epsilon: Q]}{[P]\ \mathbb{C}^\star\ [\epsilon: Q]}$$

$$\textsc{Cons}\quad \frac{P' \models P \quad [P']\ \mathbb{C}\ [\epsilon: Q'] \quad Q \models Q'}{[P]\ \mathbb{C}\ [\epsilon: Q]}$$

$$\textsc{Disj}\quad \frac{[P_i]\ \mathbb{C}\ [\epsilon: Q_i] \quad \text{for all } i \in I}{[\bigvee_{i\in I} P_i]\ \mathbb{C}\ [\epsilon: \bigvee_{i\in I} Q_i]}$$

$$\textsc{Choice}\quad \frac{[P]\ \mathbb{C}_1\ [\epsilon: Q] \quad [P]\ \mathbb{C}_2\ [\epsilon: Q]}{[P]\ \mathbb{C}_1 + \mathbb{C}_2\ [\epsilon: Q]}$$

$$\textsc{Exist}\quad \frac{[\psi]\ \mathbb{C}\ [\epsilon: \varphi] \quad x \notin \mathsf{fv}(\mathbb{C})}{[\exists x.\psi]\ \mathbb{C}\ [\epsilon: \exists x.\varphi]}$$

Fig. 1. Proof rules of ISL

Assign

$$\frac{}{[\psi]\ x := t\ [ok : \exists x'.\psi[x := x'] * x \approx t[x := x']]\ [er : \mathsf{false}]}$$

Havoc

$$\frac{}{[\psi]\ x := *\ [ok : \exists x'.\psi[x := x']]\ [er : \mathsf{false}]}$$

Assume (B is a pure formula)

$$\frac{}{[\psi]\ \mathtt{assume}(B)\ [ok : \psi * B]\ [er : \mathsf{false}]}$$

Local

$$\frac{[\psi]\ \mathbb{C}\ [\epsilon : \varphi] \quad x \notin \mathsf{fv}(\psi)}{[\psi]\ \mathtt{local}\ x\ \mathtt{in}\ \mathbb{C}\ [\epsilon : \exists x.\varphi]}$$

Frame

$$\frac{[\psi]\ \mathbb{C}\ [\epsilon : \varphi] \quad \mathsf{mod}(\mathbb{C}) \cap \mathsf{fv}(\phi) = \emptyset}{[\psi * \phi]\ \mathbb{C}\ [\epsilon : \varphi * \phi]}$$

Alloc1

$$\frac{}{[\psi]\ x := \mathtt{alloc()}\ \ [ok : \exists x'.\psi[x := x'] * x \mapsto -]\ \ [er : \mathsf{false}]}$$

Alloc2

$$\frac{}{[\psi * y \not\mapsto]\ x := \mathtt{alloc()}\ [ok : \exists x'.x \mapsto - * x \approx y * \psi[x := x']]\ [er : \mathsf{false}]}$$

Free

$$\frac{\psi \in \mathsf{CF}_{\mathrm{sh}}(\mathsf{fv}(\psi) \cup \{x\}) \quad (\psi = \psi' * x \approx y * y \mapsto t \text{ for some } \psi', y, t)}{[\psi]\ \mathtt{free}(x)\ [ok : \psi' * x \approx y * y \not\mapsto]\ [er : \mathsf{false}]}$$

FreeEr

$$\frac{\psi \in \mathsf{CF}_{\mathrm{sh}}(\mathsf{fv}(\psi) \cup \{x\}) \quad (\psi = \psi' * x \approx \mathtt{null} \text{ or } \psi = \psi' * x \approx y * y \not\mapsto \text{ for some } \psi', y)}{[\psi]\ \mathtt{free}(x)\ [ok : \mathsf{false}]\ [er : \psi]}$$

Load

$$\frac{\psi \in \mathsf{CF}_{\mathrm{sh}}(\mathsf{fv}(\psi) \cup \{x, y\}) \quad (\psi = \psi' * y \approx z * z \mapsto t \text{ for some } \psi', z, t)}{[\psi]\ x := [y]\ [ok : \exists x'.\psi[x := x'] * x \approx (t[x := x'])]\ [er : \mathsf{false}]}$$

LoadEr

$$\frac{\psi \in \mathsf{CF}_{\mathrm{sh}}(\mathsf{fv}(\psi) \cup \{x, y\}) \quad (\psi = \psi' * y \approx \mathtt{null} \text{ or } \psi = \psi' * y \approx z * z \not\mapsto \text{ for some } \psi', z)}{[\psi]\ x := [y]\ [ok : \mathsf{false}]\ [er : \psi]}$$

Store

$$\frac{\psi \in \mathsf{CF}_{\mathrm{sh}}(\mathsf{fv}(\psi) \cup \{x, t\}) \quad (\psi = \psi' * x \approx z * z \mapsto t' \text{ for some } \psi', z, t')}{[\psi]\ [x] := t\ [ok : \psi' * x \approx z * z \mapsto t]\ [er : \mathsf{false}]}$$

StoreEr

$$\frac{\psi \in \mathsf{CF}_{\mathrm{sh}}(\mathsf{fv}(\psi) \cup \{x, t\}) \quad (\psi = \psi' * x \approx \mathtt{null} \text{ or } \psi = \psi' * x \approx z * z \not\mapsto \text{ for some } \psi', z)}{[\psi]\ [x] := t\ [ok : \mathsf{false}]\ [er : \psi]}$$

Fig. 2. Rules for variables and mutation

To demonstrate this function, we will calculate $\mathsf{CA}(y \mapsto t, \mathtt{free}(x))$ as an example. In each case, we omit $x \approx x$ and $y \approx y$ for brevity.

$$\begin{aligned}\mathsf{CA}(y \mapsto t, \mathtt{free}(x)) = \{\ &(x \approx y * y \not\approx \mathtt{null} * x \not\approx \mathtt{null} * y \mapsto t), &(1)\\ &(x \not\approx y * y \not\approx \mathtt{null} * x \approx \mathtt{null} * y \mapsto t), &(2)\\ &(x \not\approx y * y \not\approx \mathtt{null} * x \not\approx \mathtt{null} * y \mapsto t)\ \} &(3)\end{aligned}$$

Note that unsatisfiable clauses, such as $x \not\approx x * y \not\approx y * x \approx y * y \approx \mathtt{null} * x \approx \mathtt{null} * y \mapsto t$ are excluded.

Clause (1) addresses scenarios involving aliasing between x and y. Clause (2) pertains to cases of non-aliasing and the occurrence of the FreeNull error, as described in [19]. Clause (3) is also a non-aliasing scenario, leading to a FreeNull error similar to the second one. In this case, x is not $\mathtt{null}$, but $s(x)$ has not been allocated in the heap, i.e., $s(x) \notin \mathsf{dom}(h)$, even though $s(x) \neq \mathit{null}$. When $\mathtt{free}(x)$ attempts to deallocate a heap denoted by x, which does not exist, it results in an error.

We define the canonicalization function.

Definition 11. (Canonicalization cano**).** *Suppose that* $P = \bigvee_{i \in I} \exists \overrightarrow{x_i}.\psi_i$ *and* $\overrightarrow{x_i} \notin \mathsf{fv}(\mathbb{C})$.

$$\mathsf{cano}(P, \mathbb{C}) = \bigvee_{i \in I} \bigvee_{\varphi \in \mathsf{CA}(\psi_i, \mathbb{C})} \exists \overrightarrow{x_i}.\varphi$$

The result of this function is canonical and equivalent to the input assertion.

Lemma 1. *For all* P *and* $\mathbb{C}$*,* $\mathsf{cano}(P, \mathbb{C})$ *is canonical for* $\mathbb{C}$ *and equivalent to* P*.*

Proof. It is easy to see that every element in $\mathsf{CA}(\psi, \mathbb{C})$ is in $\mathsf{CF}_{\mathsf{sh}}(\mathsf{fv}(\psi) \cup \mathbb{C})$, and hence $\mathsf{cano}(P, \mathbb{C})$ is canonical for $\mathbb{C}$.

Since every symbolic heap ψ is equivalent to $(\psi * t \approx u) \vee (\psi * t \not\approx u)$ for any terms t, u, we have that ψ is equivalent to $\bigvee_{\varphi \in \mathsf{CA}(\psi, \mathbb{C})} \varphi$. Therefore, $\exists \overrightarrow{x_i}.\psi_i$ is equivalent to $\exists \overrightarrow{x_i}. \bigvee_{\varphi \in \mathsf{CA}(\psi_i, \mathbb{C})} \varphi$, and also to $\bigvee_{\varphi \in \mathsf{CA}(\psi_i, \mathbb{C})} \exists \overrightarrow{x_i}.\varphi$. Hence, P is equivalent to $\mathsf{cano}(P, \mathbb{C})$. □

3.2 Weakest Postcondition and wpo

We first define the weakest postcondition as follows.

Definition 12. (Weakest Postcondition). *The* weakest postcondition *of a precondition* P*, a program* $\mathbb{C}$*, and an exit condition* ϵ *is defined as follows.*

$$\mathrm{WPO}[\![P, \mathbb{C}, \epsilon]\!] = \{\sigma' \mid \exists \sigma. \sigma \models P \wedge (\sigma, \sigma') \in [\![\mathbb{C}]\!]_\epsilon\}$$

Next, we define the calculation of the weakest postcondition (wpo) as follows.

Definition 13. (wpo) $\mathsf{wpo}(P, \mathbb{C}, \epsilon)$ *for an assertion* P *and* $\mathsf{wpo}_{\mathsf{sh}}(\psi, \mathbb{C}, \epsilon)$ *for a quantifier-free canonical symbolic heap* ψ *are simultaneously defined as follows.*

$$\mathsf{wpo}(P, \mathbb{C}, \epsilon) = \bigvee_{i \in I} \exists \overrightarrow{x_i}.\mathsf{wpo}_{\mathsf{sh}}(\psi_i, \mathbb{C}, \epsilon) \quad (\mathit{for}\, \mathsf{cano}(P, \mathbb{C}) = \bigvee_{i \in I} \exists \overrightarrow{x_i}.\psi_i)$$

The function $\mathsf{wpo}_{\mathsf{sh}}$ *is defined in Fig. 3.*

Note that infinite disjunctions are needed only when we calculate wpo of $\mathbb{C}^\star$. Therefore, if we assume a bound of the number of iterations of $\mathbb{C}^\star$ with a finite number, i.e., we use $\mathbb{C}^n$ $(n \in \mathbb{N})$ instead of $\mathbb{C}^\star$, then we can define wpo with finite formulas.

4 Proving Relative Completeness

In this section, we prove soundness and relative completeness of ISL.

Soundness is proved in a standard way.

Proposition 1. (Soundness of ISL).

$$\mathit{For\, any}\, P, \mathbb{C}, \epsilon, Q,\ \mathit{if} \vdash [P]\ \mathbb{C}\ [\epsilon : Q],\ \mathit{then} \models [P]\ \mathbb{C}\ [\epsilon : Q].$$

For relative completeness, we will show the following two propositions. First, we prove expressiveness of the weakest postconditions (Proposition 2), that is, $\mathsf{wpo}(P, \mathbb{C}, \epsilon)$ exactly represents $\mathsf{WPO}[\![P, \mathbb{C}, \epsilon]\!]$. Secondly, we prove that the specification whose postcondition is wpo can be derived in ISL (Proposition 3).

To prove expressiveness, we show the following lemmas.

Lemma 2. *If* $x \notin \mathsf{fv}(\mathbb{C})$*, then the following holds for any* (s', h')*,* ψ*,* $\mathbb{C}$ *and* ϵ*.*

$$(s', h') \in \mathrm{WPO}[\![\exists x.\psi, \mathbb{C}, \epsilon]\!] \iff \exists v \in \mathrm{VAL}.(s'[x \mapsto v], h') \in \mathrm{WPO}[\![\psi, \mathbb{C}, \epsilon]\!]$$

Lemma 3.

$$\mathrm{WPO}[\![\bigvee_{i \in I} P, \mathbb{C}, \epsilon]\!] \iff \bigcup_{i \in I} \mathrm{WPO}[\![P, \mathbb{C}, \epsilon]\!]$$

Lemma 4. *Suppose* $\mathsf{cano}(P, \mathbb{C}) = \bigvee_{i \in I} \exists \overrightarrow{x_i}.\psi_i$*. If for all* $i \in I$*,* (s', h') *and* ϵ*,* $(s', h') \models \mathsf{wpo}_{\mathsf{sh}}(\psi_i, \mathbb{C}, \epsilon) \iff (s', h') \in \mathrm{WPO}[\![\psi_i, \mathbb{C}, \epsilon]\!]$*, then for any* (s', h') *and* ϵ*,* $(s', h') \models \mathsf{wpo}(P, \mathbb{C}, \epsilon) \iff (s', h') \in \mathrm{WPO}[\![P, \mathbb{C}, \epsilon]\!]$ *holds.*

Proof.

$$
\begin{aligned}
&(s', h') \models \mathsf{wpo}_{\mathrm{sh}}(\psi_i, \mathbb{C}, \epsilon) \iff (s', h') \in \mathrm{WPO}[\![\psi_i, \mathbb{C}, \epsilon]\!] \\
&\quad \Rightarrow \exists \overrightarrow{v_i} \in \mathrm{VAL}.(s'[\overrightarrow{x_i} \mapsto \overrightarrow{v_i}], h') \models \mathsf{wpo}_{\mathrm{sh}}(\psi_i, \mathbb{C}, \epsilon) \\
&\quad \iff (s'[\overrightarrow{x_i} \mapsto \overrightarrow{v_i}], h') \in \mathrm{WPO}[\![\psi_i, \mathbb{C}, \epsilon]\!] \\
&\quad \Leftrightarrow (s', h') \models \exists \overrightarrow{x_i}.\mathsf{wpo}_{\mathrm{sh}}(\psi_i, \mathbb{C}, \epsilon) \\
&\quad \iff (s', h') \in \mathrm{WPO}[\![\exists \overrightarrow{x_i}.\psi_i, \mathbb{C}, \epsilon]\!] \quad // \text{ Lemma 2} \\
&\quad \Rightarrow (s', h') \models \bigvee_{i \in I} \exists \overrightarrow{x_i}.\mathsf{wpo}_{\mathrm{sh}}(\psi_i, \mathbb{C}, \epsilon) \\
&\quad \iff (s', h') \in \bigcup_{i \in I} \mathrm{WPO}[\![\exists \overrightarrow{x_i}.\psi_i, \mathbb{C}, \epsilon]\!] \\
&\quad \Leftrightarrow (s', h') \models \mathsf{wpo}(P, \mathbb{C}, \epsilon) \\
&\quad \iff (s', h') \in \mathrm{WPO}[\![\bigvee_{i \in I} \exists \overrightarrow{x_i}.\psi_i, \mathbb{C}, \epsilon]\!] \quad // \text{ Lemma 3} \\
&\quad \Leftrightarrow (s', h') \models \mathsf{wpo}(P, \mathbb{C}, \epsilon) \iff (s', h') \in \mathrm{WPO}[\![P, \mathbb{C}, \epsilon]\!]
\end{aligned}
$$

□

Lemma 5.

$$\forall \sigma'.\sigma' \in \mathrm{WPO}[\![\psi, \mathbb{C}, \epsilon]\!] \iff \sigma' \models \mathsf{wpo}_{\mathrm{sh}}(\psi, \mathbb{C}, \epsilon)$$

Proposition 2 explains expressiveness concerning general command $\mathbb{C}$, i.e., the assertions derived by wpo exactly describe the weakest postconditions.

Proposition 2. (Expressiveness).

$$\forall \sigma'.\sigma' \in \mathrm{WPO}[\![P, \mathbb{C}, \epsilon]\!] \iff \sigma' \models \mathsf{wpo}(P, \mathbb{C}, \epsilon)$$

Proof. This proposition holds by applying Lemmas 2, 3, 4 and 5. □

We show the following lemmas to prove the second proposition.

Lemma 6. *For any P, $\mathbb{C}$, ϵ, let us say* $\mathsf{cano}(P, \mathbb{C}) = \bigvee_{i \in I} \exists \overrightarrow{x_i}.\psi_i$. *Then, the following holds:*

$$\forall i \in I. \vdash [\psi_i] \ \mathbb{C} \ [\epsilon : \mathsf{wpo}_{\mathrm{sh}}(\psi_i, \mathbb{C}, \epsilon)] \implies \vdash [P] \ \mathbb{C} \ [\epsilon : \mathsf{wpo}(P, \mathbb{C}, \epsilon)]$$

Proof. We can assume that $\overrightarrow{x_i} \notin \mathsf{fv}(\mathbb{C})$ for each $i \in I$. Then, $[P] \ \mathbb{C} \ [\epsilon : \mathsf{wpo}(P, \mathbb{C}, \epsilon)]$ is derivable as follows.

$$
\dfrac{\dfrac{\dfrac{\forall i \in I.[\psi_i] \ \mathbb{C} \ [\epsilon : \mathsf{wpo}_{\mathrm{sh}}(\psi_i, \mathbb{C}, \epsilon)] \quad (\overrightarrow{x_i} \notin \mathsf{fv}(\mathbb{C}))}{\forall i \in I.[\exists \overrightarrow{x_i}.\psi_i] \ \mathbb{C} \ [\epsilon : \exists \overrightarrow{x_i}.\mathsf{wpo}_{\mathrm{sh}}(\psi_i, \mathbb{C}, \epsilon)]} \ \textsc{Exist}}{[\bigvee_{i \in I} \exists \overrightarrow{x_i}.\psi_i] \ \mathbb{C} \ [\epsilon : \bigvee_{i \in I} \exists \overrightarrow{x_i}.\mathsf{wpo}_{\mathrm{sh}}(\psi_i, \mathbb{C}, \epsilon)]} \ \textsc{Disj}}{[P] \ \mathbb{C} \ [\epsilon : \mathsf{wpo}(P, \mathbb{C}, \epsilon)]}
$$

□

Lemma 7. *For any* $\psi, \mathbb{C}, \epsilon$, *we have* $\vdash [\psi]\ \mathbb{C}\ [\epsilon : \mathsf{wpo}_{\mathsf{sh}}(\psi, \mathbb{C}, \epsilon)]$.

Proof. We prove this lemma by induction on $\mathbb{C}$. Here, we only prove the case of Choice.

$$\dfrac{\text{Choice}\ \dfrac{[\psi]\ \mathbb{C}_1\ [\epsilon : \mathsf{wpo}_{\mathsf{sh}}(\psi, \mathbb{C}_1, \epsilon)]}{[\psi]\ \mathbb{C}_1 + \mathbb{C}_2\ [\epsilon : \mathsf{wpo}_{\mathsf{sh}}(\psi, \mathbb{C}_1, \epsilon)]} \quad \dfrac{[\psi]\ \mathbb{C}_2\ [\epsilon : \mathsf{wpo}_{\mathsf{sh}}(\psi, \mathbb{C}_2, \epsilon)]}{[\psi]\ \mathbb{C}_1 + \mathbb{C}_2\ [\epsilon : \mathsf{wpo}_{\mathsf{sh}}(\psi, \mathbb{C}_2, \epsilon)]}\ \text{Choice}}{\dfrac{[\psi]\ \mathbb{C}_1 + \mathbb{C}_2\ [\epsilon : \mathsf{wpo}_{\mathsf{sh}}(\psi, \mathbb{C}_1, \epsilon) \vee \mathsf{wpo}_{\mathsf{sh}}(\psi, \mathbb{C}_2, \epsilon)]}{[\psi]\ \mathbb{C}_1 + \mathbb{C}_2\ [\epsilon : \mathsf{wpo}_{\mathsf{sh}}(\psi, \mathbb{C}_1 + \mathbb{C}_2, \epsilon)]}}\ \text{Disj}$$

□

Proposition 3. *For any* $P, \mathbb{C}, \epsilon$, $\vdash [P]\ \mathbb{C}\ [\epsilon : \mathsf{wpo}(P, \mathbb{C}, \epsilon)]$

Proof. By leveraging Lemmas 6 and 7, this proposition is established. □

By Propositions 2 and 3, we prove relative completeness of ISL.

Theorem 1. (Relative Completeness). *For any* $P, \mathbb{C}, \epsilon, Q$, *if* $\models [P]\ \mathbb{C}\ [\epsilon : Q]$, *then* $\vdash [P]\ \mathbb{C}\ [\epsilon : Q]$.

Proof. Since $[P]\ \mathbb{C}\ [\epsilon : Q]$ is valid, we have $\forall \sigma' \models Q.\sigma' \in \mathsf{WPO}[\![P, \mathbb{C}, \epsilon]\!]$ by the definition of the validity of ISL triples. By Proposition 2, we have $\forall \sigma' \models Q.\sigma' \models \mathsf{wpo}(P, \mathbb{C}, \epsilon)$, which is equivalent to $Q \models \mathsf{wpo}(P, \mathbb{C}, \epsilon)$.

Then, $[P]\ \mathbb{C}\ [Q]$ is derivable in ISL as follows.

$$\dfrac{\text{Proposition 3}\ \dfrac{}{\vdash [P]\ \mathbb{C}\ [\epsilon : \mathsf{wpo}(P, \mathbb{C}, \epsilon)]} \quad \dfrac{\models [P]\ \mathbb{C}\ [\epsilon : Q]}{Q \models \mathsf{wpo}(P, \mathbb{C}, \epsilon)}\ \text{Proposition 2}}{\vdash [P]\ \mathbb{C}\ [\epsilon : Q]}\ \text{Cons}$$

□

5 Related Work

Proving Relative Completeness for Graph Manipulation. Poskitt et al. demonstrate soundness and relative completeness for an under-approximation program logic for a graph manipulation language using the calculation of the weakest postconditions [18]. Therein, they prove relative completeness of an extensional logic with semantic predicates. This setting is similar to that of IL [16] in that there is no need to prove expressiveness. Relative completeness of the intensional logic, which does not allow for semantic predicates and requires proof of expressiveness, remains unknown.

Unifying Correctness and Incorrectness. Efforts to integrate correctness and incorrectness reasoning within a unified program logic are demonstrated by the work of Bruni et al. [3,4]. They introduce the Local Completeness Logic, which imposes constraints on the rule of consequence to thereby guarantee the recoverability of an over-approximation of states that are reachable from the

$$\mathsf{wpo_{sh}}(\psi, \mathtt{skip}, \epsilon) = \begin{cases} \psi & \epsilon = ok \\ \mathsf{false} & \epsilon = er \end{cases}$$

$$\mathsf{wpo_{sh}}(\psi, \mathtt{error}, \epsilon) = \begin{cases} \mathsf{false} & ok \\ \psi & er \end{cases}$$

$$\mathsf{wpo_{sh}}(\psi, \mathtt{local}\ x\ \mathtt{in}\ \mathbb{C}, \epsilon) = \bigvee_{j \in J} \exists x'', \overrightarrow{x_j}.\varphi_j$$

$$\text{where } \mathsf{wpo}(\psi[x := x'], \mathbb{C}, \epsilon)[x := x''][x' := x] = \bigvee_{j \in J} \exists \overrightarrow{x_j}.\varphi_j$$

$$\mathsf{wpo_{sh}}(\psi, \mathtt{assume}(B), \epsilon) = \begin{cases} \psi * B & \epsilon = ok \\ \mathsf{false} & \epsilon = er \end{cases}$$

$$\mathsf{wpo_{sh}}(\psi, \mathbb{C}_1; \mathbb{C}_2, ok) = \mathsf{wpo}(\mathsf{wpo_{sh}}(\psi, \mathbb{C}_1, ok), \mathbb{C}_2, ok)$$

$$\mathsf{wpo_{sh}}(\psi, \mathbb{C}_1; \mathbb{C}_2, er) = \mathsf{wpo_{sh}}(\psi, \mathbb{C}_1, er) \vee \mathsf{wpo}(\mathsf{wpo_{sh}}(\psi, \mathbb{C}_1, ok), \mathbb{C}_2, er)$$

$$\mathsf{wpo_{sh}}(\psi, \mathbb{C}^\star, ok) = \bigvee_{n \in \mathbb{N}} \Upsilon(n) \text{ where } \Upsilon(0) = \psi \text{ and } \Upsilon(n+1) = \mathsf{wpo}(\Upsilon(n), \mathbb{C}, ok)$$

$$\mathsf{wpo_{sh}}(\psi, \mathbb{C}^\star, er) = \bigvee_{n \in \mathbb{N}} \mathsf{wpo}(\Upsilon(n), \mathbb{C}, er)$$

$$\mathsf{wpo_{sh}}(\psi, \mathbb{C}_1 + \mathbb{C}_2, \epsilon) = \mathsf{wpo_{sh}}(\psi, \mathbb{C}_1, \epsilon) \vee \mathsf{wpo_{sh}}(\psi, \mathbb{C}_2, \epsilon)$$

$$\mathsf{wpo_{sh}}(\psi, x := t, \epsilon) = \begin{cases} \exists x'.\psi[x := x'] * x \approx t[x := x'] & \epsilon = ok \\ \mathsf{false} & \epsilon = er \end{cases}$$

$$\mathsf{wpo_{sh}}(\psi, x := *, \epsilon) = \begin{cases} \exists x'.\psi[x := x'] & \epsilon = ok \\ \mathsf{false} & \epsilon = er \end{cases}$$

$$\mathsf{wpo_{sh}}(\psi, x := \mathtt{alloc()}, \epsilon) = \begin{cases} \exists x'.(\psi[x := x'] * x \mapsto -) \vee & \epsilon = ok \\ \bigvee_{j=1}^{n} \exists x'.((*_{i=1}^{n} y_i \not\mapsto)[y_j \not\mapsto := y_j \mapsto -] * x \approx y_j * \psi'[x := x']) & \\ //\ \psi = (*_{i=1}^{n} y_i \not\mapsto) * \psi' \text{ (here, } \psi' \text{ does not have atoms with } \not\mapsto) & \\ \mathsf{false} & \epsilon = er \end{cases}$$

$$\mathsf{wpo_{sh}}(\psi, \mathtt{free}(x), ok) = \begin{cases} \psi' * x \approx y * y \not\mapsto & \text{if } \psi = \psi' * x \approx y * y \mapsto t \text{ for some } \psi', y, t \\ \mathsf{false} & \text{otherwise} \end{cases}$$

$$\mathsf{wpo_{sh}}(\psi, \mathtt{free}(x), er) = \begin{cases} \psi & \text{if } \psi = \psi' * x \approx \mathbf{null} \text{ or } \psi = \psi' * x \approx y * y \not\mapsto \text{ for some } \psi', y \\ \mathsf{false} & \text{otherwise} \end{cases}$$

$$\mathsf{wpo_{sh}}(\psi, x := [y], ok) = \begin{cases} \exists x'.\psi[x := x'] * x \approx (t[x := x']) & \text{if } \psi = \psi' * y \approx z * z \mapsto t \text{ for some } \psi', z, t \\ \mathsf{false} & \text{otherwise} \end{cases}$$

$$\mathsf{wpo_{sh}}(\psi, x := [y], er) = \begin{cases} \psi & \text{if } \psi = \psi' * y \approx \mathbf{null} \text{ or } \psi = \psi' * y \approx z * z \not\mapsto \text{ for some } \psi', z \\ \mathsf{false} & \text{otherwise} \end{cases}$$

$$\mathsf{wpo_{sh}}(\psi, [x] := t, ok) = \begin{cases} \psi' * x \approx z * z \mapsto t & \text{if } \psi = \psi' * x \approx z * z \mapsto t' \text{ for some } \psi', z, t' \\ \mathsf{false} & \text{otherwise} \end{cases}$$

$$\mathsf{wpo_{sh}}(\psi, [x] := t, er) = \begin{cases} \psi & \text{if } \psi = \psi' * x \approx \mathbf{null} \text{ or } \psi = \psi' * x \approx z * z \not\mapsto \text{ for some } \psi', z \\ \mathsf{false} & \text{otherwise} \end{cases}$$

Fig. 3. $\mathsf{wpo_{sh}} : \textsc{Sh} \times \textsc{Comm} \times \textsc{Exit} \to \mathrm{ISL}$

postcondition. Additionally, they propose a concept of local completeness that ensures that no false alarms are generated relative to some fixed input.

Similarly, Maksimovic et al. [12] propose Exact SL, whose operational semantics is complete; their aim is to unify correctness and incorrectness considerations. However, it encounters challenges that stem from the limitations of the rule of consequence. Exact SL introduces explicit specifications of both "*ok*" and "*er*" cases in postconditions, and it has advantages in addressing correctness (over-approximation) and incorrectness (under-approximation) of programs. However, this approach introduces a trade-off, as it involves a more restrictive coverage of proof rules, such as the rule of consequence, which is applicable only to equivalent formulas.

Outcome Logic [24] and Outcome SL [25] stand out in unifying over and under-approximate reasoning for heap-manipulating and probabilistic programs. Outcome Logic combines and generalizes standard over-approximate Hoare triples with forward under-approximate triples. In [23], relative completeness of Outcome Logic is discussed.

6 Conclusions and Future Work

In this study, we have proven relative completeness of ISL. Our objective was to maintain relative completeness of RHL while expanding to include exit conditions and heap manipulation within ISL. The calculation of the weakest post-conditions in our ISL and the demonstration of its expressiveness are key to this proof. However, this requires a trade-off by allowing for infinite disjunctions, as is done in the proof of RHL.

For our future work, we are exploring the possibility of demonstrating relative completeness for ISL within a finite syntax extended by some arithmetic theory. Although infinitary syntax aligns with our research goals to prove relative completeness, it may not be the best fit for constructing a practical automatic theorem prover.

Acknowledgments. We would like to express our gratitude to Professor Shoji Yuen for providing thoughtful guidance on our research. We also extend our thanks to Professor Hiroyuki Seki and Professor Yuichi Kaji from our research group for their valuable remarks. Additionally, we are grateful to the three anonymous referees of APLAS 2024 and an expert reviewer for their insightful comments and suggestions.
This work was supported by JSPS KAKENHI Grant Number JP22K11901. Furthermore, Yeonseok Lee is financially supported by TMI, one of the WISE programs established by MEXT Japan, as well as by JST SPRING under Grant Number JPMJSP2125. The authors also thank the Interdisciplinary Frontier Next-Generation Researcher Program of the Tokai Higher Education and Research System.

References

1. Berdine, J., Calcagno, C., O'Hearn, P.W.: A decidable fragment of separation logic. In: FSTTCS 2004: Foundations of Software Technology and Theoretical Computer Science: 24th International Conference, Chennai, India, December 16–18, 2004. Proceedings, vol. 24, pp. 97–109. Springer (2005)
2. Berdine, J., Calcagno, C., O'Hearn, P.W.: Symbolic execution with separation logic. In: Programming Languages and Systems: Third Asian Symposium, APLAS 2005, Tsukuba, Japan, November 2–5, 2005. Proceedings, vol. 3, pp. 52–68. Springer (2005)

3. Bruni, R., Giacobazzi, R., Gori, R., Ranzato, F.: A logic for locally complete abstract interpretations. In: 2021 36th Annual ACM/IEEE Symposium on Logic in Computer Science (LICS), pp. 1–13. IEEE (2021)
4. Bruni, R., Giacobazzi, R., Gori, R., Ranzato, F.: A correctness and incorrectness program logic. J. ACM **70**(2), 1–45 (2023)
5. Calcagno, C., Distefano, D.: Infer: an automatic program verifier for memory safety of C programs. In: NASA Formal Methods Symposium, pp. 459–465. Springer (2011)
6. Calcagno, C., Distefano, D., O'Hearn, P.: Open-sourcing facebook infer: identify bugs before you ship (2015). https://engineering.fb.com/2015/06/11/developer-tools/open-sourcing-facebook-infer-identify-bugs-before-you-ship/
7. Cook, S.A.: Soundness and completeness of an axiom system for program verification. SIAM J. Comput. **7**(1), 70–90 (1978)
8. De Vries, E., Koutavas, V.: Reverse Hoare logic. In: International Conference on Software Engineering and Formal Methods, pp. 155–171. Springer (2011)
9. Echenim, M., Iosif, R., Peltier, N.: The Bernays-Schönfinkel-Ramsey class of separation logic with uninterpreted predicates. ACM Trans. Comput. Log. (TOCL) **21**(3), 1–46 (2020)
10. Gödel, K.: Über formal unentscheidbare sätze der principia mathematica und verwandter systeme i. Monatsh. Math. Phys. **38**, 173–198 (1931)
11. Hoare, C.A.R.: An axiomatic basis for computer programming. Commun. ACM **12**(10), 576–580 (1969)
12. Maksimović, P., Cronjäger, C., Lööw, A., Sutherland, J., Gardner, P.: Exact separation logic: towards bridging the gap between verification and bug-finding. In: 37th European Conference on Object-Oriented Programming (ECOOP 2023). Schloss Dagstuhl-Leibniz-Zentrum für Informatik (2023)
13. Nakazawa, K., Tatsuta, M., Kimura, D., Yamamura, M.: Cyclic theorem prover for separation logic by magic wand. In: ADSL 18 (First Workshop on Automated Deduction for Separation Logics) (2018)
14. Nakazawa, K., Tatsuta, M., Kimura, D., Yamamura, M.: Spatial factorization in cyclic-proof system for separation logic. Comput. Softw. **37**(1), 1_125–1_144 (2020)
15. Nguyen, H.H., David, C., Qin, S., Chin, W.N.: Automated verification of shape and size properties via separation logic. In: International Workshop on Verification, Model Checking, and Abstract Interpretation, pp. 251–266. Springer (2007)
16. O'Hearn, P.W.: Incorrectness logic. Proc. ACM Program. Lang. **4**(POPL), 1–32 (2019)
17. Peltier, N.: Testing the satisfiability of formulas in separation logic with permissions. In: TABLEAUX 2023 32nd International Conference on Automated Reasoning with Analytic Tableaux and Related Methods. Springer (2023)
18. Poskitt, C.M., Plump, D.: Monadic second-order incorrectness logic for GP 2. J. Log. Algebraic Methods Program. **130**, 100825 (2023)
19. Raad, A., Berdine, J., Dang, H.H., Dreyer, D., O'Hearn, P., Villard, J.: Local reasoning about the presence of bugs: incorrectness separation logic. In: Computer Aided Verification: 32nd International Conference, CAV 2020, Los Angeles, CA, USA, July 21–24, 2020, Proceedings, Part II 32, pp. 225–252. Springer (2020)
20. Reynolds, J.C.: Separation logic: a logic for shared mutable data structures. In: Proceedings 17th Annual IEEE Symposium on Logic in Computer Science, pp. 55–74. IEEE (2002)
21. Tatsuta, M., Chin, W.N., Al Ameen, M.F.: Completeness of pointer program verification by separation logic. In: 2009 Seventh IEEE International Conference on Software Engineering and Formal Methods, pp. 179–188. IEEE (2009)

22. Tatsuta, M., Kimura, D.: Separation logic with monadic inductive definitions and implicit existentials. In: Programming Languages and Systems: 13th Asian Symposium, APLAS 2015, Pohang, South Korea, November 30–December 2, 2015, Proceedings, vol. 13, pp. 69–89. Springer (2015)
23. Zilberstein, N.: A relatively complete program logic for effectful branching. arXiv preprint arXiv:2401.04594 (2024)
24. Zilberstein, N., Dreyer, D., Silva, A.: Outcome logic: a unifying foundation for correctness and incorrectness reasoning. Proc. ACM Program. Lang. **7**(OOPSLA1), 522–550 (2023)
25. Zilberstein, N., Saliling, A., Silva, A.: Outcome separation logic: local reasoning for correctness and incorrectness with computational effects. Proc. ACM Program. Lang. **8**(OOPSLA1), 276–304 (2024)

OBRA: Oracle-Based, Relational, Algorithmic Type Verification

Elizaveta Vasilenko[1], Niki Vazou[1(✉)], and Gilles Barthe[1,2]

[1] IMDEA Software Institute, Madrid, Spain
niki.vazou@imdea.org
[2] MPI-SP, Bochum, Germany

Abstract. Relational logics aim to stablish properties of two expressions by combining synchronous proof rules, which reason about structurally equivalent expressions, with asynchronous proof rules, which only reason about one of the two expressions. As a result, relational logics are not syntax-directed and their algorithmic implementation is challenging. In this work, we design OBRA an algorithmic, relational, and bidirectional type system that only has synchronous rules to preserve predictability and relies on an external oracle to handle syntactic differences. We formalize OBRA and prove that it is equivalent to Relational Higher-Order Logic (RHOL). We implement OBRA by extending Liquid Haskell with synchronous relational rules and using user-provided unary proofs as the external oracle. Further, OBRA automatically translates relational properties to unary theorems with proof templates that can be manually augmented, debugged, and verified using Liquid Haskell. We evaluate OBRA on 12 benchmarks out of which 7 were proved automatically and the rest required smaller or equal proofs than the unary case.

Keywords: Refinement types · Relational types · Liquid types

1 Introduction

Relational higher-order type systems [6] and logics [4,13] have been designed to simplify the verification of relational properties, *i.e.* properties that relate two programs or two runs of the same program. Such systems have been developed to reason about a wide variety of properties, including cost analysis [10], differential privacy [7], and information flow control [17]. As a simple relational property, below we relate how `map` and `filter` modify the length of their input lists:

```
filter ~ map |  ∀f1 ∼ f2. true ⇒ ∀xs1 ∼ xs2. len xs1 ≤ len xs2
                ⇒ len (r1 f1 xs1) ≤ len (r2 f2 xs2)
```

The property states that for each pair of functions `f1` and `f2` and pair of lists `xs1` and `xs2` such that the length of `xs1` is less than or equal to the length of `xs2`, the length of `filter f1 xs1` is less than or equal to the length of `map f2 xs2`, where the special symbols `r1` and `r2` are used to refer to the related functions.

O. Kiselyov (Ed.): APLAS 2024, LNCS 15194, pp. 283–302, 2024.
https://doi.org/10.1007/978-981-97-8943-6_14

Relational verification of such statements proceeds by unfolding the left-hand side and right-hand side expressions, in our example `filter f1 xs1` and `map f2 xs2`, according to the rules of an inductive system. In type-based systems, the rules are usually *synchronous* and relate expressions of the same structure, *e.g.* they relate a function application to a function application or an if-expression to an if-expression, but not a function application to an if-expression. Such rules add up to a syntax-directed type system that can automatically establish very precise properties when comparing two similar expressions, like two runs of the same function. However, analysis of syntactically different expressions via type systems is limited [6]. Some works, such as [10] use example-driven heuristics to deal with program differences in common cases, but as a drawback, such systems lose predictability and hence, user-friendly error reporting.

To systematically analyze expressions of different structure, the Relational Higher-Order Logic (RHOL) [2–4] supports *asynchronous* rules. Such rules can choose just one of the related expressions for unfolding, *e.g.* they can compare an application to an if-expression, as required to relate the `map` with the guarded `filter` in our example. The co-existence of both synchronous and asynchronous rules in RHOL leads to a set of typing rules that is not syntax directed, thus reasoning in RHOL is non-algorithmic. Such systems focus on the theoretical aspects of relational logics and are inherently not syntax directed. As a consequence, their implementations have not yet been really explored.

Yet, the proofs conducted in RHOL can be translated to and checked by an algorithmic system, such as the unary refinement type system of LIQUID HASKELL [25]. In theory, this is possible because RHOL is equivalent to HOL (Theorem 3 of [4]) and HOL proofs can be encoded in LIQUID HASKELL (Theorem 3.1 of [26]). In practice, both [14,23] manually encoded RHOL proofs in LIQUID HASKELL and found that the process is feasible but tedious. Most of the times the syntax directed reasoning is used to deconstruct the related terms. Thus, we conjectured that the extension of LIQUID HASKELL with algorithmic, synchronous rules would ease the proof process of relational properties.

In this work, we design and implement OBRA, an oracle-based, relational, and algorithmic verifier that extends LIQUID HASKELL with synchronous relational rules. OBRA has a bidirectional, relational type system that not only verifies relational properties, but also translates them to unary LIQUID HASKELL theorems and automatically generates synchronous proofs templates for them. These proofs are developed using LIQUID HASKELL as theorem-prover [24] and can be interactively adjusted as necessary. This interaction of unary and relational systems, established a novel method of proving relational properties that takes the best of both worlds: our system has the full expressiveness of RHOL via unary proofs, yet supports automation of synchronous reasoning. Moreover, OBRA is the first relational system that generates proofs for relational properties and utilizes an underlying existing unary system. To measure the automation of our method, we used OBRA to prove 12 properties and compared our proof sizes against the existing manual proofs in plain LIQUID HASKELL [14].

Concretely, our contributions are the following:

1) We design an algorithmic, bidirectional, relational, refinement type system on top of a unary refinement type checker that uses a novel oracle rule (rule T-OBL of Fig. 4) to make the system complete (Theorem 1) *w.r.t.* RHOL.
2) We design a translation from the relational typing statements to unary theorems (Sect. 3.3) to ease the development of relational proofs. Our system reduces the proof of a relational property to the verification of an equivalent unary theorem.
3) We implement our system on top of LIQUID HASKELL and evaluate it on 12 examples (Table 1). Our evaluation shows that the synchronous rules are sufficient to prove 58% of our benchmarks, while for the rest, our translation generates unary theorems that can be manually completed. In total, our method reduces manual proof effort by 36%, compared to purely manual unary proofs.

2 Overview of OBRA

OBRA receives from the user a pair of expressions and a relational property (Sect. 2.1), then generates for the property a unary proof term that is potentially incomplete (Sect. 2.2), and returns it to the user who completes the proof as an oracle (Sect. 2.3). Section 2.4 summarizes the workflow of OBRA.

2.1 Relational Properties

Relational properties express relations between two expressions or two runs of the same expression. As an example, consider the following `map` function such that `map f xs` applies `f` to all the elements of `xs`:

```
map :: (a → b) → [a] → [b]
map f []     = []
map f (x:xs) = f x : map f xs
```

Our first relational property is that `map` preserves the length inequality when applied to two different lists, expressed as a *relational signature*:

```
relational map ˜ map :: (Int → Int) → [Int] → [Int]
                      ˜ (Int → Int) → [Int] → [Int]
  | ∀f1 ∼ f2. (true ⇒ true) ⇒ ∀xs1 ∼ xs2. len xs1 ≤ len xs2
  ⇒ len (r1 f1 xs1) ≤ len (r2 f2 xs2)
```

where `len` is inductively defined to return the length of a list. Reading the relational signature from left to right, the `relational` keyword declares that a relational specification follows. Then, `map ˜ map` states that the property relates two runs of the `map` function. Next, we provide unary types of related expressions separated by a tilde. To keep our system simple (and reducible to RHOL Sect. 3.4), these types are monomorphic. So, here, we relate two runs of `map` on integers. The final part of the signature is the assertion that states the preservation of length inequality. The assertion is of the form $\forall \texttt{x1} \sim \texttt{x2}.\phi_x \Rightarrow \phi$ and contains one pair of quantifiers for each pair of arguments of the related functions. The first assumption $\forall$f1 $\sim$ f2. (true $\Rightarrow$ true) relates the pair of functions f1 and f2 and it is trivial, meaning that their input and output values can be arbitrarily related. Next is the non-trivial assumption $\forall$xs1 $\sim$ xs2. len xs1 $\leq$ len xs2 about xs1 and xs2. Under this condition, we prove len (r1 f1 xs1) $\leq$ len (r2 f2 xs2) where r1 and r2 are reserved variables for the left and right instances of the related expressions, which here are the two runs of map.

Automatic verification of the above relational assertion is very challenging. RELSTLC [10] is an automatic verifier that relies on synchronous rules and will fail to prove the above property. Since the assumption len xs1 $\leq$ len xs2 does not ensure that the length of the two input lists are equal, there is no guarantee that the two runs of map have the same syntactic structure thus, the synchronous rules of RELSTLC will fail to apply. RELSTLC would trivially prove a length preservation property for map that assumes equal length of the two input lists, but fails for inequality. Similarly, the synchronous rules of RHOL [4] will fail to apply, since the input lists do not have the same structure. However, it is still possible to complete the proof in RHOL using asynchronous rules. Concretely, one can first case split on the left list and, at each case, case split on the right list, and at all the four cases evoke higher-order logic to prove the property.

OBRA adopts this exhaustive case split approach as the default synchronous rule and is able to prove the map property. Concretely, the T-CASE rule of Fig. 4 of Sect. 3 will generate four cases for all the structure combinations of the two input lists. Thus, our system is more general than RELSTLC, and still algorithmic.

Hence, OBRA verifies the map property by case splitting on all combinations of the input list structure. This information alone is not enough to understand why the property holds and, more importantly, how to repair a potentially failing proof. To gain understanding and repair capabilities, OBRA generates a unary proof term that can be checked by LIQUID HASKELL and inspected by the user.

2.2 Unary Verification of Relational Properties

As evidence that the map~map property holds, OBRA automatically generates a unary theorem, named mapRmap with its proof term. Using LIQUID HASKELL as a theorem prover [24], the theorem is encoded as a refinement type of the mapRmap function and its proof as the body definition of mapRmap.

Relational to Unary Specification Below is the generated unary theorem mapRmap.

```
mapRmap :: f1:(Int → Int) → f2:(Int → Int)
        → f1f2:(x1:Int → x2:Int → x1x2:() → ())
        → xs1:[Int] → xs2:[Int] → xs1xs2:{len xs1 ≤ len xs2}
        → {len (map f1 xs1) ≤ len (map f2 xs2)}
```

In general, for a relational assertion $\forall$x1 $\sim$ x2.$\phi_x \Rightarrow \phi$, OBRA will generate three arguments. The first two arguments are the quantification binders x1 and x2 that turn the universal quantification of the relational assertion into a lambda abstraction in the classic "propositions as types" [27] style. The third argument

captures the assumption ϕ_x, it is named as the combination of the names of the two quantified variables, *i.e.* `x1x2`, and we call it *relational argument.* The type of the relational argument depends on the types of the arguments it relates. For example, in the refinement type of `mapRmap`, the relational argument for the list arguments `xs1` and `xs2` is `xs1xs2:{len xs1 ≤ len xs2}` , which is a shorthand for `{() | len xs1 ≤ len xs2}` . The relational argument for the function arguments `f1` and `f2` is itself a function. In general, relations on non functional arguments are captured by a refined unit type. Relations on functional arguments are captured by a function that has three arguments, two for the arguments of the related functions and one for the relation between them. The generation of the unary theorem proceeds until it reaches the non-quantified base case of the relational assertion, which is encoded as a refined unit type. Note that, this encoding of the relational assertion as a unary type eliminates all the relational quantifiers, thus the derived refinement type belongs in the decidable logic of LIQUID HASKELL. The relational to unary translation is formalized in Sect. 3.4.
The Unary Proof Term Next, let's see how one can prove the `mapRmap` property. The below HASKELL definition gets accepted by LIQUID HASKELL, *i.e.* providing a proof of the `mapRmap` property.

```
mapRmap f1 f2 f1f2 []     []     xs1xs2 = ()
mapRmap f1 f2 f1f2 []     (x:xs) xs1xs2 = () ? map f2 xs
mapRmap f1 f2 f1f2 (x:xs) []     xs1xs2 = ()
mapRmap f1 f2 f1f2 (x:xs) (y:ys) xs1xs2 = mapRmap f1 f2 f1f2 xs ys ()

(?) :: x:a → b → { v:a | x == v }
x ? _ = x
```

We split four cases comparing the structure of the input lists. In the first case both lists are empty, because LIQUID HASKELL knows that `map f [] = []` and `len [] = 0`, the property holds trivially. Trivial proofs are encoded using the `()` value and are automated using LIQUID HASKELL's SMT-logic and restricted function unfolding (via the PLE algorithm [26]). In the second case we need to prove `0 ≤ len (map f2 (x:xs))` . There, the missing piece for the proof is that the length of `map f2 xs` is non-negative and to complete the proof we need to write the expression `map f2 xs` and let LIQUID HASKELL infer its properties. This help is provided by the question mark operator `?` which strengthens the proof environment. The third case is trivial, since the assumption `len (x:xs) ≤ len []` is a contradiction under which the property holds. The last case is completed by an inductive call to `mapRmap`, with a trivial proof as its last argument. Thus the proof is complete.
The Generated Proof Term OBRA generates a proof term for the `mapRmap` theorem that is similar to the above. Before presenting the proof term, we need to emphasize an integral feature of how refinement type checking operates. Unlike type theory style theorem provers, LIQUID HASKELL is an SMT-based verifier, meaning that the proof term will type check, if the SMT is given enough information to decide the property. Taking this into account, OBRA's automatically

generated terms collect all the information gathered by the two related terms, even if they are not required to show the validity of the property.

The generated proof term for mapRmap is verbose, but has the same structure and contains the same information as the previous, user-defined proof.

```
mapRmap f1 f2 f1f2 xs1 xs2 xs1xs2
  = case xs1 of
      [] → case xs2 of
        [] → () ? [] ? []
        x2 : xs2 → () ? [] ? (f2 x2 : map f2 xs2)
      x1 : xs1 → case xs2 of
        [] → () ? (f1 x1 : map f1 xs1) ? []
        x2 : xs2 →
          (\x1 x2 x1x2 x3 x4 x3x4 → () ? x1x2 ? x3x4 ? (x1:x3) ? (x2:x4))
          (f1 x1) (f2 x2) (f1f2 x1 x2 (() ? x1 ? x2))
          (map f1 xs1) (map f2 xs2)
          (mapRmap f1 f2 f1f2 xs1 xs2 (() ? xs1 ? xs2))
```

The proof case splits on the four potential structures of the input lists. In the first three cases, OBRA ensures that all the subexpressions that appear in the related expressions, *e.g.* `f2 x2:map f2 xs`, `[]`, *etc.*., appear in the proof. In the last case, generated by the rule T-App of Fig. 3, a lambda abstraction strengthens the proof environment with both the higher-order relational argument and the inductive hypothesis, both fully applied. The proof term is machine generated, thus it is verbose, but it is validated by Liquid Haskell. The complete generation rules are presented in Sect. 3 and follow the program product method of [8].

2.3 Oracle-Based Proofs

In many cases (5 out of the 12 benchmarks in Table 1), synchronous rules are not sufficient to prove the relational property. This happens when the two related programs have different control flows. For example, let's compare `map` to `filter`:

```
filter :: (a → Bool) → [a] → [a]
filter _ []     = []
filter f (x:xs) = if f x then x : filter f xs else filter f xs
```

Now we can revisit the relational property of `map` and `filter`, from Sect. 1:

```
relational filter ~ map :: (Int → Bool) → [Int] → [Int]
        ~ (Int → Int) → [Int] → [Int]
        | ∀f1 ∼ f2. (true ⇒ true) ⇒ ∀xs1 ∼ xs2. len xs1 ≤ len xs2
        ⇒ len (r1 f1 xs1) ≤ len (r2 f2 xs2)
```

The above property of length inequality preservation holds, but its proof is not possible using only synchronous rules. Thus, OBRA will translate the relational signature to a refinement type that is equivalent to the relational property, and will also provide an inhabitant of this type that is "incomplete" because the inductive step is proved by calling the below lemma `oblig`:

```
oblig :: f1:(Int → Bool) → f2:(Int → Int) → (Int → Int → () → ())
       → x1:Int → xs1:[Int] → x2:Int → xs2:[Int]
       → xs1xs2:{len (x1:xs1) ≤ len (x2:xs2)}
       → {len (filter f1 (x1:xs1)) ≤ len (map f2 (x2:xs2))}
```

The generated proof term is similar to the `mapRmap` proof term in that it also has four cases and the three cases follow the same pattern. The difference is that in the last case, *i.e.* when both lists are non-empty, the structure of the `filter` and `map` expressions is different thus no synchronous rule can be applied. In this case (rule T-OBL of Fig. 4), OBRA generates a call to the `oblig` lemma.

Generation of Obligations The obligation is an expression that proves the missing requirement. In our example, an expression that proves that `len (filter f1 (x1:xs1)) ≤ len (map f2 (x2:xs2))` . This proof can be done in the current proving environment, *i.e.* using all the arguments of `filterRmap`, the inductive hypothesis, and the variables introduced by the case splitting. For user interactivity, instead of requiring an in-place proof, OBRA captures this current proving environment as arguments of the obligation lemma and asks the user to complete the proof, without the need to understand the complete proof term.

In this example, the user can complete the proof manually, as follows:

```
oblig f1 f2 f1f2 x1 xs1 x2 xs2 xs1xs2 =
  if f1 x1 then filterRmap f1 f2 f1f2 xs1 xs2 ()
           else filterRmap f1 f2 f1f2 xs1 xs2 ()
```

The body of the obligation handles the structural difference between `filter` and `map`, namely the branching that is only present in `filter`. In the case of the branching when `f1 x1` is true, both `filter` and `map` append a new element to the recursive results. Hence, the property is reduced to the comparison between lengths `len (filter f1 xs1) ≤ len (map f2 xs2)` . This holds by the inductive hypothesis `filterRmap` which concludes the proof. In the other case, only `map` appends the element to the list, while `filter` skips the element for which `f1 x1` is false. The same inductive hypothesis can be used here to show that `len (filter f1 xs1) ≤ len (map f2 xs2)` and thus `len (filter f1 xs1) ≤ len (map f2 xs2) + 1` which is the desired property in the second case.

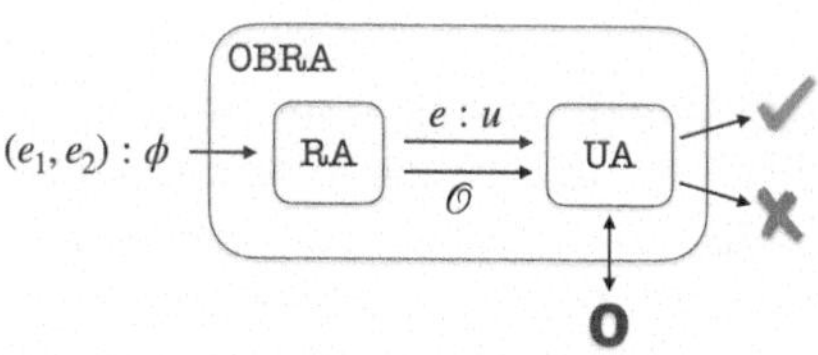

Fig. 1. OBRA workflow. `RA` is relational analysis, `UA` is unary refinement type checking, *e.g.* LIQUID HASKELL, and `O` is the oracle, *e.g.* a user.

2.4 OBRA Workflow

Figure 1 presents the workflow of OBRA that given a pair of expressions $e_1 \sim e_2$ and a relational property ϕ interacts with an oracle to decide if the pair satisfies ϕ. First, OBRA is using a relational analysis system (RA; which is essentially the synchronous subset of RHOL) to generate a unary refinement type u, a unary proof term e, and a set of proof obligations O. Second, a unary analysis system (UA; *e.g.* Liquid Haskell) is used to check that e has type u. In this step also, OBRA interacts with the oracle to provide inhabitants for the proof obligations O. The final result of OBRA is the result of UA.

The translation is designed so that e has type u, so when the proof obligations O are empty, *i.e.* in synchronous proofs, OBRA is automatic.

In Sect. 3.4 we show that if the oracle has the proof power of higher-order logic, then OBRA is equivalent to RHOL. Yet, compared to RHOL, OBRA is algorithmic and reduces to a quantifier-free, unary refinement type checking. We claim that this reduction generates proof obligations that are simpler than the original relational property and thus, the proof effort is reduced. To evaluate this claim, in Sect. 4, we use OBRA to prove 12 relational properties and conclude that OBRA can automatically prove 58% of them and reduces the proof effort by 36% in lines of code compared to the unary proofs of the same properties.

3 Formalization of OBRA

Here, we formalize OBRA as the core calculus λ_{OBRA} that is *relational*, *synchronous*, *bidirectional*, and *SMT-aided.* Section 3.1 and Sect. 3.2 respectively present the syntax and typing rules of λ_{OBRA}. In Sect. 3.3 we translate λ_{OBRA} to a unary, refined system. Finally, in Sect. 3.4 we prove that λ_{OBRA} is equivalent to the sound RHOL.

3.1 Syntax

Figure 2 introduces the syntax of λ_{OBRA}. We define expressions, unrefined and refined types, assertions, and five environments. We use magenta color for elements of the language that only appear in the translation, described in Sect. 3.3.

Constants in λ_{OBRA} include booleans, unit, integers and operators for arithmetic $(+, -, *, /)$, equality $(=)$, and boolean logic ($\wedge$ and $\neg$). Finally, constants include the type indexed list constructors $\mathtt{nil}_t$ and $\mathtt{cons}_t$.

Expressions include constants and variables, including the special relational variables $\mathbf{r_1}$ and $\mathbf{r_2}$ and variables o that capture proof obligations. Expressions are in A-normal form (ANF), *i.e.* function arguments and branching conditions must be variables. Recursive and lambda functions are type annotated.

Types of λ_{OBRA} are either unrefined or refined. *Unrefined types* t, s can either be the base types b, that is, unit, boolean, integer, and list or function types. In *refined types* u, v the base type $b\{\nu : p\}$ is refined by a predicate p that comes from the language of expressions and in the function type $x : u_x \rightarrow u$ the argument

$$
\begin{array}{rl}
\textit{Constants} & c ::= \mathit{true} \mid \mathit{false} \mid () \mid i \in \mathbb{Z} \mid +,-,*,/,=,\wedge,\neg \mid \mathtt{nil}_t \mid \mathtt{cons}_t \\
\textit{Expressions} & e, p ::= c \mid x, f, o, \mathbf{r_1}, \mathbf{r_2} \in V \mid \mathtt{let}\ x = e\ \mathtt{in}\ e \mid \mathtt{rec}\ f = (\lambda x.e) : t \\
& \quad \mid \lambda x : t.e \mid e\ x \mid \mathtt{if}\ x\ \mathtt{then}\ e\ \mathtt{else}\ e \mid \mathtt{case}\ x\ \{\mathtt{nil} \mapsto e; \mathtt{cons}\ x\ x \mapsto e\} \\
\textit{Base types} & b ::= \mathtt{unit} \mid \mathtt{bool} \mid \mathtt{int} \mid \mathtt{list}\ t \\
\textit{Unrefined types} & t, s ::= b \mid t \to t \\
\textit{Refined types} & u, v ::= b\{\nu : p\} \mid x : u \to u \\
\textit{Assertion} & \phi, \psi ::= p \mid \forall x_1 : t_1, x_2 : t_2 . \phi \Rightarrow \phi \\
\textbf{\textit{Environments}} & \\
\textit{Typing} & \Gamma ::= \emptyset \mid \Gamma; x : t \\
\textit{Relational} & \Phi ::= \emptyset \mid \Phi; x_1 \sim x_2 : t_1 \sim t_2 \mid \phi \\
\textit{Refined} & \mathrm{R} ::= \emptyset \mid \mathrm{R}; x : u \\
\textit{Translation} & \mathrm{T} ::= \emptyset \mid \mathrm{T}; x_1 \sim x_2 \rightsquigarrow x \\
\textit{Obligation} & \mathrm{O} ::= \emptyset \mid \mathrm{O}; \mathrm{R} \vdash o : u
\end{array}
$$

Fig. 2. Syntax of λ_{OBRA}.

is bound by a variable x that is used in the refinement of the return type u. *Notation:* We use an unrefined type to denote the corresponding refined type with only *true* refinements, *e.g.* unit is shorthand for $\mathtt{unit}\{\nu : \mathit{true}\}$.

Assertions ϕ, ψ are logical predicates that encode relational properties. As such, they are always quantified by two typed variables x_1, x_2 that represent the two sides of the relation. The body of the assertion is an implication and its base case a boolean expression. Since two expressions can be related by two unary types and an assertion, we call the triplet $t_1 \sim t_2 \mid \phi$ a *relational type. Notation:* We write $\forall x_1 x_2 . \phi \Rightarrow \psi$ for $\forall x_1 : t_1 x_2 : t_2 . \phi \Rightarrow \psi$ when the types are implied.

λ_{OBRA} has five *environments.* The typing environment Γ binds variables to unrefined types $x : t$ and the refined environment R binds variables to refined types $x : u$. The relational environment Φ binds the pair of variables $x_1 \sim x_2$ to their relational type, while the translation environment T binds pairs of variables to a new variable, that captures their relation. Finally, the obligation environment O collects a set of obligations, each of which is a unary typing judgment.

Synthesis and Translation $\boxed{\Gamma \mid \Phi \mid \mathrm{T} \vdash e_1 \sim e_2 \Rightarrow t_1 \sim t_2 \mid \phi + e : u \mid \mathrm{O}}$

$$
\frac{\mathrm{constTy}(c_1) = t_1 \quad \mathrm{constTy}(c_2) = t_2 \quad \mathrm{constPr}(t_1, t_2, \mathbf{r_1} = c_1 \wedge \mathbf{r_2} = c_2) = \phi}{\Gamma \mid \Phi \mid \mathrm{T} \vdash c_1 \sim c_2 \Rightarrow t_1 \sim t_2 \mid \phi + \mathrm{constTr}(t_1, t_2) : \mathbf{trTy}(t_1, t_2) \mid \emptyset}\ \textsc{T-Const}
$$

$$
\frac{x_1 \sim x_2 : t_1 \sim t_2 \mid \phi \in \Phi \quad x_1 \sim x_2 \rightsquigarrow x \in \mathrm{T}}{\Gamma \mid \Phi \mid \mathrm{T} \vdash x_1 \sim x_2 \Rightarrow t_1 \sim t_2 \mid \phi + x : \lceil \phi \rceil [x_1 / \mathbf{r_1}][x_2 / \mathbf{r_2}] \mid \emptyset}\ \textsc{T-Var}
$$

$$
\frac{\begin{array}{c}\Gamma \mid \Phi \mid \mathrm{T} \vdash x_1 \sim x_2 \Leftarrow s_1 \sim s_2 \mid \psi[\mathbf{r_1}/x_1][\mathbf{r_2}/x_2] + e_t : u_t \mid \mathrm{O}_2 \\ t_t \doteq x_1 : s_1 \to x_2 : s_2 \to x_t : u_t \to u \quad \phi' \doteq \phi[\mathbf{r_1}\ x_1 / \mathbf{r_1}][\mathbf{r_2}\ x_2 / \mathbf{r_2}] \\ \Gamma \mid \Phi \mid \mathrm{T} \vdash e_1 \sim e_2 \Rightarrow s_1 \to t_1 \sim s_2 \to t_2 \mid \forall x_1 : s_1, x_2 : s_2 . \psi \Rightarrow \phi' + e : t_t \mid \mathrm{O}_1\end{array}}{\Gamma \mid \Phi \mid \mathrm{T} \vdash e_1\ x_1 \sim e_2\ x_2 \Rightarrow t_1 \sim t_2 \mid \phi + e\ x_1\ x_2\ e_t : u \mid \mathrm{O}_1, \mathrm{O}_2}\ \textsc{T-App}
$$

Fig. 3. Relational typing synthesis and translation.

Checking and Translation $\boxed{\Gamma \,|\, \Phi \,|\, \mathrm{T} \vdash e_1 \sim e_2 \Leftarrow t_1 \sim t_2 \,|\, \phi + e{:}u \,|\, \mathrm{O}}$

$$\frac{\begin{array}{c}\Gamma; x_1{:}s_1; x_2{:}s_2 \,|\, \Phi; x_1 \sim x_2{:}\psi \,|\, \mathrm{T}; x_1 \sim x_2 \rightsquigarrow x \vdash e_1 \sim e_2 \Leftarrow t_1 \sim t_2 \,|\, \phi + e{:}u \,|\, \mathrm{O}\\ e_t \doteq \lambda x_1{:}s_1,\ x_2{:}s_2,\ x{:}\mathtt{trTy}(s_1,s_1).e \quad \phi' \doteq \phi[\mathbf{r_1}\ x_1/\mathbf{r_1}][\mathbf{r_2}\ x_2/\mathbf{r_2}]\\ u_t \doteq x_1{:}s_1 \to x_2{:}s_2 \to x{:}\lceil\psi[x_1/\mathbf{r_1}][x_2/\mathbf{r_2}]\rceil \to u\end{array}}{\Gamma \,|\, \Phi \,|\, \mathrm{T} \vdash \lambda x_1{:}s_1.e_1 \sim \lambda x_2{:}s_2.e_2 \Leftarrow s_1 \to t_1 \sim s_2 \to t_2 \,|\, \forall x_1 x_2.\psi \Rightarrow \phi' + e_t{:}u_t \,|\, \mathrm{O}}\ \textsc{T-Lam}$$

$$\frac{\begin{array}{c}t_1 = s_{x1} \to s_1 \qquad t_2 = s_{x2} \to s_2 \qquad \mathrm{Def}(f_1, x_1, e_1) \qquad \mathrm{Def}(f_2, x_2, e_2)\\ \Gamma_r \,|\, \Phi_r \,|\, \mathrm{T}_r \vdash e_1 \sim e_2 \Leftarrow s_1 \sim s_2 \,|\, \phi + e{:}u \,|\, \mathrm{O} \qquad \Gamma_r \doteq \Gamma; f_1{:}t_1; f_2{:}t_2; x_1{:}s_{x1}; x_2{:}s_{x2}\\ \phi_r \doteq \forall y_1, y_2.(|y_1|, |y_2|) < (|x_1|, |x_2|) \wedge \psi[y_1/x_1][y_2/x_2] \Rightarrow \phi\\ \Phi_r \doteq \Phi; f_1 \sim f_2{:}\phi_r; x_1 \sim x_2{:}s_{x1} \sim s_{x2} \,|\, \psi \qquad \mathrm{T}_r \doteq \mathrm{T}; f_1 \sim f_2 \rightsquigarrow f; x_1 \sim x_2 \rightsquigarrow x\\ e_r \doteq \mathtt{rec}\ f = (\lambda x_1{:}s_{x1}, x_2{:}s_{x2}, x{:}\mathtt{trTy}(s_{x1}, s_{x2}).e){:}t_r\\ t_r \doteq x_1{:}s_{x1} \to x_2{:}s_{x2} \to x{:}\lceil\phi[x_1/\mathbf{r_1}][x_2/\mathbf{r_2}]\rceil \to u\\ \phi_t \doteq \forall x_1{:}s_{x1}, x_2{:}s_{x2}.\psi \Rightarrow \phi[\mathbf{r_1}\ x_1/\mathbf{r_1}][\mathbf{r_2}\ x_2/\mathbf{r_2}]\end{array}}{\Gamma \,|\, \Psi \,|\, \mathrm{T} \vdash \mathtt{rec}\ f_1 = (\lambda x_1.e_1){:}t_1 \sim \mathtt{rec}\ f_2 = (\lambda x_2.e_2){:}t_2 \Leftarrow t_1 \sim t_2 \,|\, \phi_t + e_r{:}t_r \,|\, \mathrm{O}}\ \textsc{T-Rec}$$

$$\frac{\begin{array}{c}\Gamma \,|\, \Phi \,|\, \mathrm{T} \vdash e_{x1} \sim e_{x2} \Rightarrow s_1 \sim s_2 \,|\, \psi + e_x{:}u_x \,|\, \mathrm{O}_1 \qquad e_t \doteq \mathtt{let}\ (x_1, x_2, x) = (e_{x1}, e_{x2}, e_x)\ \mathtt{in}\ e\\ \Gamma; x_1{:}s_1; x_2{:}s_2 \,|\, \Phi; x_1 \sim x_2{:}s_1 \sim s_2 \,|\, \psi \,|\, \mathrm{T}; x_1 \sim x_2 \rightsquigarrow x \vdash e_1 \sim e_2 \Leftarrow t_1 \sim t_2 \,|\, \phi + e{:}u \,|\, \mathrm{O}_2\end{array}}{\Gamma \,|\, \Psi \,|\, \mathrm{T} \vdash \mathtt{let}\ x_1 = e_{x1}\ \mathtt{in}\ e_1 \sim \mathtt{let}\ x_2 = e_{x2}\ \mathtt{in}\ e_2 \Leftarrow t_1 \sim t_2 \,|\, \phi + e_t{:}u \,|\, \mathrm{O}_1, \mathrm{O}_2}\ \textsc{T-Let}$$

$$\frac{\begin{array}{c}\Gamma \,|\, \Phi \,|\, \mathrm{T} \vdash x_1 \sim x_2 \Rightarrow \mathtt{bool} \sim \mathtt{bool} \,|\, p + x{:}u_x \,|\, \mathrm{O}_x\\ \Gamma \,|\, \Phi; x_1 \sim x_2{:}\mathtt{bool} \sim \mathtt{bool} \,|\, p \wedge x_1 \wedge x_2 \,|\, \mathrm{T} \vdash e_{t1} \sim e_{t2} \Leftarrow t_1 \sim t_2 \,|\, \phi + e_{tt}{:}u \,|\, \mathrm{O}_{tt}\\ \Gamma \,|\, \Phi; x_1 \sim x_2{:}\mathtt{bool} \sim \mathtt{bool} \,|\, p \wedge x_1 \wedge \neg x_2 \,|\, \mathrm{T} \vdash e_{t1} \sim e_{f2} \Leftarrow t_1 \sim t_2 \,|\, \phi + e_{tf}{:}u \,|\, \mathrm{O}_{tf}\\ \Gamma \,|\, \Phi; x_1 \sim x_2{:}\mathtt{bool} \sim \mathtt{bool} \,|\, p \wedge \neg x_1 \wedge x_2 \,|\, \mathrm{T} \vdash e_{f1} \sim e_{t2} \Leftarrow t_1 \sim t_2 \,|\, \phi + e_{ft}{:}u \,|\, \mathrm{O}_{ft}\\ \Gamma \,|\, \Phi; x_1 \sim x_2{:}\mathtt{bool} \sim \mathtt{bool} \,|\, p \wedge \neg x_1 \wedge \neg x_2 \,|\, \mathrm{T} \vdash e_{f1} \sim e_{f2} \Leftarrow t_1 \sim t_2 \,|\, \phi + e_{ff}{:}u \,|\, \mathrm{O}_{ff}\\ e_t \doteq \mathtt{if}\ x_1\ \mathtt{then}\ (\mathtt{if}\ x_2\ \mathtt{then}\ e_{tt}\ \mathtt{else}\ e_{tf})\ \mathtt{else}\ (\mathtt{if}\ x_2\ \mathtt{then}\ e_{ft}\ \mathtt{else}\ e_{ff})\\ \mathrm{O} \doteq \mathrm{O}_x, \mathrm{O}_{tt}, \mathrm{O}_{tf}, \mathrm{O}_{ft}, \mathrm{O}_{ff}\end{array}}{\Gamma \,|\, \Phi \,|\, \mathrm{T} \vdash \mathtt{if}\ x_1\ \mathtt{then}\ e_{t1}\ \mathtt{else}\ e_{f1} \sim \mathtt{if}\ x_2\ \mathtt{then}\ e_{t2}\ \mathtt{else}\ e_{f2} \Leftarrow t_1 \sim t_2 \,|\, \phi + e_t{:}u \,|\, \mathrm{O}}\ \textsc{T-If}$$

$$\frac{\begin{array}{c}\Gamma \,|\, \Phi \,|\, \mathrm{T} \vdash x_1 \sim x_2 \Rightarrow \mathtt{list}\ s_1 \sim \mathtt{list}\ s_2 \,|\, p + e{:}\_ \,|\, \mathrm{O}_x\\ \Gamma_t \doteq \Gamma; y_1{:}s_1; y_2{:}s_1; z_1{:}\mathtt{list}\ s_1; z_2{:}\mathtt{list}\ s_2 \qquad \Phi_t \doteq \Phi; y_1 \sim y_2{:}\mathit{true}; z_1 \sim z_2{:}\mathit{true}\\ \mathrm{T}_t \doteq \mathrm{T}; y_1 \sim y_2 \rightsquigarrow y; z_1 \sim z_2 \rightsquigarrow z\\ \Gamma_t \,|\, \Phi_t; x_1 \sim x_2{:}p \wedge x_1 = \mathtt{nil} \wedge x_2 = \mathtt{nil} \,|\, \mathrm{T}_t \vdash e_{n1} \sim e_{n2} \Leftarrow t_1 \sim t_2 \,|\, \phi + e_{nn}{:}u \,|\, \mathrm{O}_{nn}\\ \Gamma_t \,|\, \Phi_t; x_1 \sim x_2{:}p \wedge x_1 = \mathtt{nil} \wedge x_2 = \mathtt{cons}\ y_2\ z_2 \,|\, \mathrm{T}_t \vdash e_{n1} \sim e_{c2} \Leftarrow t_1 \sim t_2 \,|\, \phi + e_{nc}{:}u \,|\, \mathrm{O}_{nc}\\ \Gamma_t \,|\, \Phi_t; x_1 \sim x_2{:}p \wedge x_1 = \mathtt{cons}\ y_1\ z_1 \wedge x_2 = \mathtt{nil} \,|\, \mathrm{T}_t \vdash e_{c1} \sim e_{n2} \Leftarrow t_1 \sim t_2 \,|\, \phi + e_{cn}{:}u \,|\, \mathrm{O}_{cn}\\ \Gamma_t \,|\, \Phi_t; x_1 \sim x_2{:}p \wedge x_1 = \mathtt{cons}\ y_1\ z_1 \wedge x_2 = \mathtt{cons}\ y_2\ z_2 \,|\, \mathrm{T}_t \vdash e_{c1} \sim e_{c2} \Leftarrow t_1 \sim t_2 \,|\, \phi + e_{cc}{:}u \,|\, \mathrm{O}_{cc}\\ e_t \doteq \mathtt{case}\ x_1\ \{\mathtt{nil} \mapsto e_{tn}; \mathtt{cons}\ y_1\ z_1 \mapsto e_{tc}\}\\ e_{tn} \doteq \mathtt{case}\ x_2\ \{\mathtt{nil} \mapsto e_{nn}; \mathtt{cons}\ y_2\ z_2 \mapsto e_{nc}\}\\ e_{tc} \doteq \mathtt{case}\ x_2\ \{\mathtt{nil} \mapsto e_{cn}; \mathtt{cons}\ y_2\ z_2 \mapsto e_{cc}\}\\ \mathrm{O} \doteq \mathrm{O}_x, \mathrm{O}_{nn}, \mathrm{O}_{nc}, \mathrm{O}_{cn}, \mathrm{O}_{cc}\end{array}}{\begin{array}{c}\Gamma \,|\, \Phi \,|\, \mathrm{T} \vdash \mathtt{case}\ x_1\ \{\mathtt{nil} \mapsto e_{n1}; \mathtt{cons}\ y_1\ z_1 \mapsto e_{c1}\}\\ \sim \mathtt{case}\ x_2\ \{\mathtt{nil} \mapsto e_{n2}; \mathtt{cons}\ y_2\ z_2 \mapsto e_{c2}\} \Leftarrow t_1 \sim t_2 \,|\, \phi + e_t{:}u \,|\, \mathrm{O}\end{array}}\ \textsc{T-Case}$$

$$\frac{\Gamma \,|\, \Phi \,|\, \mathrm{T} \vdash e_1 \sim e_2 \Rightarrow t_1 \sim t_2 \,|\, \psi + e{:}\_ \,|\, \mathrm{O} \quad \Gamma \,|\, \Phi \vdash t_1 \sim t_2 \,|\, \psi \prec: \phi}{\Gamma \,|\, \Phi \,|\, \mathrm{T} \vdash e_1 \sim e_2 \Leftarrow t_1 \sim t_2 \,|\, \phi + e{:}\lceil\phi\rceil[e_1/\mathbf{r_1}][e_2/\mathbf{r_2}] \,|\, \mathrm{O}}\ \textsc{T-Sub}$$

$$\frac{\text{no other rule applies} \qquad \Gamma \vdash e_1 : t_1 \qquad \Gamma \vdash e_2 : t_2 \qquad \text{fresh } o \qquad u = \lceil\phi[e_1/\mathbf{r_1}][e_2/\mathbf{r_2}]\rceil}{\Gamma \,|\, \Phi \,|\, \mathrm{T} \vdash e_1 \sim e_2 \Leftarrow t_1 \sim t_2 \,|\, \phi + o{:}u \,|\, \mathrm{O}; \lceil\Gamma; \Phi; \mathrm{T}\rceil \vdash o : u}\ \textsc{T-Obl}$$

Fig. 4. Relational typing checking and translation.

3.2 RA: Relational Algorithmic Typing

OBRA's main typing judgment $\Gamma \mid \Phi \mid \mathrm{T} \vdash e_1 \sim e_2 \Leftarrow t_1 \sim t_2 \mid \phi + e{:}u \mid \mathrm{O}$ checks that under the typing environment Γ and the relational environment Φ, the expressions $e_1 \sim e_2$ have, *resp.* types t_1 and t_2 and satisfy the relational property ϕ. The judgement further keeps track of the translation environment T to generate a unary expression e of refinement type u that is equivalent to the relational property ϕ, assuming the set of proof obligations O holds. For clarity of exposition, we separate the two functionalities of the judgements. Here, we describe the relational part of the judgement, in Sect. 3.3 we describe the translation part (marked with magenta color in the rules and for simplicity omitted in this subsection), and in Sect. 3.4 we combined them again to prove correctness of OBRA.

Figures 3 and 4 present the rules of OBRA which are a bidirectional and synchronous variant of RHOL [4]. If the translation is ignored, our rules comprise a subset of RHOL: a weakening rule as well as all synchronous (two-sided) rules. Our branching (rule T-IF) and pattern-matching (rule T-CASE) rules are modified to be more permissive. That is, the T-IF rule has 5 premises, one that derive the guard predicate p, and 4 that handle the four possible cases of the guard, unlike RHOL, where the cases of the guard should match. The same applies to the T-CASE rule that has 5 cases in OBRA and 3 cases in RHOL. This design choice allows us to type more programs while maintaining the system syntax-directed. Both rules are still derivable in RHOL.

Unlike RHOL, our rules are *bidirectional* [11], namely the typing judgment is split into two judgments: type synthesis $\Gamma \mid \Phi \vdash e_1 \sim e_2 \Rightarrow t_1 \sim t_2 \mid \phi$ in fig. 3 and typechecking $\Gamma \mid \Phi \vdash e_1 \sim e_2 \Leftarrow t_1 \sim t_2 \mid \phi$ in fig. 4. Both of the judgments establish that type $t_1 \sim t_2 \mid \phi$ can be assigned to a pair of expressions $e_1 \sim e_2$ under Γ and Φ. Our bidirectional system is in the spirit of unary refinement types [16], which enabled decidable checking of properties within quantifier-free logic of linear arithmetic and uninterpreted functions (QF-EUFLIA) [25].

The second property of our system is that it is *synchronous*. All checking and synthesis rules of our system assume the same syntactic structure of expressions on the left- and right-hand side, *e.g.* it is possible to relate two variables or two lambda-expressions, but not a lambda to a variable.

Relational Subtyping Fig. 5 describes relational subtyping. Informally, the judgment $\Gamma \mid \Phi \vdash t_1 \sim t_2 \mid \psi \prec: \phi$ states that the relational type $t_1 \sim t_2 \mid \phi$ is less specific than the type $t_1 \sim t_2 \mid \psi$, *i.e.* two expressions related by $t_1 \sim t_2 \mid \psi$ could also be related by $t_1 \sim t_2 \mid \phi$ with some loss of information.

Rule S-BASE applies to base types related by quantification-free predicates p_1 and p_2. In the premise, an SMT-automated procedure checks that the predicate p_1 implies p_2 under the quantifier-free interpretation of the relational environment Φ. To get this interpretation, we conjunct all the predicates of the base types in Φ, after substituting the aliases $\mathbf{r_1}$ and $\mathbf{r_2}$ with the variables x_1 and x_2:

$$(\!|\Phi|\!) \doteq \bigwedge \{ (\!| p[x_1/\mathbf{r_1}][x_2/\mathbf{r_2}] |\!) \mid x_1 \sim x_2 : b_1 \sim b_2 \mid p \in \Phi \}$$

Subtyping $\boxed{\Gamma \mid \Phi \vdash t_1 \sim t_2 \mid \psi \prec: \phi}$

$$\frac{\mathsf{SmtValid}((\!|\Phi|\!) \Rightarrow (\!|p_1|\!) \Rightarrow (\!|p_2|\!))}{\Gamma \mid \Phi \vdash b_1 \sim b_2 \mid p_1 \prec: p_2}\text{S-BASE}$$

$$\frac{\begin{array}{c}\Gamma \mid \Phi \vdash t_{x1} \sim t_{x2} \mid \phi_x[\mathbf{r_1}/x_1][\mathbf{r_2}/x_2] \prec: \psi_x[\mathbf{r_1}/x_1][\mathbf{r_2}/x_2] \\ \Gamma; x_1 : t_{x1}; x_2 : t_{x2} \mid \Phi; x_1 \sim x_2 : \phi_x \vdash t_1 \sim t_2 \mid \psi \prec: \phi\end{array}}{\begin{array}{r}\Gamma \mid \Phi \vdash x_1 : t_{x1} \to t_1 \sim x_2 : t_{x2} \to t_2 \mid \forall x_1 : t_{x1}, x_2 : t_{x2}. \psi_x \Rightarrow \psi[\mathbf{r_1}\ x_1/\mathbf{r_1}][\mathbf{r_2}\ x_2/\mathbf{r_2}] \\ \prec: \forall x_1 : t_{x1}, x_2 : t_{x2}. \phi_x \Rightarrow \phi[\mathbf{r_1}\ x_1/\mathbf{r_1}][\mathbf{r_2}\ x_2/\mathbf{r_2}]\end{array}}\text{S-FUN}$$

Fig. 5. Relational Subtyping.

To ensure SMT-decidable implication checking, we further use a logical embedding for the predicates that substitutes the functions and the recursive definitions with uninterpreted functions and is a homomorphism for all other cases:

$$(\!|\lambda x : t.e|\!) \doteq f \quad (\!|\texttt{rec}\ f = (\lambda x.e) : t|\!) \doteq f \quad (\!|e\ x|\!) \doteq (\!|e|\!)\ x \quad \ldots$$

Rule S-FUN follows the contravariant behavior of function types, where the relational variables $\mathbf{r_1}$ and $\mathbf{r_2}$ are substituted to capture the related types.
Relational Type Synthesis Fig. 3 summarizes the rules of relational type synthesis. Rule T-VAR fetches the relation between the variables from the relational environment and rule T-APP handles function application. Rule T-CONST produces a relational type for two constants of compatible types. The function constTy returns the type of a constant. To both check the type compatibility of the constants and generate the relational predicate the T-CONST rule uses the partial function constPr that is defined as follows:

$$\begin{aligned}\text{constPr}(b_1, b_2, p) &\doteq p \\ \text{constPr}(t_{x1} \to t_1, t_{x2} \to t_2, p) &\doteq \forall x_1 x_2.\text{constPr}(t_{x1}, t_{x2}, \mathit{true}) \Rightarrow \text{constPr}(t_1, t_2, p)\end{aligned}$$

For two base types, constPr produces a trivial predicate $\mathbf{r_1} = c_1 \wedge \mathbf{r_2} = c_2$ that says that the constants are equal to themselves. For a pair of function types, constPr generates fresh variables x_1, x_2 to bind the arguments and inductively calls itself on the argument types with the predicate *true*. In the return types of the inductive call the predicate p is unchanged. When the two types do not have the same structure, the function is undefined, thus the T-CONST rule fails.
Relational Type Checking Fig. 4 presents the type checking mode of the system. Rule T-LAM validates a pair of functions against the relation $\forall x_1 x_2.\psi \Rightarrow \phi$. We propagate ϕ to a checking judgment between the bodies e_1 and e_2 while extending the environments Γ and Φ with the assumptions about the arguments. In a similar manner, rule T-REC handles definitions of recursive functions f_1 and f_2. We add f_1 and f_2 to the typing environment and extend Φ with a relational inductive hypothesis $f_1 \sim f_2 \mid \forall x_1 x_2.\psi \Rightarrow \phi$. For brevity, we omit the respective types $s_1 \to t_1$ and $s_2 \to t_2$ of f_1 and f_2 from the full syntax of relational typing. As in RHOL, the rule requires that the recursive functions terminate using the predicate Def that verifies that the function's domain is an inductive type or an integer and that the recursive call is made on a smaller argument.

Rule T-IF analyses synchronous branching on x_1 and x_2 in the two compared programs respectively. There are four possible scenarios: conditions in both programs pass, only the condition on the left passes while the right one fails, only the right condition passes, and both conditions fail. In each of the cases, the rule preserves any additional relation p that was known about x_1 and x_2 prior to branching. All in all, the rule has five premises, the first of which is used to synthesize p. In the other four premises, the rule extends Φ with an assumption about x_1 and x_2 in which p gets strengthened by the (un)satisfied branching conditions. Then, the rule contraposes the branches of the two programs according to the triggered conditions. Finally, it checks that all four resulting configurations conform to the relation ϕ. The premises of the rule T-CASE comprise a very similar cross-product, but on the list constructors `nil` and `cons` instead of the booleans *true* and *false*. In the premises that correspond to the matching of pattern `cons` y_1 z_1 (or *resp.* `cons` y_2 z_2), the binders for the head y_1 (*resp.* y_2) and the tail z_1 (*resp.* z_2) of the list are added to the typing environment Γ.

Rule T-LET compares two let-expressions and rule T-SUB ascribes $t_1 \sim t_2 \mid \phi$ to e_1 and e_2 as long as ϕ subsumes the relation ψ, produced by synthesis.

Finally, rule T-OBL is used when no other rule applies and its only premises $\Gamma \vdash e_1 : t_1$ and $\Gamma \vdash e_2 : t_2$ require that the expressions have the correct unrefined types. Using relational type checking alone, *i.e.* while ignoring the translation, this rule is not correct, since the assertion ϕ is totally ignored. Essentially, reaching this rule means that the relational rules of OBRA failed and an oracle, called via the translation mechanism, is needed to prove the relational property.

3.3 OB: Oracle-Based Translation

Now, we revisit the OBRA judgment $\Gamma \mid \Phi \mid \mathrm{T} \vdash e_1 \sim e_2 \Leftarrow t_1 \sim t_2 \mid \phi + e : u \mid \mathrm{O}$ with a focus on the magenta translation-related parts. Intuitively (as formalized in Sect. 3.4), the judgement generates an expression e, a refinement type u, and a set of obligations O; the expression e has type u and the obligations O are satisfiable *if and only if* the expressions $e_1 \sim e_2$ satisfy the relational predicate ϕ. The output e, also known as *program product* [8], combines e_1 and e_2 into a common control flow that simulates the simultaneous execution of the two programs. Similarly, we produce a proof of the relational property that is sensitive to mutual branching and case-splitting in the compared expressions.

The crux of the translation is the rule T-OBL. When nothing else can be done, T-OBL generates a refinement type u that translates the relational predicate ϕ. To turn assertions into refinement types, we follow [26,27] and turn forall-quantification and implication into functional arguments, and boolean predicates into refinements of the unit type, using the function $\lceil \phi \rceil$:

$$\lceil p \rceil \doteq \mathtt{unit}\{\nu{:}p\} \quad \lceil \forall x_1{:}t_1, x_2{:}t_2.\psi \Rightarrow \phi \rceil \doteq x_1{:}t_1 \rightarrow x_2{:}t_2 \rightarrow x{:}\lceil \psi \rceil \rightarrow \lceil \phi \rceil$$

The translated refinement type is added to the set of obligations O with a fresh obligation variable o under a refinement environment that captures the current state of the translation. The definition of o should be later (Fig. 6) guessed by the oracle. To capture the state of the translation, we use the operator $\lceil \Gamma; \Phi; \mathrm{T} \rceil$ that returns a refinement type environment as follows:

$$\lceil \Gamma; \Phi; \mathrm{T} \rceil \doteq \{\, x_1 : t_1, x_2 : t_2, x : \lceil \phi[x_1/\mathbf{r_1}][x_2/\mathbf{r_2}] \rceil \mid x_1 \sim x_2 \rightsquigarrow x \in \mathrm{T}, \\ x_1 : t_1 \in \Gamma, x_2 : t_2 \in \Gamma, x_1 \sim x_2 : \phi \in \Phi \}$$

Namely, for each binding $x_1 \sim x_2 \rightsquigarrow x$ in the translation environment T, we add the bindings $x_1 : t_1, x_2 : t_2, x : \lceil \phi \rceil$ to the refinement type environment, where the types of the variables x_1 and x_2 are taken from the typing environment Γ and the relation between them from the relational environment Φ.

In the implementation, the refinement type environment is turned into arguments of the proof term e. For example, in the `filterRmap` example of Sect. 2.3, the proof function `obligation` contains all the relevant arguments in the proof environment, while relational arguments with true refinements are omitted.

Translation Rules Figs. 3 and 4 present the the translation rules, which are combined with the relational typing.

Rule T-VAR looks up the translated expression from the context—that exactly translates a pair of variables to a unary variable—and generates the translated type by lifting the relational property to a unary type.

Rule T-CONST produces a proof term $\mathrm{constTr}(t_1, t_2)$ that proves ϕ. By the definition of constPr, ϕ is equivalent to $\mathbf{r_1} = c_1 \wedge \mathbf{r_2} = c_2$ which trivially holds when $\mathbf{r_1}$ is in fact c_1 and $\mathbf{r_2}$ is c_2. However, to be compatible with the rest of the translation, we generate a proof via $\mathrm{constTr}(t_1, t_2)$:

$$\begin{aligned} \mathrm{constTr}(b_1, b_2) &\doteq () \\ \mathrm{constTr}(t_{x_1} \to t_1, t_{x_2} \to t_2) &\doteq \lambda x_1 : t_{x_1}, x_2 : t_{x_2}, x : \mathtt{trTy}(t_{x_1}, t_{x_2}).\mathrm{constTr}(t_1, t_2) \\ \mathtt{trTy}(b_1, b_2) &\doteq \mathtt{unit} \\ \mathtt{trTy}(t_{x_1} \to t_1, t_{x_2} \to t_2) &\doteq t_{x_1} \to t_{x_2} \to \mathtt{trTy}(t_{x_1}, t_{x_2}) \to \mathtt{trTy}(t_1, t_2) \end{aligned}$$

The function constTr is defined inductively. For constants of base types, it returns a trivial unit proof. Constants of function types are translated to lambda expressions with three arguments: the initial x_1 and x_2, and the relational argument x that carries the proof of a relational precondition about x_1 and x_2. The unary type u of the proof terms is constructed by `trTy` which is defined inductively and converts two base types into a unit. Two function types become a function type with three arguments: the initial x_1 and x_2, plus their relation.

Rule T-APP translates function applications and is using a third argument e_t that relates the two arguments. Dually, rule T-LAM handles lambda-abstractions and it composes two lambda functions into a new lambda with three arguments. Rule T-REC translates the recursive functions f_1 and f_2 to a new recursive function f and it adds the fresh symbol f to the relational context. Similarly, rules T-LET, T-IF, and T-CASE translate let-bindings, if-then-else, and case-expression respectively, by combining the two expressions into a single expression and generating the proof of the relation between them. Finally, rule T-SUB propagates the translated proof to the weaker property.

In short, the judgement $\Gamma \mid \Phi \mid \mathrm{T} \vdash e_1 \sim e_2 \Leftarrow t_1 \sim t_2 \mid \phi + c : u \mid \mathrm{O}$ turns the property ϕ into a unary refined type u, following "propositions as types" [27], and generates a proof term e that proves ϕ. The term e may be open because it can contain some obligation variables that should be guessed by an oracle.

3.4 Metatheory of OBRA

We combine the type checking rules of Sect. 3.2 with the translation of Sect. 3.3 to design OBRA as an oracle-based, relational, algorithmic type checker that behaves as RHOL. Here, we describe OBRA and claim that it is equivalent to RHOL (Theorem 1), the proofs are in the supplementary material.

$$\frac{}{\emptyset \dashv \emptyset}\text{O-EMP} \qquad \frac{\mathrm{O} \dashv \theta \qquad \exists e_o.\mathrm{R} \vdash e_o : u}{\mathrm{O}; \mathrm{R} \vdash o : u \dashv \theta, [e_o/o]}\text{O-VAR}$$

$$\frac{\Gamma \,|\, \Phi \,|\, \mathrm{T}(\Phi) \vdash e_1 \sim e_2 \Leftarrow t_1 \sim t_2 \,|\, \phi + e{:}u \,|\, \mathrm{O} \qquad \mathrm{O} \dashv \theta \qquad \lceil \Gamma; \Phi \rceil \vdash \theta \cdot e : u}{\Gamma \,|\, \Phi \vdash_{\mathrm{OBRA}} e_1 \sim e_2 : t_1 \sim t_2 \,|\, \phi}\text{T-OBRA}$$

Fig. 6. OBRA type checking.

Figure 6 presents the rule that designs the OBRA system. To check that the expressions $e_1 \sim e_2$ satisfy the relational refinement type $t_1 \sim t_2 \mid \phi$, OBRA has only one rule, T-OBRA, that performs three steps. First, it is using the bidirectional translation to generate the translated expression e, the unary type u, and the environment of proof obligations O. Next, it checks that the proof obligations O are satisfiable. The relation $\mathrm{O} \dashv \theta$ checks that the proof obligations O are satisfiable and returns a model, *i.e.* a substitution θ that maps each proof obligation variable to a witness expression: $\theta ::= \emptyset \mid \theta, [e/o]$. Satisfiability of O is defined by the two inductive rules O-EMP and O-VAR that ensure, using unary refinement typing, that the model θ is indeed a valid witness. The final check ensures that the expression $\theta \cdot e$, *i.e.* the expression e under the substitution θ, indeed has the translated type u under the typing environment Γ refined with the relational predicates in Φ. In the absence of a translation environment, we turn the relational environment into a refined environment as follows:

$$\lceil \Gamma; \Phi \rceil \doteq \lceil \Gamma; \Phi; \mathrm{T}(\Phi) \rceil \qquad \mathrm{T}(\Phi) \doteq \{x_1 \sim x_2 \rightsquigarrow x \mid x_1 \sim x_2 {:} \phi \in \Phi, \text{fresh } x\}$$

Equivalence with RHOL Soundness of OBRA is shown by equivalence to RHOL, a relational type system that is sound and equivalent to HOL [4].

Let $\Gamma \mid \Psi \vdash_{\mathrm{RHOL}} e_1 \sim e_2 : t_1 \sim t_2 \mid \phi$ be the RHOL judgment. The judgment is very similar to OBRA apart from that it is keeping track of an assertion environment Ψ instead of our relational environment Φ. We define the operation $\lfloor \cdot \rfloor$ that converts a relational environment to a set of assertions:

$$\lfloor \emptyset \rfloor \doteq \emptyset \qquad \lfloor \Phi; x_1 \sim x_2 {:} \phi \rfloor \doteq \lfloor \Phi \rfloor; \phi[x_1/\mathbf{r_1}][x_2/\mathbf{r_2}]$$

With this, we state soundness and completeness of OBRA *w.r.t.* RHOL.

Theorem 1. OBRA *is equivalent to* RHOL*:*

1. *If* $\Gamma \mid \Phi \vdash_{\text{OBRA}} e_1 \sim e_2 : t_1 \sim t_2 \mid \phi$, *then* $\Gamma \mid \lfloor \Phi \rfloor \vdash_{\text{RHOL}} e_1 \sim e_2 : t_1 \sim t_2 \mid \phi$.
2. *If* $\Gamma \mid \lfloor \Phi \rfloor \vdash_{\text{RHOL}} e_1 \sim e_2 : t_1 \sim t_2 \mid \phi$, *then* $\Gamma \mid \Phi \vdash_{\text{OBRA}} e_1 \sim e_2 : t_1 \sim t_2 \mid \phi$.

4 Evaluation

We implemented OBRA as an extension to LIQUID HASKELL. Concretely, we added two new features. First, the keyword `relational` allows the user to ascribe relational signatures to functions. OBRA will verify these signatures using the rules of Sect. 3. The second feature is the flag `--relational-hints`, which tells LIQUID HASKELL to generate unary proof templates from relational signatures.

Table 1. Summary of Benchmarks.

	Benchmark	Code	Unary		Relational		
			Spec	Proof	Spec	User	Auto
Toy	`Increment`	3	2	1	3	0	17
	`Map`	15	10	9	6	0	36
	`Filter map`	6	3	16	5	16	29
	`Higher-order map`	12	8	16	6	16	29
Tick	`2D count`	22	2	21	9	0	113
	`Binary counters`	36	5	45	19	0	60
	`Boolean expressions`	35	1	27	4	21	257
	`Constant-time comparison`	13	5	1	4	0	112
	`Memory allocation`	22	1	1	3	0	50
	`Insertion Sort`	39	3	90	5	90	44
	`Merge sort`	30	6	73	5	52	186
	`Square and multiply`	14	8	9	9	0	240
	Total	247	54	309	78	195	1173

`Toy` are toy examples and `Tick` are the relational benchmarks of [14]. **Code** is the number of lines of executable code. In **Unary** columns, **Spec** is the number of lines of the refinement type specification and **Proof** is the number of lines of code to verify the specification. In **Relational** columns, **Spec** is the number of lines of the relational specification, **User** is the number of lines of code to verify the proof obligations, and **Auto** is the number of lines of auto-generated code.

Benchmarks Table 1 evaluates our implementation using two sets of benchmarks. The first set, `Toy`, contains small examples like the `Map` and `Filter map` presented in Sect. 2. `Increment` asserts the monotonicity of the increment function and `Higher-order map` tests function mapping with bounded differences. The second set, `Tick`, contains all the relational benchmarks from [14]. `2D count` compares two implementations of a 2D count function. `Binary counters` asserts that if two boolean lists are dual, then incrementing and decrementing them would result in the same cost and a dual value. `Boolean expressions` compares two implementations of a boolean expression evaluator. `Constant-time comparison` asserts that a cryptographic safe function that compares an input with a secret password, has the same cost for inputs of the same length. `Memory allocation` compares memory usage between lazy and forced evaluation. `Insertion sort` and `Merge sort` both assert that the difference of the cost of sorting two lists is bounded by the difference of the number of unsorted elements in the lists. Finally, `Square and multiply` asserts that the difference of the cost of two square and multiply runs is bounded by the difference of their list inputs.

Code Size Table 1 summarizes the number of lines of code (LoC) required for unary and relational verification. The **Code** column contains the number of lines of executable code, used both for the unary and relational verification. **Spec** is the number of lines required to express the main specification. In total, the relational specifications (78 LoC) are more verbose than the unary ones (54 LoC). This was expected, since in the relational form the types are separated from the properties. The column **Proof** contains the user provided LoC that prove the unary specifications. In the relational case, **Auto** contains the LoC automatically generated and **User** is the LoC the user provided to prove the generated obligations. Out of the 12 benchmarks, 7 were proved automatically, *i.e.* requiring 0 lines of user provided proof code. In all the benchmarks, the generated proofs are big, totalling 1173 LoC. This proof code is neither optimized nor is meant to be read by the user. Instead, when user code is required, the translation is generating top level proof obligations. In the 5 benchmarks that did require user proofs the user-provided proof size is smaller or equal to proofs in the unary case. In total the user provided proof code reduced from 309 to 195 LoC, *i.e.* a reduction of 36%. In short, the relational specifications are a little more verbose but the lines of user provided proof code is smaller.

Expressiveness Compared to RELSTLC ([10]), which is the main implemented relational system, OBRA offers three key advantages. Firstly, it is more expressive. Unlike RELSTLC, which only supports indices-based predicates making it impossible to express properties required by the `Boolean expressions` benchmark, OBRA supports arbitrary relational properties. Secondly, OBRA generates unary proofs and provides local error reporting, enabling easier debugging of relational proofs. Although RELSTLC may automatically prove more relational proofs through heuristics, such as in the `merge sort` benchmark, it lacks debugging information when these heuristics fail. Finally, the generated proofs are checked by LIQUID HASKELL, increasing confidence in their validity.

5 Related Approaches

Our work is inspired by the rich literature on relational verification of higher-order programs. System R [1] is an early example of type-based relational verification for a polymorphic λ-calculus. However, its focus is limited to parametricity. Information flow typing [15,19] provides another case of type-based relational verification. However, it is limited to non-interference properties. Another example of a relational type system is Fuzz [21] and its dependently typed version Dfuzz [12]. Fuzz and Dfuzz use a rich system of linear types to reason about program sensitivity and differential privacy. In the case of DFuzz, types can be indexed over arithmetic expressions, making the type checking algorithm highly non-trivial. However, the type systems are syntax-directed (with the obvious exception of the subtyping rules, for which classic techniques can be used) and as a consequence typing can be algorithmically reduced to constraint solving over natural numbers and the reals [5]. RelCost [9] makes a similar use of indexed types to reason about relational cost. In contrast to sensitivity, which can be proved for many examples without the use of non-synchronous rules, relative cost requires asynchronous rules, which are therefore an integral part of RelCost. This makes algorithmic typing for RelCost challenging. Nevertheless, [10] develops mechanisms to perform algorithmic typing, at the cost of losing completeness *w.r.t.* the declarative type system. Our approach avoids losing completeness, by generating proof obligations that need to be discharged in a unary type system.

The first general purpose relational logic for higher-order (stateful) programs is Relational Hoare Type Theory (RHTT) [18]. RHTT is implemented within the Coq proof assistant, giving its users great flexibility to interleave synchronous and asynchronous reasoning. To our best knowledge, the problem of algorithmic verification for RHTT has not been studied. Another example of general-purpose relational type system is RF$*$ [6]. RF$*$ is built on top of F$*$ [22], and follows similar principles. Type-checking generates proof obligations that are delegated to SMT-solvers. One limitation of RF$*$ is that it is primarily restricted to synchronous reasoning. In contrast, our approach allows combining synchronous and asynchronous reasoning via the generation of proof obligations.

Our work is most closely related to Relational Higher-Order Logic (RHOL) [4]. RHOL differs from previously mentioned approaches by imposing a stratification between computations, that are expressed in a type system, and properties, that are expressed in a higher-order logic over the type system. The stratification is key for achieving soundness and completeness *w.r.t.* standard HOL. Our work allows us to combine expressiveness of RHOL with algorithmic verification that comes for free with other approaches. There are several extensions of RHOL, in particular with probabilities [2] and monadic cost R^C [20]. Like RHOL, these systems are not supported by algorithmic verification.

An alternative approach is to carry out relational reasoning using an extrinsic proof approach. In this approach, relational properties are captured as non-relational properties, typically over unit types, and the proofs are constructed manually relying on a proposition-as-types encoding customized to the language at hand. This is the approach used in [13] for F$\star$ and in [14] for Liquid Haskell. The latter work was later extended to probabilistic computations in [23]. Our work builds upon [14] by providing additional automation while similarly using SMT-aided refinement types to reason about quantitative specifications.

6 Conclusion

OBRA is an oracle-based, relational, algorithmic type checker that proves relational properties of higher-order, functional programs. We formalized OBRA as a core calculus, λ_{OBRA}, and proved it equivalent to RHOL. Further, the system automatically translates relational properties to unary theorems with a proof template. We implemented OBRA as an extension of LIQUID HASKELL and evaluated it on 12 benchmarks and out of which 7 were proved automatically.

Acknowledgments. This work is founded by the Horizon Europe ERC Starting Grant CRETE (GA: 101039196), and the DECO grant PID2022-138072OB-I00, funded by MCIN/AEI/10.13039/501100011033/ FEDER, UE.

References

1. Abadi, M., Cardelli, L., Curien, P.: Formal parametric polymorphism. In: POPL (1993). https://doi.org/10.1145/158511.158622
2. Aguirre, A., Barthe, G., Birkedal, L., Bizjak, A., Gaboardi, M., Garg, D.: Relational reasoning for markov chains in a probabilistic guarded lambda calculus. In: ESOP (2018). https://doi.org/10.1007/978-3-319-89884-1_8
3. Aguirre, A., Barthe, G., Gaboardi, M., Garg, D., Katsumata, S., Sato, T.: Higher-order probabilistic adversarial computations: categorical semantics and program logics. In: ICFP (2021).https://doi.org/10.1145/3473598
4. Aguirre, A., Barthe, G., Gaboardi, M., Garg, D., Strub, P.: A relational logic for higher-order programs. In: ICFP (2017). https://doi.org/10.1145/3110265
5. de Amorim, A.A., Arias, E.J.G., Gaboardi, M., Hsu, J.: Really natural linear indexed type checking. In: Implementation and Application of Functional Languages (2014). https://dl.acm.org/doi/10.1145/2746325.2746335
6. Barthe, G., Fournet, C., Grégoire, B., Strub, P., Swamy, N., Béguelin, S.Z.: Probabilistic relational verification for cryptographic implementations. In: POPL (2014). https://doi.org/10.1145/2535838.2535847
7. Barthe, G., Gaboardi, M., Arias, E.J.G., Hsu, J., Roth, A., Strub, P.: Higher-order approximate relational refinement types for mechanism design and differential privacy. In: POPL (2015). https://doi.org/10.1145/2676726.2677000
8. Barthe, G., Grégoire, B., Hsu, J., Strub, P.Y.: Coupling proofs are probabilistic product programs. In: POPL (2017). https://doi.org/10.1145/3093333.3009896
9. Çiçek, E., Barthe, G., Gaboardi, M., Garg, D., Hoffmann, J.: Relational cost analysis. In: POPL (2017)
10. Çiçek, E., Qu, W., Barthe, G., Gaboardi, M., Garg, D.: Bidirectional type checking for relational properties. In: PLDI (2019). https://doi.org/10.1145/3314221.3314603
11. Dunfield, J., Krishnaswami, N.: Bidirectional typing. ACM Comput. Surv. (2021). https://doi.org/10.1145/3450952
12. Gaboardi, M., Haeberlen, A., Hsu, J., Narayan, A., Pierce, B.C.: Linear dependent types for differential privacy. In: POPL (2013). https://doi.org/10.1145/2429069.2429113
13. Grimm, N., Maillard, K., Fournet, C., Hritcu, C., Maffei, M., Protzenko, J., Ramananandro, T., Rastogi, A., Swamy, N., Béguelin, S.Z.: A monadic framework for relational verification: applied to information security, program equivalence, and optimizations. In: CPP (2018). https://doi.org/10.1145/3167090

14. Handley, M.A.T., Vazou, N., Hutton, G.: Liquidate your assets: reasoning about resource usage in liquid Haskell. In: POPL (2019). https://doi.org/10.1145/3371092
15. Heintze, N., Riecke, J.G.: The SLam calculus: programming with secrecy and integrity. In: POPL (1998). http://doi.acm.org/10.1145/268946.268976
16. Jhala, R., Vazou, N.: Refinement types: a tutorial. In: Foundations and Trends in Programming Languages (2020). https://doi.org/10.1561/2500000032
17. Nanevski, A., Banerjee, A., Garg, D.: Verification of information flow and access control policies with dependent types. In: S&P (2011). https://doi.org/10.1109/SP.2011.12
18. Nanevski, A., Banerjee, A., Garg, D.: Dependent type theory for verification of information flow and access control policies. In: TOPLAS (2013). http://doi.acm.org/10.1145/2491522.2491523
19. Pottier, F., Simonet, V.: Information flow inference for ML. In: POPL (2002). http://doi.acm.org/10.1145/503272.503302
20. Radicek, I., Barthe, G., Gaboardi, M., Garg, D., Zuleger, F.: Monadic refinements for relational cost analysis. In: POPL (2018). http://doi.acm.org/10.1145/3158124
21. Reed, J., Pierce, B.C.: Distance makes the types grow stronger: a calculus for differential privacy. In: ICFP (2010). https://doi.org/10.1145/1863543.1863568
22. Swamy, N., Hritcu, C., Keller, C., Rastogi, A., Delignat-Lavaud, A., Forest, S., Bhargavan, K., Fournet, C., Strub, P., Kohlweiss, M., Zinzindohoue, J.K., Béguelin, S.Z.: Dependent types and multi-monadic effects in F. In: POPL (2016). http://doi.acm.org/10.1145/2837614.2837655
23. Vasilenko, E., Vazou, N., Barthe, G.: Safe couplings: coupled refinement types. In: ICFP (2022). https://doi.org/10.1145/3547643
24. Vazou, N., Breitner, J., Kunkel, R., Van Horn, D., Hutton, G.: Theorem proving for all: equational reasoning in liquid Haskell (functional pearl). In: Haskell (2018). https://doi.org/10.1145/3242744.3242756
25. Vazou, N., Seidel, E.L., Jhala, R., Vytiniotis, D., Peyton-Jones, S.: Refinement types for Haskell. In: ICFP (2014). https://doi.org/10.1145/2692915.2628161
26. Vazou, N., Tondwalkar, A., Choudhury, V., Scott, R.G., Newton, R.R., Wadler, P., Jhala, R.: Refinement reflection: complete verification with SMT. In: POPL (2017). https://doi.org/10.1145/3158141
27. Wadler, P.: Propositions as types. Commun. ACM (2015). https://doi.org/10.1145/2699407

Verification

A Formal Verification Framework for Tezos Smart Contracts Based on Symbolic Execution

Thi Thu Ha Doan(✉) and Peter Thiemann

University of Freiburg, Freiburg, Germany
{doanha,thiemann}@informatik.uni-freiburg.de

Abstract. We developed SCV, a verification tool geared towards contracts implemented in Michelson, the smart contract language of the Tezos blockchain. SCV utilizes symbolic execution to derive verification conditions that can be checked automatically against user specifications using an SMT solver. These specifications are written in a domain-specific language. We present the fundamental principles behind the design and development of SCV. By pruning states during symbolic execution, SCV effectively addresses the problem of state explosion. This approach has enabled us to conduct two case studies on real-life contracts, demonstrating the expressiveness of our tool.

Keywords: Smart Contract · Blockchain · Formal Verification · Symbolic Execution

1 Introduction

Once a smart contract is deployed on the blockchain, it becomes permanent and cannot be altered. Regrettably, numerous cases have been documented where vulnerabilities in smart contracts were identified and exploited by bad actors in the blockchain community, resulting in substantial financial losses [7,30]. The distinctive execution model of smart contract languages has given rise to unforeseen errors due to a lack of familiarity with their complexities. These factors, combined with the immutability of contracts, underscore the need to ensure their correctness prior to deployment.

We have developed SCV, a formal verification tool for smart contracts on the Tezos blockchain [10], written in Michelson [18]. SCV relies on symbolic execution backed by an SMT solver to simulate the implementation of the smart contract language, helping to detect subtle errors. Additionally, SCV includes a domain-specific language for precisely specifying smart contract properties, tailored to Michelson's execution model and informed by the capabilities of Z3. Each specification consists of Michelson code, a precondition, and a postcondition with the usual partial correctness semantics. Our symbolic interpreter calculates a postcondition predicate from the specified precondition. The SMT solver Z3 [21] then checks that this predicate implies the specified postcondition.

O. Kiselyov (Ed.): APLAS 2024, LNCS 15194, pp. 305–324, 2024.
https://doi.org/10.1007/978-981-97-8943-6_15

While there is already a considerable body of work applying symbolic execution to the verification of smart contracts [12,20,24,27] (see Section 7 for details), most of these efforts are targeted at Ethereum, where standard techniques for symbolic execution of imperative programs are applicable. Such groundwork does not exist for Michelson, which is a functional language running on a stack machine (see Sect. 2) with a sophisticated instruction set that includes high-level loops. For that reason, we had to develop symbolic execution for Michelson from scratch.

Besides the Mi-Cho-Coq framework that relies on interactive theorem proving [5], HELMHOLTZ [23] is another automatic verifier for Michelson. However, the approach of HELMHOLTZ is significantly different from ours. HELMHOLTZ defines a refinement type system to keep track of the properties of values in the storage and on the stack, so that verifying a program corresponds to type-checking against a specification type. Furthermore, the reported experiments with these tools consider sample smart contract codes of about one hundred instructions. The HELMHOLTZ experiments primarily replicate issues previously identified by Mi-Cho-Coq. Although HELMHOLTZ analyzes one real-world contract, it only examines a portion of the code. In contrast, our tool is capable of handling entire contracts with hundreds or even thousands of instructions.

SCV utilizes an SMT solver to eliminate invalid states during symbolic execution, addressing the problem of state explosion. This capability enabled us to conduct two case studies involving real-world smart contracts that have been operational on the Tezos blockchain for quite some time. A flaw was reported in the Kolibri oracle contract. In conclusion, SCV streamlines the process of uncovering hidden errors and validating user-defined properties. It provides a comprehensive solution to mitigate potential pitfalls in blockchain-based applications.

Our contributions are as follows.

1. Design and implementation of the SCV specification language.
2. Design and implementation of a symbolic interpreter for a significant subset of Michelson.
3. Two case studies verifying smart contracts deployed on the Tezos blockchain:
   - USDtz, an implementation of the FA 1.2 standard for financial applications;
   - Kolibri, an oracle contract that injects currency exchange rates from an external system.

Several high-level languages for smart contracts, such as LIGO [15], SmartPy [26], and Liquidity [16], support writing smart contracts for Tezos. Our tools are applicable to all these languages because they compile to Michelson.

2 Michelson

Michelson is a stack-based, statically typed functional programming language. A program is defined by the type S of its storage, the type P of its single parameter,

cpt ::= unit | never | bool | int | nat | string | chain-id | bytes | mutez | key-hash
| key | signature | timestamp | address | option **cpt** | or **cpt cpt** | pair **cpt cpt**
T, U ::= cpt | option T | list T | set **cpt** | operation | contract T
| pair T U | or T U | lambda T U | map **cpt** T | big-map **cpt** T

Fig. 1. Types

```
parameter int;
storage   int;
code {                     (* pair int int :: [] *)
  DUP; UNPAIR;             (* int :: int :: pair int int :: [] *)
  COMPARE; GE;             (* bool :: pair int int :: [] *)
  IF {UNPAIR; SUB} {PUSH string 'Unexpected Pair'; FAILWITH};
                           (* int :: [] *)
  NIL operation; PAIR (* pair (list operation) int :: [] *)}
```

Listing 1.1. A Michelson program

and a typed list of instructions for the underlying stack machine. It starts on a stack with one element containing a pair of the current storage value (taken from the blockchain) and the parameter value specified by the contract invocation. When the program finishes, the stack must contain a single element with a pair of the final storage value (to be saved on the blockchain) and a list of operations. These operations are syntactic commands, such as token transfers or contract invocations, among other possibilities. Thus, the program computes a function $P \times S \to O^* \times S$, where O is the type of operations.

Besides the standard datatypes (e.g., numbers, lists, pairs, sums, functions) with the expected operations, Michelson supports a number of types and operations specific to blockchain applications (e.g., `mutez` for tokens) as shown in Fig. 1, where **cpt** denotes comparable types. The type system does not support quantification over types and there are no user-defined types.

Listing 1.1 contains a short example of a Michelson program. The code is interspersed with comments indicating the types of values currently on the stack. This program first duplicates its input (DUP), decomposes the pair $P \times S$ into its components (UNPAIR), compares the two values on top of the stack (COMPARE), and transforms the result into a boolean (GE). The IF instruction pops the boolean and either executes the first (for true) or second (for false) list of instructions. At this point, only the initial pair remains on the stack. In the true branch, UNPAIR decomposes the pair, and SUB subtracts the two components. In the false branch, the PUSH instruction puts a string message on the stack. The FAILWITH instruction aborts the contract execution: the tokens provided with the invocation are consumed, but the storage and balance of the contract remain unchanged. Finally, the NIL instruction pushes an empty list of operations, and PAIR creates the required pair of type $O^* \times S$.

A contract may have several entrypoints. Entrypoints are encoded by using a sum type (called "or type" in Michelson). Each (nested) alternative in a sum type can be given a name, which is used as the name for an entrypoint. A call to an entrypoint automatically adds the required LEFT and RIGHT constructors of the sum type to the parameter.

3 SCV: A Domain Specific Language For Smart Contract Property Specification

SCV comes with a domain-specific language for specifying smart contract properties, which is user-friendly for non-experts and compatible with SMT solvers.

3.1 Basic syntax

Listing 1.2 shows the specification of the `sub` contract in the SCV language. Here, mcontract, spec, code, input, output, pre−condition, and post−condition are keywords. The input and output fields specify the input and output patterns, which are terms on Michelson values.

Figure 2 contains the syntax of terms: A term **t** can consist of constants of the sort nat (natural number), int (integer), string (string), and b (bytes) along with their respective types. The type annotation may be omitted except for the type nat to distinguish from integers. It also encompasses all blockchain constants **c**. When a variable appears for the first time, it must be accompanied by its type declaration. Subsequent mentions can omit the type declaration.

As Michelson operates on a stack, we assume that the input stack and the output stack each have exactly one element, as specified in the input term and the output term, respectively. The syntax allows us to specify either a fragment of Michelson code or a complete program. For a complete Michelson program, the output should be a pair consisting of an operation list and the state of the storage after code execution, as described in Sect. 2. For verification purposes, we elide the operation list and represent the output solely by the term of the value in the storage after execution concludes.

The pre- and postcondition instances are formulas in first-order logic that can be handled by an SMT solver (specifically, Z3 in our case). There are several predefined functions including get_map(e1, e2), which accesses an element in a map. If there is no key e1 in the map e2, the function returns None; otherwise, it returns Some(v) where v is the mapped value. Another function, get_contract(T, e), converts the address e to a contract on the Tezos blockchain. If no contract with an entrypoint of type T is associated with the address e, it returns None; otherwise, it returns the contract as Some(c).

Certain functions are defined as predicates, such as transfer_token(e1, e2, e3). This predicate holds true if, after executing the smart contract code, there is an operation in the operation list indicating the transfer of e2 tokens to address e3 along with parameter e1[1].

[1] Additional predicates can be added if a mapping to Z3 formulas is defined.

```
1  mcontract sub = spec
2    code := {DUP; UNPAIR; COMPARE; GE; IF {UNPAIR; SUB}
3            {PUSH string 'Unexpected Pair'; FAILWITH}}
4    input := Pair (x : int) (y : int)
5    output := (z : int)
6    pre-condition := (x >= y)
7    post-condition := (z = x - y) && (z >= 0)
```

Listing 1.2. Specification of the sub contract

c ::= pre_Balance | post_Balance | Amount | Sender | Source | Now | Level
| Chain_id | Self_address
t ::= **n** : nat | **i** : int | **s** : string | **b** : bytes | **c** | x | x : T | Unit | Never | True
| False | Pair t1 t2 | Left t T | Right T t | Some t | None T | {t ; ... } : list T
| {t ; ... } : set T | { Elt t1 t2 ; ... } : map T U | { Elt t1 t2 ; ... } : big_map T U
e ::= **t** | **e** + **e** | **e** - **e** | **e** * **e** | **e** / **e** | **e** % **e** | **e** rem **e**
| get_map(**e1**, **e2**) | get_big_map(**e1**, **e2**) | mem(**e1**, **e2**) | get_contract(T, **e**)
| abs(**e**) | to_int(**e**) | from_int(**e**) | len(**e**) | cons(**e**, **e**) | size(**e**) | **e** ∧ **e**
p ::= **e** = **e** | **e** ! = **e** | **e** > **e** | **e** >= **e** | **e** < **e** | **e** <= **e**
| transfer_token(**e1**, **e2**, **e3**) | is_nat(**e**) | contain(**e1**, **e2**) | forall(**e1**, **e2**) | exist(**e1**, **e2**)
| **p** && **p** | **p** or **p** | not **p** | **p** −> **p**

Fig. 2. Syntax of constants, **c**, terms, **t**, expressions, **e**, and predicates, **p**

In Listing 1.2, the program takes as input a stack with one element, which is a pair of two integer variables x and y, symbolically specified in the input field. The specification continues by defining the output term as a variable z of type integer, a precondition stating that the integer x is greater than or equal to y, and a postcondition asserting that the result z is equal to the subtract of x and y, which is greater or equal to zero. The symbol && stands for conjunction.

3.2 Multiple Entrypoints

The design of SCV enables us to verify all entrypoints at once and to describe relationships between entrypoints. The entrypoint name is written after the % symbol and is followed by a property specification for the entrypoint. The specification finishes with specifying entrypoint relations, which we explain next. For a smart contract, the input term includes the storage term before, and the output term represents the storage after the execution. Thus, there are two options of the syntax. The first option is similar to the basic syntax with the entrypoint specific. In the second option, the input term is then the pair of the parameter term and the storage term. The prefix post_ is used before the variables from the storage term to indicate the corresponding storage value after the execution.

```
1  mcontract auction = spec
2   storage := Pair (open: bool)
3                   (Pair (highest: address) (owner: address))
4   entrypoint %bid
5    code := {...}
6    parameter := Unit
7    pre-condition := open = true && Amount > pre_Balance
8     && get_contract (unit, highest) = Some (c: contract unit)
9    post-condition := open = true && post_highest = Sender
10    && post_Balance = Amount && post_owner = owner
11    && transfer_token (Unit, pre_Balance, c);
12  entrypoint %close
13    ...
14  (%create -> %bid) with ...
15  | (%create  -> %close) with ...
16  | (%bid -> %bid) with (Amount > pre_Balance)
17   && get_contract (unit, highest) = Some (c: contract unit)
18  | (%bid -> %close) with (Sender = owner)
19   && get_contract (unit, owner) = Some (c: contract unit)
20  | not (%close -> %bid) | not (%close -> %close)
```

Listing 1.3. Auction contract specification

Let us have a look at the specification for the auction contract that models an online auction in Listing 1.3. The contract has two entry points, %bid and %close , which serve as functions for bidding and closing the contract, respectively. The smart contract storage is a pair containing, as its first element, a boolean value open that indicates whether the contract is still open for bidding or already closed. The second element is another nested pair, where the element highest stores the highest bidder's address, and the element owner is the contract owner's address. The current highest bid is reflected in the balance of the contract before the next bid is invoked. We omit the Michelson code of the smart contract due to its length. For the %bid entrypoint, the parameter is Unit of type unit. The current storage is described by the storage phrase.

Closing the contract transfers the balance to the owner and is restricted to the owner. Both closing and bidding operations must fail if the auction is already closed. If bidding is open and the amount of tokens accompanying the bid exceeds the current highest bid, the current bidder replaces the previous highest bidder, and the previous highest bidder is reimbursed. Otherwise, bidding fails. Upon deployment, the owner deposits an initial balance to indicate the minimum bid. The contract should be deployed with the storage value Pair True (Pair owner owner), indicating that bidding is allowed, and the contract owner is currently the highest bidder.

The first property is that if a user calls the %bid entrypoint when the contract is still open for bidding and the bid is higher than the current bid (as specified in the pre−condition field at line 7), and the address of the highest bidder

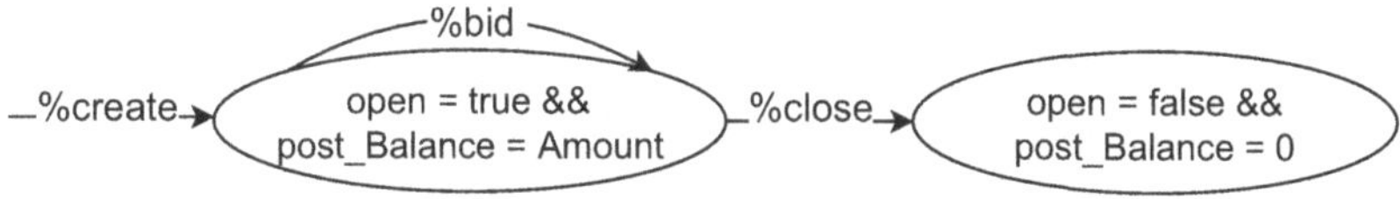

Fig. 3. Auction contract life cycle

can be cast to a real contract represented by the variable c of type contract unit on the blockchain (line 8), then the bid should succeed. In this case, the highest bidder must be updated to the sender, which is the address of the caller (line 9 in the post–condition field), and the balance of the contract should be the amount sent along with the call (line 10). Moreover, the previous highest bidder should receive their bid back, which means the auction contract should transfer the pre_Balance to the previous bidder, highest (line 11). Another property guarantees that the auction owner's address should not be changed after calling the bid entrypoint (line 10) and the auction should be still open (line 9).

3.3 Entrypoint relations

Since the order of smart contract calls can be crucial, we specify ordering constraints among calls with entrypoint relations. An entrypoint relation can be specified as %a –> %b with p , which starts with the name %a of the entrypoint and is followed by the keyword with in case conditions are specified as predicates. The following symbol –> indicates that after invoking the entrypoint %a , it is possible to call the entrypoint %b if the condition p holds. One specification can contain several entrypoint relations concatenated by |. There is a special entrypoint named create that indicates the contract state after deployment.

Let us return to the auction contract. It is important to guarantee that the bid call can happen successfully after another if the new bid is higher than the previous one (lines 16-17). The %close entrypoint can be called anytime after bidding if the caller is the contract owner (lines 18-19). However, it should not be possible to call the %bid entrypoint after the auction is closed, and, of course, it cannot be closed again if it is already closed (line 20). Furthermore, contract deployment sets the open flag to True, indicating that the contract is open for bidding, i.e., users should be able to bid on the contract or the contract owner should be able to close it. Otherwise, the owner's original deposit is lost. This sequence illustrates the life cycle of the auction contract, which is depicted in Figure 3. Other properties related to the %close entrypoint and the life cycle are omitted here due to space limitations.

4 Symbolic Execution Model

We already learned about Michelson, the low-level smart contract language for the Tezos blockchain, and its stack-based nature in Sect. 2. Here we address the changes needed for symbolic execution of Michelson programs, focusing on a selection of instructions.

4.1 System Model

Our symbolic model of a program state consists of a stack where each element is a symbolic value, represented as a pair comprising a Michelson term and its type. Thus, we write a stack as $S = (t_1, ty_1) :: (t_2, ty_2) :: \ldots :: [\,]$. Here, $[\,]$ represents the empty stack, and *hd*::*tl* denotes a stack with *hd* as the top element and *tl* as the remaining stack. Let $I = i_1; i_2; \ldots; i_n$ be a sequence of instructions, and P be a path predicate expressed in conjunctive form, capturing the branching conditions.

Definition 1. *A symbolic execution state is represented by a tuple* $ST = [I, S, P]$. *A system configuration,* $SE = \{ST_1, ST_2, \ldots, ST_n\}$, *is a set of states.*

4.2 Rules

An instruction is defined by rules on a system configuration. There are two kinds of transitions: (1) $\longrightarrow_S$ internal transitions of a state, which are non-deterministic, and (2) $\longrightarrow$ system transitions, which pick any state and replace it with all distinct states reachable by internal transitions, exploiting the non-determinism of the $\longrightarrow_S$ relation.

A state is unreachable if its predicate P is not satisfiable. The following rule drops unreachable states.

$$\frac{\text{unsat } P}{\{[I, S, P]\} \cup SE \longrightarrow SE}$$

The symbolic interpreter works on a graph with states as nodes and transitions as edges. This representation simplifies performing multi-step sub-transitions needed for some operations.

The semantics of the symbolic rules for the instructions adhere to the formal definition of the Michelson language as outlined in [18,19]. In our model, these instructions are classified based on how we handle them into one-step, multi-step, blockchain, cryptographic, branch, and loop instructions.

One-step instructions directly modify the system state without branching, have a localized effect, and are modeled with a single rule.

Multi-step instructions involve the execution of a sub-sequence of instructions before returning to the main execution. The rule below models the EXEC instruction, which executes a function specified as a sequence of instructions denoted by I_1 in the rule. This instruction applies the code of the function to the first element of the stack and then places the result back into the main execution.

$$\frac{[I_1, (s_1, ty_1)::[\,], P] \longrightarrow_S^* [[\,], (s_1', ty_2)::[\,], P']}{[(\text{EXEC}; I), (\{I_1\}, ty_1 \ \rightarrow \ ty_2)::(s_1, ty_1)::S, P] \longrightarrow_S \ [I, (s_1', ty_2)::S, P']}$$

Here, $\longrightarrow_S^*$ represents the execution of multiple steps in a sequence of internal transitions.

Blockchain instructions, such as the AMOUNT instruction make implicit use of data from the transaction, the block and the current state of the blockchain. As these values are constant during the execution of a contract, we model them as fixed variables.

Branch instructions, such as IF$\{I_1\}\{I_2\}$ consume a value at the top of the stack. If the branch condition is True, it executes I_1; otherwise, it executes I_2.

$$\frac{}{[(\text{IF } I_1\ I_2; I), (s_1, \text{bool})::S, P] \longrightarrow_S \{[I_1; I, S, P \wedge s_1], [I_2; I, S, P \wedge \neg s_1]\}}$$

The loop instructions, including LOOP check the loop condition by examining the top of the stack. These loop instructions may not terminate, just like while-loops. There are further loop instructions, like ITER and MAP, specialized to traverse data structures like lists, sets, and maps. There are also some instructions that implicitly require looping like CONCAT, and SIZE. The latter kinds of loop instructions do always terminate.

We first look at the terminating loops, such as the ITER instruction, which iterates over a list. The typing rule for the ITER instruction is as follows:

$$\frac{\Gamma \vdash I : ty::A \rightarrow A}{\Gamma \vdash \text{ITER } I : \text{list } ty::A \rightarrow A}$$

This rule ensures that if the loop body I has the type $ty :: A \rightarrow A$, then the entire ITER instruction, when applied to a stack with the top element of type ty list and the rest of the stack of type A, produces a result stack of type A.

The following rule handles the ITER loop for the non-empty list[2], while the ITER loop terminates when the list is empty.

$$\frac{hd, tl \text{ fresh} \qquad [I_1, (hd, ty)::S, P] \longrightarrow_S^* [[\,], S', P']}{[(\text{ITER } I_1; I), (s_1, \text{list } ty)::S, P] \longrightarrow_S \qquad [(\text{ITER } I_1; I), (tl, \text{list } ty)::S', P' \wedge (s_1 = \{hd; tl\})]}$$

It symbolically executes the instructions I_1 within the ITER block with the head of the list (hd) replacing the list. The resulting state transitions to a new stack (S') and an updated predicate (P' $\wedge$ ($s_1 = \{hd;\ tl\}$)), where tl represents the rest of the list.

If the list is concrete, the instruction terminates as it simply loops over the elements of the list. How do we deal with ITER if the list is a symbolic value? One solution could involve running the loop a certain number of times to obtain the symbolic value. However, we can defer that decision by abstracting the result.

The loop body I_1 can be considered as a function, say f, applied to a stack of type $ty :: A$, resulting in a stack of type A. If the first element of the stack is a list l, and the rest of the stack is $S_0 = s_1 :: s_2 :: \ldots :: s_n$. Assuming the size of the list l is m, the ITER I_1 instruction applies the function f to the stack m

[2] ITER can also iterate over sets and maps, but the details are very similar to the list case and hence omitted.

times, once for each element of the list l. By unfolding the list once as $\{hd;\ tl\}$, the result after the first iteration is $S_1 = s_1^1 :: s_2^1 :: ... :: s_n^1 = f\ hd\ S_0$, and so on.

We can represent the value of the stack after running the instruction ITER as the result of a fold function that applies the function f to the list.

$$S' = fold\ f\ S_0\ l$$

The *fold* function also can be used to express the result of other loop instructions, such as CONCAT and SIZE, symbolically.

The similar strategy can be employed for the MAP I_1 instruction.

$$\text{MAP } \{I_1\}\ /\ l :: S$$

The outcome of the MAP $\{I_1\}$ instruction is the result of a map function that applies the function f representing the sequence of instructions I_1 to the list l.

$$(map\ f\ l) :: S$$

Finally, we consider a loop instruction that may not terminate, such as LOOP. When the input to the symbolic execution consists of concrete values, an unbounded loop causes the interpreter to iterate for a significant number of times until it halts with an exception indicating an unfinished loop. This mirrors the behavior observed in the actual execution of smart contracts, where the loop continues until it runs out of gas, terminating the computation with an out-of-gas error.

For a symbolic value, the stack type is determined before the loop is executed. We unfold the symbolic value once, execute the loop to determine the operation function, and then abstract the result of the loop and loop condition as function results. This abstraction helps detect whether the loop is unbounded, such as when the abstract function of the loop condition always results true.

In separate work [3], we have designed a dynamic logic tailored to Michelson as a formal foundation for the implementation of SCV. We have formalized a soundness proof of this logic in the Agda proof assistant.

5 Static Checker

The architecture of the static checker is illustrated in Figure 4. Users write specifications in the SCV language, which are then parsed into an Abstract Syntax Tree (AST) in OCaml. The input term along with the code is passed to the symbolic interpreter, while the output term and the pre- and postconditions are fed to the static checker. The symbolic interpreter then runs the code with the provided input, where the initial stack is derived from the input term.

When a branch occurs, the interpreter sends the path condition to the Z3 converter to convert it into Z3 formulas, which are then passed to the Z3 solver to check whether the path conditions are satisfied. The result of this check determines the interpreter's action; if satisfied, the branch is added, otherwise, it is

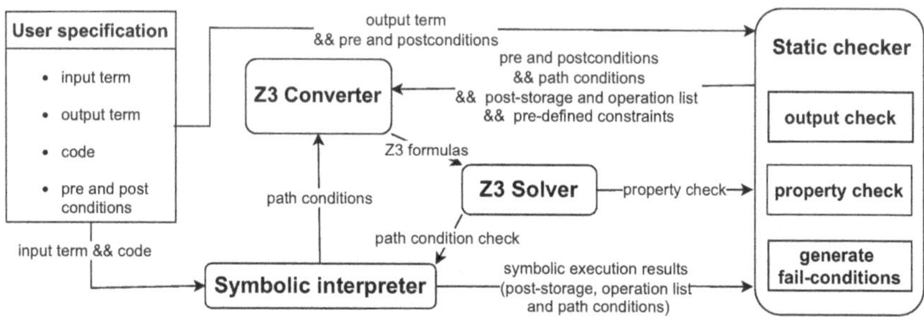

Fig. 4. The architecture of the static checker

abandoned. This branch check significantly reduces the number of execution states, especially for stack-based languages like Michelson, where the programmer may need to perform the same check multiple times.

Once the symbolic execution finishes, the results (i.e., all reachable states) are sent to the static checker. Each state contains the post-storage updated after execution, the list of operations to emit, and the path conditions. The static checker then performs the following tasks: output check, property check, and generation of all fail conditions.

We utilize the Z3 library in OCaml to construct the Z3 converter. Some adjustments are necessary to convert these terms into Z3 formulas. For instance, since Z3 does not have a natural number type (nat), it is mapped to Z3's integer type with an additional constraint asserting that the value is greater than or equal to zero. Several constants, such as amount and balance, as well as cryptographic functions are predefined in the environment that applies to any smart contract specifications.

We have implemented approximately 85% of the Michelson instructions, including the most frequently used instructions. The remaining instructions were not implemented due to time constraints rather than technical limitations.

Consider the specification of the sub contract, the results of the symbolic execution are either a failwith state with the path condition x < y, or a state in which the final stack has only one element, which is a symbolic variable sbvar of type integer, with the path condition stating that the variable x is greater than or equal to y and sbvar is equal to the subtract of x and y.

5.1 Output check

For a fragment of Michelson code, the output term of the symbolic execution has the form of a term t and its type ty. For a complete smart contract, it takes the form Pair opl stg, pair (list operation) ty_2, where opl represents the operation list and stg represents the storage. Given an output term specified as τ, the checker scans all reachable final states that do not contain a failwith stack and checks whether τ matches the output term. In the former case, it matches τ with the term t. In the latter case, it matches with stg.

```
1  1. not (open = true): 'Already closed'
2  2. (open = true) && not (Amount > pre_Balance):
3     'Not higher than the current highest bid'
4  3. (open = true) && (Amount > pre_Balance) &&
5     get_contract (unit, highest) = None: 'Invalid address'
```

Listing 1.4. Fail condition for auction contract bid entrypoint

For instance, in the sub contract, the output check ignores the states where the failwith occurs and verifies whether the output term z matches the symbolic output term sbvar in the other state. It succeeds for this example as expected. However, this test could fail if, for example, the output term is incorrectly specified as a variable of a type that does not match the actual result.

5.2 Fail conditions

A Michelson contract can fail due to conditions introduced by the programmer, triggered by the FAILWITH instruction along with an error message. Failures play a crucial role in smart contract programming to ensure that certain conditions lead to contract termination, such as unauthorized caller attempts (access control properties) or invalid arguments. Various smart contract standards, including [8,9], mandate specific fail conditions.

The static checker includes a feature to generate all fail conditions encountered in a smart contract. SCV identifies all instances where execution terminates due to the FAILWITH instruction, collecting the associated path conditions and error messages. Users receive a comprehensive report detailing each fail condition along with its corresponding message. This capability enables verifying access control properties and other critical aspects across different smart contracts.

For instance, the entrypoint bid has three fail conditions, as shown in Listing 1.4: (1) If the auction is closed, (2) if the auction is open but the bid amount is less than or equal to the current balance, and (3) if the auction is open, the bid amount exceeds the balance, but the address of the highest bidder is invalid.

5.3 Property check

A property is specified with the clause: pre−condition := && Φ_i followed by post−condition := && Ψ_j. This specification asserts that if all preconditions Φ_i hold before smart contract execution, then all Ψ_j must hold after successful (i.e., without failure) termination. To verify this property, the tool explores all the paths Π with the path condition Θ such that $(\bigwedge \Phi_i \wedge \Theta)$ is satisfiable. It then check that for every path Π, $\neg (\bigwedge \Phi_i \wedge \Theta \rightarrow \bigwedge \Psi_j)$ is unsatisfiable in the context given by the input for the entrypoint and its final state. For example, for the sub contract, the failwith branch is discarded because the precondition does not satisfy the path condition, and then z is matched to the symbolic variable sbvar in the other branch. In this example, the checker finds that $\neg$ ((x >= y) $\wedge$ (z = x − y) $\rightarrow$ (z = x − y) $\wedge$ (z >= 0)) is unsatisfiable.

5.4 Life-cycle check

An entrypoint relation can be defined as (%a −> %b) with p , indicating that after invoking the entrypoint %a , it is permissible to call the entrypoint %b if the condition p holds. The presence of the keyword not at the beginning signals an impossibility. The suffix with p may be omitted when no condition is needed.

Let S_a represent the set of all reachable states resulting from the execution of the call to the entrypoint %a . Each s_i in S_a is associated with a path condition Θ_i and is represented as a stack containing a single element—a pair consisting of an operation list (opl_i) and the storage stg_i. For each s_i, symbolic execution is performed on the entrypoint %b using input as a pair of the parameter and the storage stg_i, constrained by Θ_i and the condition p. In the execution state space, a state s_j with the path condition Θ_j is considered reachable if (Θ_i $\wedge$ p $\wedge$ Θ_j) is satisfiable, and $\neg$ (Θ_i $\wedge$ p $\rightarrow$ Θ_j) is unsatisfiable. Let S_b denote the set of these reachable states. If S_b is empty or contains only failwith states, then it is impossible to invoke the entrypoint %b from the state s_i. Otherwise, it is considered a success. Let R be the set containing all such states s_i in S_a where it is successful to call the entrypoint %b with the condition p. If R is non-empty, then (%a −> %b) with p holds. Otherwise, it is false, signifying not (%a −> %b) with p .

6 Case Studies

This section reports two case studies which are taken from the realm of financial applications deployed on the Tezos blockchain.

6.1 USDtz

In a blockchain ecosystem, tokens function as digital assets that can be transferred between accounts. These tokens come in various types, which include native tokens (cryptocurrencies) like Bitcoin and Tezos, as well as digital tokens created through smart contracts on an existing blockchain.

It is advisable to implement tokens that adhere to established standards, such as ERC-20 [8] for Ethereum [6], ensuring interoperability and compatibility across different platforms. A token standard specifies a set of rules and an interface that smart contracts must adhere to. The Tezos blockchain has its own set of standards known as Financial Applications (FA) in which FA 1.2 [9] is designed for fungible tokens.

Any contract aiming to implement the FA 1.2 standard must incorporate the functions specified in Listing 1.5, where view a r = pair a (contract r) implies an view entrypoint. A view is an entrypoint that takes an argument of type a

```
1 pair (address:from, pair (address:to, nat:value)) %transfer
2 pair (address:spender, nat:value)                 %approve
3 (view pair (address:owner, address:spender) nat) %getAllowance
4 (view (address:owner) nat)                        %getBalance
5 (view unit nat)                                   %getTotalSupply
```

Listing 1.5. FA 1.2 interface

```
1 not (paused = true)
2 && get_big_map (from, ledger) = Some sbvar
3 && sbvar = Pair sbvar1 sbvar2
4 && not (sbvar1 >= value) : 'NotEnoughBalance'
```

Listing 1.6. The NotEnoughBalance fail condition for the transfer entrypoint

and a contract to callback that receives in a value of type r. We verify USDtz [28,29], an implementation of the FA 1.2 standard. The goal is to ensure that the implementation aligns with the standard, verifying its correctness. USDtz is designed to maintain a stable value by pegging it to a fiat currency like USD or EUR. It has been operational on the Tezos blockchain for a significant time.

The implementation consists of approximately 1000 instructions, covering the five required entrypoints for the FA 1.2 standard and four additional ones. The storage contains a ledger (ledger), which is a substantial map linking user addresses (user) to a pair consisting of their balance (balance) and a map (approvals) associating addresses (spender) with the amount of tokens (value) allowed to be transferred from that user's account. It also includes additional information such as the admin address (admin), total supply (totalSupply), and the smart contract state (paused).

The transfer entrypoint credits the account associated with the address provided in the to parameter while debiting the account corresponding to the from parameter with the specified value amount. According to the FA 1.2 standard, this call must fail under two specific conditions: (1) The entrypoint must fail with the error NotEnoughBalance if the sender's account lacks sufficient funds. (2) If the sender's account does not have permission to withdraw the specified value amount, the call will fail with the NotEnoughAllowance error. To verify these requirements, we utilize the failwith condition feature of our tool and examine the returned results, one of which is outlined in Listing 1.6. The fail condition results confirm these stipulations.

Another essential property is ensuring that the allowance of the sender's account is decremented and the receiver's account is incremented by the value that has been sent. This specification is verified to ensure compliance with the contract's intended behavior.

The approve entrypoint grants the spender the right to transfer a specified amount from the owner's account. The contract prohibits changing the allowance value from a non-zero value to another non-zero value to prevent a known attack

```
1 not (paused = true)
2 && get_big_map(Sender, ledger) = Some sbvar
3 && sbvar = Pair sbvar1 sbvar2
4 && get_map(spender, sbvar2) = Some sbvar3
5 && not(value = 0) && not(sbvar3 = 0): 'UnsafeAllowanceChange'
```

Listing 1.7. The non-zero value fail condition for the approve entrypoint

vector [4]. This attack exploits the ability to spend the entire allowance before an update and then again after, resulting in a larger amount being spent than allowed. Therefore, the contract call must fail if both the parameter value and the current allowance of spender are non-zero. We verify this critical property by generating fail conditions to check whenever such a non-zero value update results in a fail condition as Listing 1.7.

When the update is allowed, the updated value must be correctly recorded in the storage. This can be divided into two sub-properties: (1) if the parameter value is zero, then the corresponding allowance value of the spender from the owner (which is SENDER in this call) should be zero, and (2) if value is non-zero and the allowance of the spender is zero, then the value should be recorded in the storage after the call. We specify these properties using pre and postconditions, as illustrated in Listing 1.8 for the first property.

The getAllowance, getBalance, and getTotalSupply entrypoints are view entrypoints that retrieve information from the storage without altering the state of the smart contract. For a view entrypoint implementation, it's crucial to return the TRANSFER_TOKENS operation targeted at the specified contract with accurate details. Another important property is that all Tezos tokens passed to a view entrypoint should be forwarded to the callback contract, and there should be no modifications made to the ledger. This ensures that view entrypoints maintain their non-modifying nature, strictly adhering to the expected behavior in blockchain environments.

We specified and verified all the properties mentioned above and others. The results confirm that these properties are guaranteed, ensuring the correctness of the smart contract code.

6.2 Kolibri Oracle Contract

The potential of smart contracts is constrained by their inability to access external data sources. To address this limitation, oracles play a pivotal role in providing external data for smart contracts. Since certain essential properties must be satisfied by an oracle contract, including data accountability, this case study illustrates the process of specifying and verifying an oracle contract using SCV, with the Kolibri oracle contract [14] as an example.

The Kolibri oracle contract ensures the accuracy of external data for the Tezos-based stablecoin Kolibri by leveraging the Harbinger Price Feed. The contract initiates calls to a Harbinger Normalizer contract, checks the returned val-

```
1  entrpoint %approve
2   parameter := Pair (spender: address) (value: nat)
3   pre-condition := not (paused = true)
4    && get_big_map (Sender, ledger) =
5       Some (v: pair nat (map address nat))
6    && v = Pair (n: nat) (m: map address nat)
7    && get_map (spender, m) = Some (k: nat)
8    && not (k = 0) && (value = 0)
9   post-condition := get_big_map (Sender, post_ledger) =
10     Some (post_v: (pair nat (map address nat))
11   && post_v = Pair (post_n: nat) (post_m: map address nat)
12   && get_map (spender, post_m) = Some (post_k: nat)
13   && (post_k = 0) ;
```

Listing 1.8. Specification of the approve entrypoint (Property 1)

ues, normalizes them to suit the Kolibri system, and subsequently relays them to the client. Key attributes stored by the oracle include: the address of the Harbinger contract (harbinger) [3], the current state of the contract (state), a callback contract awaiting Harbinger data (client), the address of the governor contract (governor), and the maximum acceptable age of data received from Harbinger (maxDelay). The oracle contract offers various entrypoints, including:

- getXtzUsdPrice: Processes the client request and calls the Harbinger contract.
- getXtzUsdPrice_callback: Relays the Harbinger price to the client.
- setMaxDelaySec: Resets the maxDelay attribute.
- setGovernorContract: Allows setting the Governor's address.

The Kolibri oracle maintains a state machine with two states: (1) IDLE and (2) WAITING_FOR_HARBINGER. The getXtzUsdPrice entrypoint is permissible only when the oracle is in the IDLE state; invoking this entrypoint transitions the oracle to the WAITING_FOR_HARBINGER state. Conversely, the getXtzUsdPrice_callback entrypoint is allowable solely when the oracle is in the WAITING_FOR_HARBINGER state; invoking this entrypoint results in the oracle transitioning back to the IDLE state. The value of client is always set to none in the IDLE state and to some in the other state. We verify this property by examining the fail conditions of these two entrypoints and verifying the entrypoint relations between getXtzUsdPrice and getXtzUsdPrice_callback.

The two subsequent properties dictate that if getXtzUsdPrice is successfully executed, the parameters must be stored in the client attribute.
If getXtzUsdPrice_callback is successful, there must be a transaction transferring the data to the client at the client. These properties are checked by using pre and postconditions. Furthermore, the critical access control property is that the entrypoints setGovernorContract and setMaxDelaySec must only be invocable

[3] Here, we shortened the names of the variables for the storage.

```
1 entrypoint %setMaxDataDelaySec
2  code := {...}
3  parameter := delay: nat
4  pre-condition := Sender = governor
5  post-condition := post_harbinger = harbinger
6  && post_governor = gover
7  && post_maxDelay = delay && post_maxDelay <= 1800
```

Listing 1.9. The specification of the setMaxDataDelaySec entrypoint

by the governor. Any attempts by unauthorized callers to these entrypoints should result in failure.

When verifying the entrypoint setMaxDataDelaySec, we noticed an unmatched statement. According to [14], the Kolibri oracle is expected to perform two checks on data returned from Harbinger: (1) confirming the asset returned is 'XTZ-USD' and (2) verifying the asset was updated within the last 30 minutes. We conducted fail condition checks for both the setMaxDelaySec and getXtzUsdPrice_callback entrypoints, but these conditions were not enforced. Specifically, upon examining the failwith conditions, we detected that there is no failwith when the data is more than 30 minutes (equal to 1800 seconds).

We then add the predicate post_maxDelay <= 1800 in the postcondition of the entrypoint setMaxDataDelaySec as shown in Listing 1.9, but then the pre and postcondition test fails. This means there is no constraint enforcing that the data must be less than or equal to 30 minutes. This constraint is possibly set up by the governor and specified in the MaxDataDelaySec field. However, users calling this contract should be aware that it is possible for the governor to set any value (>= 0) as desired. This could lead to providing out-of-date rates.

The complete specifications and experimental results for the examples and case studies can be accessed online at [25].

7 Related Work

In this section, we discuss some key approaches, particularly those employing symbolic execution in the context of smart contracts. P. Tsankov et al. introduced SECURIFY [27], a tool that utilizes symbolic execution to perform practical security analysis on Ethereum smart contracts. It targets common vulnerability security patterns specified in a designated domain-specific language. Similarly, Manticore [20] and KEVM [12] also target Ethereum smart contracts. KEVM is an executable formal specification built with the K Framework. Since tokens can hold a significant amount of value, they are often targeted for attacks. Therefore, several tools [12,24] conduct case studies for the implementations of token standards.

Several approaches use existing formal verification frameworks to ensure the correctness and security of smart contracts. Amani et al. [1] proposed the formal verification of Ethereum smart contracts in Isabelle/HOL. Hirai [13] formalizes the EVM using Lem, a language to specify semantic definitions.

There are existing tools for automated verification include solc-verify [11], VerX [2], and Oyente [17]. solc-verify processes smart contracts written in Solidity and discharges verification conditions using modular program analysis and SMT solvers. While these approaches differ, they share a focus on common bugs (such as reentrancy, overflow or underflow, and frozen funds). Our tool provide an environment where users can reliably specify their own properties and identify contract-specific bugs. Our tool aims to rich specifications to supports manually specified full correctness specifications.

Close to our approach are HELMHOLTZ [23] and Mi-Cho-Coq [5], as discussed in Sect. 1. In HELMHOLTZ, properties are annotated inside the code by the developer, which requires modifying the code. In contrast, we provide a separate specification language, so users do not need to modify the code. Similar to our tool, iContract [22] utilizes symbolic execution and pre and postconditions to specify user properties, but the iContract work and our work differ in target language, DSL design, and functionality.

8 Conclusion

Symbolic execution is well known to suffer from challenges related to state explosion, particularly when applied to large systems. To address this problem, our tool mitigates state explosion and has been applied to two real case studies of running blockchain contracts, focusing on significant subjects such as token standards and oracles.

Our tool has several limitations. SCV relies on Z3, which may struggle with very large or complex problems, potentially returning `unknown` if it cannot determine satisfiability. Additionally, the tool does not yet handle gas consumption or support external calls.

In future work, we want to extend SCV in two directions. First, we want to address the interaction of several entrypoints by extending the specification language to state allowed sequences of contract invocations. Second, a Michelson program returns a list of instructions, which may contain further contract invocations. Dealing with this kind of contracts requires an extension to the symbolic interpreter so that a sequence of contract invocations can be processed in one run.

References

1. Amani, S., Bégel, M., Bortin, M., Staples, M.: Towards verifying Ethereum smart contract bytecode in Isabelle/HOL. In: Proceedings of the 7th ACM SIGPLAN International Conference on Certified Programs and Proofs (CPP), pp. 66–77 (2018). https://doi.org/10.1145/3167084
2. Anton, P., Dimitar, D., Petar, T., Drachsler-Cohen, D., Vechev, M.: Verx: safety verification of smart contracts. In: 2020 IEEE Symposium on Security and Privacy (SP), pp. 1661–1677 (2020). https://doi.org/10.1109/SP40000.2020.00024

3. Arvay, B., Doan, T.T.H., Thiemann, P.: A dynamic logic for symbolic execution for the smart contract programming language michelson. In: European Conference on Object-Oriented Programming (ECOOP 2024). To appear (2024)
4. Erc20 api: An Attack Vector on the Approve/Transferfrom Methods. https://docs.google.com/document/d/1YLPtQxZu1UAvO9cZ1O2RPXBbT0mooh4DYKjA_jp-RLM/edit#heading=h.m9fhqynw2xvt
5. Bernardo, B., Cauderlier, R., Hu, Z., Pesin, B., Tesson, J.: Mi-Cho-Coq, a framework for certifying Tezos smart contracts. In: Formal Methods. FM 2019 International Workshops - Porto, Portugal, 7–11 Oct 2019, Revised Selected Papers, Part I. Lecture Notes in Computer Science, vol. 12232, pp. 368–379. Springer, Heidelberg (2019)
6. Buterin, V.: A Next-Generation Smart Contract and Decentralized Application Platform (2013). https://ethereum.org/en/whitepaper/
7. Understanding the DAO Attack. https://www.coindesk.com/learn/understanding-the-dao-attack/
8. ERC-20. https://ethereum.org/en/developers/docs/standards/tokens/erc-20
9. FA1.2 Tokens. https://docs.tezos.com/architecture/tokens/FA1.2
10. Goodman, L.: Tezos-a Self-amending Crypto-Ledger (2014). https://www.tezos.com/static/papers/white-paper.pdf
11. Hajdu, A., Jovanovio, D.: solc-verify: a modular verifier for solidity smart contracts. In: Chakraborty, S., Navas, J.A. (eds.) Verified Software. Theories, Tools, and Experiments, pp. 161–179. Springer International Publishing (2020)
12. Hildenbrandt, E., Saxena, M., Rodrigues, N., Zhu, X., Daian, P., Guth, D., Moore, B., Park, D., Zhang, Y., Stefanescu, A., Rosu, G.: KEVM: a complete formal semantics of the Ethereum virtual machine. In: 2018 IEEE 31st Computer Security Foundations Symposium (CSF), pp. 204–217 (2018). https://doi.org/10.1109/CSF.2018.00022
13. Hirai, Y.: Defining the Ethereum virtual machine for interactive theorem provers. In: Financial Cryptography and Data Security, pp. 520–535. Springer International Publishing (2017)
14. Kolibri Oracle Contract. https://kolibri.finance/docs/components/oracle
15. Ligo: Smart Contract Language for Tezos. https://ligolang.org/
16. Liquidity. https://liquidity-lang.org/
17. Luu, L., Chu, D.H., Olickel, H., Saxena, P., Hobor, A.: Making smart contracts smarter. In: Proceedings of the 2016 ACM SIGSAC Conference on Computer and Communications Security (CCS), pp. 254–269 (2016)
18. Michelson: The Language of Smart Contracts in Tezos. https://tezos.gitlab.io/alpha/michelson.html
19. Michelson Reference. https://tezos.gitlab.io/michelson-reference/
20. Mossberg, M., Manzano, F., Hennenfent, E., Groce, A., Grieco, G., Feist, J., Brunson, T., Dinaburg, A.: Manticore: a user-friendly symbolic execution framework for binaries and smart contracts. In: 2019 34th IEEE/ACM International Conference on Automated Software Engineering (ASE), pp. 1186–1189 (2019). https://doi.org/10.1109/ASE.2019.00133
21. de Moura, L., Bjørner, N.: Z3: an efficient SMT solver. In: Ramakrishnan, C.R., Rehof, J. (eds.) Tools and Algorithms for the Construction and Analysis of Systems, pp. 337–340. Springer, Berlin Heidelberg, Berlin, Heidelberg (2008)
22. Nguyen, T.D., Pham, L.H., Sun, J., Le, Q.L.: An idealist's approach for smart contract correctness. In: Li, Y., Tahar, S. (eds.) Formal Methods and Software Engineering, pp. 11–28. Springer Nature Singapore, Singapore (2023)

23. Nishida, Y., Saito, H., Chen, R., Kawata, A., Furuse, J., Suenaga, K., Igarashi, A.: HELMHOLTZ: a verifier for Tezos smart contracts based on refinement types. N. Gener. Comput. **40**, 507–540 (2022). https://doi.org/10.1007/s00354-022-00167-1
24. Park, D., Zhang, Y., Saxena, M., Daian, P., Rou, G.: A formal verification tool for Ethereum VM bytecode. In: Proceedings of the 2018 26th ACM Joint Meeting on European Software Engineering Conference and Symposium on the Foundations of Software Engineering (ESEC/FSE), pp. 912–915 (2018). https://doi.org/10.1145/3236024.3264591
25. SCV: A Formal Verification Framework for Tezos Smart Contracts Based on Symbolic Execution. https://zenodo.org/records/11363663
26. SmartPy: Smart Contracts on Tezos. https://smartpy.io/
27. Tsankov, P., Dan, A., Drachsler-Cohen, D., Gervais, A., Bünzli, F., Vechev, M.: Securify: Practical security analysis of smart contracts. In: Proceedings of the 2018 ACM SIGSAC Conference on Computer and Communications Security, pp. 67–82 (2018). https://doi.org/10.1145/3243734.3243780
28. Tzstats: USDtz. https://tzstats.com/KT1LN4LPSqTMS7Sd2CJw4bbDGRkMv2t68Fy9
29. USDtz Whitepaper. https://docs.usdtz.com/usdtz-whitepaper
30. The Parity Wallet Hack Explained. https://blog.openzeppelin.com/on-the-parity-wallet-multisig-hack-405a8c12e8f7

Mode-based Reduction from Validity Checking of Fixpoint Logic Formulas to Test-Friendly Reachability Problem

Hiroyuki Katsura[1(✉)], Naoki Kobayashi[1], Ken Sakayori[1], and Ryosuke Sato[2]

[1] The University of Tokyo, Tokyo, Japan
{h.katsura,koba,sakayori}@is.s.u-tokyo.ac.jp
[2] Tokyo University of Agriculture and Technology, Tokyo, Japan
rsato@acm.org

Abstract. A logical approach to automated program verification has been drawing attention recently, where various program verification problems are transformed into formulas of fixpoint logics such as CHC and νHFL(Z), so that a given program satisfies a property just if the corresponding fixpoint formula is valid. In this paper, we show a kind of converse transformation, converting fixpoint logic formulas to programs so that a formula is valid just if the resulting program never evaluates to an (error) value. This, together with the aforementioned transformation from programs to formulas, allows us to go back and forth between logical formulas and programs. In particular, our transformation enables us to use random testing to disprove a given formula, implying that the original program does not satisfy the specified property. As the programs generated by a naive transformation are not suitable for random testing, we employ mode analysis to generate more test-friendly programs. We have implemented the mode-guided transformation and confirmed its effectiveness through experiments.

1 Introduction

A logical approach to automated program verification has been extensively studied, where various program verification problems are expressed as formulas of fixpoint logics such as CHCs (Constrained Horn Clauses) [2], Higher-order CHC [5], and HFL(Z) [24], and then the validity of the formulas is automatically proved [10,12,18,24,26]. Various tools have been developed to automatically check the validity of fixpoint logic formulas. Such tools serve as language-independent, unifying tools for automated verification.

In this paper, we propose a novel method for disproving formulas of νHFL(Z), a higher-order fixpoint logic with greatest fixpoint operators and integer arithmetic. It is a sublogic of HFL(Z) and equi-expressive with HoCHC [5], subsuming CHCs as the first-order case. Using higher-order predicates and fixpoint operators, one can easily express various safety properties of higher-order programs

O. Kiselyov (Ed.): APLAS 2024, LNCS 15194, pp. 325–345, 2024.
https://doi.org/10.1007/978-981-97-8943-6_16

with recursion [24]. The functionality to disprove a νHFL(Z) formula can thus be used to prove that a given program does not satisfy a safety property. Existing solvers for νHFL(Z) [5,16,19,22] and CHCs [6,14,15,25] also provide the functionality for disproving formulas, but they were not fully satisfactory. They are often too slow for invalid formulas with only "deep" counterexamples (for which fixpoint formulas need to be unfolded many times to find contradiction). Although some methods have been proposed to address this problem [3,11] for the case of CHCs, they were neither fully satisfactory nor easily applicable to the higher-order case.

Our method is based on random testing. Given a formula of νHFL(Z), we convert it into a non-deterministic functional program, which tries to find a counterexample to the validity of the formula. We explain our approach by using the (invalid) formula $\varphi \triangleq \forall x.\forall y.\, x > 0 \land y > 5 \implies P\,x\,y$, where the predicate P is the greatest predicate that satisfies the equation:

$$P\,x\,y = \ (x = 0 \Rightarrow y \neq 0) \land P\,(x-1)\,(y-1).$$

$P\ x\ y$ may be understood as the (infinite) formula $(x = 0 \Rightarrow y \neq 0) \land (x - 1 = 0 \Rightarrow y - 1 \neq 0) \land (x - 2 = 0 \Rightarrow y - 2 \neq 0) \land \cdots$, obtained by rewriting P according to the equation. Although the formula φ above is artificial, chosen for the sake of simplicity, this kind of formula containing greatest fixpoint equations naturally arises from verification problems for recursive programs [2,24].

Figure 1(a) shows a naive program (which we call p_a) that tries to disprove the formula φ. Here, the function p takes x and y, and tries to disprove $P\ x\ y$. The main expression on the third line randomly picks integers x and y, asserts that $x > 0 \land y > 5$ holds, and then calls p to disprove $P\ x\ y$. In the body of p, it first tries to assert $x = 0 \land y = 0$ (to disprove the subformula $x = 0 \Rightarrow y \neq 0$), and if the assertion fails, proceeds to disprove $P\ (x-1)\ (y-1)$.[1] Thus, φ is invalid if and only if the program p_a in Figure 1(a) *may* terminate successfully. (In other words, p_a;**error** may reach the error point **error** if and only if φ is invalid.)

The problem of the program p_a in Fig. 1(a) is that it is not *test-friendly*; there are too many non-deterministic choices. The probability of successfully disproving φ by randomly testing p_a is quite low because the value chosen for y by `rand_int ()` must be equal to that chosen for x.

To address this issue, we employ a *mode analysis* to infer an input-output relation for each predicate, and use that information to generate more deterministic programs. For the example above, we can infer that the value of y such that $P\ x\ y$ is invalid can be uniquely determined from x. Based on such "mode" information, we obtain the program p_b in Fig. 1(b). Notice that p is now a function of type `int` $\rightarrow$ `int`, not `int` $\rightarrow$ `int` $\rightarrow$ `unit`. It takes an integer x and returns an integer y such that $P\,x\,y$ does not hold. Thanks to this transformation, the main expression on the third line no longer needs to generate a random number for y, and successfully terminates as long as the random number chosen for x is greater than 5.

[1] Here, `try` e_1 `with` e_2 first evaluates e_1, and if an exception (such as an assertion failure) occurs, e_2 is evaluated.

(a) Program p_a obtained by a naïve transformation

```
let rec p x y = try assert(x = 0 && y = 0) with p (x - 1) (y - 1)
let () = let x = rand_int () in let y = rand_int () in
         assert(x > 0 && y > 5); p x y
```

(b) Program p_b obtained by our mode-guided transformation

```
let rec p: int -> int = fun x ->
  try assert(x = 0); x with p (x - 1) + 1
let () = let x = rand_int () in let y = p x in assert(x > 0 && y > 5)
```

Fig. 1. Transformed programs

The contributions of this paper are summarized as follows.

- We have formalized a mode-guided transformation, and proved its soundness and completeness (Sect. 4).
- We have implemented a prototype falsification tool for νHFL(Z) and CHCs based on the proposed method.
- We have evaluated our approach and compared the results with the state-of-the-art CHC and νHFL(Z) solvers (Sect. 5.3).

The rest of the paper is organized as follows. Section 2 reviews the target fixpoint logic νHFL(Z). Section 3 gives an overview of our framework. Section 4 formalizes the mode-guided transformation. Section 5 reports experimental results. Section 6 discusses related work, and Sect. 7 concludes the paper.

2 Preliminaries: νHFL(Z)

In this section, we first introduce the syntax and semantics of νHFL(Z), a higher-order logic with integers and greatest fixpoints.

We first introduce types for formulas. The syntax of simple types is defined by

$$\begin{aligned} &(\textit{simple types for formulas}) && \kappa ::= \bullet \mid \eta \to \kappa \\ &(\textit{simple types for arguments}) && \eta ::= \mathbf{Int} \mid \kappa. \end{aligned}$$

Here, $\bullet$ denotes the type of propositions, and $\eta \to \kappa$ denotes the type of predicates that take an argument of type η as its argument and return a formula of type κ.

The syntax of fixpoint-free formulas, fixpoint equations and equational systems is defined by

$$\begin{aligned} &(\textit{fixpoint-free formulas}) && \varphi ::= \mathbf{p}(\overrightarrow{\mathbf{a}}) \mid X \mid \varphi_1 \wedge \varphi_2 \mid \varphi_1 \vee \varphi_2 \\ & && \qquad \forall x.\, \varphi \mid \lambda x : \eta.\, \varphi \mid \varphi\, \mathbf{a} \mid \varphi_1\, \varphi_2 \\ &(\textit{fixpoint equations}) && D ::= \{ x_1 =_{\kappa_1} \varphi_1, \ldots, x_l =_{\kappa_l} \varphi_l \} \\ &(\textit{equational systems}) && \mathcal{E} ::= (D, \varphi). \end{aligned}$$

Here, $\mathbf{p}$ is a metavariable for primitive predicates such as $\neq$ and $\mathbf{a}$ is a metavariable for arithmetic expressions. We assume that the set of primitive predicates is closed under negation; for example, if $\neq$ is in the set of predicates, $=$ should also be in the set. We assume a denumerable set of variables, ranged over by $x, y, \ldots$. Lambda abstractions $\lambda x. \varphi$ and universal quantifiers $\forall x. \varphi$ are the only binders of the fixpoint-free formulas, and we implicitly allow α-renaming of the bound variables. The fixpoint equations $\{ X_1 =_{\kappa_1} \varphi_1, \ldots, X_l =_{\kappa_l} \varphi_l \}$ define the greatest predicates $X_1, \ldots, X_l$ that satisfy the equations. An *equational system* is defined as a pair of fixpoint equations and a fixpoint-free formula, and we often call it a *νHFL(Z) formula*. We refer to φ of (D, φ) as the *goal formula* of the νHFL(Z) formula. We also write **true** for $0 \neq 1$ and **false** for $0 \neq 0$. We use θ as a metavariable for *constraint formulas*, which are fixpoint-free formulas of type $\bullet$ that contain no lambda abstractions and applications. We write $\theta \implies \varphi$ for $\neg\theta \vee \varphi$ where $\neg\theta$ is de Morgan dual of θ. We also write **if** θ **then** φ_1 **else** φ_2 for $(\theta \implies \varphi_1) \wedge (\neg\theta \implies \varphi_2)$.

A simple type judgment is of the form $\mathcal{K} \vdash_H \varphi : \kappa$, where $\mathcal{K}$ is a simple type environment, a finite map from variables to simple types for arguments. Refer to the full version [21] for typing rules. Let D be $\{ X_1 =_{\kappa_1} \varphi_1, \ldots, X_l =_{\kappa_l} \varphi_l \}$ and $\mathcal{K}$ be $\{ X_1 : \kappa_1, \ldots, X_l : \kappa_l \}$. The fixpoint equation D is well-typed under $\mathcal{K}$ if $\mathcal{K} \vdash_H \varphi_i : \kappa_i$ for each $i \in \{ 1, \ldots, l \}$, and a νHFL(Z) formula (D, φ) is well-typed if $\mathcal{K} \vdash_H \varphi : \bullet$ and D is well-typed under $\mathcal{K}$. In the sequel, we only consider well-typed νHFL(Z) formulas. We also assume that there is no predicate that takes a proposition as its argument for the simplicity of our transformation.[2]

Remark 2.1. Note that νHFL(Z) can be seen as the dual logic of HoCHC [5], which is a higher-order extension of constrained Horn clauses. Therefore, our approach can directly be applied also to falsifying constrained Horn clauses.

Example 2.2. Let us consider an invalid νHFL(Z) formula $(D, P\,10000)$ where D is a singleton set of

$$P =_{\mathbf{Int} \to \bullet} \lambda x.\, x \neq 0 \wedge (x > 10000 \vee P\,(x - 1)).$$

The semantics of P is defined as the greatest P such that the above equation holds. Note that P is in fact equivalent to $\lambda x. x < 0 \vee x > 10000$, and $P\,10000$ is invalid. Instead of semantic reasoning, we can confirm the invalidity of $P\,10000$ by expanding the fixpoint more than 10,000 times as follows:

$$\begin{aligned}
P\,10000 &\equiv 10000 \neq 0 \wedge (10000 > 10000 \vee P\,(10000 - 1)) && \text{(expansion of } P\text{)} \\
&\equiv P\,9999 && \text{(simplification)} \\
\cdots &\equiv P\,0 && \\
&\equiv 0 \neq 0 \wedge (0 > 10000 \vee P\,(0 - 1)) && \text{(expansion of } P\text{)} \\
&\equiv \mathbf{false} && \text{(simplification)}
\end{aligned}$$

[2] Note that we can easily remove such predicates by transforming each proposition φ in a formula to $\bullet \to \bullet$ predicates.

For those who are familiar with constrained Horn clauses (CHCs), we note that the CHCs equivalent to this formula are

$$\Rightarrow P(0) \qquad x \leq 10000 \land P(x-1) \Rightarrow P(x) \qquad P(10000) \Rightarrow \bot.$$

In contrast, νHFL(Z) formula $(D, P\,(-1))$ is valid since no matter how many times we apply β-reductions and simplifications to such formula, we never obtain **false**.

Example 2.3. Let us see a higher-order formula, which will be used as the running example in Sect. 4. Let φ be $\mathrm{Loop}\,(\lambda x.\, x < 1000)\,\mathrm{Dec}\,1000$ and D be:

$$\begin{aligned} \mathrm{Dec} &=_{\mathbf{Int}\to\mathbf{Int}\to\bullet} \lambda n.\, \lambda r.\, n - 1 \neq r \\ \mathrm{Loop} &=_{(\mathbf{Int}\to\bullet)\to(\mathbf{Int}\to\mathbf{Int}\to\bullet)\to\mathbf{Int}\to\bullet} \lambda g.\, \lambda f.\, \lambda n. \\ &\qquad \mathbf{if}\ n = 0\ \mathbf{then}\ g\,n\ \mathbf{else}\ \forall m.\, f\,n\,m \lor \mathrm{Loop}\,(\lambda x.\, g\,(x+1))\,f\,m. \end{aligned}$$

This formula encodes the safety property of the following program:

```
let dec n = n - 1
let rec loop g f n =
  if n = 0 then g n else let m = f n in loop (fun x -> g (x+1)) f m
let () = loop (fun x -> assert(x < 1000)) dec 1000
```

The formal semantics of νHFL(Z) is given in the full version of this paper [21]. For a closed formula φ of type $\bullet$, we write $\models \varphi$ when φ is valid. For (possibly open) constraint formulas, we also write $\models \theta$ when the universal closure of θ is valid. If a νHFL(Z) formula (D, φ) is valid, we write $\models (D, \varphi)$. The *validity checking problem* of νHFL(Z) is to decide whether $\models (D, \varphi)$ holds or not for a given well-typed νHFL(Z) formula (D, φ).

3 Overview of Our Transformation

In this section, we discuss how our overall framework transforms νHFL(Z) formulas to functional programs. We first introduce a simplified version of our transformation, which we call Basic Transformation in the sequel, to provide an overview and the intuition behind our approach in Sect. 3.1. After that we point out the problem of the Basic Transformation, illustrating its limitations with an example in Sect. 3.2. Finally, we exemplify how our mode-guided transformation can overcome the limitations of Basic Transformation in Sect. 3.3.

3.1 Basic Transformation

Recall the νHFL(Z) formula $(D, P\,10000)$ in Example 2.2. We refuted the formula by unfolding and simplifying fixpoint formulas until it is reduced to **false**. Our main idea is to transform a formula to a non-deterministic functional program so that the formula is invalid if and only if the program *may* terminate successfully. Thus, the problem of disproving a formula is reduced to the may-reachability problem. For example, $(D, P\,10000)$ can be reduced to the program:

```
let rec p x = try assert(x = 0) with (assert(x <= 10000); p (x - 1))
let () = p 10000
```

Here, the target language is a non-deterministic functional programming language with exceptions. In this program, the fixpoint P is transformed to a recursive function `p`, and the goal formula is transformed to the entry point `p 10000`. The expression `p 10000` terminates successfully since it can finally be evaluated to `assert(0 = 0)` after the iterations of the recursive function 10,000 times, which implies the invalidity of the original formula.

We formalize the Basic Transformation $[\![\cdot]\!]$ as a map from fixpoint-free formulas φ to expressions such that $\not\models \varphi$ if and only if $[\![\varphi]\!] \longrightarrow^* ()$, defined by (we omit the higher-order cases)

$$\begin{aligned} [\![\theta]\!] &= \texttt{assert}(\neg\theta) \\ [\![\varphi_1 \vee \varphi_2]\!] &= [\![\varphi_1]\!] ; [\![\varphi_2]\!] \\ [\![\theta \wedge \varphi]\!] &= \texttt{try } [\![\theta]\!] \texttt{ with } [\![\varphi]\!] \\ [\![\varphi_1 \wedge \varphi_2]\!] &= [\![\varphi_1]\!] \oplus [\![\varphi_2]\!] \\ [\![\forall x.\, \varphi]\!] &= \texttt{let x = } \star \texttt{ in } [\![\varphi]\!]. \end{aligned}$$

Here, a constraint formula θ is transformed to the assertion statement that raises an exception when θ holds. For a disjunction $\varphi_1 \vee \varphi_2$, to confirm both of φ_1 and φ_2 are invalid, we run $[\![\varphi_1]\!]$ and $[\![\varphi_2]\!]$ sequentially to disprove both φ_1 and φ_2 are invalid, we run $[\![\varphi_1]\!]$ and $[\![\varphi_2]\!]$; if one of them never terminates successfully (either by raising an exception or diverging), it means the disjunction is valid. A conjunction $\varphi_1 \wedge \varphi_2$, on the other hand, is transformed to a non-deterministic choice of $[\![\varphi_1]\!]$ and $[\![\varphi_2]\!]$, because it suffices to disprove one of the conjuncts to disprove $\varphi_1 \wedge \varphi_2$. Similarly, $\forall x.\, \varphi$, is transformed to an expression that picks an integer x in a non-deterministic manner, and then tries to disprove φ. For an optimization, a conjunction of the form $\theta \wedge \varphi$ (where one of the clauses is a constraint) is treated in a special manner, and transformed to an expression that first tries to disprove θ, and then tries to disprove $[\![\varphi]\!]$ upon failure.[3]

Given a νHFL(Z) formula (D, φ) where $D = \{ P_1 =_{\kappa_1} \varphi_1, \dots, P_k =_{\kappa_k} \varphi_k \}$, we generate a sequence of mutually recursive functions $\mathtt{p}_1, \dots, \mathtt{p}_k$ such that

$$\texttt{let rec } \mathtt{p}_1 = [\![\varphi_1]\!] \quad \texttt{and} \quad \cdots \quad \texttt{and} \quad \mathtt{p}_k = [\![\varphi_k]\!].$$

From the goal formula φ, we also generate an entry point `let () =` $[\![\varphi]\!]$. After the transformation, we apply random testing to the transformed program to find a counterexample.

As we confirm in Sect. 5.3, this naive transformation is already effective for some formulas (such as $(D, P\,10000)$), but problematic in general, as discussed below.

[3] Note that $[\![\varphi_1 \wedge \varphi_2]\!]$ cannot be transformed to `try` $[\![\varphi_1]\!]$ `with` $[\![\varphi]\!]$ in general, because $[\![\varphi_1]\!]$ may not terminate.

3.2 Problem of Basic Transformation

The main problem with Basic Transformation is that it can often introduce too many non-deterministic choices. As we defined, every time Basic Transformation encounters a universal quantifier $\forall x.\,\varphi$, it introduces a non-deterministic generation of integers. Recall the formula φ in Introduction. The output of the Basic Transformation is shown in Fig. 1.(a), where x and y are non-deterministically generated. Such non-determinism is problematic for the efficiency of random testing.

Non-deterministic choices become even more problematic when introduced to the body of a recursive function, as it leads to the infamous path explosion problem. For example, consider the invalid νHFL(Z) formula (D, φ) where D is a singleton set of:

$$\begin{array}{l} \text{fib} =_{\mathbf{Int}\to\mathbf{Int}\to\bullet} \lambda c.\lambda n. \\ \quad \textbf{if } n < 2 \textbf{ then } c \neq 0 \textbf{ else} \\ \qquad \forall c'.\forall c''.\, c' + c'' + 2 \neq c \vee \text{fib}\, c'\,(n-1) \vee \text{fib}\, c''\,(n-2) \end{array}$$

and $\varphi \triangleq \forall c.\forall n.(n > 0 \wedge c \geq 2 * n) \implies \text{fib}\, c\, n$. The predicate $\text{fib}\, c\, n$ means that `fib` function in Fig. 2(a) does not terminate for n with c recursive calls. Therefore, the νHFL(Z) formula is valid if and only if `fib` n either terminates within $2n$ recursive calls or diverges.[4] If we apply Basic Transformation to this formula, we obtain the program shown in Fig. 2(b). Although the may-reachability to () is equivalent to the invalidity of the νHFL(Z) formula, it is unlikely to find a counterexample using this transformed program through random testing. Every time `fib_b` is called with the argument $n \geq 2$, `c` must be precisely distributed to `c'` and `c''` so that in each leaf call we can eventually reach `assert`$(c = 0)$ with $c = 0$; otherwise, the program raises an exception, failing to disprove the original formula.

3.3 Mode-Guided Transformation

To address the problem of Basic Transformation discussed above, we introduce *mode-guided* transformation. In this section, we explain a basic idea through the example of fib; the concrete formalization is given in Sect. 4.

The problem of the program Fig. 1(b) obtained by Basic Transformation was that it contains too much non-determinism on the choice of c' and c''. The key observation to address this problem is that, the value of c that falsifies fib c n can actually be uniquely determined from n. To see this, recall the definition of the predicate fib. If $n < 2$, it suffices to falsify $c \neq 0$, so we can set c to 0. If $n \geq 2$, then we need to find c that falsifies $\forall c'.\forall c''.\, c' + c'' + 2 \neq c \vee \text{fib}\, c'\,(n-1) \vee \text{fib}\, c''\,(n-2)$. Assuming that c' and c'' that falsify $\text{fib}\, c'\,(n-1)$

[4] We can remove the latter possibility by conjoining $c > 0$ at the body of fib, but we omit this part for simplicity.

```
let rec fib n = if n < 2 then n else fib (n - 1) + fib (n - 2)
```

(a) Fibonacci function

```
let rec fib_b c n =
  if n < 2 then assert(c = 0)
  else
    let c' = * in let c'' = * in
    assert(c' + c'' + 2 = c);
    fib_b c' (n - 1); fib_b c'' (n - 2)
```

(b) A function transformed from predicate fib by BASIC TRANSFORMATION

```
let rec fib_m n =
  if n < 2 then 0
  else
    let c' = fib_m (n - 1) in
    let c'' = fib_m (n - 2) in
    c' + c'' + 2
```

(c) One obtained by our mode-guided transformation

Fig. 2. Comparison of the original and the functions obtained by different transformations

and fib c'' $(n-2)$ can be uniquely determined respectively from $n-1$ and $n-2$, we can let c be $c' + c'' + 2$ for such c' and c''.

Based on the observation above, we can obtain the program in Fig. 1(c). Here, the function `fib_m` takes an integer n, and returns an integer c that falsifies fib $c\,n$. Note that the original predicate fib was a binary predicate (of type $\mathbf{Int} \to \mathbf{Int} \to \bullet$), but the corresponding function `fib_m` has type `int` $\to$ `int`. Additionally, Fig. 1(c) no longer contains non-deterministic generation of integers.

To generalize the observation above, we assign an input ($-$) or output ($+$) mode to each integer argument of a predicate, and transform a given formula according to the mode assignment. For example, the predicate fib above is assigned a mode $+ \to - \to \bullet$, meaning that the value of the first argument that falsifies fib can be determined from the second argument. Based on that mode, fib is transformed to a function of type `int` $\to$ `int` as discussed above. If $- \to - \to \bullet$ were instead assigned to `fib`, then fib would be transformed to the function `fib_b` in Fig. 1(c).

The problem of statically finding a consistent mode assignment, known as mode analysis, has been studied in the context of logic programming. We adopt and extend such mode analysis for higher-order fixpoint logic formulas, and formalize a mode-guided transformation from formulas to test-friendly programs.

4 Mode-Guided Transformation

We formalize our mode-guided transformation for νHFL(Z) formulas.

4.1 Mode

A mode of a predicate represents how its arguments are used in the body of the predicate. The syntax of modes is defined by

$$(\textit{modes}) \quad \mathtt{m} ::= \bullet \mid - \to \mathtt{m} \mid + \to \mathtt{m} \mid \mathtt{m}_1 \to \mathtt{m}_2.$$

Here, $-$ and $+$ are used for integer arguments. We call $-$ an *input mode* and $+$ an *output mode*. For a predicate, its arguments with an output mode are determined by the other arguments with an input mode to falsify the predicate. We also consider modes for higher-order predicates $\mathtt{m}_1 \to \mathtt{m}_2$, and they represent that when predicates take an argument of mode $\mathtt{m}_1$, they return a predicate of mode $\mathtt{m}_2$. We use $\bullet$ for the mode of propositions. We define a mode erasure $\lfloor\cdot\rfloor$ from modes to simple types for formulas inductively by:

$$\lfloor\bullet\rfloor = \bullet \qquad\qquad \lfloor - \to \mathtt{m}\rfloor = \mathbf{Int} \to \lfloor\mathtt{m}\rfloor$$
$$\lfloor + \to \mathtt{m}\rfloor = \mathbf{Int} \to \lfloor\mathtt{m}\rfloor \qquad\qquad \lfloor\mathtt{m}_1 \to \mathtt{m}_2\rfloor = \lfloor\mathtt{m}_1\rfloor \to \lfloor\mathtt{m}_2\rfloor$$

A mode environment Γ is a finite map from variables to modes. We write $\lfloor\Gamma\rfloor$ for $\{\, x\colon\lfloor\mathtt{m}\rfloor \mid x\colon\mathtt{m} \in \Gamma \,\}$. In the mode-guided transformation that we introduce below, we maintain two sequences of integer variables: one for integer variables used in input mode and the other for those used in output mode. We often specify the former as Θ and the latter as Σ. For a mode environment Γ and a sequence of variables Θ, we write $\lfloor\Gamma;\Theta\rfloor$ for $\lfloor\Gamma\rfloor \cup \{\, x : \mathbf{Int} \mid x \in \Theta \,\}$.

Example 4.4. Recall the νHFL(Z) formula (D, φ) in Example 2.3. One possible mode for the predicate Dec is $- \to + \to \bullet$ because we can determine r to be $n-1$ to falsify the condition $n - 1 \neq r$. Note that there can be multiple valid modes; for example, Dec also has modes $- \to - \to \bullet$ and $+ \to - \to \bullet$.

Modes are associated with simple types for expressions. As we have seen, the mode of a first-order predicate corresponds to the type of the corresponding function that takes integers and returns multiple integers. We generalize this idea and for a mode $\mathtt{m}$ and a non-negative integer k, we define the type $\langle\mathtt{m}, k\rangle$ by:

$$\langle\bullet, k\rangle = \overbrace{\mathtt{int} \times \ldots \times \mathtt{int}}^{k} \qquad \langle - \to \mathtt{m}, k\rangle = \mathtt{int} \to \langle\mathtt{m}, k\rangle$$
$$\langle + \to \mathtt{m}, k\rangle = \langle\mathtt{m}, k+1\rangle \qquad \langle\mathtt{m}_1 \to \mathtt{m}_2, k\rangle = \langle\mathtt{m}_1, 0\rangle \to \langle\mathtt{m}_2, k\rangle.$$

Here, k represents how many integers are assumed to be returned so far. We often abbreviate $\langle\mathtt{m}, 0\rangle$ to $\langle\mathtt{m}\rangle$, and write $\langle\Gamma\rangle$ for $\{\, x : \langle\mathtt{m}, 0\rangle \mid x : \mathtt{m} \in \Gamma \,\}$. In addition, for a sequence Θ of variables, we write $\langle\Gamma;\Theta\rangle$ for $\langle\Gamma\rangle \cup \{\, x : \mathtt{int} \mid x \in \Theta \,\}$.

4.2 Mode-Guided Transformation

We now define the mode-guided transformation relation $\Gamma;\Theta \vdash \varphi : \mathtt{m} \rightsquigarrow e \mid \Sigma$ for a mode environment Γ, two sequences of variables Θ and Σ, a fixpoint-free formula φ, an expression e, and a mode $\mathtt{m}$ such that $\lfloor\Gamma;\Theta\cup\Sigma\rfloor \vdash_H \varphi : \lfloor\mathtt{m}\rfloor$. The sequence Θ represents variables with input mode, and Σ represents variables with output mode. As proved in Lemma 4.7, the output e of the transformation has type $\langle\mathtt{m}, |\Sigma|\rangle$ under $\langle\Gamma;\Theta\rangle$.

Intuitively, $\emptyset;\emptyset \vdash \varphi : \bullet \rightsquigarrow e \mid \Sigma$ means that e gives the values of variables in Σ that falsify φ. That is, if $e \longrightarrow^* (v_1,\ldots,v_k)$, then $\not\models [v_1/x_1,\ldots,v_k/x_k]\varphi$ for $\Sigma = x_1,\ldots,x_k$. For example, we have $\emptyset \vdash x \neq 1 \rightsquigarrow 1 \mid x$, as the assignment $[x \mapsto 1]$ makes the formula $x \neq 1$ false. Note that, in general, the expression e obtained by the translation may raise an exception or may not terminate (especially when φ is valid and hence cannot be falsified).

The mode-guided transformation rules are shown in Fig. 3. Here, we write $\mathbf{set}(\Sigma)$ for the set of variables in Σ, and $\Sigma^\flat$ for $(x_1,\ldots,x_{|\Sigma|})$, a $|\Sigma|$-tuple expression of variables, where $\Sigma = x_1,\ldots,x_{|\Sigma|}$. If we assume all the integer arguments of predicates have input mode, the transformation matches the BASIC TRANSFORMATION in Sect. 3.

The rule M-NEQ is for the case where the given constraint formula θ is logically equivalent to an inequality $x \neq \mathbf{a}$ for an output variable x, and $\mathbf{a}$ contains only input variables. In this case, we can falsify the formula by the assignment $[x \mapsto \mathbf{a}]$, and this is the only way to falsify the formula; thus we translate θ to $\mathbf{a}$. The rule M-PRED is for primitive predicates. In this case, we just try to falsify the formula by asserting the negation. The assertion successfully terminates if the formula is false indeed; otherwise, an exception is raised. The rule M-CONJ is for conjunctions. To falsify $\varphi_1 \wedge \varphi_2$, it suffices to falsify either φ_1 or φ_2. Thus, we non-deterministically run e_1 and e_2, which try to falsify φ_1 and φ_2 respectively. In the rule M-ITE for conditionals, we try to falsify φ_1 or φ_2 depending on whether θ is valid or not. Conditionals can actually be expressed by a combination of conjunctions and disjunctions, but we have prepared the specialized rule for an optimization purpose.

The rules M-DISJL and for M-DISJR are for disjunctions. To falsify $\varphi_1 \vee \varphi_2$, we need to find values (of output variables) that falsify both φ_1 and φ_2. In M-DISJL, we first run e_1 to find values of Σ_1 that falsify φ_1 and then run e_2 to find values of Σ_2 that falsify φ_2, and output a combination of the values of Σ_1 and Σ_2. The rule M-DISJR is for the reverse order; we choose one of the rules to maximize the number of variables in output mode.

In the rule M-APP for applications $\varphi\,\psi_1,\ldots,\psi_k$, we assume that all the arguments of mode $+$ are variables. This does not lose generality, because $\varphi \cdots \psi \cdots$ with $\psi : \mathbf{Int}$ can be replaced by $\forall x.x \neq \psi \vee \varphi \cdots x \cdots$. For the predicate φ, we just recursively apply the transformation and obtain an expression e. The translation of each argument ψ_i depends on its mode. If ψ_i has input mode, then we just pass ψ_i to e; note that in this case, ψ_i is an arithmetic expression, which is a valid expression of the target language. Similarly, if ψ_i is a predicate, then we pass its translation e_i to e. If ψ_i has output mode (and in this case, ψ_i is a variable x_i by the assumption above), then it becomes an output of e, as its value that falsifies $\varphi\,\psi_1 \cdots \psi_k$ can be determined from the other arguments. For example, consider $X\,x\,(y+1)$ with $X : + \to - \to \bullet$. It is translated to $\mathtt{let}\ x = X\,(y+1)\ \mathtt{in}\ x$.

$$\frac{\models \theta \Leftrightarrow x \neq \mathbf{a} \qquad \lfloor\Theta\rfloor \vdash_H \mathbf{a} : \mathbf{Int}}{\Gamma; \Theta \vdash \theta : \bullet \rightsquigarrow \mathbf{a} \mid \{x\}} \quad \text{(M-NEQ)}$$

$$\frac{}{\Gamma; \Theta \vdash p(\tilde{\mathbf{a}}_i) : \bullet \rightsquigarrow \texttt{assert}(\neg p(\tilde{\mathbf{a}}_i)) \mid \emptyset} \quad \text{(M-PRED)}$$

$$\frac{\Gamma; \Theta \vdash \varphi_1 \rightsquigarrow e_1 : \bullet \mid \Sigma \qquad \Gamma; \Theta \vdash \varphi_2 \rightsquigarrow e_2 : \bullet \mid \Sigma}{\Gamma; \Theta \vdash \varphi_1 \land \varphi_2 : \bullet \rightsquigarrow e_1 \oplus e_2 \mid \Sigma} \quad \text{(M-CONJ)}$$

$$\frac{\lfloor\Theta\rfloor \vdash_H \theta : \bullet \qquad \Gamma; \Theta \vdash \varphi_1 \rightsquigarrow e_1 : \bullet \mid \Sigma \qquad \Gamma; \Theta \vdash \varphi_2 \rightsquigarrow e_2 : \bullet \mid \Sigma}{\Gamma; \Theta \vdash \mathbf{if}\ \theta\ \mathbf{then}\ \varphi_1\ \mathbf{else}\ \varphi_2 : \bullet \rightsquigarrow \mathbf{if}\ \theta\ \mathbf{then}\ e_1\ \mathbf{else}\ e_2 \mid \Sigma} \quad \text{(M-ITE)}$$

$$\frac{\mathbf{set}(\Sigma_1) \uplus \mathbf{set}(\Sigma_2) = \mathbf{set}(\Sigma) \qquad \Gamma; \Theta \vdash \varphi_1 : \bullet \rightsquigarrow e_1 \mid \Sigma_1 \qquad \Gamma; \Theta, \Sigma_1 \vdash \varphi_2 : \bullet \rightsquigarrow e_2 \mid \Sigma_2}{\Gamma; \Theta \vdash \varphi_1 \lor \varphi_2 : \bullet \rightsquigarrow \texttt{let}\ \Sigma_1^\flat = e_1\ \texttt{in let}\ \Sigma_2^\flat = e_2\ \texttt{in}\ \Sigma^\flat \mid \Sigma} \quad \text{(M-DISJL)}$$

$$\frac{\mathbf{set}(\Sigma_1) \uplus \mathbf{set}(\Sigma_2) = \mathbf{set}(\Sigma) \qquad \Gamma; \Theta, \Sigma_2 \vdash \varphi_1 : \bullet \rightsquigarrow e_1 \mid \Sigma_1 \qquad \Gamma; \Theta \vdash \varphi_2 : \bullet \rightsquigarrow e_2 \mid \Sigma_2}{\Gamma; \Theta \vdash \varphi_1 \lor \varphi_2 : \bullet \rightsquigarrow \texttt{let}\ \Sigma_2^\flat = e_2\ \texttt{in let}\ \Sigma_1^\flat = e_1\ \texttt{in}\ \Sigma^\flat \mid \Sigma} \quad \text{(M-DISJR)}$$

$$\frac{\begin{array}{c}\Gamma; \Theta \vdash \varphi : m_1 \to \cdots \to m_k \to \bullet \rightsquigarrow e \mid \emptyset \\ \{o_1, \ldots, o_a\} = \{i \mid m_i = +, 1 \leq i \leq k\} \qquad o_1 < \cdots < o_a \\ x_{o_j} = \psi_{o_j} \qquad \mathbf{set}(\Sigma) = \{x_{o_1}, \ldots, x_{o_a}\} \\ \{l_1, \ldots, l_b\} = \{i \mid m_i \neq +, 1 \leq i \leq k\} \\ e_i = \psi_i \text{ and } \lfloor\Theta\rfloor \vdash_H \psi_i : \mathbf{Int} \text{ for each } i \text{ s.t. } m_i = - \\ \Gamma; \Theta \vdash \psi_i : m_i \rightsquigarrow e_i \mid \emptyset \text{ for each } i \text{ s.t. } m_i \notin \{-, +\}\end{array}}{\Gamma; \Theta \vdash \varphi\, \psi_1 \cdots \psi_k : \bullet \rightsquigarrow \texttt{let}\ (x_{o_1}, \ldots, x_{o_a}) = e\, e_{l_1} \cdots e_{l_b}\ \texttt{in}\ \Sigma^\flat \mid \Sigma} \quad \text{(M-APP)}$$

$$\frac{\Gamma; \Theta \vdash \varphi : \bullet \rightsquigarrow e \mid \Sigma, x}{\Gamma; \Theta \vdash \forall x.\, \varphi : \bullet \rightsquigarrow \texttt{let}\ (\Sigma, x)^\flat = e\ \texttt{in}\ \Sigma^\flat \mid \Sigma} \quad \text{(M-UNIV)}$$

$$\frac{\Gamma; \Theta, x \vdash \varphi : \bullet \rightsquigarrow e \mid \Sigma_1, \Sigma_2}{\Gamma; \Theta \vdash \varphi : \bullet \rightsquigarrow \texttt{let}\ x = \star\ \texttt{in let}\ (\Sigma_1, \Sigma_2)^\flat = e\ \texttt{in}\ (\Sigma_1, x, \Sigma_2)^\flat \mid \Sigma_1, x, \Sigma_2} \quad \text{(M-WEAK)}$$

$$\frac{}{\Gamma, X : \mathtt{m}; \Theta \vdash X : \mathtt{m} \rightsquigarrow X \mid \emptyset} \quad \text{(M-VAR)}$$

$$\frac{\Gamma; \Theta \vdash \varphi : \mathtt{m} \rightsquigarrow e \mid \Sigma, x}{\Gamma; \Theta \vdash \lambda x.\, \varphi : + \to \mathtt{m} \rightsquigarrow e \mid \Sigma} \quad \text{(M-POS-ABS)}$$

$$\frac{\Gamma; \Theta, x \vdash \varphi : \mathtt{m} \rightsquigarrow e \mid \Sigma}{\Gamma; \Theta \vdash \lambda x.\, \varphi : - \to \mathtt{m} \rightsquigarrow \lambda x.\, e \mid \Sigma} \quad \text{(M-NEG-ABS)}$$

$$\frac{\Gamma, x : \mathtt{m}_1; \Theta \vdash \varphi : \mathtt{m}_2 \rightsquigarrow e \mid \Sigma}{\Gamma; \Theta \vdash \lambda x.\, \varphi : \mathtt{m}_1 \to \mathtt{m}_2 \rightsquigarrow \lambda x.\, e \mid \Sigma} \quad \text{(M-HO-ABS)}$$

Fig. 3. Mode-guided transformation for fixpoint-free formulas

In the rule M-UNIV for $\forall x.\varphi$, we first try to find a value of x that falsifies φ by translating φ with x in output mode. Then we just remove x from the output. The rule M-WEAK is for switching between input/output modes. When we wish to translate φ with x in output mode but the value of x actually cannot be determined, we apply M-WEAK and non-deterministically generate a value for x, and then translate φ with x in input mode. The BASIC TRANSFORMATION for universal quantifiers can be seen as a combination of M-WEAK and M-UNIV.

There are three rules for lambda abstractions depending on the mode of the argument. The rules M-NEG-ABS and M-HO-ABS are standard: predicates are translated into functions. In M-Pos-Abs, the argument x of the predicate becomes an "output" in the result of the transformation; hence the abstraction disappears in the resulting expression. For example, if $\varphi \equiv x \neq 1$, then $\lambda x.\varphi$ becomes $\lambda x.\mathtt{assert}(x = 1)$ if it has mode $- \to \bullet$, while it becomes 1 if it has mode $+ \to \bullet$.

Example 4.5. Consider the body of fib in the motivating example in Sect. 3.2. Assuming that Γ is $\mathrm{fib} : + \to - \to \bullet$, we have the following derivation:

$$\frac{\Gamma; n, c', c'' \vdash c' + c'' + 2 \neq c : \bullet \rightsquigarrow c' + c'' + 2 \mid c \qquad \Pi}{\Gamma; n \vdash c' + c'' + 2 \neq c \vee \mathrm{fib}\, c'\,(n-1) \vee \mathrm{fib}\, c''\,(n-2) : \bullet \rightsquigarrow e \mid c, c', c''}$$

where Π is:

$$\frac{\dfrac{\Gamma; n \vdash \mathrm{fib} : + \to - \to \bullet \rightsquigarrow \mathrm{fib} \mid \emptyset}{\Gamma; n \vdash \mathrm{fib}\, c'\,(n-1) : \bullet \rightsquigarrow \mathrm{fib}\,(n-1) \mid c'} \quad \dfrac{\Gamma; n \vdash \mathrm{fib} : + \to - \to \bullet \rightsquigarrow \mathrm{fib} \mid \emptyset}{\Gamma; n, c' \vdash \mathrm{fib}\, c''\,(n-2) : \bullet \rightsquigarrow \mathrm{fib}\,(n-2) \mid c''}}{\Gamma; n \vdash \mathrm{fib}\, c'\,(n-1) \vee \mathrm{fib}\, c''\,(n-2) : \bullet \rightsquigarrow e' \mid c', c''}$$

and $e \triangleq \mathtt{let}\ (c', c'') = e'\ \mathtt{in}\ \mathtt{let}\ c = c' + c'' + 2\ \mathtt{in}\ (c, c', c'')$ and $e' \triangleq \mathtt{let}\ c' = \mathit{fib}\,(n-1)\ \mathtt{in}\ \mathtt{let}\ c'' = \mathit{fib}\,(n-2)\ \mathtt{in}\ (c', c'')$.

Finally, we define the translation relation for a νHFL(Z) formula (D, φ). Suppose that (D, φ) is well-typed under $\lfloor \Gamma \rfloor$ and $D = \{x_1 =_{\kappa_1} \varphi_1, \ldots, x_n =_{\kappa_n} \varphi_n\}$. We write $\Gamma \vdash (D, \varphi) \rightsquigarrow (\mathcal{F}, e)$ if (i) $\mathcal{F} = \{x_1 =_{\langle \Gamma(x_1) \rangle} e_1, \ldots, x_n =_{\langle \Gamma(x_n) \rangle} e_n\}$ that satisfies $\Gamma; \emptyset \vdash \varphi : \Gamma(x_i) \rightsquigarrow e_i \mid \emptyset$ for each $i \in \{1, \ldots, n\}$ and (ii) $\Gamma; \emptyset \vdash \varphi : \bullet \rightsquigarrow e \mid \emptyset$. The mode environment Γ is inferred in practice. The details of the mode inference are provided in the full version of the paper [21].

Example 4.6. Let us see how the formula in Example 2.3 is transformed to a program. Under a mode environment $\Gamma = \{\mathrm{Dec} : - \to + \to \bullet, \mathrm{Loop} : (- \to \bullet) \to (- \to + \to \bullet) \to - \to \bullet\}$, we have the program $(\mathcal{F}, \mathrm{Loop}\,(\lambda x.x < 1000)\,\mathrm{Dec}\,1000)$ where $\mathcal{F}$ is a set of function definitions:

$$\mathrm{Dec} = \lambda n.n - 1$$

$$\mathrm{Loop} = \lambda g.\lambda f.\lambda n.\mathbf{if}\ n = 0\ \mathbf{then}\ g\,n\ \mathbf{else}\ \mathtt{let}\ m = e\ \mathtt{in}\ ()$$

$$\text{where } e \triangleq \mathtt{let}\ m = f\,n\ \mathtt{in}\ \mathtt{let}\ () = \mathrm{Loop}\,(\lambda x.g\,(x+1))\,f\,m\ \mathtt{in}\ m.$$

We conclude this section by presenting important properties of the transformation. The proofs are given in the full version of the paper [21]. The transformed program is well-typed and the translation is sound.

Lemma 4.7. *If* $\Gamma; \Theta \vdash \varphi : \mathtt{m} \rightsquigarrow e \mid \Sigma$, *then* $\langle \Gamma; \Theta \rangle \vdash_P e : \langle \mathtt{m}, |\Sigma| \rangle$.

Theorem 4.8. (Soundness and Completeness of mode-guided transformation). *Suppose that* $\Gamma \vdash (D, \varphi) \rightsquigarrow (\mathcal{F}, e)$. *There exists a reduction* $e \longrightarrow^*_{\mathcal{F}} ()$, *if and only if* $\not\models (D, \varphi)$.

5 Evaluation

We have implemented a νHFL(Z) invalidity checker, named ModeHFL, based on the proposed method. It takes a fixpoint logic formula (expressed in the CHC or νHFL(Z) format) as an input, converts it to an OCaml program, and then applies random testing to disprove the given formula. A Docker image containing the implementation and benchmark suite is publicly available [20].

5.1 Implementation

The implementation of ModeHFL can be divided into four parts: preprocessing, mode inference, transformation, and testing.

Given a νHFL(Z) formula, we first apply some preprocessing procedures to eliminate or modify some parts of formulas to make the further analyses more efficient. These include predicate inlining, removing unnecessary universal quantifiers, detecting if-then-else structures, and so on. By detecting if-then-else structures, we mean transforming a (sub) formula like $\forall y.\ (x \leq 0 \wedge y \neq 1) \vee (x > 0 \wedge y \neq 2)$ to $\forall y.\, \textbf{if}\ x \leq 0\ \textbf{then}\ y \neq 1\ \textbf{else}\ y \neq 2$. This allows us to identify where to apply the transformation rule M-ITE, a rule that is used to avoid inserting unnecessary non-deterministic choices.

Following preprocessing, we infer modes of predicates. We adopt a constraint-based mode inference (which is similar to [27]), and try to find modes that minimize the number of non-deterministic choices in the transformed program (since there might be multiple modes for a predicate). Along with the inferred modes, we apply the transformation rules in Fig. 3. Further details of the mode inference is given in the full version [21].

Finally, we apply random testing to the transformed program. Since our tool is a proof-of-concept implementation, we simply apply a naive random testing; it makes non-deterministic choices uniformly at random. A test is run with a limit on the number of recursive calls so that ModeHFL does not keep on executing a non-terminating path of a program that may terminate. Random tests are repeated until ModeHFL finds a terminating path.

5.2 Experimental Setup

We used the following four benchmark sets.[5]

- *Unsafe AE-VAL* benchmark. This benchmark is from Blicha et al. [3] (available at https://github.com/chc-comp/aeval-unsafe), consisting of 54 unsatisfiable linear CHC instances,[6] many of which have deep counterexamples that existing CHC solvers tend to struggle to find.

[5] Mode and higher-order benchmarks are in https://github.com/hopv/benchmarks.
[6] CHCs are linear if the body of each clause contains at most one predicate variable. When expressed in νHFL(Z), disjunctions occur only in the form $\theta \vee \varphi$.

- *Mode* benchmark, consisting of 13 non-linear CHC instances. Since the *Unsafe AE-VAL* benchmark above contains only linear CHCs, we have prepared non-linear CHCs, by encoding verification problems for typical functions containing non-linear recursive calls. Many of the instances in this benchmark set also have deep counterexamples.
- *Higher-order* benchmark, consisting of 29 invalid νHFL(Z) formulas. This has been taken from the existing benchmark sets for higher-order program verification [22,23]. We have used this to compare the effectiveness of our tool with previous automated verification tools for higher-order functional programs.
- *CHC-Comp* benchmark. This has been taken from CHC-COMP 2023 [7], composed of satisfiability checking problems of constrained Horn clauses, the LIA-lin and LIA-nonlin tracks. Most of the CHC instances are larger than the *Unsafe AE-VAL* and *Mode* benchmarks above; thus, we have used this as a kind of stress test to evaluate the scalability of the current implementation of our tool. To focus on invalid instances, we excluded instances proven valid by other CHC solvers. The numbers of the LIA-lin and LIA-nonlin instances are respectively 200 and 193.[7]

Evaluation Configuration We have conducted our experiments on a machine with an Intel(R) Xeon(R) Gold 6242 CPU @ 2.80GHz and 64GB of memory. We set the timeout for each instance to 180 seconds.

We compared our method with the CHC solvers, Spacer [25], Golem [3], ELDARICA [15] and HOICE [6] for CHC instances. For the higher-order instances, we compared our method with νHFL(Z) solvers HoPDR [22] and RETHFL [19], and the state-of-the-art higher-order model checker MOCHI [23]. Additional information about the solvers such as some specific options is provided in the full version [21] of this paper.

5.3 Results

Evaluation on Unsafe AE-VAL Benchmark The results are shown in Fig. 4. Our solver could solve all 54 instances, which was the best among the five solvers. As the preprocessor (including the mode analysis) has not been fully optimized, our solver tends to be slower than Spacer and Golem for easy problems, but is much faster for difficult problems.

Evaluation on Mode Benchmark The result is shown in Table 1. The column labeled 'w/o mode' shows the result for the variant of our tool where the mode analysis is completely disabled (and assign the mode – for every integer argument). The result clearly shows the effectiveness of our mode-based transformation; our tool (with mode analysis) could solve all the instances, while none

[7] Some of those instances may actually be valid.

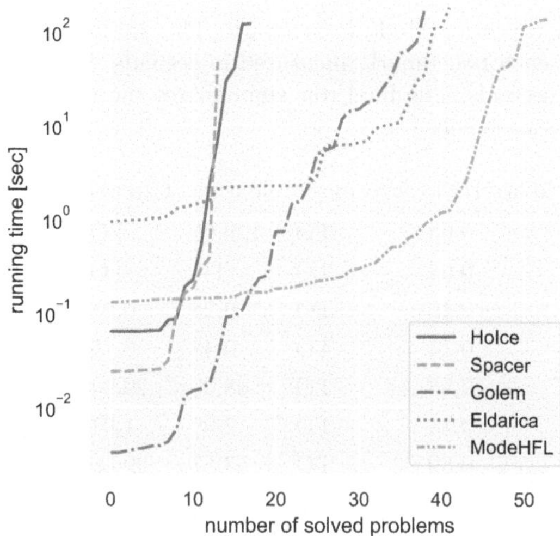

Fig. 4. Cactus plot of Unsafe AE-VAL Benchmark; the x-axis represents the accumulated number of benchmark instances, and the y-axis represents the time taken to prove the invalidity.

of the instances could be solved without the mode analysis. Our tool also outperformed other solvers for CHCs: Spacer, the most successful among the other solvers, failed to solve 4 instances.

Evaluation on Higher-order Benchmark The results are summarized in Table 2. Again, our solver ModeHFL could solve all the instances in the benchmark. This result was superior not only to the existing νHFL(Z) validity checkers such as HoPDR and ReTHFL but also to the state-of-the-art higher-order functional program model checker MoCHi. This result indicates that our method is effective even for higher-order problems.

Evaluation on CHC-COMP Benchmark The results are summarized in Table 3. As this table shows, unfortunately our method performed poorly on the problems in CHC-COMP 2023. We should note, however, that there were 9 unique instances in the LIA-lin track that our method solved, which were not solved by any other solvers.

We believe that the poor performance of our tool for this benchmark set is mainly due to the immaturity of the current implementation, not due to a fundamental limitation of our approach. Many of the instances in this benchmark are quite large, which makes the preprocessor of our tool (executed before the mode-guided transformation) quite slow. This can be confirmed by the statistics shown in Table 4, as most of the instances ended up with a timeout during preprocessing.

Table 1. Execution times for Mode Benchmark. This table presents the time taken to obtain results for each benchmark, measured in seconds. 'TO' means timeout (180 s). The units are in seconds. The final row summarizes the total number of instances successfully solved by each solver.

Instance	ModeHFL	w/o mode	Spacer	Golem	HoIce	Eldarica
Ackermann1	0.64	TO	120.95	TO	TO	TO
Ackermann2	0.64	TO	TO	TO	TO	TO
Ackermann3	0.19	TO	0.28	0.08	4.77	1.33
Factorial	0.14	TO	0.48	0.15	TO	5.09
Fibonacci1	0.53	TO	88.00	29.94	10.26	61.98
Fibonacci2	0.18	TO	2.99	1.01	0.64	5.52
Fibonacci3	0.69	TO	53.57	29.56	33.78	TO
Fibo-Cnt	0.18	TO	0.04	0.01	0.09	1.16
Addition	28.54	TO	TO	TO	TO	TO
McCarthy91	0.18	TO	0.43	0.73	TO	3.72
MC91 Sum	4.38	TO	145.59	24.91	61.30	TO
Square Sum	0.26	TO	TO	TO	TO	7.84
Tarai-2arg	0.72	TO	TO	TO	TO	TO
# solved	13	0	9	8	6	7

Table 2. Number of solved instances in experiments on Unsafe Higher-order Benchmark. Timeout is set to 180 seconds. 'Unknown' means that the solver terminated without answering valid or invalid due to the incompleteness of their formalization. ReTHFL failed to solve one instance due to its bug.

	ModeHFL	HoPDR	ReTHFL	MoCHi
# solved	29	23	21	21
# timeout	0	6	2	3
# unknown	0	0	5	5
# fail	0	0	1	0

Table 3. Number of solved instances in experiments on CHC COMP 2023 (LIA Tracks) Benchmarks. Note that we only count invalid cases. Timeout is set to 180 s.

Instance	ModeHFL	Spacer	Golem	HoIce	Eldarica
# solved	50	41	71	29	65
# solved	23	135	114	52	126

Table 4. Statistical results from experiments on CHC COMP 2023 (LIA Tracks) Benchmarks. Each number represents the count of instances for which ModeHFL resulted in a timeout, but was able to reach at least preprocessing, mode inference, and random testing, respectively.

	< preproc	< mode infer	< random test
LIA-lin	150	34	27
LIA-nonlin	170	38	15

In addition, constraints occurring in each CHC-COMP instance tend to be too complex for the current implementation to handle, which makes the mode analysis imprecise. As a simple example to illustrate a source of the problem, let us consider a formula $x > 1 \vee x < 1$. To make the rule Neq for our mode-guided transformation applicable, we have to solve the constraint with respect to x; i.e., $x \neq 1$. This case is easy, but many of the instances in this benchmark set contain the inequality information in a much more complex form, and require semantic analyses of constraint formulas using SMT solvers. We expect that the problem can be overcome by further engineering efforts. Anyway, the existence of unique instances indicates that our tool, even in the present immature form, can play a complementary role to state-of-the-art CHC solvers.

6 Related Work

Several techniques have been proposed for automatic νHFL(Z) validity checking (or equivalent formalism such as HoCHC [5]) [5,16,19,22], but they mainly focused on proving the validity of a fixpoint formula, struggling to disprove a formula with a deep counterexample efficiently. Thus, our technique for quickly disproving a formula should serve as a complement to the previous techniques.

Satisfiability checking of constrained Horn clauses (CHC) can be considered a restriction of νHFL(Z) validity checking to the first-order case. Various approaches to CHC solving have been proposed [6,14,15,25], but many of them are not good at finding deep counterexamples. Blicha et al. [3] addressed this problem by exponentially reducing the number of approximations required for refuting given CHCs. For linear CHCs, Frohn and Giesl [11] also proposed a technique called *acceleration*, to compress multiple transitions over clauses into one transition, to quickly find deep counterexamples. Although the goal is common, our approach is quite different; we have employed random testing by transforming logical formulas (or CHC as a special case) to test-friendly programs.

The idea of translating first-order fixpoint logic formulas into programs has previously been explored in the context of program verification. Jhala et al. [17] reduced a refinement type inference problem to the satisfiability of linear CHCs, which are then transformed to the unreachability problem for first-order imperative programs. According to the CHC COMP 2023 competition report [7], some CHC solvers such as Ultimate Unihorn [9] and Theta [30] transform CHCs to programs or control-flow automata for model checking. In those studies, since the resulting programs are passed to an automated verification tool, the translations are not designed to generate test-friendly programs. Also, higher-order predicates were not considered in those studies.

Mode analysis has been extensively studied in the field of logic programming [8,27], for compiler optimizations [28,29,32] and for translation from functional logic programming languages to functional programs [13,31]. Besides technical differences arising from the need for handling higher-order predicates and integer arithmetic, the use of mode analysis to generate test-friendly programs is novel, to the best of our knowledge.

Random testing has also been used for theorem provers and proof assistants [1,4]. The target logic is quite different from ours (i.e., νHFL(Z)); as a result, the techniques are also quite different.

7 Conclusion

We have proposed a transformation from fixpoint logic formulas to functional programs with non-determinism and exceptions, which allows us to use random testing to disprove a logical formula (which represents a certain property of a program). As a naive transformation introduces too much non-determinism, we have employed a mode analysis to minimize non-determinism and obtain "test-friendly" programs. We have implemented a prototype falsification tool for νHFL(Z). Experimental results show the effectiveness of our approach and suggest that our tool can play at least a complementary role to existing solvers, even though more engineering work is need for large and complex inputs. Integrating more sophisticated testing strategies such as symbolic execution and coverage-guided graybox testing is left for future work.

Acknowledgments. We would like to thank anonymous reviewers for useful comments. This work was supported by JSPS KAKENHI Grant Numbers JP23KJ0546 and JP20H05703.

References

1. Berghofer, S., Nipkow, T.: Random testing in Isabelle/HOL. In: 2nd International Conference on Software Engineering and Formal Methods (SEFM 2004), 28–30 September 2004, Beijing, China, pp. 230–239. IEEE Computer Society (2004). https://doi.org/10.1109/SEFM.2004.36
2. Bjørner, N., Gurfinkel, A., McMillan, K.L., Rybalchenko, A.: Horn clause solvers for program verification. In: Fields of Logic and Computation II—Essays Dedicated to Yuri Gurevich on the Occasion of His 75th Birthday. LNCS, vol. 9300, pp. 24–51. Springer, Heidelberg (2015). https://doi.org/10.1007/978-3-319-23534-9_2
3. Blicha, M., Fedyukovich, G., Hyvärinen, A.E.J., Sharygina, N.: Transition power abstractions for deep counterexample detection. In: Fisman, D., Rosu, G. (eds.) TACAS 2022, Part I. LNCS, vol. 13243, pp. 524–542. Springer, Heidelberg (2022). https://doi.org/10.1007/978-3-030-99524-9_29

4. Bulwahn, L.: The new Quickcheck for Isabelle—random, exhaustive and symbolic testing under one roof. In: Hawblitzel, C., Miller, D. (eds.) CPP 2012. LNCS, vol. 7679, pp. 92–108. Springer, Heidelberg (2012). https://doi.org/10.1007/978-3-642-35308-6_10
5. Cathcart Burn, T., Ong, C.L., Ramsay, S.J.: Higher-order constrained Horn clauses for verification. Proc. ACM Program. Lang. **2**(POPL) 11:1–11:28 (2018). https://doi.org/10.1145/3158099
6. Champion, A., Chiba, T., Kobayashi, N., Sato, R.: ICE-based refinement type discovery for higher-order functional programs. J. Autom. Reason. **64**(7), 1393–1418 (2020). https://doi.org/10.1007/S10817-020-09571-Y
7. De Angelis, E., Govind V.K.H.: CHC-COMP 2023: competition report. Electronic Proc. Theor. Comput. Sci. **402**, 83–104 (2024). https://doi.org/10.4204/eptcs.402.10
8. Debray, S.K., Warren, D.S.: Automatic mode inference for logic programs. J. Log. Program. **5**(3), 207–229 (1988). https://doi.org/10.1016/0743-1066(88)90010-6
9. Dietsch, D., Heizmann, M., Hoenicke, J., Nutz, A., Podelski, A.: Ultimate treeautomizer (CHC-COMP tool description). In: Angelis, E.D., Fedyukovich, G., Tzevelekos, N., Ulbrich, M. (eds.) Proceedings of the Sixth Workshop on Horn Clauses for Verification and Synthesis and Third Workshop on Program Equivalence and Relational Reasoning, HCVS/PERR@ETAPS 2019, Prague, Czech Republic, 6–7th April 2019. EPTCS, vol. 296, pp. 42–47 (2019). https://doi.org/10.4204/EPTCS.296.7
10. Esen, Z., Rümmer, P.: Tricera: verifying C programs using the theory of heaps. In: Griggio, A., Rungta, N. (eds.) 22nd Formal Methods in Computer-Aided Design, FMCAD 2022, Trento, Italy, October 17–21, pp. 380–391. IEEE (2022). https://doi.org/10.34727/2022/ISBN.978-3-85448-053-2_45
11. Frohn, F., Giesl, J.: Accelerated Bounded Model Checking. CoRR **abs/2401.09973** (2024). https://doi.org/10.48550/ARXIV.2401.09973
12. Gurfinkel, A., Kahsai, T., Komuravelli, A., Navas, J.A.: The SeaHorn verification framework. In: Kroening, D., Pasareanu, C.S. (eds.) Computer Aided Verification—27th International Conference, CAV 2015, San Francisco, CA, USA, July 18–24, 2015, Proceedings, Part I. Lecture Notes in Computer Science, vol. 9206, pp. 343–361. Springer, Heidelberg (2015). https://doi.org/10.1007/978-3-319-21690-4_20
13. Hanus, M.: From logic to functional logic programs. Theory Pract. Log. Program. **22**(4), 538–554 (2022). https://doi.org/10.1017/S1471068422000187
14. Hoder, K., Bjørner, N.: Generalized property directed reachability. In: Theory and Applications of Satisfiability Testing—SAT 2012—15th International Conference, Trento, Italy, June 17–20, 2012. Proceedings, pp. 157–171 (2012). https://doi.org/10.1007/978-3-642-31612-8_13
15. Hojjat, H., Rümmer, P.: The ELDARICA horn solver. In: Proceedings of FMCAD 2018, pp. 1–7. IEEE (2018). https://doi.org/10.23919/FMCAD.2018.8603013
16. Iwayama, N., Kobayashi, N., Suzuki, R., Tsukada, T.: Predicate abstraction and CEGAR for $\nu\mathrm{HFL}_{\mathbb{Z}}$ validity checking. In: Pichardie, D., Sighireanu, M. (eds.) Static Analysis—27th International Symposium, SAS 2020, Virtual Event, November 18–20, 2020, Proceedings. Lecture Notes in Computer Science, vol. 12389, pp. 134–155. Springer, Heidelberg (2020). https://doi.org/10.1007/978-3-030-65474-0_7
17. Jhala, R., Majumdar, R., Rybalchenko, A.: HMC: verifying functional programs using abstract interpreters. In: Gopalakrishnan, G., Qadeer, S. (eds.) Computer Aided Verification—23rd International Conference, CAV 2011, Snowbird, UT, USA, July 14–20, 2011. Proceedings. Lecture Notes in Computer Science,

vol. 6806, pp. 470–485. Springer, Heidelberg (2011). https://doi.org/10.1007/978-3-642-22110-1_38
18. Kahsai, T., Rümmer, P., Sanchez, H., Schäf, M.: Jayhorn: a framework for verifying Java programs. In: Chaudhuri, S., Farzan, A. (eds.) Computer Aided Verification—28th International Conference, CAV 2016, Toronto, ON, Canada, July 17–23, 2016, Proceedings, Part I. Lecture Notes in Computer Science, vol. 9779, pp. 352–358. Springer, Heidelberg (2016). https://doi.org/10.1007/978-3-319-41528-4_19
19. Katsura, H., Iwayama, N., Kobayashi, N., Tsukada, T.: A new refinement type system for automated $\nu\mathrm{HFL}_{\mathbb{Z}}$ validity checking. In: Oliveira, B.C. (ed.) Programming Languages and Systems—18th Asian Symposium, APLAS 2020, Fukuoka, Japan, November 30–December 2, 2020, Proceedings. Lecture Notes in Computer Science, vol. 12470, pp. 86–104. Springer, Heidelberg (2020). https://doi.org/10.1007/978-3-030-64437-6_5
20. Katsura, H., Kobayashi, N., Sakayori, K., Sato, R.: Artifact: Mode-based Reduction from Validity Checking of Fixpoint Logic Formulas to Test-Friendly Reachability Problem (2024). https://doi.org/10.5281/zenodo.13484589
21. Katsura, H., Kobayashi, N., Sakayori, K., Sato, R.: Mode-based Reduction from Validity Checking of Fixpoint Logic Formulas to Test-Friendly Reachability Problem (2024). A longer version of this paper, available from http://www.kb.is.s.u-tokyo.ac.jp/~katsura/papers/aplas24.pdf
22. Katsura, H., Kobayashi, N., Sato, R.: Higher-order property-directed reachability. Proc. ACM Program. Lang. **7**(ICFP), 48–77 (2023). https://doi.org/10.1145/3607831
23. Kobayashi, N., Sato, R., Unno, H.: Predicate abstraction and CEGAR for higher-order model checking. In: Proceedings of PLDI 2011, pp. 222–233. ACM Press (2011). https://doi.org/10.1145/1993498.1993525
24. Kobayashi, N., Tsukada, T., Watanabe, K.: Higher-order program verification via HFL model checking. In: Proceedings of ESOP 2018. LNCS, vol. 10801, pp. 711–738. Springer, Heidelberg (2018). https://doi.org/10.1007/978-3-319-89884-1_25
25. Komuravelli, A., Gurfinkel, A., Chaki, S.: SMT-based model checking for recursive programs. Formal Methods in System Design **48**(3), 175–205 (2016). https://doi.org/10.1007/s10703-016-0249-4
26. Matsushita, Y., Tsukada, T., Kobayashi, N.: RustHorn: CHC-based verification for rust programs. In: Müller, P. (ed.) Programming Languages and Systems—29th European Symposium on Programming, ESOP 2020, Held as Part of the European Joint Conferences on Theory and Practice of Software, ETAPS 2020, Dublin, Ireland, April 25-30, 2020, Proceedings. Lecture Notes in Computer Science, vol. 12075, pp. 484–514. Springer, Heidelberg (2020). https://doi.org/10.1007/978-3-030-44914-8_18
27. Overton, D., Somogyi, Z., Stuckey, P.J.: Constraint-based mode analysis of mercury. In: Proceedings of the 4th International ACM SIGPLAN Conference on Principles and Practice of Declarative Programming, October 6–8, 2002, Pittsburgh, PA, USA (Affiliated with PLI 2002), pp. 109–120. ACM (2002). https://doi.org/10.1145/571157.571169
28. Roy, P.V., Despain, A.M.: High-performance logic programming with the aquarius prolog compiler. Computer **25**(1), 54–68 (1992). https://doi.org/10.1109/2.108055
29. Somogyi, Z., Henderson, F., Conway, T.C.: The execution algorithm of mercury, an efficient purely declarative logic programming language. J. Log. Program. **29**(1–3), 17–64 (1996). https://doi.org/10.1016/S0743-1066(96)00068-4

30. Somorjai, M., Dobos-Kovács, M., Ádám, Z., Bajczi, L., Vörös, A.: Bottoms up for CHCs: novel transformation of linear constrained horn clauses to software verification. Electronic Proc. Theor. Comput. Sci. **402**, 105–117 (2024). https://doi.org/10.4204/eptcs.402.11. Apr
31. Verbitskaia, E., Engel, I., Berezun, D.: A case study in functional conversion and mode inference in minikanren. In: Keller, G., Wang, M. (eds.) Proceedings of the 2024 ACM SIGPLAN International Workshop on Partial Evaluation and Program Manipulation, PEPM 2024, London, UK, 16 January 2024, pp. 107–118. ACM (2024). https://doi.org/10.1145/3635800.3636966
32. Warren, D.H.: Implementing prologcompiling predicate logic programs. Research Reports 39 and 40, Department of Artificial Intelligence, University of Edinburgh (1977)

Efficiently Adapting Stateless Model Checking for C11/C++11 to Mixed-Size Accesses

Shigeyuki Sato[1(✉)], Taiyo Mizuhashi[2], Genki Kimura[2], and Kenjiro Taura[2]

[1] The University of Electro-Communications, Tokyo, Japan
sato.shigeyuki@uec.ac.jp
[2] The University of Tokyo, Tokyo, Japan

Abstract. Stateless model checking (SMC) is crucial for productivity in verified concurrent programming, and its recent developments for C/C++ and weak memory models are remarkable. The state-of-the-art SMC for C, GenMC, efficiently verifies C programs based on C11 atomics and pthreads. However, it does not support mixed-size accesses, accesses to the same memory region with different-sized types, even though they are ubiquitous in C/C++, particularly the code for memory management. As a result, GenMC does not work for C/C++ programs containing memory management. To resolve this problem, we develop a method of adapting GenMC to mixed-size accesses preserving its optimality. We experimentally evaluate the efficiency of our extended implementation of GenMC and its efficacy for memory management programs.

Keywords: Stateless model checking · C11/C++11 · Mixed-size accesses

1 Introduction

Model checking plays a crucial role in verified concurrent programming. Given a system model and a specification typically in logics and finite automata, model checkers formally verify the conformance of the specification over the model. However, it generally has two major problems. One is that programmers have to write system models in modeling languages by abstracting actual implementations. This modeling in itself is burdensome and involves the risk of introducing bugs. The other is the state explosion in model checking. The models of actual concurrent programs on real-world systems, which often adopt weak memory models, often result in large-scale automata so that model checking does not end in a realistic timeframe.

The original version of the chapter has been revised. Figure 9 is added and its citation is corrected. A correction to this chapter can be found at
https://doi.org/10.1007/978-981-97-8943-6_19

O. Kiselyov (Ed.): APLAS 2024, LNCS 15194, pp. 346-364, 2024.
https://doi.org/10.1007/978-981-97-8943-6_17

Stateless model checking (SMC) [12,13] deals with these problems. It directly interprets a given program and verifies its properties without the burden of modeling it. It caches visited program states in state-space exploration to suppress revisiting the same state in different transitions. As a result, SMC generally has lost the power to verify liveness properties (i.e., those that will eventually happen) but can verify safety properties (i.e., those that never happen) efficiently with less burden on users.

Recently, SMC for C/C++ has made significant advances [1,2,15–17,21,23, 24]. It was largely due to the development of axiomatic memory models [6,8,20] and dynamic partial order reduction [3,4,10]. GenMC [17,19], the state-of-the-art algorithm for SMC and its implementation, performs optimal state-space exploration by using a graph-based compact representation of program traces. It can thus efficiently verify concurrent C/C++ programs in different weak memory models. However, GenMC and similar modern SMC implementations for C/C++, focused on handling C/C++ atomics, which are elaborate, well-studied APIs [8,20]. Simple, clean C code rather than actual, tricky C/C++ code is assumed for non-atomic accesses. Mixed-size accesses [11], which is to access a memory region by different sizes, is one of the significant features of C/C++ but not supported in these modern SMC implementations for C/C++.

Non-atomic mixed-size accesses in C/C++ are not so hard to handle in theory because it is sufficient to split all the non-atomic accesses into per-byte ones [11]. However, it incurs so awful overhead as to be an obstacle to verifying programs in practice. Although splitting all the non-atomic accesses is apparently redundant, mixed-size access code is ubiquitous, and it is hard to exactly identify where mixed-size accesses will occur beforehand. For example, not limited to the use of union types, `memcpy` and zero-filling, which compilers besides programmers may introduce, result in type-erased byte-wise accesses to any typed regions. More practically, C/C++ is oftentimes used to implement memory management, of which the verification [7,27] is crucial. Memory allocators reuse memory regions as objects of different sizes. Implementation techniques of garbage collection are full of mixed-size accesses, such as forwarding pointers. A conservative approximation of possible mixed-size accesses therein would be very imprecise. To apply the state-of-the-art SMC to these code fragments, regardless of whether they will make mixed-size accesses, we end up splitting substantially all the non-atomic accesses, incurring considerable overhead.

To bridge the gap between the state-of-the-art SMC and the reality of C/C++ programming, in this paper, we extend the state-of-the-art SMC algorithm of GenMC [17] to efficiently handle programs that *may* involve mixed-size non-atomic accesses in C11/C++11. Our approach is simple and clear; we incorporate footprints [11] into execution graphs [8,20], which GenMC is based on, and adaptively split relations among read/write events as modestly as possible, preserving the core part of the GenMC algorithm as-is. Thus, our approach preserves the optimality (i.e., single visit per equivalence class) with little overhead. We experimentally demonstrate that our extended implementation of GenMC handles non-mixed-size accesses as efficiently as the original GenMC does and offers significant usability in C/C++ programming for memory management such that it can verify free lists more efficiently than conservative per-byte splitting. Our approach is not limited to the GenMC algorithm but is applicable to other algorithms for SMC based on execution graphs. Our extended GenMC implementation is available as a reusable open-source tool.

Our main contributions are summarized as follows:

- We have developed an approach to dealing with non-atomic mixed-size access in state-of-the-art SMC for C11/C++11 (Section 3). Our approach adaptively splits relations among events together with footprints [11]. It enables us to extend the GenMC [17] algorithm without breaking the optimality and with little overhead. Our implementation is provided as an open-source tool: https://github.com/satoshigeyuki/genmc.
- We have experimentally demonstrated the practical efficacy of our extension of the GenMC implementation (Sect. 4). In the non-mixed-size case, our extended implementation verified the test suite of GenMC, with little overhead over the original GenMC. In the mixed-size case, it outperformed the one based on conservative per-byte splitting by more than a factor of two for a practical scenario using a memory allocator based on free lists.

2 GenMC: Stateless Model Checking for C

2.1 Execution Graphs

We briefly introduce execution graphs for model checking under axiomatic memory models [6,8,20] through an example program W+WR+W shown in Fig. 1.

`x = 1;`	`r = x;` `if (r == 0) { y = 1; }`	`x = 2;`

Fig. 1. Example program W+WR+W, where three threads are running, and shared variables `x` and `y` are supposed to be initialized with 0.

Execution graphs represent program traces. An execution graph is an edge-labeled graph of which vertices are read and write events labeled R and W respectively. Basic relations represented by edges are program-order (`po`-labeled), read-from (`rf`-labeled), and modification-order (`mo`-labeled) relations. For example, by running W+WR+W up to termination, we obtain six execution graphs as shown in Fig. 2.

Each read/write event except for initialization (o) corresponds to a program point of any of the threads. Program-order relations mean the order of program points for each thread. Read-from relations mean to which value yielded at a source write event is captured at a target read event. Modification-order relations mean a total order of write events per location. We omit `po` labels if they are

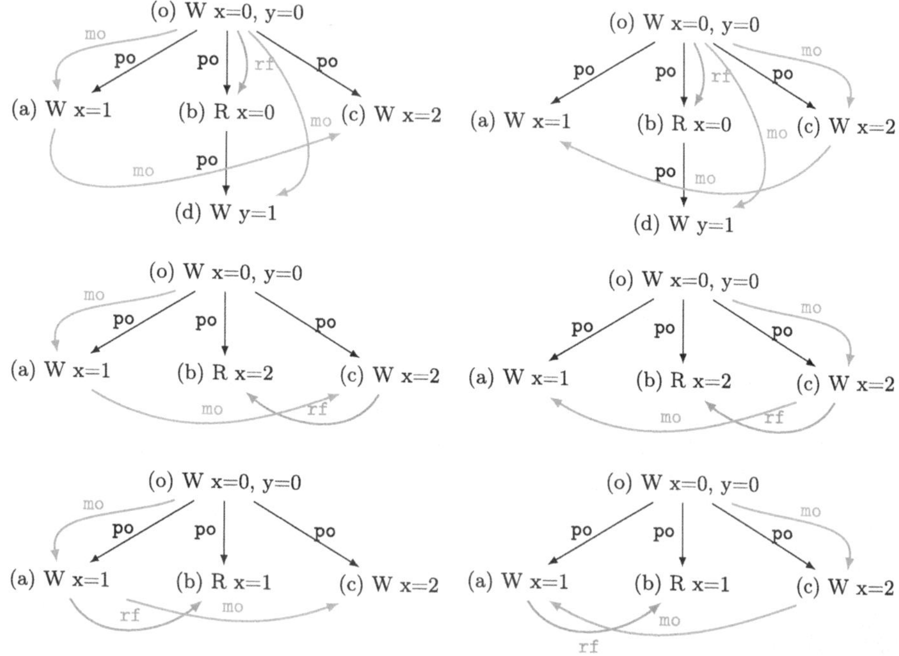

Fig. 2. Six eventual execution graphs of W+WR+W, where (o) denotes initialization.

obvious. Letting G be an execution graph, G.rf and G.mo respectively denote its read-from relations and modification-order ones. Where G is not specific, we omit G and simply write rf and mo.

2.2 C/C++ Memory Model

The C/C++ memory model (introduced in [9] and formalized in [8,20]) is based on the atomic APIs of the C/C++ standard libraries, which consist of atomic data types and atomic operations for them. Atomic operations can take various memory-ordering constraints (i.e., consistency models) such as sequential consistency (SC), release consistency, and relaxed consistency, where relaxed accesses are intended to compile to plain load/store instructions at the machine level. Race conditions for non-atomic data types, called data races, result in undefined behaviors. In the verification of C11/C++11, non-atomic accesses are not so worth tracking their behaviors once we detect their data race.

In the formalizations of C11/C++11, several derived relations are defined. Happen-before (hb) relations intuitively mean the order of events in multi-threading and are defined as a transitive closure of program-order relations and synchronizes-with relations, which means a read by one thread captures a write by another thread.

The C11/C++11 consistency is based on coherence (or SC-per-location) and atomicity per atomic data type. Coherence roughly means that 1) the order of writes to the same location according to mo does not contradict hb, 2) reads capture neither values written in the future nor ones already overwritten, and 3) two hb-related reads from the same location do not capture two writes in the reverse order of mo. RC11 [20] formalizes consistency conditions as relational properties on execution graphs. In this paper, we focus particularly on coherence[1]:

Coherence $(\texttt{mo} \cup \texttt{rf} \cup (\texttt{rf}^{-1};\texttt{mo}))^{+};\texttt{hb}$ is irreflexive,

where R^{-1} denotes the inverse of R, R^{+} denotes the transitive closure of R, and $R_1; R_2$ denotes the composition of R_1 and R_2 from left to right. This condition is one of the requirements of being RC11-consistent for any memory order.

Atomic data types in C11/C++11 have their own distinct memory regions, and no overlap of atomic data regions happens. Mixed-size accesses, which are described later, are supposed to arise only in non-atomic accesses.

2.3 GenMC Algorithm

GenMC [17] is a state-of-the-art stateless model checking algorithm for RC11. Given a program, it efficiently enumerates execution graphs by executing it with multiple threads for all the possible schedules and checks if they are RC11-consistent. We here briefly outline it. See the appendix of [17] for the details.

VERIFY shown in Fig. 3 is the entire algorithm of GenMC. Intuitively, it enumerates execution graphs by exploring in a depth-first search manner. VISITONE invoked from VERIFY explores the current execution graph by extending it up to being stuck (specifically, terminating or blocked) under the current thread schedule, where the RC11 consistency of G is checked in cons(G). During exploration, minimal events to be revisited are recorded in a worklist L. After reaching a stuck state, in VERIFY, the current execution graph rolls back up to a past event in L, and the exploration restarts for another option of thread schedules. Note that $\text{next}_P(G)$ yields a next event while managing examined thread schedules in a fixed order, enumerating all the possible schedules eventually.

The exploration algorithm of GenMC is so efficient that it is unnecessary to keep all the possible execution graphs but sufficient to keep the current graph and a minimal set of revisits that enable us to reconstruct other possible graphs unexplored from the current one. Note that this efficiency is due to the lack of verifiability of temporal properties, such as liveness. The GenMC algorithm is optimal in the sense that it explores each possible execution graph only once. Hence, no redundant checking of the RC11 consistency occurs.

2.4 Implementation Details of GenMC

We describe two implementation issues (not described in [17] but found in the implementation).

One is a way of managing mo relations. As seen from the use of $G.\texttt{mo}[\text{loc}(e)]$ in VISITONE, in calculating mo and rf relations for a new event, we would like

[1] We adopt a simplified definition used in the appendix of [17].

```
1: procedure VERIFY(P)
2:     (G, L) ← VISITONE(P, G_0, ∅)
3:     while L contains events to be revisited do
4:         e ← popMostRecent(L)
5:         Rollback G until e
6:         Update L for residual options
7:         (G, L) ← VISITONE(P, G, L)
8:     end while
9: end procedure
10: function VISITONE(P, G, L)
11:     while cons(G) ∧ ¬stuck(G) do
12:         e ← next_P(G)
13:         if e is an error then
14:             abort "erroneous program"
15:         end if
16:         Append e to G
17:         if e is a read then
18:             Pick a write w from G.mo[loc(e)]
19:             G.rf[e] ← w        ▷ mapping G.rf represents rf^{-1} relation
20:             Update L for residual options
21:         end if
22:         if e is a write then
23:             Append e to G.mo[loc(e)]
24:             Update L for residual options
25:         end if
26:     end while
27:     return (G, L)
28: end function
```

Fig. 3. The GenMC algorithm [17] (simplified for presentation).

to efficiently identify write events corresponding to a given location (address in the implementation). The GenMC implementation maintains `mo` relations per location as a list of write events (owing to total order per location) and manages a hash map from locations to such `mo` lists, corresponding to $G.\mathtt{mo}$. We call it the *location map*. Only with the location map, we can identify latest write events (in terms of `mo` relations) for any locations as well as check the existence of writes in constant time.

The other is a way of handling racy non-atomic accesses. As mentioned earlier, every racy non-atomic access is considered as data race, which result in undefined behaviors. In the GenMC algorithm, revisits are designed to handle the situation where different `rf` edges $(r, w_1) \in \mathtt{rf}$ and $(r, w_2) \in \mathtt{rf}$ for $w_1 \neq w_2$ are valid to extend execution graphs. If these are non-atomic, such situations are exactly data races and incur undefined behaviors. Therefore, in updating L, the implementation first enumerates racy accesses regardless of whether they are atomic or non-atomic. Then, it detects data race for non-atomic ones. After that, it handles revisits for racy atomic accesses over execution graphs. If the race detection option is disabled, this checking is skipped, and non-atomic accesses are handled similarly to atomic ones.

2.5 Problem with Mixed-Size Accesses

GenMC does not support mixed-size accesses, which is to access a memory region by different sizes. Mixed-size accesses generally cause overlaps between reads and writes as shown in Mixed[2] (Figs. 4 and 5); this is problematic to RC11 and GenMC.

```
int8_t *p = ...;
*(int32_t*)(p)   = 0;          // (o)
*(int16_t*)(p)   = 0xDEAD;     // (a)
*(int16_t*)(p+1) = 0xBEAF;     // (b)
int16_t v = *(int16_t*)(p);    // (c)
```

Fig. 4. Program Mixed with mixed-size access: 2-byte writes (a) and (b) overlap, and 2-byte read (c) overlaps (a) and (b), where (o) denotes initialization.

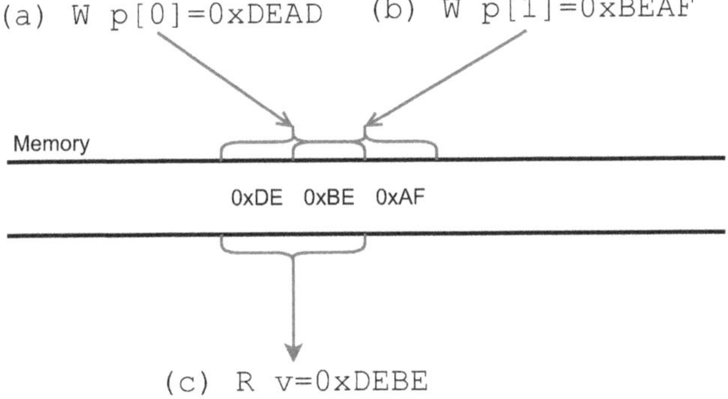

Fig. 5. Eventual memory image of Mixed under big-endian.

A critical change is that `rf` and `mo` relations are no longer ones over events but ones over address ranges of memory. Because the RC11 consistency is defined in terms of relational properties, this change immediately makes RC11 consistency checking broken.

To make execution graphs amenable to RC11, we can encode these mixed-size accesses into ordinary ones by splitting all the non-atomic accesses per byte [11], as shown in Fig. 6. With this preprocessing, which we call split-RW, GenMC can

[2] Precisely, Mixed incurs undefined behaviors because of the violation of the strict aliasing rule in the C/C++ standards. Similar overlapping situations can happen within the C/C++ standards in a more complicated form. Moreover, strict conformance to the strict aliasing rule is unrealistic for programming in system software [28]. We intentionally use Mixed for conciseness and practicality.

handle programs containing mixed-size accesses. However, letting k be word size in byte, it increases the program size, the number of steps, and hence the execution graph size by a factor of k. Assuming RC11 consistency checking (cons(G) in VISITONE) be in linear time with respect to execution graph size, it incurs $O(k^2)$ overhead in time regarding non-atomic accesses on VISITONE. Furthermore, in the presence of racy non-atomic accesses, the increase in the number of steps can increase the possibility of interleaving. Specifically, it increases the number of iterations in VERIFY, of which the overhead is hard to bound precisely. In total, the split-RW approach can slow down more than one order of magnitude impact in practice.

```
int8_t *p = ...;
p[0] = 0;        // (o1)
p[1] = 0;        // (o2)
p[2] = 0;        // (o3)
p[3] = 0;        // (o4)
p[0] = 0xDE;     // (a1)
p[1] = 0xAD;     // (a2)
p[1] = 0xBE;     // (b1)
p[2] = 0xEF;     // (b2)
int8_t v[2];
v[0] = p[0];     // (c1)
v[1] = p[1];     // (c2)
```

Fig. 6. Mixed-S, where all non-atomic accesses in Mixed are split per byte.

Assuming that mixed-size accesses arise in limited part, we could avoid such awful overhead if we identified mixed-size accesses exactly in advance. It is, however, difficult and contradicts the design of dynamic partial order reduction [10], a crucial basis of modern SMC including GenMC. We should handle C/C++ code in which mixed-size accesses *may* arise efficiently within SMC.

3 The Proposed Approach

We present our approach to efficiently adapting GenMC to mixed-size accesses.

3.1 Adaptive Footprint Splitting

The basic idea of our approach is to split `mo` and `rf` relations as modestly as possible without splitting events, while we keep the GenMC algorithm as it is.

As seen from Fig. 5, mixed-size access can be formalized as read/write from a specified address with a specified size, called footprints [11]. A footprint `store/size` denotes a memory region of `size` bytes starting from `store`, where `store` can be a pointer expression or a variable. Now, we extend execution graphs by assigning footprints to read/write events and `rf`/`mo` relations. For example, we formalize the eventual execution graph of Mixed as shown in Fig. 7.

An important change is that the `mo` relation to (b) and the `rf` relation to (c) are split according to resultant mixed-size accesses in Mixed; i.e., `rf` and

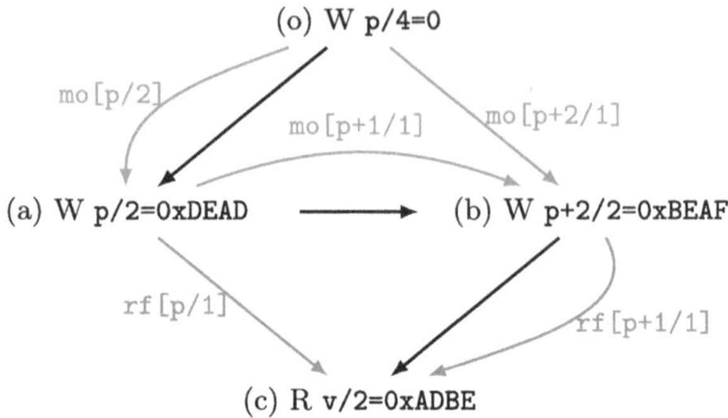

Fig. 7. Footprint extension for the eventual execution graph of Mixed.

mo relations become many-to-one relations augmented with split footprints. To conform to the RC11 consistency, it is reasonable to split the footprints of rf and mo relations. If their footprints are not split, their relational compositions become imprecise, which inevitably causes false violations of RC11 consistency, particularly for coherence. To keep the relational formalization of RC11 strict for data flow over memory regions, adaptive splitting of rf and mo footprints are simple, intuitive, and efficient.

A key point of this approach is that footprint splitting occurs only for rf/mo relations and not for read/write events. As a result, once a rf/mo edge is constructed, it will not split afterward in running the GenMC algorithm. It is sufficient to construct rf/mo edges with split footprints regarding execution graphs.

3.2 Location Interval Map

It is obvious that augmenting events and relations with footprints does not change GenMC algorithmically. The main issue is how to implement adaptive footprint splitting, more specifically, how to construct rf/mo edges with split footprints efficiently.

The location map plays the primary role in constructing rf/mo edges, as seen from that the lookup of $G.\mathtt{mo}[\mathrm{loc}(e)]$ occurs to update $G.\mathtt{rf}$ and $G.\mathtt{mo}$ in VISITONE. Originally, it is sufficient that $G.\mathtt{mo}$ only manages mapping from addresses (more precisely, pointer values) to lists of write events. In our approach, because read/write events and rf/mo relations have footprints rather than addresses, querying with footprints to identify write events is demanded. Furthermore, split footprints are to be dynamically maintained to implement adaptive footprint splitting efficiently. To meet these desiderata, interval-based data structures are an appropriate choice for the location map. Now, we thus call $G.\mathtt{mo}$ the *location interval map*.

We employ `interval_map` of Boost Interval Container Library[3] for the location interval map. It can naturally represent a mapping from footprints to lists

[3] https://www.boost.org/doc/libs/release/libs/icl/

of write events and offers updates based on the *aggregate on overlap* principle, which implicitly splits footprints recorded in its domain on adding write events.

For example, in Mixed, the location interval map $G.\texttt{mo}$ of `interval_map` mapping from footprints to lists of events is constructed at the initialization (o) such that

$$G.\texttt{mo} = \{\texttt{p/4} \mapsto [(\mathrm{o})]\}.$$

When adding write event (a) to $G.\texttt{mo}$, the domain of $G.\texttt{mo}$ is automatically split, accompanying aggregate on overlap such that

$$G.\texttt{mo} = \{\texttt{p/2} \mapsto [(\mathrm{a}), (\mathrm{o})], \texttt{p+2/2} \mapsto [(\mathrm{o})]\}.$$

When adding (b), the domain of $G.\texttt{mo}$ is again split such that

$$G.\texttt{mo} = \{\texttt{p/1} \mapsto [(\mathrm{a}), (\mathrm{o})], \texttt{p+1/1} \mapsto [(\mathrm{b}), (\mathrm{a}), (\mathrm{o})], \texttt{p+2/1} \mapsto [(\mathrm{b}), (\mathrm{o})], \texttt{p+3/1} \mapsto [(\mathrm{o})]\}.$$

When adding (c), by querying the footprint `p/2` of (c) onto $G.\texttt{mo}$, we can identify the `rf` relations to (c) with split footprints as follows.

$$(\mathrm{a}) \xrightarrow{\texttt{rf [p/1]}} (\mathrm{c}) \qquad (\mathrm{b}) \xrightarrow{\texttt{rf [p+1/1]}} (\mathrm{c})$$

Thus, `interval_map` enables us to implement adaptive footprint splitting simply yet efficiently.

A tiny patch to the GenMC algorithm is sufficient to implement our approach. In Line 18 of Fig. 3, we obtain through querying $G.\texttt{mo}[\mathrm{footprint}(e)]$ a set W of write events of which the footprints are exclusive. Then, in Line 19, we record W into $G.\texttt{rf}[e]$ to construct a many-to-one `rf` relation. Note that an algorithmic change on the extension of $G.\texttt{mo}$ is implicit because it is confined within the append operation of the location interval map.

3.3 Optimality and Overhead

One major advantage of our approach is to preserve the GenMC algorithm as-is with the optimality for free. In contrast, the split-RW approach incurs twofold overhead: it expands the size of execution graphs and increases the number of execution steps. It breaks the optimality in theory and incurs significant overhead in practice. Our approach creates additional `mo`/`rf` relations for mixed-size accesses but never changes the size of execution graphs and the number of execution steps. It thus enjoys the as-is efficiency of the GenMC algorithm.

We then focus on the practical overhead of our approach. The footprint of the `mo` relation to a write event is split by the number of overlapping patterns on it. If all the non-atomic accesses make per-byte mixed-size accesses, our approach results in `mo`/`rf` splitting of the same degree as split-RW. However, practically, mixed-size accesses occur only at a specific part of the entire program, on the whole, and are far fewer than non-mixed-size ones. Because the footprints of `rf` relations are split according to the footprints of `mo` relations, less `mo` splitting leads to less `rf` splitting. Because read/write events themselves are not split, `po` relations are not split, and the number of execution steps does not increase over the original.

In our implementation, we do not recover the domain splitting of the location map even after removing the footprints causing the split. It can cause redundant splitting of footprints, but it is merely a matter of implementation choice. We can avoid redundant splitting by using data structures that can recover states completely, including their split domains. However, from our observation, simply using `interval_map` and keeping its split domain is practically more efficient than recovering domain splitting.

3.4 Extensibility to Mixed-Size Atomics

In this work, we focus on non-atomic mixed-size accesses because of the RC11 semantics. However, the C++20 standard has `atomic_ref`, which is a wrapper that enables atomic accesses via a specified pointer. In the C11 standard, atomics take pointers to atomic data types and, to the best of our knowledge, no special restriction on type punning on these pointers. In this sense, the C/C++ standards do not rule out the potential of mixed-size atomic accesses.

Meanwhile, the formal model of mixed-size concurrency is still a major open problem. Flur et al. [11] presented the formal model at the ISA level, but later, Alglave et al. [5] revealed its unsoundness with respect to the hardware implementation of the Arm architecture. Although their work significantly clarified mixed-size concurrency in the Arm architecture, as the authors concluded therein, their model was a work in progress. In a nutshell, in the present situation, even what is to be model-checked for mixed-size atomics is unclear.

While the semantics of mixed-size atomics in C/C++ is so challenging, we conjecture that our approach is extendable towards atomic mixed-size accesses in the flat memory model under SC. Assuming SC for each contiguous memory region on which mixed-size accesses overlap, all the write events thereon are totally ordered and can be managed in the location interval map as in the non-atomic case. Our approach splits `rf`/`mo` relations adaptively but does not split events themselves, preserving the atomicity of read/write. Therefore, the flat memory model under SC seems to be a sufficient assumption to make our approach effective for mixed-size atomics. However, it is not evident that the GenMC algorithm could work as is for such cases.

4 Evaluation

We experimentally demonstrate the practical feasibility of the proposed adaptation of GenMC to mixed-size accesses and evaluate the overhead for mixed-size and non-mixed-size cases.

4.1 Experimental Setting

We extended GenMC version 0.5.3[4] on top of LLVM 10.0.0. It took straightforward modifications of 2,000 LOC, of which most were due to footprints. For a reference, we also implemented the split-RW version.

We used the test suite bundled with GenMC, which consisted of more than 300 tests, to evaluate the overhead of our extension in the non-mixed-size case. We excluded the tests of file systems (named FS) for persistency semantics [15], for which a special treatment of `memcpy` is implemented. We used the default parameter setting (e.g., the number of threads) for all the tests. We additionally prepared a benchmark program MWF (in 127 LOC) to evaluate the overhead in the mixed-size case. It iterates a series of the allocation, write, and free of a single `int` with multiple threads, by using a hand-coded memory allocator based on K&R free lists, which naturally cause mixed-size access and the overlap of reads and writes because next pointers and allocated objects are generally of different types. See Appendix A for the details.

We ran all the versions of GenMC under RC11 with MO. We used a laptop equipped with an AMD Ryzen 5 PRO 4650U processor and 32-GB PC4-25600 memory. Our experiment was conducted on Ubuntu 20.04 on Docker Desktop on Windows 11. The artifact to reproduce the experiments is available; see the supplementary material [26].

4.2 Experimental Results

Non-Mixed-Size Case Figure 8 shows the execution time of GenMC on the test suite for the proposed approach and split-RW compared to the original. We can find two groups of tests in Fig. 8a: one is near to the original and the other is far from it. The former group contains no or little non-atomic access and the latter contains non-atomic access significantly. For the former group, we observed no significant difference between the proposed approach and split-RW. In several tests, split-RW slightly outperformed the proposed approach. We attribute this result to the overhead of the use of footprints. For the latter group, the proposed approach outperformed split-RW by a few folds because of the gap in the size of execution graphs as expected.

We observed significant differences between the proposed approach and split-RW particularly in data structure tests, which are relatively large, practical ones in the test suite. Table 1 summarizes their results by listing the execution time, the number of complete execution graphs, and the number of blocked ones, which denote the states of thread blocking. As clearly presented, the proposed approach and the original had identical results in any sense. In contrast, split-RW had different results for dq, dq-opt, and qu-opt; the number of complete executions significantly blew up, increasing execution time accordingly. It was because they involved intentionally racy non-atomic accesses, and splitting their events incurred additional possibilities of thread scheduling. In these cases, split-RW hurt the optimality and thus incurred considerable overhead.

[4] https://github.com/MPI-SWS/genmc/releases/tag/v0.5.3

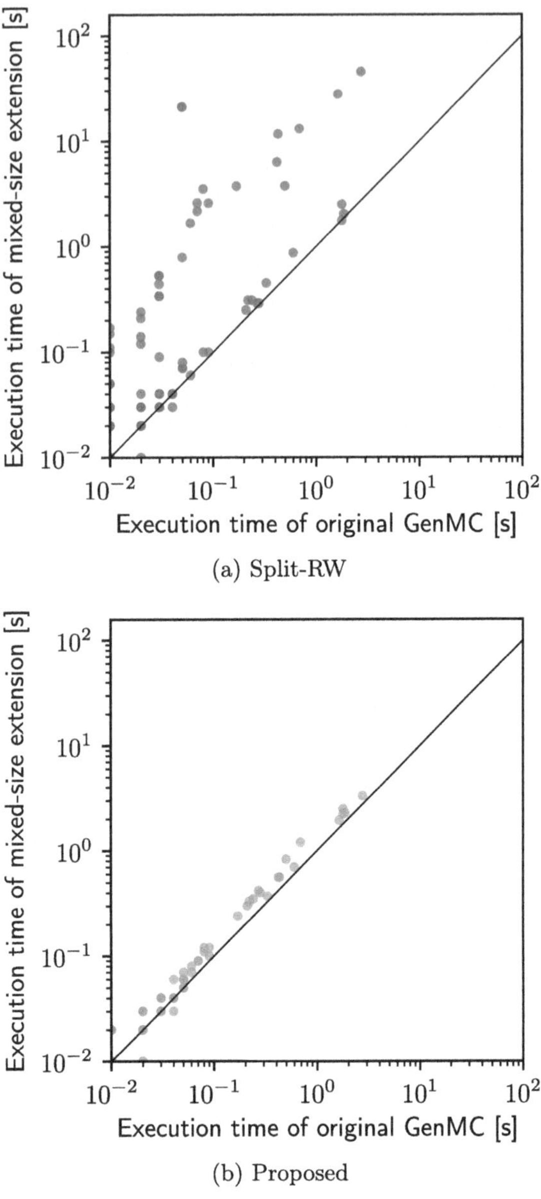

Fig. 8. Execution time of GenMC on the test suite: nearer to the diagonal line, less overhead in time.

Table 1. Results of data structure tests: T denotes execution time in second, $|E|$ denotes the number of complete executions explored, $|B|$ denotes the number of blocked executions, and the suffix n to each test denotes the number of threads.

	Original			Proposed			Split-RW		
Test$_n$	T	$\|E\|$	$\|B\|$	T	$\|E\|$	$\|B\|$	T	$\|E\|$	$\|B\|$
barrier$_2$	0.01	2	2	0.01	2	2	0.01	4	2
chase-lev$_2$	0.01	59	0	0.02	59	0	0.02	59	0
dq$_3^*$	0.05	1802	0	0.05	1802	0	21.80	557046	0
dq-opt$_3^*$	0.05	1802	0	0.05	1802	0	21.19	557046	0
linuxrwlocks$_2^*$	0.02	222	116	0.02	222	116	0.02	222	116
mcs_spinlock$_2$	0.01	10	18	0.01	10	18	0.01	10	18
mpmc-queue$_2$	0.01	6	8	0.01	6	8	0.01	6	8
ms-queue$_2$	0.03	114	64	0.04	114	64	0.04	114	64
qspinlock$_2$	0.02	6	2	0.02	6	2	0.02	6	2
qu$_3^*$	0.02	75	0	0.02	75	0	0.02	75	0
qu-opt$_3^*$	0.02	132	0	0.02	132	0	0.04	594	0
seqlock$_2$	0.01	2	0	0.01	2	0	0.01	2	0
seqlock-atomic$_2$	0.01	6	3	0.01	6	3	0.01	6	3
stc$_3$	0.02	37	0	0.02	37	0	0.03	37	0
stc-opt$_3$	0.03	183	0	0.04	183	0	0.09	183	0
treiber-stack$_4$	0.01	22	0	0.01	22	0	0.01	22	0

barrier A barrier implemented as a global flag adapted from [23, 24]
chase-lev An implementation of the Chase-Lev deque adapted from [23, 24]
dq An implementation of the Chase-Lev deque adapted from [25]
linuxrwlocks A reader-writer lock ported from the Linux kernel adapted from [23, 24]
mcs_spinlock An implementation of the MCS lock extracted from the Linux kernel [17]
mpmc-queue A multiple-producer multiple-consumer queue adapted from [23, 24]
ms-queue An implementation of the Michael-Scott queue adapted from [23, 24]
qspinlock Queued spinlocks (1.2 KLOC) extracted from the Linux kernel [17]
qu An implementation of the Michael-Scott queue adapted from [25]
seqlock Sequential locks (1.0 KLOC) extracted from the Linux kernel [17]
stc An implementation of the Treiber stack adapted from [25]
* The race detection was disabled because of intentionally racy non-atomic accesses.

These results have confirmed that the proposed approach has little overhead over the original in the non-mixed-size case, unlike split-RW.

Mixed-Size Case Figure 9 shows the execution time of GenMC on MWF with different threads for the proposed approach and split-RW. From 4 threads, the proposed approach outperformed split-RW by twofold or more. It is worth noting that the performance advantage over split-RW in mixed-size cases is generally lower than that in non-mixed-size cases because splitting for mixed-size accesses takes place both in the proposed approach and split-RW.

We thus have confirmed that our approach makes GenMC feasible for the realistic mixed-size accesses for memory management, and the handling for the mixed-size case is much more efficient than that of split-RW.

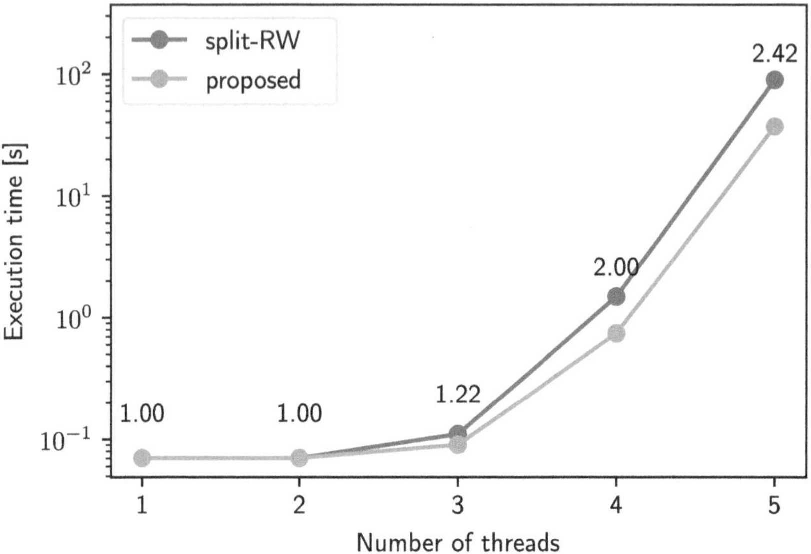

Fig. 9. Execution time of GenMC on MWF scaling the number of threads, where numbers above points denote the relative speed of the proposed over split-RW.

5 Related Work

SMC [12,13] have been well studied and the literature [1,2,15–17,21,23,24] on SMC for C/C++ presented different algorithms and tools. However, case studies on applying these tools to actual C/C++ software were very limited.

Musuvathi and Qadeer [22] developed the Chess model checker and empirically evaluated it through C++ benchmark applications including ones in more than ten thousand LOC. They did not describe the handling of mixed-size access although the benchmark applications might possibly contain it. Kokologiannakis and Sagonas [18] used Nidhugg [1,2] to verify the read-copy-update (RCU) of a Linux kernel. They ported the core part of Linux's RCU to the one tractable for Nidhugg and did not verify actual Linux code as-is.

Mixed-size access is important not only for memory management but for persistency handling because of bytewise read/write from persistent memory or storage. Kokologiannakis et al. [15] developed the PerSeVerE algorithm for model checking under persistency semantics and implemented it into the GenMC checker, where memcpy was interpreted as a primitive of typed memory copying. Gorjiara et al. [14] developed the Jaaru model checker for persistent memory/storage on x86-TSO at the binary level. Jaaru dealt with mixed-size access through the bytewise splitting of memory access without footprints; it corresponds to split-RW in our work.

6 Conclusion

In this paper, we have presented an approach to efficiently adapting GenMC to mixed-size accesses in C11/C++11. It adaptively splits the footprints of rf/mo relations so that the conditions of RC11 consistency keep checkable with the GenMC algorithm as-is. We have experimentally demonstrated that our approach has significantly less overhead than split-RW does.

Atomic mixed-size accesses are an important issue on real-world C/C++ programs. Although they are basically beyond the scope of this paper, as discussed in Sect. 3.4, our work could be a practical basis for dealing with them. For efficient SMC of atomic mixed-size accesses, we should define their formal semantics with a reasonable compromise and extension. For example, to adopt the suggested assumption on semantics described in Sect. 3.4, the C/C++ languages should allow programmers to specify the SC ordering onto an arbitrary memory region. Otherwise, even if we find problems, we would not be allowed to enforce mixed-size atomics to be safe in a reasonable effort. We leave it for future work.

A MWF benchmark

```
#include <pthread.h>

#define FREE_LIST_SIZE 10

typedef struct header {
    struct header *next;
    unsigned size;
} header_t;
struct free_list {
  union { // Source of mixed-size access
    _Alignas(header_t) char buffer[FREE_LIST_SIZE*sizeof(header_t)];
    header_t data[FREE_LIST_SIZE];
  };
  header_t *freep;
  pthread_mutex_t mtx;
};
static struct free_list freeList =
  {{.buffer = {0}}, NULL, PTHREAD_MUTEX_INITIALIZER};

void *my_malloc(size_t nbytes);
void my_free(void *ptr);
```

```
// The number of thereads N is specified with the -D option
pthread_t p[N];

#define NITER 1 // single iteration

void* malloc_write_free(void* arg) {
  for (int i = 0; i < NITER; ++i) {
    int* p = my_malloc(sizeof(int));
    if (p != NULL) {
      *p = 100;
      my_free(p);
    }
  }
  return NULL;
}

int main() {
  for (int i = 0; i < N; ++i)
    if (pthread_create(&p[i], NULL, malloc_write_free, NULL))
      return -1;
  for (int i = 0; i < N; ++i)
    pthread_join(p[i], NULL);
  return 0;
}
```

References

1. Abdulla, P.A., Aronis, S., Atig, M.F., Jonsson, B., Leonardsson, C., Sagonas, K.: Stateless model checking for TSO and PSO. In: Tools and Algorithms for the Construction and Analysis of Systems: 21st International Conference, TACAS 2015, Held as Part of the European Joint Conferences on Theory and Practice of Software, ETAPS 2015, London, UK, April 11–18, 2015, Proceedings. Lecture Notes in Computer Science, vol. 9035, pp. 353–367. Springer, Heidelberg (2015). https://doi.org/10.1007/978-3-662-46681-0_28
2. Abdulla, P.A., Aronis, S., Atig, M.F., Jonsson, B., Leonardsson, C., Sagonas, K.: Stateless model checking for TSO and PSO. Acta Informatica **54**, 789–818 (2017). https://doi.org/10.1007/s00236-016-0275-0
3. Abdulla, P.A., Aronis, S., Jonsson, B., Sagonas, K.: Optimal dynamic partial order reduction. In: Proceedings of the 41st ACM SIGPLAN-SIGACT Symposium on Principles of Programming Languages, pp. 373–384. POPL '14, ACM (2014). https://doi.org/10.1145/2535838.2535845
4. Abdulla, P.A., Aronis, S., Jonsson, B., Sagonas, K.: Source sets: a foundation for optimal dynamic partial order reduction. J. ACM **64**(4), 25:1–25:49 (2017). https://doi.org/10.1145/3073408
5. Alglave, J., Deacon, W., Grisenthwaite, R., Hacquard, A., Maranget, L.: Armed cats: Formal concurrency modelling at Arm. ACM Trans. Program. Lang. Syst. **43**(2), 8:1–8:54 (2021). https://doi.org/10.1145/3458926
6. Alglave, J., Maranget, L., Tautschnig, M.: Herding cats: Modelling, simulation, testing, and data mining for weak memory. ACM Trans. Program. Lang. Syst. **36**(2), 7:1–7:74 (2014). https://doi.org/10.1145/2627752

7. Appel, A.W., Naumann, D.A.: Verified sequential malloc/free. In: Proceedings of the 2020 ACM SIGPLAN International Symposium on Memory Management, pp. 48–59. ISMM '20, ACM (2020). https://doi.org/10.1145/3381898.3397211
8. Batty, M., Owens, S., Sarkar, S., Sewell, P., Weber, T.: Mathematizing C++ concurrency. In: Proceedings of the 38th Annual ACM SIGPLAN-SIGACT Symposium on Principles of Programming Languages, pp. 55–66. POPL '11, ACM (2011). https://doi.org/10.1145/1925844.1926394
9. Boehm, H.J., Adve, S.V.: Foundations of the C++ concurrency memory model. In: Proceedings of the 29th ACM SIGPLAN Conference on Programming Language Design and Implementation, pp. 68–78. PLDI '08, ACM (2008). https://doi.org/10.1145/1375581.1375591
10. Flanagan, C., Godefroid, P.: Dynamic partial-order reduction for model checking software. In: Proceedings of the 32nd ACM SIGPLAN-SIGACT Symposium on Principles of Programming Languages, pp. 110–121. POPL '05, ACM (2005). https://doi.org/10.1145/1040305.1040315
11. Flur, S., Sarkar, S., Pulte, C., Nienhuis, K., Maranget, L., Gray, K.E., Sezgin, A., Batty, M., Sewell, P.: Mixed-size concurrency: ARM, POWER, C/C++11, and SC. In: Proceedings of the 44th ACM SIGPLAN Symposium on Principles of Programming Languages, pp. 429–442. POPL '17, ACM (2017). https://doi.org/10.1145/3009837.3009839
12. Godefroid, P.: Model checking for programming languages using VeriSoft. In: Proceedings of the 24th ACM SIGPLAN-SIGACT Symposium on Principles of Programming Languages, pp. 174–186. POPL '97, ACM (1997). https://doi.org/10.1145/263699.263717
13. Godefroid, P.: Software model checking: the VeriSoft approach. Form. Method Syst. Des. **26**, 77–101 (2005). https://doi.org/10.1007/s10703-005-1489-x
14. Gorjiara, H., Xu, G.H., Demsky, B.: Jaaru: efficiently model checking persistent memory programs. In: Proceedings of the 26th ACM International Conference on Architectural Support for Programming Languages and Operating Systems, pp. 415–428. ASPLOS '21, ACM (2021). https://doi.org/10.1145/3445814.3446735
15. Kokologiannakis, M., Kaysin, I., Raad, A., Vafeiadis, V.: PerSeVerE: persistency semantics for verification under ext4. Proc. ACM Program. Lang. **5**(POPL), 43:1–43:29 (2021). https://doi.org/10.1145/3434324
16. Kokologiannakis, M., Lahav, O., Sagonas, K., Vafeiadis, V.: Effective stateless model checking for C/C++ concurrency. Proc. ACM Program. Lang. **2**(POPL), 17:1–17:32 (2018). https://doi.org/10.1145/3158105
17. Kokologiannakis, M., Raad, A., Vafeiadis, V.: Model checking for weakly consistent libraries. In: Proceedings of the 40th ACM SIGPLAN Conference on Programming Language Design and Implementation, pp. 96–110. PLDI '19, ACM (2019). https://doi.org/10.1145/3314221.3314609, full paper with the technical appendix: https://plv.mpi-sws.org/genmc/full-paper.pdf
18. Kokologiannakis, M., Sagonas, K.: Stateless model checking of the linux kernel's read-copy update (RCU). Int. J. Softw. Tools Technol. Transfer **21**, 283–306 (2019). https://doi.org/10.1007/s10009-019-00514-6
19. Kokologiannakis, M., Vafeiadis, V.: GenMC: a model checker for weak memory models. In: Computer Aided Verification: 33rd International Conference, CAV 2021, Virtual Event, July 20–23, 2021, Proceedings, Part I. LNCS, vol. 12759, pp. 427–440. Springer, Heidelberg (2021). https://doi.org/10.1007/978-3-030-81685-8_20

20. Lahav, O., Vafeiadis, V., Kang, J., Hur, C.K., Dreyer, D.: Repairing sequential consistency in C/C++11. In: Proceedings of the 38th ACM SIGPLAN Conference on Programming Language Design and Implementation, pp. 618–632. PLDI '17, ACM (2017). https://doi.org/10.1145/3062341.3062352
21. Lång, M., Sagonas, K.: Parallel graph-based stateless model checking. In: ATVA 2020: Automated Technology for Verification and Analysis. Lecture Notes in Computer Science, vol. 12302, pp. 377–393. Springer, Heidelberg (2020). https://doi.org/10.1007/978-3-030-59152-6_21
22. Musuvathi, M., Qadeer, S.: Iterative context bounding for systematic testing of multithreaded programs. In: Proceedings of the 28th ACM SIGPLAN Conference on Programming Language Design and Implementation. pp. 446–455. PLDI '07, ACM (2007). https://doi.org/10.1145/1250734.1250785
23. Norris, B., Demsky, B.: CDSCheker: checking concurrent data structures written with C/C++ atomics. In: Proceedings of the 2013 ACM SIGPLAN International Conference on Object Oriented Programming Systems Languages & Applications, pp. 131–150. OOPSLA '13, ACM (2013). https://doi.org/10.1145/2509136.2509514
24. Norris, B., Demsky, B.: A practical approach for model checking C/C++11 code. ACM Trans. Program. Lang. Syst. **58**(3), 10:1–10:51 (2016). https://doi.org/10.1145/2806886
25. Pulte, C., Pichon-Pharabod, J., Kang, J., Lee, S.H., Hur, C.K.: Promising-ARM/RISC-V: a simpler and faster operational concurrency model. In: Proceedings of the 40th ACM SIGPLAN Conference on Programming Language Design and Implementation, pp. 1–15. PLDI '19, ACM (2019). https://doi.org/10.1145/3314221.3314624
26. Sato, S., Mizuhashi, T., Kimura, G., Taura, K.: Efficiently Adapting Stateless Model Checking for C11/C++11 to Mixed-Size Accesses (Supplemental Material) (2024). https://doi.org/10.5281/zenodo.13624833
27. Ugawa, T., Abe, T., Maeda, T.: Model checking copy phases of concurrent copying garbage collection with various memory models. Proc. ACM Program. Lang. **1**(OOPSLA), 53:1–53:26 (2017). https://doi.org/10.1145/3133877
28. Yodaiken, V.: How ISO C became unusable for operating systems development. In: Proceedings of the 11th Workshop on Programming Languages and Operating Systems, pp. 84–90. PLOS '21, ACM (2021). https://doi.org/10.1145/3477113.3487274

Effective Search Space Pruning for Testing Deep Neural Networks

Bala Rangayah[1], Eugene Sng[2], and Minh-Thai Trinh[3](✉)

[1] Singapore University of Technology and Design, Singapore, Singapore
[2] Ministry of Defence of Singapore, Singapore, Singapore
[3] Illinois Advanced Research Center at Singapore, Singapore, Singapore
minhthai.t@iarcs-create.edu.sg

Abstract. Dynamic symbolic execution is widely used for test case generation and software bug/vulnerability detection because of its two advantages: high coverage and low false positives. It has also been used in the context of testing Deep Neural Networks (DNNs). Here, each activation value of a neuron is modelled as a decision/choice point (similarly to the way a conditional program statement is handled). However, the main challenge is still the *exponential* number of combinatorial cases of activated neurons. In this paper, we propose to develop an *effective pruning* method to deal with this problem. Firstly, we propose to construct a *better symbolic tree representation* of DNNs for effective search space pruning both in test case generation and in bug/vulnerability detection. Secondly, we propose a novel unsatisfiable core extraction technique, based on the *binary search* algorithm and *variable dependency graph*, to support that method. Finally, we demonstrate their impact via a thorough experimental evaluation and promising results.

1 Introduction

On the robustness of DNNs, existing works can be loosely divided into two groups. In the offensive approaches, the focus is on heuristic search algorithms, which are mainly guided by the forward gradient or cost gradient of a DNN [5, 34, 41], in order to find adversarial examples that are as close as possible to a correctly classified input. These works may be able to find adversarial examples efficiently, but are not able to provide any guarantee (akin to verification) or any certain level of confidence (akin to testing) about the nonexistence of adversarial examples when the algorithm fails to find one. This becomes problematic when DNN models are used in critical systems [2, 23, 32], which motivates the defensive approaches (such as verification and testing).

For DNN testing, existing works [27, 35, 39, 42, 45] are usually inspired by software testing methodologies and employ coverage criteria to guide the generation of test cases; the resulting test suite is then searched for adversarial examples by querying an oracle. There is also the application of dynamic symbolic execution

O. Kiselyov (Ed.): APLAS 2024, LNCS 15194, pp. 365–387, 2024.
https://doi.org/10.1007/978-981-97-8943-6_18

(DSE) to DNN testing [10,40], where each activation value of a neuron is modelled as a decision point (similarly to the way a conditional program statement is handled).

Unfortunately, despite being able to handle complicated coverage criteria, state-of-the-art DNN verification and testing techniques are not yet scalable. Similarly to the case of using formal methods for program reasoning, DNN reasoning also copes with the exponential number of combinatorial cases of activated neurons. This problem is more serious with the widespread use of activation functions such as `ReLU` [31] for hidden neurons.

In this paper, we propose a novel method for *effectively* pruning the search space in test case generation for DNNs. Our method is inspired by the use of unsatisfiable cores in formal verification and is also applicable to the verification of DNNs. Specifically, when solving a symbolic path constraint, if the constraint is unsatisfiable, we can extract a core reason for the unsatisfiability; this is usually known as an *unsatisfiable core*. Later, when dealing with other symbolic paths/traces, if the corresponding path constraints can imply one of the collected unsatisfiable cores, we can safely skip exploring these paths since these are also infeasible. However, a naive application of this idea to DNN reasoning is not effective. Since the unsatisfiable cores are usually generated by constraint solvers, which do not know about the symbolic tree representation of DNNs and the domain knowledge of DNNs, every constraint will be treated equally. As such, constraint solvers cannot guarantee to generate a *good* unsatisfiable core that can help skip exploring a large search space.

To achieve an effective yet sound pruning method,[1] we start with our novel construction of a symbolic tree to represent DNNs, which enables us to prune more search space than a naive one. Next, among different unsatisfiable cores, each element of which corresponds to a node in the tree, we prioritize the core whose lowest node is highest. This allows us to soundly prune a larger sub-tree rooted at that node. We call it *local* pruning since it is only applicable locally to that node. To further speed up the tree exploration and thus the overall performance of the symbolic executor, we also introduce the concept of *global* pruning to deal with the dependency on local constraints.

Formal reasoning about DNNs usually relies on general-purpose solvers that do not take into account the setting of DNN reasoning. Though the cores generated by these solvers can be minimal, it does not mean they can be helpful for pruning the search space. To demonstrate that the domain knowledge is necessary, we propose a simple yet powerful unsatisfiable core generation technique to support the pruning method for testing DNNs. Specifically, our algorithm tries to derive better unsatisfiable cores by first splitting the constraints into two parts: i) the constraints representing the DNN and coverage requirements, and ii) the constraints relevant to the input (e.g. to ensure the closeness between the newly-generated input and the seed input). For the first part, among different unsatisfiable cores, we prioritize the core whose lowest node is highest, which enables us to soundly prune a larger sub-tree rooted at that node. For the sec-

[1] Soundness proof is available in our technical report [36].

ond part, we try to remove as many constraints as possible from it to generalize unsatisfiable cores so that their dependency on the concrete input is minimal. This enables us to prune other subtrees that are not local to that node.

Finally, we implemented our symbolic tree construction, search-space pruning, and unsatisfiable core generation methods in DeepConcolic [40], a state-of-the-art DSE framework for DNNs. Our new framework is called DC_{BS}. We conducted different experiments to evaluate our new framework with respect to 4 complicated coverage criteria and 3 different DNN datasets (and models). For every experiment, our tool DC_{BS} significantly outperforms the other tools under comparison. The performance speed-up is more than 10 times while the coverage of test cases is remarkably improved (wrt. the same running time). We also compared our unsatisfiable core generation algorithm with state-of-the-art techniques. The results show that the unsatisfiable cores generated by our algorithm are much more useful. Their subsumption rate, which is the number of pruned paths for each unsatisfiable core, is 10 times more than the second best in our comparison. With the above promising results, we have moved one step closer to addressing the scalability of DSE-based testing techniques for DNNs.

2 Preliminaries

We first give an overview of Deep Neural Networks (DNN) and their components. Then we discuss existing coverage criteria for testing DNNs and their relationship with each other.

2.1 Deep Neural Networks

A DNN can be defined as a tuple $N = (L, C, \phi)$ such that:

- $L = \{L_k \mid k \in [1, K]\}$ is a set of layers,
- $C \subseteq L \times L$ is a set of connections between (neurons in) layers, and
- $\phi = \{\phi_k \mid k \in [2, K)\}$ is a set of activation functions.

where K is the number of layers. We use $[a, b]$ to denote a range of integer numbers from a to b and (a, b) to denote a range from $a + 1$ to $b - 1$.

Each layer L_k consists of s_k neurons, and the i-th neuron of the layer k is denoted by $n_{k,i}$. We use $v_{k,i}$ to denote the value of $n_{k,i}$. Values of neurons in hidden layers (i.e. with $k \in (1, K)$) need to pass through an activation function. In this paper, we focus on the most popular one `ReLU` though our technique is applicable to others as well. We explicitly denote the activation value before a `ReLU` as $u_{k,i}$ such that $v_{k,i} = u_{k,i}$ if $u_{k,i} \geq 0$ and $v_{k,i} = 0$ if $u_{k,i} < 0$. We next describe each $C_{i,j}$ for two layers i and j. If it is a fully connected and convolutional layer then every neuron is connected to neurons in the preceding layer by pre-defined weights such that $u_{k,i} = \sum_{1 \leq j \leq s_{k-1}} w_{k-1,j,i} \cdot v_{k-1,j} + b_{k,i}$, where $k \in [2, K]$, $i \in [1, s_k]$, $b_{k,i} \in \mathbb{R}$ is the bias, and $w_{k-1,j,i}$ is the pre-defined weight for the connection between the j-th neuron of the layer $k-1$ and the

i-th neuron of the layer k. Finally, for any input $t \in \mathbb{R}^{s_1}$, the neural network assigns a label, that is, the index of the neuron of the output layer that has the largest value. The result of the classification function, which is dependent on t is $label_t = \text{argmax}_{1 \leq i \leq s_K} \{v_{K,i}\}$. The above description can also be extended to handle other popular layers such as convolutional, max-pooling, flatten.

2.2 Testing Coverage Criteria

Software testing methodologies has recently been used to evaluate DNN robustness. The evaluation is highly dependent on the test suite's representativeness. Testing criteria are thus required to characterize a test suite's quality and toward which the input mutations can comprehensively explore DNN behaviors.

Our technique is not dependent on the coverage criteria that are used since as long as they can be represented as constraints, our technique would be applicable. This section is thus to provide some background on existing coverage criteria.

The safety coverage criterion M_S is introduced in [45], where the input space is discretized with a set of hyper-rectangles, inside which the inputs share the same pattern of ReLU, and then one test case is generated for each hyper-rectangle. Though the criterion closely reflects the DNN robustness, such a scheme is computationally intractable due to the high-dimensionality of DNNs. Therefore, [14,39] have recently proposed 4 coverage criteria, which are inspired by established practices in software testing, in particular MC/DC test criterion [21], but are designed for the specific attributes of DNNs. These are sign-sign (M_{SS}), value-sign (M_{VS^g}), sign-value (M_{SV^g}), and value-value coverage ($M_{VV^{g1,g2}}$). In [39], the authors also present the proofs for the relationship between common structural coverage criteria. The other 4 common criteria are neuron coverage (M_N) [35]; multisection neuron coverage (M_{MN^m}) [27]; neuron boundary coverage (M_{NB}) [27]; top neuron coverage (M_{TN^m}) [27]. All of them are subsumed by the above set of four MC/DC coverage criteria.

3 Testing Deep Neural Networks

We present our symbolic tree representation for DNNs and two optimizations in order to achieve a *sound* and more *effective* pruning method for testing DNNs.

3.1 Symbolic Tree Representation

We represent a DNN N (whose neurons are $n_{k,i}$) as a labeled directed acyclic graph (DAG) $T = (V, E, \Sigma_V, \Sigma_E, s, t, l_V, l_E)$ where

- V is a set of vertices or nodes,
- E is a set of ordered pairs of vertices called directed edges, arcs or arrows,
- Σ_V is a set of labels including the label *root*, the values $v_{k,i}$ of the neurons $n_{k,i}$, the activation values $u_{k,i}$ before a ReLU, and dummy values $x_{u_{k,i}}, y_{u_{k,i}}$,
- Σ_E is a set of labels including constraint θ_w that corresponds to the target vertex labeled w,

```
function CONSTRUCT(a DNN N = (L, C, φ))
⟨1⟩ Let T be a dummy node root
⟨2⟩ for k = 2 to K do
⟨3⟩     foreach neuron n in the layer L_k
⟨4⟩         T_{k,n} ← CREATEGRAPH(n, C, φ)
⟨5⟩         T ← APPEND(T, T_{k,n})
⟨6⟩ return T
end function
```

Fig. 1. Graph representation construction of a DNN

- $s : E \to V$, $t : E \to V$ are maps indicating source/target vertex of an arc,
- $l_V : V \to \Sigma_V$, $l_E : E \to \Sigma_E$ are two maps describing the labeling of the vertices and arcs.

A root node is one which is not the target of any arc, while a leaf node is one which is not the source of any arc. There is only one root node and one leaf node. Each node of T is labelled with a variable name in Σ_V. The set of variables is denoted by $\texttt{Var}(T)$; we also use $\texttt{Var}(p)$ where p is a path in the DAG. Note that though we use a DAG to represent a DNN, we will keep using the term "symbolic tree" for consistency with the existing literature on DSE. To avoid any confusion, we will only use (directed acyclic) graph to refer to the concrete representation of DNNs.

In Figure 1, the function CONSTRUCT shows us how to construct the graph representation of a DNN N from the dummy node labelled *root* as in line 1 and expands it using the function APPEND in line 5. We will expand the current DAG with new (directed) edges representing the constraints relevant to neurons in the DNN layers (from the second to the last layer as in line 1). There are two auxiliary functions which are not defined in Fig. 1. The function APPEND is used to append the graph T with a graph $T_{k,n}$ by setting the root node of $T_{k,n}$ to be the current leaf node of T. So it is essentially a graph union, plus merging root nodes of the graphs. Meanwhile, the function CREATEGRAPH is used to create a graph $T_{k,n}$ to represent the constraints relevant to each neuron n in the layer L_k. We illustrate two instances of CREATEGRAPH as follows.

Linear Graph: As an example, to represent a max-pooling layer, we need to specify the relationship between some j-th neuron $n_{k-1,j}$ of the layer $k-1$ and the first neuron $n_{k,1}$ of the layer k. Suppose we have a dummy node labelled with x in Fig. 2a. We will create a new edge from that node to a new node labelled with $v_{k,1}$. The edge is then labelled with $\theta_1 \equiv v_{k,1} = \max_{j \in \kappa}\{v_{k-1,j}\}$ where $\kappa \subseteq [1, s_{k-1}]$, $k \in [2, K]$. We will refer to these nodes as the node x and the node $v_{k,1}$ for short.

DAG: As stated above, for a dense layer, since every neuron is connected to neurons in the preceding layer by pre-defined weights, we have $\theta_2 \equiv u_{k,i} = \sum_{1 \le j \le s_{k-1}} w_{k-1,j,i} \cdot v_{k-1,j} + b_{k,i}$ where $k \in [2, K]$, $i \in [1, s_k]$. Also, based on the

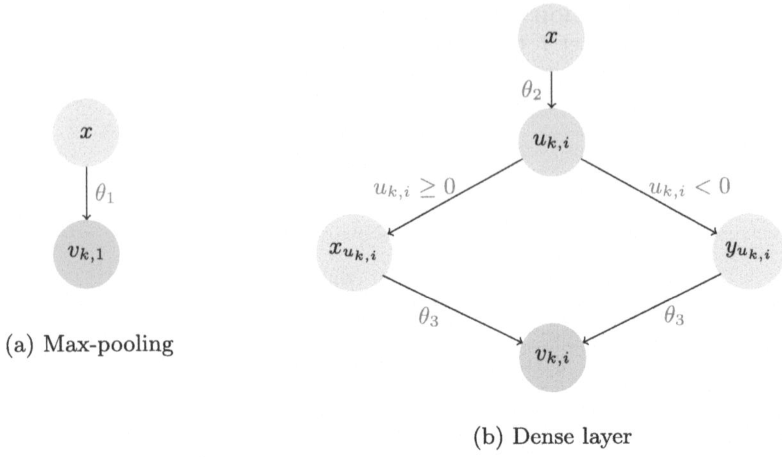

(a) Max-pooling

(b) Dense layer

Fig. 2. Graph representation for different neurons

activation function, we have $\theta_3 \equiv (u_{k,i} \geq 0 \Rightarrow v_{k,i} = u_{k,i}) \wedge (u_{k,i} < 0 \Rightarrow v_{k,i} = 0)$. In Fig. 2b, the node labelled with $u_{k,i}$ is called a *branching point.* (If $k = K$ then the graph will end at that node.) There is an edge, labelled with θ_2, from a dummy node x to $u_{k,i}$. To create the two branches, we introduce 2 dummy nodes, labelled with fresh variables $x_{u_{k,i}}$ and $y_{u_{k,i}}$. There are two edges, labelled with $u_{k,i} \geq 0$ and $u_{k,i} < 0$, from $u_{k,i}$ to $x_{u_{k,i}}$ and $y_{u_{k,i}}$ resp., and two edges, labelled with θ_3, from $x_{u_{k,i}}$ and $y_{u_{k,i}}$ to the node labelled with $v_{k,i}$. Note that x will be removed when calling APPEND while $x_{u_{k,i}}$ and $y_{u_{k,i}}$ will remain. In fact, we can also merge the two nodes $x_{u_{k,i}}$ and $y_{u_{k,i}}$ into one and the DAG becomes a *multidigraph.* However, for clarity, we just use the two nodes separately.

The resulting graph representation over-approximates the DNN. Specifically, if we traverse each path and collect the constraints along it, the models/solutions of all path constraints will cover all possible concrete inputs of the DNN. The more precise the constraints (e.g. θ_1) that we use to model the DNN are, the more precise the over-approximation is. If we can model exactly behaviours of a DNN using precise edge constraints then there is no approximation. In the current paper, we do not have to use over-approximation but in general we can support that in order to handle other types of activations functions, for example.

We now present the two optimizations to further improve the effectiveness and efficiency of our pruning method later. The first contribution is the application of our dependency analysis, which results in the dependency group and graph in Sect. 3.2. The second, which involves the order in which the graph is constructed for test case generation, is presented in Sect. 3.3.

3.2 Dependency Analysis

The purpose of the dependency group and graph is to speed up the binary search algorithm that we use in our unsatisfiable core generation technique in Sect. 4.

Dependency Group. We try to group relevant constraints together. For example, in the case of a separate activation layer such as in Keras, we will group this activation layer and its preceding layer (e.g. a (pure) convolution/dense layer) as if they are merely a convolution/dense layer with the activation function. This avoids the fragmentation of related constraints and helps speed up our binary search algorithm whose performance relies on a variable dependency analysis.

Dependency Graph. We also apply the variable dependency analysis to the graph representation of a DNN. Note that these dependency edges are not part of the representation of a DNN. Instead, we use them (in the function WEAKEN2 in Fig. 4) to enable a more efficient pruning method, which is presented in Sect. 4. However, since the dependency graph is relevant to the constraints representing DNNs, and can also be annotated on top of the DAG representation, we present it here for clarity.

Based on the constraints in the DNN representation, we can easily construct dependency edges as follows. Normally, if there is a connection between a j-th neuron of the layer $k-1$ and an i-th neuron of the layer k, then there is a dependency edge from the node $v_{k,i}$ to the node $v_{k-1,j}$. However, for activation functions, the dependency edges are slightly different. We summarize them as follows. For the linear graph, if we have a constraint $v_{k,1} = \max_{j \in \kappa}\{v_{k-1,j}\}$, we will have dependency edges from the node $v_{k,1}$ to all the nodes $v_{k-1,j}$, where $j \subset \kappa$. For the DAG, if we have a constraint θ_2, we can construct edges from the node $u_{k,i}$ to the *root* node (if $k = 2$) or all the nodes $v_{k-1,j}$ (if $k > 2$). For the constraint θ_3, we have dependency paths from $v_{k,i}$ to $u_{k,i}$ via the dummy node $x_{u_{k,i}}$ (and $y_{u_{k,i}}$) in the left (and right).

In general, there exists a dependency edge from a lower node labeled x to a higher node labeled y if there is an edge in the DAG representation of the DNN whose label is in the form of $x = f(\tilde{y})$, where f is a function over variables including y. The edge from $u_{k,i}$ to the *root* node (if $k = 2$) follows this idea if we consider *root* as the representative for the neurons in the input layer. The edges wrt. θ_3 also do if we use multidigraph to avoid the use of dummy nodes.

3.3 Test Case Generation with Coverage Criteria

When testing the robustness of a DNN, we need to use coverage requirements to address the quality of the testing method. Such coverage requirements can be represented as constraints and encoded in the DNN graph representation.

Many coverage criteria have been proposed so far in the context of DNN testing. Here, we use sign-sign coverage (SSC) [39], which is inspired by MC/DC coverage in conventional software testing, as an illustrative example. Similar representation can be done for other criteria such as Neuron coverage [35] and other variants of MC/DC coverage for DNNs [39]. Before formalizing the SSC criterion, we need to define the following auxiliary functions.

Definition 1 (Node-to-Constraint Function). *Given a path p in the DAG representation of a DNN, and an internal node (labelled with) x in the path p, we define the function $p[x]$ to be a mapping from x to the constraint on the edge starting from x. The function $p[x]$ returns true if x is a leaf node and* `undefined` *if x does not belong to p.* □

We also write $u^p_{k,i}$ to denote that the node $u_{k,i}$ belongs to p. Moreover, we can refer to a path via its path constraint.

Definition 2 (Path Constraint). *A path constraint pc for a path p is defined as the list of constraints, which are the results of applying the node-to-constraint function to every node in the path p; that is $pc =_{def} \{p[x] \mid x \in \mathtt{Var}(p)\}$.* □

We can also refer to a path using a partial path constraint by applying the node-to-constraint function to only the nodes which are branching points (i.e. $u_{k,i}$) since other constraints are the same for every path. This (along with our graph construction) allows an efficient implementation for our pruning method.

Finally, we can access the ending node of any constraint θ in pc.

Definition 3 (Path-Constraint-to-Node Function). *Given a path constraint pc for a path p, the function $pc[\theta]$ is a mapping from a constraint θ in the path constraint pc to the ending node of the edge labelled with θ in p.* □

To satisfy an SSC requirement, we need to find a new test case t' such that wrt. the seed input t, the activation signs of two neurons $n_{k+1,j}$ and $n_{k,i}$ are negated, while other signs of other neurons are equal to those for the input t (see e.g. [39]). The SSC criterion is formalized as follows.

Definition 4 (Sign-Sign Coverage). *A pair of path $p{=}(p_1, p_2)$ is Sign-Sign-covered if the following conditions are satisfied for some k, i, j:*

- $p_1[u^{p_1}_{k,i}] = \neg p_2[u^{p_2}_{k,i}]$
- $p_1[u^{p_1}_{k+1,j}] = \neg p_2[u^{p_2}_{k+1,j}]$
- $p_1[u^{p_1}] = p_2[u^{p_2}]$ *for all* $u^{p_1} \not\equiv u^{p_1}_{k,i} \wedge u^{p_1} \not\equiv u^{p_1}_{k+1,j}$ □

To achieve this, given the current path p, we negate two constraints, $p[u_{k+1,j}]$ and $p[u_{k,i}]$, in the corresponding path constraint pc while keeping other constraints unchanged. (Note that every node $u^p_{k,i}$ is a branching point in the symbolic tree.) Then we check the satisfiability of the conjunction of the new path constraint pc'. If $\bigwedge pc'$ is satisfiable, it means that we can find a new input t' that witnesses a different path p' and can improve the Sign-Sign coverage. This newly-generated input t' will then be added to the test suite τ.

So DSE combines both concrete execution and symbolic analysis on the symbolic tree representation. Each concrete execution corresponds to a running of the DNN with a concrete input t. Meanwhile, the symbolic analysis is responsible for generating a new test input t' to explore a different path. To make sure that the obtained test case is meaningful, we also need to add an objective function (to the path constraint pc' to get pc'') that minimizes the distance between the seed input and the newly-generated input. If we use linear constraints to model the DNN, we need to make sure that the distance metric is also linear. So we use the distance constraint that applies to the L_∞-norm (the Chebyshev distance).

Since the objective function is relevant to a seed input, the above *distance constraints* are parameterized by seed inputs and will be generated and expanded to the *leaf* of the DAG. (This will help achieve a more effective pruning method as shown in Sect. 4.) Firstly, we need to specify the constraint θ_4 on the distance between the generated input t' and the seed input t via some variable d. Then we need to specify the constraint θ_5 to minimize d. For example, if we have θ_4 is $d = ||t - t'||_\infty \wedge d \in [lb, ub]$ and θ_5 is $minimize(d)$ then $\theta_4 \wedge \theta_5$ must also be satisfied when solving the above formula $\bigwedge pc'$ to generate t'.

4 Effective Search Space Pruning

We present how to effectively prune the search space in testing DNNs. We start with the limitation of existing techniques, then the principles of an effective pruning method and finally a novel unsatisfiable core generation method.

4.1 Limitation of Existing Techniques

The main existing approach to tackling the state explosion problem is based on Craig interpolation. The idea is that given an unsatisfiable formula $A \wedge B$, where B is a target constraint, we would like to find a Craig-interpolant I such that $A \rightarrow I$ (meaning A implies I) and $I \wedge B$ is also unsatisfiable (see [17,18,29])). So in order for the Craig interpolation to work, we need to have a target constraint and ideally, it should be shared among all program paths. This requirement is usually fulfilled by verification techniques since the target constraint in the context of verification is some assertion that needs to be satisfied in all program paths.

However, in the context of DNN *testing*, the target constraints are usually dynamic. For example, for test case generation, they can only be distance constraints. Furthermore, those distance constraints will be likely to be different for each path since the current seed input might be changed. Note that even if the unsatisfiability of a new path constraint (e.g. the above pc'') is not relevant to distance constraints, we cannot simply remove those distance constraints since they are the target of the Craig interpolation. As a result, this prevents existing interpolation based techniques from being applicable, which leads to our proposal of an unsatisfiable core based algorithm in the following. Our technique is built inside constraint solvers and can be used for both verification and testing.

4.2 Dynamic Symbolic Execution with Pruning

In Fig. 3, we present a generic and top level function DSE for testing DNNs based on dynamic symbolic execution. Starting with a list of seed inputs τ, we choose

```
function DSE(τ, r, T)
⟨1⟩ λg ← [ ], M ← [ ]
⟨2⟩ while ¬COVERED(τ,r) do
⟨3⟩     t ← CHOOSE(τ)
⟨4⟩     γ ← SYMBOLIC(t,T)
⟨5⟩     ω ← SEARCH(γ,t,r,λg,T,M)
⟨6⟩     τ ← τ ∪ ω
⟨7⟩ return τ
end function
function EXTRACT(λg, t)
⟨8⟩ λl ← [ ]
⟨9⟩ foreach (label,dist) ∈ λg do
⟨10⟩    if t satisfies dist
⟨11⟩        λl ← λl ∪ {label}
⟨12⟩ return λl
end function
function PRUNE(L, Γ, T)
⟨13⟩ foreach last ∈ L do
⟨14⟩    Γ ← ADD(last,T,Γ)
⟨15⟩ return Γ
end function
function SEARCH(γ0, t0, r, λg, T, M)
⟨16⟩ λl ← EXTRACT(λg,t0)
⟨17⟩ Γ ← [ ]
⟨18⟩ foreach label ∈ λl do
⟨19⟩    Γ ← PRUNE(M[label], Γ, T)
⟨20⟩ while ¬ISCOMPLETE(Γ,T) do
⟨21⟩    γ ← NEXT(γ0,r,Γ)
⟨22⟩    Γ ← Γ ∪ {γ}
⟨23⟩    (ω0,issat) ← SOLVE(⋀γ)
⟨24⟩    if ¬issat
⟨25⟩        (l,p,d) ← GEN(γ,γ0)
⟨26⟩        λg ← λg ∪ {(l,d)}
⟨27⟩        f ← PARTIAL(γ,l)
⟨28⟩        λf ← ENUM(f,p)
⟨29⟩        foreach fi ∈ λf do
⟨30⟩            M[l] ← M[l] ∪ {l^fi}
⟨31⟩        Γ ← PRUNE(M[l], Γ, T)
⟨32⟩    else
⟨33⟩        return {ω0}
⟨34⟩ return [ ]
end function
```

Fig. 3. Testing DNNs with search space pruning

one input t from τ in line 3 (possibly with some heuristics) and construct the symbolic path constraint γ corresponding to that input t (based on the graph representation T of the DNN) in line 4. We keep on trying to generate a list of new test inputs ω via the SEARCH function in line 5 and add it to τ in line 6. This loop ends when we reach the full coverage wrt. the type of coverage r and τ. In other words, the condition COVERED(τ, r) is satisfied in line 2. For each kind of coverage r, COVERED is implemented differently. For example, neuron coverage means for any hidden neuron, there exists a test case $t \in \tau$ such that the neuron is activated. We refer readers to the previous work such as [11,40] for the details. Finally, the algorithm returns the list of all test inputs τ in line 7.

Let us give an overview of our contribution. The main difference between ours and the existing DSE algorithms (e.g. as in [11,40]) is the SEARCH function and its capability of *pruning* the search space both *locally* and *globally*. (Instead, the existing ones simply use the NEXT function in line 21 to generate a new test input.) This is done using the global variable λ_g in line 1 (for global pruning), and the local variable λ_l in line 16 (for local pruning). We extract λ_l (of type *label list*) from λ_g (of type *(label, constraint list) list*) via the EXTRACT function in line 16. Intuitively, λ_l contains the labels of the nodes in the graph representation T of the DNN, where we can safely skip exploring the sub-graphs rooted at these nodes. In line 18, for each *label* in λ_l, we first get a list of nodes via the map M and then able to do a local pruning via the function PRUNE in line 19. To skip exploring those paths (of the sub-graphs), we add them to the list Γ of explored paths (which is initially empty in line 17) via the ADD function in line 14 (of the

PRUNE function). We will explain the PRUNE function and how to construct the map M later when revisiting them in line 30 and line 31.

The core of the SEARCH function is still the NEXT function in line 21, where we keep on generating an unexplored path with its path constraint γ as a candidate to improve the coverage for the criterion r. Similarly to COVERED, for each kind of coverage r, the NEXT function is implemented differently and we also refer readers to the previous work such as [11,40] for the details. Because the NEXT function will ensure that $\gamma \notin \Gamma$, we add γ into the list Γ in line 22.

The loop ends if ISCOMPLETE(Γ, T) is satisfied in line 20. In other words, we have finished the exploration of the whole search tree wrt. the current path γ_0 and the coverage criterion r, and we cannot improve the coverage further given the input t_0. So we return an empty list in line 34.

In the other case, the loop ends when we can find a new input that improves the coverage. In other words, we can find a path γ such that it is feasible and a concrete input that witnesses this path. So we need to check the satisfiability of the path constraint γ via the SOLVE function in line 23. If the path constraint γ is consistent, the result of solving the path constraint (i.e. the conjunction $\bigwedge \gamma$) is a new concrete input ω_0, which is returned as the result in line 33. If γ is inconsistent, we use the GEN function (defined in Sect. 4.3) in line 25 to get

- the label l of the highest node l^{γ} responsible for the infeasibility of γ
- the unsatisfiable core $p \cup d$, where d contains distance constraints and p contains the remainder. The last constraint c in the list p satisfies $\gamma[c] = l^{\gamma}$.

We then add the pair (l, d) into λ_g in line 26 for global pruning later.

For local pruning, in line 30, we first update the map M by adding the new nodes (whose label is l), at which we can safely skip exploring the subgraphs rooted. Given that a label l can appear in multiple paths of the graph T, we need to compare the constraint list p (which is obtained from the unsatisfiable core for γ) with the partial path constraint f (from the root node to the node l^{γ}) in line 27 to find out which constraint is missing. We only collect the missing constraints m_j on the edges whose starting nodes are branching points (i.e. $u_{k,i}$) since the others are the same for all the paths from the root node to a node labeled l. By enumerating all the possibilities of combinatorially negating the missing constraints m_j in f, we can collect all the partial paths f_i (including f) that satisfy the constraints in p into λ_f in line 28. The last nodes l^{f_i} of these different paths f_i will be collected into $M[l]$. Finally, we can prune all the paths that go through the collected nodes l^{f_i} by using PRUNE in line 31. In fact, the pruning step can be implemented very efficiently since a path is defined via the constraints at branching points, i.e. whether $u_{k,i} \geq 0$ or $u_{k,i} < 0$. So we only need to track the values of $u_{k,i}$ to mark the explored paths.

For global pruning, getting back to line 16, we use the function EXTRACT to filter the elements of the list λ_g. Basically, since distance constraints are dependent on the input, we need to check if these constraints are also satisfied by the current input t in order to be used in the search w.r.t. t (via the SEARCH function). For example, we check if the distance constraints $dist$ in λ_g (which corresponds to a previous input t_{prev}) can be satisfied in line 10 by the current input t. If so, we can add the corresponding *label* into the list λ_l for local pruning w.r.t. the input t in line 11. Finally, we return λ_l as the result in line 12.

4.3 Unsatisfiable Core Generation

Figure 4 presents our unsatisfiable core generation algorithm, which is the base for the GEN function used in line 25 in Fig. 3. We implemented the algorithm on top of the state-of-the-art CPLEX solver. Since this is not an open-source tool, our implementation can only be done via its public API methods [16]. Though existing optimization techniques such as the ones in [19] can be adopted to speed up our current implementation, this paper focuses more on the *effectiveness* of the pruning method and thus leaves further optimization as our future work.

The GEN function takes two lists of constraints as its inputs: the current path constraint γ and the original path constraint γ_0 (corresponding to the seed input). It will try to weaken the list of constraints γ using 3 auxiliary weakening functions (i.e. WEAKEN1, WEAKEN2, and WEAKEN3), and return $(last, \alpha, \beta)$ as the final result. We also construct a dependency graph G (line 1) on top of the DNN graph representation T as mentioned in Section 3 and use it in WEAKEN2.

```
function GEN(γ, γ0)
⟨1⟩ G: dependency graph
⟨2⟩ δ1, δ2: map from a constraint to its pref
⟨3⟩ γ1 ← WEAKEN1(γ, δ1)
⟨4⟩ (γ2, last) ← WEAKEN2(γ1, γ0, G)
⟨5⟩ (α, β) ← WEAKEN3(γ2, δ2)
⟨6⟩ return (last, α, β)
end function
function WEAKEN1(γ, δ)
⟨7⟩ (α, β) ← SPLIT(γ)
⟨8⟩ PREF(α, δ, 0)
⟨9⟩ PREF(β, δ, 1)
⟨10⟩ return REFINE(γ, δ)
end function
function WEAKEN2(γ, γ0, G)
⟨11⟩ (α, β) ← SPLIT(γ)
⟨12⟩ αf ← FILTER(α, γ0, G)
⟨13⟩ (α', αk) ← BINARY(αf, [ ], β)
⟨14⟩ return (α' ∪ β, LABEL(α'[αk]))
end function
function WEAKEN3(γ, δ)
⟨15⟩ PREF(γ, δ, 1)
⟨16⟩ γ' ← REFINE(γ, δ)
⟨17⟩ return SPLIT(γ')
end function
function PREF(γ, δ, n)
⟨18⟩ foreach cnt ∈ γ do
⟨19⟩     δ[cnt] = n
end function
function BINARY(α, ψ, β)
⟨20⟩ if SIZE(α) ≤ 1
⟨21⟩     return (ψ ∪ α, α[0])
⟨22⟩ (α1, α2) ← DIVIDE(α)
⟨23⟩ if ISSAT(⋀(α1 ∪ ψ ∪ β))
⟨24⟩     α = α2
⟨25⟩     ψ = ψ ∪ α1
⟨26⟩ else
⟨27⟩     α = α1
⟨28⟩ return BINARY(α, ψ, β)
end function
```

Fig. 4. Unsatisfiable core generation algorithm

The WEAKEN1 function uses the SPLIT function to divide the constraints γ into two lists: β containing distance constraints, and α containing the remaining. We next assign the preferences for all the constraints in the two lists with 0 and 1, where 0 means the constraints must be included while 1 means the constraints may be excluded. The preference assignment is done via the PREF function by using the mapping δ over all the constraints from γ. Finally, the REFINE function is responsible for extracting the unsatisfiable core for γ based on the preference δ. Basically, REFINE contains different algorithms provided by state-of-the-art constraint solvers such as Bound Propagation [25], Pre-solve [3], QuickXPlain [19], Irreducibly Inconsistent Set (IIS) [6], etc. Based on the constraint inputs, the solver may decide which algorithm results in the best performance. Since this is not our contribution, we just describe these algorithms (of CPLEX) as a black-box and always use the default configuration chosen by CPLEX. Also, both REFINE and PREF are API methods.

It can be seen that WEAKEN1 tries to weaken the list β while leaving α unchanged. Its purpose is to eliminate as much as possible distance constraints in order for the unsatisfiable cores to become more useful in global pruning. In the WEAKEN2 function, we also split the constraints into two lists. However, we now put our focus on the first list α and leave β unchanged. Our first task is to keep only relevant constraints in α, which are responsible for the infeasibility of γ, to get α_f. We would like to recall that the original path constraint γ_0 (corresponding to the input t_0) is feasible. To improve the coverage, we explore a new path constraint γ (via NEXT in Fig. 3) by changing some constraint(s) in γ_0. However, it results in the infeasibility of γ. So, in the FILTER function, we first identify the different constraints c_i, which are responsible for the infeasibility of γ, between two lists of constraints α (i.e. a part of γ) and γ_0. Then for each edge constraint c_i, we can obtain its ending node e_i. With the help of the *variable dependency graph* G, we can trace all the constraints on the edges of T, whose ending nodes belong to the dependency path(s) from (all the nodes) e_i to the root node. In other words, all edge constraints whose ending nodes are between two consecutive nodes in a dependency path are eliminated from α.

The next task is to find the shortest unsatisfiable prefix of the path constraint using BINARY, which has 3 parameters (α, ψ, β) and returns a pair consisting of

- a list α' containing the first k elements $[\alpha_1, \ldots, \alpha_k]$ from the list α such that α' and β are still inconsistent and
- the last element α_k.

Note that the elements in α and α' appear in the same top-down order as in the DNN graph representation T. Furthermore, another property of the list α' is that if we remove the element α_k from α', the new list $[\alpha_1, \ldots, \alpha_{k-1}]$ will become consistent with β. To achieve this, we do a binary search for α_k as follows. In line 22, we divide α into two sub-lists, α_1 and α_2. If $\bigwedge(\alpha_1 \cup \psi \cup \beta)$ is satisfiable, we need to keep searching α_k in the sub-list α_2. So we need to update α to be α_2 in line 24, while appending ψ with α_1 in line 25. Otherwise, if $\bigwedge(\alpha_1 \cup \psi \cup \beta)$ is unsatisfiable, we simply update α to be α_1 (and remove α_2) in line 27 since α_2 does not contain α_k. While the recursive case is in line 28, the base case is in line 21, when the size of α is 1 (which is exactly the case when α is $[\alpha_k]$). In the base case, we just simply return a pair $(\psi \cup \alpha, \alpha[0])$. The invariant is that the list $\psi \cup \alpha$ is always a superset of the return list (e.g. α' in line 13).

Getting back to WEAKEN2, in line 13, after obtaining the last constraint α_k, we need to map it to its ending node in line 14 via $\alpha'[\alpha_k]$. In short, we have found the highest node, $\alpha'[\alpha_k]$, in the graph T, that is responsible for the infeasibility of γ. We now return the label of this node (along with $\alpha' \cup \beta$) as the final result.

In WEAKEN3, we call REFINE on all the elements of γ to get its normal unsatisfiable core. Their preferences are all 1. The purpose is to simplify the final core as much as possible by removing constraints that are irrelevant to the infeasibility of γ. This allows improving the effectiveness of the subsumption checking such as lines 10 and 28 in Fig. 3. We finally use the function SPLIT to split the constraints in γ' into two parts and return them as the final result.

To summarize, we use 3 different weakening functions to first weaken the distance constraints, then the remaining constraints, and finally all of them together. While the first and third functions are mostly based on state-of-the-art conflict refiner algorithms (as shown in the above description of the REFINE function), the second one is based on our binary search algorithm, which helps us achieve better unsatisfiable cores. To reduce the search space and improve the performance of the binary search algorithm, we also use the dependency analysis to remove irrelevant constraints using the above dependency graph G.

5 Evaluation

We implemented our graph construction, search-space pruning and unsatisfiable core generation methods on top of DeepConcolic [40], a state-of-the-art DSE framework for DNNs. Our new tool is called DC_{BS} which supports search space pruning using unsatisfiable cores generated by our binary search algorithm.

We evaluated our tool using 4 different coverage criteria and 3 datasets (and models), which are also used in the experimental evaluation of DeepConcolic. The first two datasets, `MNIST` [47] and `CIFAR-10` [24], and the corresponding pre-trained models (with 17 layers) are shipped with DeepConcolic and available at https://github.com/TrustAI/DeepConcolic. The third dataset is `ImageNet` [38] and the corresponding used model is VGG16 [43].

Table 1. Description and abbreviation of each tool

Description	Abbreviation
The original DeepConcolic tool	DC
A modified version of DC which supports pruning by using the Conflict Refiner algorithm of CPLEX to generate unsatisfiable cores	DC_{CR}
A modified version of DC which supports pruning by using the Full-Solve algorithm of CPLEX to generate unsatisfiable cores	DC_{FS}
Our tool, which is also a modified version of DC, supports pruning by using our binary search algorithm to generate unsatisfiable cores	DC_{BS}

The four criteria that we used for test case generation are sign-sign coverage (SSC), value-sign coverage (VSC), sign-value coverage (SVC), and value-value coverage (VVC). For the value change, we used the setting of neuron boundary coverage. Specifically, if the activation value of a neuron exceeds either its upper bound or its lower bound, it means a value change for that neuron happens.

To demonstrate the efficiency of our proposed methods for improving the coverage, we compared our tool with 3 other ones, which are the variants of the DeepConcolic tool. All the four tools are described in Table 1. The three tools, DC_{CR}, DC_{FS} and DC_{BS}, support our effective pruning method in Sect. 4.2, but with different algorithms to generate unsatisfiable cores. While DC_{CR} uses the Conflict Refiner algorithm of CPLEX, DC_{FS} uses its FullSolve algorithm, and DC_{BS} uses our binary search algorithm in Sect. 4.3. We could not compare our tool with other DNN testing tools since they do not support passing different coverage criteria as input or they are not available [10]. Instead, we mention here previous comparison [7,39,49] between DeepConcolic and fuzzing based techniques [12,33]. They are comparable wrt. simple coverage criteria such as neuron coverage. However, [12,33] cannot handle complicated coverage criteria such as the above MC/DC variants [39] since these criteria usually require the handling of *complicated* constraints on neurons' signs and values.

The experimental results are presented in the cactus plot diagrams in Fig. 5. For each tool, we measure the running time (in second) and the mean coverage (in percentage) over time. In our experiments, we set the timeout to be 12 hours. For easier and nicer presentation, we crop the top of the graph and report 288 as the maximum coverage; the full graph is very long since the plot for DC_{BS} continues to rise up beyond the top border in Fig. 5a. The number 288 is also the maximum coverage for DC_{CR} in Fig. 5b.

Similarly to the DeepConcolic tool, based on the generated test cases, all the tools are able to generate adversarial attacks. The numbers of generated attack inputs (given the 12 hour timeout) for the `MNIST` benchmark range from 2 to 11 (depending on the coverage criterion) and those for the `CIFAR-10` and `ImageNet` benchmarks range from 10 to 121. Of course, given the provided timeout, our tool can detect more attacks than the 3 other tools. However, if we do not limit the running time, the number of malicious inputs will be the same when the tools reach the same coverage. In this case, the one that reaches that coverage more quickly will be able to find the attack faster. So our contribution is the speed-up in the performance of attack detection, which is also reflected in the below discussion on the performance of test case generation. As such, we will not discuss attack detection further and only focus on testing coverage measure.

In Fig. 5, the result data of each tool is plotted using a line of different color. The two best tools are DC_{CR} and DC_{BS} which can achieve the highest coverage. However, our tool DC_{BS} reaches the maximum coverage faster. The worst tools are DC and DC_{FS}. The performance of the four tools decreases from left to right, from top to bottom. The main reason is because of the overhead when solving more complicated constraints representing the DNN and coverage criteria. For example, the constraints for `MNIST` are simpler than e.g. `CIFAR-10`

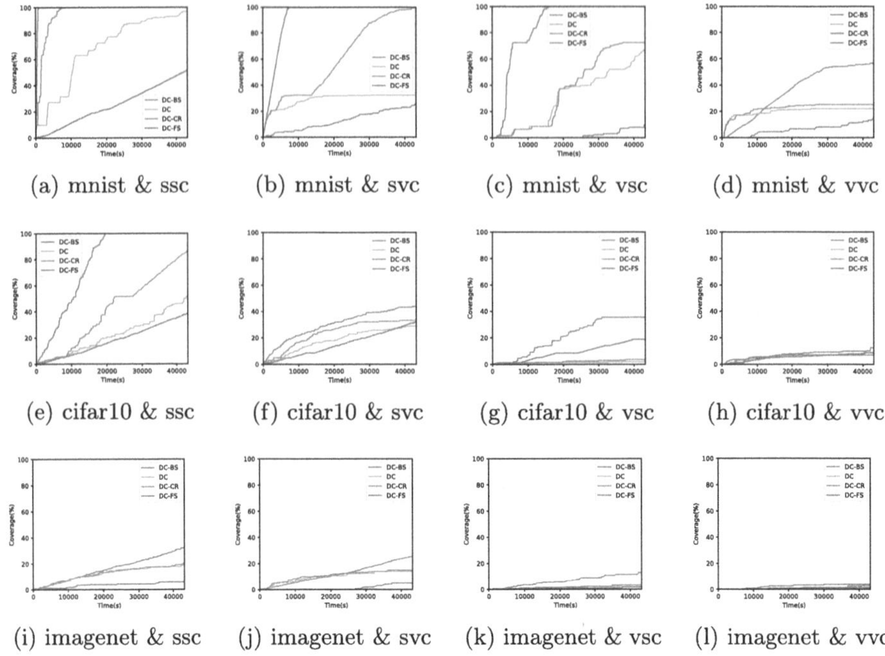

(a) mnist & ssc (b) mnist & svc (c) mnist & vsc (d) mnist & vvc

(e) cifar10 & ssc (f) cifar10 & svc (g) cifar10 & vsc (h) cifar10 & vvc

(i) imagenet & ssc (j) imagenet & svc (k) imagenet & vsc (l) imagenet & vvc

Fig. 5. Mean coverage over time when running the four different tools

and the constraints for SSC are also simpler than e.g. SVC. Now we address three research questions (RQ) by using the detailed data in Fig. 5.

RQ1: Is search space pruning helpful? When comparing *DC* with other tools, *DC* is usually the worst; we will discuss the corner case of DC_{FS} later. DC_{CR} is usually about 5 times faster than *DC*. This speed-up is even higher (more than 10 times) when comparing DC_{BS} with *DC*. Therefore, search space pruning is really helpful to speed up dynamic symbolic execution of DNNs. The main reason is because we can skip exploring the large search space, which we know for sure does not contain any test case that improves the coverage.

We note that, in some cases such as testing with the `ImageNet` benchmark, it requires more time to clearly see the efficiency of search space pruning. For example, the speed up of DC_{BS} over *DC* is about 8 times if we continue to run the tools with the SSC coverage till 30 hours. Another example is the testing with the `MNIST` benchmark and VVC coverage, where DC_{BS} is slower than *DC* at first, but later outperforms *DC*. In general, since there is an overhead in finding unsatisfiable cores and pruning a search space, DC_{BS} might be slower in the beginning, but later because of its capability of skipping exploration of a large search space, its performance will be boosted along the way.

RQ2: Is domain knowledge important? In Fig. 5, we can also see that DC_{BS} is sometimes even 10 times faster than DC_{CR}.[2] So our unsatisfiable core generation technique based on binary search algorithm is really helpful. To clearly explain the reason for such a speed-up, let us look at Table 2, which summarizes the results when running the four tools with the `MNIST` benchmark using sign-sign coverage (SSC) criterion. Here, we present the maximum coverage (over 288) and the number of pruned paths per unsatisfiable core (given 12 hour timeout).

Table 2. Testing `MNIST` with SSC

Tool	Coverage (%)	Pruning Rate
DC	97.2	Not applicable
DC_{CR}	100	2.734
DC_{FS}	51.7	4.892
DC_{BS}	100	58.136

The most efficient unsatisfiable core is generated by our method with more than 58 pruned paths for each unsatisfiable core. We call this number the pruning rate for short. (Overall, our tool can prune about 35,000 paths.) This rate is 10 times more than the second best one of DC_{FS} (4.892), where the cores are generated by the Full-Solve algorithm. Later, we will explain the reason why the pruning rate for DC_{FS} is low though the quality of unsatisfiable cores generated by Full-Solve is also very good.

The pruning rate for DC_{CR} is very small (2.734), which is as expected. This shows that the unsatisfiable cores generated by the Conflict Refiner algorithm, which does not know anything about DNN and does not make use of DNN domain knowledge, are not as useful as the ones generated by our algorithm. In contrast, since our algorithm, which makes use of the domain knowledge, can find the highest node that is responsible for the path infeasibility, it helps prune the largest sub-graph rooted at that node. In addition, it is also useful for global pruning since distance constraints are eliminated as much as possible.

It can be seen that the scalability is still an issue, especially in the experiment with VGG16. This is because the performance of the constraint solving step is not so good. Given that the domain knowledge is very helpful in pruning the search space, we plan to apply it to constraint solving as well. The implementation can be done on top of open-source solvers such as SCIP [1].

RQ3: What is an efficient implementation for unsatisfiable core generation? Though we know that exploiting the domain knowledge is very helpful in boosting DSE of DNNs, unfortunately there is no unsatisfiable core generation algorithm that can exploit such information efficiently yet.

[2] We present an illustrative example in our technical report [36].

A state-of-the-art algorithm to specify the preferences among constraints when refining the conflict among the constraints is QuickXPlain [19], also called FullSolve in CPLEX. Unfortunately, it is not really useful in our evaluation. There are two reasons for its inefficiency. Firstly, it is not appropriate for the setting of the search for the most useful unsatisfiable core. Specifically, its main purpose is to debug and explain the reason why a set of constraints is unsatisfiable. Secondly, it is a generic algorithm where each constraint can be assigned with any integer number to specify its priority. However, our purpose here is just to find the subset of nodes (in the graph representation) that is responsible for the path constraint unsatisfiability. So, using FullSolve might be overkill. In fact, FullSolve takes a lot of time to extract unsatisfiable cores and prove they are minimal, which becomes useless because the running time for unsatisfiable core generation is much longer than solving a single path constraint. This explains the poor performance of DC_{FS} in Fig. 5 and low pruning rate in Table 2 although the unsatisfiable cores generated by FullSolve is very good. By contrast, our binary search algorithm is much faster and thus can generate the unsatisfiable cores with a higher pruning rate.

6 Related Work

We discuss in more detail defensive approaches. One promising approach is automated verification, which aims to provide robustness guarantees for DNNs. The state-of-the-art use different methods to over-approximate a DNN's behavior such as layer-by-layer exhaustive search [15], constraint solving [20], global optimisation [37] and abstract interpretation [8,30]. [45] shows that Monte Carlo tree search can be used to mitigate the space explosion problem in exhaustive search. While constraint-based approaches usually work on small DNNs with hundreds of neurons, global optimisation can work with larger DNNs. However it is sensitive to the number of input dimensions to be perturbed. In general, the results of over-approximating approaches can be pessimistic due to false alarms.

Meanwhile, the problem of test input generation for DNNs is also important. [7,13,22,44] present distribution-aware DNN testing. [45] aims to cover the input space by exhaustive mutation testing. [27,35,42] apply gradient-based search algorithms to solve optimisation problems and [39] applies linear programming. Recently, [10,40] applies the methodology of DSE, which is introduced to mitigate the limitations of traditional random testing [9,33], to DNNs.

Though the application of testing techniques to DNNs is difficult, there is a lot of work that attempts to do so [26,27,35,39,42,45,46,48], to name a few, with different coverage criteria. State-of-the-art coverage-driven DNN testing tools include DeepConcolic [40], DeepCheck [10], DeepXplore [35], DeepTest [42], DeepCover [39], and DeepGauge [27]. DeepConcolic and DeepCheck are able to take coverage requirements as input while the other methods are tailored to specific requirements. DeepXplore requires a set of DNNs to explore multiple gradient directions while the other methods need a single DNN only. Apart from the other methods, DeepConcolic and DeepCheck can achieve good coverage by starting from a single input—the others need a non-trivial set of inputs.

There is also work that uses coverage-guided fuzzing (CGF) techniques for testing DNNs. TensorFuzz [33] is the first to explore the idea of CGF for neural networks. Similarly to TensorFuzz, DeepHunter [46] is another CGF based framework, which utilises the extensions of neuron coverage from [28]. Though input mutation and fuzzing are good at generating a large amount of random data, there is no guarantee that certain test objectives will be satisfied.

All the above methods suffer from the path/space explosion problem, which is addressed in this paper. To mitigate this problem, program verification techniques [29] and symbolic execution (for other domains) [17,18] introduced the idea of interpolating infeasible paths, which is inspired by conflict clause learning in a DPLL-style SAT solver. However, existing interpolation techniques are not applicable to the domain of DNN testing. These interpolation-based frameworks require the target to be static but this assumption is no longer valid in the context of testing DNNs because the target constraint is relevant to the input (thus it is dynamic). There is also work [4] that addresses the problem of pruning the search space in DNN verification. However, since it is tied to the setting of DNN verification, it is not applicable to DNN testing. In contrast, our technique is built at the level of constraint solvers and can be used for both the two contexts.

7 Conclusion

We addressed the space explosion problem for DSE of DNNs by pruning redundant paths, which do not contribute to the test coverage or bug/vulnerability detection. Our technical contributions include the construction of the tree representation for testing DNNs, an effective search space pruning method, and an efficient unsatisfiable core generation algorithm, which boost the performance of testing tools for DNNs. Ultimately, this helps improve the robustness of critical systems that are based on machine learning and deep learning algorithms.

Acknowledgment. This research is supported by the National Research Foundation, Prime Minister's Office, Singapore under its Campus for Research Excellence and Technological Enterprise (CREATE) programme.

References

1. Achterberg, T.: Scip: solving constraint integer programs. Math. Programming Comput. **1**, 1–41 (2009). https://doi.org/10.1007/s12532-008-0001-1
2. Alipanahi, B., Delong, A., Weirauch, M., Frey, B.J.: Predicting the sequence specificities of dna- and rna-binding proteins by deep learning. Nature Biotechnol. **33** (2015). https://doi.org/10.1038/nbt.3300
3. Andersen, E.D., Andersen, K.D.: Presolving in linear programming. Math. Program. **71**(2), 221–245 (1995). https://doi.org/10.1007/BF01586000, https://doi.org/10.1007/BF01586000
4. Botoeva, E., Kouvaros, P., Kronqvist, J., Lomuscio, A., Misener, R.: Efficient verification of relu-based neural networks via dependency analysis. In: Proceedings of the AAAI Conference on Artificial Intelligence, vol. 34, issue 04, pp. 3291–3299

(2020). https://doi.org/10.1609/aaai.v34i04.5729, https://ojs.aaai.org/index.php/AAAI/article/view/5729
5. Carlini, N., Wagner, D.: Towards evaluating the robustness of neural networks. In: 2017 IEEE Symposium on Security and Privacy (SP), pp. 39–57 (2017)
6. Chinneck, J.W., Dravnieks, E.W.: Locating minimal infeasible constraint sets in linear programs. ORSA J. Comput. **3**, 85–176 (1991). https://doi.org/10.1287/ijoc.3.2.157. May
7. Dola, S., Dwyer, M.B., Soffa, M.L.: Distribution-aware testing of neural networks using generative models. In: Proceedings of the 43rd International Conference on Software Engineering, pp. 226–237. ICSE '21, IEEE Press (2021). https://doi.org/10.1109/ICSE43902.2021.00032, https://doi.org/10.1109/ICSE43902.2021.00032
8. Gehr, T., Mirman, M., Drachsler-Cohen, D., Tsankov, P., Chaudhuri, S., Vechev, M.: Ai2: safety and robustness certification of neural networks with abstract interpretation. In: 2018 IEEE Symposium on Security and Privacy (SP), pp. 3–18 (2018). https://doi.org/10.1109/SP.2018.00058
9. Godefroid, P., Klarlund, N., Sen, K.: Dart: Directed automated random testing. In: Proceedings of the 2005 ACM SIGPLAN Conference on Programming Language Design and Implementation, pp. 213–223. PLDI '05, ACM, New York, NY, USA (2005). https://doi.org/10.1145/1065010.1065036, http://doi.acm.org/10.1145/1065010.1065036
10. Gopinath, D., Păsăreanu, C.S., Wang, K., Zhang, M., Khurshid, S.: Symbolic Execution for Deep Neural Networks. arXiv preprint arXiv:1807.10439 (2018)
11. Gopinath, D., Păsăreanu, C.S., Wang, K., Zhang, M., Khurshid, S.: Symbolic execution for attribution and attack synthesis in neural networks. In: Proceedings of the 41st International Conference on Software Engineering: Companion Proceedings, pp. 282–283. ICSE '19, IEEE Press, Piscataway, NJ, USA (2019). https://doi.org/10.1109/ICSE-Companion.2019.00115, https://doi.org/10.1109/ICSE-Companion.2019.00115
12. Guo, J., Jiang, Y., Zhao, Y., Chen, Q., Sun, J.: Dlfuzz: differential fuzzing testing of deep learning systems. In: Proceedings of the 2018 26th ACM Joint Meeting on European Software Engineering Conference and Symposium on the Foundations of Software Engineering, pp. 739–743. ESEC/FSE 2018, Association for Computing Machinery, New York, NY, USA (2018).https://doi.org/10.1145/3236024.3264835, https://doi.org/10.1145/3236024.3264835
13. Huang, W., Zhao, X., Banks, A., Cox, V., Huang, X.: Hierarchical distribution-aware testing of deep learning. ACM Trans. Softw. Eng. Methodol. **33**(2) (2023). https://doi.org/10.1145/3625290, https://doi.org/10.1145/3625290
14. Huang, X., Kroening, D., Ruan, W., Sharp, J., Sun, Y., Thamo, E., Wu, M., Yi, X.: A survey of safety and trustworthiness of deep neural networks: verification, testing, adversarial attack and defence, and interpretability. Comput. Sci. Rev. **37**, 100270 (2020). https://doi.org/10.1016/j.cosrev.2020.100270, http://www.sciencedirect.com/science/article/pii/S1574013719302527
15. Huang, X., Kwiatkowska, M., Wang, S., Wu, M.: Safety verification of deep neural networks. In: Majumdar, R., Kunčak, V. (eds.) Computer Aided Verification, pp. 3–29. Springer International Publishing, Cham (2017)
16. IBM: Ibm ilog cplex optimization studio (2019). https://www.ibm.com/products/ilog-cplex-optimization-studio
17. Jaffar, J., Murali, V., Navas, J.A.: Boosting concolic testing via interpolation. In: Proceedings of the 2013 9th Joint Meeting on Foundations of Software Engineering, pp. 48–58. ESEC/FSE 2013, ACM, New York, NY, USA (2013). https://doi.org/10.1145/2491411.2491425, http://doi.acm.org/10.1145/2491411.2491425

18. Jaffar, J., Santosa, A.E., Voicu, R.: An interpolation method for clp traversal. In: Gent, I.P. (ed.) Principles and Practice of Constraint Programming - CP 2009, pp. 454–469. Springer, Heidelberg (2009)
19. Junker, U.: Quickxplain: preferred explanations and relaxations for over-constrained problems. In: Proceedings of the 19th National Conference on Artifical Intelligence, pp. 167–172. AAAI'04, AAAI Press (2004). http://dl.acm.org/citation.cfm?id=1597148.1597177
20. Katz, G., Barrett, C., Dill, D.L., Julian, K., Kochenderfer, M.J.: Reluplex: an efficient smt solver for verifying deep neural networks. In: Majumdar, R., Kunčak, V. (eds.) Computer Aided Verification, pp. 97–117. Springer International Publishing, Cham (2017)
21. Kelly, J.H., Dan, S.V., John, J.C., Leanna, K.R.: A practical tutorial on modified condition/decision coverage. Tech. Rep. (2001)
22. Kim, J., Feldt, R., Yoo, S.: Guiding deep learning system testing using surprise adequacy. In: Proceedings of the 41st International Conference on Software Engineering, pp. 1039–1049. ICSE '19, IEEE Press (2019). https://doi.org/10.1109/ICSE.2019.00108, https://doi.org/10.1109/ICSE.2019.00108
23. Knorr, E.: How Paypal Beats the Bad Guys with Machine Learning (2015). http://www.infoworld.com/article/2907877/machine-learning/how-paypal-reduces-fraudwith-machine-learning.html
24. Krizhevsky, A.: Learning multiple layers of features from tiny images. Tech. Rep. (2009)
25. Leisink, M., Kappen, B.: Bound propagation. J. Artif. Int. Res. **19**(1), 139–154 (2003). http://dl.acm.org/citation.cfm?id=1622434.1622439
26. Ma, L., Juefei-Xu, F., Xue, M., Li, B., Li, L., Liu, Y., Zhao, J.: Deepct: tomographic combinatorial testing for deep learning systems. In: 2019 IEEE 26th International Conference on Software Analysis, Evolution and Reengineering (SANER), pp. 614–618 (2019). https://doi.org/10.1109/SANER.2019.8668044
27. Ma, L., Juefei-Xu, F., Zhang, F., Sun, J., Xue, M., Li, B., Chen, C., Su, T., Li, L., Liu, Y., Zhao, J., Wang, Y.: Deepgauge: multi-granularity testing criteria for deep learning systems. In: Proceedings of the 33rd ACM/IEEE International Conference on Automated Software Engineering, pp. 120–131. ASE 2018, ACM, New York, NY, USA (2018). https://doi.org/10.1145/3238147.3238202, http://doi.acm.org/10.1145/3238147.3238202
28. Ma, L., Zhang, F., Sun, J., Xue, M., Li, B., Juefei-Xu, F., Xie, C., Li, L., Liu, Y., Zhao, J., Wang, Y.: Deepmutation: mutation testing of deep learning systems. In: 2018 IEEE 29th International Symposium on Software Reliability Engineering (ISSRE), pp. 100–111 (2018). https://doi.org/10.1109/ISSRE.2018.00021
29. McMillan, K.L.: Lazy annotation for program testing and verification. In: Touili, T., Cook, B., Jackson, P. (eds.) Computer Aided Verification, pp. 104–118. Springer, Heidelberg (2010)
30. Mirman, M., Gehr, T., Vechev, M.: Differentiable abstract interpretation for provably robust neural networks. In: International Conference on Machine Learning, pp. 3575–3583 (2018)
31. Nair, V., Hinton, G.E.: Rectified linear units improve restricted Boltzmann machines. In: Proceedings of the 27th International Conference on International Conference on Machine Learning, pp. 807–814. ICML'10, Omnipress, USA (2010). http://dl.acm.org/citation.cfm?id=3104322.3104425
32. NVIDIA: Nvidia tegra drive px: Self-driving Car Computer (2015)

33. Odena, A., Olsson, C., Andersen, D., Goodfellow, I.: TensorFuzz: debugging neural networks with coverage-guided fuzzing. In: Chaudhuri, K., Salakhutdinov, R. (eds.) Proceedings of the 36th International Conference on Machine Learning. Proceedings of Machine Learning Research, vol. 97, pp. 4901–4911. PMLR, Long Beach, California, USA (2019). http://proceedings.mlr.press/v97/odena19a.html
34. Papernot, N., McDaniel, P., Jha, S., Fredrikson, M., Celik, Z.B., Swami, A.: The limitations of deep learning in adversarial settings. In: 2016 IEEE European Symposium on Security and Privacy (EuroS P), pp. 372–387 (2016). https://doi.org/10.1109/EuroSP.2016.36
35. Pei, K., Cao, Y., Yang, J., Jana, S.: Deepxplore: automated whitebox testing of deep learning systems. In: Proceedings of the 26th Symposium on Operating Systems Principles, pp. 1–18. SOSP '17, ACM, New York, NY, USA (2017). https://doi.org/10.1145/3132747.3132785, http://doi.acm.org/10.1145/3132747.3132785
36. Rangayah, B., Sng, E., Trinh, M.T.: Effective Search Space Pruning for Testing Deep Neural Networks (Technical Report) (2024). https://trinhmt.github.io/home/DNN/
37. Ruan, W., Huang, X., Kwiatkowska, M.: Reachability analysis of deep neural networks with provable guarantees. In: Proceedings of 27th International Joint Conference on Artificial Intelligence (IJCAI'18), pp. 2651–2659 (2018). https://doi.org/10.24963/ijcai.2018/368
38. Russakovsky, O., Deng, J., Su, H., Krause, J., Satheesh, S., Ma, S., Huang, Z., Karpathy, A., Khosla, A., Bernstein, M., Berg, A.C., Fei-Fei, L.: Imagenet large scale visual recognition challenge. Int. J. Comput. Vision **115**(3), 211–252 (2015). https://doi.org/10.1007/s11263-015-0816-y, https://doi.org/10.1007/s11263-015-0816-y
39. Sun, Y., Huang, X., Kroening, D., Sharp, J., Hill, M., Ashmore, R.: Structural test coverage criteria for deep neural networks. ACM Trans. Embed. Comput. Syst. **18**(5s) (2019). https://doi.org/10.1145/3358233, https://doi.org/10.1145/3358233
40. Sun, Y., Wu, M., Ruan, W., Huang, X., Kwiatkowska, M., Kroening, D.: Concolic testing for deep neural networks. In: Proceedings of the 33rd ACM/IEEE International Conference on Automated Software Engineering, pp. 109–119. ASE 2018, ACM, New York, NY, USA (2018). https://doi.org/10.1145/3238147.3238172, http://doi.acm.org/10.1145/3238147.3238172
41. Szegedy, C., Zaremba, W., Sutskever, I., Bruna, J., Erhan, D., Goodfellow, I., Fergus, R.: Intriguing properties of neural networks. In: International Conference on Learning Representations (2014)
42. Tian, Y., Pei, K., Jana, S., Ray, B.: Deeptest: automated testing of deep-neural-network-driven autonomous cars. In: Proceedings of the 40th International Conference on Software Engineering, pp. 303–314. ICSE '18, ACM, New York, NY, USA (2018). https://doi.org/10.1145/3180155.3180220, http://doi.acm.org/10.1145/3180155.3180220
43. VGG16: Vgg16 Model for Keras (2021). https://gist.github.com/baraldilorenzo/07d7802847aaad0a35d3
44. Wang, L., Xie, X., Du, X., Tian, M., Guo, Q., Yang, Z., Shen, C.: Distxplore: distribution-guided testing for evaluating and enhancing deep learning systems. In: Proceedings of the 31st ACM Joint European Software Engineering Conference and Symposium on the Foundations of Software Engineering, pp. 68–80. ESEC/FSE 2023, Association for Computing Machinery, New York, NY, USA (2023). https://doi.org/10.1145/3611643.3616266, https://doi.org/10.1145/3611643.3616266

45. Wicker, M., Huang, X., Kwiatkowska, M.: Feature-guided black-box safety testing of deep neural networks. In: Beyer, D., Huisman, M. (eds.) Tools and Algorithms for the Construction and Analysis of Systems, pp. 408–426. Springer International Publishing, Cham (2018)
46. Xie, X., Ma, L., Juefei-Xu, F., Xue, M., Chen, H., Liu, Y., Zhao, J., Li, B., Yin, J., See, S.: Deephunter: a coverage-guided fuzz testing framework for deep neural networks. In: Proceedings of the 28th ACM SIGSOFT International Symposium on Software Testing and Analysis, pp. 146–157. ISSTA 2019, Association for Computing Machinery, New York, NY, USA (2019).https://doi.org/10.1145/3293882.3330579, https://doi.org/10.1145/3293882.3330579
47. Yann, L., Corinna, C., Christopher, J.B.: The mnist Database of Handwritten Digits (1998)
48. Zhang, F., Chowdhury, S.P., Christakis, M.: DeepSearch: A Simple and Effective Blackbox Attack for Deep Neural Networks, pp. 800–812. Association for Computing Machinery, New York, NY, USA (2020). https://doi.org/10.1145/3368089.3409750
49. Zhang, J.M., Harman, M., Ma, L., Liu, Y.: Machine learning testing: survey, landscapes and horizons. IEEE Trans. Software Eng. **48**(1), 1–36 (2022). https://doi.org/10.1109/TSE.2019.2962027

Correction to: Efficiently Adapting Stateless Model Checking for C11/C++11 to Mixed-Size Accesses

Shigeyuki Sato, Taiyo Mizuhashi, Genki Kimura, and Kenjiro Taura

Correction to:
Chapter 17 in: O. Kiselyov (Ed.): *Programming Languages and Systems*, LNCS 15194,
https://doi.org/10.1007/978-981-97-8943-6_17

In the originally published version of chapter 17, Figure 9 was eliminated and its citation is renumbered to Figure 7 instead of Figure 9. They are now been corrected.

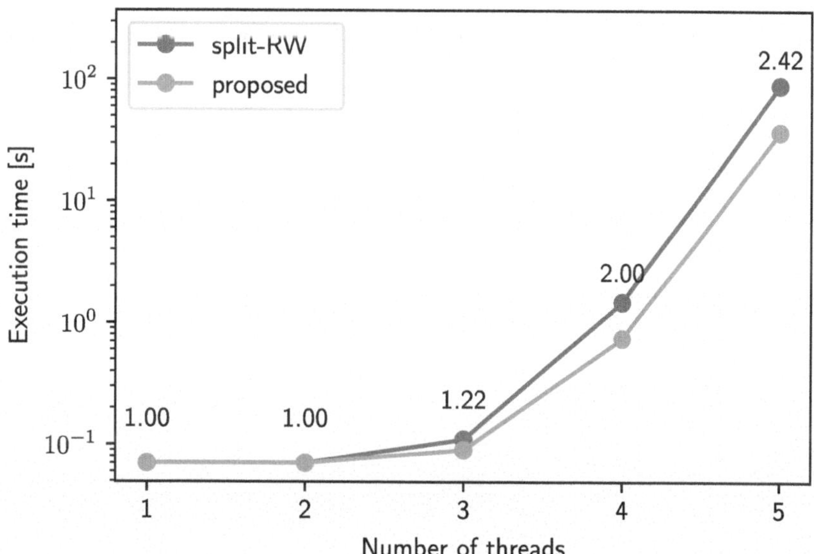

Fig. 9. Execution time of GenMC on MWF scaling the number of threads, where numbers above points denote the relative speed of the proposed over split-RW.

The updated version of this chapter can be found at
https://doi.org/10.1007/978-981-97-8943-6_17

O. Kiselyov (Ed.): APLAS 2024, LNCS 15194, pp. C1–C2, 2025.
https://doi.org/10.1007/978-981-97-8943-6_19

Author Index

O. Kiselyov (Ed.): APLAS 2024, LNCS 15194, p. 389, 2024.
https://doi.org/10.1007/978-981-97-8943-6

The manufacturer's authorised representative in the EU is Springer Nature Customer Service Centre GmbH, Europaplatz 3, 69115 Heidelberg, Germany. If you have any concerns regarding our products, please contact ProductSafety@springernature.com

Printed and bound by CPI Group (UK) Ltd, Croydon, CR0 4YY
15/07/2026
02167637-0004